W9-DDO-386

THE RECENT STUDY OF HEBREW

An I. Edward Kiev
Library Foundation Book

BIBLIOGRAPHICA JUDAICA 10

A bibliographic series of the Library of
Hebrew Union College-Jewish Insitute of Religion
3101 Clifton Avenue, Cincinnati, Ohio 45220
Edited by Herbert C. Zafren

1 Rudolf Glanz. *The German Jew in America.* An Annotated Bibliography Including Books, Pamphlets and Articles of Special Interest. 1969
2 *Judaica.* A Short-Title Catalogue of Books, Pamphlets and Manuscripts Relating to the Political, Social and Cultural History of the Jews and to the Jewish Question, in the Library of Ludwig Rosenberger, Chicago, Illinois. 1971
3 Bernard Grossfeld. *A Bibliography of Targum Literature.* 1972
4 *Judaica.* Supplement [to No. 2 above]. 1974
5 Werner Weinberg. *How Do You Spell Chanukah?* A General-Purpose Romanization of Hebrew for Speakers of English. 1976
6 Martin H. Sable. *Latin American Jewry: A Research Guide.* 1978
7 Shimeon Brisman. *A History and Guide to Judaic Bibliography* (Jewish Research Literature, Vol. 1). 1977
8 Bernard Grossfeld. *A Bibliography of Targum Literature.* Volume Two. 1977
9 Vera Basch Moreen. *Miniature Paintings in Judaeo-Persian Manuscripts.* 1985
10 Nahum M. Waldman, *The Recent Study of Hebrew: A Survey of the Literature with Selected Bibliography.* 1989.
11 Shimeon Brisman. *A History and Guide to Judaic Encyclopedias and Lexicons* (Jewish Research Literature, Vol. 2). 1987
12 *The Sino-Judaic Bibliographies of Rudolf Loewenthal.* 1988. (In association with the Sino-Judaic Institute)

THE RECENT STUDY OF HEBREW

A SURVEY OF THE LITERATURE WITH SELECTED BIBLIOGRAPHY

Nahum M. Waldman

PJ
4543
.W24
seab

Hebrew Union College Press • Cincinnati
Eisenbrauns • Winona Lake, Indiana
1989

The United Library
Garrett-Evangelical/Seabury-Western Seminaries
2121 Sheridan Road
Evanston, IL 60201

Copyright © 1989 Hebrew Union College-Jewish Institute of Religion
All rights reserved.
Printed in the United States of America

Library of Congress Cataloging-in-Publication Data

Waldman, Nahum M.
The recent study of Hebrew: a survey of the literature with selected bibliography / Nahum M. Waldman
p. cm.—(Bibliographica Judaica, ISSN 0067-6853; 10)
"An I. Edward Kiev Library Foundation book"—1st prelim. p.
Includes bibliographical references.
ISBN 0-87820-908-5
1. Hebrew language—Bibliography.
2. Hebrew language—Abstracts.
I. Title.
II. Series.
Z7070.W34 1989
[PJ4543] 89-19885
016.4924—dc20 CIP

I. Edward Kiev Library Foundation

In memory of Dr. I. Edward Kiev, alike distinguished as Rabbi, Chaplain and Librarian of the Hebrew Union College-Jewish Institute of Religion in New York, his family and friends established in September 1976 a Library Foundation bearing his name, to support and encourage the knowledge, understanding and appreciation of books, manuscripts and other efforts of scholars in Judaica and Hebraica. In cooperation with the Publications Committee of the Hebrew Union College-Jewish Institute of Religion, the Foundation offers the present study as an I. Edward Kiev Library Foundation Book.

This book is dedicated to
the memory of my beloved parents,
Irving and Rose Waldman,
my first teachers in the Hebrew language.

CONTENTS

PREFACE

The work presented here puts before the student and researcher a survey of the linguistic study of the Hebrew language during the past forty years (approximately), with a bibliography of that research. The periods under consideration are: biblical, Second Commonwealth and rabbinic, masoretic, medieval, and modern and contemporary. In addition, a chapter has been devoted to languages spoken by Jews which have a Hebrew component and which have existed alongside Hebrew, with varying hierarchical relationships and degrees of mutual influence. This chapter includes targumic Aramaic, Judeo-Arabic, Judeo-Persian, Judezmo, modern Aramaic, and Yiddish. Translation Greek also shows Hebrew influence.

Periods under consideration

This work is not intended to be a history of the Hebrew language. There have been some attempts to compose a one-volume history (Chomsky 1957, 1967; Eisenstadt 1967; Federbush 1967; Kutscher 1982). But it is clear that the time is not ripe for such a work. Much important research has been done and is continuing to be done since these one-volume histories appeared. Kutscher's attempt (1982) was published and edited posthumously by his son, Raphael Kutscher. While it contains much valuable technical and anecdotal information on periods other than the ones which were the author's great strength, Qumran and Rabbinic Hebrew, and even though some of the more recent literature was treated cursorily by specialists in various areas, this book, with all its strengths, is not the hoped-for historical survey.

History of Hebrew yet to be written

The time will be ripe for a comprehensive history of the Hebrew language when much basic research has been digested and when a team of specialists can contribute their expertise in each area of specialization. A possible model is the *Cambridge Ancient History* (3rd edition; Cambridge University Press).

The goal of this work is more modest. It is an attempt to survey studies that come to significant conclusions and to list

Goal of this work

bibliographies that will lead the student further in his work. It is also important that the various time periods appear in the same volume, to demonstrate that there is some kind of unity in the confusing diversity of phenomena of this language group through the centuries. Certainly contemporary Israeli Hebrew draws upon each of the different layers.

The choice of the time-frame

The period chosen and the materials selected for my bibliography require some explanation. The past thirty-five years or so following the end of World War II have been rich in events that have influenced the study of Hebrew. Since the Ugaritic materials became available in the 1930s, there has been a rich development of Ugaritic studies relating to Biblical Hebrew. The Dead Sea Scrolls were discovered in 1947. The emergence of the State of Israel and the resulting influx of Jews speaking different dialects have been most important. Before immigrants pass away, their language traditions are being recorded and interpreted.

Significant resources and approaches

Weiman's pioneering study in Hebrew structuralism (1950) opened new approaches for the study of modern Hebrew, as has the work of H. B. Rosén. Noam Chomsky's transformational grammar has greatly influenced current methodology. The appearance of the Aleppo Codex (facsimile published in Israel) has inspired the Hebrew University Bible Project, with much scholarly spin-off in the study of language traditions and Masorah. The *Historical Dictionary of the Hebrew Language*, now in preparation, has stimulated much lexical research. Much work has been done in Jewish languages and in the emerging field of Jewish interdialectics. The influence of Neo-Assyrian legal formulae (Muffs 1969) on Hebrew and Aramaic legal terminology has been discovered. That these developments have occurred within the last thirty to forty years appears to me to justify the selection of this period for my survey.

In some cases, however, older publications are included, either because they were republished in this period or because they are still relevant. In some cases they are included alongside more recent work by a kind of attraction. The need for dialectic, where older studies still appear in current discussion, also influenced the choice.

The sources of bibliographical entries

I do not know if it will be possible to satisfy all objections to the selection of bibliographical material. Specialized bibliographies are the ideal for each area, and where these were available or known to me, I include them. This work cannot include everything that is listed in those specialized bibliographies. A search was made of all major journals dealing with Hebrew, general linguistics, and ancient Near Eastern and biblical studies. The search included conference proceedings, *Festschriften*, dissertation abstracts, and bibliographical lists. Some items were omitted because of their brevity or narrow scope, such as brief lexical studies. An attempt was made to include in the descriptive text as many bibliographical items as possible. It was, naturally, impossible to include them all. In view of the length of time between the completion of the manuscript and the publication of this book there were items that could not be summed up in any detail. An attempt was made to at least record them in the bibliography.

Additional areas included

Certain areas not traditionally included in linguistics are nevertheless included because of their relevance to linguistic matters. These are: masoretic studies; biblical rhetoric and poetry; medieval poetry; and contemporary Hebrew styles, both literary and journalistic. The line between linguistics and literature is not always clearly defined, and I include editions or studies of the literary corpora in the case of Ugaritic, the Dead Sea Scrolls, and medieval poetry. These materials are basic for establishing linguistic facts. For obvious reasons, I do not attempt to do this for Modern Hebrew literature.

Linguistics and Literature

With its admitted limitations, I offer this work to the reader with the confidence that it will provide a sense of what is being done in the field and will stimulate further study. The simple passage of time is one justification, for *Encyclopedia Judaica*, with its valuable articles and bibliographies (1971) and the bibliography of Hospers (1973, 1974) are almost twenty years old. Furthermore, this listing is more comprehensive; there are about 1,350 authors and 3,700 items represented in this book.

Transliteration systems

The transliteration systems used in this work are those of the American National Standards Institute, approved in 1975. For the transcription of text I use the "Narrow Transliteration Style," indicated in the table as *I*, and for personal names, names of books and grammatical terms I use the "More Exact Romanization Style," indicated in the table as *II*. While style *I* does not call for capitalization, I do capitalize personal and divine names, e.g., *ʾĔlōhîm*, *Mōšeh*. Style *II* does not require the rendering of a *shewa mobile*, but I have retained it for accepted transliterations of well-known texts, e.g., *Berakhot*, *Nedarim*. In compound names only the first element is capitalized in Style *II*, unless the second element is also a proper noun, e.g., *Mishneh Torah*, *Moreh nevukhim*. In Style *II*, *alef* is not indicated at the beginning of a word, only in the middle, e.g., *amen*, *haʾarets*. As indicated in the table, the definite article and prefixes are connected in both styles, but the initial letter is doubled only in Style *I*, e.g., *habbōqer*, but *Hatsfirah*.

The transliteration of Yiddish follows Style *II* except in the bibliography, where an author has used a different system is used. Similarly, Hebrew citations in the bibliography follow the author's transliteration even if it differs from my system.

To indicate pronunciation or realization, brackets are used and the symbols follow *Style* II, with the exception of [x] for *ḥet* and aspirated *kaf*, [k] for both plosive *kaf* and *qof*, [t] for *ṭet* and [š] for *shin*.

The initial stimulus for this work was an article which I wrote for *Current Trends in Linguistics*, entitled "The Hebrew Tradition" (Vol. 13, edited by Thomas A. Sebeok [The Hague: Mouton, 1975], pp. 1285–1330). Wherever any of this material appears here with similar phrasing, the source is indicated (Waldman 1975a). I wish to thank Mouton Publishers (division of Walter de Gruyter and Co.) for permission to cite. The method of citation and bibliographical listing is based upon the practice in *Current Trends*, with some modification.

Acknowledgments

It is my pleasant duty to thank certain individuals for their help and support. It was the late Prof. William Chomsky of Gratz College, Philadelphia, who inspired me to write the original article in *Current Trends*. My late, beloved parents, Irving and Rose Waldman, were my first teachers of the Hebrew language and the values connected with it, and they inspired in me a lifelong interest in Hebrew and its cognates. To them I have dedicated this book. I wish to thank Prof. Chaim Rabin of the Hebrew University and Mr. Ben Zion Fischler of the Council on the Teaching of Hebrew for their interest and suggestions. I am grateful to have been able to make use of the library facilities of the University of Pennsylvania, Dropsie College, and the Jewish Theological Seminary. Most of my time, however, was spent in the library of my home institution, Gratz College, and I want to single out for special thanks its former librarian, and now Head of the Judaica Section of the Library of Congress, Michael W. Grunberger, for his unflagging support. I wish to thank librarians Eileen Samuelson, Elie Wise, Jack Weinstein, Hayim Sheynin, and Marcia Goldberg for their invaluable help. Special thanks are due to Dr. Herbert C. Zafren, Director of the Hebrew Union College Library, his assistant, Mr. David J. Gilner, and to Mr. James Eisenbraun and the members of his staff for their patient editing and guidance through the arduous process of making this book ready for publication. Finally, my thanks and heartfelt gratitude are extended to my beloved family—my wife, Saula, and my children, Oren and Renee, Ethan, Ilana, and Iscah and Avi Chaim—for their love, understanding, and constant support.

ABBREVIATIONS

AAJR	American Academy for Jewish Research
AAL	*Afroasiatic Linguistics*, Malibu, California
ACIL	*Actes du Congres International des Linguistes*
ACILCS	*Actes du Premier Congres International de Linguistiqie Sémitique et Chamito-Sémitique* (held in Paris, July 16–19, 1969). Paris, 1974
AcOr	*Acta Orientalia*, Copenhagen
AION	*Annali; Istituto Universitario Orientale di Napoli*
AJA	*American Jewish Archives*
AJBI	*Annual of the Japanese Biblical Institute*
AJHQ	*American Jewish Historical Quarterly*
AJSL	*American Journal of Semitic Languages and Literature*
AJSN	*Association for Jewish Studies Newsletter*
AJSR	*Association for Jewish Studies Review*
ALUOS	*Annual of the Leeds University Oriental Society*
AN	*Abr Nahrain*
AO	*Archiv Orientalni*
AOAT	Alter Orient und altes Testament
AOS	American Oriental Series
AS	Assyriological Studies, University of Chicago
ASE	*Annuario di Studi Ebraici*
A Sph	*American Sephardi*
ASTI	*Annual of the Swedish Theological Institute*
BA	*Biblical Archaeologist*
BAEO	*Boletin de la Association Espanole de Orientalistes*
BAR	*Biblical Archaeological Review*
BASOR	*Bulletin of the American Schools of Oriental Research*
BDB	F. Brown, S. R. Driver, and C. A. Briggs, *A Hebrew and English Lexicon of the Old Testament*, Oxford University Press, 1907
BH	Biblical Hebrew
BHi	*Bulletin Hispanique*, Bordeaux
BiOr	*Bibliotheca Orientalis*

BJRL	*Bulletin of the John Rylands Library*
BM	*Beth Mikra*
BSLP	*Bulletin de la Societé de Linguistique de Paris*
BSOAS	*Bulletin of the School of Oriental and African Studies*
BWAT	Beiträge zur Wissenschaft vom alten Testament
BZ	*Biblische Zeitschrift*
BZAW	Beihefte zur Zeitschrift für die alttestamentliche Wissenschaft
CAD	*The Assyrian Dictionary of the Oriental Institute of the University of Chicago*; Chicago, 1956ff.
CAH	*Cambridge Ancient History*
CBQ	*Catholic Biblical Quarterly*
CLHM	*Cahiers de linguistique hispanique médiévale*
CRB	*Cahiers de la Revue Biblique*
EE	*Europa Ethnica*
EI	*Eretz-Israel*
EIv	*Haᵓentsiqlopediyah haᶜivrit*
EJ	*Encyclopedia Judaica*
EM	*Entsiqlopediyah miqraᵓit*
EOL	*Ex Oriente Lux*
EphE	*Ephemeris Epigraphica*
E Sef	*Estudios Sefardies*, Annual of *Sefarad*, Madrid
ET	*Expository Times*
FoL	*Folia Linguistica*, The Hague
FO	*Folia Orientalia*
FY 1	*The field of Yiddish*, vol. 1, ed. by U. Weinreich, New York, 1954
FY 2	*The field of Yiddish*, vol. 2, ed. by U. Weinreich, The Hague: Mouton, 1965
FY 3	*The field of Yiddish*, vol. 3, ed. by M. Herzog, W. Ravid and U. Weinreich, The Hague and Paris: Mouton, 1969
FY 4	*The field of Yiddish*, vol. 4, ed. by M. Herzog, B. Kirschenblatt-Gimblet, D. Miron and R. Wisse, Philadelphia: Institute for the Study of Human Issues, 1980
GCA	*The Gratz College Annual of Jewish Studies*, Philadelphia
G–K	*Gesenius' Hebrew Grammar*, edited and enlarged by E. Kautzsch, Oxford University Press, 1910
GLECS	*Comptes Rendus du Groupe Linguistique d'Études Chamito-Sémitiques*, Paris

HA	*Hebrew Abstracts*
HAR	*Hebrew Annual Review*, Ohio State University
HCL	*Hebrew Computational Linguistics* (in Hebrew)
HS	*Hebrew Studies* (formerly *Hebrew Abstracts*)
HTR	*Harvard Theological Review*
HUCA	*Hebrew Union College Annual*
IC	Immediate constituent (analysis)
ICLLC	International Conference on Literary and Linguistic Computing
IEJ	*Israel Exploration Journal*
IF	*Indo-germanische Forschungen*
IJAL	*International Journal of American Linguistics*
IJMES	*International Journal of Middle East Studies*
IJSL	*International Journal for the Sociology of Language*
IMR	*International Migration Review*
IOS	*Israel Oriental Studies*
IR	R. Hestrin, Y. Yisraeli, Y. Meshorer and A. Eytan, eds., *Inscriptions Reveal* (Hebrew edition: כתובות מספרות), Jerusalem: The Israel Museum, 1972
JA	*Journal Asiatique*
JANES	*The Journal of the Ancient Near Eastern Society of Columbia University*
JAOS	*Journal of the American Oriental Society*
JBL	*Journal of Biblical Literature*
JCL	*Journal of Child Language*
JFL	*Jahrbuch für frankische Landesforschung*
JHS	*Journal of Historical Studies*
JJSoc	*Jewish Journal of Sociology*
JL	*Journal of Linguistics*
JLR	*Jewish Languages Review*
JNES	*Journal of Near Eastern Studies*
JNSL	*Journal of Northwest Semitic Languages*
JPh	*Journal of Philosophy*
JQR	*Jewish Quarterly Review*
JSI	*Journal of Social Issues*
JSJPHRP	*Journal for the Study of Judaism in the Persian, Hellenistic and Roman Periods*
JSS	*Journal of Semitic Studies*
JTS	*Journal of Theological Studies*
KAI	H. Donner and W. Röllig, *Kanaanäische und aramäische Inschriften*, 3 vols., Wiesbaden: Harrassowitz, 1962–64; second edition, 1971–76

KJS	*Kansas Journal of Sociology*
KLL	קונטרסים לעניני לשון (*The Bulletin of Language Studies*, Jerusalem, 1937–43, ed. by H. Yalon; reprinted Jerusalem, 1963
KS	*Kiryath Sepher*
LB	*Linguistica Biblica*
Les	*Leshonenu*
LLA	*Leshonenu La*ʿ*am*
LQ	*Language Quarterly*
LangS	*Language Sciences*
LS	*Language and Speech*
LXX	Septuagint; A. Rahlfs, ed., *Septuaginta*, 2 vols., Stuttgart: Württembergische Bibelanstalt, 1935, reprinted 1971
MEJ	*Middle East Journal*
MGS	*Michigan German Studies*
MH	Mishnaic Hebrew; further divided into MH^1 and MH^2
Midr.	Midrash, as in *Gen./Ex./Lev./Numb./Deut. R.* = *Rabbah*; *Cant. R.* = *Canticles Rabbah*; *Koh. R.* = *Koheleth Rabbah*; *Esth. R.* = *Esther Rabbah*
Mish.	Mishnah
ML	מחקרי לשון מוגשים לזאב בן־חיים (Language Studies in honor of Z. Ben-Hayyim), ed. by M. Bar-Asher, A. Dotan, D. Téné and G. Sarfatti, Jerusalem: Magnes Press, 1983
MRA	*Mainzer romanische Arbeiten*
MSL	*Materialen zum sumerischen Lexikon*
OA	*Oriens Antiquus*
OH	*Or Hamizrach*
OLP	*Orientalia Lovaniensia Periodica*
OLZ	*Orientalistische Literaturzeitung*
Or	*Orientalia*
OS	*Orientalia Suecana*
OTS	*Oudtestamentische Studiën*
PCLS	*Papers from the Regional Meeting of the Chicago Linguistic Society*
PEQ	*Palestine Exploration Quarterly*
PHULTP	*Publications of the Hebrew University Language Traditions Project*
PIASH	*Proceedings of the Israel Academy of Science and Humanities*
PICL	*Proceedings of the International Congress of Linguists*

PICO	*Proceedings of the International Congress of Orientalists*
PICSL	*Proceedings of the International Conference on Semitic Languages*
PICSS	*Proceedings of the International Conference on Semitic Studies* (held in Jerusalem, July 19–23, 1965), Jerusalem: Israel Academy of Sciences and Humanities, 1969
PMLAA	*Publications of the Modern Language Association of America*
POS	*Pretoria Oriental Series*
RB	*Revue Biblique*
REJ	*Revue des Études Juives*
RHR	*Revue de l'histoire des Religions*
RHPR	*Revue d'histoire et de la Philosophie Religieuses*
RIP	*Revue International de Philosophie*
RLR	*Revue de Linguistique Romane*
RMI	*Rassegna Mensile di Israel*
RN	*Romance Notes*
RPh	*Romance Philology*
RQ	*Revue de Qumran*
RTA	*Religious and Theological Abstracts*, published quarterly, Myerstown, PA
SBB	*Studies in Bibliography and Booklore*
SBF	*Studies in Bibliography and Folklore*
SBL	Society of Biblical Literature
SBLSP	Society of Biblical Literature Seminar Papers
SH	*Scripta Hierosolomytana*
SHSL	*Studies in Hebrew and Semitic Languages* (in memory of E. Y. Kutscher: מחקרים בעברית ובלשונות שמיות מוגשים לזכרו של פרופ׳ יחזקאל קוטשר, ed. by G. Sarfatti, P. Artsi, J. C. Greenfield and M. Z. Kaddari, Ramat Gan: Bar-Ilan University, 1980
StudOr	*Studia Orientalia*
TA	*Tel Aviv*
TB	*Talmud Bavli*
ThL	*Theoretical Linguistics*
TLZ	*Theologische Literaturzeitung*
TPS	*Transactions of the Philosophical Society*
TSLL	*Texas Studies in Language and Literature*
TY	*Talmud Yerushalmi*
UF	*Ugarit-Forschungen*

UJE	*Universal Jewish Encyclopedia*
VD	*Verbum Domini*
VR	*Vox Romana*
VT	*Vetus Testamentum*
WCJS	*Proceedings of the World Congress of Jewish Studies*, Jerusalem
WHJP	*World History of the Jewish People*
WLSGF	*The Word of the Lord Shall Go Forth: Essays in Honor of David Noel Freedman*, ed. by Carol L. Meyers and M. O'Connor. Winona Lake, IN: Eisenbraun, 1983.
WO	*Die Welt des Orients*
WTJ	*Westminster Theological Journal*
WZKM	*Wiener Zeitschrift für die Kunde des Morgenlandes*
YOSR	*Yale Oriental Series Researches*
YS	*Yiddish Sprakh*
ZAl	*Zeitschrift für Althebraistik*
ZAW	*Zeitschrift für die alttestamentliche Wissenschaft*
ZDMG	*Zeitschrift der deutschen morgenländischen Gesellschaft*
ZNW	*Zeitschrift für die neutestamentliche Wissenschaft*
ZPAS	*Zeitschrift für Phonetik und allgemeine Sprachwissenschaft*

Table of Transliteration Equivalences

	I	II
א	ʾ	ʾ
בּ	b	b
ב	ḇ	v
גּ	g	g
ג	ḡ	
דּ	d	d
ד	ḏ	
ה	h	h
ו	w	w
ז	z	z
ח	ḥ	ḥ
ט	ṭ	ṭ
י	y	y
כּ	k	k
כ, ך	ḵ	kh
ל	l	l
מ, ם	m	m
נ, ן	n	n
ס	s	s
ע	ʿ	ʿ
פּ	p	p
פ, ף	p̄	f
צ, ץ	ṣ	ts
ק	q	q
ר	r	r
שׁ	š	sh
שׂ	ś	s
תּ	t	t
ת	ṯ	

	I	II
◌ָ	ā	a
◌ַ	a	a
◌ֵ	ē	e
◌ֵי	ê	
◌ֶי	e	
◌ֱ	ĕ	
vocal ◌ְ	e (raised)	e, or disregard
◌ִ	i	i
◌ִי	î	
◌ֹ	ō	o
וֹ	ô	
◌ָ	o	
◌ֳ	ŏ	
וּ	û	u
◌ָה	āh	ah
◌ֶה	eh	eh
◌ָיו	āw	av
◌ַי	ay	ay
◌ָהּ	hh	h
dagesh forte	doubling	doubling
prefixes לַ-, בַּ-, הַ-	connected, doubling	connected, no doubling

I

BIBLICAL HEBREW

BASIC BIBLIOGRAPHICAL RESOURCES

Bibliographies in Judaica, Semitics, and Hebrew Linguistics

A general guide to Judaic bibliography is Brisman (1977, 1987), and general Judaica bibliographies are Shunami (1965, 2nd ed.; supplement 1975) and Cutter and Oppenheim (1983). Tronik (1974) is a guide to Israeli periodicals in English and other European languages. A comprehensive bibliography for Semitics in general is Hospers (1973, 1974). The index to periodical literature edited by B. I. Joel (1969ff., continued after his death) lists articles written in Hebrew and other languages on Jewish studies in general, as well as language and linguistics. Another resource is the *Index to Hebrew Periodicals* published by the University of Haifa (1977ff.). Hupper (1977) is a bibliography of periodical literature on Semitic grammar and syntax. Books are indexed and reviewed in *KS* (1924ff.). Articles in *Festschriften* up until 1970 have been indexed by C. Berlin (1971). Rutherford (1968) indexes American doctoral dissertations in linguistics, including material on Hebrew, Judeo-Spanish, Judeo-Arabic, and Yiddish, for the period from 1900 to 1964. *Dissertation Abstracts International*, published by University Microfilms, contains abstracts of dissertations, including those which deal with Hebrew linguistics. Bar-Asher (1978) lists masters theses and doctoral dissertations on Hebrew language and linguistics from Israeli universities between 1938 and 1977, including dissertations in progress. *Min Hasadna* 6 (Fischler, ed., 1984) has now appeared, listing 951 items: books, periodicals, articles, masters theses and doctoral dissertations published in Hebrew in Israel, from 1948 to 1980, on Modern Hebrew. This updates Bar-Asher (1978), adding, of course, much more. There is a preface by C. Rabin and an essay by M. Z. Kaddari on "The State of Research on Israeli Hebrew." In preparation is *Min hasadna* 7, which will add Hebrew items published from 1981 on and will list items parallel to the ones in the previous volume (this time in Hebrew and other languages), which were published outside Israel on the subject of Modern Hebrew.

Doctoral dissertations are also listed in *KS*. *Bibliographie Linguistique* (1952ff.) lists articles on Hebrew and related languages, including Jewish languages (Yiddish, Judezmo, Judeo-Persian, etc.). *RTA* includes abstracts of articles on Hebrew and Aramaic. Nir and Nehemias (1975) is a bibliography on the teaching of Modern Hebrew and contains items on languages and linguistics.

Journals dealing with linguistics

A journal specifically devoted to Hebrew linguistics is *Lešonenu*, and articles in this field also appear in *Tarbiz*, *HA*, *HS*, *AN*, *JJS*, *JSS*, *Word*, *Lingua*, and in journals devoted to biblical and Northwest Semitic studies: *JBL*, *JNES*, *JANES*, *CBQ*, *ZAW*, *Maarav*, *Biblica*, and *VT* and its *Supplements*. The annual indexes of these journals are also of great value.

Attention should be directed to *HAR*, the *Annual* and the *Newsletter* of the Association for Jewish Studies, *IOS*, the *Proceedings* of the International Congress of Linguists, the *Proceedings* of the World Congress of Jewish Studies, and *GLECS*.

THE WRITING SYSTEM

General treatments and bibliography

Hospers (1973: 378–83) has a bibliography on writing and the alphabet. General treatments include: the survey by Drower (CAH^3 1973 II/1: 517–19, 792–93); *EM* (*s.v.* 'Alphabet' H); J. Naveh (1965a, 1965b, 1965c, 1971, 1973a, 1979) and a comprehensive study (1982); Driver (1948, 1954^2, 1976^3); Moscati (1951); Diringer (1960, 1962, 1967); Gelb (1963); Birnbaum (1971a, 1971b, 1972). Cross (1961) and Hanson (1963) carry the study of the alphabet into the period of the Second Commonwealth. The development of the late Phoenician scripts is dealt with in a study by Peckham (1968), and the Aramaic script is surveyed by J. Naveh (1964–65, 1967 [doctoral dissertation], 1970). Early views on the alphabet are summarized in the grammars (i.e., G-K, §5).

Egyptian hieroglyphics and the acrophonic principle

The alphabet system used by the Phoenicians, the Hebrews, the Arameans, and later by the Greeks, the Etruscans and the Romans, is commonly held to have originated and developed under the direct or indirect influence of Egyptian hieroglyphics through application of the acrophonic principle. This is the principle that the phonetic value of the character is derived from the pronunciation of the initial consonant of the word depicted by the hieroglyph. This view was advanced by Gardiner in 1916, based on the paleo-Sinaitic writing discovered by Petrie in 1904–5, with more materials later found by Albright in 1948. Albright subsequently published in 1966 a more detailed study in which he attempted to interpret the inscriptions from Serabit el-Khadem.

Driver (1954: 78–197) surveys the materials which record the early stages of the Phoenician and Hebrew alphabet and evaluates the various theories that had been offered about its origin. Cross and Freedman suggest that the center of development was located somewhere in Canaan or, more probably, in Phoenicia (Cross and Freedman 1952: 9; Diringer 1962: 117–18; Naveh 1965a, 1965b, 1971). Drower (*CAH*³, II/1: 517–19), on the other hand, calls attention to scribal experimentation at Byblos in the second millennium, something which may have figured in the later development of the alphabet. Mazar (1964) suggests Philistine mediation.

One confirmation of the acrophonic principle is the fact that the *ᶜayin* from Serabit el-Khadem (Albright 1966, figs. 1, 5) has a dot, suggesting an eye and its pupil. This sign is also found in the arrowhead inscription from Al-Khadar, near Bethlehem, dating from the end of the 12th century B.C.E., which reads: *ḥṣ ᶜbdlbᵓt* 'the arrow of ᶜAbd-labiᵓat' (*IR*, no. 17; Driver 1954: 96). General studies on the alphabet are collected in Tur-Sinai (1954–59, *Halashon*, 3–43).

Akkadian cuneiform has long been rejected as a source for the first alphabets. The Egyptian pseudo-alphabet has been considered by many as the source of the Phoenician, since both alphabets include symbols only for consonants, not vowels.

The Sinaitic inscriptions

The development of writing and writing materials also indicates a relationship between the Egyptian and Phoenician alphabets. Gardiner suggested that the Sinaitic inscriptions might be the missing link between the two systems, but it must be observed that the values of similarly-shaped signs in Egyptian and Phoenician are not identical. The Egyptian sign may only have served as a stimulus.

The names of the letters

Driver regards the names of the letters as ancient and primary because in fourteen out of twenty-two cases the name of the letter agrees with the object depicted. Some names, however, may be secondary; this must be the case when there are two names, e.g., *n* is called *nun* 'fish' by the Hebrews and *naḥaš* 'serpent' by the Ethiopians. The latter term resembles the Egyptian sign and could be older. The names of the letters, however, are from different languages, e.g., *resh* 'head' is an Aramaic noun, whereas the Hebrew noun is *rōᵓš*; *mem* has a reduction of the diphthong found in Hebrew *mayim* 'water'; but *ʿayin* retains the diphthong. Driver sees this as evidence of the early relationship between Hebrew and Aramaic.

There are two classes of signs, in Driver's view. In the primary class the letters correspond to Egyptian hieroglyphs, and the letter values are reproduced by the initial letters of their Semitic names. The secondary group, on the other hand, includes those signs which were formed by modifying other signs, e.g., *ḥ* (𐤇), adapted from *h* (𐤄). The signs were then given the names of objects the letters resembled, or a suitable onomatopoeic name. In summary, several principles are thought to have combined in the naming and shaping of the letters.

Differing views on Egyptian influence

Gelb (1963: 137–53) has dissented from the prevailing view, rejecting the acrophonic principle and questioning whether there was Egyptian influence. While the names of some signs are alleged to have a recognizable meaning, e.g., *alef* 'ox,' *bet* 'house,' others, such as *he*, *ṭet*, and *tsade* bear names which cannot be explained as deriving from any known Semitic language. Some signs have different names in other dialects. (For example, *nun* 'fish' is called *naḥaš* 'serpent' in Ethiopic, as noted above.) Gelb proposes instead that the signs are not really alphabetic but syllabic and were developed consciously and arbitrarily. He supports his argument by a consideration of visual and phonetic similarities (for example, *he* and *ḥet*, *nun* and *mem*, *zayin* and *samekh*, *taw* and *ṭet*). Gelb does agree (1963: 147) that Egyptian influence is responsible for the main structural element that these scripts have in common, which is that a single sign represents only one consonant, not a vowel.

Van den Branden (1962) argued that the Proto-Sinaitic alphabet developed from Egyptian models. This in turn produced the pre-Islamic Arabic alphabet, which was adapted by the Phoenicians. In the first stages, a process of translation was involved: the Egyptian symbol for *pr* 'house' was used for the letter *byt*, *bet* ('house' in West Semitic), and the Egyptian symbol for *ʿwt* 'scepter' was used for the letter *lamed*, since the related noun *malmad* 'goad' was roughly the West Semitic equivalent. However, in many cases, the original Semitic names of the letters are lost, and only shapes are compared.

The borrowing of the Phoenician alphabet

For the date of the borrowing of the Phoenician alphabet by the Greeks, McCarter (1974, 1975) suggests 800 B.C.E., disagreeing with Naveh (1973b), who dates it around 1100 B.C.E. McCarter agrees, however, that experimentation may have taken place as early as 1100. Greek *rho* is one indication that the Greeks borrowed from the Phoenicians. Akkadian transcriptions of Ugaritic letters indicate that the name of the Ugaritic letter was pronounced [raʾš], while Greek *rho* apparently originates from the Phoenician pronunciation, [roʾš]. Greek *san* may be a clue to the original pronunciation of *sin*. Greek *zēta* may stem from a Phoenician **zen* (McCarter 1975: 76–126).

Ugarit was situated between two cultural areas, one using cuneiform writing and the other alphabetic scripts. The dual cultural influences are reflected in the development of Ugarit's alphabetic cuneiform script. Three is no apparent relationship between the alphabetic order and the graphical notation of the underlying sound system (Windfuhr 1970). C. H. Gordon (1970) has advanced a theory that alphabets in general, ranging as they do from 22 to 30 letters, are a result of both the acrophonic principle and a need to list the days of the lunar month. It may be objected, however, that there seems to be no real relationship between the original meanings of the letter names and the names of the calendar days. On the other hand, a relationship between astronomy and the alphabet was already proposed in ancient times (Driver 1954: 128). On the suggested relationship between the alphabet and the moon, see M. Eliade, *Patterns in Comparative Religion* (Cleveland/New York, 1963) 178, and the literature cited there.

Theories of astronomical influence on the alphabet

Early views of the development of Hebrew orthography are summarized in the grammars (G-K, §§5, 7) and by Cross and Freedman (1952: 2–6). Cross and Freedman's proposal (1952: 32–34) is that Hebrew writing, like Phoenician, was strictly consonantal until the 10th century B.C.E. The evolution of *matres lectionis* cannot be explained as a development from historical spellings but was a borrowing from Aramaic in the 9th century. Letters indicating vowels first were used to represent long vowels at the end of the word and later came to indicate internal vowels. *Matres* are fully developed in final position in the Moabite Mesha inscription, ca. 835 B.C.E., having been foreshadowed by earlier examples, e.g., the seal *lšmʿyhw*. The evidence of the Samaria ostraca is discussed by I. Kaufman (1966). Fitzmyer (1979: 64–66) provides a thorough survey of the debate over the thesis of Cross and Freedman, citing the dissenting views of Goodwin (1969), Garbini, Tsevat, and Segert, and giving a full listing of the literature. In his view, despite the corrections offered by Bange (see below), the thesis is valid.

The development of *matres lectionis*

Bange (1971) disagrees with Cross and Freedman. He argues that vowel letters entered Hebrew 300 years later. They began to be used, in his view, at the end (final position) and inside of the word (medial position) at the same time. Three periods are distinguished.

1) There was a period when spellings were entirely consonantal, with no diphthongs indicated anywhere in Northwest Semitic. 2) Next came a semi-consonantal stage, from the end of the 10th to the 7th century, during which *h*, *w*, and *y* indicated offglides in accented, open, long syllables, and when ʾ represented a glottal stop in accented, open, short syllables. Finally, 3) Aramaic and Hebrew, by 600 B.C.E., were written with vowel letters in medial and final positions by analogy with historically spelled forms where ʾ, *h*, *w*, and *y* once had a consonantal function.

Grintz (1972: 76–79) attempts to argue from a traditionalist point of view that *matres* are as old as the script itself and that the masoretic writing reflects the original situation, but his evidence from Ugaritic *ʾa*, *ʾu*, *ʾi* is not necessarily applicable to Hebrew. Sarfatti (1982), in a detailed survey of the grammatical and lexical significance of the extra-biblical inscriptions, also takes issue with the position of Cross and Freedman (1952) that medial vowel letters are not to be found during the First Commonwealth. He argues that, while internal *matres* are not frequent, they nevertheless do exist, as in the Siloam tomb inscription, *ʾrwr* (*ʾārûr*) 'cursed,' and in the Arad ostracon, *hbqydm* 'entrust them,' and *hʿyr* 'the city.' Note also a study by Murtonen (1974) and Zevit's monograph (1980) on *matres* in ancient Hebrew epigraphs.

The recent discovery of early writing from Izbet Sartah (biblical Eben Ezer?) provides a missing link in the evolution of the alphabet. This inscription is the oldest abecedary yet found and contains about 85 letters in the proto-Canaanite script. The order of the alphabet is interesting: the letter *zayin* follows *ḥet*, and *ʿayin* follows *pe*, as in Lamentations 2, 3, and 4 (see *Jerusalem Post*, Jan. 25, 1977). Analyses of this discovery have been written by Demsky (1977), Kochavi (1977), Dotan (1982), and Naveh (1982: 36–37). Naveh thinks this inscription was scratched by a semi-literate person who gave up writing an abecedary and etched a conglomeration of random letters. There is now opinion that the Gezer jar signs predate the paleo-Sinaitic.

Newly discovered alphabets

Further studies on writing include Pardee (1978) and Aharoni (1981) on the Arad inscriptions (paleographic discussion and tables, *ibid.*, 128–40); Vattioni (1969–78), Hestrin and Dayyagi-Mendeles (1978) and Herr (1977, doctoral dissertation) on ancient seals; Shermon (1966) on *matres* down to 135 C.E.; general surveys by Sirat (1968a) and J. Naveh (1971, 1979, 1982). Drinkard (1980, doctoral dissertation) treats the subject of vowel letters in pre-exilic Palestinian inscriptions.

The development of the use of *alef* as a *mater* in the middle of a word at Qumran and in rabbinic documents is traced by Qimron (1974–75). At Qumran, primarily in the Isaiah scrolls and the Copper Scroll, the medial *alef* indicates *a* or *e* after or before *yod* or *waw*. In Christian and Samaritan Aramaic this usage becomes more prevalent, but in Palestinian rabbinical texts this use of *alef* is rare. Freedman and Ritterspach (1967) have also discussed the *alef*.

Scripts and *matres lectionis* at Qumran

A doctoral dissertation by Mathews (1980) deals with the paleo-Hebrew Leviticus scroll from Cave 11 of Qumran. He dates the 15 fragments at 100 B.C.E. Post-exilic orthography is studied on the basis of 8 representative exemplars from Qumran. Mathews concludes that there are four spelling systems: 1) the conservative, 2) the proto-rabbinic, 3) the proto-Samaritan, and 4) the Hasmonean. Tov (1978–79) has discussed the textual nature of the Leviticus scroll.

Scribal traditions at Qumran are treated by Siegel (1971, 1972, 1974, 1975), who compares them with talmudic and masoretic practice. His conclusions are summarized below in the section on Qumran in chapter 2. Cross (1961) and R. S. Hanson (1963), as noted above, both discuss the development of the script in the period of the Second Commonwealth.

The development of the Samaritan script is surveyed by Purvis (1968: 18–69). Menachem Cohen (1975–76) disagrees with the conventional view that the Samaritan orthography is "full" and typical of the late Second Commonwealth. A careful examination convinces him that in many instances there are "defective" spellings, suggesting that a "conservative" tradition is here represented. There may have been two simultaneous traditions, the "full" writing, characteristic of 1QIsa[a], and a "conservative, defective" tradition, the evidence for which appears only later in the masoretic text. Many phenomena of the defective spelling system indicate that there was another concurrent dialect which differed from the Tiberian. Because of the multiplicity of contemporary pronunciations, scribes hesitated to use a full orthography if all dialects did not agree.

The Samaritan script

Birnbaum's *The Hebrew Scripts* (1971b, 1972) is a major contribution. In these volumes about four hundred examples of Hebrew writing are collected, from what is termed Paleo-Hebrew down to the various scripts of the present, East and West. Each letter, it is observed, developed at its own speed. The stage of development of a particular inscription or manuscript is measured by determining the ratio between the number of features linking it to an earlier model (e.g., the Gezer Calendar), and the total number of features in the inscription. Another ratio which must be considered is that between the total number of features relating to the model and the total number of letters in the inscription.

The change to Aramaic script

In his notes Birnbaum discusses the surprising change from the old alphabet to the Aramaic script. This change is particularly amazing because it resulted in the sacred literature, the Bible, being written in a "secular," borrowed script. He concludes that this was not accomplished gradually, but must have been a deliberate action, the leaders proclaiming all other forms of the script invalid. A similar development occurred in Greece when the local alphabet of Attica was replaced by the Ionic alphabet in Athens during the archonship of Eucleides (404 B.C.E.) (G. F. Moore, *Judaism*, III [Cambridge, 1940] 6).

Paleo-Hebrew script in the Second Commonwealth

Birnbaum also raises the question of the use of the Paleo-Hebrew script on the Hasmonean coins and comes to the conclusion that it was not due to an upsurge in nationalistic feeling. The old script was used because it had customarily been used on coins during the Persian period. The multiplicity of forms on the coins and the inconsistency in style indicate that this was not a living script and that the designers and coin cutters were not really familiar with it. The influence of the square script during this period is also discernible from the coins. The script on the coins of the Bar Kochba period, however, shows more Samaritan influence than Hasmonean. The Samaritan script itself, according to Birnbaum, did not develop directly from Paleo-Hebrew. On the contrary, it represents deliberate archaizing which nevertheless became accepted as the standard script in the 3rd century B.C.E. A detailed study of the coins of this period has been done by Kanael (*BA* 26/2 [1963]. 38–62). McLean (1982, doctoral dissertation) surveys the use of paleo-Hebrew in the Greek and Roman periods.

A very thorough history of Hebrew writing in all its phases has been written by W. Weinberg (1972), who in previous articles (1969–70, 1970–71) had expressed his independent views on these matters. He has also taken issue with the decisions of the Academy for the Hebrew Language (*LLA*, 1970, No. 206) on the writing of unpointed Hebrew. Weinberg (1972) traces the inconsistencies in the Academy's decisions which have persisted despite various attempts to establish rules for *plene* and defective writing. Numerous suggestions for simplifying the printing of Hebrew, in addition to proposals for transposing it into the Latin alphabet, are thoroughly covered. A series of articles (1975–80; *HUCA*, vols. 46–50) traces in depth the history of Hebrew *plene* writing and the various

Views on current plene writing

proposals of the Hebrew Language Academy. These have been collected in Weinberg (1985a).

Modern technological needs for a transliteration system and a "computer-compatible" Semitic alphabet are the basis of a study by Goldman, Smith, and Tannenbaum (1971). Landmann (1976) argues strongly for reform of the Hebrew alphabet, calling for vowels as segmental graphemes, not written above or below the line; the removal of under-differentiation and ambiguity; and the use of lower-case or small-sized characters, as in Latin or Greek. His polemic also contains material on the history of alphabet reform. Another study by Minkoff (1975) deals with the diachronic evidence offered by Hebrew cursive writing. W. Weinberg (1973) studies common features and failings of various systems of transliteration of Hebrew and proposes a universally-accepted model.

Engel and Sirat (1982) describe a method of analyzing and comparing scripts involving magnification and geometric analysis. This methodology is described in detail in the book by Colette Sirat, *L'examen des écritures: l'oeil et la machine* (Paris, 1981).

HEBREW AND ITS COGNATE RELATIONSHIPS

Hebrew and its cognates: general treatments

A general bibliography of Hebrew linguistics has been compiled by Hospers (1973), and there is much useful information in Moscati (1964). General surveys include Rabin (1970a: 304–16) and Waldman (1975a). General treatments, including a discussion of Hebrew and its cognate relationships, are: Blau (1968a, 1970a, 1971b, 1972b, 1976a); Brovender (1971); Garbini (1960); Gessman (1967); H. L. Ginsburg (1970); Goshen-Gottstein (1965a, 1965b); Grande (1972); Harris (1939); Kuryłowicz (1949, 1961, 1973a); R. Meyer (1953, 1960, 1964); Moran (1961); Moscati (1964); Murtonen (1967); Polotsky (1964a); O'Leary (1923, reprinted 1969); Rabin (1963b, 1971b); Rosén (1956a: 1–56); Schlanger (1967); Weingreen (1959); M. Greenberg (1965). Rabin (1982) surveys recent Israeli research on Biblical Hebrew linguistics. Faber (1980, doctoral dissertation) treats genetic sub-groupings of the Semitic languages.

Theories of unitary language origin

Hebrew is generally considered to be part of the Northwest Semitic group of languages. A number of attempts, however, have been made to find more far-reaching affinities. Jacobowitz (1968) argues for a unitary origin of languages, using Biblical Hebrew as his starting point. The lexical relationships he proposes are far-reaching indeed, e.g., *ʾbh* 'desire,' Japanese *aibo* 'yearn,' Korean *won* 'desire,' and Finnish *ahneus* 'lust for gain,' while Hebrew *tôʿēḇāh* 'detestable thing' is equated with Polynesian *taboo*. There is great erudition here but no system or convincing results. There are many *ad-hoc* hypotheses aimed at equating roots between which a clear relationship does not exist. Fishkin (1976) unscientifically proposes onomatopoeia as a universal basis for language, and M. Fraenkel (1970a) theorizes that III *h* roots originally had a consonant. Thus, based on the analogy of Latin *rex* and French *roi* 'king,' Hebrew *peh* 'mouth' can be equated with Latin *bucca*, and Hebrew *pōh* 'here' becomes cognate with Latin *pagus* 'village.' Hebrew can then be related to the Indo-European family.

With more attention to methodology and to the linguistic literature, S. Levin (1971) also attempts to prove that there are affinities between the Semitic and Indo-European language groups. He is concerned less with lexical items than with structural elements. Those which he finds common to Hebrew and Greek are, for example: the prefix *ti-* and the stereotyped presence of the pronoun before the verb in Greek, *se chre* 'you need,' and Latin *te pudet* 'you are ashamed'; the feminine ending in Hebrew, *-āh*, and Greek *-o*, *-e*; the Hebrew dual *-ayim*, *-ayin*, and Greek *-oiin*; Hebrew stative verbs in *-ēʾ* and Latin verb stems in *-ē*, e.g., *yārēʾ* 'he is afraid' and Latin *ueretur* 'he is afraid.' A recent study by Levin (1975) compares Greek occupational terms and Semitic counterparts, e.g., *lēwî* 'Levite' and *laios* 'people.' These affinities are considered by Levin to be due to some early contact. It is not clear, however, whether we have real affinity, borrowing, or chance resemblances. Brunner (1969) has also explored this area by collecting common Semitic and Indo-European roots. Latin-Hebrew affinities are treated by Avisar (1973).

Suggested Hebrew and Greek affinities

Possible Hamito-Semitic relationships are discussed in various studies: Marcel Cohen (1947); Helmann (1949); Thacker (1954); A. Gardiner (*Egyptian Grammar* [London, 1957] 2–3); Polotsky (1964a, 1964b); the symposium edited by J. and T. Bynon (1975); Vergote (1975) and W. Müller (1975) in the same symposium; Hodge (1971); Hospers (1978); and Newby (1972), who deals with the dependent pronouns. As described by Polotsky (1964b), Erman in 1889 was impressed by the resemblance of the Egyptian old perfective or pseudo-participle paradigms to the Semitic perfect and to the Akkadian permansive (stative). The functions, however, are not identical. Polotsky rejects the claim that the moods of the Semitic or Hamito-Semitic preformative conjugation can be correlated with the Egyptian *sḏm.f*. The claim that "imperfective" *sḏm.f*

Hamito-Semitic affinities

is the Egyptian representative of the "Afro-Asiatic present" is dubious, because the existence of "imperfective" *sḏm.f* is doubtful.

Lexical affinities between the Hamito and Semitic groups, however, have been sought and found by Rabin (1976b, 1977a). He draws upon languages such as Somali, Galla, Iraqw, Moca, Haruro, Mogogodo, and Mocha, and compares Hebrew *gôy* 'nation' and Somali *gob* 'one of noble birth' and Rendille *gob* 'family.' In the second study, Rabin draws upon the work of I. M. Diakonov, *Semito-khamitskiye yaziki* (Moscow, 1965), and relates Hebrew *pāḏer* 'fat' to Galla *furda* and *šannēn* 'teach diligently' to Daffo *sun* 'know.' The importance of this connection, according to Rabin, is that there is no need for an etymological development from *šnn* 'be sharp.'

The common elements of Semitic languages

Proto-Semitic, or Common Semitic, is a term which refers to the ensemble of elements that can be traced back from changes in the attested dialects and which may be regarded as the common property of Semitic in its earliest phase. It cannot be established, however, that this theoretical construction corresponds to any historical situation; but it does serve as a useful tool for measuring the distance of a particular element from the prototype (Moscati 1964: 1–17). Criteria for classifying a language as Semitic are discussed by Goshen-Gottstein (1965b: 869–72). Sekine (1973) and Hetzron (1974) discuss the division of the Semitic languages.

Migrations and language development

Various models have been proposed to account for the dialectical differences attested in the historical Semitic languages. Bauer and Leander, writing in 1922, assumed that Hebrew was a fusion of an indigenous Canaanite language and newer West Semitic elements brought in by invaders (Rabin 1963b: 104; 1970a: 312–13), and they were followed by Birkeland in 1940 and Driver (1936, 1969). R. Meyer (1960) holds that the *qaṭal* and *yaqṭulu* systems have different origins and represent a mixing of different dialects which took place before the entry into Canaan. The *Mischsprache* interpretation has been criticized by Goshen-Gottstein (1965a: 44). A. Bendavid (1967: 14–59) accounts for Aramaisms in biblical writing as a stylistic device used by the authors for variation. Sekine (1973), however, assumes that there were two migrations, Amorite and Aramean, both of which influenced developments in Hebrew.

Proto-Semitic features in Hebrew

Archaic features in Hebrew stemming from Proto-Semitic are enumerated by Garbini (1960: 185–86). Among these are the Qal passive, the prefixes *b* and *l* with the sense 'from,' the cohortative and jussive modes, *-t* as the indicator of the 3f.s., *-āh* as the adverbial marker, and the pronoun *ᵓānōḵî* 'I.' Later innovations are the assimilation of /ġ/ and /ᶜ/, /ḫ/ and /ḥ/, the tendency to assimilate /n/, the partial reduction of diphthongs, the change from 3f.s. *-t* to *-āh*, the *nota accusativi ᵓēṯ*, which follows upon the loss of case endings, and, later, the spirantization of /bgdkpt/.

A geographic model for linguistic diffusion

Rabin (1963b), rejecting the idea that successive invasions of different ethnic groups speaking different languages can account for the linguistic development of Hebrew, follows Friedrich, who proposed that the Canaanite dialects go back to Proto-Northwest-Semitic without an intermediate link, but that linguistic innovations and the formation of isoglosses are due to contact with other groups. Rabin divides the Semitic area into three zones: 1) the north, marginal zone: Palestine-Mesopotamia, via Ugarit (the Fertile Crescent); 2) the south marginal area: the Ethiopian group on the African mainland; and 3) a central axis: the Arabian peninsula and the Syrian home of Aramaic. He uses a geographical model to explain several examples of linguistic diffusion, originating at a center and radiating along a geographic axis. For example, the reduction of the original tertiary opposition *š/ś/s* to a binary opposition seems to have originated in the northwest corner, proceeding in time to South Arabia. The reduction of the original tertiary opposition *yaqṭul/yaqaṭṭal/qaṭala* to a binary opposition moves on a northwest to southeast axis, appearing earliest in Phoenician and Aramaic and finally reaching Arabic some time after the middle of the first millennium C.E.

Rules for diachronic change

Malone (1971) has proposed a model to account for different forms of segholates in Hebrew and Aramaic. If the traditional rules for diachronic change from a Proto-Semitic form are listed for both Hebrew and Aramaic, it can be seen that there are differences in the order of application of these rules. The differences in sequence account for different stem shapes in both languages. Changes occur across dialect lines, but not in a linearly consecutive manner. However, Malone also entertains the possibility of another model which could account for these phenomena. This model sees the changes as occurring in the common ancestor of the languages being compared.

Models for explaining linguistic differentiation

Blau in several studies (1968a, 1971–72a, 1972b) rejects any possibility of tracing the differences in the dialects back to a prehistoric Proto-Canaanite. In his view, parallel development is a model which also can account for these variations, especially since there does not seem to have been a single center of origin and a wide geographical area is involved. Both parallel development and mutual contact can explain certain changes in modern Arabic dialects, and Blau considers these instructive for the earlier development of the Canaanite dialects (1969). Canaanite is not to be located at the beginning of the process, when the languages were becoming differentiated, but at the end. At the beginning the dialects were different and became closer through contact, until Canaanite was created (1971–72). A more recent article (1978d) sums up these views. Blau contends that the "wave hypothesis," that is, a model that involves contact and parallel development, is more convincing than the family tree model. He does admit, however, that the *yaqṭulu* conjugation might be part of the verb system of Proto-Southeast-Semitic and even of Proto-Semitic.

Akkadian and Hebrew

Gelb (1969) has presented a reconstruction of Akkadian, and his work is reviewed by Bubenik (1973) and Blau (1970–71). Some of his observations are relevant for Hebrew. It is generally held that *-t* is the original feminine marker, and the anatyptic vowel *-a* developed secondarily. Gelb, however, contends that *-a* is the primary gender marker, lengthened in the plural, with the *-t-* as a secondary element, that is, a consonantal glide introduced to prevent the occurrence of two contiguous vowels, e.g., *kalb-a(t)u-m*. The basic masculine:feminine contrast is expressed by u:i/a. Intervocalic *-t-*, when used in the Akkadian pronouns *šuāti*, *šiāti*, in which the final *i* is a secondary marker of the oblique case, must have been popularly understood as a marker of the objective case. Gelb suggests that this may account for the development of the West Semitic *nota accusativi* *ʾēṯ* (Gelb 1969: 87). Another point made by Gelb is that each morpheme has only one function, and that to arrive at this stage, the Semitic languages underwent an agglutinative phase. Blau (1980b) contends that the change of final *-aṯ* in the feminine singular to *-āh* is the result of parallel development within the Semitic languages.

The grouping of Semitic dialects

The 60 to 70 identifiable Semitic dialects are normally arranged in three subgroups (putting aside the Semitic-Hamitic question): East Semitic (Akkadian), Northwest Semitic (Canaanite, Aramaic), and Southwest Semitic (Arabic, South Arabic, Ethiopic). Polotsky (1964a: 109–11) traces the development of the relationship between East and West Semitic. With the recognition by Haupt in 1878 of the affinity of Akkadian *iparras* to Ethiopic *yĕqaṭṭel*, and with the speculation about the relationship of Hebrew *waw*-conversive to Akkadian *iprus* (preterite), the two systems are now understood as closer together than once thought. Speiser (1964a: 115) concurs with this general assessment, but dissenting views on the relationship of East and West Semitic have been expressed by Marcel Cohen and Klingenheben and Rundgren (*WHJP* 1: 358, n 29).

Blau (1972b: 15) and Goshen-Gottstein (1965b: 875) present somewhat different diagrams of relationships and affinities.

A comparative model for Semitic verbal systems

Goshen-Gottstein (1969b) uses a grid system to diagram the relationship between the East and West Semitic verbal systems, with their various stems and infixes. Along the top of the grid the following stems are arranged: *D*, *Š*/*H*, *N*, *T* (infix-t), and on the vertical axis are *d* (*Piˁel*), *l* (lengthened stems) and *m* (modified forms). The horizontal line corresponds to Common Semitic, and the vertical line presents formulations which are only found in West Semitic. Goshen-Gottstein observes that the place and function of the *d* in West Semitic has been changed from that of the *D* in East Semitic. Along the horizontal axis there is a close relationship between form and function but not along the vertical. This indeterminancy is a West Semitic characteristic. The *d* in West Semitic may have served as a kind of "archepattern" for the development of other forms added to the axis, the *l* and the *m*. Goshen-Gottstein now (1985b) offers his more recent reflections on this subject.

A theoretical discussion of the problems of language grouping and the identification of foreign borrowings can be found in the collection of essays by J. Greenberg (1963: 35–85). Fronzaroli (1973) discusses the current situation by the application of statistical analysis to the study of isoglosses between language families, including Semitic.

The common Semitic lexicon and the original home of the Semites

Studies on the Common Semitic lexicon by Fronzaroli (1975) and Tyloch (1975) have shed some light on the cultural situation of the Semitic peoples before the differentiation of groups and languages. Common terms for herbs, animals, and geographic areas provide clues. The results indicate that hoe cultivation had already been superseded by a plow technology when the differentiation took place. The word for 'desert' is not common to the Semitic languages. This and other evidence strongly indicate that the Semites did not emerge from the desert. One of the early views was that the original home of the Semitic peoples was in Arabia, in a nomadic context. Other views, based on Hamitic-Semitic affinities or on the biblical account, are that the original home was either Africa or Armenia (T. Nöldeke, *Encyclopaedia Britannica*, 11th ed., 1911, vol. 24: 620). The common Semitic geographical terms suggest an area consistent with the features of the Syrian coastal plain. Because of the common terms suggesting settled agriculture, the nomadic origin of the Semites must also be reconsidered.

Rabin (1975) applies lexico-statistics, also called glottochronology, to the problem of dating the differentiation of the various Semitic dialects. In this study he follows the example of Morris Swadesh who proceeded on the theoretical assumption that items of vocabulary are replaced at a fixed rate. Rabin's results, admittedly tentative, suggest that Hebrew became separated from Ugaritic at about 1900 B.C.E., from Aramaic or Syriac around 1700, but from Akkadian as early as 3250, and from Arabic around 2400. The evidence suggests that around 2000 Northwest Semitic was one language and that Proto-Canaanite did not include Ugaritic. Critiques of these statistical methods are discussed by Fronzaroli (1973). Diakonoff (1975) treats root structure in Proto-Semitic.

Lexico-statistics

PHONOLOGY

General summaries of Hebrew phonology can be found in the standard grammars: G-K; Bauer-Leander (1922); Jouön (1923, reprinted 1965); O'Leary (1923, reprinted 1969); Moscati (1964: 22–70; bibliography 176–79); and Blau (1976a). Other studies include: Grande (1969, 1972); Murtonen (1966, 1967); Harris (1939); Rabin (1960a, 1960b, 1971a); Rosén (1953, 1961); D. Gutman (1970 [doctoral dissertation]; 1973); Kutscher (1982: 12–30); Kuryłowicz (1961, on vowel gradation; 1973a).

General summaries of phonology

One of the problems which has received much discussion but which remains unresolved is the question of the distinctiveness in Hebrew of /š/ and /ś/. Rabin (1963b: 107–8) has interpreted the reduction of an original tertiary opposition, š/ś/s, in terms of linguistic geography. Harris (1939: 33–36, 40–41, 62–64), basing his conclusions on Egyptian transcriptions from different periods, has concluded that /š/ and /ś/ were distinguished, at least in the Jerusalem dialect. Earlier transcriptions have *š* for Hebrew /š/, e.g., *ȝwšȝmm* 'Jerusalem.' Later Amarna letters from Jerusalem (in Akkadian), however, have *s* for etymological /š/, e.g., *u-ru-sa-lim*, *la-ki-si* 'Lachish,' but *š* for etymological /ś/, *ša-te-e* 'field.' This evidence is not unambiguous, for *la-ki-ši* is also attested (Brovender 1971). Moran (1961: 59) does not accept the view of Harris, who regards the anomalies in the representation of /š/ and /ś/ as

The /š/ś/ question

reflecting a complicated and unparalleled development. He tends instead toward the view of Goetze (*Language* 17 [1941] 127–38), that the anomalies are due to the unique syllabary used by the Jerusalem scribe. Moran (1975: 152) has written further on this problem, noting that the Jerusalem scribe's practice was unique in the Amarna correspondence. Moran suggests (1975: 155–56) that there are many Assyrianisms in his language, and that he came south in the service of his master, Abdi-Hepa, king of Jerusalem, from somewhere in Syria, along the border between "Reichs-akkadisch" and "Canaanite-Akkadian." If one holds this view, then, the Jerusalem letters cannot clarify the problem of the local dialect of Jerusalem, let alone that of other places and periods.

Gumpertz (1953: 33–50) has denied that there was any distinction between *š* and *ś* prior to the Middle Ages. The later articulation of orthographic š as [š] was, in his view, influenced by sound shifts in Germany in the 13th century C.E. or may have been due to Crusader contact with the Arabs. The articulation of *ś* as [s] in the Hebrew reading of medieval French and Spanish Jews (Gumpertz 1953: 1–32; Garbell 1954) is, as he interprets it, a reversion to an earlier situation. We may also compare the similar view of Tur-Sinai (1954–59, *Halashon*, 39, n 3), who denied the articulation [š] in Biblical Hebrew, Canaanite, and early Aramaic.

/š/ /ś/ and /s/ in the biblical rabbinic and medieval periods

The development of the distinction between *š* and *ś* may not be as late as proposed by Gumpertz, but one must note the many rabbinic homilies which make no distinction between historic /š/, /ś/, and /s/ (see below, chap. 2, on MH phonology). Rabin (1965: 19) suggests that in the early biblical period *š* and *ś* were distinguished in living speech even though the same orthographic symbol was used for both. A parallel would be the use of orthographic *z* in Old Aramaic for both /z/ and /ḏ/, and *š* for /š/ and /ṯ/. However, it should be noted that Psalm 119, possibly a later work (A. Hurvitz 1972a), mixes etymological *š* and *ś* in its acrostic (vv 161–68).

Garbini (1971) approaches the problem by positing three fricatives, /ṯ/, /s/, and /š/, for the earliest period. The last of these was articulated as [s], while the second may be considered [s_x]. The emergence of the [š] articulation is an innovation found not earlier than the first half of the first millennium B.C.E. It is significant that, in the earlier period, the Greeks chose the Phoenician symbol *š* to express [s]. Some biblical puns, it might be observed, suggest that /š/ and /ś/ were not distinct; compare Isa 5:7; Jer 20:7; and Qoh 7:5–6. It may be objected, however, that a pun can be effective even without total phonetic identity. The sibilants are treated in a doctoral dissertation by L. Shehadeh (1968). The views of Garbini (1971) have been challenged in an article by Beeston (*JSS* 22 [1977] 50–57) on the Proto-Semitic phonemes /s/, /ś/, and /š/. Blau (1977b) argues that /ś/ is original in Hebrew and Proto-Semitic. The subject is also treated in a masters thesis by H. Nathan (1972).

The coalescing of /ḫ/ and /ḥ/

The early coalescence of the /ḫ/ and /ḥ/ phonemes is generally accepted (Harris 1939: 40–41; Moran 1961: 49; Moscati 1964: 40). It has been held by some that distinctions between /^{c}/ and /ǵ/, /ḫ/ and /ḥ/ were maintained down to the time of the Septuagint, although the evidence is not conclusive. Wevers (1970), for example, claims to have found a consistent pattern. In a study of 318 Old Testament names, he has observed a distinction between original /ḥ/, represented as a zero-element, and /ḫ/, often represented by Greek *chi.* This holds true in 200 of the 318 cases, and Wevers concludes that the distinction was in effect down to the 2nd century B.C.E., the time of the Old Greek translation. Rabin (1965: 15) is more non-committal.

Egyptian transcriptions as evidence

Egyptian transcriptions of Canaanite place-names have been treated as important evidence for the pronunciation of Canaanite and Hebrew consonants. We have already seen some of the discussion regarding /š/ and /ś/. The main evidence comes from the Execration Texts (20th–19th centuries, B.C.E.), the list of conquered cities of Thutmose III (ca. 1468–1436 B.C.E.), three lists of conquered cities of Seti I (ca. 1303–1290 B.C.E.), Papyrus Anastasis I from the reign of Ramses II (1290–1224 B.C.E.), and the list of cities conquered by Shishak (ca. 924 B.C.E.). Basic studies in this area have been done by W. F. Albright, *The Vocalization of the Egyptian Syllabic Orthography* (AOS 5; New Haven, 1934); J. Simons, *Handbook for the Study of Egyptian Topographical Lists Relating to Western Asia* (Leiden, 1937); and W. F. Edgerton, "Egyptian Phonetic Writing" (*JAOS* 60 [1940] 473–506). Albright contended that the Egyptian foreign office developed a system for consonant correspondences which was most consistent in the period of Ramses II and then rapidly fell apart. Simon and Edgerton differ with his conclusions. A reexamination of this material by David Dorsey (in a term paper done in a course at Dropsie College, Philadelphia) leads to different conclusions. While mimation is preserved in the Execration Texts, it vanishes from the lists of Thutmose. Case endings are found in lists from the time of Thutmose, becoming irregular in Seti's time, and vanishing by the era of Shishak, replaced by *ʾi.* Therefore it appears that mimation disappeared between the 19th and the 15th and the 13th centuries [evidence cited with permission of the author].

The Egyptian transcriptions reveal something about Egyptian as well as about Semitic, and care must be taken in interpretation. For example, *g* is generally rendered by a voiceless velar, *k*; *d* is rendered by *d*, *t*, or *ṯ*; *z*, *ẓ*, *ṣ* are rendered by Egyptian *ḏ* = [dj]; *l* appears as Egyptian *ꜣ*. It is significant that *ḥ* and *ḫ* are distinguished, as are ᶜ and *ǵ*, even where the Canaanite script shows no differentiation. This may be due to the influence of Ugaritic, where these letters are distinct in the script, or to direct hearing by the Egyptians. Canaanite *samekh* (*s*) is represented by *ṯ*. It has been suggested that this may have been realized as a palatal or prepalatal stop (like [tʸ]) or an affricate, like [tˢ] (T. O. Lambdin in a personal communication to McCarter, 1975: 98, n 83).

Accent change and ấ > ṓ

The *ā* > *ō* change in Canaanite dialects is exemplified by the well-known Amarna glosses, for example: *ḫu-mi-tu* 'wall' (EA 141: 44), Hebrew *ḥōmāh*, from **ḥamītu* (read *ḥōmiyyôṯ* for *homiyyôṯ* in Prov 1:21; Phon. *ḥmyt*, Ug. *ḥmyt*); and *ru-šu-nu* 'our head' (EA 264: 18) from **raʾšunu*. Ugaritic does not show this change, a fact that leads Blau (1968a: 36) to argue that it cannot be traced to Proto-Semitic but must have been developed independently in later dialects. Blau is reiterating an earlier view (cf. Harris 1939: 43–45). The change is generally thought to be conditioned, occurring only on accented syllables. Instances where *o* occurs in unaccented syllables are explained in terms of accent shift (Harris 1939: 43–44; Rabin 1965: 34–35). Rabin (1960b) has argued as well for an *a* > *o* change occurring on unaccented syllables, this *o* later coalescing with the *o* which resulted from the reduction of the diphthong *aw* or which is the reflex of original short *u*. Blau (1970a, 1976a: 30–34) rejects this and proposes five stages in stress history: 1) Proto-Hebrew: penultimate, where the syllable is open or closed, or antepenultimate, e.g., *kấhinu* 'priest,' *lašấnu* 'tongue,' where the *ā* > *ō* change occurs; 2) generally penultimate, e.g., *dabáru* 'thing,' and elision of ʾ closing a stressed syllable; 3) same as above, but with dropping of final short vowels and consequent ultimate accent, e.g., *yašī́nu* > *yašī́n* 'sleeping' > *yāšḗn*, with compensatory lengthening of the now closed vowel; 4) a general tendency to final accent, with the lengthening of open penultimate short stressed vowels, e.g., *šᵉmārấnu* 'he has preserved us'; 5) Masoretic Biblical Hebrew: addition of auxiliary vowels on consonant clusters, e.g., *málk* > *mélek̲* 'king.' A study by Dotan (1983), which finds evidence in Tiberian manuscripts of penultimate accents differing from the general norm, suggests that the accent change came much later, in the pre-masoretic centuries.

It is possible that *ā* > *ō* shifts occurred in later periods (compare the Greek transcription *labon* of Phoenician *lbn* 'white'). While this change is unconditioned, Qimron (1970–71) presents an example from Qumran Hebrew of *a* > *o* change in the presence of a liquid, e.g., *ḥnwm* (masoretic *ḥinnām*) 'in vain,' which he reads as *ḥinnōm*.

The Proto-Semitic and the Masoretic vowel systems

Attempts have been made to relate the vowels of Masoretic Hebrew to the Proto-Semitic system. As summarized by Rabin (1970a: 311), the short vowel system of Proto-Semitic, *i*, *a*, *u*, has split into three series: short *i*, *e*, *a*, *ɔ*, *u*; lengthened *e:*, *ɔ:*, *o:*; and reduced, *ə*, realized in certain circumstances as reduced *e*, *a*, *ɔ*. These changes are related to syllabic structure and individual word stress. Birkeland (1940: 55) recognizes three short-vowel phonemes with *ə* and *shewa medium* as separate phonemes. According to Harris (1941: 147), each of the reduced vowel graphemes represents an independent phoneme.

A major study by Rabin (1960a; summarized 1965: 30–33) establishes the following relationships between Proto-Semitic and masoretic vowels (compare earlier views, G-K, §§45–54): long *i*, *a*, *u* appear as *i*, *o*, *u*; short vowels are more complex; "medium" vowels (included by other grammarians among the "long" vowels) *i*, *a*, *u* appear as *e*, *ɔ*, *o*; among the "short" vowels, original short *u* appears as *u* (*qibbuts*) and *qamets qaṭan*, while *a*, *e*, *i* can go back to either *i* or *a*. This table illustrates the relationship (Rabin 1965: 33):

Proto-Semitic	Medium	Short	Reduced
i	e	i, e, a	ə, ĕ, ă, ŏ
a	ɔ		
u	o	o u	

Formulations and reformulations of Philippi's Law

Rabin formulates a general rule embracing the law of attenuation and Philippi's law. The first states that, in a closed, unaccented syllable, original *a* is represented by *i*. The second states that, in closed, accented syllables, *i* becomes *a*. Rabin reformulates both laws into an inclusive statement in three parts: a) in closed syllables medium vowels are accented, while short vowels are accented or unaccented; b) when short vowels appear in closed syllables, the original opposition of *i* and *a* is negated; and c) the vowel which emerges from this obliteration is *a* or, occasionally, *e*, in an accented syllable, but *i* in an unaccented syllable. The phonetic environment, however, may change this to *e* or *a*. The views of Malone (1972) are also relevant to this issue. While Blau (1986b) discusses the chronology of Philippi's law, Garr (1985b) denies the existence of a law of vowel dissimilation in Biblical Hebrew.

The phonetic distinction between *i* and *a* is preserved when they are represented by a medium vowel but negated when represented by a short vowel. The fact that the phonetic environment plays such a significant role, leading to a high degree of inconsistency, indicates to Rabin that we are dealing with an indefinite phoneme, /ə/, realized in several ways, *i*, *e*, or *a*.

The *shewa* medium

Rabin's analysis equates this phoneme with the *shewa medium*. Solomon Hanau in 1733 advanced the theory that the nature of this *shewa* is determined by the vowel preceding it, termed "light" or "weak." The "weak" vowel replaces a *shewa* (thus *m^e^lāḵîm* 'kings' and *mal^e^ḵê* 'kings of'; Chomsky 1952: 39–40). Rabin proposes that *shewa medium*, resulting from the reduction of an original short vowel and the cancellation of phonemic distinctions, retains its original vocalic character, even though it is a zero-realization of *ə*. Thus, /bgdkpt/ are aspirated when they follow it. However, the zero-realization of *ə* causes the immediately preceding vowel to be realized as a short vowel, thus *mal^e^ḵê* 'kings of,' which theoretically should have been **m^e^lāḵê* (following paradigm: *m^e^lāḵîm*).

J. Fellman (1975a) proposes that *ḥaṭaf-patah*, *ḥaṭaf-segol* and *ḥaṭaf-qamets* be considered separate phonemes and that phonemic status be denied to *shewa mobile*. Further studies in this area include W. Weinberg (1968) on *qamets qaṭan* structures, Yeivin (1980a) on the changing qualities of vowels with *haṭaf* and their relationship to Proto-Semitic and Dotan (1985).

Other Proto-Semitic consonants

Other works on Hebrew phonology include Cardona (1968) on the historical development of the *tsade* and Steiner (1977), who discusses the case for fricative laterals in Proto-Semitic. Steiner (1983) argues that the affricate pronunciation of *tsade* in Hebrew and Aramaic is not a late Ashkenazic development but is an ancient variant of the fricative [s] pronunciation, as in Ethiopian Semitic and modern South Arabian. Dolgopolsky (1977) discusses emphatic consonants in Semitic and (1978) treats phonemic stress in Proto-Semitic. Eilers (1978) discusses Semitic root theory.

MORPHOLOGY

General resources on morphology

A general bibliography on Hebrew morphology can be found in Moscati (1964: 179–83) and Hospers (1973: 176–282, 400–401). Surveys can be found in the standard grammars: G-K; Bauer-Leander (1922); Jouön (1923, reprinted 1965); O'Leary (1923, reprinted 1969); Blau (1976a); Moscati (1964: 71–170); Rabin (1973a); Kuryłowicz (1949, 1961, 1973a); Kutscher (1982: 30–43); and A. S. Prince (1975; doctoral disseration) on the phonology and morphology of Tiberian Hebrew.

Studies on specific topics

Treatments of more specific topics include: Corriente (1971) on plurals in Semitic; Fontinoy (1969) on the Semitic dual; Spitaler (1954) on gemination and dissimilation; Newby (1972) on the dependent pronoun in Semitic and Egyptian; Dahood (1966) on vocative *lamed* and (1970c) on the independent personal pronoun in the oblique case; Bravmann (1961) on the genetic aspects of the genitive in Semitic; Croatto (1971) on the definite article and emphatic particles; J. Gibson (1966) on stress and vocalic change; D. Gutman on morpho-phonemics (1970); Huesman (1955, 1956) and Hammershaimb (1963) on the infinitive absolute; Blau (1974a) on pronouns; Hummel (1955, 1957) on enclitic *mem*; Austel (1969) on prepositional and non-prepositional complements with verbs of motion; Solá-Solé (1961) on the infinitive; Starinin (1963) on interrupted morphemes in the structure of the Semitic word; Aartun (1974) on the morphology of nominals; Ofek (1951, masters thesis) on nouns and genders in various stages of Hebrew; Ratner (1983; doctoral dissertation) on gender problems in Biblical Hebrew; and B. Eshel (1967, masters thesis) on the morphology of proper names.

The application of structural and transformational methods

The application of modern structural methods to Hebrew is surveyed briefly by Rabin (1970a: 310). This approach was initiated by Birkeland (1940) and developed further by Harris (1941; 1951: 314–24). Goshen-Gottstein (1964) has suggested a framework for classifying basic morphological structures in Biblical Hebrew, distinguishing, for example, between continuous and discontinuous morphemes. The former class is further subdivided into free or bound, and the free morphemes classified as joinable or unjoinable (e.g., "continuous free unjoinable morphemes" are the demonstrative pronoun *zōʾṯ* 'this' and the personal pronouns).

Transformational grammar has been applied to the language of Psalms by Battle (1969). His study deals with surface and logical deep structures, categories of sentences and elements of noun-phrases, imbedded and secondary sentences. Transformational analysis has also been used by Greenstein (1974) to demonstrate that certain types of climactic parallelism use the same word in different syntactic functions.

Biliteral and Triliteral Roots

Arguments for biliteral roots

There has been considerable discussion on nominal and verbal roots which do not conform to the triliteral theory made dominant in Hebrew grammar by Judah Hayyuj (Chomsky 1967: 161; G-K, §30). There is no reason to assume that all roots were biconsonantal, but those in that biconsonantal category were assimilated, in various ways, to the triconsonantal pattern (Moscati 1964: 72–74).

A number of attempts have been made to group roots on the basis of two radicals, with a third added. Von Soden (1952, §73b) cites **p-r* 'separate, divide' with various consonants added: *pṭr, prq, prr, prs, prk, pšr.* Driver (1936: 3–8), citing earlier writers, has suggested several groupings, e.g., *gz, ks, qs/ṣ* 'cut, sever.' Some problems exist in these groupings, such as the need to etymologize in order to fit a particular root into the pattern, e.g., Arabic *kasafa* 'cut' and Syriac *ʾetkassap* 'cut himself (in prayer).' Compare Sirat (1974) on the *ʿ-r* element in verbal roots.

Root-letter compatibility

Macdonald (1966) has argued for a Proto-Semitic biliteral origin of the triliteral root. He bases his study on the earlier work of J. Greenberg (1950), who dealt with the compatibilities of various classes of consonants occurring in different root positions. In positions I and III, identical or homo-organic consonants will generally not occur. In positions II and III homo-organic consonants will not occur, but identical ones will. There are some exceptions, e.g., Akkadian *ḫašāḫu*, Aramaic *ḥšḥ* 'need.' Positions I and II, requiring the closest juncture and the strictest rules of compatibility, correspond to the biliteral base. Where a breakdown of the rule occurs, there is evidence of an element added later to the root. It is not possible, however, to assign any specific meaning or semantic value to the added consonants (Moscati 1964: 74). Gevirtz (1982), however, considers the *ʿayin* prefixed to a verb to be a morpheme of specification and intensification.

This analysis of root-letter compatibility has been challenged by Schwarzwald (1973–74). Following Ornan (1971c), Schwarzwald rejects the idea that the root is the carrier of meaning, proposing instead the *base*, which is a combination of root letters and vowels in a specific morphological unit. This approach simplifies the grammatical explanation, obviating the need to establish compatibility on two levels, first on the level of the root and again on that of the morpheme. With the vowels included in the base it is possible to account for the exceptions which have been observed. A simple rule can be formulated: identical or homo-organic consonants can occur side by side when a vowel intervenes. There are also certain restrictions on consonant clusters: if totally identical consonants come together, they merge; if consonants identical in place of articulation come together, each will be articulated in a different manner, e.g., fricative and plosive. The same rules are applicable in the root and across word boundaries. Another detailed analysis is given by Kuryłowicz (1973a: 6–31), who observes (p. 17) that originally *immediate* contiguity is decisive, not vicinity, as thought by J. Greenberg (1950). In inflection these consonants can occur next to one another.

Consonant incompatibility

On the subject of consonant incompatibility, first raised in Hebrew grammar by Saadiah (Skoss 1955; Chomsky 1967: 161–68), it may be noted that the following dental and velar plosives are incompatible in Hebrew: *gṭ*, *ṭg*, *kṭ*, *ṭk*, *qt*, *ṭq*, but not *tq* and *qṭ* (Moscati 1964: 75). This fact may be of help in identifying foreign borrowings, where the rules do not apply, e.g.: Mishnaic *qaṯ* 'handle' < Akkadian *qātu* 'hand'; *qaṯedraʾ* < Greek *kathedra* 'seat'; *gēṭ* < Akkadian *giṭṭu* < Sumerian GÍD.DA 'document'; and *ṭgn* 'fry' < Greek *tēganon* 'frying pan.' These incompatibilities apply only within a root, excluding suffixes, e.g., *šôṭᵉḵā* 'your whip.'

Andersen (1970b) has treated a problem related to that of biradical roots. The non-realization of a weak consonant in certain phonetic environments, or in certain form classes (stems, *binyanim*) in some verbs, results in a biconsonantal alloroot. Andersen defines a verb which has no more than one alloroot as "strong," while a root realized by more than one allomorph is "weak." Weak roots overlap with other strong roots and their paradigms in specific circumstances and are attracted to the pattern of the strong roots. Thus *sabbûnî*/*sᵉḇāḇûnî* 'they have surrounded me' go back to the same root, *sbb*, but *yissōḇ*/*yāsōḇ* 'will surround' are alloroots, the first form behaving as if the root were **nsb* (cf. *yippôl* < *npl* 'fall'), and the second as if from *swb*. A form *tattî* (contrasted with *nāṯattî* 'I have given') indicates an alloroot **tn* (compare traditional views, G-K, §66). Andersen cites numerous Phoenician and Ugaritic verbs which are stable biconsonantals and are not made hollow as in Hebrew. Psalm 23:6, *wᵉšaḇtî bᵉḇēṯ YHWH*, 'and I shall dwell in the house of the Lord,' has a verb which is a byform of *yšb* 'dwell,' even though it follows the pattern of *šwb* 'return.' No emendations are necessary. The various patterns and meanings of *yšb*/*šwb* and *yṭb*/*ṭwb* are further discussed by A. Ahuviah (1974–75). Kuriakos

(1971, doctoral dissertation; book, 1973) treats the weak verb in Hebrew. Germinating-dissimilation is discussed by Spitaler (1954).

The Š-Causative Added to the Root

The š-causative as a root element

The *Š*-causative element has long been considered as an augment for biliteral or weak roots. The pitfalls of this approach can be seen by consulting some examples from M. Jastrow's *A Dictionary of the Targumim, of the Talmud Babli and Yerushalmi, and the Midrashic Literature* (New York, 1903), e.g., *škn* 'dwell' < *kwn* 'stand firm'; *šeleḏ* 'skeleton' < *ḥld* 'mold, rust' (contrast Zimmern 1917: 48, Akkadian *šalamd/tu* 'corpse' > **šaladdu* > *šeleḏ*). Nevertheless, further suggestions of *Š*-augmentation have been made. Soggin (1966) proposes the following: *šḥw* 'bow' < Hebrew and Ugaritic *ḥwy* 'make a gesture, bow' (see Gruber 1980: 90–91, who relates *ḥwy* to Aramaic *ḥiwyaʾ* 'snake,' giving it a meaning of 'curl up' > 'bend oneself [over at the waist]'); *šḥr* 'be black' < *ḥrr* 'be burnt'; *špl* 'be low' < *npl* 'fall'; *šqṣ* 'despise, loathe' < *qwṣ*. More recently Wächter (1971) has proposed *šḥq* 'grind' < *ḥqq* 'engrave'; *śgb* 'be lofty' < *gbh* 'be high.' Rabin (1969a) has proposed a source in Amorite for the origin of the rare Š-form in Hebrew, while Kutscher (1970: 354) considers it to have originated in Akkadian. More literature on the subject is cited by Van Zijl (1972: 21).

A Rule for Exceptions to the Paradigm

A comprehensive rule for accent, length, and openness of vowels

A study by Ornan (1964b) deals with the relationship between the theoretical and the real linguistic situation, and attempts to reduce some of the exceptions to rules. Ornan sets up the following relationships for syllables, which are generally valid for Masoretic Hebrew (compare a different classification of vowels, Rabin 1960): (*a*) A(ccented)/O(pen)/S(hort); (*b*) A/C(losed)/L(ong); (*c*) U(naccented)/O/L; and (*d*) U/C/S. The exceptions to these rules can be summarized as follows: 1) a syllable which is theoretically closed, but in reality open, can be treated as a closed syllable; and 2) an open syllable which does not behave as a theoretically-closed syllable, adapts itself to the vowel law, that is, it undergoes modification.

An illustration of the first exception is *dārômāh* 'to the south,' where the rule A/C/L in the second syllable is violated because it is open. This word, however, derives from *dārôm* 'south,' where rule (*b*), A/C/L, does apply. The opened second syllable is treated as if it were closed. (Compare also *mizrāḥ*, *mizrāḥāh* 'east, to the east.') The term "theoretically closed" can also apply to a diachronic analysis, where now-silent laryngeals and pharyngeals are treated as if they had consonantal value, e.g., *taᶜănûg* 'delight,' in which the first syllable is the anomalous *U/O/S, but which really goes back to **taᶜnûg*, that is, U/C/S. Ornan treats the segolates as if the first syllable was originally closed and long (final forms preceding the medial), e.g., **ʾārṣ* 'land,' following the rule (*b*) A/C/L. A form like *yāḏî* 'my hand,' in which the second syllable *A/O/L defies the rule, must go back to **yadiya* and was originally A/O/S (Harris 1939: 59), or it might represent an intermediate step, going back to **yadiy*, A/C/L.

For an illustration of adaptation to the vowel law, exception 2, compare *pērûš* 'commentary,' from **pirûš*. In *sippûr* 'story' the second consonant is doubled, but doubling cannot occur with gutturals, e.g., *niḥûm* 'consolation,' and the syllable remains open. In the case of **pirus* > *pērûš*, however, the first vowel has changed from short to long, thus following rule (*c*), U/O/L. Vowel changes are also listed, without explanation, in Moscati (1964: 67).

Different grammatical rules in Pre-masoretic Hebrew

These rules apply to Masoretic Hebrew, but in pre-masoretic Hebrew, different rules applied. (Compare Greek transcriptions of biblical names, *Ieremias* < **Yeremiah*, with masoretic *Yirmᵉyāhû*.) Blau (1971–72a), reviewing K. Beyer, *Althebräische Grammatik* (Göttingen, 1969), agrees with Beyer that it was due to Aramaic influence that short, unaccented vowels in open syllables were no longer pronounced in Hebrew and thus had to be lengthened. Thus, the phenomenon of pretonic lengthening came about during the Second Commonwealth, when Hebrew was spoken under Aramaic influence. Blau does reject Beyer's emphasis on the innovations brought about by Aramaic and by the Masoretes, with the attendant search for a pre-masoretic Hebrew. Pre-masoretic Hebrew has been treated in studies by Speiser (1925–26, 1932–33, 1933–34), an early dissertation by C. U. Wolf (1942), and Murtonen (1958, 1960, 1964, 1968a). Ben-Hayyim (1958, 1963) has argued for an original penultimate accent in pre-masoretic Hebrew. He supports his view by observations of close parallels between Samaritan and Qumran Hebrew (chap. 2).

Blau (1979a) evaluates divergent views on sound change: that of "autonomous" phonemics, that sound change is strictly phonetically controlled; and the opposing view that phonetic change may take place in "environments whose specification requires reference to non-phonetic morphophonemic and/or (superficial) grammatical structure." Paradigmatic resistance to sound change preserves a functionally-significant sound, like the final vowel of *ᵓattā* 'you' (m.), to distinguish it from *ᵓatt* 'you' (f.). It is not a question of the stability of the *a*-vowel in contrast to the feminine *i*-vowel. Another example provided by Blau, preceded by a theoretical discussion, concerns 1) a situation where allophones A_1 and A_2 exist, 2) a second stage where B shifts to A_1, and 3) a third stage where A_1 becomes C. According to the view of strict conditioning of sound change, A_1 must shift to C in all of its occurrences. This, however, does not actually happen. The shift $A_1 > C$ concerns only the phoneme A_1 that arose from B, but does not change A_1 which is the allophone of A_2. An illustration of this process, according to Blau, is the retention of /ǵ/ and /ḫ/ in Hebrew down to the time of the Septuagint. Besides the phonemes /ǵ/ and /ḫ/, there also existed, as a result of spirantization, the allophones [ǵ] and [*k*] (of /g/ and /k/ respectively). The latter were practically identical with the former. Later, when phonemes /ǵ/ and /ḫ/ shifted to /ᶜ/ and /ḥ/, the practically identical allophones were not affected (Blau 1979a: 11).

Qaṭal, Yaqṭal *and* Waw-*Consecutive*

The relationships of qaṭal, yaqṭol and yaqṭula

There has been considerable discussion on the evolution of the binary tense system, the prefixed *yaqṭulu* and the suffixed *qaṭal* form. The extent of the debate and its vigor can be seen from the literature cited in Moscati (1964: 131–37, 182–83) and Rabin (1970a: 311–12). Hebrew tenses are generally thought to express aspect: action completed (*qaṭal*) and action as yet incomplete (*yaqṭulu*). Blake (1951a) has argued that the Hebrew tenses also express time, and Hughes (1970) has compared them to the Greek Aorist, which expresses action without regard to its completeness or incompleteness. The problem of aspect and tense has been reexamined by Kuryłowicz (1973a: 79–93; and in another study 1973b). In his view, the comparison of aspect in Hebrew to the situation in Slavic languages is misleading and incorrect. As a general rule, existence of tense does not require the existence of aspect, but aspect does presuppose the existence of tense. In Semitic, the only opposition which is expressed by *yaqṭulu*:*qaṭala* is that of simultaneity:anteriority. The tense is conditioned by the context. From the basic opposition of simultaneity:anteriority, the two forms developed secondary and tertiary functions. Thus *yaqṭulu* can become imperfect and future, then imperative preterite and imperfective future, while *qaṭala* becomes *plusquamperfectum* and *futurum exactum*, as well as perfective preterite and perfective future. Other relevant studies are by Rundgren (1961a, 1961b, 1963), Rabin (1964b: 28–32), Kustar (1972), Bobzin (1963, 1974, doctoral dissertation).

Akkadian has a ternary tense system, including two prefix conjugations: 1) *iparras* for incomplete action, "present–future"; 2) *iprus* for completed action, "preterite"; and 3) a permansive or stative, *paris*. The last has an affinity with nouns and adjectives, and they too can take on stative suffixes (Von Soden 1952: 97–103, §§75–79). This three-fold situation has been understood by some as corresponding to Proto-Semitic, and Rabin (1963b) has visualized the reduction of the original ternary system to a binary along a geographic axis.

Akkadian as model for the tense system

It is generally held that the present–future *yaqaṭṭalu*, corresponding to Akkadian *iparras*, was discontinued in Hebrew and Phoenician because it could not be sufficiently differentiated from the intensive D-stem (Harris 1939: 49; Polotsky 1964: 110–11). Others have claimed, however, that the traces of the old form can be recognized in Biblical Hebrew, albeit obliterated by later vocalizers who failed to recognize it (Otto Rössler, *ZDMG* 100 [N.F. 25; 1950] 461–514; *ZDMG* 111 [N.F. 36; 1961] 445–51; Rosén 1969a: 213–14, 227). Thus, *yinṣôr* as opposed to *yiṣṣôr* 'will guard,' reflects the old *iparras* form. The non-assimilation of *-n-* in the first form is due to an intervening vowel. The elusiveness of such a form, however, is brought home by the difficulty of definitively assigning Amorite personal names such as *Ibassir* < **Yabaśśir* (?) to the *iparras* form. A derivation from the *D*-stem in Northwest Semitic is equally plausible and is sometimes preferred (Huffmon 1965: 82–85). R. Meyer (1958b) has claimed that the *yᵉqoṭel* form followed by personal endings in Qumran Hebrew is a survival of the old *iparras*.

Siedl (1971), following Rössler, also argues that there were in Hebrew two prefix conjugations which were distinguished by accentuation and which corresponded to Akkadian *iprus* and *iparras*. Hebrew *yiqṭol*, with accent toward the end of the word, corresponds to *iparras*, the Akkadian present–future, and *wayyiqṭôl*, with accent pushed to the beginning, is to be identified with the preterite *iprus*. As pointed out by Gelb (1952: 57), one of the marks of differentiation between the two tenses in Akkadian is accent, *i-párras* and *í-prus*. The doubling in *iparras* is secondary, following a consequence of the stressed vowel. This doubling is an orthographic means of representing the accent and the shortening of the previous vowel. The throwing back of the tone in *wayyiqṭôl* is evident only in certain defective forms, I *w/y*, II *w/y*, and III *h*.

Akkadian *ḫamṭu* and *marû* reflected in Hebrew

When in time other distinguishing morphological evidence disappeared, the *waw* was attached to the preterite. This *waw* was not the cause of the change in tense (as often erroneously taught) but was a means of preserving the throwing back of the tone and marking the distinctiveness of the form. Another marker is that the *wayyiqṭôl*, expressing the preterite or narrative past, appears at the beginning of a clause, while *yiqṭôl*, the present–future, is placed toward the end.

Siedl then links these two forms with Akkadian grammatical terms: 1) *ḫamṭu* 'fleet, quick,' expressing punctual action (Akkadian preterite, Hebrew *wayyiqṭôl*); and 2) *marû* 'fat, slow,' corresponding to the Akkadian present (Hebrew *yiqṭôl*). He proposes that the two prefix conjugations in Hebrew be called *ḥāmēṭ* and *mārēʾ*. D. Marcus (1975) in a review of Siedl's monograph suggests that better renderings would be *marû* 'long form' and *ḥamṭu* 'short form.'

Akkadian *ḫamṭu* and *marû* go back to a description of Sumerian verbs (*CAD* Ḫ (6): 71; Speiser, *WHJP* 1: 249; Marie-Louise Thomsen, *The Sumerian Language* [Copenhagen: Akademisk Vorlag, 1984], 115–123). As interpreted by Jacobsen (*MSL* 4: 21*), *marû* (Sumerian e) describes a process, while *ḫamṭu* (Sumerian d u) expresses a single, indivisible fact. Akkadian forms were placed alongside Sumerian forms which were perceived as equivalent. Further study of the Sumerian is by I. M. Diakonoff (AS 20 [1974] 99–121) and by M. Yoshikawa (*Or* 43 n.s. [1974] 17–39).

As noted by Marcus (1975), Siedl's view depends upon that of Rössler—that there were in Hebrew two morphologically distinct prefix forms. This view, however, has been challenged by Bloch (1963), Fitzgerald (1972), and Fenton (1970), who categorically deny the existence of a *yaqaṭṭal* in Northwest Semitic. The situation in Ugaritic, with a survey of the literature, is discussed in Van Zijl (1972:238–42).

Differing functions of *qaṭal* and *yaqṭulu* in Hebrew

W. Gross (1976), in his study of verb form and function, surveys the various views on the relation of *ḫamṭu*/*ḥāmēṭ* and *marû*/*mārēʾ* to the Hebrew tenses. His own conclusions are that *wayyiqṭol* is related to the suffix-conjugation, not the long form of the prefix conjugation, *yaqṭulu*. *Wayyiqṭôl* can serve everywhere that the suffix conjugation can, with the following exceptions: 1) the suffix-conjugation cannot indicate progression, and 2) *wayyiqṭôl* cannot be the first verb in a series where the time of an action must be established and further contemporary or subsequent action is indicated; the suffix conjugation is needed here. Furthermore, if two syndetic sentences have the same subject, and the second verb is intransitive, *wayyiqṭôl* must be in the second clause. In a chiasm (substantive + verb *w/wa* + verb + substantive), the second verb must be *wayyiqṭôl.* However, in sentences with a general–present content, or in statements of general experience, not only the suffix tense but the *wayyiqṭôl* form may be in the first position. Gross observes that there are many problematic usages in the book of Job and observes that careful study of the sequence of tenses removes the idea that they are chaotically used in the Bible.

Proto-Semitic as source of the tense-system

We have mentioned above that some think that the three-fold tense system of Akkadian reflects the original Proto-Semitic situation. This, however, is not universally agreed upon. Gelb (1952: 54–57) argues that nouns such as *balṭu* 'living one' are more primitive than the corresponding verbal form 'he lives' or 'he lived.' In the case of transitive verbs, however, it cannot be proven that *nādin* 'giver' or *nadānum* 'giving' is older than *iddin* 'he gave' or *anaddin* 'I give/will give.' Gelb holds that the primacy of the present forms over the preterite is evidenced by the fact that the vowel of the present, *a*, appears regularly in various stems—Gt *iptarras*, Gtn *iptanarras*, N *ipparris*, Ntn *ittanapras.*

E. Reiner (1970: 286–89) surveys various views on the primacy of the various opposing forms in the verbal system of Akkadian. Rundgren (1963) maintains that the basic opposition is binary in every Semitic verbal system. Von Soden (1959) argues for an original three-fold distinction, which was enlarged in Akkadian to a four-fold system with the advent of the *t*-perfect. Rabin (1963b: 110–11), as already observed, relates the three-fold opposition to Hebrew, where a reduction to a binary opposition occurred. Theoretically, however, one could derive all of the forms from a single basic form, **prus.* Reiner's own view is that there is an essential equivalence in the positions of the disputants which is obscured by differences in terminology and by the assumption that a theoretically primary form is necessarily prior in time. Thus, one can derive *i-parras* from **i-paras*, that is, from the *paras* base of the West Semitic perfect, but this is merely formal, not chronological. Reiner cites Aro to the effect that we are really in no position to make categorical statements about the situation in Proto-Semitic. On the development of forms from bases through apophony, see Kuryłowicz (1973a: 32–52).

Parallels to the *waw*-consecutive

Another overlapping between East and West Semitic is considered to be the verbal form used after *waw*-consecutive, formerly thought to be a shortened imperfect (cf. G-K, §49), now generally classified as a jussive. It has been identified with Akkadian *iprus* (as we have noted above) and Arabic *lam yaqṭul*, a jussive following a negative particle (Polotsky 1964: 109–11). Claims have been made for parallels to *waw*-consecutive in other dialects, in the Amarna letters from Byblos (Moran 1961: 64–65) and in Phoenician (Cross and Freedman 1952: 14). Speiser has suggested that Hebrew *waw*-consecutive is modeled after an Akkadian idiom in which the present form, *iparras*, is followed by the copula *-ma* and is employed after imperatives, statives and preterites to signify purpose. Moabite, too, appears to have this construction, e.g., *wʾbn* 'and I built' (Meshaᶜ, line 9), as well as Old Aramaic, e.g., *wʾśʾ ydy* 'and I lifted up my hand' (Zakir, *KAI*, I, 37; no. 202, A, 11; cf. G-K, §49, p. 132, n 1).

The evidence from Phoenician and Moabite has, however, been rejected by Siedl (1971: 123), following Friedlich. The Arabic parallel is also rejected. Maag (1953) has an alternate view of the origin of *waw*-consecutive, claiming that it originates in the root **han*. Thus an original **wᵉhanyiktob* becomes *wayyiḵtôḇ* (cf. Hughes 1970: 13, n 8).

The syntactic force of *waw*-consecutive

Doubts have been expressed about the syntactic force of the *waw* of *wayyiqṭôl*, some concluding that it is irrelevant (see above, Siedl 1971). Barnes (1965) regards the Hebrew verb as basically atemporal. The speaker places himself so vividly on the time level with which he begins his discourse that it becomes for him a present, and he can use either the stative *qaṭal* or the descriptive *yiqṭôl*. A. Sperber, too (1966: 591–92) has claimed that the Hebrew verb is temporally neutral and insists that the two forms be described solely in terms of morphological characteristics. Hughes (1970), as noted, sees the tenses as originally timeless or omnitemporal, requiring that the time element be indicated by other means.

Rosén (1956b), denying any syntactic significance to the *waw*, claims with others that the initial verb in a passage generally establishes the time of the action, and the second verb will relate to that action, depending on which of the two forms it is. Thus, if the sequence is *qaṭal-qaṭal*, the second is plusquamperfect. In *qaṭal-yaqṭul*, the second verb refers to a series of events which is part of, and leads up to, the initial past. In the series *yaqṭul-yaqṭul*, the first expresses incomplete action, the second present–future infactive action. The series *yaqṭul-qaṭal* indicates perfective action in the present and future. Biblical examples cited by Rosén indicate that the same relationships obtain with or without the initial *waw*. (Compare Kuryłowicz [1973a: 87–90].)

Rosén has expanded this thesis in a later paper (1969a), setting up certain tense sequences in consecutive clauses. Several groups of contrasts can be established between clauses, depending on the form of the verb and its position within the clause. But when this is done, the imperfect and the consecutive are never found in categorical opposition (Rosén 1969a: 221).

Waw-consecutive, the jussive, and the subjunctive

The traditional identification of the *wayyaqṭul* with the jussive is also rejected by Rosén in this study. He sets up two series, one with an original *-u* morpheme, including the Akkadian subjunctive, the Arabic "indicative," and the Hebrew "consecutive," and another series based upon an original zero-mood, including the Hebrew imperfect, the precative (unjoined jussive), Arabic *modus apocopatus*, and Akkadian present and preterite (1969a: 231).

The Evolution of the Tense System

Several accounts have been given of the evolution of the *qaṭal-yaqṭulu* opposition. Harris (1939: 45–49) dated the change between 1500 and 1365 B.C.E. in Phoenician, Hebrew, and Moabite. The *yaqṭulu* form ceased to carry a preterite sense, and the *qaṭala*, basically a noun form with personal endings, became the perfect active form. The short preterite *yaqṭul* was discontinued, retained only for the special use with the *waw*-consecutive. Rabin (1963b: 110–13) suggests a development which includes the replacement of *yaqaṭṭal* by *yaqṭulu* with a present–future/imperfective sense, and a coalescing of perfective *yaqṭul* and *qaṭal*. This left a binary opposition in place of an original ternary opposition. With the addition of *waw*-consecutive, each *Zeitstufe* had two syntactically-conditioned alloforms. A later stage shows the abandonment of the perfective use of *yaqṭul* (as used in early Hebrew poetry) and the loss of the modal use of *yaqṭul* (*wayyaqṭul*), except in cases of conscious archaizing. As to the replacement of one form by the other, Kuryłowicz (1973b) suggests that *qaṭal* replaced *yaqṭul* very gradually, with the Amarna letters and glosses illustrating an intermediate stage. At that transitional level *qaṭal* expresses *passé indefini* and *yaqṭul* served as *passé defini* or narrative tense.

Historical development of the *qaṭal-yaqṭulu* opposition

A somewhat more complicated reconstruction is given by R. Meyer (1960, 1966: 26–27). In his view, too, *yaqṭul*, belonging to the verbal realm, and *qaṭala*, essentially nominal, are not related. Meyer follows Bauer and Driver in positing two different geographic origins for these structures. The earliest opposition was *yaqṭul*/*qṭul*, the first having a jussive and preterite character, the second being the imperative. There then developed an indicative, the *yaqṭulu*, having a punctual present–future function, and a subjunctive, *yaqṭula*. At a later date, *qaṭal* transcended the boundaries of the nominal stative and began to be the affirmative conjugation. However, in addition to the preterite–narrative functions of the *yaqṭul*, *qaṭal* also took over some jussive functions from the *yaqṭul*. (Compare Ugaritic *ʿm ʿlm ḥyt* 'may you live forever.') When the *qaṭala* took over the perfect–preterite function, the tense system was altered along the lines already noted. *Yaqṭulu* took over the future sense of the *yaqaṭṭulu*, which then mainly disappeared. The old jussive *yaqṭul* remained, as noted, in the *waw*-consecutive.

Qaṭal as command and prophetic perfect

Regarding the jussive function of the *qaṭal*, Driver (1969) has expressed the view that *qaṭal* can express a command. His interpretation is essentially based on the speaker's subjectivity. The development is from actual to imminent: from what is, to what should be, and finally, to direct commands. Dahood (1965: xxxix, 19–20) finds numerous examples of the precative or optative perfect in the Psalms and cites earlier scholars such as Ewald, Böttcher, Eitan, Jouön, and Buttenwieser, who pointed out some examples. Ps 3:8 is an example of this usage: *kî hikkîṯāh ʾeṯ-kol-ʾōybay leḥî*, 'O that you yourself would smite all my foes on the jaw' (Dahood 1965: 15, 19–20, 22–23). There may also be an affinity with the Akkadian precative, which is formed from the preterite preceded by the particle *lū* (von Soden 1952: 105, §81). The transition of the *qaṭal*, identical in form with the Akkadian stative, to a perfect is foreshadowed in Akkadian. E. Reiner (1970: 288) cites Rowton (*JNES* 21 [1962] 233–303), who provides many examples of the Akkadian stative used this way. Fenton (1973) confirms this development in his study of the Hebrew tenses in the light of Ugaritic. Saydon (1962) has written on the conative imperfect and Williams (1972) on energic verbal forms. McFall (1982) has surveyed the history of study on the Hebrew verbal system.

Verbal Stems

The *Qal* passive is regarded by Garbini (1960: 185) as one of the archaic elements preserved in Biblical Hebrew. Medieval grammarians such as Samuel Nagrela (Hanagid; 993–1056) and Jonah ibn Janah (985–1040) recognized the *Qal* passive in such forms as *nuṭṭaš* 'abandoned' (Isa 32:14) and *luqqaḥ* 'taken' (Job 29:22). In modern times this category was again recognized by Böttcher in 1868 and by Barth in 1890 (Chomsky 1952: 89, 103; G-K, §§52e,

53u). Ugaritic studies have provided additional support for the identification of this form in Biblical Hebrew (Ginsburg 1970: 113). Williams (1970), on the basis of Amarna forms such as *tu-ul-qu* 'it (fem.) will be taken' and Ugaritic *yʾuḫd* 'it was kindled,' enumerates fifty-two examples which have been overlooked by the standard lexica. He suggests that original perfect **kutiba* became **kutaba* on the analogy of other passive perfects. Had the form developed naturally, it would have produced a **kotab*, but it was arrested prior to the lengthening of pretonic vowels. The original *u* was retained by the Masoretes by doubling the following consonant, producing **kuttab*. This is, of course, indistinguishable from the *Puʿal*. Imperfect **yuktabu* developed to *yuḵtaḇ* or *yoḵtaḇ*, which is identical with the *Hofʿal*. With the extension of the *Nifʿal* to the inclusion of a passive for the *Qal*, the *Qal* passive declined in frequency, many instances of its occurrence being overlooked. Poetry, with its tendency to preserve archaic forms, retains more of the *Qal* passives than prose. Chomsky (1970) also has dealt with this form. The vocalization of the *Qal* (or *Grundstamm*) has been studied by Aro (1964). Bicknell (1984, doctoral dissertation) treats passives in Biblical Hebrew.

The *Qal* passive

Several items in the historic development of the Hebrew verb are dealt with in a study by Blau (1971c). Following Moran (1960), who established that *yqṭla* forms in Amarna are not ventives (Amarna *yqṭla* and Hebrew cohortative), Blau contends that the Canaanite scribes had developed a chancellory language in which Akkadian, the language of prestige, and Canaanite, their native tongue, combined. In this language, even artificial features became productive. The Amarna *yqṭla* forms, expressing a voluntive–indicative aspect, correspond to the Biblical Hebrew cohortative.

Amarna *yqṭla* and Hebrew cohortative

Reviewing several theories on the emergence of the *Poʿel* and *Polel* themes of verbs with II *w/y* and II geminate roots, Blau concludes that multiple channels of development can be posited. The conjugation–form may have arisen in either class and spread to the other, or they may have arisen independently, exerting mutual influence. Bravmann (1971) argues that the *Qal* forms *qaṭᵉlû*, *qaṭᵉlah* could not have originated from a reduction of the second vowel to *shewa* (against Moscati 1964: 67), as this vowel would undergo pretonic lengthening instead. He prefers to see these forms as arising by analogy to the *Piʿel*, *qiṭṭᵉlāh*, *qiṭṭᵉlû*. Verbs with II *w* and II *y* stems are treated by M. Fraenkel (1970b).

Poʿel and *Polel* stems

There has been much discussion of the significance of the D-stem or *Piʿel* in Semitic and in Hebrew. Poebel (*Studies in Akkadian Grammar* [Chicago, 1939]) denied the usual view of the

History and function of D and *Piʿel*

D as "intensive" and proposed that the doubling of the second radical indicates plurality. Goetze (1942) has seen in the D a denominative–factitive function. Along these lines, Rundgren (1961a, 1961b, 1963) considers the vast majority of D forms as based upon verbally-derived substantives or as having a factitive significance, being a causative in relation to a state or condition expressed by stative verbs in the *Qal*. Thus the *Qal* of *qaṭal* would be understood literally as 'he has a killing' and the *D* as 'he has made a killing.'

Jenni (1968) considers the *Piᶜel* as a unitary stem in distinctive opposition to the other stems. It is neither intensive nor causative but expresses the effectuation of the *G*, that is, the intransitive *Qal* or G-stem becomes factitive through the D-stem. Ryder (1974) also considers the D to be denominative in origin and predominantly factitive in function. It derives from the nominal form, not from any other verbal stem. It is quadrilateral in structure, and it originated as one of several devices for expanding a triconsonantal root to quadriconsonantal proportions. While the *Qal* (in Ryder's terminology, B "base") places the emphasis upon the doer of the action, the D concentrates on the action itself.

Williams (1972) has a study on energic verbal forms in Hebrew, and a general summary can be found in Moscati (1964: 124; see also G-K, §52).

Original vowel patterns of *Piᶜel* and *Hifᶜil*

Blau (1971c) discusses the various suggestions offered regarding the original pattern of the *Piᶜel* and *Hifᶜil* stems: 1) *a-a-a*, 2) *i-a-a* (Ungnad) and 3) *i-i-a* (Tur-Sinai). Blau suggests that a single line of development from Proto-Semitic cannot be posited and that at least two patterns may have developed in a parallel manner. The declarative–estimative *Hifᶜil* is treated by Claasen (1971–72). Jenni (1973) studies the reflexive–passive stems in Biblical Hebrew.

Infix-t *Forms*

Infix-*t* forms in Akkadian and Hebrew

As represented in the schema of Goshen-Gottstein (1969b), infix-*t* forms are quite prevalent in the various dialects. Compare, for example, Akkadian *t*-stems which express reciprocity, separation, the durative (*Gt*), passivity (*Dt*, *Št*), the perfect with infix-*t*, connecting action to its immediate antecedents (*consecutio temporum*), and the iterative–habitative *tan*-stems (von Soden 1952: §§86, 91–94). There have been efforts to find a simple, common explanation for the syntactic effect of the infix-*t*. Jacobsen (*MSL* 4: 3*–50*) compares the infixes in Akkadian verbs with corresponding Sumerian elements and theorizes that the *t* expresses the relationship of two spheres of activity in the consciousness of the speaker. This might be the common theme underlying reciprocity or the *consecutio temporum* in the Akkadian perfect (von Soden 1952: §80d). A different view is that of Renger (*JNES* 71 [1972] 230), who maintains that the infix-*t* forms express emphasis, which explains their use in different contexts. Other works in this area are Blau (1957) and Wheeler (1971).

Yalon (1971: 76–79) has made an effort to find infix-*t* forms in both Biblical and Mishnaic Hebrew, and has argued for the existence of a *Hitpaᶜel* serving as a reflexive of the *Qal*. The verb *hiṯpoqᵉḏû* 'presented themselves for review' (Judg 20:17) has also been considered a *t*-stem of the *Qal* (G-K, §54l). Yalon (1971: 19–20) regards *ništāwāh* 'equal' (Prov 27:15) as an example of *Nitpāᶜāl*, while other grammarians treat it as a combination of *Nifᶜal* and *Hitpāᶜāl*. (Contrast G-K, §75x, where an emendation is offered.) In Post-biblical Hebrew, primarily in the midrashim, Yalon finds other examples of infixed-*t* forms, e.g., *niṯmāḵû* from *mwk*, *mkk* 'be brought low,' and *hiṯḥîl* 'trembled, was frightened,' from *ḥyl* (1971: 76–79).

Boyle (1969) concludes that infix-*t* forms were once a prominent feature of Biblical Hebrew but that later scribes failed to recognize them, assimilating them to other forms. The force of the infix is to give an intensive meaning in contexts of urgency and emotional involvement. While Garbini (1960: 130) holds that this element had long vanished from the Hebrew of the first millennium, Dahood(1965) argues for the existence of hitherto unrecognized infix-*t* forms of *mediae-waw* verbs, e.g., *histîr* (Ps 10:11), deriving it from *swr* 'turn away' and not from *str* 'hide,' and *ᵓepṯaḥ* (Ps 49:5) from *pwḥ* 'blow' and not from *ptḥ* 'open' (Dahood 1965: xxxviii, 64, 297; Waldman 1975a: 1287). In neighboring dialects the phenomenon is more evident, e.g., Phoenician *tḥtsp* 'let it be broken,' *thtpk* 'may it be overthrown,' Moabite *wᵓltḥm* 'I fought' (reciprocal, compare Hebrew *nilḥamtî*, in the *Nifᶜal*), Old Aramaic *htnᵓbw* 'they desired,' a *Hittanafᶜal* form (*KAI* I, no. 1: 2; no. 181: 11; no. 216: 14). Rainey (1971) interprets the infix-*t* forms in the Amarna letters, morphologically identical with Akkadian perfects, as West Semitic forms with reciprocal and reflexive meaning. The biblical evidence is much less promising except for a few survivals (compare *hištîn* 'he urinated,' not from *štn* but from **šyn*, with Akkadian *šiānum* 'urine.') On the basis of Ugaritic, *hištaḥawwāh* 'he bowed himself' is to be considered a Št from *ḥwy* (compare Ugaritic *tšthwy* 'she prostrates herself'). Boyle (1969; University

Microfilms, 1973) is reviewed by Ben-Asher (1975–76). He is most dubious about Boyle's attempts to prove the existence of infix-*t* forms and wonders why traditional analysis cannot account for the verbs he proposes or why the *t* cannot be original. For these reasons he rejects *ktp* 'shoulder' as having derived from *kwp*, *kpp* 'bend.'

The Hebrew *Hitpaʿel* and Akkadian correspondences

The *Hitpaʿel* form in Hebrew has been connected with the *Pōʿēl* of *mediae-ʿayin* and *waw* verbs or with the *Piʿel* (Chomsky 1952:93–95). It is primarily the reflexive of these verbs, although not always. Speiser (1955) argued that the *Hitpaʿel* corresponds to the Akkadian *Dt*, the passive or reflexive of the D-stem. In this study Speiser compared a number of atypical *Hitpaʿel* verbs which connote repeated or continuous action with Akkadian *tan*-forms which express durative or repeated action, e.g., *ittanallaka mitḫariš utirra*, '[chariots with their riderless horses] wandered to and fro,' Hebrew *umiṯhallēk bāhh* '[from roaming over the earth] and wandering on it to and fro' (Job 1:8; 2:2); *hiṯʾabbēl* 'mourn,' *hiṯʾannēp̱* 'become angry.' Goetze (*JAOS* 67 [1947] 7ff.) would derive the *Hitpaʿel* from an *n*-infix, which has a continuative force, e.g., **ya-ha-n-lik*, to which a further *t* is added. Thus, from a secondary D-stem would evolve a *Hitpaʿel.* Speiser favors a derivation from the *tan*-infix, e.g., **yahtanlik* > *yiṯhalleḵ*. Bean (1976, doctoral dissertation) studies the *Hitpaʿel* from a phenomenological point of view.

Secondary *t*-forms

The existence of infix-*t* forms is distinct from the phenomenon of secondary forms where *t* is prefixed to the root. In many cases this is due to the weakness of the first radical or of the middle one, including the geminates, e.g., *tbʿ* 'seek, demand' in Aramaic, from *bʿy* (Isa. 21:12); *tʿr* < *ʿwr* 'arouse,' as in *m^{e}ṯāʿēr ʾeṯ hāʿôlām* 'stirs up the world' (*Midrash Tehillim* to Ps 60:5); *tšš* < *ʿss* 'be weak'; *tkp* <*ʿkp*, *ʾkp*, Akkadian *ekēpu* 'follow hard upon, rest upon'; *tql* 'stumble,' Ugaritic *qll* 'fall'; *tqʿ* 'sound a trumpet' and *qwʿ*, *qʿqʿ* 'call, make noise.' We may compare the similar phenomenon of Akkadian *abālu* and *tābālu* 'be dry.' Other first radical *t*-forms, however, derive from nouns with *t*-preformatives, e.g., *rwm* 'lift up, make an offering' > *t^{e}rûmāh* 'heave offering' > *trm* 'make a heave offering.' Yannai (1974) has made a study of augmented verbs in general.

Litterae Compaginis

Summaries of traditional and modern views on *litterae compaginis*, "letters of connection," are given by Chomsky (1952: 81) and in G-K (§90). Dunash and Ibn Janah saw these letters as pleonastic. Some of the modern grammarians interpret them as remnants of ancient case endings, while others trace them to the analogical influence of the construct forms of *ʾāḇ*, *ʾăḇî* 'father (of),' *ʾāḥ*, *ʾăḥî* 'brother (of),' and *ḥām*, *ḥămî* 'father of the husband of.' Bauer-Leander explain the form with *-ô* as anticipatory, with the following noun in apposition, e.g., *bᵉnô Ṣippôr* 'his son, namely, Sippor's.' Loewinger (1961) has seen in these forms and in other similar ones occurring in the Qumran scrolls remnants of an early dialect which he calls a "lengthened dialect," e.g., *hammašpîlî lirʾôṯ* 'who looks far down' (Ps 113:6).

Theories on pleonastic *waw*

The current theories have been evaluated by Robertson (1969) in terms of form and function analysis. He concludes that in twenty-nine out of thirty-three cases *-y* is affixed to nouns or participles in apposition. This usage is related to *Nisbeh*, i.e., *raglî* 'foot soldier,' *noḵrî* 'stranger.' In some cases of *-y*, Robertson agrees with J. Barth that these mark bound structures. The affix *-w* occurs only in nouns and emphasizes the bound state. Wernberg-Møller (1958b) has also treated the pleonastic *waw*. Hoftijzer (1985) treats the function of the imperfect with *nun paragogicum*.

Taqṭul, Taqṭulu

Ginsberg (*Or* 5 [1936] 188n.) was the first to note that Hebrew, like Ugaritic, had a *taqṭulu* form for the 3m. pl. compare *ilm tǵrk tšlmk* 'may the gods protect you and keep you whole' (Harris 1939: 12). Albright, on the other hand, regards such a form as a 3 f. sing. with a plural subject, taken as a collective (Moran 1961: 63).

Does Hebrew have *taqṭul* and *taqṭulu*?

Van Dijk (1969) has gone further and claimed that *taqṭul* can be interpreted in Hebrew as a 3m. sing., citing the parallelism of *yᵉgallaḥ* 'will shave' and *tispeh* 'will destroy' (Isa 7:20). Some of his examples are ambiguous, however, e.g., Ps 42:2, *kᵉʾayyāl taʿărōḡ* 'as the hart cries out.' It is possible that this is not a masculine *taqṭul* at all. The subject may be *ʾayyeleṯ* (cf. Ugaritic *ʾylt*) with the *t* lost through haplography. Furthermore, abrupt shifts in person are often seen in biblical poetry, and the strict requirements of parallelism do not compel emendation or the recognition, in this case, of a masculine *taqṭul* (G-K, §144p; Gevirtz 1973b: 170–71). Dahood (1979a) has likewise argued for preformative *t-* in the 3m. sing. in Biblical Hebrew and in Northwest Semitic, e.g., Ebla *ti-ra-il* 'Il sees.' Some examples are Isa 32:13, *taʿăleh*, and Hos 5:9, *tiḥyeh*.

Particles

Juncture and the development of the definite article

Austel (1969) has dealt in his dissertation with prepositions and verbs of motion. Lambdin (1971a) has proposed a unitary theory to account for the development of the definite article in various dialects. He rejects the usual theory that Hebrew *ha-* followed by consonant doubling derives from an original **han* or **hal* (G-K, §35l). Lambdin regards the article as having developed from the phenomenon of juncture. A special closed juncture existed between a noun and certain preposed and postponed words, among them definite pronouns, e.g., **malku* + *ð* > **malkuðð* 'this king,' **malakūm/na* + *ʾill* > **malakum/naʾʾill* 'these kings.' With the loss of final short vowels before open juncture and the concomitant loss of case distinctions, the short vowels trapped in these constructions achieved a neutral state in *-a-*, e.g., **malakaðð*, pl. **malakīm/naʾʾil-*. Aramaic and Hebrew went their own ways, the resulting *-a-* developing into the postpositive article in Aramaic and the prepositive in Hebrew (Waldman 1975a: 1289–90).

The first extension of the article as such was probably due to the attributive adjective, e.g., *zeh*:*hazzeh* : : *tôḇ*:*haṭṭôḇ*. The junctural origin of the article may explain its absence in a construction like *d*^{e}*ḇarēnû zeh* 'this, our word,' just as the presence of the suffix as a terminal morpheme precludes close juncture.

Lambdin discusses other cases of junctural doubling, e.g., the *dagesh conjunctivum* (G-K, §§20c–f), as in Exod 21:31, *yēʿāśeh* + *lo* > *yēʿāśeh-llō* 'shall be done to him' and Ps 91:11, *y*^{e}*ṣawweh* + *lāḵ* > *y*^{e}*ṣawweh-llāḵ* 'he will give (his angels) charge over you.' The traditional explanation of *dagesh forte* in such constructions is that, while the *he* is written, it is disregarded phonetically, the two words being so closely joined as to be thought of as one. The normal rules for the *dagesh* then apply (Chomsky 1952: 22).

The emphatic force of *he*

Croatto (1971) has noted that there are passages where *he* prefixed to a noun or verb is neither a definite article nor a sign of the interrogative, e.g., *hăniglōh niglēṯî* (1 Sam 2:27) and *hărāṣaḥtā w*^{e}*gam yārāštā* (1 Kgs 21:19). These are interpreted as emphatics and are to be so rendered ('I did indeed reveal myself' and 'you have indeed murdered and taken possession'). Moreover, particles can be combined, e.g., *hălōʾ kî-m*^{e}*šāḥăḵā YHWH* (1 Sam 10:1). This is a double emphatic, not an interrogation, and might be rendered 'it is true that the Lord has appointed you' (*Metsudat David*). Joseph Kimchi clearly construed the example of 1 Sam 2:27 as a statement of corroboration (Chomsky 1952: 370). He was anticipated by Ibn Janah, who maintained that the *he* was for emphasis and verification (*Riqmah*, 6:5, ed. B. Goldberg [Frankfurt am Main, 1856] 43).

Other particles

Croatto (1971) compares Ugaritic *hl, hn, hlk*, and Arabic *hā huwa* 'it is he.' He suggests the development: *ha-* was originally emphatic or deictic, developing into a demonstrative, and finally into a determinative. Croatto accepts the traditional view that doubling of a following consonant is due to the assimilation of the *nun* or *lamed* of original **han* or **hal.* Earlier, Mirsky (1957–58) identified many instances of *h* as a word separator. Whitley (1972) has written on the particles *b* and *l*, and Pope (1949) treats the Ugaritic particles *w, p, m, b, l, k* and their relationships to Hebrew.

The syntactic force of *ʾēṯ*

The particle *ʾēṯ*, indicator of the definite accusative, has been studied from a number of points of view. Eitan (*AJSL* 45 [1928–29] 48ff.) distinguished between *ʾēṯ* 'with' and *ʾēṯ* as indicator of the definite accusative. The former he interpreted as a back formation from *yad* 'hand, side,' **yidti* > *itti* 'with me' (compare Akkadian *itti* 'with'). Harris (1939: 43) considered *ʾeṯ* in Hebrew and Moabite as having developed through syncope of *y* from *ʾiyāti*, as in Phoenician *ʾyt.* Saydon (1964) does not feel it represents any particular case, accusative or nominative. It was, in his view, used only with determinate nouns and was originally a substantive prefixed to a noun to give it emphasis. In time the emphatic meaning was lost. Rosén (1960) has compared Hebrew *ʾēṯ* with similar particles in Moabite and Aramaic in a structural study. After establishing the hierarchical positions of syntactic elements on the basis of their being closer to or more distant from the verbal root, Rosén defines types of sentences in which *ʾēṯ* is not required. It is required where position alone is insufficient to indicate function. Lambdin (1971a) interprets the evolution of the form of *ʾēṯ* in terms of junctural doubling, tracing it back to an original **iyata-*, thus **iyatammalk* > *ʾeṯ -hammalk* 'the king' (accusative). In archaic poetic Hebrew, e.g., Exodus 15, the absence of the article coincides with the absence of *ʾēṯ*.

Transformational analysis of *ʾēṯ*

The use of *ʾēṯ* with the nominative has been discussed by Chomsky (1952: 330), but his examples (Num 26:55; Jer 38:4; 35:14, showing *ʾēṯ* before passive *Hofʿal or Nifʿal* verbs suggest that it is a carryover from the original active counterpart of the passive construction, when the so-called nominative was an accusative. Andersen (1971), however, has demonstrated that the opposition 'active/passive' is not meaningful in Biblical Hebrew. In the usual transformation from active to passive, the object of the active verb becomes the subject of the passive verb. In Hebrew grammar, however, these transformations cannot be carried out without residue. There are cases, as noted, where ʾēṯ occurs before the "subject" of the passive verb, that is, the word which indicates the victim or recipient of the action of the verb, e.g., *ʾaḵ bᵉgôrāl yēḥālēq ʾeṯ-hāʾāreṣ* 'but the land, by lot it shall be divided' (Num 26:55). In certain passages the *ʾēṯ* and the noun connected with it appear superfluous, a relic, as it were, of the same clause with an active verb, e.g., *bᵉhimmōlô ʾēṯ bᵉśar ʿorlāṯô* 'when he circumcised himself, (that is) the flesh of his foreskin' (Gen 17:25; note v. 24, where the *ʾēṯ* is omitted). Andersen concludes that the position of the verb in relation to the object of its action appears to dictate whether the *ʾēṯ* is to be used. If the verb precedes, *ʾēṯ* is required. In Moabite, too, *ʾt* differentiates victim from agent only when both are specified in sequence after the verb (Andersen 1971: 14).

Dfferent functions of *ʾēṯ*

Traditional views of the use of *ʾēṯ* other than *nota accusativi* are found in the standard works (BDB 85; G-K, §§117i–m). It can function as a separator, permitting the emphasis upon a word or phrase in order to distinguish it from what precedes. It can emphasize the status of an item in a group or series (1 Sam 17:43), mark off appositional nouns or phrases (Exod 1:14), serve as a "breather" in a long list (Josh 17:11), or mark off the *casus pendens*, separated syntactically from the rest of the sentence (Ezek 44:3). Hoftijzer (1965) has made a thorough study of the functions of *ʾēṯ*, and his work has been critically reviewed by Barr (1974b). Certain changes in the use of *ʾēṯ* are carefully enumerated by Polzin (1976: 28–37) as a feature of late Biblical Hebrew, found frequently in Chronicles. These include the radically reduced use of *ʾēṯ* with pronominal suffix and its increased use before nouns in the nominative, that is, *ʾēṯ emphatic*. Comparison with other books of the Bible leads to the conclusion that these features emerged in the period of the sixth to the fourth centuries B.C.E. Wilch (1969) treats the uses of *ʾēṯ* in comparison with other temporal expressions. Izreʾel (1978–79) demonstrates the use of *ʾēṯ* in the sense of 'to, towards,' as well as 'with,' and compares Ugaritic *ʿm*, which has the same semantic range.

Additional particles: *p, l, n, w*

A significant number of students affirm the existence of a particle *p-* as a conjunctive in Hebrew, parallel to Ugaritic and Arabic (Van Zijl 1972: 101–2). Medieval commentators, such as Saadiah and Abraham ibn Ezra, compared the *waw* to Arabic *fa* (Chomsky 1952: 352, 369). Y. Ratzhaby (1980) documents the passages where *fa al-ʿaṭf* was perceived.

Lamed emphatic, identified by Haupt in 1894 (G-K, §143e), is used by the Chronicler before the last element of a list. This usage is not necessarily late or Aramaic-influenced. Dahood (1965: 143) has identified many instances in the Psalms. In later books of the

Bible its incidence increases. (*Lamed emphatic* and *vocative* are also studied by Ruiz (1975), Penar (1967), and Whitley (1975a). Whitley has also written on *lû* and *lōʾ* (1975b) and on the particle *šām* (1974). Muraoka (1969) has written a doctoral dissertation on emphasis in Biblical Hebrew and (1975) on the *nun energicum* and the prefix conjugation. The *waw explicativum* is treated by Baker (1980), who lists previously noted examples and suggests new uses of the *waw* with the sense 'that is.'

Plurals, Duals

Plurals and duals in Proto-Semitic and Hebrew

A description of the plurals and duals in Semitic languages is found in Moscati (1964: 86–94). Corriente (1971) observes that the barrier to proper understanding of the plural was the failure to differentiate between Semitic and Indo-European and the lack of a dynamic approach to Semitic morphology. In his view, prehistoric Semitic possessed an external inflection almost exclusively agglutinative. It had a tendency toward polysynthesis, as is evident from the fusion of subject, object, and verb in the conjugation.

Broken or internal plurals may be regarded as Proto-Semitic, but their use is regularly found only in the South Semitic area, in Arabic and Ethiopic. A dubious example of a trace of an internal plural in Hebrew is *reḵeḇ* 'cavalry,' which could possibly derive from the singular *rōḵēḇ* 'horseman' (Moscati 1964: 89).

Fontinoy (1969) has studied the dual in the Semitic languages. In his analysis, the dual existed in Proto-Semitic and preceded the development of the plural. This is more clear in the personal than in the demonstrative pronouns. There was a dual form for all three persons, but the evidence for the third person is clearer than for the second, and clearer for the second than for the first. The dual was originally used to express all aspects of duality, including polarity and occasional duals. The Akkadian dual also serves as a plural of paucity. The dual occurs extensively in Akkadian, Ugaritic, and Arabic, and its use in Hebrew at an earlier period must have been more extensive than merely to express pairing. The restriction of the dual is a later development (Moscati 1964: 93; G-K, §88).

Rendsburg (1982b) studies dual personal pronouns and dual verbs in Biblical Hebrew. The third person common dual is *hm*(*h*) and the second person common is *ʾtm*. The suffixed forms are, respectively, -(*h*)*m* and -*km*. It is Rendsburg's claim that these duals were much more common than is generally recognized, extending into the Second Commonwealth period. Sol Cohen (1982) demonstrates that dual and singular pronouns are often mixed and that the singular forms are also to be understood as duals. Examples occur in Gen 1:27 and 5:12.

The Infinitive

Comparative and functional studies of the infinitive

Solá Solé (1961) deals with the development of the infinitive in the Semitic languages. There existed, in his view, multiple verbal–nominal forms with adverbial function. Some dialects, Arabic, Modern South African, and Tigre conserved the plurality of forms. Others, such as Aramaic and Akkadian, excluded them. The infinitive as it appears in Hebrew and other Northwest Semitic languages is the synthesis of many primitive forms, showing the analogic influence of the imperfect. Traditional views of the infinitive absolute and infinitive construct are stated in G-K, §§113–14. An earlier comparative study of the infinitive absolute is that of Goddard (1950).

Hammershaimb (1963) surveys the various functions of the infinitive absolute in Hebrew and related dialects. Infinitives occupy a position intermediate between nouns, which they resemble in their formal structure, and verbs. The distinction between the infinitive absolute and infinitive construct, preserved by the Masoretes, is completely valid, despite the argument of A. Sperber that the functional distinction between them cannot be maintained. Infinitives in the Semitic languages denote in the abstract the verbal action or state or quality inherent in the verb without regard to number, agent, or gender. They are thus used for commands, or for hurried, excited speech. The infinitive precedes the finite verb, as in Akkadian, El Amarna, and Ugaritic, or it follows the verb, as in some examples from Biblical Hebrew and generally in Arabic. Wherever the infinitive stands in the construction, strengthening or intensifying the action of the verb, it is to be considered as the object of the verb. Some medieval views on the distinction, or lack of it, between *qāṭôl* and *q*^{e}*ṭôl* are summarized by Chomsky (1952: 75–76). A. J. Fox (1984, doctoral disseration) traces the evolution of the form and function of the Hebrew infinitive.

Pennacchietti (1968) classifies the demonstrative pronouns in Semitic as 1) autonomous, requiring no qualification to establish their meaning, and 2) non-autonomous, requiring a complementary element, as they are void of true semantic content.

Additional Morphological Topics

Blau (1974a), in a diachronic study of the pronouns, observed that the prepositions with final *-n*, attested in epigraphic South

Arabic and in Ugaritic, explain survivals such as *taḥtēnî* 'beneath me' and *ʿimmadî* < *immanî* 'with me.' The original stress of *hallāzeh* 'this' was penult, e.g., *hallāz* and *hallēzû*. The shift to final stress is due to the impact of *zeh*. Blau (1978c) confirms the view of M. Lambert that *n*-suffixes prevail after the historical indicative, while *h*-suffixes appear after the historical short imperfect, the jussive. Forms such as *-ennû*, *-enhû* originate in the energic of the indicative. They are secondary and are rare in biblical poetry.

Nun-suffixes

A generative approach to accent is applied by A. Gutman (1974). Azar (1977b) studies the prepositional phrase as an attribute in the Bible. Greenfield (1977) deals with the prepositions *ʿad* and *ʿal* in Hebrew and Aramaic.

The philological studies of M. Bravmann have been collected (1977), and some of the topics treated by this scholar over the years follow briefly here: the auxiliary vowel *i* replaced, not only *a* in closed syllables (attenuation), but other vowels as well; the *i* was a factor in the breakup of consonant clusters (1977: 3–93; originally published 1938); all Proto-Semitic diphthongs, regardless of position or accent, were contracted in different ways; the boundaries between monosyllability (true diphthongs) and disyllability (where the glide became lengthened) was not clear (1977: 98–123; originally published 1940). Words like *ʾāḇ* 'father' and *ʾāḥ* 'brother' are considered to be derived from an original triconsonantal structure with third radical *w* (1977: 124–30). The causative *ha-* is considered to have developed phonetically from *š*/*sa* (1977: 201–5). Words for 'suddenly' are seen to be of onomatopoeic origin, a labial-dental sequence, imitative of a stroke or blow, e.g., *peṯaʿ*, *piṯʾōm*, Akk. *ina pitti* (1977: 483–90). A review of these collected essays by Blau appears in *Les* 42 (1978) 146–51.

Bravmann's collected studies

Bar-Magen (1980) discusses the particle *-nāʾ*, which occurs about 400 times in the Bible. While traditional commentators understood it to mean 'please,' contextual analysis does not bear this out. There are phonetic reasons for the use of *-n-* to lengthen the preceding word. It generally follows a guttural or one of the *l-m-n-r* consonants. The lengthening is a means of emphasis.

The particle *-naʾ*

I. Ben-David (1982) contends that the verbal substantives of the *Nifʿal*, *Piʿel* and *Hifʿil* formations in Hebrew and the *Paʿel*, *Hafʿel*, *Afʿel* and *Hitpeʿel* formations in biblical Aramaic have a common feature: the vowel *a* which is unchanged at all times. He corrects a number of accepted ideas. For example, the name of the dividing accent should not be *ʾeṯnaḥtāʾ* but *ʾiṯnāḥaṯāʾ*. In another study (1983) I. Ben-David shows that the same word can have either a *Pēʿel* or a *Peʿel* pattern, depending upon its place in the clause. When the noun comes first in a short phrase, it has the

Verbal and nominal vowel patterns

Pēᶜel form, e.g., *śēḵel ṭôḇ* 'good understanding,' but if it comes at the end of the phrase it has the pattern *Peᶜel*, e.g., *ṭôḇaṯ śeḵel* 'having good understanding.' Nominalization in Biblical Hebrew is the subject of a doctoral dissertation by Grossberg (1977).

The Dialect Question

Interpretations of the *šibboleṯ* incident

The well known *šibbōleṯ/sibbōleṯ* episode of Judg 12:6 suggests that different dialects of Hebrew existed in the biblical period, but various interpretations of this evidence are possible. There may have been different realizations of the /š/ phoneme, or the word in question may have been *šibbōleṯ* 'stream' (Ps 69:16), perhaps going back to an original /ṯ/ which was realized in Ephraim as [s] (Harris 1939: 64; Beeston 1979). Swiggers (1981) suggests that Proto-Semitic /ṯ/ was represented in writing by the *shin* sign, but that the variant Ephraimite pronunciation of /ṯ/ as [s] had to be represented by the scribe with a *samekh*.

Northern and Southern dialects

Differences between the northern and southern pronunciations have been noted, and these are reflected in the early defective script. In the north the diphthongs *aw* and *ay* were reduced to *ō* and *ē*, showing affinities with Phoenician and Aramaic. It has been suggested that the pun in Amos 8:2 reflects the prophet's mocking use of the northern dialect (Harris 1939: 30–32; Cross and Freedman 1952: 47). Psalm 18 and 2 Samuel 22 have been treated as northern and southern recensions of the same composition (Cross and Freedman 1953; 1975: 125–58). Material external to the Bible is most relevant in this regard and is drawn upon in the study of the Gezer Calendar by S. Talmon (1963).

Some dialectical differences are seen in the Samarian ostraca where *št* (= *šatt*) is used for *šānāh* 'year,' going back to original **šantu* and **šanātu*. The dialect hypothesis has been applied to biblical exegesis by Dahood (1965: xxxviii) who finds, for example, in Ps 16:4 a contracted form of the northern dual, *middēm* 'from my hands,' parallel to the southern diphthong *-ay*. Such a radical rejection of the masoretic tradition presents problems in itself, and strictures on Dahood's method have been suggested, for example, by M. Greenberg (*JAOS* 90 [1970] 536–40).

Attempts at reconstruction of early pronunciation

There have been some attempts to reconstruct the Hebrew spoken by Jeremiah (Harris 1941), e.g., *wayyáhy dᵉḇar-YAHWÉ ᵓiláy laᵓmúr, ma ᵓattā rōᵓe Yarmᵉyáhu*, "and the word of the Lord came to me, saying, what do you see, Jeremiah?" (Jer 1:11). This reconstruction recognizes the *shewa mobile*; a different accent pattern, e.g., *wayyáhy* as against masoretic *wayyᵉhî*; the unreduced *a* in a closed, unaccented syllable, e.g., *Yarm^{e}yahu*; and unaccented *i* in place of masoretic *ē*, e.g., *ʾilay*, masoretic *ʾēlay*. Reconstructions in several stages have been offered by Birkeland (1940: 52–59), the earliest reconstruction retaining the case endings, accented *u* not yet changed to *o*, and masoretic final *h* being a later development from an earlier vocalized *y*, e.g., *wăhannăḥašu hăyayă ʿărumă mikkul ḥayyat̠ haśśădayĭ*, 'and the serpent was more sly than all the beasts of the field' (Gen 3:1). Later stages show the loss of endings and vowel change.

Personal and place names as dialectic evidence

B. Eshel (1960) makes use of personal and place names in the Bible, the Septuagint, and extra-biblical sources for the identification of dialectical variants such as *ū*/*ī* (*Y^{e}ḥûʾēl*/*Y^{e}ḥîʾēl*), *ō*/*ē* (Greek *Mōsa*/Hebrew *Mēšaʿ*, *Môʾāb̠*/*Mēʾāb̠* 'from the father,' Gen 19:37), and *š*/*ś* (*Mik̠maš*/*Mik̠maś*). The interchange *u*/*i* has been traced back into the earliest period by Chomsky (1952: 34, 83; 1971: 26) who follows Pinsker in positing an original /ü/ phoneme.

A paper by Isserlin (1971) deals with dialectical differences in place names, drawing from such sources as Jewish papyri and tombstones, Jewish and pagan literary sources, Christian materials, and administrative documents. The results are admittedly tentative. The letters *b*, *g*, *d*, *k*, *p*, *t* obey neither the masoretic rules nor demonstrate the universal softening characteristic of the Hexaplaric transcriptions. They often do appear as plosives after vowels. Short Semitic *a* is *o* or *e* in some regions, and long Hebrew *o* alternates with *u* in the hill zone. The rare form *poʿol*, not common in masoretic Hebrew, is noticeable in the south and west, e.g., LXX *Phogor* (masoretic *P^{e}ʿor*). The transcriptions of Josephus generally agree with the masoretic tradition, but there are some that the latter ultimately rejected. The Hebrew of Jerome and the Samaritans may reflect a later, vulgar southern pronunciation. These results are of more relevance for the Second Commonwealth than for the First.

Northern Israelite influence upon Judean Hebrew

Gordon (1954) has speculated that apparent Canaanite influences upon later books of the Bible are due to the migrations of northern Israelites to the kingdom of Judah after the fall of Samaria in 721 B.C.E. A similar avenue of transmission for the contents of the book of Deuteronomy has been proposed by E. W. Nicholson, *Deuteronomy and Tradition* (Philadelphia, 1967). A. Sperber (1966: 105–297) claimed that two dialects were combined to form Biblical Hebrew. The masoretic text is the Judean recension, while the Samaritan Bible is that of northern Israel (1966: 231; Waldman 1975a: 1291). His views have been challenged by Morag (1968a), who contends that the materials used by Sperber to restore Pre-masoretic Hebrew are drawn indiscriminately from different periods. The evidence points to a post-exilic origin of the Samaritan sect and a redaction of the Samaritan Pentateuch during the Hasmonean period (Purvis 1968). A critique of the views of Sperber is also found in Wheeler (1970).

Sociolinguistics and the dialect question

In addition to dialects, we may consider language on different social levels. Driver (1970) explains certain biblical difficulties in terms of colloquialisms, e.g., lack of congruence of gender and number; misuse of the article; and the use of *mî*, not for 'who,' but as in *mî ănaḥămēḵ* (not 'how can I comfort thee' but 'what? can I comfort thee?' [Isa 51:19]). Tension between current usage and a usage of higher social prestige thought to be "correct" leads to the phenomenon of hypercorrection (compare spoken English "between you and I"). This has been studied by Blau as it appears in several Semitic languages, including Hebrew (1970b). One example is the spelling of *bᵉʾēr* 'well' with *alef*, influenced by *ḥōṭᵉʾîm* 'sinners,' and *mûm* 'blemish,' hypercorrected in Dan 1:4 and spelled *mʾwm*. On the other hand, Blau discounts as hypercorrections certain phenomena which are not, e.g., the use of *sin* in place of original *samekh* alongside the change of historical *sin* to *samekh*; this is no more than a scribal vagary. Blau rejects the view of Birkeland that the Judean pronunciation of [Yerušalayim], written *Yrwšlm*, is a hypercorrection. In Birkeland's opinion, northern speakers, knowing that *ē* in their dialect corresponded to *ayi* in Judah, pronounced the name as [Yerušalayim], even though in the south, as revealed by the *ketiv*, the pronunciation was [Yerušalem]. Blau's objection is that it is highly unlikely that the Judeans would later abandon their traditional pronunciation in favor of a hypercorrect northern one. One must assume, instead, parallel traditions.

Extra-biblical inscriptions and dialects

Indications of local dialectical variations may be culled from extra-biblical inscriptions. For example, the Gezer Calendar (*IR*, no. 8; *KAI* I, 182: 3) has *ʿṣd pšt* 'harvesting of flax,' *ʿṣd* not being attested in the Bible, except for *maʿăṣāḏ* 'axe' (Jer 10:3; Isa 44:12). Aramaic has *ḥṣd*, and Akkadian has *eṣēdu* 'to harvest.' Because the Gezer Calendar also uses *qṣr* 'harvest,' it may be that *ʿṣd* is specialized for the harvesting of flax (compare the differentiation in Mishnaic Hebrew, *môsēq zêṯîm* 'harvests olives,' and Biblical Hebrew *bôṣēr ʿănāḇîm* 'harvests grapes'). It has also been suggested by Albright that *yrḥw* 'its months' be understood as *yarḥêw* < **yarḥēhû* < **yarḥaihû* (dual), and that the singular *yrḥ* be vocalized as **yarḥō*, a feature of the construct state. This would mean that an archaism survived into the 10th century (compare the name *Šᵉmuʾēl*). Furthermore, an Arad ostracon (*IR* no. 52) has *wṣrrt*

ʾtm bṣq 'you shall tie them in a bag,' the last word being a variant of *śaq* (cf. Gen 42:35). The alternation of *Yiṣḥāq*/ *Yiśḥāq* is also known in the Bible. Another Arad ostracon (*IR* no. 63; Aharoni 1981: 46) has *b* for *p* e.g., *whbqydm* 'he shall hand them over' and *bnbškm* 'for your very life.' The same variant is attested in the Kilammu inscription (*KAI* I, no. 24), *nbš*, and in Hebrew, compare Mishnaic Hebrew *heḇqēr*/*hep̱qēr* 'unowned property.' The significance of these details, however, has yet to be studied systematically in relation to dialects, and the evidence appears as yet to be scanty. Garr (1985) deals with the question of dialect geography in Syria–Palestine between 1000 and 586 B.C.E. Diringer and Brock (1968) offer lexical interpretations of the unique words in extra-biblical inscriptions, and a masters thesis by Mishor (1969) deals with the language of inscriptions from the First Commonwealth. Mali (1983, doctoral dissertation) treats conversational language in the Early Prophets.

Sarfatti (1982), in a comprehensive survey of the linguistic features of the First Commonwealth inscriptions, observes, contrary to Cross and Freedman (1952), that medial *matres* do exist. With Gordis (1937) he holds that the readings of the inscriptions parallel the *ketiv* of the masoretic text of the Bible. This leads to the conclusion that the inscriptions, as well as the *ketiv*, reflect a popular tradition, while the biblical *qere*, as well as the official seals, reflect a literary tradition. There are other features which parallel the more popular Mishnaic Hebrew dialect: the variation of *p*/*b* (*hbqydm* 'entrust them,' *bnbškm* 'at the cost of your life,' Arad inscription; compare Mishnaic Hebrew *hep̱qēr*/*heḇqēr* 'ownerless property'); the tendency to omit the definite article; the spelling *qtlth* in the 2m. sing.; and a vocalization *-āḵ* with the possessive suffix, 2m. sing. Sarfatti also discusses the lexical items that are non-biblical. The inventory is not too large, but he brings the suggestion that *pym* should be vocalized *payim* 'two parts,' that is ⅔ of a standard weight (cf. Zach 13:8). Sarfatti's conclusions parallel those of Rendsburg (1980a, doctoral dissertation), who argues for the early presence of Mishnaic Hebrew features. According to this view, diglossia existed in biblical times.

Ketiv-qere and the dialect question

Morphology and Meaning

Van Selms (1971) has offered some theories on the relationship of form and meaning. Because of the great irregularity in the relationship between gender and class in the nouns, it was maintained by earlier scholars that such a correlation was not part of

History of forms and their functions

the original structure of the Semitic languages. Van Selms, following Landsberger, holds that final *-t* indicated a single object selected out of a natural group by means of a sentence of identification, e.g., *ʾayyal-t* 'a buck thou art' (cf. Bubenik 1973). Since the greater probability was that there were more females in the herd than males, the sentence of identification came, in time, to be the feminine form. Similarly, Van Selms considers the early feminine endings in the names *Pdry*, *Ṭly*, *Arṣy*, daughters of Baal, and biblical *Śāray*, to be derived from the vocative *ya-*, as in Arabic and Ugaritic. Ben-Asher (1976b) treats 177 word pairs with masculine and feminine endings. In only five cases does this distinction differentiate between the unit and the collective (*ʾŏnî* 'fleet'/ *ʾŏniyyāh* 'boat'). Accepted views are summarized in Moscati (1964: 75–102).

Van Selms (1971: 422–23) also notes that many words indicating non-domesticated animals have a *bet* as their last radical, e.g., Hebrew *ʿaqrāb* 'scorpion'; Hebrew *ʾarneḇeṯ*, Ugaritic *ʾanhb*, Akkadian *annabu* 'hare'; Akkadian *šēlibu*, Arabic *ṯalʿab* 'fox'; Hebrew *zᵉʾēḇ* 'wolf'; Hebrew *keleḇ* 'dog'; Hebrew *zᵉḇûḇ* 'fly'; Hebrew *ḥāgāḇ* 'locust'; Hebrew *dōḇ* 'bear.' There is, however, much that remains unaccounted for: there are non-domesticated animals which do not have a *bet*, and one may ask, what do flies and wolves have in common besides this letter?

Nominal and verbal classes and specialized meanings

Other relationships between form and meaning have long been recognized, e.g., the *qaṭṭāl* class, denoting one who has made a profession of the action denoted by the corresponding verb, *gannāḇ* 'robber,' and *dayyān* 'judge.' The *qabberet* form indicates illness, e.g., *dalleqeṯ* 'inflammation,' *bahereṯ* 'white spot, skin eruption'; and the *yaqbur* class denotes animals and plants, e.g., *yaḥmûr*, 'antelope,' *yattûš* 'mosquito, gnat,' *yabruaḥ* 'mandrake.' The D or *Piʿel* includes a whole group of verbs denoting waiting, pleading, seeking, e.g., Akkadian *quʾum*, Hebrew *qawwēh* 'wait,' *buʾum*, *baqqēš* 'seek.' The durative aspect of the D is evident in nouns formed in this pattern denoting illness or bodily incapacity, e.g., Akkadian *kubburum* 'very fat,' *sukkukum*, *ṭummumum* 'deaf,' Hebrew *ʿiwwēr* 'blind,' *pissēaḥ* 'lame,' *ʾillēm* 'mute,' *ʾiṭṭēr* (*yad yᵉmînô*) 'tied in his right hand,' that is, 'left-handed' (von Soden 1952: 62, §55n; Moscati 1964: 78–79). Gevirtz (1982) offers the hypothesis that *ʿayin* prefixed to verbs, forming a new root, serves as a morpheme of specification, imparting a sense of greater forcefulness and causative meaning.

A measure of correlation between certain kinds of "weak" verbs and certain semantic categories was recognized by Landsberger (*Islamica* 2 [1926] 326ff.; Moscati 1964: 168–69). Some of these categories are: 1) verbs I *n*, where the biradical base indicates a noise, e.g., *nbḥ* 'bark,' *nhm* 'moan,' *nʿr* 'growl, bray,' or where the *nûn* has a locative meaning, e.g., *nśʾ* 'lift up,' Akkadian *nadû* 'cast down' (cf. *ydh*); 2) verbs II *w*, describing a turning or a change of condition, e.g., Hebrew *mwr* 'change,' Akkadian *târu* 'return'; 3) verbs II *y*, denoting specific physiological functions, e.g., Akkadian *šiānum* 'urinate,' *ḫiālum* 'have pain,' *ṣiāḫum* 'laugh,' Hebrew *gyl* 'rejoice,' *ḥwl* 'whirl, dance, twist, writhe.' In addition, there are *mediae geminatae* which denote a series of individual actions (*Kettendurative*), e.g., *šll*, *bzz* 'take booty,' Arabic *ʿdd* 'count' (Moscati 1964: 168–69; von Soden 1952, §§104c–e, 105a).

Nun added to the biradical base

As stimulating as this concept is, there is still much that is yet unexplained, if, indeed a full correlation between form and function can ever be found. There are verbs, apparently similar in meaning, which appear in different morpho-semantic classes, e.g., *mny* 'count,' a III *y*, and Arabic *ʿdd* 'count,' a mediae geminatae verb. Synonyms or near-synonyms which are found in parallelism in biblical poetry can be in different classes, e.g., *śmḥ* and *gyl* 'rejoice,' *dyn* and *špṭ* 'judge.' Of course, one must also take into account the different semantic histories of words which at a particular period have been conjoined in parallelism.

Gluska (1981) deals with the connection between form and meaning in nouns of the *maqtēl*/*maqtîl* pattern in Biblical and Mishnaic Hebrew. There is lack of agreement among the grammars. J. Barth (1894) maintained that the morphology of nouns was related to that of verbs, which was definitely correlated with their meaning. Tur-Sinai (1954–59, *Halashon*, 228) saw no correlation at all. Gluska shows that the biblical evidence demonstrates that there are two categories of meaning: "implement" and "abstract." In Mishnaic Hebrew there is a change away from polysemic forms; the category of "abstract" almost disappears, and the general tendency is to limit this form to implements.

A dissertation by Weinstock (1979) and a further study (1983) deal with onomatopoeia. Weinstock reviews the literature on the intelligibility of imitative words to hearers unfamiliar with a particular language. He divides the corpus of biblical roots into twenty-one categories, such as "break," "cut," "shake," "rub," "indistinct talk," "animal sounds," "murmur," "hiss" and "swallow." The presence or absence of certain consonants in each meaning class is checked for statistical significance. For example, /h/ is significantly present in the meaning class "bubble," /d/ in "friction," /h/ in "murmur," while /l/ occurs fewer times than expected

Classification of verbal roots in the basis of onomatopoeia

in "break" and /ᶜ/ is absent from "friction." An earlier dissertation in this area, by Boucher (1950), dealt with onomatopoeia in Northwest Semitic.

LEXICOGRAPHY AND SEMANTICS

Critiques of etymological theories

Commenting on the development of lexicography since the time of Gesenius, Rabin (1970a: 314–16) observes that none of the standard dictionaries does full justice to the total range of scholarly discussion over the last century. One problem that has hampered lexicography is the influence of etymology in establishing meaning, together with a search for "basic," often theologically-biased, denotations. A recent example of this criticism is a review by Blau (1973–74a) of Eisenbeis (1969), who deals with the root *šlm* 'be complete' in Biblical Hebrew. Blau takes issue with Eisenbeis' view that secular and theological uses of the root should be kept separate, and that, in the latter case, the content of the root is always fixed.

Barr (1961) offers an extensive critique of the methodology of studies in biblical semantics based upon theological considerations. The search for "root" meanings, or the treatment of words as "concepts," evident in G. Kittel, ed., *Theologisches Wörterbuch zum neuen Testament* (Stuttgart, 1933ff.; Eng. tr. *Theological Dictionary of the New Testament*, Grand Rapids, 1964ff.), is motivated in part by a reaction to source criticism of the Bible. The effort is to find a stock of basic concepts which are consistent, regardless of source or time period. Another motivation is to establish what is unique in Christian and Hebraic thought as opposed to Greek or European thought which is based upon it. Greek thought is presented as abstract, stressing static being, while Hebrew thought is concrete and dynamic. A major exponent of this type of semantics is Boman (1960), who maintains, for example, that Hebrew verbs of condition, such as *yārēᵓ* 'afraid' and *zāqēn* 'old' are not static but have the dynamic quality of progress into a condition. The influence of J. G. Herder (*The Spirit of Hebrew Poetry*, transl. by J. Marsh [Burlington, 1833], 2 vols.) is also felt here. Herder maintained that "with the Hebrew the verb is almost the whole of the language. . . . The nouns are derived from verbs, and in a certain sense are still verbs. They are, as it were, living beings, extracted and moulded, while their radical source itself was in a state of living energy . . ." (Barr 1961: 85).

Greek and Hebrew thought and grammar contrasted

Barr's extensive critique of this methodology and its theological bias has as its main thrust the idea that the two languages are not amenable to this neat dichotomy between static and dynamic. Moreover, the meanings of words are not centered in roots but in the context, in their use in a sentence. The theological formulations are not under criticism but the idea that they inhere in roots.

James Barr's views on etymolgy

A related area which Barr criticizes extensively is that of etymology. For example, *qāhāl* 'group, assembly,' translated by Greek *ekklesia*, has been connected with *qôl* 'voice'; therefore, the Church is a covenant community which hears the voice of the living God. Hebrew *dāḇār* 'word' is connected by some with Arabic *dabara* 'back' and Hebrew *dᵉḇîr* 'hindmost chamber of the temple.' The conclusion is then drawn that *dāḇār* 'word' refers to the hinterground of meaning, the inner reality of the word, and to the future, in the same way as *ʾāḥôr* 'rear' means "that which comes after" (Barr 1961: 119–40; BDB, 180). Further studies on comparative philology have been made by Barr (1968, 1969).

In a recent study Barr (1974) has isolated several types of etymological operations, evaluating the appropriateness of each for specific circumstances. For example, if one attempts a prehistoric reconstruction of the root *ʾmr*, he will discover that in Hebrew it means 'say,' in Arabic 'command,' in Ethiopic 'show, know,' and in Akkadian 'see.' He might conclude, therefore, that the Proto-Semitic sense underlying all of these may be 'be clear.' This approach is useful for comparing dialects and the development of a specific root. It becomes uncertain, however, if a meaning attested in one dialect is assigned within another; cf. Dahood (1965: 16, 24, 69) who attempts to find *ʾmr* 'see' in Hebrew. Again, only sufficient examples in clear contexts can corroborate such cross-dialect semantic shifts.

Another method involving etymology is the use of a cognate language to discover the sense in Hebrew. This approach has value in "gross semantics," giving a meaning to something hitherto not understood, but the true meaning of a biblical passage requires what Barr calls "fine semantics." A further method is simple comparison of institutions with cognate words, e.g., Hebrew *nāḇîʾ* 'prophet' and Akkadian *nabû* 'call.' This may be helpful, as is a comparison of the institutions themselves, for example, prophecy in Israel and at Mari. However, the specific meaning of a word or institution in a particular culture is not fully established in this way. Barr also devotes some attention to popular etymology and concludes with a warning. Etymology attempts to reduce the element of arbitrariness in language, but no matter how valid the processes of etymology might be, it is futile to hope that the element of arbitrariness in language in relation to reality can be overcome fully or even alleviated.

Comparative lexicography

Gates (1972) has surveyed the lexicographical resources currently available to American biblical scholarship. Chaim (H. R.) Cohen (1975) has attempted to apply a methodology to the study of *hapax legomena* and to put it on a sound basis. Using the resources of cognate languages such as Akkadian and Ugaritic, Cohen attempts to arrive at the meaning of a given word through the use of semantic equivalents in similar contexts. Considerations on comparative Semitic lexicography are offered by Segert (1960, 1969). Greenspahn (1977, a doctoral dissertation; 1980) deals with *hapax legomena*. While, in general, two- to three-fifths of the words in literary works are *hapax legomena* (poetry has more than prose), the Bible has less than one-quarter. The percentage is low due to undetected homographs and to the treatment of conjugated forms as part of their roots.

Semantic studies of specific words

The problems of biblical semantics are dealt with by Rabin (1961–62; 1968b) and a comprehensive treatment is by Kedar (1981). A significant number of studies of individual words and concepts have appeared, some of which can be noted here: Ackroyd (1950–51) on the root *bʾš* 'smell bad, act badly'; Hills (1954) on the root *kpr* 'atone'; Delcor (1967) on special meanings of the word *yāḏ* 'hand'; Pope (1964) on the word *šaḥaṯ* 'pit, grave' in Job 9:31; Rabin (1972) on *zāḥal* 'crawl, fear'; R. W. Fisher (1966) on *bśr* 'inform'; Holladay (1958) on *šûḇ* 'return'; Giesen (1981) on *šbᶜ* 'swear.' W. F. Meyer (1974) surveys the semantic range of *pāḏāh* 'redeem' which, in its context, is said to denote actions opposed to injustice, especially death. Gunnel (1980, doctoral dissertation) studies *pqd* as 'determining the destiny.' Shults (1974) distinguishes between *šlm* and *tmm* 'be whole' in Biblical Hebrew. Recognizing a distinction between 'abstract' or 'root' meaning and 'contextual meaning,' he concludes that *šlm* means 'evenness, balance,' while *tmm* indicates 'integrated togetherness.' Trevor (1963) has studied the semantic range of 'folly' in the wisdom literature. Schultz (1973) treats the different ranges of *ᶜānî* 'afflicted' and *ᶜānāw* 'humble,' the former word referring to the righteous victims of fellow Israelites. Terms for 'evildoers' are dealt with by S. N. Rosenbaum (1975): *rᵉšāᶜîm* 'wicked ones' in Psalms, meaning Israelites; *ʾôyᵉḇîm* 'enemies,' referring to non-Israelites; and *pôᶜălê ʾāwen* 'workers of iniquity,' those who upset the social order.

Semantic values of derivatives of the root *š*ʾ*r* 'remain' are discussed by Hasel (1973). Rozenberg (1963) investigated the root *špṭ* 'judge' in biblical and extra-biblical sources, and Forshey (1973) has studied *nḥl* 'inherit.' Now Mafico (1979: doctoral disseration) has studied *špṭ* with reverence to YHWH. Bronznick (1976–77) proposes to derive all the meanings of *ḥlš* 'be weak,' Mishnaic Hebrew 'cast lots,' from a basic meaning of 'cut.' When used in regard to a lot the word refers to the practice of diviners making use of cut materials. Analogously, *qôsēm* 'enchanter' is related to *qîsām* 'piece of wood, chip.' The root *ḥlš* in the sense of 'be weak' is connected with *qᵉṣar nep̱eš* 'short of breath, wretched.'

Wolff (1974), in his *Anthropology of the Old Testament*, deals with terms for the body and assumed connotations, thus, for him, *nep̱eš* connotes 'needy man,' *bāśār* 'flesh' is man in his infirmity, and *rûᵓaḥ* 'spirit' is man as he is empowered by an outside force. However, root meaning and contextual applications must be carefully distinguished, and a contextual meaning does not necessarily achieve the status of a dictionary entry. Thus, one must view Wolff's results with caution, as well as Dahood's suggestion that *ṭôḇ* 'good' is a term for 'rain' (Dahood 1965: 25–26).

Wildberger (1967) treats the semantics of *heᵓĕmîn* 'he believed, trusted,' while Lau (1970), Baltzer (1971), Greenfield (1967), Tadmor (1978–79) and Veettil (1982) have studied the terminology of covenant. The latter is a comprehensive survey with rich bibliography. Donald (1964) compares the semantic fields of 'rich' and 'poor' in Akkadian and Hebrew. Sawyer (1975) surveys the development of *yšᶜ* 'save,' equating it with Common Semitic *yṯᶜ*. Balentine (1980) studies the semantic field of 'hide,' where six verbs apply to God, man and inanimate objects. Gerleman (1973a) devotes a study to the treatment of *šlm* 'be whole,' and in a later study (1978) compares *ḥeseḏ* and *ṣedeq*. He argues that the first term expresses the idea of 'full measure.' Schmid (1971) traces *šalôm* in the ancient Near East and in the Bible. Kamchi (1973) relates *ḥlq* to Arabic *ḥalaqa* 'be high,' Cazelles (1973) deals with *bᶜr* 'be brutish,' and Healy (1976) attempts to isolate a *nṣr* II in Hebrew meaning 'chirp, lament,' a reflex of Syriac *nṣr*. Kaddari (1977–78) shows, through transformational grammatical analysis, that ambiguities in the surface structure, where *mnᶜ* 'hold back' is used, can be clarified by parallelism and reference to cultural factors. Ahuviah (1976–77) studies covenantal expressions in Second Isaiah, and a doctoral dissertation by R. Price (1977) treats terms for exile. O. E. Collins studies the stem *znh* (1977; doctoral dissertation). Chaney (1976, doctoral disseration) studies the use of the verb *ḥdl* in the Song of Deborah, and Trommer (1975, masters thesis) has written a semantic-syntactic study of *ʾmr* 'say' in the Bible.

Morag (1978), using componential semantic analysis, studies the semantic markers (sememes) in several roots which are part of the semantic field of 'movement.' There are roots where the sememe of 'speed' is associated with positive qualities such as 'ability,' 'skill,' 'power,' 'wealth,' 'success,' e.g., *mhr*, *šlḥ*, *ḥyl*/*ḥwl*, *šwḥ*, *ḥyh*. There are others where the sememe of 'speed' is associated with negative qualities, e.g., 'burning' and 'fear,' as in *bhl*, *hpz*, *mhr*.

Ben-Hayyim (1980) suggests that the different meanings of *ʿrb* that appear to be homonymous are actually polysemic, and that the semantic development of *ʿrb* can be traced. The basic meanings, which are interrelated, are 'joining,' 'accepting responsibility,' 'doing business,' 'setting (of the sun), and 'to be sweet.' Meaning 4 ('setting [of the sun]') can be challenged, as it may be related to Akkadian *erēpu* 'be dark,' while meaning 5 ('to be sweet') involves some stretching of meanings through analogy with Arabic and Aramaic.

Polysemy has been studied by a number by a number of authors: Herzberg (1979, doctoral dissertation), E. Goldberg (1977, masters thesis), and Rendsburg (1982a). Double meanings, often intentionally applied by the biblical authors, are found in many contexts, e.g., *zāmîr* 'pruning' and 'singing' (Herzberg 1979).

Demands for strict methodology in the use of cognates

A. Gibson (1981) follows the lead of Barr (1961) in demanding a rigorous methodology in the study of cognate Semitic languages and biblical semantics. The theoretical framework of his analysis is based upon the work of G. Frege (*Philosophical Writings of Gottlob Frege*, [Oxford, 1960]). Gibson cites numerous examples of hypostatization of language, where disparate forms and usages are concluded to be variations of the same concept. For example, he objects to the widely-held formulation that Ugaritic *ltn bṯn brḥ* is identical with *lwytn nḥš brḥ* (Isa 27:1). He holds with Geach (P. T. Geach, *Reference and Reality* [Cornell, 1968]) that there is no sense in saying "*x* and *y* are the same," unless one adds," they are the same *F*" (Gibson 1981: 24). Following Barr, Gibson (1981: 191–93) criticizes the methodology of scholars who, while concealing their underlying assumptions, link an alleged semantic value based on common roots found in different languages with social contexts in which the root appears. He also criticizes severely the automatic assumption that a foreign root is an acceptable Hebrew root. An example of this methodology in action is G. R. Driver's influence on passages in the *New English Bible*, where *ṣnḥ* (Josh 15:18; Judg 1:14) is taken to be the Arabic *ṣnḥ* 'break wind' (Gibson 1981: 29–33). Barr (1979) surveys and evaluates current approaches in philology and biblical semantics.

Further semantic and lexical studies

Semantic and lexicographic studies are collected in *Words and Meanings: Essays Presented to David Winton Thomas*, ed. by P. Ackroyd and B. Lindars (Cambridge, 1968). Some of the subjects included in this work are: a reinterpretation of Isa 28:1–22 by G. R. Driver (pp. 47–67); a clarification of difficult words in Genesis 49 by J. A. Emerton (pp. 81–93); a discussion of twofold aspects of Hebrew words by G. Fohrer (pp. 95–103); and a study of *ḥesed* and *tôrāh* in the Psalter by A. E. Goodman (pp. 105–15). Bach (1978) traces changes of meaning in *tôḏāh*, a sacrifice of expiation in pre-exilic contexts and one of remembrance in post-exilic texts. The work of Radday (1970a, doctoral dissertation; 1970b, 1970c, 1970–71, 1973) is based on the application of statistical methods to the problems of the language of the book of Isaiah. Silva (1983) presents an introduction to biblical lexical semantics. E. Rubinstein (1982b) discusses verbs dealing with location and (1986) descriptive words.

A recent doctoral dissertation by M. M. Kaplan (1981) traces the historical development of the lion metaphor in the classical prophets. Connecting *kᵉp̄îr* 'lion' with *kbr* 'mighty,' Kaplan concludes that the metaphor was borrowed from preclassical prophetic prose legends. Alexander To Ha Luc, in a doctoral dissertation (1982), studies *ʾhb* 'love.' It is a term that is connected with vassal relationships, and the verb can be used to express the relationship in either direction, from superior to inferior or vice versa. The noun *ʾôheb*, however, is never used of a superior, only of the inferior person. D. I. Block (doctoral dissertation, 1982) studies terms for kinship and nation in Hebrew and neighboring languages. *ʿAm* has the warmest, kinship-related connotations, while *gôy* is formal, associated with *meleḵ*; *lᵉʾôm* is poetic and archaic. Ancient language played less of a role in establishing national identity than modern languages reputedly do.

Other useful study tools in this area are the index to the lexicon of Brown, Driver, and Briggs prepared by Einspahr (1976) and an important reference for the theological meanings of Hebrew words, the dictionary edited by Botterweck and Ringgren (1973ff.); the fascicles have appeared from 1970 on. The Koehler-Baumgartner *Lexicon in Veteris Testamenti Libros* (1953) is also a major reference tool, and the new *Hebräisches und aramäisches Lexicon zum alten Testament* (Leiden 1967ff.), a cooperative venture involving various scholars, is also of importance.

Two studies in related languages are also useful for research in Hebrew lexicography. They are: Stephen J. Lieberman, *The Sumerian Loanwords in Old Babylonian Akkadian* (Harvard Semitic Studies, Missoula, MT, 1977) and Richard S. Tomback, *A Comparative Semitic Lexicon of the Phoenician and Punic Languages* (SBL Dissertation Series, Missoula, MT, 1977).

Semantic fields and biblical studies

Rabin (1968b), suggesting an approach grounded in careful methodology, stresses the need to divide the biblical vocabulary into "fields" and to formulate "areas of meaning." The problems that require study are: the extent of synonymity; the structure of the field—that is, the distinctions indicated by the vocabulary; levels of style; and emotional connotations. Only one aspect of this work, diachronic semantics, is in Rabin's view similar to traditional exegesis. Other more general treatments of root meanings and semantics in biblical research can be found in works by Sawyer (1967) and Spomer (1972).

Morag (1975a) has applied to the book of Jeremiah the concepts of "key words" (*mots-clé*) and "evidentiary words" (*mots-temoins*) developed by G. Matoré (*Le vocabulaire et la société sous Louis-Philippe*, Geneve-Lille, 1951; *La méthode en lexicologie*, Paris, 1953). A "key word" is one which signifies a concept that occupies an important place in the material and spiritual life of a society in a certain "linguistic generation." An "evidentiary word" bears witness to a change that took place in the life of a society. Some of the "evidentiary" words in Jeremiah are *šeḇer* 'destruction,' and *māgôr* 'terror.' The following words are considered to be "key words": *m^{e}šûḇāh* 'deviation,' *ša^{c}ărûrāh* 'abnormal behavior,' and *š^{e}rîrûṯ lēḇ* 'stubbornness, stiffness of heart.' This suggestive approach should stimulate more work in this area, combining the sociological aspects with the semantic.

Earlier work in Hebrew semantics which deserves mention is that of Martin Buber in his *Darko shel miqra* (Jerusalem, 1964) and of L. Liebreich, *HUCA* 27 (1956) 181–82. A recent study of Buber's exegetical methods is K. J. Illman, *Leitwort, Tendenz, Synthese: Programm und Praxis in der Exegese Martin Bubers* (Åbo, Finland, 1975). Specific terminology is treated by Milgrom (1970), who deals with levitical terms and by Delcor (1975), who seeks to identify survivals of terms which could be traced to the nomadic period of Hebrew language.

A doctoral dissertation by Y. I. Kim (1981) treats the vocabulary of oppression in the Old Testament: *ʿšq*, *ynh*, *lḥṣ*, and their congeners. Hayman (1980, doctoral dissertation) treats the meaning of *hôšîʿa* in the Old Testament. A. Brenner (1980) has studied the semantic distributions of *maṭṭeh* and *šēḇeṭ* 'tribe' and (1982) has written on color terms in Biblical Hebrew. V. Sasson (1979, doctoral dissertation) studies the lexicon and linguistic usage in early Hebrew inscriptions. The language of curses has been treated by H. Brichto (1962, 1963, reprinted 1968) and Schottroff (1969).

COGNATES AND LOANWORDS

Use and misuse of Akkadian loanwords

Distinguishing between words which are cognates and those which are borrowed from other Semitic languages is a particularly troublesome problem. Ideally, it should be possible to identify loanwords on the basis of synchronic descriptions from the source and receptor languages, so that foreign and native patterns can be distinguished. However, in a significant study of Indo-European loans in Semitic languages, Rabin (1970b: 464) has noted that historical considerations also play an important part. Chomsky, in a popular presentation (1967: 22–74), did not adequately distinguish between cognates and borrowed words. Ellenbogen's study (1962) of loanwords in Biblical Hebrew from Egyptian, Akkadian, Persian, and Indo-European is a useful summary of research up to that point, mentioning such examples as: *ʾēd* 'ground flow' < Akkadian *edû* (cf. E. Speiser, *BASOR* [1955] 140:9–11); *gōme* < Egyptian *qmꜣ* 'rush'; *sappîr* < Sanscrit *çanipriya* 'sapphire.' There are problems, however. For example, he follows Zimmern (1917) in deriving Hebrew *ʿaštê* 'one' from Akkadian *ištēn*. Ellenbogen (1962: 129) maintains that the phoneme /ʿ/, although not represented graphically, was still pronounced at the time of the borrowing. This would presuppose a very early loan, for Akkadian lost this phoneme in representation and realization after the Old Babylonian period (1950–1530 B.C.E.; von Soden 1952: 24). It is preferable to conclude with S. A. Kaufman (1970: 104) that this is not a borrowing, but that the words are cognate. E. Reiner (1970: 283–84) has questioned von Soden's practice (in his *Akkadisches Handwörterbuch*) of indicating variants by use of ʿ, e.g., *ʿadānum* 'fixed time' (Aramaic *ʿîdānāʾ*, Hebrew *ʿîdân*) without giving evidence to confirm it. This kind of notation merely indicates a spelling variation but does not correspond to any morphological or phonological reality (Waldman 1975a: 1291–92). A general survey of loan-words in Biblical Hebrew is that of Kutscher (1982: 46–53).

Arabic as source of borrowings

The heavy emphasis which was formerly given to Arabic cognates as a means of elucidating obscure Hebrew words has been superseded by a greater emphasis upon Akkadian and Ugaritic. Identifications with Arabic, however, continue to be made (compare Mani [1957] and Guillaume [1961, 1962, 1963, 1965a, and, in book form, 1965b]). An example of this approach (which also illustrates its weaknesses) is a study by Hirschberg (1961). He suggests that *rāṣûp̱ ʾahăḇāh* 'inlaid with love' (Cant 3:10) should be identified with Arabic *ʾihab* 'raw leather'; *šᵉlāḥayiḵ* 'your branches' (Cant 4:13) with Arabic *šalḥ* 'vagina'; and *kᵉp̱arîm* 'henna' (ibid.) with *ʾal kafirān* 'groin.' More serious and legitimate contributions to Hebrew lexicography on the basis of Arabic have been made by Kopf, whose collection (1976) contains articles dealing with over 120 lexical items (originally published in *VT* 8 [1958] 161–215, and *VT* 9 [1959] 247–87). A doctoral dissertation by Ababneh (1978) treats the morphophonemics of pluralization in Biblical Hebrew and Classical Arabic. Blau (1983a) also discusses Arabic-Hebrew cognates and parallels.

Southwest Semitic and Hebrew

Several authors have directed their attention to the relationships between Southwest Semitic and Hebrew. Rabin (1951) enumerated 28 examples of words common to Himyaritic and Northwest Semitic. These tend to show that a segment of the Hebrew lexicon has South Arabian affinities but has no apparent relationship to Canaanite, Aramaic, or Akkadian. Rabin suggests, in a study on Qatabanian (South Arabian) etymologies (1983a), that words in the Timnaʿ obelisk inscription can clarify terms in Hebrew and other languages. He proposes relating *ʾĂrammî* (Deut 26:5) to a word meaning 'wandering merchant,' *ʿîr* (Dan 4:10) to a term for 'demon,' and *ḥānûṯ* to a word meaning 'dug out, enclosed place.'

Ullendorff (1954, 1956, 1967) treats Ethiopic affinities to Hebrew. Leslau (1958), for example, has compared *hiṯgaddēl* 'boast' and Tigrina *gändäla* 'stalk, be proud, lord it over someone.' Other suggestions include relating Hebrew *ykḥ* 'reprove, argue' to Geʿez *wäkkeḥa* 'raise a tumult,' *täwakḥa* 'quarrel, fight' (compare *ʾîš tᵉḵaḵîm* [Prov 29:13]). Hebrew *lʿʿ* (cf. Job 6:2) 'be confused of words' may be illuminated by *Geʿez talaʿleʿa* 'speak indistinctly, stammer.' A masters thesis done in 1971 by Gavra Michael under the guidance of C. Rabin (Bar-Asher 1978: 21, no. 1) applies lexicostatistics to the problem of the relationship between Biblical Hebrew and Mishnaic Hebrew and Classical Ethiopic.

Ullendorff (1967) has suggested that since *ʾdm* 'red' means 'pleasant' in Ethiopic, *ṣaḥ weʾādôm* (Cant 5:10) can be explained as meaning 'radiant and pleasant.' Barr (1974) rightly cautions about the elucidation which these studies of cognates can offer.

Other sources for cognates and loanwords

Extensive suggestions about lexical affinity and clarification of Hebrew on the basis of the Hamitic and Cushitic languages have been made by Rabin (1976b, 1977a; referred to above, p. 11). Rabin (1971d) sees in loanwords evidence for trade between Tamil Nad and Palestine in the first millennium B.C.E. His studies in Hittite and Aryan loanwords (1963a = 1964a, 1970b) will be discussed below.

Biblical Hebrew and Mari

Zohory (1969) compares the Hebrew of the Patriarchs with the Mari dialect. One problem that influences the outcome of any such linguistic comparison, of course, is the variety of opinions about the dating of the patriarchal narratives in Genesis. The Albright school has considered these narratives to contain much early, authentic material (cf. John Bright, *A History of Israel* [Philadelphia, 1972²] 67–102). This view has been challenged by Thomas L. Thompson in *The Historicity of the Patriarchal Narratives* (Berlin, 1974) and by John Van Seters in *Abraham in History and Tradition* (Yale University Press, 1975). A rather full bibliography of the literature covering the relationships between Mari and the Bible is found in Barry F. Beitzel, *The Place Names in the Mari Texts: An Onomastic and Toponymic Study* (doctoral dissertation, Dropsie College, Philadelphia, 1976).

The role of Aramaic

The earlier view that Aramaisms in a biblical book of necessity indicate a late date cannot be maintained any longer. Prior to the time when *Reichsaramäisch* became the *lingua franca* of the ancient Near East, there was ample opportunity, through military, political, and commercial contact, for Hebrew to absorb Aramaic loanwords. Driver (1953) suggested that supposed Aramaisms in pre-exilic literature may have descended from the common Semitic stock underlying both languages (Kutscher 1970: 358). Wagner (1967) has offered a lexicographical study based on the assumption that Israel and Aram had a common ancestry (cf. Deut 26:5). On the other hand, Wagner's erudite study of Aramaic lexical and grammatical influences (1966) has been criticized by Greenfield (1968a) precisely because of its failure to consider that Aramaic loanwords, originating in Akkadian, may have entered Canaanite, then Hebrew, as early as the Amarna period (Rabin 1970a: 323).

A. Hurvitz (1965; 1967a; 1972a: 33–35) deals at length with criteria for establishing "lateness." Isolated Aramaisms are insufficient as evidence, and one must demonstrate an accumulation of linguistic features which may clearly be contrasted with corresponding forms of expression characteristic of pre-exilic books. The early poetry, such as Deuteronomy 33 and Judges 5, contains some Aramaisms, and these may be characteristic of Northern Israel, e.g., *ᶜad šaqqamtî* 'until you (*or* I) arose'; *yᵉṯannû* 'will relate, narrate'; *ʾāṯāʾ* 'came.'

Indo-Aryan and Hittite loanwords

Rabin has contributed to the discussion some significant studies on loanwords in general (1962), as well as on specific areas of borrowing, e.g., in hippology, from the Indo-Aryan languages (1970b) and from Hittite (1963a = 1964a). Biblical words which are clarified by reference to the vocabulary of the aristocratic Indo-European *maryannu* warriors include: *bᵉruddîm* (Gen 31:10; Zech 6:3) < *parittannu* 'grey, pallid'; *paʾrûr* (Joel 2:6, Nah 2:11) < *pāndura-* 'pale color'; *dhr* (Nah 2:3) < *dor* 'trot'; *resen* < *rasnu* 'rein' (proposed in 1886 by DeLagarde); *nešeq* 'weapons' < *nisanga* 'hanging something on oneself,' i.e., the quiver or sword; *ʾaddîr* 'mighty one' < *ādrta-* 'honored, revered one,' *tōp̱eṯ, top̱teh* (Isa 30:33) 'place of burning' < *tapti-* 'heat' (all derivations from Sanscrit).

Another group of words which Rabin found etymologically isolated in the Semitic languages is traceable to Hittite (1963a = 1964a), e.g., *kullupi*, Akkadian *kalabb/ppatu*, Hebrew *kēlappōṯ*, Aramaic *qulbāʾ* 'hatchet'; Luwian *mitgaimi*, Akkadian *matqu*, Hebrew *māṯôq* 'sweet'; and Hittite *turawasa*, Ugaritic *trṯ*, Hebrew *tîrôš* 'must, wine.'

Hebrew and Akkadian

S. A. Kaufman (1970; 1975) cautiously challenges commonly held views on the primacy of Akkadian as a source of loanwords in Biblical Hebrew. A significant number of words, etymologically isolated in Akkadian, are considered by Kaufman to have originated elsewhere and to have been borrowed simultaneously by Akkadian and by the West Semitic forerunner of Aramaic and Hebrew. Other words, commonly thought to be loans, are considered by Kaufman to be cognates. The following words, for example, are assigned a non-Akkadian origin: *agammu/ʾaggām* 'marsh,' *agannu/ʾaggān* 'bowl,' *bību/bīḇ* 'drainage opening, gutter,' *gallābu/gallāḇ* 'barber,' *ittimali/ʾeṯmôl* 'yesterday,' *kimtu* 'family'/ *kîmāh* 'the Pleides' (see discussion in Waldman 1975a: 1292). On Akkadian–Hebrew affinities there have been numerous studies, a few of which we list here: Landsberger (1967), Held (1961, 1965b, 1970–71, 1973, 1974), Waldman (1969, 1970, 1971,

1972b, 1973, 1974a, 1974b, 1975b, 1976, 1977a, 1977b, 1979a, 1979b, 1979c, 1981, 1982, 1984), S. E. Loewenstamm (1982), and Chaim (H. R.) Cohen (1982). M. Weinfeld (1983) compares Akkadian and Hebrew idioms for defilement (of what is holy, or a woman), using the image of 'treading' (*kabāsu*, *kubbusu*, *kbs*, *drs*). Garfinkel (1983, doctoral dissertation) evaluates Akkadian influence on Ezekiel (see now Lipinski, *ZAl* 1 [1988], 61–73).

Other sources of loanwords

Grintz (1974–76) sought Egyptian derivations for certain ancient terms in the Priestly Code, e.g., *ʾaḇnēṭ* 'girdle' < *bnd*; *nôp̱eḵ* 'carbuncle' < *mkpt*; *piṭᵉḏāh* 'topaz' < **pḏdt*; *šānî* 'scarlet' < *šní* 'fur'; and *ʾep̱ôḏ* 'special garment' < *ʾipd*. The reflex of the last-mentioned word in Akkadian is *epattum* and in Ugaritic, *ʾipd*, although these words may not be native in either language. Rabin (1974–75a) has dissented from some of these proposals, suggesting instead a source in Dravidian for *piṭᵉḏāh* 'topaz,' namely, *pitha-* 'yellow.' Other possible loanwords from Sanscrit in Hebrew may be *kinnôr* 'harp' and *qôp̱* 'monkey.'

BIBLICAL HEBREW AND UGARITIC

Ugaritic studies have contributed greatly to the clarification of words and features of syntax and style in Biblical Hebrew. It is impossible to survey all of the vast literature on this subject, but we can list some basic resources. Good bibliographies can be found in Van Zijl (1972), Hospers (1973: 127–45), and G. R. Driver, *Canaanite Myths and Legends* (Edinburgh, 1956). A major bibliographic tool is *Ugarit-Bibliographie 1928–1966*, edited by M. Dietrich, O. Loretz, P. Berger, and J. Sanmartín (AOAT 20; Neukirchen-Vluyn, 1973). Literature in the field of Ugaritic is regularly listed in the *Newsletter for Ugaritic Studies*, edited by P. C. Craigie of the University of Calgary. The many articles by Mitchell J. Dahood have been indexed by Martinez (1967, 1981). Dahood's *Ugaritic-Hebrew Philology*, based on a series of articles appearing in *CBQ*, was published in 1976. The collected studies of S. E. Loewenstamm appeared in 1980. Articles in this field appear regularly in *Ugarit-Forschungen*. Biblical parallels with Ugaritic literature are treated in detail in Fisher (vol. 1, 1972; vol. 2, 1975) and Rummel (vol. 3, 1981). The texts are to be found in G. R. Driver's *Canaanite Myths and Legends* (see above); A. Herdner, *Corpus des tablettes en cunéiformes alphabétiques* (Paris, 1963); C. Virolleaud, *Le Palais royal d'Ugarit* II and V (Paris, 1957, 1965), *Ugaritica* V and VI (Paris, 1968, 1969); C. Gordon, *Ugaritic*

Basic resources

textbook (Rome, 1965). The dictionary by J. Aistleitner (Berlin, 1965) and *A Concordance of the Ugaritic Literature* by R. Whitaker (Cambridge, 1972) are also useful reference tools. Svi and Shifra Rin (1968) have produced an edition of the mythological texts with Hebrew transcription. Segert (1984) has written a basic grammar with texts and glossary.

Studies on specific topics

Important pioneering work was done by H. L. Ginsburg (1936), T. H. Gaster (*Thespis*; New York, 1950), and Cassuto (1951). Many stimulating philological suggestions can be found in the articles by Dahood (see Martinez 1967, 1981) and in his commentary on the Psalms (Anchor Bible; *Psalms*, vol. 1, 1965; vol. 2, 1968; vol. 3, 1970a); in numerous articles by Held (1953a, 1953b, 1959, 1961, 1962, 1965a, 1965b, 1968, 1973); Gevirtz (1963); Gray (1965); Rin (1963, 1967); S. E. Loewenstamm (1973–74; 1974; 1980, collected studies); Van Zijl (1972); Hummel (1955); A. Wieder (1965); Loretz on Psalms (1971a, 1973, 1974); Watson on verse patterns (1975); Avishur (1980a, 1980b, 1981, 1985); Fenton (1980); Craigie, comparing various philological approaches in the past fifty years (1981).

Ugaritic and Hebrew as related dialects: different views

The place of Ugaritic in the family of Northwest Semitic and in relationship to Hebrew has been much debated (cf. Goetze, *Language* 17 [1941] 127–38). Ginsburg (1970) and Greenfield (1969a) have also written on this matter. Dahood (1965: xxxviii–xliii, 197) has taken the position that Hebrew and Ugaritic are so closely related that they may be considered dialects of the same language.

M. Greenberg (1970) has criticized Dahood's method, in which the consonantal text is strictly maintained and revocalized according to a strictly applied rule of synonymous parallelism and with heavy dependence upon Ugaritic. Dahood (1971a) has defended his approach against the charge of "Pan-Ugariticism." Rainey, in his *A Social Structure of Ugarit* (Hebrew; Jerusalem, 1967) 15–16, maintains that Ugaritic is not Hebrew—not even an ancient stage of Hebrew—and that Biblical Hebrew did not develop out of Ugaritic. Rin (1971), reviewing Rainey's book, denies that most Ugaritologists consider Hebrew and Ugaritic to be identical. He holds, however, that many, such as Albright, Ginsberg, Cassuto, Friedrich, and Harris, consider Ugaritic and Biblical Hebrew to be dialects of one general "language of Canaan."

Many doctoral dissertations which explore Ugaritic literature and discuss the linguistic affinities between Hebrew and Ugaritic have been written in the interim. For example, the study by Clifford (1972) on the cosmic mountain theme contains stimulating ideas on philology; Khanjian (1974) has written on wisdom literature; Knutson (1971) on literary parallels; D. Marcus (1970a) on the Ugaritic verb in the light of comparative Semitics; W. D. Michel (1970) on Ugaritic philology and the book of Job; Parker (1967) on the grammar of prose texts; Pope (1949) on particles shared by Ugaritic and Hebrew, such as *w*, *p*, *b*, *l*, *k*; Tsumura (1973) on the *Drama of the Good Gods*; Watson (1970) on Mot, the god of death in Ugaritic literature and in the Bible. Other works in this field are a monograph by Blommerde (1969) on Northwest Semitic and the book of Job and the commentary of Marvin Pope (*Job*; Anchor Bible [New York, 1965]). D. Sivan (1983) considers the influence of Akkadian texts from Ugarit upon Ugaritic and Biblical Hebrew.

Contributions of Ugaritic to Hebrew studies

An excellent survey by Moran (1961) on the impact of Ugaritic studies on the understanding of Hebrew shows that evidence from Ugaritic has forced scholars to reconsider the view that Hebrew retains traces of obsolete case endings. For example, the final *he* in *šamaimāh* 'toward heaven' can no longer be regarded as *he-locale*, since it occurs in the purely consonantal Ugaritic script. Another result of comparison with Ugaritic is the recognition that enclitic *mem* occurs more frequently in Hebrew (as it does in Ugaritic) than once thought. This discovery has resulted in fewer emendations attempting to obliterate the *mem*; examples of the occurrence of enclitic *mem* in Ugaritic and Biblical Hebrew are, respectively, *bn-m-ᵓil* 'the son of El' and *mik̲t̲ᵉb̲ê-m-ᶜāmāl* 'writings of iniquity' (Isa 10:1). The particle *kî*, as in *kî-rabbāh* 'indeed great' (Gen 18:20), and the asseverative use of *l-* are now recognized in Hebrew, e.g., *kî l-YHWH māginnēnû* 'indeed Yahweh is our shield' (Ps 89:18). The *l*-vocative also exists in Hebrew, as can be seen in a comparison between Ugaritic *lbn ilm mt* 'O, son of El, Mot' and Hebrew *l-rōk̲ēb̲* 'O, rider' (Ps 68:34).

Ugaritic and Hebrew morphology

The *waw* of apodosis, found in literary materials from Mari and in Canaanite, also occurs in Hebrew and Ugaritic. The indefinite pronoun *mn*, discovered by Albright, must be added to the Hebrew lexicon; an example is found in Deut 33:11, emended to **umiššonᵉᵓāw mn yᵉqûmûn* 'and of his enemies whoever rises up.' The archaic use of the demonstrative in expressions like *zeh Sinay* 'the one of mercy' and in Mari personal names, e.g., *Zu-sumim* (Moran 1961: 61). The accepted view that *b*, *l*, and *m* are interchangeable in Ugaritic, Phoenician, Hebrew, and epigraphic South Arabic (cf. Dahood 1965: xxvi) has, however, been challenged by Zevit (1975).

Ugaritic and new lexical understanding in Hebrew

Gray (1965) includes in his general survey of the contribution of Ugaritic studies a chapter on lexical and grammatical relationships (1965: 259–311). He notes that many such relationships have already been observed, e.g., *ǵzr* 'hero,' cf. *ᶜōzrê hammilḥāmāh* 'the warriors' (1 Chr 12:1). Some of Gray's comparisons are speculative and open to question, e.g., *ᶜšr* 'serve with drink,' Ps 65:10, parallel to *watᵉšōqᵉqehāh* 'you watered it.' Earlier, Brown, Driver, Briggs held that *šqq* was identical with Assyrian *šūqu* 'abundance' (BDB, 1003). Dahood has argued for the existence in Hebrew of independent personal pronouns in the oblique case such as those existing in Ugaritic (1965: 156–57; 1970b). Kutler (1980) has recently made a study of the various terms in Phoenician, Hebrew, and Ugaritic for leaders and different social classes. There is further useful information in the study of personal names from Ugarit by Gröndahl (1967). Avishur (1980a) has proposed, on the basis of Ugaritic, to add *šnn* 'cry' to the Hebrew lexicon, noting that medieval poets used the root in this sense (based on Ps 73:21). He also finds (1981) many examples of the root *rwm* meaning 'build' and *rāmāh* 'religious structure' on the basis of the parallelism *bny*//*rmm*. Saur (1974) and Bornemann (1970; doctoral dissertation) discuss Ugaritic and Hebrew poetry.

Methodology and the value of Ugaritic-Hebrew comparisons

There has been some discussion about the proper and improper use of comparisons between Ugaritic and biblical material and the propriety of the comparative method in general. Simon B. Parker, in *Maarav* 2/1 (1981) discusses methodological principles in Ugaritic philology at length. Loewenstamm (1974) discusses the limits of parallels. Dietrich and Loretz (1977) sound a caution against excessive dependence upon Ugaritic lexicography while it is yet in flux. And finally, Fenton (1980), on the fiftieth anniversary of Ugaritic studies, has examined some of H. L. Ginsburg's major contributions (based on Ugaritic) to Hebrew lexicography. While questions have been raised over the years regarding some of Ginsburg's ideas, suggestions such as *spsg* 'glaze' and *šrᶜ thmtm* 'upwelling of the deeps' remain undisputed. Fenton also responds to the challenge of S. Talmon (*EI* 14 [1978] 117–240), who maintains that the internal linguistic unity of the canonical books is a firmer basis for textual emendation than Ugaritic. Morag, however, (*Leš* 45 [1981] 317–18) argues against Fenton that the emendation by Ginsberg of *śᵉdê tᵉrûmōṯ* 'fields of offerings' to *šrᶜ tᵉhōmōṯ* 'upwelling of the deeps' is not necessary (*Revised Standard Version*, 1951, translates according to the emendation).

OTHER LANGUAGES AND HEBREW

Gelb (1977) offers a preliminary evaluation of the position of the language of Ebla in relation to other Semitic dialects. The

The position of Eblite

Semitic language of Ebla appears to have the following features: retention of the initial *w*; a unique pattern of sibilants; the vowel change *a* >*e* in the environment of *ḫ*, as in Akkadian; the absence, as in Ugaritic, of the *ā́*>*ṓ* change; the 1 pl. pronoun *ʾana*, instead of *ʾănaḥnû*; the 3 sing. pronoun *šuwa*, similar to Akkadian; a *ŠD* stem and possibly a *DŠt*; and the non-operation of the Barth-Ginsberg law. This law, operative in Ugaritic and to some extent in Hebrew, states that the relationship of the prefix to the thematic vowel in the *Qal* imperfect is 1) *yaqtul*/*yaqtil*, e.g., *ʾamluku* 'I will rule' and 2) *yiqtal*, e.g., *ʾiqraʾ* 'I will call.' In Eblite, however, we find *yiqtul*, as in the personal name *Ipṭurni* [Yipṭurni] 'he has redeemed me/us' and *yiqtil*, as in *Igriš-Ḫalam* [Yigrish-Ḫalam] 'Halam has come'(?). In addition, Eblite has the infix-*t* formation, as in the name *Aštame-šarri.* A table of the various linguistic features indicates that Eblite is closest to Old Akkadian and Amorite and is most distant from Hebrew and Canaanite. Eblite script has affinities with the scribal traditions of Abu Ṣalabikh, post-Ur III Mari, and Kish. The publication of more texts, however, may modify these preliminary conclusions.

Dahood (1978b, 1979b, 1982) also discusses relationships between Eblite, Ugaritic, and Biblical Hebrew. His studies are indexed in Martinez (1981). His afterword to Pettinato (1981: 271–321) offers a sample of his method. He bases his method on the evidence from personal names, assumed cognates, and Sumerian-Eblite lexical lists. Thus, *nāḥāš bāriaḥ* is translated 'evil serpent,' because of an equation of *ba-rí-um* = ḪUL 'evil,' and Delilah means 'day' because of the equation of *da-la-lum* = UD 'day.' These lexical conclusions must be approached with caution because they are not based on occurrences of the words in extended contexts. A group of studies in this area has been edited by Fronzaroli (1984). A useful tool is now *The Tablets of Ebla, Concordance and Bibliography*, by S. Beld, W. W. Hallo and P. Michalowski (Winona Lake, IN: Eisenbrauns, 1984).

The Deir-ʿAlla inscriptions

The plaster inscriptions of Deir-ʿAlla have been published in a work edited by Hoftijzer and Van der Kooij (1976), which includes philological and grammatical analysis. Caquot and Lemaire (1977) have also dealt with these texts. B. Levine (1981) proposes new word divisions and readings, suggesting many affinities with Biblical Hebrew. Certain sound shifts and words characteristic of Aramaic occur in the inscriptions but there *waw*-consecutive also is present, as well as other affinities to Biblical Hebrew (B. Levine 1981: 195). M. Weinfeld (1982a) draws comparisons with phrases in the biblical Balaam story and other prophetic literature.

Ammonite is the subject of studies by Horn and Cross (*BASOR* 193 [1969] 2–13, 13–19), Cross (1969a, 1973a, 1975), H. O. Thompson and F. Zayadine (1973, 1974), Garbini (1970), Baldacci (1978), Puech and Rofé (1973), Krahmalkov (1976, an Ammonite lyric poem), Fulco (1978, 1979), Shea (1978, 1979, 1981), Veenhof (1972, 1973) and Jackson (1980, doctoral dissertation; 1983). Jackson, in his dissertation, attempts an analysis of the orthographic system, the morphology, and the lexicon, with a recognition of the limitations stemming from the fragmentary na-

Ammonite and Hebrew

ture of the corpus. The conclusions remain vague: there are similarities to contemporary Phoenician, Israelite, Judahite, and Moabite, but the isoglosses are not sufficient to show a clear linguistic affinity (revised book form, 1983).

Amorite

Amorite is known only from personal names. Huffmon (1965) dealt with 900 names, providing grammatical analysis and a lexicon. Now Gelb, Bartels, Vance, and Whiting (1980) have published a computer-aided analysis of Amorite, based upon 6662 names.

Phoenician, Aramaic, and Moabite

Other languages studied in the light of their relationship to Hebrew are Phoenician (Dahood 1971a), the dialect of Byblos (Moran, doctoral dissertation, 1950), and Moabite (Segert 1961; Andersen 1966). B. Haines (1966) has done a palaeographical study of Aramaic inscriptions antedating 500 B.C.E. Tawil demonstrates the relationship of Aramaic royal inscriptions to Akkadian prototypes and discusses the influence of these formulas upon the Bible (*Or* 40 [1974] 40–65; *JNES* 32 [1973] 477–82). The studies by Fitzmyer on the Sefire inscriptions (1961, 1967) contain much material on biblical affinities. A doctoral dissertation by Brauner (1974) deals with the Akkadian sources of Old Aramaic expressions, with material that is relevant for Biblical Hebrew. Aufrecht (1975) has prepared a concordance of Aramaic inscriptions. Segert (1960) discusses comparative Semitic lexicography and (1969) computer-aided research of this subject. Cathcart (1973) studies the book of Nahum in the light of Northwest Semitic, and Kuhnigk (1974) does the same with Hosea. Penar (1975) compares the Hebrew of Ben Sira with Northwest Semitic. The last three studies are in the spirit and method of Dahood. Grabbe (1977) applies comparative philology to the book of Job. Moabite ostraca have been studied by Cross (1969b, 1973b, 1976) and by Shea (1977).

An Akkadian-Aramaic bilingual

The Akkadian-Aramaic bilingual inscription of King *Hds*^{c}*y* from Tell Fekherye has been published by P. Bordreuil, A. R. Millard, and A. Abou Assaf (Paris, 1982). A study by Greenfield and Shaffer (1982) deals with the writing, phonology, morphology, and biblical affinities of the Aramaic inscription, and a study by

J. Naveh (1978–79) reviews briefly the development of Phoenician and Aramaic script. Naveh argues that the date of the writing is the 11th century B.C.E., against the view of the editors of the *editio princeps* that it is from the 9th century. He rejects their arguments that the uncharacteristic script is the result of archaizing or a special development. The texts are dealt with by S. A. Kaufman (1982), Zadok (1982), and by Gropp and Lewis (1985).

SYNTAX

Syntactic functions of verbal forms

The standard grammars deal with syntax, e.g., G-K, §§106–12. Recent treatments include Rabin (1964b), Watts (1964), Williams (1965), Diethelm (1977), and Thorion (1984). Lambdin (1971b) classifies verb and clause sequences as follows: Imperfect + *w^e* + perfect expresses future or habitual/durative action. In general, there are two types of clause-relationship among those joined by *w^e*: 1) consecutive sequential, where the second clause is temporally or logically posterior to or consequent to the first, signaled by *w^e* (or wa-) + verb, and 2) disjunctive, signaled by *w^e* + non-verb. Types of disjunctive clauses include those which indicate contrast, describe an attendant situation or circumstance, serve as additional explanation, or constitute a parenthesis. Initial or terminative clauses, indicating the completion of one episode or the beginning of another, also take the disjunctive form, e.g., *w^e* + definite subject + perfect. There are also conjunctive, consecutive sequences: perfect + *w^e* + unconverted perfect and imperfect + *w^e* + unconverted imperfect. These latter are seldom used in punctual narrative but occur in simple listings of clauses without any temporal or logical consecution (Lambdin 1971b:107–8, 119, 162–64).

Tense consecution

Rosén (1969a) has also studied tense consecution, and some of the patterns he has identified may overlap with those outlined by Lambdin and summarized above: 1) clause-initial jussive in the second clause expresses consequence of the preceding clause; 2) perfect + negation (*lōʾ*) + imperfect expresses consequence of the preceding clause; 3) consecutive (*wa-*) in clause-initial position in the second clause expresses continuation of a reported series of events; and 4) perfect in clause-initial position in the second clause expresses intent; 5) jussive in non-initial position in the second clause expresses volition; 6) perfect + imperfect, in non-initial positions, expresses occurrence contemporaneous with the first clause; 7) pausal form + imperfect, in non-initial position: the second clause is antithetical to the first; and finally, 8) perfect in non-initial position in the second clause describes situation, background, and circumstances relating to the first. Further study in this area has been done by Rosén (1985).

The verbless clause

Earlier views of the verbless clause or nominal sentence have been subjected to severe criticism by Andersen (1970a) in a significant study. The commonly held view that the normal order is S(ubject + P(redicate) and that the exception P + S emphasizes P as the dominant idea or psychological subject is rejected by Andersen. In establishing a set of rules and patterns, he makes use of immediate constituent analysis and transformational grammar. The conclusion is that it is possible to formulate a set of rules which can generate all the clauses actually found in Biblical Hebrew and many others which would be accepted by the "native speaker" as "grammatical." Based upon a corpus of 555 specific examples, the following patterns are said to emerge. When the predicate is definite (a clause of identification), the order is S + P. When the predicate is indefinite (a clause of classification), the sequence is P + S. Where the predicate is a suffixed noun, S + P and P + S are about equally distributed. S + P is the order where a definite subject has a participle or a participial phrase as predicate. When marginal modifiers are placed before, after, or within the clause nucleus, there is no peturbation of the normal clause structure.

A critique of Andersen's study and of some of his classifications has been written by Blau (1972–73). A masters thesis by Biran (1977) deals with the nominal sentence in the Former Prophets. A doctoral dissertation by Thorion (1977) treats the complex sentence in the prose of the First Commonwealth. Andersen (1974) has done a further study of the verbal sentence in Biblical Hebrew.

The particle *kî*

Bandstra (doctoral dissertation, 1982) studies the syntax of the particle *kî* in Biblical Hebrew and Ugaritic. He establishes the following relationships: if the *kî*-clause follows the main clause, its function is to indicate complementation, consequence, adversion, or causation. If the *kî*-clause precedes the main clause, it indicates temporal circumstances, condition, or concession. He rejects the commonly held view that *kî* before the verb at the end of the clause is an indicator of emphasis. Variations in word order within the clause are a function of discourse strategy and are not due to emphasis.

ʾAšer-clauses and Aramaic

Watts (1959) has studied *ʾăšer*-clauses, affirming their attributive or secondary nature. He recognizes three levels of development: 1) *ʾăšer* + fully developed verbal or substantive clause; 2) no *ʾăšer*, but a fully developed verbal or substantive clause acting as a contact or naked relative clause; and 3) *ʾăšer* + prepositional phrase. The last level is not a primary syntactical construct (that is, one based upon the indicative clause) but a tertiary one. In a second stage of development it is converted to a secondary construction (attributive) by prefixing the particle *ʾăšer*. In a third stage, it tends to become a full clause by the insertion of *yēš* or *hāyāh*. Qimron (1981) demonstrates that a hitherto unrecognized use of *ʾăšer*, *še*, and Aramaic *dî* is at the beginning of a main clause before the imperfect or infinitive absolute to indicate command or obligation. Kogut (1981–82) classifies three pleonastic uses of the pronoun: postposited, proleptic, and doubled.

Diverse syntactic topics

Radday and Schor (1977) demonstrate that the use of the *waw-conjunctivum* as a criterion for distinguishing between authors of biblical materials is statistically inconclusive. Azar (1977b) treats the prepositional phrase as an attribute in Biblical Hebrew. Markovitz (1970), in a masters thesis, deals with formulas of introduction to direct speech in the book of Genesis. A masters thesis by A. Tene (1972) deals with negation in Genesis.

Sadka (1980) evaluates two views on the use of *hûʾ* in a sentence such as *kî haddām hûʾ hannapeš*, 'for the blood is the soul.' One is that the pronoun is a copula and the other is that it is the subject of an imbedded sentence. He shows that these views are not mutually exclusive.

E. Rubinstein (1975–76) treats *lipnê* 'before' in its appearances before a noun phrase. Proceeding from the surface to the deep structure, it is possible to show that these combinations can be divided into several groups which show a historical progression from *lipnêe*, marking the locative, to *lipnê*, an indicator of "the one who thinks" and "the one who causes." Haneman (1975–76) historically surveys the use of *bēn . . . bēn* 'between . . . between' in Biblical Hebrew and Mishnaic Hebrew. Brin (1982) analyzes the formula *mi- . . . ulᵉmaʿălāh/wāhālʾāh* 'from . . . and above/beyond' in the Bible. M. Kaddari (1973, 1976), in his studies in biblical syntax, analyzes many topics on the basis of transformational grammar. These topics include: the double object, the double adverb, the order of adverbs, the ergative, and a syntactic-semantic analysis of the verb *ntn* 'give' in Biblical Hebrew.

Blau (1971d) discusses the frequent repetition of the predicate in Biblical Hebrew, e.g., "and (he shall) burn it on wood with fire; where the ashes are poured out shall it be burnt" (Lev 4:12). The reason for the repetition may be to avoid the use of too many periods in the sentence or it may be due to the process of adding the complement as an afterthought. Von Gabelenz expressed the view that every word in a sentence becomes a psychological predicate of those words which precede it. Blau discusses Biblical Hebrew and *piyyuṭ* Hebrew in the light of this process. Ben-Asher (1978) uses a transformational grammar approach in his analysis of causative *Hifᶜil* verbs with double objects in Biblical Hebrew. His observation is that one of the objects may be an imbedded clause or an anaphoric pronoun. W. Gross (1974) discusses the relationship of formulas to syntax and (1978) syntactic phenomena in narrative. Sappan (1980) analyzes nominal sentences with an abstract noun at the head of the predicate phrase. Qimron (1983) studies the negation *ᵓal* in Biblical Hebrew, Mishnaic Hebrew, and the Qumran literature. The use of the negative with the 2nd person consistently indicated the same thing, namely, a negative command. With the 1st and 3rd person there was a change: at Qumran *ᵓal* was equivalent to *lōᵓ* and was used for literary effect. In Mishnaic Hebrew it expressed a valuation, not a wish.

Labuschagne is the editor of *Studies in Hebrew Syntax and Biblical Exegesis* (1973), which includes his own paper on *hēn* and *hinnēh*, papers by Van Leeuwen on *ᵓim*, by Mulder on *yaᶜan*, by Brongers on *lᵉmaᶜan*, and by Jongeling on *raq*. Earlier, Muilenberg (1961) treated the linguistic and rhetorical usages of the particle *kî*. Blau (1977a) studies sentence adverbials, that is, those adverbials that refer to the whole sentence and stand in frontal position, separated from the rest of the sentence. The material is drawn from all periods of Hebrew and is compared with Arabic.

Blau (1979b) expands upon a suggestion made by Bravmann concerning the "pregnant" use of possessive pronouns in an impersonal context, e.g., *wᵉdāḇaq bᵉᵓištô* 'and he cleaves unto his wife,' instead of . . . *bᵉᵓiššạ* 'unto a woman.' Blau offers more examples of redundant possessive pronouns attached to nouns which indicate intrinsic possession and/or have a tendency to concreteness, e.g., *qārûᶜa kuttontô* 'with his coat rent' (2 Sam 15:32), *lāṯēṯ ᵓoḵlām bᵉᶜittô* 'to give (their) food in due time' (Ps 104:27) and *ᵓim yihye nᵉḇîᵓăḵem* 'if you have a prophet' (Num 12:6).

Kogut (1979–80) reviews critically a work on biblical syntax by Rottenberg (1979), who proposes various rules of exegesis based on the assumption that ellipsis plays a major role in Biblical Hebrew. He criticizes the debatable classifications of parts of speech and proposes alternate analyses of the verse. Hoftijzer (1981) has produced a study of the syntactic use of *he-locale*. The verbal clause in Jeremiah 37–45 and Esther 1–10 is treated diachronically in a doctoral dissertation by Guenther (1977), and D. L. Thompson

(1973, doctoral dissertation) surveys the order of adverbial modifiers in Genesis and Proverbs.

RHETORIC AND POETRY

General studies on rhetoric

Recently there have been many studies on Hebrew rhetoric, the most outstanding work being by: Lundbom (1973), who deals with rhetorical devices in Jeremiah, among them *inclusio* and *chiasmus*; Perlitt (1969); Lau (1970); Baltzer (1971); Greenfield (1967); M. Weinfeld (1972: 59–157, 320–65) and Tadmor (1982) on covenantal rhetoric, the last two making comparison with Mesopotamian treaties; M. Fox (1973) on the word *ṭôḇ* in covenant terminology; Broida (1973) on Deuteronomic imagery and rhetorical devices; and Rimbach (1972) and Dahood (1967) on animal imagery. Greenfield (1979) finds poetic devices, including parallelism, in Daniel and in Old Aramaic inscriptions. Adams (1984) examines the diachronic development of narrative and exhortation discourse structures in Hebrew epigraphical sources.

Work on biblical poetry includes: D. N. Freedman (1960); Cross and Freedman (1975); Loretz (1971a, 1971b, 1973, 1974), who uses a comparative approach to biblical poetry; A. Hurvitz (1961, masters thesis) on the language of biblical poetry; and Robertson (1966) and W. Watson (1984). Broadribb (1972) presents a historical review of studies of Hebrew poetry. Robertson (1966) distinguishes between early and standard poetic Hebrew, some of the markers of the earlier stage being the suffixes *-anhû*, *-annû*, *-ēmô*, and enclitic *mem*. Robertson also attempts to set criteria for distinguishing between genuinely early and later archaizing material. Applying these criteria to Exodus 15, he shows it to be early. An illustration of the uncertainty in this area, however, is the fact that different students arrive at different conclusions. D. N. Freedman (1975), treating Exodus 15 thematically, dates it in the 12th century B.C.E., while Butler (1971), on the other hand, concludes that the allusions to Yahweh's abode, the elements of confessional praise, and traditional oral formulaic language reveal a late date. He sees in the poem evidence of a long development finally shaped by the Deuteronomic school in the late exilic period.

Specific topics

Yoder (1972) provides a general treatment of poetic devices in Hebrew. Word pairs occurring in Ugaritic and Hebrew have been studied by Cassuto (1951), Gevirtz (1963), and Held (1953b). Based on a knowledge of these studies, Yoder (1970, 1971) has analyzed word pairs and formulaic expressions. He concludes that if 50% of the parallelism in a poem results from formulas, the poem can be regarded as orally composed. Thus, oral composition is indicated by higher formulaic density. The presence of fixed pairs gives the poem a stylized character so that, no matter how close to the time of the historical event is was composed, the high proportion of traditional compositional units precludes its being a faithful rendering of that event.

Whitley (1975c) deals with poetic diction, while W. Watson (1975) compares verse patterns in Hebrew, Ugaritic, and Akkadian. Sirat (1968b) surveys the evolution of poetic language. Alphabetic acrostics are studied from a form-critical approach by K. C. Hanson (1984, doctoral dissertation).

Many problems remain in establishing clearly that Hebrew poetic literature was originally oral rather than composed in written form. A useful bibliography and discussion is found in Culley (1976). The application of transformational grammar to Canaanite and biblical parallelism can yield interesting results. For example, Greenstein (1974) concludes that the same words in different segments of a "staircase parallelism" grouping have different syntactic functions. Bronznick (1979) discusses metathetic or proleptic parallelism. T. Collins discusses line forms in Hebrew poetry (1978).

Theories of parallelism and semantics

The relationship of parallelism to semantic units has been investigated by Kaddari (1967–68). He argues that parallel metric structures may have impact on the meaning of semantic units, but only in synonymous or antithetical parallelism, and a number of restrictions must be observed: 1) constituent semantic units have to be established within their proper boundaries, 2) surrounding words and subject matter must be carefully considered, and 3) parallel semantic units have to be found in identical semantic structures. In most cases, parallel structure emphasizes common semantic features of the units. Sometimes, however, stereotyped phrases are split up into their constituents, without impairing their semantic unity, a feature earlier observed by Yellin (1933–34). These considerations apply to antithetical and synonymous parallelism. In the general category of "synthetic parallelism," however, the parallelism is formal. While there is no semantic parallelism between the constituent units in this category, there is a common semantic field which embraces them; e.g., in Ps 5:3 the common field is theophany, and in Ps 69:10 it is concern for the destruction of the temple. Kaddari also asks what precedes—does meaning depend upon parallelism or vice versa? He concludes that, at the outset, semantic boundaries must be established, thus indicating that semantic considerations take precedence.

Adele Berlin, in a doctoral dissertation (see *JBL* 96 [1977] 567–68, n 6) observes that parallelisms can be generated on several grammatical levels. The syntactic level governs the arrangement of the parallel terms, while the lexical level provides the word or phrase pairs used. There are also shifts on the morphological level, e.g., changes in tense, in subject, and in mood. The various types of parallelism, grammatical and morphological, are classified in a further study (1979). These types include: noun//pronoun; noun, pronoun//relative clause; substantive//verb; and word pairs of different tense, gender or quality, such as positive//negative and nominal//verbal. Another study (1978) explores similarities between biblical and Sumerian parallelism. Berlin (1985) has recently published a full treatment of parallelism, where she connects word-pairing with processes of word association.

A doctoral dissertation by Galbraith (1981) attempts to show quantitatively the change in parallel structures through time. The study establishes a relative time scale and uses five control areas: lines of more than four words, series, semantic and grammatical incongruity, ballast structures, and the ratio of classical patterns to metric units.

Sappan (1974) deals with the correspondence between the comprehensive semantic parallelism of linguistic strings and their structures. Sappan recognizes several classes: 1) complete correspondence, 2) lesser correspondence (i.e., noun vs. pronoun, adjective vs. noun in genitive in the parallel clauses), 3) lesser correspondence (two different types of phrases), 4) lesser correspondence (a single word in one clause corresponds to a syntactic or lexical phrase in the other, and 5) different construction in both clauses. In categories 1 and 2, semantic units coincide with the semantic constituents of their respective classes down to all levels of independent constituent analysis. In types 3 and 4, however, corresponding semantic units occupy syntactically equivalent positions only at a relatively higher level of independent constituent analysis. So what is the common denominator between types 3 and 4? The common denominator is the fact that differently-structured semantic units do occur in the same syntactical frame or context. They can be substituted for each other, and the new string is linguistically acceptable. In part of the corpus in section 5, such substitution is also possible. However, other cases in category 5 can be shown to be equivalent in their deep structure by means of transformation.

Geller (1979) follows the lead of Roman Jakobson (*Language* 42 [1966] 423) in seeking to establish a rigorous methodology for

Parallelism and transformational grammar

the analysis of parallelism. The corpus is analyzed with appropriate symbols according to the following categories: text, translation, metrical units, grammatical units, syllabic symmetry, grammatical structure, and transformation. Transformation is important when semantically parallel units are grammatically incompatible. A reconstructed sentence which embraces both parts of the parallelism, is then formulated. The result of the analysis is stated symbolically, presenting the steps of deletion-compensation, parallelism, or transformation by which the B line was hypothetically generated by the A line.

Assonance and alliteration

Poetic features such as rhyme and assonance have been discussed by Rankin (1930) and Yellin (1933–34). Glück (1971) has done further work on assonance in relation to the emotional impact of a poem, showing, for example, the way in which rhyme in a curse (Gen 3:14–15) makes it more ominous or how the prevalence of gutturals may heighten the feeling of anger. In his study of Psalm 137, D. N. Freedman (1971) finds a relationship between assonance and emotion. We may offer some preliminary observations. An A-clause may be dominated by a consonant group, while in the B-clause this consonant group is sparsely represented, if at all (e.g., *lû šāqôl yiššāqēl kaʿśî w*^{e}*hawwāṯî b*^{e}*mōʾznayim yiśś*^{e}*ʾû-yāḥaḏ*, 'O that my vexation were weighed and all my calamity laid in the balance.' A different pattern is *w*^{e}*rûaḥ al-pānay yaḥălōp̱ t*^{e}*sammēr śaʿăraṯ b*^{e}*śārî*, 'a spirit glided past my face; the hair of my flesh stood up' (Job 6:2, 4:15; *RSV*). However, in other verses, even within the same poem, there is no apparent pattern. See now A. Berlin (1985; 103–126) on sound pairing. Another poetic feature, paronomasia, is discussed by Glück (1970).

Resources and theories of metrics

Bibliographies on Hebrew metrics are to be found in Eissfeldt (1965: 57–64, 81–127, 731–72), in the prolegomenon by Freedman (1972a) to the reissued volume, *The Forms of Hebrew Poetry*, by George Buchanan Gray, and in Stuart (1976: 239–45). Various theories of Hebrew metrics have been proposed, and a historical survey is found in Eissfeldt (1965: 57–64) and in Stuart (1976: 1–10). Those Stuart includes in what he calls "traditional school," including Bellermann, Saalschütz, Ley, Budde, and Sievers, described the poetry in terms of units of stress. Ley, for example, counted the accented syllables, ignoring the number of unaccented syllables. Bellermann thought Hebrew poetry followed a roughly hexameter pattern, with words accented on the ultima, while Saalschütz place the accent on the penult. Sievers, affirming the anapestic character of Hebrew verse, considered the unaccented syllables to be quite important and part of a pattern, measured in four-time, with two unaccented syllables in each foot. What Stuart terms the "semantic parallelism" school, including Lowth, Gray, and Robinson, subordinated considerations of stress and tone and emphasized instead units of indivisible words and word elements. Gray (1915, reprinted 1972), on the other hand, counted the number of stressed words, holding that if they are equal in both cola the line is balanced. He goes on to explain that the *qinah* meter is "incomplete parallelism without compensation." Semantic parallelism is considered the main factor, and phonetic considerations are treated as secondary.

A third group of scholars, labeled the "alternating meter" school by Stuart, includes Horst, Mowinckel, and Segert. They were anticipated by Bickell, who believed that all Hebrew poetry was either iambic or trochiac: a colon with an even number of syllables was iambic, while one with an uneven number was trochaic. Mowinckel stressed the iamb as the basic unit, and his scansions add one more stress to that of the "semantic parallelism" school. The extra factor is comprised of meaningful units which are not independent, such as suffixes, pronouns, and prepositions.

Syllable-counting in metric analysis

Recently, Culley (1970) has defended the view that individual syllables are to be counted in determining the meter. The number of syllables per colon is high in comparison with the number of stresses or words. Culley's view is that definite restrictions were imposed on biblical poetry and that lines and cola tend to a typical length. He treats the *shewa medium* as vocal, agreeing with Bergsträsser in opposition to Harris, who considered it silent.

D. N. Freedman (1972a) rejects the position of Gray (1915) and favors counting the syllables, including the unstressed ones. He also rejects the category of synthetic parallelism (in Gray's terminology, "incomplete parallelism"), considering it a non-specific catchall. He contents that, if rhythm with all of its deliberate variety and irregularity is the fundamental criterion of Hebrew verse, then parallelism is a stylistic device and not a necessary characteristic of biblical verse. There are numerous examples of complementary or "overlapping" non-synonymous parallelism in which sequential actions or further amplification are clothed in parallel form. Parallelism is also partly influenced by metric considerations. This view should be contrasted with that of Kaddari (1967–68), who makes the semantic field the unifying factor.

Cross and Freedman (1975), following the lead of Albright and Haupt, have emphasized the total number of syllables in the line, pointing to the large measure of symmetry that exists in Hebrew and Ugaritic poetry. This approach involves either emendation of the consonantal text or a revocalization in a manner differing from the received Masoretic Text. Stuart (1976) applies the method of syllable-counting to selected examples of Hebrew and Ugaritic poetry, showing that couplets and triplets are largely symmetrical. To obtain these results, however, he attempts to arrive at a "pre-masoretic" vocalization, which, following A. Sperber (1959a, 1966), he considers preferable to the masoretic. D. N. Freedman (1978), using similar methods, assigns Psalm 113 to the earliest period of Hebrew poetry, the pre-monarchic.

Metric accent and parallelism

Kuryłowicz (1973a: 66–77) discusses Hebrew metrics in the context of comparison with Greek, Old Germanic, Arabic, and Akkadian metrics (1973a: 158–87). Hebrew metric accent is closer to the colloquial than the quantitative meter of Arabic, but it is still not identical with the normal accent of the spoken word. Kuryłowicz maintains that a distinction exists between the metric pattern and the phonetic transcription of the text. In the metric analysis, secondary and even primary accents are replaced by the primary accent in the word-complex which is part of the hemistich; thus, a metric analysis of Ps 2:12 shows: *ʾašrḗ* | *kol-ḥôsê ḇṓ* 'happy are all who trust in him.' The word-complexes can be readily identified by the lenition (aspiration) of /bgdkpt/ when following a vowel. This is true within the word-complex, but they are plosive when beginning a new one. In realization, however, the phonetic accent cannot be overlooked, and the secondary accents (marked ̀-, rather than with the metric accent ́-) appear: *ʾašrḗ* | *kol-ḥȏsê ḇṓ*. The difference between the metrical pattern and its realization parallels the difference between the phoneme and its realization. Rejecting the analysis of Sievers, who maintained that no accented syllable of the colloquial language can remain unaccented in poetry, Kuryłowicz holds that the accented syllable of the foot is always represented by a colloquial accent, but that there are many primary and secondary accents which are overlooked in metric accentuation. In this way he rejects Segert's hypothesis (*AO* 21 [1953] 481ff.) of alternating meters. This alternation can take place as a secondary development, but arbitrary assumptions regarding accent shift and syncope, with textual change, must be avoided.

Free rhythm and Hebrew poetry

De Moor (1978) evaluates the various theories of Hebrew metrics in the light of research in Ugaritic, noting, as a caution, that there is no unanimity on the interpretation, vocalization, and metric analysis of Ugaritic poetry. The diversity of conflicting theories of Hebrew poetry is well known. He arrives at the conclusion that West Semitic poetry did not know any kind of meter, not even a free meter. The smallest unit in Ugaritic and Hebrew poetry is not the syllable but the word or cluster of words bearing a main stress (foot). Both the Hebrew and Ugaritic poetic traditions were based upon a free rhythm similar to that of Jewish cantillation and Gregorian chant, and the poetic rhythm must be considered together with the rendition of the poem in song. The prominence of the syllable bearing the stress was expressed by drawing out the tone or distributing it over a series of notes, thus lending it a great deal of flexibility. In parallel stiches the number of feet was usually the same. The singers had many devices to restore an appearance of symmetry when parallel stiches were not in perfect rhythmical balance.

Different bases for metric analysis

Pardee (1981) evaluates the current situation in the study of Hebrew and Ugaritic metrics. It is his contention that the term "meter" is arbitrarily used and largely inapplicable to both these literatures because they lack a predominant form of rhythm, and metric predictability is problematic. He rejects the metric scansion of Stuart (1976) as based on an artificial regularity. B. Margalit (1975) proposes a system of metrics based on "word-meter" and the "verse-unit." Pardee, however, holds that only the latter term has any validity and that the ancient poet sensed intuitively the proper length of his line.

Further study in parallelism includes the doctoral dissertation of A. M. Cooper (1976). O'Connor (1980) examines current theories from the vantage point of modern linguistics. He rejects the metrical hypothesis and maintains that parallelism is not a single feature but a "congeries of phenomena." Demolishing Lowth's categories of synonymity and antonymity, he attempts to reconstruct the "standard description." He rejects the idea of Culley and Freedman that a typical number of syllables governs the meter of A and B. Instead, he posits a matrix of syntactic constraints that are visible in the base and surface structure of the line. The metrical component is replaced by a system of syntactic constriction, and parallelism is demoted to a series of tropes which bind the lines together into groups of twos, threes, or more. This approach is surveyed and criticized by Kugel (1981: 315–23).

Kugel (1981) surveys the history of thought about parallelism from ancient times, through the medieval and renaissance periods, and down to modern times. It is his contention that Lowth was original, not in his concepts, but in the combining of earlier ideas into a synthesis. Kugel rejects synonymity and antonymity. He sees the poetic line as a sequence: first part—pause—next part—greater pause. The B part of the line is subjoined and emphatic. It does not merely repeat A, but carries it further, emphasizing, expanding, echoing, and defining. Geller (1982) offers a detailed critique of both Kugel (1981) and O'Connor (1980). He regards them as two opposite extremes, the latter rejecting all subjective and esthetic factors and the former rejecting description, considering the Bible to be more than literature.

Parallelism and chiasm

W. Watson (1975) compares verse patterns in Ugaritic, Hebrew, and Akkadian; Whitley (1975c) discusses poetic diction. Chiasm in the Bible and other literatures is treated by Ceresko (1975, 1976, 1978), Di Marco (1975, 1976), Kogut (1977), Willis (1979), and Boadt (1975). Welch (1981) has edited a group of studies in chiasm. Tsumura (1983) treats extensively insertions in a parallelistic structure which bears a relationship to both the A and B elements. Avishur has dealt extensively with parallel pairs in the Bible and parallel literatures, in a doctoral dissertation (1974) and other studies (1971–72, 1974 [book version, 1977a], 1975–76b, 1977b, 1979b, 1984, 1985). In another study (1975–76a) Avishur traces the influence of biblical parallelism in the later *piyyuṭ*, and (1973) he also discusses patterns of repetition of numbers in biblical and parallel literatures.

Papers by Geller, Greenstein and A. Berlin, delivered at a Dropsie College symposium (May 11, 1982) have been published as a *Jewish Quarterly Review* supplement by Eisenbrauns under the title: *A Sense of Text: The Art of Language in the Study of Biblical Literature*.

2

THE SECOND COMMONWEALTH AND RABBINIC HEBREW

ARAMAIC INFLUENCE AND LANGUAGE CHANGE

The change in importance of Aramaic

The incident described in 2 Kgs 18:26, in which the officials of the Judean king understand Aramaic while the populace does not, indicates that official Aramaic (or Reichsaramäisch) was used mainly as a medium of diplomatic exchange. When we compare this text with Neh 8:7–8, in which the Torah must be interpreted and, possibly, translated (cf. *t.b. Ned.* 37b) and Neh 13:24, in which so many are unable to speak the language of Judah, we can see the dramatic change which took place during the intervening 250 years. While Aramaic influence is not necessarily an indication of lateness in a biblical book, as we have noted above (Driver 1953; Greenfield 1968a), these influences become more extensive at this time.

General resources on Second Commonwealth Hebrew

General discussions of this later stage in the Hebrew language can be found in the bibliographies listed for individual biblical books such as Jonah, Job, Daniel, Ezra–Nehemiah, Chronicles, Esther, the Song of Songs, and Koheleth (Eissfeldt 1965). There is important discussion and citation of literature in Rabin (1970a: 316–20) and Kutscher (1970: 358–60; 1982: 71–77). The general characteristics of late biblical prose are treated by Polzin (1976) and will be referred to below, as will be the criteria posited by A. Hurvitz (1972a; on the prose tale of Job, cf. idem, 1974).

The changes between identical historical sources in Samuel and Kings, on the one hand, and Chronicles, on the other, are easily seen in the handy parallel column edition of Bendavid (1965; Rabin 1970a: 316, n 65). Japhet (1966–67) has described some of the dynamics of change. Little known roots, for example, are replaced in Chronicles by better-known ones, one reason being that changes have occurred in the meaning of the older roots. The new root may bear some graphic similarity to the one it replaces. Some Aramaic influence is discernible here, e.g., *heḥĕzîq* 'took hold,' in the specialized sense of 'consolidated authority' is Aramaic in influence (cf. *heḥĕsînû*, Dan 7:22). Similarly, *nṣḥ* comes to mean 'dominate, rule,' replacing an earlier *rdh* (Dan 6:4). This type of scribal change, reflecting a changed linguistic situation, is an early example of the process of popularizing and vulgarizing later seen in the Qumran Isaiah Scroll, the Samaritan Bible, and in the Hebrew *Vorlage* of the Septuagint (Kutscher 1959: 23–34, 57–65).

Linguistic features of Chronicles

Japhet has argued (1968) that Ezra–Nehemiah is an earlier example of post-biblical Hebrew than Chronicles, but this view has been challenged by Newsome (1975: 202). Bendavid (1967: 71–72) cites examples of Aramaic influence in Chronicles, among them *ᶜal* 'on' for *ᵓel* 'to' (but compare the Arad ostracon: Aharoni 1981: 17–18, no. 3, lines 3–4, following the view of Rainey, *ibid.,* 18, n. 2; *IR* no. 52:3) the use of *l* before the direct object, and a change in word order, the verb moving to the end of the clause. The construction *ᵓănî hûᵓ ᵓăšer* 'I am the one who' represents a translation of Aramaic phrases with *di* (see Kutscher 1970: 352–53). In earlier Biblical Hebrew the pronoun *ᵓānōḵî* 'I' would have been repeated; later Biblical Hebrew has *ᵓănî hûᵓ ᵓăšer* 'I am the one who' (2 Sam 24:17, 1 Chr 21:17; cf. Talshir, *VT* 38, 165–93).

Dates of Ezra–Nehemiah and Chronicles

A. Hurvitz (1967a, doctoral dissertation; 1967b, 1971, 1972) has enumerated various linguistic features which must be present in concert for a piece of literature to be identified as post-exilic, and he has assigned Psalms 103, 117, 119, 124, 125, and 145 to a later period. These features include: the double plural, also present in Mishnaic Hebrew, e.g., *ḥorošê ᶜēṣîm* 'craftsmen in wood' (1 Chr 14:1); *ᵓēṣel* 'at' for *beṯôḵ* or *beqereḇ* 'in'; *āmar tehillāh* 'recite, tell the praise of'; *beḵol dôr wāḏôr* in place of *dōr dōr* 'in every generation, eternally'; *lakkōl* 'to all' instead of *leḵol* + noun; *ᶜolāmîm* 'forever,' in place of *ᶜôlām*; *maleḵûṯ* in place of *mamlāḵāh* 'kingdom,' *šabbēaḥ*, replacing *hallēl* 'to praise'; and *raḥēm ᶜal* 'have mercy upon' instead of earlier *raḥēm ᵓeṯ* or *raḥēm* + pronominal suffix.

Specific features of Post-Exilic Hebrew

Polzin (1976) enumerates the linguistic features which distinguish the book of Chronicles and that part of Nehemiah which is distinct from the memoirs of the historical figure, Nehemiah. These features, enumerated in terms of frequency, include: radically reduced use of *ʾēṯ* with pronomial suffix, increased use of *ʾēṯ* before a noun in the nominative (*ʾēṯ* emphatic), the construing of collectives as plurals, abandonment of the use of infinite absolute in immediate connection with a finite verb of the same stem, the total non-use of the infinite absolute as a command, the repetition of a single word (e.g., *ʿîr weʿîr* 'each city'), the 3 f. pl. suffix in final *mem*, obsolescence of the cohortative *-āh*, reduction in the use of *wayyehî*, the placing of the substantive before the numeral and in the plural (in distinction to the older usage), and increased use of infinitive construct with *le*.

Chronology of biblical sources and their linguistic features

Polzin also establishes a typology of biblical narrative, ordering the biblical documents in the following historical arrangement: the JE document, the Davidic court history, Deuteronomy, all of which share a similar linguistic type; the ground of the P document, which begins to show incipient changes and is linguistically later than Deuteronomy; the additions to P, which approximate the later stages of Hebrew; the memoirs of Nehemiah; and, finally, Chronicles, Ezra, and the rest of Nehemiah. Lexical features of the Chronicler include the use of *ʾăḇāl* in the sense of 'but, however,' the absence of *ʾaḵ* with an asseverative force, the use of *ʾalgummim* 'kind of wood,' *ʾiggereṯ* 'letter,' the *Nifʿal* form *niḇdāl* 'be separated,' *bihal* 'hastened,' *bîrāh* 'castle, fort, *berûrîm* 'chosen ones,' *darḵemôn* 'a unit of money,' *ganzaḵ* 'treasury,' the *Hifʿil* use of *lʿg* 'mock,' *hilʿîg*, and *hēḵ* 'how' for earlier *ʾēḵ*.

Use of *ʾēṯ* in late biblical sources

The grammatical criteria which Polzin (1976) used in establishing the features of a distinctive late Biblical Hebrew are seriously challenged by Rendsburg (1980c) in a critical review. He contends that the use of *ʾēṯ* before a noun in the nominative case (*ʾēṯ* emphatic) appears 28 times in the earlier books, suggesting that the ratio of its use is the same in early and late Biblical Hebrew. While the use of infinitive absolute with a finite verb is lacking in Chronicles (as Polzin notes), it is very frequent in Esther. It may be concluded that this feature is not related to lateness but to a particular style. Polzin notes that the lengthened imperfect (cohortative) with *-āh* is rare in Chronicles. It is, however, frequent in Ezra, Nehemiah, and Daniel. Rendsburg suggests that its absence in Chronicles is due to the paucity of first person expression in Chronicles or to the fact that colloquial Hebrew (like Mishnaic Hebrew) never used it. Thus Chronicles shows the influence of the colloquial language. Polzin also contends that in Chronicles the order is material weighed/measured + the weight/measure, while Rendsburg argues, on the basis of Chronicles and the other late books, that the order is optional. There are other criteria that are challenged in Rendsburg's review.

If Rendsburg's challenge has validity, it forces a revision of the periodization of the language adopted in this chapter. Rendsburg (1980c: 73) admits that there are differences between early and late Biblical Hebrew and suggests that the conservatism of the latter was due to the geographical isolation of its speakers in the hills of Judah and Samaria.

The priestly source

A. Hurvitz (1982a) discusses the linguistic relationship between the Priestly source and Ezekiel. He also (1983a) studies an innovative phase in Ezekiel and argues for an early date for P (1983b). B. Levine (1982, 1983), on the other hand, argues that the language of P is late. Y. Hoffman (1986) further discusses the dating of P. The language of Malachi is studied by A. E. Hill (1982, doctoral dissertation), and Bergey (1983, doctoral dissertation) assesses the historical position of the language of Esther.

Ginsberg (1970: 114) and Kutscher (1970: 352–53) have dealt with the replacement of *ʾăšer* 'that, which' by *še*, tracing it back to Aramaic *zy*/*dy*. Kutscher argues that *zy*/*dy*, used with an undetermined antecedent where formerly only a construction with *l*- was possible, is based upon Akkadian *ša*. Kutscher rejects Rabin's view (1969a) of an "Amorite" origin for the *Šafʿel*, arguing for an Akkadian source. Rabin contends that the few *Šafʿel* forms which exist in Aramaic and Hebrew are borrowings in themselves, but the *ša* as a freely generative construction is not borrowed. Soggin (1966) has also studied the causative *Š* of the *Šafʿel*.

Development of *še*-

Aramaic calques

Aramaic calques in Hebrew have received treatment by Kutscher (1963–64), among them *k*^{e}*ʾeḥāḏ* 'together,' replacing *yaḥdāw*, going back to Aramaic *kaḥăḏāʾ* and Akkadian *ištēniš*. A new meaning was given to Hebrew *ʾḥz* 'hold, seize' which reflected the influence of the Aramaic word *ʾḥd* 'close' (cf. Neh 7:3). Similarly, Hebrew *zāḵar* in Mal 1:14 should not be rendered 'male' but 'ram'; compare Aramaic *diḵrāʾ*.

Aramaic borrowings rejected by Mishnaic Hebrew

Despite the many instances of Aramaic influence, not all of these survived in later Rabbinic Hebrew. A. Bendavid (1967: 132–34) demonstrates how a Hebrew word was retained in Mishnaic Hebrew in preference to the Aramaic, e.g., *ʾîš* 'man' in place of *geḇer* < *gaḇrāʾ*, *tēn* 'give' instead of *haḇ*. This may be a measure of the vitality of Mishnaic Hebrew which, in the view of M. H. Segal (1927: 10–11; 1936: 4–15), was a living dialect during the First Commonwealth. Other examples of loans which did not survive are *gallāḇ*, Akkadian *gallabu* 'barber' (Ezek 5:1), Aramaic *glb* 'scrape, shave,' as opposed to Mishnaic Hebrew *sappār* 'barber';

and *ṭll* 'cover' (Neh 3:15), Ugaritic *mẓll* 'cover, ceiling,' Aramaic *ṭll* 'cover, roof' (vb.), *ṭᵉlālāʾ* 'shade, ceiling,' but Mishnaic Hebrew *mᵉqāreh* 'lays ceiling beams' as in Biblical Hebrew. Nationalistic factors cannot be ruled out—we may compare Rabbi Judah the Patriarch's preference for Greek and Hebrew and his rejection of Aramaic (*t.b. Soṭa* 49b; Lieberman 1942: 41).

Steps in the weakening of laryngeals and pharyngeals

Blau (1980a) traces the stages in the process of the weakening of laryngeals and pharyngeals. The first stage is attested around 1300 B.C.E., where initial *n* is retained so as not to double the guttural, e.g., *yinḥal* 'will inherit' as opposed to *yippôl* 'will fall.' All other attestations of the process are from the Second Commonwealth, when Hebrew existed side by side with Aramaic. Words like *ʾaḥîm* 'brothers' and *ʾaḥēr* 'other' reflect pretonic vowel-lengthening. Because of the difficulty of articulating *ḥ* after *ʾalef*, and in order to prevent its weakening, pretonic doubling was preferred to pretonic lengthening. At this period *ḥ* could still be doubled. The phenomenon is related to the changes induced by Aramaic influence. An open, short, unaccented syllable (e.g., **kataba*) was possible in an earlier period, but Aramaic, which shortened vowels into *ḥaṭaf*, forced other means of preserving the syllable. A word like *haʿirōṯî* 'I aroused' exhibits the lengthening of *ḥaṭaf-pataḥ* to permit the existence of a short, unstressed, open syllable. A short *segol* came to precede a laryngeal/pharyngeal with *qamets*. This *segol* developed through the partial assimilation of *pataḥ* to *qamets ā*. This is evident in the interrogative particle before a guttural, e.g., *heʾānōḵî* 'did I . . .'? In this case, for the lack of doubling to be replaced by lengthening, the partial assimilation occurs. In words like *hāhār* 'the mountain,' the *qamets* after the *he* is not due to lengthening in order to omit doubling, but it is a case of total assimilation because of the force of the stressed *qamets*.

SPIRANTIZATION

Hebrew spirantization and parallels

Spirantization is a case of partial assimilation, in which the plosive articulation of the consonant is influenced by the continuant articulation of the foregoing vowel. It occurs in various dialects, e.g., Arabic *dič* for *dik* 'cock,' and it can be retained after the elision of the vowels which originally caused it, e.g., Syriac *dahḇāʾ* from **dahaḇāʾ* 'gold' (Moscati 1964: 57–58). There is evidence of spirantization in Phoenician, as seen from the transliterations, e.g., *rufe* < **rapiʾu* 'healer,' *sufet* < **šapiṭu* 'judge'

(Harris 1939: 66–67). According to Harris, spirantization made its appearance after the changes *d̲* > *z*, *t̲* > *š*, *ḫ* > *ḥ*, and *ǵ* > ᶜ, since there is no confusion between these spirantic phonemes and the later, non-phonemic spirantization.

Hebrew spirantization and Akkadian: different theories

There has been considerable discussion regarding possible outside influences upon the spirantization of /bgdkpt/ in Hebrew. Tur-Sinai (1954–59, vol. *Halashon*: 165–74) claimed Akkadian influence, basing his theory on Greek transcriptions of Akkadian, e.g., *ikû*, Greek transcription *eich*; *palgu*//*phalag*, and *attapû*// *athaph*, all meaning 'canal.' Kutscher (1970: 374, 386, 392), assessing various views, has rejected Speiser's view (*BASOR* 74 [1939] 4–7) that spirantization originated with Hurrian influence. He cites Eilers, who found this phenomenon localized in the Akkadian of the sixth century, and Knudsen, who claimed a wider distribution in time and space. An example is *tamāku*/*tamāḫu* 'hold,' *kanāšu*/ *ḫanāšu* 'submit' (von Soden 1952: 26, §25d). Kutscher tends toward the view of Eilers.

The hypothesis of Akkadian influence on Hebrew spirantization has not gone unchallenged. One detail which supported this view has been reevaluated by Batto (1971). Sumerian DINGIR.IŠ.ḪI has been read as ^{d}*Mil-ḫi*, thought to be a spirantized form of West Semitic *Milku*, a divine name. Batto questions this, proposing instead a reading ^{d}*Iš-šár*. The evidence cited in Coogan's study of West Semitic personal names (1976) indicates that in names such as *Abdi-Milḫi*, *Milḫi-taribi*, and *Nuḫi-Milḫi* the *Milḫ* element is a spirantized form of *Milk* (Coogan 1976: 16–19, 32, 53, 64, 95–104). On the other hand, in names such as *Barak-šameš*, *Barik*, *Baruka*, *Barikia*, *Barik-el*, *Barik-ellil*, and *Barik-bēl*, there is no evidence of a variant *ḫ* for *k̲*.

Knudsen (1969) discusses the spirantization of velars in Akkadian and its relationship to this phenomenon in Aramaic and Hebrew. He observes (1969: 149) that ^{d}*Milḫi* represents a pronunciation [milik/miliḫ], and that the final consonant is postvocalic, one of the conditions required for spirantization in Akkadian. He concludes that a plosive:spirantized alternation did exist in Akkadian in the articulation of the velars, but that the long consonants /gg, kk/ and the emphatic /q/ were never spirantized. The alternation in Akkadian was free, not positional. Nevertheless, Knudsen raises the question of possible Akkadian influence on Aramaic.

S. A. Kaufman (1970: 134–36, 295–99) disagrees with Knudsen's view that the alternation in Akkadian is generally free but that spirantization is more likely to follow a vowel or occur in the presence of a velar. Kaufman cites, instead, the *k*/*ḫ* interchange in the presence of an unvoiced sibilant (von Soden 1952: 26, §25d) and Neo-Babylonian intervocalic *m*, which was pronounced as [w], e.g., the month-name *Simānu*, Hebrew *Sîwān*. Spirantization occurs in Akkadian under different circumstances than in Aramaic or Hebrew, and the conclusion must be drawn that spirantization in Aramaic and Hebrew is an internal phenomenon, not influenced from the outside. A further extensive study of spirantization has been made by Corriente (1969–70).

Moscati (1964: 27) claims that there is no evidence for the occurrence of this phenomenon in Hebrew earlier than the Christian era, since neither Egyptian nor Greek or Latin transcriptions of Northwest Semitic names give sufficient indication of this variant. It appears to be more correct to say that evidence of spirantization is present in Septuagint transcriptions of names but that there is no consistent positional pattern. Blau (1979a: 11), on the other hand, argues that spirantization had already occurred by the time of the Septuagint. A recent study by Y. Lerner (1981) on the Elephantine letters suggests another interpretation. In ancient Aramaic inscriptions /ṯ/ and /ḏ/ are represented graphically by *shin* and *zayin*, but in the Biblical Aramaic texts they are represented by *taw* and *dalet*. In the Elephantine letters, which come from the period between the old Aramaic inscriptions and those from Elephantine, there are almost 1,000 cases where /ḏ/ is represented graphically by *zayin* and 57 by *dalet*. Lerner rejects the common view that the "errors" are evidence of the transition of /ḏ/ from [z] to [d]. He suggests instead that the *dalet* developed a second allophone, [ḏ], leading to scribal uncertainty and demonstrating that spirantization of /bgdkpt/ was present in the Elephantine period. However, the existence of forms like *whbqydm* 'he shall hand them over' and *bnbškm* 'for your very life' at Arad (Aharoni 1981: 46–48), implying that weak *b* and *p* could be pronounced similarly, indicates that spirantization was operative in Judah during the First Commonwealth (cf. E. Y. Kutscher, *JSS* 10 [1965] 21–51, who assigns a date around the 10th or 9th centuries B.C.E. for the beginning of the phenomenon).

Greek transcriptions and non-masoretic rules for /bgdkpt/

Isserlin (1971), in a study of place names, has reached a tentative conclusion that /bgdkpt/ neither obey the masoretic rules nor demonstrate the universal softening characteristic of Hexaplaric transcriptions. The evidence from Septuagint transliterations of personal and place names, for example, gives the impression of indeterminateness. One finds *Kittim* and *Kitioi* (Gen 10:4), *Karmel* as *Karmelou* (1 Sam 25:5), but *Karmi* as *Charmi* (1 Chr 2:7) and *Keśed* as *Chasad* (Gen 22:22). The same variation is found in the case of *p* in initial position. While *Pôṭîp̱ar* appears as *Petephres* (Gen 39:1), *Pinḥās* is transcribed as *Phinees* (Exod 6:25) and *Pîšôn* as *Phison* (Gen 2:11). A study of transcriptions was made by Speiser (1925–26, 1932–33, 1933–34), and similar evidence resulted, e.g., *kallôṯām* 'they were consumed' (Ps 18:38), transcribed as *chellotham* (the *dagesh forte*, however, is preserved in the doubling), and *tiṯpattāl* 'act perverse' (Ps 18:27), transcribed as *thethphaththal*.

Aspiration in Mishnaic Hebrew

At a later period, in Mishnaic Hebrew, both earlier (Tannaitic) and later (Amoraic), aspiration is clearly attested. There are numerous illustrations in the major work of J. N. Epstein (1948) on the text of the Mishnah, e.g., *ʾăwîr/ʾăḇîr* 'air,' *ʾawwāz/ʾaḇāz* 'goose,' *tarwād/tarḇāḏ* 'spoon.' Sokoloff (1968–69: 30–33) provides examples of the same situation in the later phase, Mishnaic Hebrew², based upon the Vatican manuscript of *Midrash Genesis Rabbah, Vatican 30*. One finds *šiwwar* 'jumped' and *hišḇîr* 'caused to jump' and *niḵbaʾ* for *niḵwaʾ* 'was burned.'

Latin borrowings as evidence for spirantization

There are a number of examples which show that *b* at the beginning of a syllable was not plosive as the masoretic rules require, e.g., the above-cited *niḵḇāʾ* 'was burned,' and the borrowed word *bîlôn/wîlôn* 'curtain,' Latin *velum*, Greek *bēlon*. It may be argued that the loanword was pronounced in accord with the masoretic rules (despite the spelling) and the initial consonant realized as a plosive, or that the word reflects the Latin; compare, however, a personal name, *Rabbî Ḥiyyāh bar Wwāh*, the last element of which goes back to *Baʾ*, *ʾAbbāʾ*, the plosive pronunciation (*dagesh*) not observed. Some interesting problems are raised by Aramaic *piwwlāʾ* 'clasp,' also attested as *piḇlāʾ*, Latin *fibula*. The second consonant is obviously aspirated, but the first may also have been aspirated, based on the Latin pronunciation, or might be plosive, perhaps through dissimilation.

Bilabial articulation of *b* and *p*

Related to this problem is a talmudic injunction regarding the reading of the *Shema*. Words which end in the same consonant as the first consonant of the following word must be kept distinct, e.g., *ʿal lᵉḇāḇᵉḵā* 'upon your heart' (Deut 6:6), *ʿēśeḇ bᵉśāḏᵉḵā* 'grass in your field' (Deut 11:15), and *ʿal-ṣiṣṣîṯ hakkānāp̱ pᵉṯîl tᵉḵēleṯ* 'a cord of blue upon the tassal of each corner' (Num 15:38; *t.b. Ber.* 15b). If the masoretic rules were in force at this period, there could be no question of aspirated and plosive consonants being assimilated to each other. One could only conclude that both were plosive or both were aspirated. Segal (1928: 25) and Garbell (1954) have rejected both possibilities in favor of a third, that both plosive and aspirate *b* and *p* were articulated as bilabials. Thus, even granting the existence at this time of plosive/aspirate articulation, in accordance with masoretic rules, the assimilation against which the talmudic law warns could take place. The usual labio-dental articulation of *b* and *p* would make the rabbinic injunction meaningless.

POSTBIBLICAL LITERATURE

Postbiblical literature provides important landmarks for the history of the Hebrew language. General literature is cited in Eissfeldt (1965: 571–668; 770–78) and A. Bendavid (1967: 73–74). Rabin (1970a: 319–20) sees in Ben Sira (Ecclesiasticus) and other documents, not evidence of an irregular and unstable transition between a decaying late Biblical Hebrew and a rising tendency to write the Mishnaic colloquial, but rather of a short-lived literary language enjoying a period of stability and incorporating the features of both (Waldman 1975a: 1294).

General resources

The authenticity of the Hebrew fragments of Ben Sira from the Cairo Geniza has often been questioned since their discovery (Segal 1958: 47–66). Some scholars have maintained that the Hebrew of Ben Sira was later reconstructed from Syriac and other versions. Segal (1958: 66) maintained that the Hebrew versions all go back to a single archetype and are distinct from the Hebrew reversions of the Greek and Syriac. Di Lella (1962, 1966) has argued for the originality of the Hebrew, admitting, however, that it contains many reversions from the Syriac. There is a recent study of the subject by Rüger (1970). The discovery of fragments of a Hebrew text from Masadah (Yadin 1967) confirms the originality of the Hebrew. This text corresponds closely to version B from the Genizah. The tension between an attempt to emulate the biblical style, on the one hand, and the popular language, influenced by Aramaic, on the other, is seen by comparing the Massada fragments with the Genizah text, e.g., *ʿilʿûl ṣāp̱ôn* (Massada) in place of *zalʿāp̱ôṯ ṣāp̱ôn* 'north wind' (43:19), *śīmāh* for *ʾôṣār* 'treasure' (41:18), and *šuttāp̱* for *ḥôḇēr* 'partner, friend' (the latter is derived through Aramaic from Akkadian *tappû, šūtapû*). Patteson (1967) argues that another Hebrew text-type stands between Cairo Hebrew B and the Massada fragments and that the basic integrity of Cairo Hebrew B is established.

Ben Sira versions

Other examples of Aramaic influence and elements of the Mishnaic style are given in the edition by Segal (1948), e.g., *tāḇuʿa* 'rejoice' (16:2), *lᵉhištaʿôṯ* 'speak' (44:10, margin, for text: *lᵉhištaʿă-nôṯ*), *tᵉqālāh* 'obstacle' (31:10), *ḥayyāḇîm* 'sinners' (8:7), and *kay-yôṣēʾ bāhem* 'similar to them' (10:29). The Massada text and the

Aramaic influences on Ben Sira

margin read *mardûṯ* 'chastisement' (Mishnaic) in place of Biblical Hebrew *mûsār* (42:9). I. Rabinowitz (1971) has studied the concluding acrostic on wisdom in the Qumran Hebrew version, and Penar (1975) surveys the Hebrew fragments in the light of Northwest Semitic philology. Philological studies have been contributed by Kister (1983). In addition, there is a masters thesis by Sappan (1967) which is a dictionary of new linguistic forms in Ben Sira. Another reference tool is the concordance of the Hebrew Ben Sira by Barthélemy and Rickenbacher (1973).

Greek influence on Ben Sira

Possible Greek influence upon Ben Sira has been suggested by Lowe (1971), based on the following features: the frequency of *ᶜelyôn* 'most high' as a term for God, reflecting Greek *hypsistos*; the frequent omission of the definite article with the subject, common in Greek poetry; the sparing use of suffixes with nouns; and a reflexive use of the second person suffix with verbs.

Apocrypha and Pseudepigrapha: general resources

On the question of lost Hebrew originals for apocryphal and pseudepigraphic books, see the standard edition edited by Charles (Oxford University, 1913, 2 vols.) and Eissfeldt (1965) on *Maccabees* (576–82), *Tobit* (583–85), *Judith* (585–87), *Additions to Daniel* (588–90), *Baruch* (592–94), *Wisdom of Solomon* (600–603), *Jubilees* (606–8), *Psalms of Solomon* (610–13), *Enoch* (617–22), *The Assumption of Moses* (623–24), *IV Ezra* (= *II Esdras*, 624–27), *The Testaments of the Twelve Patriarchs* (631–36), and the *Life of Adam and Eve* (636–37). These discussions contain bibliographical material, supplemented on pp. 771–75. Now, the introductions and translations in J. Charlesworth (1983, 1985) are most valuable.

Different views on Judith

Grintz (1957) has concluded that the primary linguistic influence on Judith is Biblical Hebrew, contradicting Jouön, who claims that the main influence is Aramaic (Eissfeldt 1965: 585–86; cf. F. Zimmerman, *JBL* 57 [1938] 67–74). Dubarle (1966: 1.48–79) argues that Hebrew texts of Judith are independent of the Vulgate and represent an authentic tradition, not being re-translations. This view is rejected by Grintz (1957). Burke (1974), in a doctoral dissertation, reconstructs the original Hebrew text of Baruch 3:9–5:9. Harrington (1980) reviews recent study of the pseudepigrapha.

Geniza and Qumran sources

The discovery of Hebrew fragments of *Jubilees*, *Enoch*, and the *Testament of Naphtali* at Qumran strengthen the view that there are Hebrew originals of these books. The bibliographical materials are collected in Fitzmyer (1975, 1977[2]). The history of research in the *Testaments* is summarized in de Jonge (1978) and in Slingerland (1977). The Aramaic text of *The Testament of Levi*, from the Cairo Geniza, is discussed by Greenfield and Stone (1979).

Various literary, theological, and linguistic aspects of the *Testament of Abraham* are studied in the collection of articles *Studies on the Testament of Abraham*, edited by George W. E. Nickelsburg, Jr. (Missoula, Montana, 1976, Scholars Press). The article in this book by Martin on syntax (1976) concludes that where recensions A and B have parallel material, according to the seventeen criteria of syntax criticism (Martin 1974: 1–43), B is more Semitic. Two possible diagrams can account for the relationships: 1) a direct line runs from the Semitic *Vorlage*, through the Greek translation, Recension B, and Recension A, or 2) Recensions A and B derive independently from the Greek translation of the Semitic *Vorlage* (Martin 1976: 102). The discussion and bibliography by E. P. Sanders in Charlesworth (1983: 871–902) are also very helpful.

The Testament of Abraham

The *Apocalypse of Abraham*, known only in an Old Slavonic translation, with several Russian redactions, is also thought to have a Hebrew original, as it exhibits hebraisms. It has been studied by A. Rubinstein (1953, 1954) and R. Rubinkiewicz (1977, doctoral dissertation; 1980, 1983).

THE SEPTUAGINT AND TRANSLATION GREEK

A general survey of the role of Greek in Jewish life is by Sevenster (1968). The bibliography by Brock, Fritsch, and Jellicoe (1973) is a useful tool which also contains a section on language (pp. 21–36, 41–42). Various writers have discussed translation technique and the question of Hebrew influence on the Greek of the Septuagint. Gehman (1951) sees definite evidence of "Jewish Greek," e.g., *kai* for *w-* 'and'/'then'; *ton* for *ʾēṯ*; *ʾen* for *b-*; *epanothen* for *meʿal* 'above.' Greek words were adapted to new meanings corresponding to the Hebrew terms they were used to translate, e.g., *thalassa* 'sea' used for 'west' (Gen 12:8) and *ischos* 'strength' used for *koaḥ* 'wealth' (Job 6:22). Jellicoe (1968: 324–27) collects more examples of outside influence. S. Daniel (1983) discusses the translation of phrases with 'head,' 'mouth,' and 'heart.' Within these phrases she finds flexibility: where the translator felt that the expression was archaic in Hebrew, he rendered it literally; but where the expression was still in use, he used a Greek equivalent. Further work on Hebrew influence in Greek compositions has been done by D. Hill (1967), Martin (1974), Fitzmyer (1979: 1–27); Maloney (1981; doctoral dissertation, 1979), and G. Howard (1982).

Translation techniques in the Septuagint and Hebrew influence

Fritsch (1977) discusses homophony of the sort in which Greek words were chosen because they sounded like a Hebrew word, e.g., *qallaḥaṯ* 'vessel' and *kalkion* 'copper vessel' and *thalassa* 'sea' for *tᵉᶜālāh* 'channel' (1 Kgs 18:32). Caird (1976) also deals with the phenomenon of homophony, citing earlier observations by Wellhausen and S. R. Driver. Some examples are: *drepanon* 'sickel' for *dorḇān* 'goad,' *alalos* for *ᵓillēm* 'dumb'; *mōmos* 'blame, disgrace' for *mûm* 'blemish.'

Sailhamer (1981; doctoral dissertation) discusses the technique of the Septuagint translator of Psalms 3–41 and concludes that he was guided by a dynamic equivalency approach. He was well informed about the range of meaning possible for each Hebrew verbal form, and he invoked the principle of equivalency when dealing with difficult forms. Sailhamer maintains that there was a theological motivation in the choice of the Greek tense. The motivation was a hope that the future would be the time of God's reward of the righteous and punishment of the wicked. Nysse (1984, doctoral dissertation) and Varughese (1984, doctoral dissertation) seek to restore the Hebrew tests underlying the Greek versions.

A doctoral dissertation by Zlotowitz (1981) on the Septuagint translations of Hebrew terms relating to God in the book of Jeremiah comes to the conclusion that the translators reproduced the Hebrew terms correctly; they were *not* swayed by a desire to avoid anthropomorphisms. A dissertation by Sollamo (1979) deals with the renderings of Hebrew semi-prepositions in the Septuagint. Other literature in this area includes: C. Fritsch, *The Anti-anthropomorphisms of the Greek Pentateuch* (Princeton Oriental Texts, No. 10, 1943); D. Gard, *The Exegetical Method of the Greek Translator of the Book of Job* (JBL Monograph Series 8, 1952); G. Gerleman, *Studies in the Septuagint*, I: *Book of Job* (Lunds Universitets Årsskrift, N.F., Avd. 1, Bd. 43, Nr. 2, 1943); M. Hurwitz, "The Septuagint of Isaiah 36–39 in relation to that of 1–35, 40–66" (*HUCA* 28 [1957] 75–83); J. Janzen, *Studies in the Text of Jeremiah* (Harvard Semitic Monographs 6, Cambridge, 1973); H. M. Orlinsky, "The Treatment of Anthropomorphisms and Anthropopathisms in the Septuagint of Isaiah" (*HUCA* 27 [1956] 193–200), and the same author, on the Septuagint of Job (*HUCA* 30 [1959] 153–67; 32 [1961] 239–68); A. Soffer on anthropomorphisms in the Septuagint of Psalms (*HUCA* 28 [1957] 85–107). Fritsch (1982) considers the Septuagint translation technique employed with Hebrew verbs for 'see' when used with the Deity. The interest of these studies is theological as well as linguistic.

Hebrew phonology as reflected in the Septuagint

On the subject of the phonological situation of Hebrew as reflected in the Septuagint, we may refer to the observations of Kutscher (summarized in 1982: 106–7) that short [i] in biblical Hebrew (as attested in the masoretic text) is nearly always transliterated by *e*, e.g., *Hillēl*, *Hellēl*, and that short [u] is replaced by *o*, e.g., *Y^{e}p̱ûneh*, *Iephonne*. The Septuagint has a tendency to color a half-vowel by the quality of the following vowel, e.g., *ʿAdullām*, *Odollam*, and *S^{e}dôm*, *Sodoma*. These features are also present in the Dead Sea Scrolls. The Septuagint often has *a* where the masoretic text has *i*: *Bilʿām*, *Balaam*. The evidence of the transcription of Hebrew names in the Septuagint was treated earlier in a doctoral dissertation by Lisowsky (1940). In certain instances of nouns of the *qutl* pattern, the second vowel can be *o*, as in *Moloch*. This would never happen in Masoretic Hebrew, e.g., *Mōleḵ*. In the personal name *Yišay*, there is no doubling of the second consonant in the masoretic text, but there is in the Septuagint *Iessai* and the common *Jesse*. This feature has also been preserved in some Sephardic prayerbooks (Yalon *KS* 32 [1957] 98–99; see 1971: 183).

The work of E. Tov

The important work of Tov should be noted, including: studies on the language of the Septuagint (1975b); the three dimensions of Septuagint words (1976a); the Septuagint translation of Jeremiah and Baruch (1975a, 1976b); on translation technique and vocabulary (1978). Tov's comprehensive work on the text-critical use of the Septuagint in biblical research (1981) deals with problems of methodology in assessing reversions from the Greek to a presumed *Vorlage*. He enumerates various factors that may have influenced the translators, among them linguistic ones: confusions of *š*/*ś*, ʾ/ʿ, ʿ/*ḥ*; the treatment of *w*-ʾ or ʾ-*w* as in the Dead Sea Scrolls; and the reading of final *ḏ* as final [ṯ] (1981: 167, 201–3, 206, 231–32; see *Midrash Genesis Rabbah* 9:5, מות / מאד).

HEBREW, ARAMAIC, TARGUM, AND NEW TESTAMENT

Sociolinguistic factors in the emergence of Mishnaic Hebrew

Rabin (1976c) reviews the situations of Hebrew and Aramaic in the first century C.E., with attention to historical development and sociolinguistic factors. The following facts in his presentation are of significance: the Hebrew of the post-exilic books was classical Biblical Hebrew in intention, but the re-use of traditional material obliterated the distinction that had existed earlier between prose and poetry. Features resembling the later Mishnaic Hebrew make their appearance, although it is clear that some of these had existed from earliest times in the north of Israel (cf. the verb *tnh* in place of *šnh* 'repeat' and *ša-* instead of *ʾăšer* in the Song of Deborah). Late Biblical Hebrew persisted down to the first century and is seen in the Dead Sea Scrolls.

It is Rabin's opinion (1957: 67, 1958: 160–61, 1976c: 1015–16) that the Pharisees abandoned the biblical style in order to set off their teaching from that of the sectarians. What emerged was a mixed style, in which the grammar and syntax was largely Mishnaic and the vocabulary was a mixture of Mishnaic and Biblical. The mixed language, based upon the spoken language of the Judean population, was used for historical works in the Hasmonean period. The Qumran sect regarded this language as "halting," "uncircumcised," and "blasphemous" (*Hymns* 2:18–29; 4:16–17; *Damascus Document* 5:11–12).

Mishnaic Hebrew: an artificial or living dialect?

In the nineteenth century some scholars regarded Mishnaic Hebrew as an artificial attempt by Aramaic-speaking scholars to express themselves in Biblical Hebrew, but this view is now rejected. In addition to the evidence cited by Segal (1927), Rabin (1976c: 1023) cites more to show that Mishnaic Hebrew was a living dialect or combination of dialects. Included in his evidence are the facts that mishnaisms existed in the Aramaic of a Melkite community in southern Judea from the sixth to the ninth centuries B.C.E., there are involuntary deviations from Biblical Hebrew in the Qumran scrolls, and the Septuagint translators understood certain Hebrew words in their Mishnaic sense.

The roles of Hebrew and Aramaic

The situation of Aramaic is different. During the Assyrian and Neo-Babylonian empires, and on through the Persian domination, Aramaic became the *lingua franca* of the Near East. The various dialects of Middle Aramaic are to be regarded as developments from Official or Imperial Aramaic. These dialects include Syriac, Mandean, Jewish Babylonian (talmudic) Aramaic, Galilean Aramaic, Samaritan, and Christian Palestinian Aramaic. The situation in Palestine at that time may be characterized as one of *diglossia*, a term coined by C. A. Ferguson (*Word* 15 [1959] 325–40). In any one community, two languages or two forms of one language were used, one for formal communication (upper) and one for familiar communication (lower, or "home-language"). In the Hasmonean period Hebrew was in a healthy state, being a symbol of the struggle against foreign influences. However, Galilean and foreign Jews gradually flocked to Jerusalem and Judea, increasing the number and influence of Aramaic speakers and diminishing the influence of Hebrew. In Judea, Aramaic took second place to

Hebrew, while in Galilee the situation was reversed. There, Aramaic and Greek were the dominant languages. After the destruction of 70 C.E., speakers of Mishnaic Hebrew became a minority among the majority Aramaic speakers, and gradually Hebrew retired to the status of a language of learning (Rabin 1976c: 1035–36).

Periodization of Aramaic

In an important study, Fitzmyer (1979: 57–84) surveys the various terms that have been proposed for the periods of Aramaic, criticizes the ambiguities in many of them, and proposes his own periodization: 1) Old Aramaic, 925–700 B.C.E.; 2) Official Aramaic (rather than the terms *Reichsaramäisch*, Imperial or Standard), 700–200 B.C.E.; 3) Middle Aramaic, 200 B.C.E.–200 C.E.; 4) Late Aramaic, 200–700 C.E.; 5) Modern Aramaic, spoken today in various locations in Syria, Lebanon, Iran, and Iraq. Fitzmyer is not ready to accept Kutscher's attempt to divide Official Aramaic into an eastern and a western branch, because there is insufficient evidence.

Aramaic, standard, and substandard Hebrew dialects

The question of which languages dominated in Judea and Jerusalem has generated much discussion. Kutscher (1959: 57–65) maintained that in Jerusalem the dominant language was Aramaic, not Hebrew, although the upper classes spoke Greek. He terms the Hebrew dialect which shows affinities with later Mishnaic Hebrew "substandard," in contrast with the "standard" dialect used in the scriptures. The interference of the "substandard" and of the Aramaic is seen in the Isaiah scroll (1QIsa[a]).

A "Jerusalem Aramaic" dialect

Rabin (1976c: 1028–32) deals with the social position of Aramaic documents such as the *Genesis Apocryphon*, *Megillat Taᶜanit*, the traditional *geṭ* 'divorce,' and the *ketuvah* 'marriage contract.' They are written in the dialect termed by Kutscher "Jerusalem Aramaic." Rabin suggests that these were not written for an uneducated class but for the many foreign Jews whose language was Aramaic. He believes that the substratum of Josephus' *War* was also composed in this dialect.

Roles of Hebrew, Aramaic, and Greek

A thorough survey by Fitzmyer (1979: 29–56) examines the position of Hebrew, Aramaic, and Greek in Palestine in the first century C.E. in the light of the most recent epigraphic finds. He rejects the view of Birkeland, who maintained that Hebrew was the language of Jesus and of the common people. Fitzmyer maintains that the most commonly used language was Aramaic but that many spoke Greek as a second language. There were pockets where Hebrew was spoken, but they were not widespread. Nonliterary Hebrew was subject to foreign influences, from Aramaic, Greek (but not extensively), and Phoenician, in the form of *t* as the sign of the accusative instead of biblical ʾēṯ. Fitzmyer's study is important also for its detailed survey of the scholarly literature.

The question of Targumim as witnesses to the language of Jesus

Opinion has been divided on the relationship of the Targumim to the language situation of the first century C.E. Rabin (1976c: 1029–32) suggests that the Targum was designed to be heard by listeners who spoke Mishnaic Hebrew, as some words in its lexicon are not accounted for by Official Aramaic. These words are "sacred," based on the original Hebrew. A paraphrase into Hebrew would have created the erroneous impression that it was part of the original text. The compromise was a type of Aramaic which resembled both Hebrew and spoken Aramaic but was distinct from Hebrew.

A summary of current views on the reliability of the various Targumim as witnesses to the language of the period is given by Black (1968). The Kahle school maintains that the Genizah Targum fragments reflect a Palestinian tradition, while Targum Onkelos is a Babylonian product brought to Palestine no earlier than 1000 C.E. The Genizah Targum fragments are a collection of midrashic material from the Palestinian Targum which was preserved after Targum Onkelos became authoritative in Palestine. Geiger, Berliner and Dalman believed that Targum Onkelos had a Palestinian origin (Kahle 1959: 192–95, 200–203; Eissfeldt 1965: 696–98).

An article by M. Klein (1983) presents the most up-to-date description of the production of editions of Palestinian Targumim.

Targum Neofiti

Díez-Macho announced in 1956 the discovery of the complete text of a Palestinian Targum in the Vatican library. This had been acquired in 1891 from the *Pia Domus Neophytorum*, an institution established in 1577 for the instruction of converts from Judaism and Islam (in Italian, *neofiti*). The manuscript is a copy of an Aramaic Targum which was copied in 1504. For a long time it remained unrecognized because it had been erroneously labeled as *Targum Onkelos*. In articles subsequent to the discovery, Díez-Macho has maintained his position that this codex is an authentic early witness to the language of Jesus in the first century (e.g., 1960a). The entire text was published in five volumes during the years 1968–1978. The volumes contain introductions and translations as well as some lists of parallel rabbinic passages (M. Klein 1983: 88–89). Díez-Macho's views have been opposed by other scholars, for example, by Fitzmyer (*CBQ* 30 [1968] 417–28; *JBL* 91 [1971] 575–78; *JBL* 95 [1976] 315–17), who rejects the connection Díez-Macho seeks to establish between this targum and the supposed substratum of the Gospels and Acts. Komlosh (1971–72) reviews critically the contention that *Neofiti* underlies all the

Palestinian Targumim and that its *Vorlage* is based upon a premasoretic text, a view that reverts to Geiger (see also Wernberg-Møller, *VT* 12 [1961] 312ff.).

J. R. Miller (1979, doctoral dissertation) studies the grammar of the type II marginalia in *Codex Neofiti I*. B. Levy (1974, doctoral dissertation) also treats the grammar of *Neofiti I*, and a grammar of *Targum Neofiti* has been written by Golomb (1985). Lund and Foster (1978) deal with the problems of variant versions of targumic traditions within *Neofiti I*.

Editions of Targumim

Díez-Macho (1977–80) has published four volumes of the *Biblia Polyglotta Matritensia*, which includes *Neofiti I* and the Pseudo-Jonathan based upon the edition of Rieder (1974). The appendix lists variants from various sources, such as the *ʿArukh* and Elija Levità's *Meturgeman*. A review of the first volume has been written by E. Tov (*JQR* 72 [1981] 67). Publications of Pseudo-Jonathan and the Geniza Fragment Targum are discussed by M. Klein (1983). M. Klein (1979) has published the Fragment-Targums.

Studies in Targum

Díez-Marinos (1977) summarizes achievements in the study of Targum Onkelos, and another survey is that of Kaddari (1971). Dodi (1973, masters thesis) has prepared a grammar of Targum Onkelos on the basis of Geniza fragments and (1983) a study of III *y* verbs. Aberbach and Grossfeld (1982) have prepared a translation and critical analysis of Targum Onkelos.

Interrelation of Targumim

Black (1954 [1967[3]], 1968) adopts a compromise position on the question of the Targumim. In his view, Onkelos, while admittedly showing traces of Babylonian influence, appears to have been an authoritative redaction of the same kind of Palestinian Targum tradition which is preserved, in a more fluid state, in the Geniza Targum fragments, in *Pseudo-Jonathan* on the Torah, and in *Codex Neofiti I*. Some of the problems inherent in Black's attempt to arrive at the language of Jesus through the Targumim are discussed at length in a review by Greenfield (*JNES* 31 [1972] 58–61). An important point made by Greenfield is that Aramaic Qumran material, rather than targumic material, should be the primary evidence in attempting an Aramaic approach to the New Testament. Fitzmyer (1979: 85–113), in a detailed survey of the literature and the various theories, offers some specific examples where Qumran Aramaic illuminates the New Testament.

Studies by Tal (1978–79, 1979) deal with specific features of Aramaic in the Qumran, targumic, and talmudic eras. The nasalizing *nun* attached to verbs is one feature which helps to establish the sequence of these three periods. In the Qumran texts, it is sparse and inconsistent; in targumic Aramaic, it is standard; in

Periodization of Targumic material

talmudic Aramaic the *nun* was removed from forms in which it followed the diphthong *ay*. This historical development enables Tal to reject an early dating for *Targum Neofiti* and also to reject the idea that the Aramaic of the Palestinian Targum is either "pre-Christian" or "pre-tannaitic." This is because targumic Aramaic occupied the historical period between Qumran and talmudic Aramaic. Another study (1979) arrives at a similar conclusion based on the demonstrative pronouns. He agrees with Greenfield that Qumran Aramaic is standard literary Aramaic, but with a uniquely Palestinian quality, as shown by Kutscher. With the destruction of the Temple, this form of Aramaic gave way to targumic Aramaic. A further study (1983) on the infinitive absolute in the three periods—Qumran targumic, and talmudic—leads to similar historical conclusions. Studies on the Samaritan Targum by Tal (1976, 1978) are prolegomena to his edition of the Samaritan Targum (1980–1983). Morag (1983a) deals with diphthongs in talmudic Aramaic; see now Beyer (1984).

Various studies in Targumim and Aramaic

Some other literature in the field can be listed: A. Zimels (1972, doctoral dissertation), comparing *Neofiti I*, Pseudo-Jonathan, and Onkelos; Komlosh (1973a) on Targumim to the Torah, (1973b) to Job, (1980) to the Minor Prophets, and (1983) to Amos; Rappel (1982) on deviations in Onkelos; Tal (1971, doctoral dissertation; 1975) on the Former Prophets; A. Sperber's editions of Targumim (1959b, 1959c, 1962, 1968) and collected studies (1973); Sapir (1973, masters thesis) on the Aramaic of the Tannaim; a grammar of Babylonian Aramaic in Yemenite manuscripts by Kara (1974, masters thesis; 1983). Editions of Targumim include Schneekloth (1977, doctoral dissertation) on Song of Songs and various editions by E. Levine, which are the Targum on Ruth (1973), Jonah (1975), and Lamentations (1976b). Grossfeld and Schiffman (1978) have produced a critical commentary to *Neofiti I* on Genesis. Grossfeld has a bibliography of Targum literature in two volumes (1972, 1977). Another important addition to the literature is Boyarin's edition of Targum Onkelos fragments from the library of the Jewish Theological Seminary, in four volumes (1976a). And a masters thesis by Mali (1975) compares literal translations in Onkelos, Pseudo-Jonathan, and *Neofiti I* of Exodus 1–5. Now, a major tool for study is the work by Clarke (1984), the text and a concordance of Targum Pseudo-Jonathan.

An entire issue of *JNES* (vol. 37, 1978) contains papers on the current status of Aramaic studies. Franz Rosenthal (1978) reviews the progress of Aramaic studies in the past thirty years. Sokoloff (1978) discusses the difficulties and advances in the study of Galilean Aramaic, an area in which the late E. Y. Kutscher made important contributions (see Kutscher 1976, 1977). Segert (1978) discusses vowel letters in early Aramaic, Jonas Greenfield (1978a) treats early Aramaic dialects, and Daniel Boyarin (1978) offers a new theory of the development of the /a/ and /ā/ phonemes in the Babylonian and Yemenite traditions of Aramaic.

Goshen-Gottstein (1978a) reviews the various theories on the Babylonian or Palestinian origin of Targum Onkelos, some with extra-linguistic, theological biases. Both models pose problems, and neither is fully satisfying. Goshen-Gottstein maintains that there is no reason to reject a model maintaining that Targum Onkelos is a Babylonian revision of a Palestinian Proto-Onkelos. We must assume, then, that literary diglossia existed in Babylonia, a literary style existing alongside a popular one. Similar ground is covered in the Hebrew article by Goshen-Gottstein (1978b).

A study by Bailey (1982) includes a treatment of the Persian origin of *naḥšîrḵān* 'hunter' in Aramaic, and E. S. Rosenthal (1982) deals with numerous Aramaic expressions of Persian origin. M. Klein (1982) demonstrates the presence of associative translation methods in the Targumim, and Greenfield (1982) studies the Arsham letters.

The language of Jesus; Aramaic and Hebrew influence on the New Testament

The question of the language of Jesus has generated much controversy and can be considered still unsolved (Rabin 1976c: 1033; see the bibliography on the subject, ibid., 1037–39). Kutscher (1959: 10–11), sharing the view of Birkeland (1954), maintained that Hebrew was common in the time of Jesus and that Aramaic was spoken only by the upper classes. The writings of Black (1954[2], 1967[3], 1956, 1965, 1968) should be noted here. Black (1968) cites the views of Argule, that *koine* Greek was the second language of Jesus, and of M. Wilcox (*The Semitism of Acts*, 1964), that Hebrew was at that time a spoken language. Black (1968), however, argues that Hebrew was limited to the circles of the learned. Gundry (1964) summarizes the various positions: the Aramaists, such as Meyer, Dalman, Wensinck, Jeremias, Kahle, Black, and Torrey; and the Hebraists: Segal, Grintz, and Birkeland. Further studies done in this area—and this list is not intended to be exhaustive—are: Jouön (1930), Feigin (1943), S. Brown (1964), Rüger (1968), Barr (1970), and Emerton (1973). M. Smith (1950, 1951) deals with Hebrew and Aramaic elements in the Gospels. A survey article by Fitzmyer (1980) treats Aramaic and the study of the New Testament. S. Thompson (1985) treats the Apocalypse and Semitic syntax. We have referred above to Fitzmyer's comprehensive study (1979: 29–56) and must also note that he has dealt with the question of the language of Jesus in another study (1979: 1–27, especially 6–10). The consensus is that Jesus spoke Aramaic but would also use Hebrew and Greek on occasion.

As an example of the attempt to find a Mishnaic Hebrew substratum in the Gospels, we cite Grintz (1960), who finds in Matt 28:1 the influence of *ʾôr l^eyôm* 'the night before' (cf. *Pesaḥ*. 1:1) in what is translated 'as it began to dawn toward the first day of the week.'

Fitzmyer (1971, 1974²), in his collection of essays on the Semitic background of the New Testament, gives specific examples of phrases in Qumran texts that influenced the New Testament. Examples are: *bḥyr ʾlhʾ* 'the elect of God' (4QMess ar; some MSS of John 1:34) and *bʾnwš rʿwth* 'among men of good will' (4QHazut ʿAmramaʾ; Luke 2:14 (Fitzmyer 1974: 127–60). This evidence tends to confirm a widely-held view that the source of Luke's first two chapters is a Hebrew composition (Fitzmyer 1974: 101–4). On Aramaic origins we may cite Zimmerman's studies of biblical books, which he maintains are translated from Aramaic (1975), and of the Gospels, for which he posits an Aramaic origin (1978).

Relevant to the question of the age of targumic material is the study by McNamara (1978). He demonstrates that aggadic material present in the Palestinian Targum is reflected in the New Testament. The implication is that this material, heard orally in the synagogues by Paul as part of the translation-elaboration process (midrash), has great antiquity. These conclusions refer, of course, to the contents of the Targum, not to the age of any specific recension or to the linguistic aspects.

Tal (1982) discusses problems of Samaritan Targum lexicography. Talshir (1982) proposes quantitative methods of measuring the linguistic relationship of the various Targum dialects. Onkelos is close to the Palestinian Targumim, with the Samaritan standing on the opposite extreme from Onkelos. His doctoral dissertation (1983b) is a study of names of animals in the Samaritan Targum.

New Aramaic texts from Saqqara are described by J. B. Segal (1983). Kaddari (1983) treats the verb *hwh* in Imperial Aramaic. Muraoka (1983) argues for the authenticity of infinitive *maqtāl* in the Geniza fragments of the Palestinian Targum. Naveh and Shaked (1985) have published a corpus of Aramaic incantations. Z. Talmon (1984, doctoral dissertation) investigates linguistic aspects of Talmudic Aramaic proverbs.

THE DEAD SEA SCROLLS

A major source of information on the linguistic situation of Hebrew in the first pre-Christian century is the body of biblical books and sectarian writings which have been discovered since 1947 in the caves of Qumran, near the Dead Sea. These have generated a great volume of historical, theological, and linguistic discussion. The full range of the literature cannot be covered here, but attention can be called to the following bibliographies and tools for research: Eissfeldt (1965: 637–38, 645, 652, 654, 657–60); Yizhar (1967); the concordances of Kuhn (1960) and Edwards (1975); the bibliography by Jongeling (1971; on linguistics, 11–21); and, by the same author, in Hospers (1973: 214–65). Fitzmyer (1975, 1977[2]) has a useful guide to published materials and texts.

General resources

A selected group of studies of the Hebrew of Qumran is: Kutscher (1959), with a general summary of his views in *EJ* 1971a); Goshen-Gottstein (1951b, 1958, 1959, 1960a); M. Mansoor (1958, 1961, 1962); Wernberg-Møller (1957, 1958a, 1964); Ben-Hayyim, on the affinities between Samaritan and Qumran Hebrew (1953 = 1954, 1957–58, 1958); Brønno (1954); R. Meyer (1958a); S. De Vries (1965); Rabin (1957; reprinted 1975; 1958; translated into Hebrew in Bar-Asher 1972: 355–82); the collected essays of Yalon (1967); Yadin (1969) on the tefillin from Qumran; Kaddari (1968a) on semantic fields; Suder (1973) on the functional syntax of the verb clause in the sectarian scrolls from cave 1; the doctoral dissertation of Qimron (1976) on the Hebrew grammar of the scrolls and a further study (1986); Fabry (1975) on the root *šûḇ*; Nebe (1972) on the word *ʾušên*; Kosovsky, a masters thesis on the scrolls and the Damascus Covenant (1953); S. Talmon (1968) on the Psalms scroll; Murtonen (1963–64), a general survey; Bush (1960), an argument for penultimate accent in Hebrew on the basis of the *War Scroll*; Carmignac (1986) on the infinitive absolute in Ben Sira and Qumran; and Thorion (1982) on the language of the Temple Scroll and Chronicles.

Selected specific studies

Editions of the texts, with philological discussions, include: Holm-Nielsen (1960) on the *Hodayot*; Licht (1957) on the *Hodayot* and (1965) on the *Manual of Discipline*; *The Genesis Apocryphon* edited by Avigad and Yadin (1956) and by Fitzmyer (1966, 2nd ed. 1971), also treated by Kutscher (1958); J. van der Ploeg (1959) and Yadin (1962a) on the *War Scroll*. General information can be found in Burrows (1956, 1958).

The relationship between the biblical scrolls and the masoretic text has been a major topic of discussion. S. Talmon (1955) holds that the deviations are not due to a lapse of memory on the part of the scribe but to a different text, and that these deviations reflect the indeterminate situation prior to the establishment of the masoretic text. He rejects the view of Orlinsky (*JBL* 69 [1950] 165) that the Isaiah scroll is an unreliable variation on the Urtext of the Masorah. Elsewhere, Orlinsky has argued (1966) against a single

Qumran scrolls and the Masorah

Masorah. The relationship of the masoretic text, the Septuagint, and the Qumran scrolls has been discussed by Skehan in various studies (1954, 1957, 1959, 1969), Wernberg-Møller (1958a, 1964), in studies edited by Cross and Talmon (1975), as well as in articles in *Textus* and *Revue de Qumran*.

Qumran Hebrew as "substandard"

Addressing the problem of the social position of the language of Qumran, Kutscher (1959: 57–65) theorized that 1QIsa[a] was a vulgar text designed to facilitate the reading of the Bible by people unable to cope with archaic and defective spelling. The Hebrew of the scribe and of his readers is a late form of Hebrew strongly influenced by Aramaic. Kutscher calls this dialect, closely related to the later Mishnaic Hebrew, "substandard." It is to be contrasted with the "standard" language reserved for the reading of scripture. According to Kutscher's view (cited above), the dominant language in Jerusalem was Aramaic, and the language of the Isaiah scroll shows its influence. Among other characteristics, gutturals are severely attenuated. The dialect of the scribe also has definite relationships with the Samaritan dialect which was prevalent north of Jerusalem and with the popular Hebrew which prevailed in Judea.

The social position of Qumran Hebrew

Goshen-Gottstein (1958) maintains that the unusual *plene* orthography of the Qumran documents does not permit any conclusions about dialect boundaries. Morag (1961) objects to the idea of "upper" and "lower" languages. In his opinion a struggle was taking place between living Aramaic, spoken late Hebrew, and a classical Biblical Hebrew that had been restricted to a liturgical status. Rabin (1970a: 319–20) finds in the scrolls a stable language combining elements of Biblical and Mishnaic Hebrew, whose dominance, however, was brief. He finds in this language some "involuntary" mishnaisms, such as *nāśā᾿ w^{e}nāṯan* 'engaged in commerce,' *mámôn* 'money,' *b^{e}p̱ērûš* 'specifically,' and *galgal haššemeš* 'the orb of the sun,' a thinly disguised translation of *galgal ḥammāh* (Rabin 1958: 146–48). Rabin has elsewhere (1957 = 1975) expressed the view that the Qumran community was not Essene but a diehard Pharisaic group which opposed most vigorously the change to Mishnaic or Rabbinic Hebrew. Rabin interprets polemic references to an "uncircumcised language" or a "halting tongue" in the light of this traditionalism (1975: 68–69). The view that the people of Qumran were Pharisees is not widely held as it is generally felt that the people of Qumran were Essenes. Another question might also be raised regarding the place the mishnaic language of the *Copper Scroll* (3Q15) occupied in the life of this group.

What is of most interest, however, is the parallelism that can be seen between two dialects, e.g., Mishnaic *dînê n^e^p̱āšôṯ* / Qumran *d^e^ḇar māweṯ* 'capital cases,' *b^e^mēzîḏ* / *b^e^yāḏ rāmāh* 'presumptuously, with a high hand,' and *haṯrāʾāh* / *b^e^hôḵēaḥ* 'with reproof, advance warning by the witnesses to an offense' (Rabin 1975: 106–11). The tension between allowing a new form of the language to emerge and a need to retain the archaic biblical usage which can be discerned in this literature parallels the situation noted above in the discussion of the various texts of Ben Sira. A response to Rabin's identification of the Qumran sect as Pharisees rather than Essenes can be found in R. De Vaux, *Archaeology and the Dead Sea Scrolls* (London, 1973) 126–38.

Parallels between Mishnaic and Qumran Hebrew

The unusually full orthography of the scrolls has led to various interpretations. Yalon (1967: 14–22; first appeared in *Sinai* 20 [1949–50] 267–82) sees in the *plene* writing, not a text for the uneducated, but evidence of the reliability of the masoretic tradition. Writings like *-kh* in place of masoretic *-k* (read *-ḵā*), the 2 m.s. suffix, confirm that the reading was *-kā* and not *-āḵ*, as claimed by Kahle, the scholar who had made available the basic texts of the Babylonian and Palestinian Masorah. He expressed the view in 1921, later summarized in his work on the materials from the Cairo Geniza (1959: 149–71), that masoretic *-kā* is an artificial reconstruction influenced by Arabic (compare also A. Sperber [1966: 191]). Yalon (in Kutscher [1959: 34–39]) and Ben-Hayyim (1953 = 1954) have argued against this view, using the evidence from the scrolls to buttress the reliability of masoretic tradition.

Qumran and the reliability of the Masoretic tradition

Goshen-Gottstein (1958) notes that the elision of laryngeals and pharyngeals brought about several results in orthography: 1) their omission in spelling, 2) the adding of a letter because it is silent anyway, and 3) the change of place of the *waw* with historically preceding *alef*, e.g., masoretic *nʾwm* = *n^e^ʾûm*, Qumran *nwʾm* 'speech.' Because a silent *alef* may be added at the end of a word, it is not to be regarded as consonantal. Goshen-Gottstein is willing to consider the possibility of a double paradigm of the personal pronoun, *hûʾ*/*hûʾa* 'he' and of the 2 m.s. suffix, *-āk*/*-kā*. In his comments on method, he rejects "atomism," the basing of linguistic and historic considerations on isolated pieces of evidence, and calls for a thorough tracing of each feature in each document and across the entire range of available Qumran material.

Phonetic changes and orthography

Kutscher's masterful study of the Isaiah scroll (1959) treats in great depth the phonetic features of that document and their general development in the language of the period. Only a small

Kutscher's studies of Qumran phonology

part of the vast material collected in this work can be referred to here. Kutscher (1959: 356–91) illustrates the change of the vowel *u* to *i* in various Hebrew dialects, showing that the change may be due to dissimilation, e.g., *ḥûṣ* 'outside' > **hûṣôn* > *ḥîṣôn* 'external'; the change also may be free. The dialect of the scrolls shows that this process of vowel change is not yet completed, cf. a *qutul* form such as *ʿuzûz* 'might' as opposed to masoretic *ʿizzûz*. There are many instances of the change of the vowel *a* to *u* in a closed syllable and in the environs of a labial or of *r*. This is a case of assimilation, e.g., Semitic **libb* > Arabic *lubb* 'heart' (Moscati 1964: 58). In the scroll *Rᵉmalyāhû* is *Rumalyāh*, *Šeḇnāʾ* is *Sūḇnaʾ*, and *qiḇrēḵ* is *quḇrēḵ* 'your grave.'

The phonemes /bgd/ in final position were articulated in a voiceless manner, e.g., *gaṯ* 'winepress' written as *gd*. Greek and Latin transcriptions reveal the same situation, e.g., *Doek* for *Dôʾēg* and *Phalek* for *Pāleg* (Kutscher 1959: 108–9). Orthographic final *m* was articulated as [n]; compare *Miḏyān*, written as *Mdym*. This is also true in later, Rabbinic Hebrew, e.g., *ʾdn* for *ʾāḏām* 'man' (Kutscher 1959: 45, 82, 409; 1963b: 258).

Pausal forms are primary

In the area of morphology, a notable encroachment of the "substandard" upon the "standard" is the use of pausal forms in context, e.g., *ʾpʿwlh* (= *ʾepʿôlāh*) 'I will act.' Such forms also occur in Mishnaic Hebrew, e.g., *huttārû habbāmôṯ* 'the high places were permitted.' These forms also suggest that accent was penultimate. Imperfect forms with suffixes occur without any reduction, e.g., *wylkdw* (= *wayyilkôdāh*) 'he captured it' in place of reduced *wayyilkᵉḏāh*. Such forms also occur in the Greek and Latin transcriptions, e.g., *iezbuleni* 'he will uplift me.' A. Sperber (1966) considered such forms to be material for a non-masoretic grammar. Morag (1961) comes to a different conclusion, maintaining that the final form may be written but not pronounced. He cites other examples in which the orthography represents a long vowel when short vowels are intended. A methodological critique of A. Sperber has been written by Murtonen (1982). Brønno (1954), noting that the *kutb* form is short in the first Isaiah scroll, both in pausal and contextual positions, concludes that masoretic *yiḵtôḇû* (pausal) and *yiḵtᵉḇû* (contextual) are not different linguistic forms but different phonetic realizations of one form, namely, the pausal, which is normal, the context form being secondary (see Rosén 1974).

Qimron (1970–71), in his study of the Psalms scroll from Qumran Cave 11 (Sanders 1965, 1967), notes a consistency in the use of the *waw* as a *mater lectionis* (contrast Morag 1961) and suggests that, where one does find a defective spelling, a reading differing from the masoretic is intended. Where the Psalms scroll has *ḥnwm* (masoretic *ḥinnām*) 'without cause,' Qimron proposes a reading *ḥinnôm*, based on a conditioned *ā* > *ō* change influenced by the liquid consonant. In the case of attested *tʿmd*, Qimron suggests that there was a *Qal yaqṭîl* form, contrasting with masoretic *taʿămôḏ*. In the form spelled *ʾwhl* 'tent,' Kutscher (1971a: 1587) finds a *quṭul* form, realized as *qoṭol*.

Morphology in the Psalms scroll

R. Meyer (1958a) sought to find in forms like *mhwrsyk* (masoretic *mᵉhorsayiḵ*) 'your destroyers' evidence of an *ā* > *ō* change such as occurs in Phoenician, where *lbn* 'white' is transcribed in Greek characters as *labon* (Moscati 1964: 49). He suggests that the vowel was articulated as long *ō* or long *ā*. This view is rejected by Kutscher, who sees *mhwrsyk* as an instance of the change of *a* (masoretic *ā*) to *u* in a closed syllable in the vicinity of an *r* (Kutscher 1959: 391). Morag (1961: 30) accepts Meyer's suggestion, citing the well-known, though rare, transcription of *bāśār* 'meat' by Jerome as *bosor*. If the *qamets* was articulated somewhere between [a] and [o] it would have been transcribed sometimes by the symbol for one and at other times by the symbol for the other. Chomsky (1971a: 22) has used this evidence from the scrolls and from Jerome to argue for an early dating of the "Ashkenazic" pronunciation of *qamets*.

Ā/*ō* and *u* changes

Yalon (1967: 59) considered the 2 f.s. forms ending in *-tî*, like those which occur in the *ketiv* of the Masorah (e.g., Jer 2:20, 4:19) and often in the Isaiah scroll, to be early (compare Akkadian *attī*, Arabic *ʾanti*, and Ethiopic *ʾantī*). This view is not shared by Kutscher (1959: 20–22) or Hurvitz (1972a: 116–19), who consider such forms to be Aramaisms and their presence in biblical books to be limited to the period of the destruction of the First Temple and following.

R. Meyer (1958b) finds in the *yᵉqôṭēl* + suffix forms evidence of the survival of the old Semitic present-future *yaqaṭṭal*, e.g., *yʿwšqnw* 'he will oppress him,' *ydwršhw* 'he will seek him.' Yalon (1967: 42; 1971: 253–59) saw these as *Pōʿēl* forms, a variant of the *Piʿel*. Wernberg-Møller (1957: 8–10) relates them to the *G* rather than to the *Piʿel*. Various medieval and modern views on the status of the *Pōʿēl* (cf. the masoretic text, Job 9:15, 20:26; Ps 101:5) are summarized by Chomsky (1952: 92–93, 105) and Yalon (1971: 253–59). Kutscher (1959: 254–61) suggests that three forms of the *Qal* imperfect existed at this time: 1) the form characteristic of the Masorah, accented on the ultima, *yiqṭᵉlû*, 2) the substandard form *yiqṭôlû*, with penultimate accent, and 3) the same form with

Tense forms in Qumran

ultimate accent, found in the Babylonian Masorah and in scattered places in the Tiberian Masorah. Thorion–Vardi (1985) surveys the use of tenses in the Zadokite documents. Passoni Dell'Aqua (1984) analyzes the root *ydʿ* 'know' in Qumran documents.

I. Yeivin (1971) argues that the Babylonian masoretic tradition for *Qal* verbs is the closest parallel to Qumran Hebrew, in which such verbs have an extra *waw* after the first or second radical. These are accented on the ultima, e.g., *ʾeqṭôlāh, q*^{e}*ṭôlû*. He rejects Kutscher's view that these are pausal forms parallel to Mishnaic Hebrew. The *waw* in *y*^{e}*qôṭlenû* is not auxiliary, but *qutl* and *qtul* are two parallel structures, as in Babylonian and Tiberian Masoretic Hebrew.

Greek influence on Qumran

The question of the possible influence of Greek upon the scrolls has been raised by Lowe (1971) and A. Bendavid (1967: 92–94), although the evidence does not permit final conclusions. The best point of comparison may be the Greek borrowings in Daniel, *qaṯrôs, p*^{e}*sanṭērîn, sûmpōnyāh* (3:7, 10, 15). But ideological factors may have been operative in the composition of Daniel and the scrolls, since a definite effort was made to emulate a "biblical" style, and this may have militated against the use of loanwords (U. Weinreich 1953: 99–103; Kutscher 1982: 100). A. Bendavid (1967: 92–94) suggests that the use of *daʿaṯ* in place of biblical *lēḇ* 'heart, mind' reflects Greek *gnṓme* and that *bāʿûl* 'qualified,' lit. 'servant' is a translation of *oikeios*. Yalon (1967: 32), however, thinks that this use of *bāʿûl* is a natural Hebrew development.

Military terms in the *War Scroll*

Military terms used in the *War Scroll* may with more probability be traced to outside influence, e.g., *beṭen* 'stomach' > 'case, scabbard,' reflecting Greek *koilía*. Bendavid proposes that *ḥaḏ* 'sharp' > 'quick, fast' reflects Greek *ozus*, but *qal* and *ḥaḏ* 'light, swift' and 'sharp, fast' are already found in parallelism in Hab 1:8. The use of *yaḏ* 'hand' to mean 'military unit' may reflect Greek *cheir* and Latin *manus*, but Yalon (1967: 34) again suggests a Hebrew derivation.

A tendency to change the expression of an impersonal subject by the 3 s. passive to the 3 s. active is present in the books of Chronicles, in the Isaiah Scroll (Kutscher 1959: 303–4), and has also been noted in the *Manual of Discipline* by Sarfatti (1967–68a). Kaddari (1964–65b, 1968a) has contributed a significant study of semantic fields in the Qumran literature.

Several authors have concentrated on the Temple Scroll, and an edition of the scroll itself was produced by Yadin (1977). Brief notes on the orthography (1977, 1:21–29) and the linguistic aspects (1977, 1:29–34) indicate that the scroll has many features in

Morphology in the Temple Scroll

common with the other scrolls. There is a clear affinity with Rabbinic Hebrew characteristic of the later Mishnah. Thus, *matres lectionis* include *waw*, e.g., *ʾădoršennu* (*ʾdwršnw*) 'I will inquire after it'; *alef-waw* or *waw-alef*, e.g., *w*^{e}*zôʾṯ* (*wzwʾt*) 'and this,' which is more frequent than *zʾwt*. The form *gwyym* alternates with *gwʾym* 'gentiles.' The gutturals are often eliminated, e.g., *rwyh* in place of *rʾwyh*, *r*^{e}*ʾûyāh* 'suited.' *Yod* is substituted for *he*, e.g., *ʾšy* for *ʾšh* 'woman'; and a *samekh* is written in place of a *shin*, e.g., *mnsh* for *mnšh* 'Menasseh.'

The scroll uses the compound verb, already seen in the *Manual of Discipline* and the *War of the Sons of Light*, e.g., *yih*^{e}*yû yoṣ*^{e}*ʾîm* 'will go out.' There is a tendency to draw upon the vocabulary of the later biblical books, e.g., *niškāh* (*nškh*) 'chamber' and *hakkôl* 'all.' Certain technical terms connected with the temple, familiar from later rabbinic literature, are also frequent. Rabbinic phrases such as *miṯʾanḥîm* 'sighing' and *y*^{e}*ḵabb*^{e}*ḏû ʾeṯ habbayiṯ* 'will sweep the house' are found. Yadin dates the scroll to the Hasmonean era, the second half of the second century B.C.E. Qimron (1977–78a, 1977–78b, 1980b) also discusses textual, orthographic, and phonetic features of the scroll, elaborating upon the phenomena presented briefly by Yadin. Sharvit (1966–67) has discussed the lexicon of the scroll. The noun form *haqṭîlāh*, as opposed to Mishnaic Hebrew *haqṭālāh*, occurs in the scroll, but it has also has been found in Mishnaic Hebrew (see Berggrün, *Leš* 18 [1951–52] 13–14; M. Zeidel, *Leš* 22 [1977–78] 181–82; *Leš* 23 [1958–59] 128; A. Bendavid, *LLA* 16 [1964–65] 33; A. Lowenstamm, *Leš* 42 [1977–78] 46–47).

Scribal traditions at Qumran

The scribal traditions of the Dead Sea Scrolls have been compared with talmudic and masoretic practice by Siegel (1971, 1972, 1974, 1975), who notes some basic agreement between them. Divine names in the scrolls, for example, were written in paleo-Hebrew letters, while a talmudic tradition records the practice of Alexandrian Jews who wrote the Tetragrammaton in gold letters (*t.b. Menaḥ.* 30b). Siegel compares the Qumran convention for use of initial-medial *mem* in final position with survivals in the masoretic text of Isa 9:6 and Neh 2:3 and with the variants in the Severus scroll and in *Midrash Bereshit rabbati* of Rabbi Moshe Hadarshan. The convention followed by the Qumran scribes, prior to the establishment of the talmudic halakhah (*t.y. Meg.* I:9; *Soferim* 2:20), is: monosyllabic words terminating in *mem* are usually written with initial-medial *mem* in final position when the word has no prefix. When prefixed, the same words are written with final *mem* (Siegel 1975: 1–14). This description is based on

Orlinsky's view (1960) that *ketiv-qere* variants arose from discrepancies in basic texts, where the scholars chose the reading of two of them as the vocalized *qere* and relegated the third to the status of *ketiv*. Siegel also notes that a number of midrashic variants, such as the well-known variants of Rabbi Meir (*Midrash Genesis Rabbah* 9:5), existed in the "vulgata" type of text represented by the first Isaiah scroll and the Severus scroll (Kutscher 1959: 64–65; Lieberman 1950: 23–26).

SAMARITAN, QUMRAN, AND RABBINIC HEBREW AFFINITIES

General resources

Surveys of the progress of Samaritan studies include: Bowman (1959), Rainey (1969), and Pummer (1976–77). A bibliography of the Samaritans by Crown (1984) and a historical linguistic survey of the development of Samaritan Hebrew by Mandel (1978) have recently appeared. There is valuable historical information in Purvis (1968), and a treatment of the development of the script there and in Birnbaum (1971b, 1972). Menachem Cohen (1975–76), as summarized above in chapter one (p. 7), believes the Samaritan writing tradition to be a mixed one, reflecting both *plene* and defective traditions and mixed dialects. Studies in Samaritan grammar and lexicography include those of Diening (1938), Murtonen (1958, 1959, 1960, 1964), and Macuch (1969, 1973). Of greatest significance for the future study of Samaritan Hebrew and Aramaic is the publication by Ben-Hayyim of a corpus of Samaritan literature (1957–77). The importance of Ben-Hayyim's work is pointed out by Greenfield (1964).

Hebrew, Arabic, and Aramaic at Qumran

In numerous articles Ben-Hayyim has demonstrated the importance of the Samaritan material for the better understanding of the vernacular of the Second Commonwealth, including Qumran and Mishnaic Hebrew. In a brief popular article Ben-Hayyim (1958–59) surveys the history of Samaritan Hebrew. The commonly held view that the separation between Jews and Samaritans was absolute must be rejected. As mentioned, there are many affinities between Samaritan Hebrew and other dialects of the Second Commonwealth. During the long period between the demise of spoken Hebrew and the 14th century C.E., Hebrew was replaced by Aramaic for liturgical purposes—that is, prayer and *piyyuṭ*. Arabic gained dominance in the secular sphere, in biblical commentary, grammar, legal, and historical writing. H. Shahade (1983) now discusses the processes leading to the adoption of

Arabic in the 11th century as the spoken language. However, in the 14th century there was a revival of Hebrew creativity in and around Nablus. According to Shahade, the Hebrew used for *piyyuṭ* was heavily influenced by Aramaic in its lexicon and grammar. Ben-Hayyim, on the other hand, sees this Hebrew as integrally related to the family of Hebrew dialects and not in any way separate from it. The sources for this upsurge include Hebrew writings produced prior to the 14th century (which did not survive) and the competitive need to be well-versed in Scripture so as to counter the polemic of the Jews. In recent years Samaritan Hebrew has come more and more under the influence of modern Israeli Hebrew and may soon be lost irrevocably.

Samaritan Hebrew and other dialects

Some examples of the affinity of Samaritan Hebrew to other dialects, taken from Ben-Hayyim's studies (1957–58, 1958, 1963, 1967, 1969, 1970a), are cited here. Samaritan Hebrew is characterized by the use of *u* and *o* as allophones, not as distinct phonemes. The same situation exists in a fragment of the Bible with Palestinian vocalization published by Murtonen (1958) where the same symbol is used for *u* and *o*. The interchange of *g* and *k*, the *-tî* ending for 2 f.s., and the ending *-mh* for 3 pl. are common both in Samaritan and in the language of Qumran. Samaritan is noted for the absence of the *shewa*, including the *shewa mobile*, e.g., *dḗbāri* (masoretic *diḇrê*) 'the words of,' *ā́dāmat* (*ʾaḏmaṯ*) 'the land of,' and *ā́mēri* (*ʾimrê*) 'the words of.' A similar situation is seen in Greek and Latin transcriptions, e.g., Septuagint *Araboth-Moab* for *ʿAr-ḇōṯ Môʾāḇ* (Num 26:63). Not only is final *m* pronounced [n], as in the Septuagint (*Madiam* = *Midian*) and the Dead Sea Scrolls, but medial *m* as well, e.g., *ʾarkmy* for *ʾrkny*, the Aramaic rendering of *haṭṭî* 'incline' (Gen 24:14; Kutscher 1959: 45, 82, 409). According to Ben-Hayyim (1957–58: 233), a Samaritan vowel which precedes final *m* or *n* becomes nasalized. By analogy, other vowels in this position, even where there is no historic *m* or *n*, become nasalized, as well. This may explain forms in Rabbinic Hebrew, such as *Yûdān* (= *Yᵉhudāh*) and *lᵉmaʿălān* (= *lᵉmaʿălāh*) 'above.' The penultimate accent is characteristic of Samaritan and also appears in *Qal* imperfect forms in the Dead Sea Scrolls, in which the final form appears in context. As in the Scrolls and in Aramaic, a short vowel such as *a*, or the short vowel represented by the masoretic *shewa mobile*, is changed to *u* (compare Samaritan *šū́meyya* [= *šᵉmayyāʾ*] 'heavens'). The presence of a labial may account for this change.

It must be noted, however, that despite the affinities, Samaritan Hebrew does represent a *later* development than the Scrolls. In

Mishnaic Hebrew and Samaritan affinities

the Scrolls historic *u* is preserved as *u/o*, but in Samaritan it has become *a/e*, e.g., Qumran *swdm* for masoretic *Seḏôm* (Greek *Sodom*), but Samaritan *sắdem*. Samaritan exhibits the use of the *Piᶜel* where *Qal* might be expected, with no differentiation in meaning, a phenomenon also encountered in Rabbinic Hebrew. Ben-Hayyim attributes this to a need for more expression of emotion in the popular language. Finally, the *Pāᶜēl*, an alternative to the *Pōᶜēl* (*Qal*), is used in Samaritan, and may explain a form found in the Mishnah (*Pesaḥ.* 10:6), which should not be read *gāᶜal Yiśrāʾēl* 'who has redeemed Israel' but *gāʾēl Yiśrāʾel* 'who redeems Israel.' Zurawel (1984) traces the process of abandonment of the *Qal* in Samaritan Hebrew. Brønno (1968) also explores relationships between Samaritan Hebrew and Origen's *Secunda*, and a masters thesis by J. Yaron (1976) evaluates the contribution of Samuel Cohen to Samaritan lexicology.

Ben-Hayyim (1977) surveys the history of the study of the Hebrew tenses, participle, "past"/"future" or "perfect"/"imperfect," as an introduction to a description of the status of the tenses in Samaritan Hebrew. Early Hebrew grammarians could not describe the tense system adequately because they saw all levels of Biblical Hebrew as of one piece. In addition, the Sephardim, influenced by Arabic, saw the *ḥireq* and *tsere* as one unit, similar to the *ḥolem* and *shureq*. Thus, medieval poets used *yap̱ᶜîl* and *yap̱ᶜēl* interchangeably.

The Samaritan Targum remains close to the sense of the original Hebrew. It may use the Aramaic tense that corresponds to the original Hebrew or it may use an imperfect to render an original perfect. However, in religiously sensitive passages, where it is important to emphasize that an event or promise took place in the past, the perfect will be used to render the imperfect in the original, e.g., with respect to the place chosen by God, *yibḥar* 'will choose' is rendered by *diḇeḥar* 'which he has chosen' (Deut 12:26). It becomes clear from the writings of Samaritan grammarians and the present-day pronunciation that the differentiation between verb forms with *wᵉ-* and *wa-* was not recognized. The tendency of Samaritan to accent the first syllable also contributes to this, since no differentiation can be recognized. A similar situation also occurs in Origen's *Hexapla*, e.g., *wyedabber*. Certain verbs, however, have forms that are an exception to the simple "past" and "future" of Samaritan Hebrew. Ben-Hayyim suggests that such forms, with preformative *ā*, reflect traces of the Barth-Ginsberg law, before it was displaced through analogical processes. In summary, because Samaritan Hebrew was so close to Mishnaic Hebrew, it cannot contribute to the reconstruction of original Hebrew; it simply reflects its own time.

Phonological changes in Samaritan Hebrew

Ben-Hayyim (1979) seeks to explain processes operating in the evaluation of forms of mono- and bisyllabic middle guttural nouns in Samaritan Hebrew. He deplores the tendency to dismiss the data by reference to grammatical "laws" or by a comparison with Masoretic Hebrew. Samaritan Hebrew has an extra long vowel, common in both open and closed syllables. A Samaritan monosyllabic noun with a long vowel, e.g., *lām* 'bread,' can be the counterpart of a masoretic segolate, originally bisyllabic. Ben-Hayyim concludes that all middle guttural nouns pronounced today as single syllables were originally bisyllabic nouns. For example, when an *alef* (historical ᵓ, *h*, *ḥ*, ᶜ) standing between two different vowels disappeared, a single extra-long vowel was formed. Another phenomenon is the secondary dividing of an extra-long vowel, recreating the original situation prior to the contraction. This may account for the pronunciation of *rēᵓōš* 'head.' These changes took place while Samaritan was still being spoken.

THE HISTORIC POSITION OF MISHNAIC HEBREW

Earliest traces of Mishnaic Hebrew

Features of Mishnaic Hebrew are adumbrated in earlier periods, in the later books of the Bible, and in the scrolls of Qumran. The use of *ša*, the relative pronoun, in place of *ᵓăšer*, occurs as early as the Song of Deborah (Judges 5), and A. Hurvitz (1972a: 40–46) has suggested that Mishnaic Hebrew *zô* 'this' did not replace Biblical Hebrew *zōᵓṯ* but antedated it. Geiger's early view that Mishnaic Hebrew was an artificial dialect created by scholars for use in the academies has long been rejected. M. H. Segal (1927: 10–11; 1936: 4–15) stressed the relative independence of Mishnaic Hebrew from Aramaic influences and considered it to be a direct descendent of the spoken, not literary, language of biblical times. Rabin (1958: 156–61), as noted above, posits the emergence of a stable dialect involving elements from both Biblical and Mishnaic Hebrew prior to the formation of the Qumran sect, and before, him, Klausner (in *SH* [Jerusalem 1923], cited in M. H. Segal 1927: 14, n 2) expressed his view that Mishnaic Hebrew was a dry version of the popular speech used in Hasmonean courts. Albeck (1959: 128, 132) also agrees that Mishnaic Hebrew is a natural development from Biblical Hebrew, and he documents this view by his lists of uniquely mishnaic words which have no apparent Semitic cognates. He also assigns to Aramaic an important role as the medium through which Greek and Latin words entered Hebrew. J. Fellman (1977a) traces the various views regarding the independence of Mishnaic Hebrew and notes a swing back to the view of Geiger. He proposes that Mishnaic Hebrew is a *langue melangée.* For a summary of various views, one should consult Kutscher (1982: 115–20).

The Bar Kokhba letters and Mishnaic Hebrew

The Bar Kokhba letters are, in the opinion of Rabin (1970a: 317–18, n 72), strong vindication of M. H. Segal's views on the vitality and independence of Mishnaic Hebrew (Kutscher 1960–61, 1961–62), although some differences between the letters and the language of the Mishnah have been enumerated by A. Bendavid (1967: 99–101). Bendavid finds in them a trace of the late biblical style. This may be due to a conservative Judean dialect which preserved ancient features, noticeable also in the talmudic passages written in archaic style which preserve the *waw*-conversive but have a mishnaic verbal noun in place of the biblical infinite construct. These passages date from the Second Commonwealth (*t.b. Qidd.* 66a; *Ned.* 9b; *m. Yebam.* 16:7; Rabin 1958: 155). It is also possible that letters tend to preserve a more archaic style. One of the letters, containing the expression *wdql hṭwbh wtḥṣd šbkpr* 'the fine date and the *ḥāṣād̲* in the village,' verifies a reading in the Kaufmann Manuscript of the Mishnah and in *t.y.* as against *ḥāṣāb̲* of *t.b.* (Yadin 1962b: 255). The multilingualism of the community in the mishnaic period is made clear by the discovery of Greek and Aramaic as well as Hebrew documents.

Selected studies on Mishnaic Hebrew

Kutscher, while accepting in essentials the view of M. H. Segal regarding the independence of Mishnaic Hebrew, attaches greater weight to the Aramaic influence, especially in morphology. In his opinion, Segal's grammatical works (1927, 1936) were vitiated by his reliance upon the printed texts of the Mishnah, which has been "corrected" in the direction of Tiberian Masoretic Hebrew. More reliable results would have been obtained by the judicious use of the most reliable manuscripts, which would have yielded valuable information about the unique characteristics of this phase of the language, despite the fact that they date from a later period. Another valuable resource is the oral tradition of the historic Jewish communities. Important work was done along these lines by Yalon, in articles in *KLL, The Bulletin of Language Studies* (reissued in 1963), and in other very important studies collected in subsequent volumes, which appeared in 1967 and 1971. His introduction to the Mishnah edition of Albeck (Jerusalem-Tel

Aviv, 1958–59) is reproduced with additional material in his *Introduction to the Vocalization of the Mishnah* (1964). Variant traditions in the reading of Mishnaic Hebrew were discussed by Shivtiel (earlier: Damti; Ashbat; 1937, 1938–39a and b, 1944, 1963), Murtonen (1956–57), Kahle-Weinberger (1935), and Porath (1938). The festschrift in Yalon's honor, edited by Saul Lieberman and others in 1963, contains an evaluation of his work by Kutscher (1963a) and a bibliography up to that time, compiled by S. Esh.

General descriptions of Mishnaic Hebrew are given by Har Zahav in the first volume of his historical grammar (1951), by Chomsky (1957: 157–71; 1967: 137–57), Kutscher (1963b, 1971b), M. H. Segal (1927, 1936), Matmon-Cohen (1934–38), and Sznejder (1933–35, 1935–36). The earlier studies in the area of the linguistics of Rabbinic Hebrew are listed in H. L. Strack, *Introduction to the Talmud and Midrash* (Philadelphia, 1931; reprinted New York and Philadelphia, 1959, 159–63. A more recent survey of the literature is found in Rabin (1970a: 320–26) and Waldman (1975a: 1292–1302). There is also a relevant bibliography in Hospers (1973, 1974). The monumental work by J. N. Epstein (1948) is of great importance for the phonology of Mishnaic Hebrew, as well as for textual matters, and A. Bendavid (1967, 1971) provides significant descriptions of the development and syntax of Mishnaic Hebrew. There are important studies in the two volumes of the *Archive of the New Dictionary of Rabbinical Literature*, published by Bar Ilan University, Ramat Gan, Israel, vol. 1 (1972) edited by E. Y. Kutscher, and vol. 2 (1974) by M. Z. Kaddari. Articles on Mishnaic Hebrew have been collected by Moshe Bar-Asher (1972, 1980a).

When and where Hebrew was spoken

The question of the extent to which Hebrew was a spoken language at this time has been discussed by several writers, among them Chomsky (1951–52); Margaliot (1962–63), who also discusses the relationship of Aramaic and Mishnaic Hebrew (1970); and A. Bendavid (1967: 153–65; 1972). According to Bendavid, the influence of Aramaic increased during the Second Commonwealth, and Jerusalem was a stronghold of Aramaic (cf. Kutscher 1959: 65–70). The surrounding area of Judah, however, retained Hebrew as a spoken language. There was a decline after the Bar Kokhba rebellion, but pockets of Hebrew speakers are attested until the year 330 C.E. in southern Palestine. In time Hebrew was pushed out of its last stronghold and became the academic language of the house of study. Kutscher (1972b) suggests that the demise of Mishnaic Hebrew as a spoken language is not due to the overpowering influence of Aramaic, since Mishnaic Hebrew shows signs of being a very vigorous language. The reason for its demise was that its speakers were uprooted or exterminated. The area in which it was spoken was limited to the territory which was inhabited by the exiles returning from Babylon, primarily Judea. After the Bar Kokhba revolt, the rabbis fled to Galilee, an Aramaic-speaking area long cut off from the rest of Palestine. The transplanted rabbis spoke Mishnaic Hebrew; their children did not.

Different levels of Mishnaic Hebrew

The general category of Mishnaic Hebrew (*lᵉšôn ḥăḵāmîm*) must be further subdivided into Mishnaic Hebrew[1], the living language of Judah, and Mishnaic Hebrew[2]. This second level, however, cannot be identified exclusively with Amoraic, post-Mishnaic Hebrew. It is to be related to the Hebrew of the transition generation of rabbis who migrated to Galilee (ca. 140–165 C.E.). Kutscher (1971b) proposes a further subdivision: 1) the language of the Tannaim, as transmitted in Palestine, 2) that of the Tannaim as transformed by the Amoraim of Babylonia, 3) the Mishnaic Hebrew of the Amoraim of Palestine, 4) the Mishnaic Hebrew of the Amoraim of Babylonia, 5) the language of prayers and benedictions, and 6) loans from Biblical Hebrew and Mishnaic Hebrew which do not properly belong to Mishnaic Hebrew (Kutscher 1967b, 1969a, 1971b, 1972b; Sokoloff 1968–69: 26–27). Masters theses by M. Vardy (1950) and Y. Margalit (1950) compare *baraytot* in the *Bavli* and *Yerushalmi* with the *Tosefta* and the halakhic midrashim for linguistic purposes. Studies by Moreshet (1972b, 1974a, 1974b) trace the changes in *baraytot* (tannaitic material not in the Mishnah) quoted in the *Bavli* and *Yerushalmi* in comparison to their form in the *Tosefta* and the halakhic midrashim. The changes are in the direction of Mishnaic Hebrew[2]. The influence of Biblical Hebrew becomes stronger in Mishnaic Hebrew[2], as shown by Kutscher and Moreshet. Much has been made of the revealing story of the scholars who had to consult the maid of Rabbi Judah the Patriarch in order to get an explanation of difficult biblical words which were in her spoken dialect but unknown to them (*t.y. Meg.* II:5).

An important survey of the achievements, resources, problems, and prospects of the study of Mishnaic Hebrew has been made by Kutscher (1972a). A masters thesis by Truper (1941) deals with the writing of the halakhic midrashim, while a masters thesis by Schneid (1945) treats the linguistic aspects of tannaitic interpretations in the halakhic midrashim.

The rabbinic period records the beginnings of an awareness of language and a naive sense of cognates. The rabbis recognized a distinction between Biblical and Mishnaic Hebrew, e.g., "the languages of Scripture and of the sages are distinct" (*t.b. Qidd.* 2b; *ʿAboda Zar.* 58b; *Ḥul.* 137b). This statement by Rabbi Johanan is explained (Morag 1961: 26–27; Kutscher 1968: 230–31; 1972b) as reflecting the fact that the language was alive in Judea but not in Galilee or Babylonia. There biblical grammar and lexicon again became dominant. Borrowings from Biblical Hebrew in Mishnaic Hebrew^2 have been demonstrated by Kutscher (1967b) and Haneman (1968). Abramson (1974) shows that the expression *m^{e}hallēḵ biss^{e}p̱înāh* 'travels in a boat' is strictly Mishnaic Hebrew^2, influenced by Aramaic, whereas Mishnaic Hebrew^1 has a variety of expressions, e.g., *m^{e}p̱āreš/niḵnās/rôḵēḇ biss^{e}p̱înāh*. Bar-Adon (1982) compares creative processes in Mishnaic Hebrew^1 with similar creativity in children's speech.

Rabbinic language consciousness

Some other rabbinic reflections on language are: "Four languages are of value: Greek for song, Latin for war, Aramaic for dirges, and Hebrew for speech" (*t.y. Soṭa* VII:2); "Adam spoke Aramaic" (*t.b. Sanh.* 38b); "the first language was Hebrew, and through it the world was created" (*Midrash Tanḥuma, Noaḥ*, 19); "Abraham came from across the Euphrates and spoke Hebrew" (*Midrash Genesis Rabbah* 42:13); "do not regard Aramaic lightly, for it is used in the Torah, the Prophets and the Writings" (*t.y. Soṭa* VII:2); "the Holy One, Blessed be He, exiled Israel to Babylonia because their language is similar to the language of the Torah" (*t.b. Pesaḥ.* 89b); "this shows that *śāḏeh* ('field') is masculine in the holy tongue" (Biblical Hebrew, as against Mishnaic Hebrew, where it is feminine; *Midrash Sifra, Beḥuqqotay*, §4, ch. 11); "when God came to reveal the Torah to Israel he revealed himself not in one tongue but in four . . . Hebrew . . . Latin . . . Arabic . . . Aramaic" (*Midrash Sifre, Berakhah*, 343). The rabbis held the idea that the Hebrew Bible contains elements of other languages, such as Greek, Arabic, Aramaic, and even Egyptian, enabling them to explain difficult words in terms of imagined cognates (Wechter 1964: 1–2, 126–28).

The rabbis distinguished between *l^{e}šôn ḥăḵāmîm* 'the tongue of the sages' and *l^{e}šôn heḏyôṭ* 'speech of the common person.' It is not clear just what this latter term denotes. It may mean legal formulas commonly used but at variance with those established by the rabbis, or a language which is a mixture of Hebrew and Aramaic. A number of proverbs, however, called *māšāl heḏyôṭ* 'common proverbs' are in perfect Hebrew (A. Bendavid 1967: 170–71). Arend (1960) treats rabbinic language consciousness in a masters thesis, based on *Midrash Genesis Rabbah*, and Gottlieb deals with the topic in a doctoral dissertation (1972) based on *Sifre* on Deuteronomy.

Basic manuscripts as sources for Mishnaic Hebrew

Sokoloff (1968–69) follows the lead of Kutscher (1963b) in seeking basic texts which can serve as reliable evidence of Mishnaic Hebrew tradition, uncorrupted by "correctors" who imposed biblical rules of grammar upon mishnaic and midrashic material. Kutscher regarded the Kaufmann manuscript of the Mishnah as such a text (Beer 1929), and Sokoloff has treated a Vatican manuscript of *Midrash Bereshit Rabbah* (Ms. Vat. Ebr. 30) as a primary text which has preserved many authentic forms (also discussed by L. Barth [1973]). As already noted by Kutscher (1963b), Biblical Hebrew words and forms not appearing in Mishnaic Hebrew^{1} reappear in Mishnaic Hebrew^{2}, e.g., Mishnaic Hebrew^{1} uses exclusively *ʾatt* 'you' (m.s.) and *ʾānû* 'we,' but Mishnaic Hebrew^{2} interchanges these with biblical *ʾattāh* and *ănaḥnû*.

The Parma manuscript (De Rossi 138) has been studied by Haneman for its phonology (1965–66). His morphological studies of this manuscript will be enumerated in the following section. He has also dealt with the script of Rome Ms. 66 of the *Sifra* (1974a). Geniza fragments of Mishnah and Talmud now in the Soviet Union have been published by A. I. Katsh (1970, 1975–77), providing material for linguistic and textual study. Z. M. Rabinovitz (1976) has published early midrash fragments from the Geniza.

THE PHONOLOGY OF MISHNAIC HEBREW

Manuscript evidence for Mishnaic Hebrew phonology

Some evidence for the phonology of Mishnaic Hebrew^{1} is available in Epstein (1948), e.g., the aspiration of *b*, as seen from the variants *ʾăḇîr*/*ʾăwîr* 'air,' *ʾawwāz*/*aḇāz* 'goose.' Voiced consonants are assimilated to neighboring unvoiced ones, e.g., *heḇqēr*/*heqēr* 'ownerless property,' *sāgap̱*/*sākap̱* 'plague, afflict. Contrary to the accepted masoretic rule, there is evidence that initial *b* was aspirated, e.g., *gāmāl ʿôḇēr wᵉrôḵᵉḇô*, variant: *ḇᵉrôḵᵉḇô* 'a passing camel and its rider' (J. N. Epstein 1948, 2.1220–34). At an earlier time the distinction between *ś* and *s* was obliterated, cf. *sōḵrîm* 'hiring' (Ezra 4:5), from original *śkr*.

Similar evidence can be drawn from Sokoloff's (1968–69) analysis of Mishnaic Hebrew^{2} in Vat. Ms. Ebr. 30 (see also L. Barth 1973). Variants *b*/*w*, *k*/*q*, *b*/*p*, *ṣ*/*s*, *z*/*ṣ* (*qôp̱zîm*/*qop̱ṣîm* 'they jump'), *z*/*s* (*azḵārôt*/*askārôṯ* 'divine names') and *m*/*n* in final position (*ʾādām*/*ʾādān*; cf. Kutscher 1963b: 250–51) are found. The alternation *d*/*z* (*šiḏrāh*/*šizrāh* 'spinal column') may go back to original Semitic *ḏ*, but it is, on the other hand, hardly likely that the distinction between *d* and *ḏ* was maintained at so late a period. The *d*/*z* alternation may be no more than dialect or phonetic variants. An interchange of *l*/*r* is found (*Borsîp̱*/*Bolsîp̱* 'Borsippa,' *kallaqṭērîn* < Greek *charakteres* 'features of the face'). There is evidence that *h* disappeared and was confused with ʾ, e.g., *ʾaśāmaṯ ʿayin* for *hăśāmaṯ ʿayin* 'laying one's eye upon.' Laryngeals and pharyngeals are attenuated and confused with one another (*ʾôšer* is written for *ʿôšer* 'wealth' and *ḥôqîr* written for *hôqîr* 'increased in value'; compare the discussion by Kutscher for the earlier Qumran period (1959: 399–403).

Galilean pronunciation

It cannot be assumed that the loss of *ḥ* and ʿ was universal. There is the well-known rabbinic passage mocking the Galileans who fail to distinguish between ʾ, ʿ, and *ḥ*. This suggests that even in the later Amoraic period there were those who retained the distinctions (*t.b. ʿErub.* 53b). There is a source which forbids the men of Haifa, Beisan, and Tivʿon from leading the prayers because they pronounce *h* as *ḥ*, and ʿ as ʾ (*t.y. Ber.* II:4). A variant reverses the direction of the change, *ḥ* to *h*. It is also stated that the students of Rabbi Eliezer ben Jacob indiscriminately confused ʿ and ʾ (*t.b. Ber.* 32a), but in *t.b. Meg.* 24b this is attributed to the residents of the aforementioned towns. Now, a paper by Beyer (1986) seeks to establish the pronunciation of Galilean Aramaic on the basis of Geniza fragments with Palestinian and Tiberian pointing.

The same attenuation of gutturals and the interchange of *š*/*ś* is attested in numerous rabbinic homilies, mainly from Mishnaic Hebrew², e.g., the equation for homiletic purposes of *hillûlîm* 'praise' and *ḥillûlîm* 'profanation, secularization' and the statement that the rabbis do not refrain from interpreting *h* as if it were *ḥ* (*t.y. Maʿaś. šeni* V:2; *t.y. Šabb.* VII:2). Even in gematria, the homiletic technique of assigning numerical values to letters, *h* is treated as if it were *ḥ* = 8 (*t.y. Šabb.* VII:2). Biblical *wayyiḥaḏ* 'he rejoiced' (Exod 18:9) is interpreted as if it were *wayyihaḏ* 'he became a Jew' (*Midrash Tanḥuma*, *Yitro*, 7), but there is no evidence of this in the *Mekhilta* on the passage, Mishnaic Hebrew¹. On the other hand, the Torah of Rabbi Meir, from the earlier period, had *ʾôr* 'light' for *ʿôr* 'skin' (Gen 3:21; *Midrash Genesis Rabbah* 20:12). There are numerous instances of *š* being treated as if it were *ś* or *s* in Mishnaic Hebrew² homilies, e.g., the equating of *šāmayim* 'heaven' with *śāʾ mayim* 'bear water' (*Genesis Rabbah* 4:9), *māšḵēnî* 'pull me' understood as *maskinnannî* 'makes me poor' (Cant 1:4; *Midrash Cant. Rabbah* 1:29).

The development of the vowels has been treated by Kutscher (1968; summary, 1971b: 1595–96). Biblical *i* becomes *e*, e.g., *Binyāmîn* > *Benyāmîn*, *Milkāh* > Greek *Melcha*, and *u* is changed to *o*, e.g., *ʿAdullam* > Greek *Odollam* place-name). The short high vowels, *u* and *i*, were replaced by short, low vowels, *o*, *e*, in unaccented closed syllables. Homiletic evidence is much less reliable for establishing actual vowel quality, but it might be noted that *ʿôšeq* 'oppression' is interpreted as *ʿēśeq* 'contention' (Qoh 7:7; *Midrash Qoh. Rabbah* 7:14) and *pōh* 'here' as if it were *peh* 'mouth' (Gen 19:12; *Midrash Yalquṭ Shimʿoni*, Proverbs 1, §932). At a later period, in south Yemenite poetry, the same kind of change occurred, namely, *ḥolem* and *tṣere* are rhymed (Ratzhaby 1968: 28; Morag 1963: 92–99). It has been suggested by Eshel (1960) that even in Biblical Hebrew such a variation existed; compare the pun on the name of *Moab* based upon *mēʾāḇ* '(born) from the father' (Gen 19:37). A variant *u*/*i* is suggested by the pun on *y^{e}hûdî* 'man from Judah' and *y^{e}ḥîdî* 'alone' (*Midrash Esther Rabbah* 6, on Esth 2:5) and the case of *tāšûrî* 'you will gaze,' treated as if it were *tā-šîrî* 'you will sing' (Cant 4:18; *t.y. Šeb.* VI:1). This alternation is known from later dialects (Chomsky 1971a: 25–27). There are also numerous examples of *ketiv* and *qere* reflecting this interchange, e.g., Num 1:16, 14:36, 16:11, 26:9, 32:7; Jer 4:19, 15:11, 48:5, 49:39.

Vowel changes in Mishnaic Hebrew

THE MORPHOLOGY OF MISHNAIC HEBREW

A general discussion of the morphology of Mishnaic Hebrew is found in Chomsky (1967: 137–57) and in M. H. Segal (1927; 1936). Among the significant developments which occurred in Mishnaic Hebrew were the establishment of a three-tense system; a leveling out of the *tiqṭôlnāh* (3 f.p.) to the m. *yiqṭôlû*; the use of the verb "to be" before the participle to indicate continued or habitual action; the dropping of the *ʾ* in *primae-alef* verbs, e.g., *leʾěḵôl* > *lôḵal* 'to eat'; the dropping of initial *n* in the imperative of *primae-nun* verbs, e.g., *nāṭal* 'he took,' *ṭôl* 'take'; the *plusquamperfect*: *mi* + *še* + past tense (Loewenstamm 1966–67); and the indication of previous action in the future, *li* + *ḵ^{e}* + *še* + future tense, e.g., *liḵ^{e}šeyibbāneh bēṯ hammiqdāš* 'when the temple will have been rebuilt.' Kutscher (1963b), basing his evidence on the Kaufmann Manuscript (Beer 1929), enumerates morphological points such as the alternation of *m*/*n* in final position; the Aramaic influence apparent in the use of *ʾatt* for 'you' (m.s.), *naḥnû*

Mishnaic morphology contrasted with biblical

for *ʾănaḥnû* 'we,' the possessive suffix *-îḵ*, e.g., *baʿălîḵ* 'your husband' contrasted with masoretic *baʿălēk*; the suffix *-āḵ*, e.g., *ʾištāḵ* 'your wife,' as compared with masoretic *išteḵā*; the form *rabbûn* or *rabbôn* 'master' (now see N. Wieder, 1964 on *rabbûn*); the form *ribbî* 'master, teacher'; and finally the change to the *qityah* form from *qetiyāh*, e.g., *piryāh weribyāh* 'being fruitful and multiplying.' The periphrastic imperative, e.g., *hĕwēh dān* 'judge,' has been traced to Aramaic inscriptions by Greenfield (1969b).

The most thorough presentation of the distinctive morphological and syntactic features of Mishnaic Hebrew are the two volumes by Bendavid (1967, 1971). The first is a historical treatment, and the second contains numerous examples of Mishnaic Hebrew constructions illustrating the differences between Biblical Hebrew and Mishnaic Hebrew. The development is not presented diachronically, but the two languages are presented side by side in the second volume for purposes of comparison. It may be noted that Bendavid's study grew out of the intense ideological discussion over which of the two styles, Biblical or Mishnaic, should dominate Modern Hebrew (Bendavid 1967: 1–12; 248–328). The title of his first volume, published in 1951, was, significantly, *Biblical Hebrew or Mishnaic Hebrew?* (written in Hebrew), but the sharpness of this opposition was modified in the title of the later edition (1967). The bulk of the material is derived from literary sources, and the work has been criticized for its neglect of the spoken language, as far as the spoken can be recovered (Blau 1968b). Even within the limitations imposed by the literary nature of the material it should be possible to differentiate further between different types of discourse, including reproduction of colloquial speech, legal formulas, and language influenced by the biblical idiom of which is interpreted in midrashic exegesis. Another review of Bendavid has been written by Sarfatti (1967–68b). B. Levine (1978) comments on Bendavid's views regarding Canticles as a link between the spoken language in the late biblical and mishnaic periods.

Bendavid's contribution

The distinctive nominal forms of Mishnaic Hebrew have been treated in several places (Segal 1927; 1936; Bendavid 1971: 442–52). There is a bias toward the *qeṭîlûṯ* form, e.g., Biblical Hebrew *ḥeseḏ* > Mishnaic Hebrew *ḥăsîḏûṯ*; Biblical Hebrew *šikkārôn* > Mishnaic Hebrew *šiḵrûṯ* 'drunkenness.' Another widespread form, replacing biblical segolates and preformative *mem* forms, is *qeṭîlāh*, e.g., *begeḏ* > *begîḏāh* 'treason, betrayal,' *beḵî* > *beḵiyyāh* 'weeping' (or possibly: *biḵyāh*), *mišmereṯ* > *šemîrāh* 'guarding.' Names of professions are found in the *qāṭôl* form instead of *qôṭēl*, e.g.,

Unique nominal forms

ṭôḥēn > *tāḥôn* 'miller,' but Biblical Hebrew *qattāl* is also used. The *Piᶜel qiṭṭûl* and *Hifᶜil haqṭālāh* forms are distinctive, e.g., *qiwwûy* 'hoping,' *haggāḏāh* 'telling.' The difference between *Hafᶜel* and *Afᶜel* forms may reflect different degrees of Aramaic penetration and may be associated with different geographic areas. It is difficult to systematize the evidence, e.g., *ᵓaggāḏāh* 'telling,' *ᵓaḇṭāḥāh* 'promising,' which are associated with Palestinian literary sources, while the corresponding *h*-forms come from Babylonia. On the other hand, *hônāyāh* 'oppression' comes from Babylonia and *ᵓônāyāh* from Palestine (Bendavid 1967: 214–15).

There is a detailed study by Kutscher (1969a) of nominal forms as they appear in the Kaufmann manuscript (Beer 1929). According to his enumeration, there are sixteen normal forms and a few others of doubtful category. Some are extensions and developments of forms found in Biblical Hebrew, e.g., *qᵉṭîlāh*, *qᵉṭēlāh*, *qᵉṭālāh*, all based on the *Qal*. In some cases these replace other biblical forms based on the same root. In other cases, they do not, and in these there is a differentiation in meaning. The form *qᵉṭûl* is not Biblical Hebrew and seems to be limited to legal contexts in Mishnaic Hebrew. The *qāṭēl* is also uniquely Mishnaic Hebrew and is confined to legal terminology, e.g., *gāzēl* 'robbery,' *kārēṯ* 'early death.' Forms in Mishnaic Hebrew which were less productive than the above were the segolates and the *-ûṯ* forms, e.g., *zᵉḵûṯ* 'right,' 'merit,' *gālûṯ* 'exile.' In summary, Kutscher points out that there was a strong tendency toward nominalization in Mishnaic Hebrew and a consequent abandonment of the biblical infinitive absolute. A doubtful form is *qᵉṭillāh* which, it is suggested, may derive from biblical *qᵉṭullāh* through the vocalic change *u* > *i* (Kutscher 1968). Mettinger (1971) has attempted to connect biblical *qᵉṭullāh* with the Akkadian *purussûm* form.

Other studies in morphology

Other studies in the area of morphology are: Bar-Asher (1968, masters thesis) on the grammar of *Ṭohorot* in the Parma manuscript, De Rossi 497; M. Elitsur (1977, masters thesis) on the geminates in Mishnaic Hebrew; B. Z. Gross (1971, doctoral dissertation) on nouns ending in *-ān*, *ôn* in Biblical Hebrew and Mishnaic Hebrew.

The morphology of Mishnaic Hebrew as represented in the Parma Manuscript, De Rossi 138, has been studied by Haneman (1962, masters thesis; 1965–66; 1972, doctoral dissertation; 1980a). It has been shown by Cuomo (1977; summarized by Sarfatti 1981) that this manuscript dates from the 11th century.

Gender changes between Biblical and Mishnaic Hebrew are quite dramatic. The rabbis were aware of the differences, e.g., the *rᵉḥēlîm/rᵉḥēlôṯ* 'ewes' variant which led to the observation that Biblical Hebrew and Mishnaic Hebrew are distinct (*t.b. Hul.* 137b), and that *śāḏeh* 'field' is masculine in the biblical tongue (*Midrash Sifra, Behuqqotay*, §4, chap. 11). There is also a clear tendency to break up the bound formation, and instead of using the dual *-ayim*, to use the numeral two with the plural, e.g., *ʾammāṯayim* > *šᵉtê ʾammôṯ* 'two cubits.' The Biblical Hebrew collective (singular) is always made into a plural, posing problems for homileticians when they approach biblical language with language habits of another age (A. Bendavid 1971: 449–51; *Midrash Genesis Rabbah* 75:7).

Gender change and the break up of bound formation

Sarfatti (1980a) discusses determination of fixed phrases in Mishnaic Hebrew. In printed editions of the Mishnah there are three fixed patterns: 1) indetermination in both singular and plural; 2) determination in both singular and plural, and 3) determination in singular but indetermination in the plural. In Geniza fragments and reliable manuscripts there is greater flexibility, consistent with syntactic position and semantic value. For example, *ʿereḇ šabbāṯ* 'the eve of Sabbath' (Friday) is always undetermined in printed editions, but in manuscripts one finds also *ʿereḇ haššabbāṯ*. Sarfatti reaches no conclusions about this variation.

Determination in Geniza manuscripts

Schwarzwald (1980b) sees parallels between Mishnaic Hebrew and Modern Hebrew. Both dialects of the language have weakened the spirantization rule (/bgdkpt/) and have treated weak verbs in similar ways. Processes of analogy, restructuring, and simplification in both dialects attest to a living language.

Haim Cohen (1983) demonstrates that, while Biblical Hebrew has both *qᵉṭālô* or *qāṭal ʾōṯô*, Mishnaic Hebrew knows only the first. Only when it is impossible to use the first pattern does Mishnaic Hebrew use the second, e.g., *qôṭlîn ʾoṯô*. Exceptions to this rule are III *y* verbs, e.g., *rāʾāh ʾôṯān* 'he saw them,' not *rāʾām/n*.

The verbal system shows significant development. The cohortative has vanished and is replaced by *yaqṭûl*, e.g., *naʿbrā-nāʾ* > *naʿăḇôr* 'let us cross.' Mishnaic Hebrew differs from Biblical Hebrew in having final *-t* in the 3 f.s. form in III *y* forms, e.g., *hayᵉṯāh* > *hāyāṯ* 'she was.' There are traces of this in Biblical Hebrew, e.g., *wᵉʿāśāṯ* 'it will produce' (Lev 25:21; G–K, §75m). Weak verbs show changes due to the vanishing of the weak consonant, e.g., *maṣāʾnû* > *māṣînû* 'we have found,' but there is also a reverse phenomenon, *ʿāśûnî* > *ʿăśāʾûnî* 'they have made me,' a kind of hypercorrection. Middle weak and final *-he* verbs

Development of verbal stems

interchange their patterns of conjugation, e.g., *nāḥîm/nôḥîm* 'they rest,' and some weak verbs add a consonant and assimilate to the triradical pattern, e.g., *mûl* > *mhl* 'circumcise,' *sāḏ* > *Piᶜel siyyēḏ* 'whitewashed.'

Changes in the use of the stems are most striking. *Piᶜel* often replaces the *Qal* with no differentiation of meaning, e.g, *hôlēḵ* > *mᵉhallēk* 'going, walking.' Ben-Hayyim (1957–58) describes a similar pattern in Samaritan Hebrew and cites the significant observation in the Talmud that Rabbi Nathan, a Babylonian dependent upon the written Biblical Hebrew, makes a distinction between *Qal* and *Piᶜel*, while the Palestinian Tanna of the Mishnah uses the *Piᶜel* with no difference in meaning from the *Qal* (*t.b. Git.* 65b). *Qal* may be replaced by *Hifᶜil*, especially in II *w* verbs, and the effect is to fill out the weak root, e.g., *sāḥ/mēsîaḥ* 'speaks, tells,' *śam/hēśîm* 'placed.' The *Qal*, however, is by no means obsolete. There is a shift to the use of the *Hifᶜil* in verbs indicating a change of state, e.g., *yeḥkam* > *yaḥkîm* 'will become wise.' *Nitpaᶜel* replaces biblical *Hitpaᶜel* and also replaces *Qal* statives, e.g., *gāḇar* > *niṯgabbēr* 'became strong.' Various biblical passives, *Hofᶜal*, *Puᶜal*, and, in some cases, the *Nifᶜal*, are leveled out and replaced by the *Nitpaᶜel*, e.g., *neʾĕnāḥ* > *niṯʾannēaḥ* 'sighed,' *pôrāš* > *niṯpārēš* 'was explained, clarified,' *huraq* > *niṯrôqēn* 'was emptied.' Another method of replacing the biblical passive and reflexive is to break up the construction into one using an active verb and the appropriate pronouns, e.g., *miṯlaḥăšîm* > *lāḥăšû ʾēlû lᵉʾēlû* 'they whispered one to another.' The *Nitpaᶜel* appears to be a fusing of the *Hitpaᶜel* and the *Nifᶜal*, but its range is not identical with the biblical *Hitpaᶜel*, despite the artificial similarity, e.g., *hiṯᶜaššēr* 'pretended to be rich' but *niṯᶜaššēr* 'became rich.'

Further study of the *Nitpaᶜel* has been done by Bar-Asher (1976–77) and Qimron (1976–77). Bar-Asher considers many examples of the *Nitpaᶜel* to be present participles, and, allowing for incorrect texts and corrections by later copyists, regards the *Nitpaᶜel* as a regularly attested form in Mishnaic Hebrew. The similarity in function between the *Hitpaᶜel* and *Nifᶜal* resulted in the transfer of the *n*-element to the *Hitpaᶜel* and the birth of the *Nitpaᶜel* form. Qimron surveys the views of earlier writers on Hebrew grammar regarding this matter. It is his conclusion that *Mitpaᶜel* was still the standard present participial form in Mishnaic Hebrew and that *Nitpaᶜel* in the participle was a byform, perhaps dialectic. Kaddari (1978c), who studied the form in the post-talmudic responsa literature, concludes that the *Nitpaᶜel* as a present participle is not the present of the past tense *Nitpaᶜel*, as

Mitpaᶜel is the present participle of past tense *Hitpaᶜel*. The so-called present participle *Nitpaᶜel* is only apparently so. In reality it is the passive participle *Paᶜul* of *Nitpaᶜel*.

The *Nufᶜal* stem

Moreshet (1980b) defends the view of H. Yalon that there is a *Nūfᶜal* stem in Mishnaic Hebrew. Examples are: *nûgʾălû* 'were redeemed' (not *nigʾălû*) and *nûldāh* 'was born' (not *nôldāh*). The cause of this phenomenon was not phonetic but was a subconscious factor, the feeling that passive actions were expressed with the vowel *u*, as in the Biblical Hebrew *Puᶜal* and *Qal paᶜul*. Elements of the *Nifᶜal* and *Puᶜal* merged. The vowels *i*, *o*, and *e* (as in *nigʾălû*, *nôldû*, *neḥlaq*) merged into *u* (*nûgʾălû*, *nûldû*, *nûḥlaq*).

The iterative past

In the article mentioned above, Bar-Asher (1976–77) also recovers some lost forms in Mishnaic Hebrew. For example, alongside of *swk* 'anoint' there was a byform *ysk*. The *Paᶜol* of the *Qal* served in Mishnaic Hebrew as a present participle and also as a noun, e.g., *ʾāsôr* 'forbids' (often rejected as an error for *ʾôsēr*).

As noted above, the use of the verb "to be" with the present participle indicates the iterative past, but from some examples given by A. Bendavid (1971: 541–42), it appears that this construction can also serve as a narrative past, indicating actions contemporary with or even prior to the time of the narration, but with a durative aspect inherent, e.g., *hûʾ šôlēaḥ yāḏ lîṭôl ʾeī hassakkîn weᶜênāw môrîḏôṯ demāᶜôṯ . . . wehāyû hammalʾāḵîm miṯqabṣîn*, 'he (Abraham) was reaching to take the knife, and his eyes were running with tears . . . and the angels were gathering' (*Midrash Genesis Rabbah* 56:8). As the narration is in the present tense (see F. Rosenthal 1961: 55, §177, for this phenomenon in Aramaic), the action of the angels is contemporary with it. The punctual sense of the perfect would not fit here, because there is a continuous aspect in their action. Another example is *kešeyāṣeʾû Yiśrāʾēl mimmiṣrayim hāyû bāhem baᶜălê mûmîm meᶜăḇôḏaṯ pāreḵ, šehāyû ᶜôśîm beṭîṭ uḇileḇēnîm*, 'when Israel departed from Egypt there were among them cripples from the hard labor, for they had been working (pluperfect) with mortar and bricks' (*Midrash Tanḥuma, Yitro*, 8).

Mishor (1979) discusses the use of the *yaqtul* form in expressing modality. Modality includes that which is desirable, possible, doubtful, or astonishing. With the loss of sensitivity to the modal *yaqtul* form, the printed editions preferred to use more explicit circumlocutions.

Sharvit (1980) discusses the overall pattern of the tenses in Mishnaic Hebrew. Since *qôṭēl* expresses present-future, futurity is emphasized when needed by *ᶜaṯîḏ liqṭôl*. Regarding aspects, *hāyāh qôṭēl* denotes either repeated, habitual, or durative actions in all tenses, including the imperative. The tense system in Mishnaic Hebrew is treated in a doctoral dissertation by Mishor (1983). Blau (1983b) regards 3 f.s. forms such as *hāyāṯ* 'was' as a late development in Mishnaic Hebrew, to be separated from similar forms in Biblical Hebrew. The form *hāyāṯ* developed from the pausal *hāyā́ṯāh*.

THE LEXICON OF MISHNAIC HEBREW

General studies in lexicography

Numerous studies on the lexicon of Mishnaic Hebrew have appeared in *KLL*, *Leš*, *LLA*, and elsewhere. Notable among them are: Abramson (1956–57, 1974); Berggrün (1932, 1948–49, 1949–50, 1962–63, 1967–68, 1972–73, 1974, 1975–76); Yalon, in numerous articles collected and reprinted in 1971; S. A. Kaufman (1970, 1974); D. Sperling (1969, 1972, 1973a, 1973b); N. Wieder (1964); E. and H. Guggenheimer (1971–75); R. Weiss (1962–64); Kaddari (1970b); Moreshet and Klein (1975–76); Greenfield (1956, doctoral dissertation); Wartsky (1970); R. Pines (1963, masters thesis) on terms for colors; Moreshet (1972a, 1974a, 1974b, 1980); D. Sperber (1971–72, 1973–74, 1974, 1974–75, 1975–76, 1980, 1982, 1984, 1986); and Boyarin (1980–81, 1982–83, 1986). Numerous lexical items have been elucidated in the studies of Saul Lieberman (1942, 1950, 1965, 1967–68, 1968, 1970a, 1970b) and in his authoritative edition of the *Tosefta* (1955–73, *Zeraᶜim*, *Moᶜed*, *Nashim*) and the accompanying *Ṭosefta kifshutah* (1955–73).

The replacement of Biblical Hebrew words

The question of the replacement of Biblical Hebrew words by new ones is discussed by A. Bendavid (1967: 355–66), who gives lists of such replacements, a small proportion of which appear to derive from Aramaic. What is lacking in Bendavid's presentation is a full discussion of the effects of the entry of a new lexical item on the rest of the existing inventory. Total replacement or obsolescence of the former item is not the only option (for a theoretical discussion see H. Hoenigwald, *Language Change and Linguistic Reconstruction* [University of Chicago Press, 1960]). Since much of this literature is biblical exegesis, the language of the academy and old terms may be retained, at least in a specialized sense. New terms will be based upon biblical sources. Moreover, there are different strata in the Mishnah and Tosefta, and more archaic words may be retained in certain levels, e.g., *pārûr* 'pot' is replaced by *qᵉḏērāh*, but at least once *pārûr* is used (*m. Beṣa* 1:7). Biblical *sēp̱er*, Elephantine Aramaic *spr*, is replaced by *šᵉṭār* and *gēṭ*, both derived ultimately from Akkadian and entering via Aramaic. However, in *m. ᶜEd.* 1:12 *sēp̱er* appears in the sense of 'document,' e.g., *sēp̱er kᵉṯubbāṯāhh* 'the document of her marriage contract.' This may merely reflect the biblical idiom of Deut 24:1 or an earlier stratum of Hebrew. Both examples are quoted by the school of Shammai, whose conservatism is well known and may also extend to the linguistic sphere. Albeck's view, as stated in his commentary on the Mishnah (*Neziqin*, Tel Aviv-Jerusalem, 1959, 275–79) is that *ᶜEduyot* is the earliest collection of *mishnayot*.

Changing semantic boundaries resulting from the entry of new words can be illustrated by the replacement of *gᵉḇûl* 'boundary' by *tᵉḥûm* and *meṣer*, Assyrian *taḫūmu* and Akkadian *miṣru*, as well as *sᵉp̱ār*. The word *gᵉḇûl*, in the plural, designates areas outside of the Temple in Jerusalem, but, at least in Mishnaic Hebrew[2], it is still found in its original meaning. Mishnaic Hebrew *nāṭal* 'take' replaces Biblical Hebrew *lāqaḥ* which now has the sense 'buy' (already present in Biblical Hebrew; see Prov 31:16). The blessing over the *lûlāḇ*, based on Lev 23:40, has *ᶜal nᵉṭîlaṯ lûlāḇ* 'for the taking of the *lûlāḇ*.' Had the biblical *lqḥ* been used it would have meant 'for the purchasing' (Kutscher 1961: 55–56).

New lexemes in Mishnaic Hebrew

A significant part of the lexicon of Mishnaic Hebrew[1] cannot be traced to cognates. Albeck (1959: 128–215a) provides three lists of words which are new in the Mishnah or are homonymous with Biblical Hebrew but with a different meaning. The first list has Aramaic cognates, the second has no Semitic cognates, indicating the vitality of Mishnaic Hebrew, and the third lists Greek loanwords. The Aramaic component is significant as is the further semantic development of roots present in Biblical Hebrew.

Moreshet, in his doctoral dissertation (1972a), later published as a book (1980a), takes up the question of the new verbs which have entered the lexicon of Mishnaic Hebrew. Disagreeing with M. H. Segal, who found 300 new verbs, Moreshet counts 580. Moreshet also maintains that Aramaic influence on Mishnaic Hebrew[1] is quite intensive, and in this he again opposes Segal, who argued for the autonomy of Mishnaic Hebrew. Only one-third of all the new verbs have a link with Biblical Hebrew or are of an obscure, non-Aramaic origin. The rest, and by far the greater part, are known from Aramaic dialects. Some of Moreshet's methods are questioned in Sarfatti's (1980c: 74) review of Moreshet's book (1980a). According to Sarfatti, Moreshet's guiding but unarticulated assumption is that etymological homonyms alone constitute distinctive lexemes, while semantic homonyms do not. This introduces a diachronic measure on a single synchronic level. Thus, one might object that even if biblical *spr* 'tell, count' and mishnaic *spr* 'cut the hair' are not shown to be distinctive etymologically, they are sufficiently distinctive semantically to count *spr* in Mishnaic Hebrew as a new root. In general, however, Sarfatti's review is quite favorable and includes much praise for the thorough research.

M. Bar-Asher (1983) elucidates a number of forms in the Kaufmann manuscript which differ from the printed editions, such as *p*^{e}*ṯîlāh* = *b*^{e}*ḏîlāh* 'piece of tin'; *haggāhāh* = *hagbāhāh* 'lifting, correcting'; and he treats errors of vocalization in the Kaufmann manuscript (1984b). G. Birnbaum (1984–85) surveys vocalization of /b k l/ in the manuscript. A. Goldberg (1983) discusses the lexical implications of a confusion of *ʿrb/ʿbr* in the Mishnah. Talshir (1983) discusses *ʾănāqāh* 'she-camel.' E. S. Rosenthal (1983) offers lexical studies in Mishnaic Hebrew. Sarfatti (1983) shows that scribal variants acquired independent lexical meaning, proving that Mishnaic Hebrew was a living *literary* language. Legal terminology is analyzed by H. Nathan (1986).

AKKADIAN LOANWORDS AND INFLUENCE

A small fragment of the mishnaic lexicon can be traced to Akkadian, with Aramaic as the intermediary. Identifications of late Hebrew and Akkadian words were made quite early (Waldman 1972a: 13–23). Schrader (*Die Keilinschriften und das Alten Testament*, 2nd ed., Giessen, 1883) related *ṣ*^{e}*ḇāṯ* 'tongs' to *ṣabātu* 'seize,' *qaṯ* 'handle' to *qātu* 'hand,' and *š*^{e}*ṭār* 'document' to *šaṭāru* 'write.' Oppert (*ZA* 1 [1886] 304–6) connected *maškôn* with *maškānu* 'pledge' and Feuchtwang (*ZA* 5 [1890] 90; *ZA* 6 [1891] 437–43) identified *k*^{e}*rî* 'heap,' *šôḇār* 'receipt,' and *hep̱qēr* 'ownerless property' with Akkadian counterparts. Meissner (*ZA* 6 [1891] 289–98) identified plant names occurring in both languages. Barth (*Wurzeluntersuchungen* [Leipzig, 1902] 3, 11, 32, 53) identified *bēl dabābi* > *baʿal d*^{e}*ḇāḇāh* 'enemy,' *dalāḫu* > *dlḥ* 'trouble,' *taqānu* > *tqn* 'set in order,' and *sakāpu* 'strike down > *skp/sgp* 'afflict.' Delitzsch's *Assyrisches Handwörterbuch* (Leipzig, 1896) included a number of lexical identifications, among them *qalāpu/qlp* 'peel off, skin' and *ziʾipu* > *zayyēp̱* 'mold, forge.'

Earlier studies of Akkadian loanwords

Pick, in his *Talmudische Glossen* (Berlin, 1903), referring to Delitzsch's dictionary, discussed personal and place names, talmudic legends originating in Babylonian myths, lexical identifications, and legal formulas that survived past the talmudic period until the Middle Ages. A major landmark was Zimmern's monograph, *Akkadische Fremdwörter* (Leipzig, 1915, 2nd ed., 1917). Of the approximately 400 words discussed, about fifty are in Mishnaic Hebrew and not attested in Biblical Hebrew. Many of Zimmern's identifications are valid, but his method has severe limitations. As seen by the full title, the monograph sought to demonstrate Babylonian cultural influence; the excess and tendentiousness of this "Pan-Babylonism" have long been rejected. There is no philological discussion, merely a listing, and no effort is made to distinguish between true loans and common Semitic. Making this distinction properly is no doubt the major challenge to all studies in this area.

Akkadian loanwords in Syriac and Mishnaic Hebrew

Brockelmann's *Lexicon Syriacum* 2nd ed., Göttingen, 1928) contains numerous Akkadian loanwords which are also found in the mishnaic lexicon, among them *askuppatu* > *ʾisqûpāʾ* 'threshold,' *gassu* > *gēṣāʾ* > *gēṣ* 'gypsum,' *kisibirru* > *kusbartaʾ* 'coriander,' *marru* > *marraʾ* > *mar* 'hoe,' and *taḫūmu* > *tᵉḥûmāʾ* > *tᵉḥûm* 'boundary.' Eitan (*AJSL* 46 [1929] 31–32) sought to derive *ʾep̱šār* (variant: *ʾip̱šār*) 'it is possible' from Akkadian *ippašar* 'it is loosened,' root: *pšr*, *pašāru*, although this could be common Semitic, rather than a loanword. Tur-Sinai (ספר איוב [Tel Aviv, 1954] 232) related Hebrew *šᵉp̱îr* 'sac of the foetus' with *saparu* 'net,' finding it concealed in Job 26:13.

Current debate on Akkadian loanwords

Kutscher has related numerous mishnaic words to Akkadian in his popular work (1961) and in various articles, e.g., *ʾēmāṯay*/*ʾimmāṯayi* < *immati*, *ina mati* 'when' (1963b: 267–68), *ʾappār* (not *ʾăp̱ār*) to *apparu*, Sumerian AM.BAR 'meadow, swamp' (1966–67a: 108–9), and *kûḵ* 'sepulchral chamber,' through Nabatean *gwḥ* and Palmyrene *gmḥ* to *kimaḫḫu*/*gimaḫḫu*, Sumerian KI.MAḪ 'preeminent place' (1967a). Some phonological problems related to the last identification have been raised by S. A. Kaufman (1970: 69, 160, 238). Kutscher (1967a) has also related *qamṣûṣ* 'bent (as a corpse)' with Akkadian *kamāṣu*/*kamāsu* 'crouch,' but the relationship may be a cognate one, as two emphatics cannot occur in the same word in Akkadian (Geers' law), and *q* in the Hebrew word may be original. It is harder to establish that the word was borrowed without the emphatic and that a secondary emphaticization took place later in the Hebrew. B. Levine (1962) has connected Ugaritic *dqt* and *gdlt* with mishnaic *bᵉhēmāh daqqāh* and *bᵉhēmāh gassāh* 'light cattle, heavy cattle,' and has proposed a relationship between *targēm* 'recite, translate' and Akkadian *ragāmu* 'call.' Levine also sees a connection between *mulugu* and *mᵉlôg*, a type of property arrangement in marriage, but he is challenged by Kaufman (1970) concerning the Akkadian origin of the last two terms.

Legal language and Akkadian influence

Legal terminology has been traced through Aramaic to Akkadian and Assyrian prototypes; notable studies in this area are those by Kutscher (1954) and Falk (1956–57, 1967, 1969). Driver and Miles make several identifications in their *Babylonian Laws* (Oxford University Press, 1935). R. Yaron (1961: 90–91) sees a wide-ranging translation loan in various reflexes of the image of 'shining, pure' in the sense of 'innocent, clear of obligation,' e.g., Akkadian *ubbubu*, *zukkû*, *murruqu*, Egyptian *wʾb*, mishnaic *zky*, and Greek *katheropoio*.

Muffs (1969) has treated at length legal formulas from peripheral Akkadian and from Neo-Assyrian which found their way to the Aramaic of the Elephantine documents. Some of these have been absorbed into Hebrew as well, e.g., *ṯuppa waṣû* > *hôṣîʾ š^{e}ṭār* 'produce a document,' and *qāta eṭēru* 'remove the seller's hand,' i.e., 'pay off a debt' > *sillēq ʾeṯ yad* X. Kutscher (1970: 385–86) accepts Muff's conclusions but cautions that the possibility of reverse borrowing, from Aramaic to Assyrian, is also to be considered, since in some cases Neo-Assyrian has the first occurrence of certain legal formulas. Oppenheim (1955) has traced *ṣōʾn barzel* 'iron sheep' to Akkadian *alpē ul imutti* 'those bulls do not die' and *ša* AN.BAR *šunu* 'they are made of iron'; cf. Greek *zōon sidēreion* 'iron animal,' medieval *pecora/bestiae ferri*. Falk (1956–57) has also dealt with this expression.

Weisberg (1968) also lists proposed loanwords, some of which, however, can just as easily be explained as resulting from parallel development, e.g., *mizru* 'wool material' > *mizrān* 'girth of material spread under a bed,' *ritta šaṭāru ana* 'to inscribe the hand to' > *muḵtāḇ l^{e}mal^{e}ḵûṯ* 'marked with the royal mark,' and *ṣalmāt qaqqadi* 'the black-headed ones,' i.e., 'mankind' *š^{e}ḥôrê hārōʾš*. These may not be loans, however, since *mzr* 'spin wool' can underlie *mizrān*, and *ritta šaṭāru*, while paralleling Isa 44:5, may not be the origin of *mûḵtāḇ l^{e}mal^{e}ḵûṯ*. Latin *conscribere* and Greek *grapho* 'enroll' may be the source. Also, *š^{e}ḥôrê hārōʾš* is not completely identical in range with its proposed Akkadian counterpart.

Further study on Akkadian influence

Akkadian loanwords and parallels in Mishnaic Hebrew, with Aramaic as the medium of transmission, are treated by S. A. Kaufman (1971, 1974), Waldman (1972a), and Sperling (1969, 1972, 1973a, 1973b). Some examples of Akkadian loanwords which have found their way into Mishnaic Hebrew are: *arad ekalli* 'servant of the palace' > *ardîḵal* 'architect, builder,' *arḫu* > *ʾārîaḥ* 'half brick,' *nat/dbaku* > *nidbāḵ* 'course of bricks,' *tamkaru* > *taggar* 'merchant,' *kiššû* 'bundle of reeds' > *k^e^šûṯ* 'tuft, fine hairs,' *rukkubu* > *harkîḇ* 'pollinate the date palm,' *ḫaṣṣinu* > *ḥăṣînāʾ* 'axe,' *ṣilbu* 'bandage or wood arranged crosswise' > *ṣ^e^lāḇ* 'cross,' *susapīnu* > *šuš^e^ḇîn* 'attendant of the bride or groom.' Other examples of lexical influence, not lexical transfer, are: *išāta šūḫuzu* > *haʾăḥîz ʾeṯ hāʾûr* 'ignite a fire,' *ubān amūtim* > *ʾeṣbaʿ hakkāḇēḏ* 'finger of the liver,' and *kiṣir tāḫāzi* > *qišrê milḥāmāh* 'ranks (lit. bonds) of war.' Moreshet and Klein (1975–76) have demonstrated the Akkadian origin of Mishnaic Hebrew *knn* 'wrap' < *kanānu*, but some objections to their methodology have been voiced by Rabin (*Leš* 40 [1975–76] 291–92). Other parallels and possible influences between Akkadian and Rabbinic Hebrew have been noted in studies by Waldman: *ʿṭr/eṭēru* 'snatch, save' (1971); *hmm/ḫamāmu* 'sweep away'; *etēqu/ʿbr, hipḇîg* 'pass, overlook, disdain' (1973); words for heat and emotion (1974c); and *ragāmu/qôrēʾ tiggār, miṯrāʿēm, m^e^ʿarʿēr* 'challenge, litigate' (1975b). There are also other works in this area by Waldman (1969, 1974b). Sharvit (1974b), referring to J. N. Epstein (1948), clarifies some lexical items, including *ʿāśāh milḥāmāh* < Akkadian *ṣalta epēšu* 'make war,' *heḥĕzîq badderek* < *ḫarrānam ṣabātum* 'take the road, begin to go.' Abramson (1974) suggests that *rôḵēḇ biss^e^p̱înāh* 'traveling in a boat' reflects Arabic, but one might consider a comparison with Akkadian, e.g., *irkabū elippi* 'rode/boarded the boat' (*Gilgameš* XI:256).

Contractual formulae and Akkadian

Skaist (1980) traces back to cuneiform sources the contractual formula *hakkōl šārîr w^e^qayyām* 'everything is true and valid.' This formula served at first to endow the document with absolute reliability, to prevent any legal challenges. It is to be compared to Neo-Assyrian, Neo-Babylonian, Nuzi, and Ugarit formulas invalidating any challenging document and to the term *ṭuppu dannatu* 'valid document,' which Skaist prefers to translate as 'a conclusive document.' Aramaic *dnt* '(valid/conclusive) document' and Greek *kuria* 'valid' are all to be traced back to cuneiform sources. Skaist (1983) also discusses the *clausula salvatoria* in Elephantine and Neo-Assyrian conveyances.

GREEK INFLUENCE ON MISHNAIC HEBREW

Mishnaic Hebrew is rich in Greek loanwords (Albeck 1959: 203–15). The publications of Krauss (1898, 1900) in this area are useful but greatly in need of revision (Kutscher 1972a). Zuntz

General resources in Greek influence

(1956) is also quite critical of Krauss's work and cites the earlier critique of Fraenkel. He notes that Krauss was wrong in believing that Greek *digamma* was reproduced in Hebrew as *s*. A number of masters theses deal with aspects of Greek influence: A. Blum (1945) on Greek and Latin loanwords as understood by the Geonim and later commentators; M. Hurvitz (1945) on Greek and Latin loanwords appearing in Talmud and Midrash fragments from the Geniza; and Thorion (1968) on transliterations of Hebrew names in Greek and Latin papyri and inscriptions. Kutscher (1966–67b) also has written on Greek influences. Much additional material of significance is found in the masterful studies by Saul Lieberman (1942, 1950) and in his definitive edition of and notes to the *Tosefta* (1955–73). Lexical studies of Greek loanwords include those by E. and H. Guggenheimer (1971–75), D. Sperber (1971–72, 1973–74, 1974, 1974–75, 1975–76, 1980, 1982, 1984, 1986 [nautical terms]) and Berggrün (1972–73).

S. Lieberman's studies of Greek influence

According to Lieberman (1942: 1–67), there was a high level of Greek culture among the rabbis, and this fact may be demonstrated by means of several examples. For instance, the members of the Sanhedrin and the court at Yabne were expected to know foreign languages (*t. Sanh.* 8:1; *t.b. Sanh.* 17b). Aquila, the proselyte, presented his Greek translation of the Torah to Rabbis Eliezer and Joshua. Rabbi Jonathan of Eleutheropolis noted that Greek is most suitable for *zemer* 'song,' Latin for war, Syriac for dirges, and Hebrew for speaking (*t.y. Meg.* I:11, 71b). (This remark is of interest also as evidence that Hebrew was spoken.) The rabbis often interpreted biblical words as if they were Greek, Aramaic, or Arabic (Wechter 1964: 1–2; 126–28). In their homilies the rabbis used Greek proverbs, many of which, missed by the dictionaries, have been clarified through recovery of the original text by Lieberman. In fact, the frequency of Greek words in the speech of the rabbis has led Lieberman to conclude that such words were no longer foreign but an integral part of the vocabulary.

Phonetic and accentual changes in borrowed words

A number of phonetic and accentual changes occurred when Greek and Latin words became part of the Mishnaic Hebrew vocabulary. The prosthetic vowel was used when two consonants begin a word, thus avoiding a consonant cluster, e.g., *ʾizmēl* < *smílē* 'scalpel,' *ʾalûnṭîṯ* < *lention*, Latin *linteum* 'linen cloth, sheet.' Non-initial *s* becomes *ṣ*, e.g., *parṣûp̱* < *prósōpon* 'face.' There are various forms of Latin *castra* 'camp': *qaṣrāh*, *gastrāh*, *qaṣṭrāʾ*. The change *s* > *ṣ* here may be due to some assimilation to the emphatic *q*, but this cannot explain the change in other words. The final ending in Greek is dropped and a Hebrew noun pattern is adopted, e.g., *s^e^p̱ôg* < *spongos* 'sponge,' *sandlār* < *sandalarios* 'sandal-maker.' There are accent changes and corresponding lengthening and shortening of vowels when a borrowed word is adapted to Hebrew patterns, e.g., *mēlopépōn* 'melon, squash' > *m^e^lap̱^e^p̱ṓn*, *kappadókia* > *qappṓṭqîyāh* 'Cappadocia.'

Greek loanwords distorted in Babylonian sources

Distance from the Greek speech area also affects the form of the words as found in the literary sources. Numerous examples of change in the Babylonian sources are cited by A. Bendavid (1967: 183–90), e.g., *libelários* > Pal. *liḇlār* Bab. *laḇlār* 'scribe'; *diegma* > Pal. *dîgmāʾ*, Bab. *dûgmāh* 'proof, example'; *kotúlē* > Pal. *qôṭlîṯ*, Bab. *qaṭlîṯ* 'cup or socket of the hip-bone.' These examples illustrate interchanges of short vowels familiar in Hebrew generally. There are consonant changes, e.g., *kóllix* > Pal. *q^e^lûsqîn*, Bab. *g^e^lusqîn* 'long roll of coarse bread'; Latin *quaestor* > Pal. *qûsṭôr*, Bab. *qasdôr* 'investigator'; Latin *annona* > Pal. *ʾannônāʾ*, Bab. *arnônāh* 'tax' (note dissimilation, using *r*). Babylonian sources sometimes demonstrate a serious misunderstanding of the Greek word and a folk etymology or assimilation to known Hebrew words, e.g., *archeion* > Pal. *ʾarḵîyôṯ*, Bab. *ʿarkāʾôṯ* 'courts'; and *lēstēs* > Pal. *lîstēs*, but Bab. *lisṭîm* 'robber, bandit.' Compare also the verb *m^e^lasṭēm* 'plunders.' The confusion may be due to the graphic similarity between *s* and final *m*. Interesting examples of such cases, Hebrew expressions born of misunderstanding, are presented by Tur-Sinai (1954–59, *Halashon*, 361–92). His materials are drawn from the various stages of the language.

Greek calques

It is somewhat more difficult to demonstrate Greek influence without lexical transfer. A. Bendavid (1967: 135–49) argues for a large number of such cases, e.g., *mûḇhāq* < Greek *phaenomenos* 'outstanding,' from the basic meaning of 'shining' in both languages; *mikkôl māqôm* 'by all means' < Greek *ʾek pantòs trópou*; *pereq* 'age' < Greek *hora*; *maʿ^a^leh śāḵār* 'to pay, credit to one's account' < Greek *timē pherein*. Proverbial expressions are translated from the Greek, e.g., *hinîaḥ maʿôṯāw ʿal qeren haṣṣ^e^ḇî* < Greek *katorussómenon hupò ton ʾelaphon kéras*, 'he put all his money on the horn of the deer,' i.e., he lost it. Other examples are enumerated by Saul Lieberman (1942: 144–60). J. Rabinovitz (1951–52) has written on *mup̱lāg* / Greek *nomophulax*. D. Sperber (1980) derives *pôyṭînôn* from Greek *phoitēnon* 'one who struts about to show his person.'

There remain some ambiguous areas, as noted by A. Bendavid (1967: 149–50). Various derivations and outside influences have been suggested. Bendavid regards Hebrew *ʾmd* 'estimate' as influenced by Greek *histēmi* 'stand, balance, weigh.' On the other hand, Kutscher (1939) derived it from Akkadian *emēdu* 'impose upon, obligate,' noun: *imittu* 'estimate.' Bronznick (1977) seeks internal semantic developments in Hebrew and rejects the idea of calques in the following examples. Hebrew *šāweh*, meaning 'immediately' was regarded by Lieberman (1942: 177) as a translation of Greek *euthos*. Bronznick, instead, traces a semantic development from 'straightness' to temporal immediacy, in a manner parallel to the development of *kēn*, *naḵôn*, *kēwān še-*. Hebrew *ᶜmd* in Mishnaic Hebrew has the meaning 'cost, be worth.' The development is internal, from 'rising' to 'be worth'; a parallel is *ᶜlh* 'go up' and 'cost.' Kutscher's derivation from Akkadian (1939) is rejected by Bronznick.

MISHNAIC HEBREW SYNTAX

A. Bendavid (1971) gives numerous examples of mishnaic syntax contrasted with the same content expressed in Biblical Hebrew. Only a few examples from the abundance of material he presents can be cited here. A noticeable characteristic of Mishnaic Hebrew is the breaking up of the closely bound syntactic structures found in Biblical Hebrew, one of which was the construct. In Biblical Hebrew the *nomen regens* and the *nomen rectum* are so closely bound together that there is a shift of accent from the former to the latter. Biblical Hebrew also prefers to avoid a series of several coordinate genitives depending upon a single *nomen regens*, repeating instead the *nomen regens* for each separate and closely bound construct (Gen 24:4; G–K, §89, 128).

The use of *šel*

The situation in Mishnaic Hebrew is different, and this is related to the introduction of a new particle, *šel* 'of.' In many Mishnah manuscripts this particle is written as part of the following word, and this was the procedure followed by Yalon in his vocalization of Albeck's edition of the Mishnah. In the Bar Kokhba letters from Wadi Murrabbaᶜat, however, one finds *šel* written separately from the following word, but *ᵓeṯ*, the *nota accusativi*, is reduced to *t-* and assimilated with the article *h*, e.g., *wḥzq tmqwm* 'and strengthen the place' (Kutscher 1960–61, 1961–62).

Various syntactic studies

Rosén (1955a: 45–47; 1957: 117–37) has pointed out that Mishnaic Hebrew gained greater syntactic flexibility through the use of constructions with *še*, which replaced biblical *ᵓăšer* and was connected with *l* 'to, of.' Biblical Hebrew *sûsî* can mean 'my horse' (definite) or 'a horse of mine' (indefinite), but Mishnaic Hebrew can contrast *sûs šelî* 'a horse of mine' with *hassûs šelî* 'my horse.' The origin of Hebrew *še* and *še* + *l* has been debated, some connecting it with Phoenician *ʾaš* and others with Akkadian *ša* (Chomsky 1952: 52–53). Ginsburg (1970: 114) argues that *še* reflects Aramaic *dî*, and Kutscher (1970: 352–53) contends that *zy/dy* used with a determined antecedent, where formerly only a construction with *l-* was possible, is based on the syntax of Akkadian *ša*. The Aramaic counterpart of *šellô* 'his' occurs in Biblical Aramaic, e.g., Dan 2:20, *dî lēh* 'his.' A form like *bayṯāʾ dî ʾĔlāhāʾ* 'the house of God' originally came into being to break up long strings of successive genitives but in Biblical Aramaic was used indiscriminately alongside the construct (F. Rosenthal 1961: 20, 24, §§31, 48).

The construct state and Mishnaic alternatives

Rosén's view that a noun with a possessive suffix in Biblical Hebrew is ambiguous, that it can be understood as both definite and indefinite, is problematic. The accepted view of the grammars is that a pronominal suffix attached to a substantive is considered to be a genitive determinate (G–K, §127a). Biblical Hebrew has other means of indicating the indefinite, e.g., *ʾeḥāḏ mēʾeḥāw* 'one of his brothers' (Lev 25:48), *ʾeḥāḏ meʿaḇāḏāw* 'one of his servants' (2 Kgs 6:12), although one might object that the use of a number makes this construction definite. In Mishnaic Hebrew, too, *ḥăḇērô* 'his friend,' *śāḏî* 'my field,' *ʾištô* 'his wife' (*B. Meṣ.* 1:3–5) are all definite, as in Biblical Hebrew. Rosén's thesis needs to be revised. Nevertheless, it is true that certain biblical constructions were ambiguous to the Rabbis, e.g., *ʿeḇeḏ ʿiḇrî* (Exod 21:2), which might mean 'a slave who is a Hebrew' or 'the slave of a Hebrew,' equivalent to *ʿaḇdô šel ʿiḇrî* (*Mekhilta, Nez.* 1). The double indication of possession is absent in Biblical Hebrew, rare in Biblical Aramaic (Dan 2:20, 3:25, 4:23), and common in Mishnaic Hebrew. It does not, however, replace the construct state, e.g., *šôr hāʾiššāh* 'a woman's ox,' *šôr hayyᵉṯômîm* 'the ox of orphans' (*B. Meṣ.* 4:7), *baʿal haśśāḏeh* 'the owner of the field' (ibid., 6:3), The double possessive may have as its function the clarification of possession and the breaking up of construct chains, e.g., *bᵉhemtô sellᵉḇaʿal haśśāḏeh* 'the animal of the owner of the field' (ibid.).

Other biblical constructs, indicating attributes rather than possession, were also broken up and paraphrased, e.g, *yôḏēʿa naggēn* (1 Sam 16:18) becomes *mî šeyôḏēʿa lᵉnaggēn* 'one who knows how to play music.' Another method used was to treat the former *nomen rectum* as an adjective, e.g., *ruaḥ ṣāpôn* > *ruaḥ ṣᵉp̄ônîṯ* 'north wind.' Note, however, that there is a semantic shift in this case, and in Mishnaic Hebrew *rûʾaḥ* means 'direction,' thus *ruaḥ ṣᵉp̱ônît̲* means 'northern side' or 'direction.' Clearly defined rules for the use of a construct or a paraphrase are not yet formulated. In cases of *termini technici* in which close juncture is needed, the rule may be to use the construct, while longer constructions or those with unfamiliar terms are to be broken up, using *še* + *l-* (A. Bendavid 1971: 460–69; Segal 1936, §§75, 371).

Changes in the use of the definite article

There is a change in the use of the definite article in Mishnaic Hebrew. The use of *ha-* is limited, a phenomenon perhaps derived from Aramaic and paralleled in Syriac (A. Bendavid 1967: 129); compare Biblical Hebrew *wᵉʾim yāšûḇ hannegaᶜ* 'if the affliction returns' (Lev 14:43) and Mishnaic Hebrew *ḥāzar negaᶜ labbayit̲* 'the affliction returned to the house' (*m. Nega.* 13:5). The lessened use of *ha-* in Mishnaic Hebrew led the rabbis to find homiletic interpretations for what was (to them) an unusual presence of the article. Their basis of interpretation was the belief that no letter or particle is ever superfluous (*t.b. Qid.* 66b; *t.b. Men.* 66a).

In Mishnaic Hebrew the definite article can indicate a general class, while in Biblical Hebrew this is left indefinite, e.g., *bēn yᵉḵabbeḏ ʾāḇ wᵉᶜeḇeḏ ʾădōnāw* 'a son honors his father and a slave his master' (Mal 1:6) as compared with *hāʾāḇ gôleh ᶜal yᵉdê habbēn* 'a father must go into exile because of a son' (*m. Mak.* 2:3). This is also true in Mishnaic Hebrew where the particle *ʾet̲* is followed by the article, e.g., *wᵉḵî-yiggaḥ šôr ʾet̲-ʾîš ʾô ʾet̲-ʾiššāh* 'if a bull gores a man or a woman' (Exod 21:28), but *šôr šenāgaḥ ʾet̲ hāʾādām wāmēt̲* 'if a bull gored a human and he died' (*m. B. Qam.* 4:5). There is some biblical precedent for this usage, where the article is used to denote a single person or thing, unknown and not capable of being defined, e.g., *hāʾărî* 'a lion' (Amos 5:19; G–K, §126r). G. Birnbaum (1986) discusses determination of nouns in Mishnaic Hebrew. The demonstrative pronouns in Mishnaic Hebrew can also indicate a general class, e.g., *ᶜal yᵉhî hammāšāl hazzeh qal bᵉᶜēneḵā* 'let not the parable [lit. this parable] be insignificant in your eyes' (*Midrash Cant. R.* 1:8).

Mishnaic sentence order

A. Bendavid has assembled much material illustrating the order of the nominal sentence and the verbal sentence (1971: 704–69, 785–855). Various factors operate in these sentence types, as in sentence order generally: modification of normal order for reasons of emphasis, negation, contrast, and differentiation of meaning. Normal order is S(ubject) + V(erb) + P(redicate). However, a sentence which is a continuation can invert, e.g., *ʾAnṭônînûs šāʾal ʾet̲ rabbēnû* 'Antoninus asked Rabbi (Judah the Patriarch),' S + V + P, but *wᵉᶜôḏ šāᶜal ʾAntoninus lᵉrabbēnû* 'Antoninus further asked Rabbi Judah,' V + S + P. Differences of word order may depend on the tense of the verb, e.g., S + V(past) + P, which, in conditions of inversion, becomes P + V(past) + S, but, on the other hand, S + V(present) + P inverts to P + S + V, e.g, *ʿad kaʾn ʾāmᵉrû kᵉšērîm šebāhem* 'this is as much as the righteous among them said' but *ʿad kaʾn rûaḥ haqqôdeš ʾômereṯ* 'till here the Holy Spirit speaks.' There are exceptions to these rules which must be studied in greater depth; some may be due to dialectic and local conditions.

The shorter member of a pair comes first

Rhythmic and stylistic factors must be taken into account in the Mishnah, which was learned and transmitted orally and by rote. S. Friedman (1970–71) has studied the "law of increasing members" in Mishnaic Hebrew. It has already been shown that in Biblical Hebrew approximately 80% of pairs of words in hendiadys have the shorter member first. Friedman shows that this also applies to series of items in the Mishnah. The exceptions to the rule can in large part be accounted for by reference to manuscript variants. In addition, diphthongs are not to be counted as two syllables, and this is borne out by reference to Greek and Latin inscriptions; e.g., *šāmayim* 'heavens' is transcribed by Hieronymus as *samaim* (A. Sperber 1966: 163). The second vowel of a segolate is a helping vowel, not original, and was so treated in Mishnaic Hebrew. Thus, *batteḇen uḇaqqaš* 'with straw or stubble' would be an exception to the 'law of increasing members' unless it is read *battebn uḇaqqaš*. We may compare *resen* 'rein,' which appears in Greek transliteration as *resn*, and *qešeṯ* 'bow,' which is transliterated *kesth* (A. Sperber 1966: 198, 202).

He as separator of accents

Sarfatti (1980b) elaborates on earlier work by Livni (*Lashon kehilkhatah* [Jerusalem, 1957]) and Mirsky (1957–58) on the euphonic use of the definite article and carries the research much further. In construct combinations, the definite article tends to be present when the second term is accented on the first syllable, e.g., *ʾôṯāhh hāʿîr* 'that city.' In other words, the function of the *he* is to separate two accents which otherwise would be contiguous. Sarfatti expands his survey to include combinations other than those with demonstrative pronouns, and using statistics, comes to the following conclusion: when there is no problem of contiguous accents, the *he* is absent 2 to 2½ times more than it is present; when there is a danger of contiguous accentation, the changes of the *he* being present are 3 to 3½ times as great as its being absent.

Sarfatti reviews the uses of the definite article in Mishnaic Hebrew, including its use in objectifying or concretizing an abstract, e.g., *hārāʿāh, haṭṭôḇāh* 'evil, good,' and in expressing concrete vividness, e.g., *hammᵉṣîʾāh* 'a lost object' (*m. B. Meṣ.* 2:3). The evidence in this study points to the euphonic or prosodic use of the article. The article is also involved by attraction, under the influence of a phrase earlier in the sentence. Sarfatti finds examples in S. Friedman (1970–71) and in an unpublished study by Moreshet. An example of another kind of attraction, gender change (from Moreshet), is: *ḥammāṯāhh m^{e}rubbāh miṣṣillāṯāhh*, 'its (the Sukkah's) sunlight is greater than its shade' (not *ṣillāhh*, as grammar would require; *m. Sukk.* 1:1).

Sokoloff (1968–69) has noted the differences between Mishnaic Hebrew^1 and Mishnaic Hebrew^2 as they appear in *Ms Vat. Ebr. 30*, a manuscript also studied by L. Barth (1973). The phonetic aspects were discussed above. In Mishnaic Hebrew^2 the distinctive features and lexicon of Mishnaic Hebrew^1 tend to disappear, due to the retreating influence of the spoken language and the greater influence of the Bible. Forms like *hallālû, hallîlû* replace *ʾēlû, hāʾēlû* 'these.' There is an interchange of *ʿal*/*ʿaḏ*, the first form showing Aramaic influence, e.g., *ʿal šelōʾ maltî*/*ʿaḏ šelōʾ maltî* 'before I was circumcized.' The conflated construction *qôdem ʿaḏ šelōʾ* replaces *ʿaḏ šelōʾ* 'before, prior to.' In Mishnaic Hebrew^2 one finds the participle substituting for the future tense and also serving as the narrative past, after the time has been established by an initial perfect, e.g., *hakkôl qilq^{e}lû maʿăśēhen b^{e}ḏôr hammabûl, hakkeleḇ hôlēḵ* . . . 'everyone corrupted his deeds in the generation of the flood, the dog goes. . . .' Aramaic influences are apparent here, since the participle is used in Biblical Aramaic as a narrative tense; compare Dan 3:3ff. (F. Rosenthal 1961: 55, §177).

Changes in Mishnaic Hebrew^2

The form *niqṭôl* (1 com. pl.) is used in place of *ʾeqṭôl*, showing the influence of Galilean Aramaic. Significantly, however, the final form in contextual position appears only once, contrary to Kutscher's observations for Mishnaic Hebrew^1 and the Isaiah scroll (1963b: 277). A number of unique forms also occur: the *Nufʿal* as opposed to the *Nifʿal*, e.g., *nûgāp̱* 'was beaten'; and the retention of *mediae w/y* in the *Qal* participle, e.g., *kammāh malʾaḵîm hāyû ḥālîm . . . šiššîm rîbôʾ malʾāḵîm hāyû ḥôlîm* 'how many angels were dancing? . . . 600,000 angels were dancing.' The *Nifʿal* is the passive of the *Piʿel* (in Biblical Hebrew the *Puʿal* would be), e.g., *ʾap ʿal pî šeʾat hôlēḵ um^{e}p̱ayyesô w^{e}hûʾ nîpôs* 'even if you are going to appease him and he is appeased.' One also encounters here the transposition of a *ḥolem* within a word, e.g., *Sôdmî* in place of *S^{e}dômî* 'from Sodom,' *maḥlāqôṯ* for *maḥlôqeṯ* 'dispute.' This is also characteristic of the Isaiah scroll, indicating that there is continuity in Mishnaic Hebrew^2 as well as discontinuity (Kutscher 1959: 83–84; *t. Šabb.* 7:24).

Unique verbal forms and syntax

An observation on syntax made by Blau (1956–57) is that a series of clauses indicating alternatives beginning with *ʾô* 'or' are felt to be isolated and must be re-bound by repetition of the conjunction which served in the first clause, thus, *ʾim* 'if' . . . *ʾô ʾim* 'or if' . . . , and *ʿad še-* 'until' . . . *ʾô ʿaḏ še-* 'or until.' This usage led to an analogical formation, the use of *še* to introduce the second clause even when it is not a repetition of the introduction to the first, e.g., *ʾim* 'if' . . . *ʾô še-* 'or that.' This phenomenon is not seen when the clauses are short or felt to be one unit. A. Goldberg (1961–62) observes that in MH the word *wᵉḵēn* 'and thus' functions as a coordinating conjunction and can even have a contrastive sense, the Talmud occasionally paraphrasing it by *ʾap̱ ʿal pî* 'even though.' Kaddari (1974b) examines sentences of interrogation in which *mah lᵉ*, followed by a noun phrase as predicate, is used. A study by Moreshet (1976) follows the use of rabbinic *Hifʿil* for *Qal* in medieval Hebrew literature and responsa. A masters thesis by Fatihi (1971) deals with the structure of rabbinic maxims. Ouellette (1980) takes note of the construction with *sôp̱* + pronomial suffix for expressing the future.

Syntax of various formulae

A study by Azar (1981a) deals with the syntax of formulas of commitment in Biblical Hebrew and Mishnaic Hebrew. Among the categories he treats are oaths, vows, substitute formulas for vows (*kinnûyê nᵉḏārîm*) and formulas for taking on *nazir*-status. Another study by Azar (1982) describes various uses of *ʾelāʾ* in different sentence positions. These include the expression of exclusiveness, the rejection of an opinion, and the response to a question. Azar (1983) discusses the "pseudo casus pendens" in Mishnaic Hebrew (e.g., *m. ʿAbod. Zar.* 5:2), where the resumptive pronoun in the *comment* (the second part) is not coreferential with the *topic* (the first part), but with a noun, itself a verb-complement of a relative clause. This kind of sentence is possible only when the head of the nominal phrase serving as the topic is a generic noun. A masters thesis by Ambar (1980) treats semantically the verbs in constructions such as: noun phrase + verb + noun phrase$_2$ + infinitive absolute. Braverman (1986) contrasts the language of the Mishnah and the Tosefta.

3
THE MASORETES

GENERAL SURVEYS AND BASIC TEXTS

General resources on Masorah

General surveys of the methods and achievements of the Masoretes are found in Chomsky (1957: 139–54; 1967: 75–94), Roberts (1948), Dotan (1971a), Morag (1969; the last two are rich in bibliography), Eissfeldt (1965: 678–93, 781–82), and Würthwein (1979: 12–41). Roberts (1979) surveys the current state of research in the Masorah. Because of the discovery of the Dead Sea Scrolls and other texts, there has been an upsurge of interest in the work of the Masoretes.

The revival of interest in The Masorah has been accompanied by the reissuing by Ktav, New York, of earlier major studies, each with a prolegomenon updating the field. These works, under the general title *Library of Biblical Studies*, are edited by Harry M. Orlinsky and include the following: C. D. Ginsburg's *Introduction to the Massoretico-Critical Edition of the Hebrew Bible*, with prolegomenon by Orlinsky (1966); Jacob ben Chayim ibn Adoniyah's *Introduction to the Rabbinic Bible*, edited by C. D. Ginsburg, with prolegomenon by Snaith (1968); Wickes' *Two Treatises on the Accentuation of the Old Testament*, with prolegomenon by Dotan (1970); Butin's *The Ten Nequdoth of the Torah*, with prolegomenon by S. Talmon (1969); and C. D. Ginsburg's four volume *The Massorah*, edited, with lists of identified sources, by Dotan (1975).

Weil (1963a, 1964) has written on Elijah Levità. Important also is *The Canon and the Masorah of the Hebrew Bible*, an anthology of articles on canonization, Qumran materials, and Masorah, edited by Sid Z. Leiman (New York, 1974). In addition, Strack's edition of the Petrograd Babylonian Codex has been reissued with an introduction by Wernberg-Møller (New York, 1970). L. Lipschutz (1964, 1965) has edited Mishael ben Uzziel's account of the differences between the schools of Ben Asher and Ben Naphtali. *Okhlah weʾokhlah*, Codex Paris, Bibliothèque Nationale 148, has bene issued in limited facsimile edition by Loewinger (1978).

The prolegomena mentioned are useful introductions to the study of the Masorah in this and previous generations. The earlier work of scholars like Jacob ben Chayim ibn Adoniyah, Elijah Levità, Baer, Heidenheim, Luzzatto, C. D. Ginsburg, Wickes, and others, Christian and Jewish, is surveyed and evaluated by Snaith (1968), Dotan (1970), Weil (1968), and S. Talmon (1969).

The *Biblia Hebraica*, 3rd edition, edited by Kittel, is based on the Leningrad manuscript, B19A, and the fourth edition, *Biblia Hebraica Stuttgartensia*, edited by K. Ellinger and W. Rudolph (in fascicles, 1968ff.; as a volume, 1977), is also based on that manuscript. Snaith in 1958 prepared an edition based on Or 2626-8 and Or 2375 of the British Museum and upon the Shem Tob Bible, Ms. Sassoon 82. The Hebrew University Bible Project, directed by M. Goshen-Gottstein, is described in articles in *Textus* (vol. 1, 1960; 2, 1962; 3, 1963; 4, 1964; 5, 1966; 6, 1968; 7, 1970; 8, 1973; 9, 1981; 10, 1982) and is based on the Aleppo Codex (Goshen-Gottstein 1960b). All of these are considered to be manuscripts of the Ben Asher school. Initial results of the Hebrew University Bible Project have appeared in a sample edition with introduction (Isaiah 2, 5, 11, 51; Goshen-Gottstein 1965c) and two volumes covering Isaiah 1:1–44:28 (Goshen-Gottstein 1975, 1981).

Ben Asher manuscripts

Orlinsky argues (1966) that there is not a single Masorah but various local traditions. Snaith (1968) and B. Levine (1971) disagree with this opinion, and Breuer (1976) argues for a unitary Masorah. Tov (1980) evaluates the *Biblia Hebraica Stuttgartensia*.

Other significant contributions to the study of the Masorah include the doctoral dissertation by Dotan (1964a) which was later published as a book (1967). This is an edition of *Diqduqe haṭeʿamim*, attributed to Aaron ben Moses ben Asher. We may also mention Dotan's survey of the field in *EJ* (1971a), his (1971b) edition of the Bible according to the Aaron ben Asher text of the Leningrad manuscript, and his (1977a) *Thesaurus of the Tiberian Masorah*, containing the *Masora Parva* and the *Masora Magna* notes in the margin of Genesis in the Leningrad Codex, with explanatory notes.

Diqduqe haṭeʿamim

Among the important works of I. Yeivin are the following: his study of the linguistic situation reflected in the Babylonian pointing (1965, 1973a), his detailed study of the Aleppo Codex and its Masorah (1969), his thorough introduction to the accents and

I. Yeivin's studies

technical terminology of the Tiberian Masorah (9173b), and several other articles in the field (1958–59, 1960, 1962, 1963, 1972–73, 1974a). A recent study (1980a) deals with the relationship of the half-vowels, *shewa* and *ḥaṭaf*, to the Proto-Semitic originals.

A new organization that shows much promise for future study has been formed under the leadership of Harry M. Orlinsky—the International Organization for Masoretic Studies. Orlinsky has published the papers which were delivered in the 1972 and 1973 proceedings under the title *ʾOḵlā w*^{e}*oḵlāh*: *Masoretic Studies* I (1974). In addition, we cite the editing by Ortega (1977) of a Spanish Bible manuscript which forms a part of the Biblia Polyglotta Matritensia project.

G. Weil

Weil (1968) has written the prolegomenon to the *Massora Magna* of S. Frensdorff and has edited the *Masorah gedolah* of Ms. Leningrad B 19A. A study of his on Masorah appeared in 1972, as well as a concordance of cantillation of the Pentateuch and Megillot (1978b). A masters thesis by Edrei (1976) deals with the text, Masorah, vocalization, and accents in Ms. Leningrad 18 (Firkovitch collection A, 59).

Ketiv-qere

The problem of *ketiv-qere* has been examined by numerous authors. Gordis (1937, reissued 1971) has argued that the *qere* is not a correction or emendation of the *ketiv* and has traced several stages in the development of the marginal readings. At first, the *qere* was a guide intended to guard the reader against blasphemy, the use of the Tetragrammaton, and indecency of expression. At a second stage, it became the guide to correct reading before the invention of vowel signs. Later, it was a method of preserving variants. When the reading of two out of three manuscripts in the Temple was adopted (*t.y. Meg.* IV:2; *Soferim* 6:4), the excluded reading was consigned to oblivion. To preserve it, the rejected reading was then included in a conflated and, therefore, confusing text. When one basic text was adopted as an archetype, around 135 C.E., the *qere*, noted in the margin, became the repository of many variants thought to be worth preserving. Gerleman (1948) has concluded that some of the *qere*-s represent popular variants. He observed that the *qere*-s in Samuel and Kings are found in the text of Chronicles, a more popular type of text (Würthwein 1979: 18, n 12). Orlinsky (1960) has traced the origin of the *ketiv-qere* variants to the practice of the early Masoretes (about 600 C.E.), who would select the majority reading out of the three best manuscripts available to them. Breuer's views on *ketiv* and *qere* will be cited below.

THE ALEPPO CODEX AND THE BEN ASHER SCHOOL

Diqduqe haṭeᶜamim

The authenticity of the Aleppo Codex has been defended by several writers, who see it as a product of the Ben Asher school and identify it with the codex endorsed by Maimonides in his code (*Mishneh Torah*, *Sefer Torah* VIII:4; Goshen-Gottstein 1960b, 1963, 1979; Loewinger 1960). The *Diqduqe haṭeᶜamim* was reissued in the form of a photographic offprint of the early edition by Baer and Strack, with a prefatory note and appendix by Loewinger (1970).

Relationship of Ben Asher, *Diqduqe haṭeᶜamim*, and the Aleppo Codex

Dotan (1967), however, has produced a critical edition of this work, a major contribution, based on 51 manuscripts, considerably more than the 16 used by Baer and Strack. His conclusion is that only 26 of the chapters can be attributed to Ben Asher. Earlier scholarship had based its understanding of Ben Asher's masoretic, phonological, and grammatical views on the entire work as edited by Baer and Strack (Leipzig, 1879; Bacher 1895: 23–38; M. H. Segal 1928: 108–13). The grammar of *Diqduqe haṭeᶜamim* differs from what is embodied in the vocalization of the codex, and the marginal Masorah of the codex is contradicted by the vocalization of the biblical text. In concluding that Ben Asher is the author of part of the masoretic-grammatical work, Dotan (1967) rejects the view that the codex is from the hand of Ben Asher. The attack of Loewinger (1968–69) on this position has been responded to by Dotan (1971–72). Allony (1974–75), on the other hand, reviews the work of Dotan (1967) and points out its significance. Allony's article is also valuable for its information about bibliography and manuscripts, about the forgeries of Firkovitch in the last century, and for its clarification of terminology. Allony comments on the versification of masoretic and early grammatical treatises and relates the appearance of these treatises to a cultural counter-reaction by minority groups against the Arab emphasis on the superiority of their language (*Šuᶜubiyah* versus *ᶜArabiyah*).

Allony (1983) has published several geniza pages of *Kitab al-muṣawwitāt* of Moses ben Asher, TS Ar 32/17 and TS Ar 33/6. He considers this to be the first grammatical work to be written in Judeo-Arabic, valuable for early grammatical views and for traditions concerning the reading and cantillation of Mishnaic Hebrew.

Breuer (1976) takes a traditional position in the scholarly debate over the reliability of the various manuscripts and their affinity with the Ben Asher tradition. Compared to Leningrad B19

Various traditions in the Aleppo Codex

and the Cairo manuscript of the Prophets, the Aleppo Codex has the least amount of deviation from the traditional, accepted masoretic text. Comparing basic manuscripts and Meir Halevi ben Todros Abulafia, Breuer concludes that there is an orthographic text based upon the Masorah. This version is not found in the known manuscripts but is found in the accepted, halakhic version of the Torah and in the Aleppo Codex. The variations in the other manuscripts are due to faulty knowledge by the scribes.

Breuer observes that vocalization and the consonantal text are consistent in all the manuscripts, but the spelling (defective or *plene*) is not. In contrast, the spelling in the accepted version is consistent with the Masorah, while the vocalization is not always so. Elsewhere (1981) he maintains that the *ketiv* represents the tradition of scribes and copyists and the *qere* is the tradition of the readers. In the period before the Masorah, the consonantal text and vocalization were known, but spelling was unsettled. The Masoretes decided how the accepted reading should be written. If the writer of the Aleppo Codex was not Aaron ben Moses ben Asher, then, in the opinion of Breuer, he is another, unknown genius.

The contents of *Diqduqe haṭeᶜamim* (Dotan 1967) deal primarily with the musical aspect of the accentuation system, not so much with the syntactic function. They also treat certain rules regarding the *shewa*. For example, one rule (1967 I:34) maintains that a *shewa* in the middle of a word has no fixed status. It may be vocal or silent in identical circumstances, and its articulation will depend upon melody and accent, not upon historical development or specific morphological conditions.

Further study on Aleppo Codex

Yeivin (1969), in a major work, has thoroughly examined the Masorah of the Aleppo codex. His method is itself a continuation of the painstaking approach of the Masoretes. In his analysis great emphasis is placed upon the musical properties of the accents, the function of the conjunctive accents, and shifts between various disjunctive accents (Breuer 1970–71). Yeivin found in the codex a high degree of accuracy, marred by no more than fifty errors at the most. The codex is unique in its abundant use of *ḥaṭaf*-vowels in non-guttural letters and in its use of the "light *gaᶜya*." There were fixed rules for the "heavy *gaᶜya*," that is, one occurring in a closed syllable, whereas the "light *gaᶜya*," appearing in an open syllable, was handled in a more flexible manner. Where both appeared in the same word, the "light *gaᶜya*" was often omitted (Breuer 1970–71: 96–97). The Aleppo codex, edited with a critical apparatus by M. H. Goshen-Gottstein, has recently appeared in a limited facsimile edition (1976). Beit-Arié (1982) describes the recovery of a lost page of the Aleppo Codex, and its vocalization and accents are described by Yeivin (1982a).

Was Ben Asher a Karaite?

There has been continued controversy over the affiliation of the Ben Asher family: were they Karaites? Pinsker, Kahle (1959: 77), and Ben-Hayyim (*EJ*, 4:465–67) have maintained that they were Karaites, while Jacob Mann and Dotan (*EJ*, 4:467–69) deny this. Dotan (1957–58, 1977b) has written on the history of this controversy. Allony (1974–75: 238–39) provides useful information on the Ben Asher family line. F. Reiner (1974) has suggested a method of determining whether a manuscript derives from a Karaite or Rabbanite source, by comparing unusual sentence divisions with rabbinic midrashim. The literature on the role of the Karaites in the transmission of biblical texts and variant versions is cited by J. P. Siegel (1975: 55–57).

*Horayat haqore*ᵓ (*The Direction of the Reader*) was first edited by Derenbourg as *Manuel du Lecteur* (Paris, 1870; cf. the review by A. Bendavid [*BM* 3 (1957–58]). Allony (1982) considers Judah ibn Balaam to be its author. Now Eldar (1981b) has published a section of the Arabic version, entitled *Hidāyat al qāri.* It is a masoretic-grammatical composition from the first half of the eleventh century. Its author also prepared a shorter version (*al-Muḫtaṣar*), and there are abbreviated Arabic and Hebrew versions, very popular in Yemen. The section published by Eldar deals with the points of articulation of the consonants, beginning with the throat and proceeding upward and forward to the lips. In this, the author follows Arabic and Indian grammar. The author's conception was that the unique quality of a letter is the sound it represents. Wherever *alef* is given a *dagesh* (four times in the Bible), the sound is artificial and forced. Fricative *k* and *g* are given a post-velar articulation, while /r/ is realized as uvular *r*, since it is classified with *g*, *y*, *k*, *l*. This treatise is unique in its statements on these matters, and it provides a clue to the pronunciation of the Tiberian Masoretes. All together, there are six points of articulation. Eldar (1983) examines a three-fold classification of the vowel-articulation of the masoretes in the light of Arabic theories. An edition of *Horayat haqore*ᵓ has been recently edited by Busi (1984).

*Horayat haqore*ᵓ

VARIOUS SYSTEMS OF MASORAH

Differences between the Masorah of the Ben Naphtali and Ben Asher schools have been examined in detail by L. Lipschutz

Ben Naphtali and Ben Asher: phonological and graphic differences

(1964, 1965), A. Bendavid (1957), and Goshen-Gottstein (1963). The variations are limited to minutiae and do not concern the basic text. Ben Naphtali manuscripts, for instance, do not have *pataḥ futivum* with final ᶜ or *ḥ*; all consonants with the exception of ᶜ and *r* can have *dagesh forte* or *lene*; the name *Yiśśāḵār* is so written, not as *Yiśśāśḵār*; and the treatment of initial *y* with the *i*-vowel is exemplified by forms like *biyśrāʾēl* 'in Israel,' not *bᵉyiśrāʾēl*. Ben Naphtali manuscripts also use the *gaᶜyaʾ* to give added emphasis to the word. Breuer (1980) enumerates in great detail the differences between the two schools in matters of vocalization with respect to the variants *ḥolem*/*qamets qaṭan*; *pataḥ*/*qamets*; *tsere*/*segol*; *ḥaṭaf* with a non-guttural consonant; *waw*, *yod*, *bet*, and *lamed* before *yod* with *ḥireq*; the vocalization of the name *Issakar*; and *dagesh rafe*. Ben Naphtali considered each occurrence of *wayᵉhî* 'and it came to pass' to be a separate sentence, and the *kaf* of the following *kî* was given a *dagesh*. Ben Naphtali also inserted a *dagesh* in the *qof* of *Yaᶜăqōḇ*.

Studies on Tiberian and non-Tiberian traditions

Allony (1972), in evaluating the work of Díez-Macho (1971), provides useful information about the discovery of the Cairo Geniza, noting discoverers prior to Schechter, and summarizes what is known about the four vocalization systems: 1) Palestinian, 2) Tiberian-Palestinian, 3) Babylonian and Babylonian-Tiberian (the latter used by Yemenite Jews) and 4) Tiberian. Systems 2 and 3 are mixed.

There have been numerous works written about non-Tiberian and mixed Masorah, and a continuous effort is made to publish the manuscripts: Díaz (1974), Hebrew and Targum texts from the Geniza with Babylonian pointing; Díez-Macho (1957a, 1957b, 1958, 1960b, 1968, 1971), texts from various traditions, including the Babylonian; Dietrich (1968), Bible fragments with Palestinian vocalization; Morag (1959a) on the vocalization of Codex Reuchlinianus, (1961–62) a fragment of Mishnah with mixed Babylonian-Tiberian pointing, (1962b) on the vowel system of Babylonian Aramaic as preserved in the Yemenite tradition, (1968b) on the vocalization of the Babylonian Talmud in the gaonic period, (1974a) on some terms of the Babylonian Masorah, (1974d) a manuscript of the book of Daniel of Babylonian-Yemenite origin; Eldar (1976) on the Tibero-Palestinian tradition and its transplanting to central Europe, as evidenced by *maḥzorim*; Yeivin (1982b) describing the Babylonian Masorah for the Prophets; Murtonen (1956–57), Mishnah fragments with Babylonian pointing; Y. Ratzhaby (1970–71) on survivals of Babylonian pointing in a Yemenite Torah codex; Revell (1969, 1970a, 1970b, 1972, 1973, 1974a, 1977) on Palestinian pointing; Weil (1962, 1963–65) on the

Babylonian Masorah; Allony (1973a), Geniza fragments of rabbinic texts with Palestinian pointing; A. Van Der Heide (1974), a fragment with Palestinian-Tiberian pointing (Pseudo-Ben Naftali).

Relative dates of Palestinian and Tiberian Hebrew and pointing

The Tiberian and Palestinian traditions of pointing are compared by Revell (1970a: 104–9, 1970b, 1974a). Revell's opinion is that Palestinian Hebrew represents a later form of language which has developed beyond the original parent common to it and to Tiberian. This theory is in contrast to the theory of Díez-Macho (1963), who has argued that Tiberian pointing is an outgrowth of Palestinian, the intermediate "proto-Tiberian" stage being represented by the so-called "Ben Naphtali" manuscripts. Revell, on the other hand, maintains that Palestinian pointing must have developed earlier than, or in isolation from, Tiberian. There was a period when both systems were used contemporaneously, but the Tiberian system became more popular, exerting influence upon the Palestinian. This influence is evident in Palestinian attempts to specialize a sign to correspond in function to the Tiberian *shewa*. In time Palestinian scholars used the Tiberian system to reproduce their own pronunciation. The Palestinian tradition was less well-preserved and underwent linguistic change. The Palestinians were inhibited by the principle of economy of sign form (Revell 1974a; Eldar 1976).

Tiberian and Palestinian accents compared

Revell (1972) disputes the commonly held view, first promulgated by Kahle, that the Palestinian accent signs do not mark the stress syllable. The general tendency is to place the accent sign in Palestinian manuscripts closer to the beginning of the word than in the Tiberian tradition, represented by Kittel's *Biblia Hebraica* (3rd ed., 1937, based on Leningrad B19A). In the Tiberian tradition, there is a tendency toward penultimate accent position, or, more generally stated, toward accenting one of the last three syllables of the word. There are, however, many instances where the Palestinian accents do appear on the same syllable as in *Biblia Hebraica*. These divergences have been explained as showing a development from Palestinian use to Tiberian. As we have seen above, Revell argues that there is no unilinear development from Palestinian to Tiberian but the two different traditions developed separately. Palestinian pointing reflects a stage of the language which has developed further from the common origin than Tiberian. An older pattern of the language, represented by *Biblia Hebraica*, was undergoing change, hence the instability of accent position in Palestinian manuscripts.

Letters for cantillation signs

Yeivin (1962) analyzes a biblical manuscript which was written in abbreviated form, with small letters on the tops of the words to indicate the cantillation sign, e.g., *t* for *tevir*, *ḥ* for *ḥazar* = *reviᶜa*.

The first word of a line is written in full, but subsequently only the first letters are written, and representative letter is accented. Only 25 out of 3000 accents deviate from the Tiberian, but the pronunciation is a hybrid of Babylonian and a late stage of Tiberian. The pausal form of the verb prevails, however, with ultimate, not penultimate accent, e.g., *yumāṯū́* 'they will be put to death,' not *yumā́tû*. The use of letters for accent signs in Babylonian manuscripts is also described by Yeivin (1973a: 17–18). A masters thesis by H. Horowitz (Grebel; 1944) deals with the development of the three accentual systems. Palestinian vocalization is treated in a masters thesis by R. Nir (1959).

ORIGINS OF THE MASORETIC SIGNS

Greek and Syriac models for the accents

There are numerous theories about the external derivation of the accents. Lieberman (1950: 38–46) has compared the inverted *nuns* and the dots over certain letters with similar marks devised by Alexandrian Greek grammarians. For further discussion, see Sid Z. Leiman (*JBL* 93 [1974] 348–55) and B. Levine (*JBL* 95 [1976] 122–23). S. Talmon (1969) agrees that the points did not indicate a spurious reading but were a kind of *nota bene*. Specific matters indicated by the superimposed points include doubtful words, words to be deleted, and the necessity of avoiding pronunciation of the Tetragrammaton. Talmon agrees that the parallel with Greek practice is significant.

The accents have been compared to Greek models in the writings of Praetorius and to Syriac by Merx and Graetz (Dotan 1970, 1974). An important study of Syriac accents has been made by J. B. Segal (1953). Dotan (1974) attacks the long-accepted view of Graetz that masoretic accentuation is derived from the Syriac diacritical points above and below the line. According to this view, *mil^{c}el* 'above,' indicating upper vowels, is represented by a supralinear point, while *milra^c* 'below,' signifying lower vowels, corresponds to an infralinear point. Dotan shows, however, that corresponding terms do not exist in Syriac and that in no Hebrew manuscript is vowel quality indicated by such points. He interprets the terms *mil^{c}el* and *milra^c* in light of contemporary theories of vowels, using for example, the theory of Saadiah Gaon, who ranked the vowels on a scale at the top of which was *ḥolem* ($\bar{o}$), with *ḥireq* ($\bar{\imath}$) at the bottom (Morag 1962a; Ben-Hayyim 1952–53a; M. H. Segal 1928: 92–144).

MASORAH, PHONOLOGY, AND PHONEMICS

Status of Tiberian Masorah: new norm or tradition

The linguistic and grammatical position of the Tiberian Masorah has been discussed from several points of view: 1) What was the underlying dialect? 2) What were the grammatical and linguistic assumptions of the Masoretes? 3) What was the relationship of the Tiberian language tradition to earlier, pre-masoretic forms of Hebrew? A study by Schramm (1964) seeks to establish the phonemes of Tiberian Hebrew and to determine their relationship to the orthography. Schramm lists phonemic oppositions and treats the distribution of the phonemes. A major conclusion of the study is that Tiberian Hebrew reflects a transitional stage in which various pronunciations which were formerly allophonic gradually came to be given phonemic status and were given symbols reflecting this. Differing with Kahle (1959), Schramm concludes that the aim of the Masoretes was not to establish a norm but to record and transmit a traditional pronunciation. This appears to be in agreement with Wernberg-Møller (1974), who has contrasted the Arabic vocalization system, which demonstrates a development of the phonemic principle, with the masoretic vocalization system, which was phonetic. The Masoretes, in his opinion, did not attempt to indicate vowel quantity, long or short, but intended to represent vocalic quality with a limited range of symbols. It follows, therefore, that the masoretic notation cannot be used to support conclusions about the relationship of this stage of Hebrew to Common Semitic. Stress and syntactic position, not word class, would determine vowel quantity. On the phonetic nature of masoretic notation, see also Rabin (1960a). Schramm's study (1964) was well received by Rabin (1970a: 310–11) but was criticized by Morag (1967b) for the omission of relevant literature available at that time. Morag's article is itself a good survey of the literature on the traditional pronunciations of the various historic Jewish communities. Corré (1966–67) treats phonemic problems in the Masorah.

Musical aspects of *maqqef*

Yeivin (1958–59) has shown that musical considerations are relevant in the use of *maqqef*. Small words, e.g., *kî*, *ʾô*, *ʾăšer* 'for, when, that' are connected to relatively short words with florid musical patterns, e.g., *kî-tirʾeh* 'when you see,' the second word having the trope *gershayyim,* contrasted with *kî hammāqôm* 'for the place,' which is not joined because the second word is longer. In certain words, such as *ʾanōḵî* 'I,' *šāmᵉrû* 'they guarded,' the *gaʿya* indicates a secondary accent, thus having a musical function.

In more complex words the *gaʿyot* signify the slowing down of the word (Yeivin 1981).

Breuer (1979a) seeks new formulations of rules for the occurrence of the *gaʿya* in words which have the *zaqef-qaṭon* accent. His study (1979b) on the classes of *gaʿya* shows that there seven types of phonetic *gaʿya* and three euphonic types.

Morag (1962a), in his treatment of the vocalization system, divided the Tiberian signs into two classes, univalent and bivalent. The first class included the seven vowels, *pataḥ*, *segol*, *ḥireq*, *qibbuts*, *qamets*, *tsere*, and *ḥolem*, together with *ḥaṭaf-qamets*. To all of these he assigned a phonemic status. the other two univalent signs represent *ḥaṭaf-pataḥ* and *ḥaṭaf-segol*, which he regarded as allophones of the *shewa*. This analysis presupposes that the distinction between long and short vowels, introduced by the Kimchis in the twelfth and thirteenth centuries (Chomsky 1952: 31–32d; 1967: 178; 1971b; A. Bendavid 1957–58b), was not known to the Masoretes or early grammarians, but reflected the Latin grammar known in Provence. Morag (1962a) considers the two ambivalent signs to be *shewa*, representing the phoneme /ĕ/ and zero, and the *dagesh*, indicating both the feature of gemination and the plosive articulation of /bgdkpt/. J. Gibson (1974) disagrees, arguing for the univalence, not ambivalence, of these two signs as well, with implications for methods of transliteration. Morag understands the *shewa* to be a murmured sound and transcribes it linearly, e.g., *deḇar* 'the word of,' while Gibson, resting on the etymology *shewa* < *šāwʾ* 'nothing,' transcribes it as *dᵉḇar*.

Phonemic status of the vowels

Gibson treats the *dagesh*/*rafeh* notation as primarily and originally distributional, that is, *dagesh* in a consonant indicates either gemination or a closed syllable preceding it. In both cases the *dagesh* indicates syllable division. The *rafeh* on the other hand, occurs in a letter which follows a full vowel or a vocalic *shewa*.

In the Codex Reuchlinianus, the *dagesh*/*rafeh* notation customarily limited to /bgdkpt/ is used for all letters in the positions indicated above. A. Sperber (1966: 557–59) regarded this codex as pre-masoretic, and J. Gibson (1974: 92–93) agrees that its practice antedates the Tiberian Masorah. Later, the Masoretes limited the practice only to those consonants in which the phonetic factor of plosive/fricative was involved. Morag (1959a) has argued that the codex is post-masoretic, and that the scribe extended the *dagesh*/*rafeh* notation by false analogy. Yeivin (1983) discusses the group of manuscripts which includes Codex Reuchlinianus and "so-called Ben Naphtali" manuscripts (Díez-Macho 1963), focusing on

Historical position of Codex Reuchlinianus

the "separative" *dagesh*, a strong *dagesh*, and its phonetic significance in lengthening the consonant.

Malone (1979) presents some variant forms in Tiberian Hebrew and formulates rules for their generation. This article is based on his *Tiberian Hebrew Phonology* (MS, 1978). Malone observes that when words like *ʾĔlōahh* 'God' and *ʾaḏôn* 'lord' are combined with proclitics (e.g., *w*, *l*) morphologically coalesced forms (*wēlōhê*, *wāḏōnî*) exist alongside morphologically discrete forms (*leʾĕlōahh*, *waʾăḏōnēnû*). One rule that accounts for the latter phenomenon he has named Group Simplification, which means that in the combination *Vʾ V̆* (*V̆* = vocalic *shewa* or *ḥaṭaf-pataḥ*), the second two segments of the group are lost. This is a minor rule applying to limited lexical items. Another rule is formulated, the rule of Vowel Closing: short atonic open-syllabic *e* may not occur when the immediately following vowel is other than open-mid, otherwise the *e* is raised to *ē*. Vowel Closing (VC) after Group Simplification (GS) occurs, thus: *weʾĕlōhê* > (GS) *welōhê* > (VC) *wēlōhê*. Other rules Malone formulates are: Shewa Intrusion (in the maverick *haʿăḇartā* 'thou hast brought over,' Josh 7:7, in place of expected *heʿĕḇartā*) and Atonic Opening (*ē* is lowered to *e* and *o* to *ɔ*).

Rules for generating variant forms

THE SYNTACTIC SIGNIFICANCE OF THE MASORAH

The accents and their pausal significance have been described in numerous studies. A. Schlesinger (1954) compares the accents of the twenty-one books with the accents of Psalms, Proverbs, and Job. Exposition of the pausal and syntactic function of the accents have been presented by Breuer (1958), Miles B. Cohen (1969, 1972), D. B. Freedman and Miles B. Cohen (1974), S. Weinfeld (1972), and, in great detail, Yeivin (1973b: 109–207).

Analyses of pausal function of the accents

Dotan (1970) surveys the development of research on the pausal strengths of the accents, evaluating scholars such as Luzzatto, Levità, Bohlius, Lederbuhr, Wasmuth, Weimar, Hanau, Baer, Wickes, Ackermann, and Spanier. One view prominent among students of Masorah was that the accents were to be ranked in terms of their pausal strength, "caesars, kings, dukes, etc." Wickes, in 1881 and 1887, following the lead of Florinus and Ewald, who, in 1667 and 1863, respectively, advanced the principle of dichotomy, developed this further. A biblical verse is divided into segments, and certain signs are used to mark each segment, not according to any presumed pausal strength but by a conventional assignment of a sign to particular location in the verse. The main caesura in the twenty-one books is marked by *ʾetnaḥta* (֑). The main division of the *ʾetnaḥta* segment is marked by *segol* (֒), and the other caesurae are indicated by *zaqef-qaṭon* (֔) and finally by *ṭifḥa* (֖) and so on. As pointed out by Dotan (1970), Spanier in 1927 made a significant contribution by exploring the accent-sentence relationship.

Principle of line segmentation

Yeivin (1973b: 117–18) summarizes perspectives on verse segmentation and supplies a simplified schema of the line segments and their associated disjunctive accents, which are ranked in four groups. A segment marked by an accent from level I (*silluq* and *ʾetnaḥta*) will be subdivided by another accent from level II (*segol*, *shalshellet*, *zaqef*, *ṭifḥa*). A segment from level II will be subdivided by an accent from level III (*zarqa*, *pashṭa*, *tevir*, *reviʿa*), and, of course, this level can only be divided by means of signs from level IV (*pazer*, *telishah gedolah*, *geresh* and *legarmeh*). There can be no crossing of levels; in other words, a segment marked by a level I sign cannot be divided by one from level III. Revell (1971) examines the oldest evidence for the accents.

Aramaic masoretic terms

Aramaic terms coined by the Masoretes of Babylonia and Tiberias are interpreted by Morag (1973–74; 974a). For example, the Babylonian term *nigra* 'penultimate' derives from an Aramaic root *ngr* 'be extended,' indicating that stress in the penultimate syllable was considered to be a phenomenon of length. The opposing term, *digra* 'ultimate stress' derives from *dgr* 'bring together' (compare Syriac *degara de ʿayna* 'a twinkling of the eye' that is, 'a fraction of a second'). When *digra* is used for 'utmost brevity' in the penultimate syllable, the ultima is then lengthened (stressed). Morag also discusses the function of the *gaʿya* in the Tiberian Masorah (1973–74: 75–77), a mark which serves to indicate secondary accentuation, ensuring that a syllable will not be overlooked. The *maqqef*, on the other hand, joins two words, indicating that one of them is not accented.

Further syntactic study of accents

Levenson (1972: 46–47) has pointed out a historical fact not noted in Dotan's survey (1970), namely, that the principle of dichotomy, which is in contrast to the hierarchical ranking of the accents, was anticipated by Moses Mendelssohn in his *Biur*, well in advance of Wickes. A study by Lavian (1975, 1978) explores the relationship of vocalization and accentuation to exegesis. B. Ben Yehudah (1974–75) has identified a tonal aspect of accentuation which he calls *qofets qadimah* 'jumping ahead'; that is, alongside the well-known retardation of accent *nāsōg aḥor*, an accent will be advanced so that two beats will not be contiguous.

MASORETES AND PRE-MASORAH

Work on pre-Masoretic Hebrew has been done by Murtonen, who has collected and published early materials (1958, 1960, 1964, 1968a, 1968b, 1986), and Lehman (1971), who has dealt with the antecedents of the Tiberian system of vocalization. R. Meyer (Díez-Macho and R. Meyer 1965: 79–80) argues that the *dagesh* was originally a diacritical point, signifying, not the quality of a consonant, but its quantity. It indicated the shortness of the vowel in a preceding open or closed syllable. In later times it lost its original character.

Tiberian Masorah as preservation of a tradition

In view of the publication of pre-masoretic material, a major question for debate is whether the Masoretes were preservers of an existing tradition or the creators of a "correct" pronunciation which had no relationship to reality. As noted above, Schramm (1964), Wernberg-Møller (1974), and Rabin (1960a) have argued that the Masoretes were merely describing an existing phonetic situation. The opposite view was taken by Kahle, whose voluminous research and publication of texts (*Masoreten des Osten*, 1913; *Masoreten des Westens*, 1927–30) have dominated the field. According to view, summarized in *The Cairo Geniza* (1959: 150), the Masoretes suppressed variant pronunciations and texts. They also imposed an unreal pronunciation, restoring gutturals which had long vanished and archaizing the 2 m.s. suffix *-āḵ* to *-ḵā*. They were influenced in this endeavor by Moslem scribes who were establishing definitive editions and readings of the Koran (Waldman 1975a: 1302).

One source of support for Kahle's contention is the Greek and Latin transcriptions, e.g., *eromemech* for *ʾăromimᵉḵā* 'I will extol thee' and *orech* for *ʾôrᵉḵā* 'your light' (Kahle 1959: 171–79; A. Sperber 1966: 191). Zulay (1936: 244–48) has shown that in the early poetry of Yannai (seventh century) a rhyme could be formed between *ʾ*, *h*, *ḥ*, and *ʿ*, and between *ʿaḇdāḵ* 'your servant' and *dāḵ* 'humble.' There is also evidence that rhymes could be made with the plosive and aspirated forms of *b* and *p*, suggesting that the masoretic rules for their pronunciation were not observed at this time.

A. Sperber (1959a, 1966) has even challenged the validity of the standard Hebrew grammars, such as Gesenius, Bauer-Leander, and Bergsträsser, which are based on the masoretic text. On the basis of the transcriptions, he posits a totally different grammar; his support is found in Greek transcriptions, e.g., *phadith* for masoretic *pāḏîṯā* 'you have redeemed,' *tharak* for *tirḥaq* 'you are distant,' and Latin transcriptions, e.g., *iezbuleni* with unreduced second vowel for *yizbᵉlēnî* 'he will elevate me' (Waldman 1975a: 1303). Sperber's views are discussed by Meyer (Diéz-Macho and Meyer 1965: 63–84). Murtonen (1982), however, raises serious methodological objections to Sperber's work. He rejects Sperber's idea that the nominal stem is unchangeable in inflection and contends that Sperber ignores frequency of occurrence. Murtonen holds, furthermore, that the Greek transcriptional system is basically phonological, opposing Sperber, who maintained that the Greek vowels in transcription are interchangeable and go back to /i/.

Gumpertz (1953: 87–130) has argued for the restorative nature of masoretic grammar. He contends that the gutturals had disappeared, and forms of the verb "to be" indicate that the *he* was not pronounced, e.g., the Greek transcriptions *aea* for *hāyāh* 'he was' and *ieie* for *yihyeh* 'he will be.' Gumpertz suggests that the Masoretes revived the pronunciation of the gutturals by several means: the use of compound *shewa* under them, the use of *dagesh* in /bgdkpt/ following them, and the use of *meteg* under the prefixes in words like *yihyeh* 'he will be' and *yiḥyeh* 'he will live.' He also proposes that the original pronunciation of the *r* was uvular, thus accounting for a change in vowels in its environment similar to that encountered in the environment of gutturals. The change was not sudden, but, under the influence of Arabic, Hebrew returned to its Oriental roots, so to speak. In the earliest stages the vocalization shows that the gutturals were not present. But the Masoretes began to emphasize them by use of the compound *shewa*, then by use of the *meteg*, and finally, the vowels were modified in the vicinity of gutturals.

This view presupposes too much, namely, that a small group of Masoretes (great though their prestige might be) could reverse the reading habits of the widespread Jewish community. It is well-known that, while the masoretic accentuation and vocalization were widely accepted and even replaced Babylonian texts in Yemen and penetrated Babylonian accentuation itself, the phonemic structure the Masoretes so carefully transcribed never displaced those in use by other communities (Morag 1963: 289–90). Moreover, there are scholars who claim that the gutturals were pronounced in the time of Origen and Hieronymus and that the transcriptions bear this out (Sutcliffe 1948; Barr 1967; Brønno 1967, 1970). Brønno, following earlier work by Kutscher (1965), claims that the gutturals were pronounced and that this fact is reflected in the transcriptions of Hieronymus. In his opinion, Kahle (1959) and A. Sperber (*HUCA* XII/XIII [1937–38] 103–274), who considered the gutturals to be only vowel indicators at that time, used the evidence selectively and omitted what was unfavorable to their case. Examples given by Brønno include *Ahihod* (*ʾĂḥîhûḏ*) *Chodorlahomer* (*Kᵉdārlāʿōmer*), *aheberim* (*hāʿibrîm* 'the Hebrews'), *hissa* (*ʾiššāh* 'woman'), and *Hiras* (*ʿÎrāʾ*).

Janssens (1982) has drawn historical linguistic conclusions on the basis of Origen's *Secunda*. He denies the aspiration of /bgdkpt/ and claims that final position lengthening is not reflected in the *Secunda*. These views and others concerning the transcriptions of vowels are rejected in a review by Blau (1983–84).

Ben-Hayyim (1953–1954) has challenged the views of Kahle. By classifying all the occurrences of *-āk* and *-kā*, he concludes that Tiberian, Palestinian, and Babylonian readings of scripture should be grouped separately from Samaritan, Latin, and Greek transcriptions. These two groups represent two different traditions of scripture reading. The Masoretes sought to preserve one of these, an existing traditional pronunciation known to them, and they were consistent in refraining from Aramaisms. The presence in the Dead Sea Scrolls of readings like *-kh*, realized as [ka], is evidence that the Masoretes were not merely engaging in archaizing (Yalon 1967: 16–18; Kutscher 1959: 34–39; 1971a: 1586). Goshen-Gottstein (1960b, 1963) has also argued that oral tradition must be given its proper weight (1963: 90) in any consideration of this problem.

Phonological explanation of *-āḵ*/*-ḵā* variants

Steiner (1979) takes a different approach to the problem of *-āḵ* and *-kā*. Ben-Hayyim (1954: 37) had noted that, in post-biblical texts, the suffix is *-ḵā* in words which ended in a vowel. Conversely, bases ending in a consonant generally take *-āḵ* as the suffix form, although *-ḵā* is also found. Ben-Hayyim laid down the general principle that the absence of the final vowel is not a feature of original Hebrew but is an Aramaism. Steiner's objection is that this description fails to explain why *-āḵ* occurs in pausal position in Masoretic Hebrew. Moreover, *-āḵ* is an apocopated form, and apocope is a pausal phenomenon in both Semitic and non-Semitic languages. Steiner believes that the increase in the use of *-āḵ* must be dated to a time when Hebrew was still a living language. He does not agree with Ben-Hayyim that the *-āḵ*/*-kā* alternation is related to different reading styles of a dead language but proposes instead that the distribution of *-āḵ*/*-ḵā* in Mishnaic Hebrew follows the same rule as *-āh*/*-hā*. Analogical development blocked the spread of *-āḵ* in some environments, while encouraging it in others. The reason that apocopation is not found is that in certain environments it would cause an impermissible cluster. Steiner (1979: 172) summarizes: the two Proto-Hebrew environments in which **-hā* is found are those in which apocope was blocked to avoid impermissible clusters. The loss of final short vowels and the resultant metanalysis caused a split in phonetic environments, giving *-āh* and *-hā* anomalous distributions in Masoretic Hebrew. In Mishnaic Hebrew these distributions were extended by analogy to *-āḵ* and *-ḵā*.

Harviainen (1977) has contributed a study of the vocalization of unstressed closed syllables in Hebrew, basing his research on the transcriptions of Jerome and texts with Palestinian pointing. He compares this material with the original etymological vowel and its Tiberian counterpart. Harviainen does not claim that the Tiberian system was inherently purer but instead suggests that the Masoretes sought to create a text which would be acceptable over a wide range of local reading traditions. The text had to be most accurate, it had to incorporate features common to various traditions, and its graphemes had to be realizable in different local manners (1977: 218–28).

Dotan (1983) argues from the accentuation of personal names and other words in various manuscripts that, in contrast to the normative Tiberian tradition, there is evidence of penultimate accentuation. If this is true, then the date of the accent shift posited by many grammarians must be set later, in the sixth century C.E. or the centuries immediately preceding.

4

COMMUNAL TRADITIONS AND JEWISH LANGUAGES

This chapter is concerned with the various traditions of pronunciation of Hebrew in liturgical contexts, such as the reading of the Torah, the recitation of the prayers, and the vocalization of rabbinic texts. In many cases, these traditions were influenced both by the languages shared by the Jews with their non-Jewish neighbors as well as the languages Jews spoke among themselves. This brings us to another area of research surveyed here: Jewish languages in which Hebrew and non-Hebrew words and structures are fused. The study of the various communal traditions, facilitated by massive immigration to Israel since 1948, is of great importance in establishing patterns of influence between different Jewish communities as well as between the Jewish minority and the non-Jewish majority; it has also facilitated restoration of earlier levels of the language (Morag 1956–57b; 1968c). There is a real urgency to recording and collecting facts about these languages, since in time the older generation will pass on and the various local languages will be abandoned in favor of standard contemporary Israeli Hebrew.

Spoken Hebrew

The revolt of Bar-Kokhba marked the beginning of a sharp decline in the speaking of Hebrew itself, although it did not entirely cease to be spoken (Bendavid 1967: 53–65; Morag 1956–57a; Chomsky 1951–52). There were special ceremonial occasions, Sabbaths and the delivery of a sermon, when Hebrew was used (Morag 1963: 30–31; Chomsky 1967: 243–53; Federbush 1967:

325–27). Federbush (1967: 130–33) describes how spoken Hebrew facilitated communication between Jews from different communities and how, in the seventeenth and eighteenth centuries, individuals spoke Hebrew and won rabbinical approval (1967: 311–17). Murtonen (1961–62), studying the vocalization of a tenth-century Bible manuscript (JTS 512 = ENA 2118, fols. 14–15), sees evidence of the interference of the spoken language. The deviation from masoretic standard vocalization that he notes is that the vowel in the open syllable immediately preceding the stressed syllable was not lengthened. Allony (1967–68, 1970–71) also has published some early examples of spoken Hebrew.

Classification of Jewish languages

Problems of classification and nomenclature exist in the study of Jewish languages. A major article by Wexler (1981) raises problems common to all Jewish languages and is a contribution to the study of Jewish interlinguistics. The Jewish people have been unique in adoption-cum-adaptation of a coterritorial language, this tradition going all the way back to the time when Aramaic was the first language adapted by Hebrew-speaking people. Wexler notes that only Yiddish, Judeo-Arabic, and Judezmo (Judeo-Spanish) have been well researched and provided with adequate bibliographical tools.

Classification is also a problem. In the *Bibliographie Linguistique*, from 1953 to 1957, Jewish languages were classified with "pidgins" and "creoles" and Gypsy languages. From 1958 to 1967 they were given separate listings. At present, since 1968, Jewish languages have been deprived of independent status and are classified under the cognate language supplying the base component, Yiddish under German, and Judezmo under Spanish. Even in collective studies of Jewish languages, interlinguistics is neglected. Research is further hampered by an over-emphasis on the dependency of the Jewish languages upon their non-Jewish base (e.g., Judezmo is a frozen form of Castilian Spanish) and by overemphasis on a monogenetic model. These languages should be treated as independent language systems, and heterogeneous influences should be sought at the very outset of the lives of these languages.

Wexler also raises objection to the prevailing view that segregation and religious separatism were the main reasons for creating Jewish languages, because most Jewish languages were created when Jews had free access to Non-Jewish linguistic norms. Actually, voluntary acts of linguistic creativity on the part of Jews brought about the new languages, while social oppression was a contributing stimulus.

Wexler proposes four types of Jewish-language-creation:

1) Jewish languages linked by a chain of shifts back to spoken Palestinian Hebrew—such languages are characterized by the merger of a coterritorial non-Jewish language with heterogeneous imported components. One example is Yiddish.

2) Jewish languages originating in the absence of any Jewish substratum, but which acquire a Jewish identity because of dialect shifts which affect either the Jewish or the non-Jewish population, but not both—this "Jewish" speech may resemble non-Jewish speech in another part of the country. An example is Baghdadi Judeo-Arabic.

3) Jewish languages developed for certain forms of written expression, such as Bible translations or exegesis—such languages have large numbers of calques on Hebrew-Aramaic patterns.

4) Languages spoken by Jews and non-Jews alike, but to which Jews have added occasional Hebrew-Aramaic or Jewish elements—one example of this may be the English spoken by some New York Jews recently removed from a Yiddish-speaking community. Wexler argues that Israeli Hebrew belongs in this category.

Wexler proposes designating the first two types with the prefix "Judeo-" attached to the non-Jewish variant (Judeo-Arabic) unless there exists a native name (Yiddish, Judezmo). Numbers 1 and 2 are "primary" and "secondary" respectively. Number 3 should be designated "Judeo-calque" languages, and Number 4 could be designated as "Jewish-English" or "Jewish-German." Further discussion in the article is devoted to types 1 and 2, establishing facts, and conceiving a framework for the processes of genesis and development. The bibliography is also of importance.

A new journal devoted to Jewish languages is *JLR* (vol. 1, 1981; vol. 2, 1982; vol. 3, 1983). Gold (1981) offers a critique of recent studies in Jewish languages which is quite comprehensive but is also somewhat programmatic. A response by Blau appears in *Leš* 46 (1982) 153–57.

TIBERIAN, PALESTINIAN, BABYLONIAN, AND YEMENITE HEBREW

Yemenite tradition and Babylonian connections

Criteria for evaluating the evidence of oral tradition have been proposed by Morag (1965). Taking the Yemenite Jewish tradition as an example, Morag divides the oral traditions into two categories, a) traditional reading of texts with authorized vocalization, i.e., Biblical Hebrew and Targum Aramaic, and b) unvocalized texts, such as post-Biblical Hebrew and Babylonian Aramaic. The second category yields more significant phonologic and morphologic data. The Yemenite tradition of reading Babylonian Aramaic reflects a living dialect which derived from Gaonic Babylonia. The Yemenite reading tradition is, in many cases, independent of the printed text of the Talmud and forms a consistent dialect, features of which are described by Morag. It shares a number of characteristics with Syriac, Mandaic, and Targum Aramaic, yet it emerges as an independent entity the development of which from other East Aramaic dialects can be described diachronically.

Yemenite and Babylonian reading of the Mishnah

Babylonian and Yemenite phonology and morphology have been described by various writers, among them Porath (1938), who treats Babylonian traditions of pronunciation of the Mishnah; Yalon, in significant articles (1963, 1964–65); and Shivtiel (formerly Ashbat, Damti; 1937, 1938–39a and b, 1944, 1963) on verbal forms in the reading of the Mishnah distinct from Tiberian Hebrew. Some examples are: *Pā^{c}āl* of stative verbs in place of *Pā^{c}ēl*, e.g., *yāšān* 'slept'; *Pi^{c}al* in place of *Pi^{c}el*, e.g., *zimman* 'invited'; *Mefā^{c}el*, instead of *Mefa^{c}el*, e.g., *m^{e}ḵāmmēn* 'hides'; *Nitpā^{c}el* in place of *Nitpa^{c}el*, e.g., *miṯrāgēl* 'becomes accustomed'; and the *Nitpi^{c}al* form for the *Nitpa^{c}el*, e.g., *Niṣṭi^{c}artā* 'you were troubled.' The forms unique to the Yemenite tradition are evident in the edition of *Mishnah Sanhedrin* published by Shivtiel (1963). A collection of Yemenite materials has been edited by Nahum (1971), who has also edited a catalogue of Yemenite manuscripts (1986).

Morag's studies

A significant contribution to the study of the linguistic tradition of the Yemenite Jews is a series of studies by Morag: a doctoral dissertation (1956), articles (1956–57b, 1956–58, 1960, 1965, 1975b), and his book (1963), a major work. The mystical *Book of Creation* counts *r* as one of the letters which have a twofold pronunciation, along with /bgdkpt/ (Chomsky 1952: 24–25, 44; M. H. Segal 1928: 30–33). The Tiberians, according to Saadiah's commentary on that book, doubled the *r* when reading scripture, while the Babylonians did so only in their daily speech. Saadiah formulated a rule for the doubling of *r*, namely: when *d, z, ṭ, k, ṣ, s* stand before the *r*, and they or the *r* have a *shewa*, the *r* is doubled (Bacher 1895: 22–23).

The doubling of the *r*

Morag (1960) accounts for the differing circumstances under which *r* can be doubled in the two traditions of Tiberian and Babylonian. He also accounts for the disappearance of doubled *r* in the Tiberian tradition. An important historical fact is that Saadiah commented on the phenomenon, not in terms of the Babylonian tradition in which he participated, but in terms of the dissimilar Tiberian grammar, showing that the Tiberian system penetrated into Babylonian (Waldman 1975a: 1306). Morag (1963: 30–36) notes that Yemenite readers doubled the *r* in scripture wherever the Tiberian notation indicates a *dagesh*, albeit inconsistently. He does not consider this to be evidence of an independent linguistic tradition.

There is a different system, however, for the reading of post-biblical materials. After the particle *ša*, for instance, the *r* is doubled, e.g., *mišarrāḇû hāraṣḥānîm* 'when the murderers increased in numbers' (*m. Soṭah* 9:9), and in *qattāl* forms which indicate professions, e.g., *garrādî* 'weaver' and *harrāgîn* 'murderers' (*m. Dem.* 1:4; *m. Nĕd.* 3:4). There is much evidence to demonstrate that the Yemenite tradition was dependent on the Babylonian.

Stages in Babylonian Aramaic

Boyarin (1978), in an important study, attempts to revise accepted theories on the relationship between various traditions of reading Babylonian Aramaic, illustrated by the relationship between the phonemes /a/ and /ā/. Earlier, Morag (*Phonetica* 7 [1962] 217–39) had suggested that the Yemenite reading of the Aramaic of the Babylonian Talmud stemmed from a spoken Babylonian Aramaic dialect. But Boyarin suggests, instead, that there were three stages: 1) an archaic stage, represented by the Babylonian pointing of the Targumim; 2) a later stage of the spoken language, represented by the pointing of *Halakhot pesuqot*; and 3) an archaizing tradition, as represented by the Gaonic fragments from the Geniza, *Halakhot gedolot*, and the Talmud reading of the Yemenite Jews. In the first stage, /a/ and /ā/ were phonemically distinct. In the second, they merged, but the new phoneme /a/ also had an allophone, [ə] (*miqpats puma*, *qamets*). Despite this development, the learned elite maintained the old phonemic opposition in their reading of the Bible and the Targum. In the third stage there was a partial reform where the opposition between /a/ and /ə/ was rephonologized. Disagreeing with Kutscher and Yalon, who maintained that *miqpats puma* (*qamets*) was a front vowel, Boyarin holds that it was a back, round vowel.

Multiple traditions in Yemen

Presumably because of Maimonides' endorsement of the Bible codex of Ben Asher (*Mishneh Torah*, *Sefer Torah* VIII:4; Goshen-Gottstein 1963), the Tiberian tradition began to penetrate Yemen. In his major study, Morag (1963) indicates that this penetration first appears in certain centers, radiating outward. Yemenite Bible manuscripts are vocalized with the supralinear Babylonian system but are read according to the Tiberian tradition. Ratzhaby (1970–71) has published a portion of a Yemenite Bible codex with remnants of Babylonian vocalization, and Morag (1974d) has brought to light a Babylonian-Yemenite manuscript of the book of Daniel, to cite some examples. The reading of post-biblical texts, as noted, was not affected by this standardization and remained closer to the Babylonian model.

Unique features of Yemenite Hebrew

Poetry also provides evidence for a divergent linguistic tradition, e.g., the rhyming of *ḥolem* (Tiberian *ô*) with *tsere* (Tiberian *ē*) in south-Yemenite poetry, and the rhyming of *segol* (TIberian *e*) with *patah* (Tiberian *a*), the last two undistinguished in the Babylonian tradition underlying the Yemenite (Ratzhaby 1968: 28; Morag 1963: 92–99, 119–20). Ratzhaby (1968: 26, 27) provides examples of Aramaic and Arabic verbs which were treated as Hebrew and of the coinage of new verbs from unusual noun forms. The vocabulary and grammar of the noted Yemenite poet, Rabbi Shalem Shabazzi, have been described by Ratzhaby (1974; bibliographical, 1971). Idioms in the Hebrew currently spoken and written by Yemenite Jews are collected by Ratzhaby (1969–71, 1973–74a, 1973–74b, 1975–76). He has also compiled a lexicon of Yemenite Hebrew, illustrating unique words and forms and indicating their origin. Tobi (1966–67) discusses the pronunciation of *tsere* and *ḥolem* by Yemenite Jews. Avizemer (1983) offers a general survey of the contribution of Yemenite Jewry to Hebrew language and culture.

Linguistic interference in Yemenite Hebrew

Morag (1963) attempts to formulate patterns of interference between the spoken language and what he terms the liturgical language. Various patterns are observed. The vernacular may influence the elimination of phonemic contrasts in the liturgical language, or the contrasts may be maintained, but the realization of the consonants will shift to sounds characteristic of the vernacular. With all the influence of the Masoretes, they never succeeded in imposing upon any community the phonemic structure they so laboriously transcribed. A certain dualism between orthography and grammar on the one hand, and pronunciation, on the other, existed in Yemen, Spain, France, and Germany (Morag 1963: 289–90). Morag's study (1963) has been critically reviewed by Garbell (1965b) and Kutscher (1966).

Babylonian and Tiberian Hebrew compared

The Hebrew dialect which is recoverable from the vocalization of Babylonian Bible-manuscripts has been painstakingly described by Yeivin (1965, 1973a, 1985), who also treats masoretic signs and vocabulary. Unique to the supralinear Babylonian vocalization is the fact that the same sign, a truncated *ʿayin*, corresponds both to Tiberian *a* and *e*. There is much that both B(abylonian) and T(iberian) have in common. It will be possible here to enumerate only a few of the many differences which Yeivin has collected. For example, in final weak verbs ending with *alef*, T moves the vowel back in the word and leaves the *alef* quiescent, but in B it is articulated, e.g., *biṣ*ʾ*ēṯām* 'when they went out' (T *b*^{e}*ṣe*ʾ*ṯām*). Often a *dagesh* is placed over an *alef* merely to emphasize that it is a consonant. Frequently the vowel after final *w* is *u*, especially when the preceding vowel is *i*, e.g., *biqqaštîwû* 'I sought him' (Cant 3:1; T *biqqaštîw*), ʾ*āḇîwû* 'his father,' ʾ*āḥîwû* 'his brother.'

Similar phenomena are observed in the Yemenite dialect, e.g., statives such as *zāqan* 'was old' (T *zāqēn*), *šālam* 'was complete' (T *šālēm*, Gen 15:16; Shivtiel [Damti, Ashbat] 1937, 1938–39a, 1938–39b, 1944, 1963). In the Babylonian dialect the *Hof*ᶜ*al* form appears as *Huf*ᶜ*al*, e.g., *w*^{e}*huškaḇ* 'will be made to lie down' (Ezek 32:32). The *Polal* form corresponds to T *Polel*, e.g., *sôrar* (T *sôrēr*, 'turned aside [my ways],' Lam 3:11). The *Pi*ᶜ*al* form *niggan* 'played an instrument' contrasts with T *niggēn*, and the *Hitpolal* contrasts with T *Hitpolel*, e.g., *hiṯbônān* 'examine' (Job 37:14).

Yemenite and Babylonian compared

Kara (1979) analyzes a sixteenth-century Yemenite manuscript of *Mo*ᶜ*ed*, published in 1976 by Y. Nahum, with introduction by S. Morag. Kara also notes the publication of other Yemenite *mishnayot* (pp. 26, 27). This manuscript bears evidence of three traditions: the supralinear Babylonian, the Tiberian, and one expressed by the consonantal writing. This evidence indicates that in Yemen different traditions existed side by side. Some of the features in this manuscript include: the absence of *pataḥ furtivum*, in many instances; *shewa* and *pataḥ* are often interchanged; the signs for *segol* and *pataḥ* are interchanged, a feature of the Babylonian tradition; the vowel *a* becomes *u* before *r*; the *resh* is doubled, as we have noted elsewhere; verbs with ᶜ or *ḥ* are treated as regular verbs, e.g., *hiḥšîḵ* 'became dark' (not *heḥšîḵ*); the vowel in the second radical of the verb is often *a* instead of *ē*, e.g., *biṭṭal* 'canceled' (not *biṭṭēl*); a *Nuf*ᶜ*al* form exists, e.g., *nuldāh* 'laid (of an egg), born'; the nominal for *Pe*ᶜ*āl* replaces segolates used in other traditions, e.g., *n*^{e}*p̄āš* 'monument' (in place of *nep̄eš*).

Kara has done considerable work in the area of the dialect reflected in the Yemenite manuscripts of the Talmud (1974, masters thesis; 1982, doctoral dissertation; 1983). A summary of his most recent work (1983: 21–29) demonstrates that the Yemenite manuscripts retained a Babylonian, Gaonic tradition, with early Palestinian features. In contrast to the printed editions of the Talmud, there are unique orthographic features, such as *-yy* for final *-*ʾ*ay*, e.g., *myy* 'what/' instead of *m*ʾ*y*. A final *he* is used in place of the *alef* e.g., Rabbi *Ḥyyh*, instead of *Ḥyy*ʾ. Gutturals are weakened, e.g., ʾ*hwy* showed,' instead of ʾ*ḥwy*. There is an interchange of *š*, *ś*, and *s*, e.g., *sbwr mlk* 'King Shapur,' Final consonants are dropped and there is widespread interchange of vowels, *e/i*, *ā/a*, *o/u*, *i/u*, and *ā/a* with *u/o*. Vocalic *shewa* appears as *i*. The traditions in these manuscripts—the vocalization considered a separate tradition from the consonantal writing—do not correspond to those studied by Morag, who concentrated on Sanʿah traditions. Kara's manuscripts reflect traditions outside that center and also have affinities with the various editions of the Yemenite *Midrash hagadol.* Kara (1986) discusses the Arab dialect of the Yemenite Jews.

Studies in various traditions

Other material from various dialects include: examples of early spoken Hebrew collected by Murtonen (1961–62) and Allony (1967–68, 1970–71); Y. Yahalom's discussion (1969–70) of Palestinian vocalization in the *piyyuṭim* of Hedwata; Mishor's publication (1968–69) of a manuscript in Tiberian vocalization without an *o/u* opposition; a manuscript of *Pesiqta de-Rav Kahana* with Palestinian vocalization (Allony [1958–59], with Díez-Macho); Mishnah fragments with Babylonian pointing (Murtonen 1956–57); Geniza fragments of rabbinic literature with Palestinian pointing (Allony 1973a); a Palestinian fragment of Haftarot with mixed pointing (Yeivin 1963); Mishnah fragments from the Geniza with Babylonian pointing (Yeivin 1974b); Mishnah and Talmud fragments from the Geniza of various origins (Katsh 1970, 1975–77).

Examples of Babylonian vocalization in a Yemenite Torah manuscript are provided by Y. Ratzhaby (1970–71). They include deviations from the masoretic such as *ḥamʾāh* 'butter' (T *ḥemʾāh*), *ʿĕlî* b^{e}*ʾēr* 'spring up, o well' (T *ʿălî*), *mēʾznê ṣedeq* 'righteous scales' (T *mōʾznê*; cf. Ratzhaby 1968: 28).

Different realizations of *a* and *e*

Revell (1970a: 99–121; 1970b) has identified two groups among manuscripts with Palestinian pointing. The general theory is that Palestinian Hebrew had only one realization of *a* and *e* and that the differentiation came about under the influence of the Tiberian Ben Asher tradition. A. Bendavid, on the other hand (1957–58c), claimed that there is no differentiation between Palestinian and Ben Asher Tiberian but that they have the same pronunciation expressed in different signs. Revell, however, observes that Palestinian manuscripts with only one realization of *a* and *e* are rare. There are texts with two clear realizations of *a* and *e*. In her view, the distinction are maintained in the earlier group and are broken down in a later group. The Palestinian tradition is later than the Ben Asher and it was used only for the reading of biblical texts and not for biblical quotations in liturgical texts. In the latter Aramaic influence is apparent. Revell also suggests that the group of texts in which the distinctions are no longer maintained may be assigned to an "Egyptian" dialect group, reflecting the pronunciation of Jews who were subject to more foreign influence.

Some of the differences between the Palestinian (P) and the Tiberian (T) Ben Asher traditions and the conditions under which they occur are as follows: 1) in a stressed or unstressed syllable preceding a laryngeal or a doubled consonant, T *u* corresponds to P *ō*, *roḥaṣt* 'you were washed' (*ruḥaṣt*); T *a* corresponds to P *ā*, e.g., *n^eṯāṯîḵā* 'I have made you' (Jen 1:5; cf. *n^eṯattîḵā*; other changes include *i*/*e*, *ē*; *ā*/*e*; and 2) in open, unstressed syllables T *ō* corresponds to P *u* e.g., *naḇšûṯēnû* 'our souls' (cf. *naḇšoṯēnû*; other changes include *ā*/*e*, *ē*; *ā*/*a*, *ă*/*o*).

Palestinian and Tiberian Hebrew compared

Important historical information was collected by Klar (1942, 1947a, 1950–51; collected writings 1954). In his 1950–51 study Klar disagreed with the position of Samuel David Luzzatto and suggested that *qamets* in Babylonian and Tiberian was pronounced like Swedish [å]. Transcriptions of incantations from Nippur have *bwrwk* = *buruk* 'blessed' instead of *bārûḵ*. Perhaps Tiberian *qamets* is related to Syriac *a*, which was realized as [o]. Klar offered the evidence from Kirkisani and Persian transcriptions as confirmation. While in the Middle Ages the Tiberian pronunciation was held to be the most ancient, he suggests that the Egyptian-Sephardic might really occupy this position. The Tiberian texts where *qamets*/*pataḥ* and *segol*/*tsere* are completely confused provide clear evidence of the interference of the "Sephardic" pronunciation. In this area Chomsky (1941–42; 1952: 34, 77; 1971a) has suggested a hypothesis for the rise of the Sephardic pronunciation and for the *u*/*i* variation between the pronunciations of Lithuanian and Ukrainian Jews. He reverts to the position put forth earlier by S. Pinsker, that underlying both is a /ü/ phoneme.

Studies of Klar

K. Fellman (1982) examines nouns of the *qôṭel* formation in the traditions of Bible and Mishnah reading of the various communities—Tiberian, Babylonian, Spanish, Aleppo, and others. She concludes that the biblical tradition is quite conservative in retaining the *qôṭel* formation. Mishnaic Hebrew, however, is quite fluid, open to many influences, among them that of Aramaic. There is a trend to use the form *quṭlîn* for the plural *qôṭālîn*, and there is a variety of forms resulting from *qôṭēl* + suffix. Moreover, a parallel variety is seen when the suffix is attached to *kôṯēl,* 'wall,' e.g., *k^eṯālô*, *kôṯālô*, *koṯlô*, *kitlô* 'his wall.'

Qôṭel formations in the dialects

JUDEO-ARABIC AND ARABIC INFLUENCE ON HEBREW

The relationships between classical Arabic, middle Arabic, Judeo-Arabic, and Hebrew have been explored in significant studies by Blau (1957–58, 1961–62, 1974b), who also surveys the current situation of research into Judeo-Arabic (1973b). His grammar of medieval Judeo-Arabic appeared in 1961, and his study *The Emergence and Linguistic Background of Judeo-Arabic* was published in 1965. In this work Blau traces the process of the acceptance of Arabic by the Jews in Arab-dominated lands, who in accepting Arabic dropped attachment to Aramaic or Greek. The acceptance of Arabic was widespread, extending to the writing of religious and halakhic text. Poetry in Arabic, on the other hand, was not cultivated by Jews. This may be due to the difficulties of the language and their imperfect command of it, as well as to the alien spirit of that poetry.

Socio-linguistics of Judeo-Arabic

A *koine* developed among Jews, who wrote in a dialect which omitted any local idioms, the intention being that the work by understandable to Jews in other lands. Generally, however, the spoken language of the Jews was similar to that of their non-Jewish neighbors. A different situation obtained in Egypt in the time of Maimonides, where Jews from the Maghreb of high culture were the dominant element. The Arabic used by Jews was middle Arabic which expressed concepts by use of a single words. This was different from the rich ornateness of classical Arabic, but an effort was made to upgrade the language by drawing from classical Arabic, which often led to hypercorrection. Blau, disagreeing with Halper, maintains that Judeo-Arabic was influenced by Hebrew and incorporated many Hebrew words from the very outset. It was a distinctive language and it was so perceived by the Jews of that period. Corré (1982) analyzes the later development of Judeo-Arabic, when it became a language of the masses only and failed to develop standards of grammar and lexicon. He discusses the influence of other languages under these circumstances.

Various studies in Yemenite and Baghdadi dialects

The terminology "merged Hebrew" (M. Weinreich 1954) has been applied as a description of the speech of other Jewish communities. An early study of the Hebrew elements in the daily speech of Yemenite Jews was made by Goitein (1930–31), and, more recently, Ratzhaby (169–71, 1973–74a) has compiled a list of expressions currently used by Yemenite speakers. Blanc (1964b, 1964c) has studied the dialects and literary idiom of Baghdad Jews. Mansour (1955–56, 1974–75, 1975–83, 1980) has dealt extensively with the Judeo-Arabic dialect of Baghdad, including the questions of anaptyxis (1974–75) and vowel phonemes (1980). Saig (1981, master thesis) describes syndetic clauses. Poetic materials of Babylonian Jewry have been assembled by Ben Yaacov, Semah and Tobi (1970). Khayyat (1972) has collected Iraqi Jewish proverbs on family life. In his dissertation (1975) Khayyat deals with Arabic folk songs sung among Iraqi Jews and also considers the question of merged Hebrew. Examples he provides include: *il-ʾabot* 'the ancestors' (with Arabic article), *mizzāla* 'her good luck,' *winzūru linnābi* 'we will visit the prophet,' with the accusative particle *l*, which also occurs in Aramaic and occasionally in the Bible. Khayyat concludes that, apart from words expressing religious and ritual concerns, such as *mafṭîr* 'the prophetic portion' and *il-mîlah* 'circumcision,' the amount of Hebrew words in this dialect is less than in Ladino or Yiddish. Further studies by Khayyat deal with proverbs (1968) and folksongs (1979).

In the work of David Rabi (Rabeeya; 1974, doctoral dissertation, 1975, 1978) there is special emphasis upon the Hebrew element in the Baghdadi dialect. The dissertation is a linguistic analysis of proverbs and idioms of Baghdad Jews. A later study (1978) emphasizes that Hebrew was very much a part of Jewish life in Baghdad, present in names, religious objects and occasions, names of institutions, and in social gatherings. Rabi has collected many examples of phonetic change in Baghdadi Hebrew that can be contrasted with Tiberian and with current Israeli speech, e.g., *Šmil, Šemmel* (*Š^{e}muʾel*), *Miʾir* (*Mēʾîr*), *ṣeṣid* (*ṣiṣṣîṯ* 'fringes'), *hasuwušalôm* (*ḥas w^{e}šālôm* 'God forbid'), *qerban* (*qorban* 'offering'), *sendiq* (*sandāq* 'the one who holds the child at a circumcision'), *baṣar* (*bāśār* 'meat'), *labas* (*lăḇaš* 'wore'), *Ġaḥēl* (*Rāḥēl* Rachel), *reššana* (*Rōʾš ha-šānāh* 'New Year'), *maḥveġet* (*maḥbereṯ* 'notebook') and *emmaḥa-ʾesmu* (*yimmaḥ š^{e}mô* 'may his name be obliterated,' Arabicized). Schramm (1956) and Blanc (1964b) have also and there are others who have made contributions: the work of Mansour (1955–56, 1974–75, 1975, 1980) is referred to above; Morag (1977) has edited a monograph on the phonology; Eldar (1978–79b) treats the plosive realization of /bgdkpt/ and the Arabic, Tiberian, and Spanish Hebrew influences on the dialect.

North African dialects

David Cohen (1964b, 1975) has collected examples of the Hebrew of the Jews of Tunis from various spheres, both religious and cultural. Volume 1 (1964b) presents text of ethnographic material, and Volume 2 (1975) is a linguistic analysis of phonology, morphology, syntax, and lexicon. Some Hebrew examples from ritual terminology are: *massut* 'unleavened cakes' (*maṣṣôṯ*), *marûr* 'bitter herbs' (*mārôr*), *ḥrušûṯ* 'paste of nuts, wine and fruits used at the Passover Seder' (*ḥărōseṯ*), *qaddūš* 'sanctification over the wine' (*qiddûš*), and *biṣiṯ ʾIsraʾil* 'when Israel went forth' (from the *Hallel*, Ps 114:1). The bibliography of North African Jewry by Attal (1973) is important in this context.

Moroccan Hebrew and Judeo-Arabic

The dialect of the Jews of Morocco has also received some attention. The collection of texts by Brunot and Malka (1939) was a pioneer effort, as was the study by Leslau (1946) which was based on it. A number of shorter studies are mentioned in the comprehensive article by Bar-Asher (1977–78). He notes that Hebrew played an important role in the spoken Arabic of the Moroccan Jews, although only the learned group used Aramaic expressions as well. Literary sources played a role, so that the Ashkenazic *Yahrzeit* (anniversary of death) became [yaʾerṣyaṭ] or [larsyat]. Vowels in unaccented, closed syllables were attenuated or pushed out, e.g., [n^{e}fṭar] or [nfṭar] 'departed,' and the Arabic article was often attached, e.g., [lbarzil] 'iron' and [rr^{e}hmanot] 'compassion.' The main realm of such Hebrew terms was that of religion and piety, but there was also occasionally a deliberate use of Hebrew in order to conceal meaning from non-Jews, e.g., [l^{e}mmd qameṣ] 'no' (Arabic *lā*) and [xalab] 'dog' in place of Arabic *kalb*. Bar-Asher also discusses changed in meanings of the Hebrew elements. Ben-Asher (1984–85) analyzes the Hebrew elements in the *šarḥ*, the Arabic translation of the Bible and some extra-biblical works, of the Moroccan Jews. The number of Hebrew words is limited, and *Targum Onkelos* is also a source. Ben-Ami (1970) has collected 1001 proverbs from Morocco. Benoliel (1977) has reissued some earlier studies in this dialect. Zafrani (1971) surveys Judeo-Arabic and Judeo-Berber in a brief article in the *EJ*.

K. Katz, in a doctoral dissertation (1975) and in a study which is part of the PHULTP series (1977), has treated the traditions of reading the Bible and the Mishnah in the Jewish community of Djerba. K. Katz (1981) has also contributed a study of the phonology of the language tradition of the Jews of Aleppo (*Aram Tsova*) in reading Bible and Mishnah (PHULTP 7).

Studies on interaction of Hebrew and Arabic

General descriptions of the influence of Arabic on medieval Hebrew are given by Chomsky (1967: 194–99), Y. Avinery (1946: 81–88) and Federbush (1967: 238–39). Rosén (1956a: 67–71) cites some examples of philosophical terms which entered Hebrew from the original Sanskrit, with Arabic as intermediary. Extended meanings present in the donor language were thus imported into Hebrew, extending the range of the Hebrew word. The doctoral dissertation of Goshen-Gottstein (1951a) deals in depth with Arabic influence, citing many examples. Current research into medieval Hebrew is surveyed by E. Goldenberg (1971). Jarden (1956) and Kaddari (1970a) traced current idioms back to medieval philosophy or Kabbalah. Wechter (1964) edited and translated Ibn Barun's works on comparative Arabic and Hebrew grammar and lexicography. There is further discussion by Becker (1980). Goodstein (1960), in a doctoral dissertation, has analyzed Judah ibn Quraish's Judeo-Arabic book of Hebrew, Aramaic, and Arabic comparisons known as the *Risala*. This work has also been studied by Becker (1977, 1984). Early comparative Semitics of the medieval period is described by Gil (1973–74).

Various levels of Hebrew influenced by Arabic

Goshen-Gottstein's study of loanwords (1951a) in Hebrew texts which are directly dependent upon an Arabic original does not take into account loanwords in literature which is not translation. The reason there are more loanwords in a work of translation is that a translation is more bound to the original. This is especially true if the original work is philosophical or technical in nature, and corresponding Hebrew terms are nonexistent. An illustration of word-borrowing during translation is given in the translator's introduction to Bachya ibn Paqudah's *Duties of the Heart*, in which he contrasts the richness of Arabic with the depleted resources exemplified by the vocabulary of the Bible; the Bible, of course, is but a small remnant of the vast treasures on which it drew. He is apologetic for his translation, saying: "Let the reader of this translation not blame me because, in a few places, I created noun and verb formations which do not exist in Hebrew, for the complexity of the matter and the inadequacy of the (Hebrew) language brought me to this." Goshen-Gottstein (1968) has made a plea for linguistic study of Hebrew under Arabic influence in terms of the following categories: 1) early Arabicized Hebrew documents, including non-literary Geniza fragments; 2) Arabicized Hebrew writings, grammar, and sciences, of the pre-classical period; 3) translations of the pre-classical period, from Ibn Gikatilla to the Tibbonides; 4) translations and writings of the post-Tibbonide period; and 5) works of Hebrew writers who did not know Arabic but modeled their work on classical arabicized Hebrew literature. Sarfatti (1975, masters thesis; 1958–60; 1963, doctoral dissertation; 1968a, book form of the previous has treated Hebrew mathematical terminology influences by Arabic (Waldman 1975a: 1309).

Studies by Kopf

Kopf's *Studies in Arabic and Hebrew Lexicography* (1976), edited by M. H. Goshen-Gottstein, contains essays published earlier. One of the studies demonstrates the dependence of Hebrew dictionaries on the principles of arrangement used in Arabic lexicography (original: *Leš* 34 [1979] 106–24; Kopf 1976: 116–34, Hebrew). Another study seeks to identify the sources of the non-Hebrew terms used in the medieval dictionary of Gershon ben Solomon of Arles (second half of the thirteenth century), *The Gate of Heaven* (Venice, 1547; Rödelsheim 1801, translated by F. S. Bodenheimer, Jerusalem 1953). This was originally published as a series of articles (*Tarbiz* 24 [1955] 150–66, 274–89, 410–25; 25 [1956] 36–43). A small portion of these are of Arabic origin, the rest deriving from Greek, Latin, and the romance languages.

JUDEO-ARAMAIC AND OTHER LANGUAGES

Judeo-Aramaic of Kurdistan and Azerbaijan

J. B. Segal (1955) has collected proverbs of the Jews of Zakho. The poetry of Kurdistani Jews was published by Rivlin (1959), who termed them "Jews of the Targum," and who also studied the Hebrew words in their dialect (1956–57). Sabar (1973–74) has studied the phonology and the Hebrew elements in the neo-Aramaic dialect of Zakho in Kurdistan. A number of interesting features are: *ṯ* is pronounced as [s] and *ḏ* as [z], the latter reflecting the general Aramaic articulation in the area; the consonants [f], [g], and [v] occur only in Hebrew and in loanwords, not in the spoken Aramaic; the consonants *ḥ* and ʿ are retained only in Hebrew words, for in the Aramaic dialects *ḥ* has become *h*, and ʿ has become ʾ. There are secondary doublings, e.g., [kummar] 'priest,' from *kômer*, *kûmrāʾ*; there is assimilation to voiced consonants, e.g., [haz-u-salom] 'no indeed,' from *has w^{e}šālôm*; *o* and *u* interchange, e.g., [roslayim] 'Jerusalem' (*Y^{e}rušalayim*); and initial vocalic *shewa* is pronounced as [a], e.g., [šaxina] 'the Divine presence' (*š^{e}ḵînāh*). Borrowed Hebrew words are given Aramaic grammatical endings, in a manner analogous to Yiddish, and they often receive extended meanings, e.g., [peʿullos] (*p^{e}ʿullôṯ* 'actions') in this dialect means 'foolish actions' and [ʿasamos] (*ʿăṣāmôṯ* 'bones') signifies 'a stubborn person.'

Sabar (1965–66) has presented Aramaic translations of the Bible and *piyyuṭim* of the Kurdestani Jews and (1976) a homiletic interpretation of a biblical portion (*Vayehi beshallaḥ*). Both works contain surveys of the oral and written literature of this community. Sabar (1976) has been reviewed enthusiastically by Boyarin (1982), who notes the significance of this dialect for the general study of Aramaic. Sabar (1981) has also edited a homiletic commentary to Jonah, has published two homiletic commentaries to the *Haftarah* of *Tishʿa beʾav* (1983a) and has written on the factors that determine deviations from literalism in neo-Aramaic Targumim (1982a, 1983b). He has also compiled a bibliography of secondary literature on New Aramaic (1981–82) which has appeared in *JLR*, vols. 1 and 2 (his term is "New Aramaic"). I. Avinery (1968, masters thesis) has studied the Arabic elements in the Aramaic dialect of Zakho and (1974, 1977) has published folk tales in that dialect.

A study by Sabar (1974–75), which continues the pioneering efforts of Garbell (1965a), deals with the Hebrew elements in the Aramaic dialects of Azerbaijan. In this article there is an important bibliography on the subject of dialectology (Sabar 1974–75: 272–74). Sabar uses a comparative, interdialectical approach in comparing the similarities of Yiddish, Ladino, and Judeo-Persian. He notes that the consonants of the Hebrew component were not affected by the changes that occurred in the Aramaic component, possibly because the Aramaic dialect of Azerbaijan is not a direct descendant of the Aramaic spoken by the Jews in Talmudic and Gaonic times but was borrowed in a later period. There is a phonemic distinction between the "simple" and the "flat" or emphatic articulations, e.g., [tora] 'Torah, the law' and [TORA] 'bull.' Only /bgkp/ retain two articulations, with aspirated /b/ realized as [w]. The initial vocalic *shewa* is pronounced as [a], e.g., [tafillim] 'phylacteries' (*t*^{e}*p̱illîn*). Aramaic grammatical elements are grafted onto the Hebrew word, e.g., the abstract ending [-uta]), as in [aniyula] 'poverty.' Sabar (1974a) also treats the sociological aspects of bilingual Hebrew and neo-Aramaic contact in Israel.

Merchants' Argot

H. Goldberg (1973–74) has written an introductory study of the language and culture of the Jews of Tripolitania, now transplanted to Israel. He notes a merchants' argot, used to conceal communication from non-Jewish competitors, e.g., the verb [qat] 'bring' from Talmudic *qāʾ ʾāṯā* 'he has come' (1973–74: 139). A similar phenomenon is attested by Sabar (1973–74: 216), e.g., [ḥāṣi šilli ḥāṣi šillox] 'half is mine, half is yours', that is, 'let us divide the profits.' Similar phenomena occur in Yiddish (U. Weinreich 1959–61; Guggenheim-Grünberg 1954) and in Judeo-Persian (Yarshater 1977). Linguistic matters are also considered in the memoir edited by H. Goldberg (1980), *The Book of Mordecai.*

Georgian Jews

Babalikshvili (1979) describes the phonology and pronunciation of Hebrew of the Georgian Jews. Their Hebrew is influenced by the language of their daily speech, Georgian, although recently Ashkenazic Jewish influences have been noted. There is no distinction between plosive and aspirated *b*, or between *ḥ* and *ḵ*. The pronunciations of ʿ and *q* approach each other. Pre-velar aspirate *k* and glotalized *q* are distinguished and correspond to Georgian consonants. *Alef* is not pronounced at all, while *ṭ* and *t* are distinguished, again under the influence of Georgian. Glotalized *ṭ* corresponds to a Georgian consonant. Moskovich and Ben-Oren (1982) reject the claim that a separate Judeo-Georgian does not exist. At the present stage of their research, they have gathered a file of more than a thousand elements of Hebrew, Aramaic, and Georgian origin that are specific to Judeo-Georgian speech.

JUDEO-PERSIAN

General resources in Judeo-Persian

Paper (1978b) describes the current status of studies in Judeo-Persian. While the symbiosis of Jews and Persians dates back to the sixth century B.C.E., the materials to be studied cover the last ten or eleven centuries. The geographic range of Judeo-Persian is wider than the boundaries of Iran: it includes Afghanistan, part of the Caucasus, and much of central Asia, Uzbekistan, and Tajikistan. It reached at one time as far as the Jewish community of Kai Feng Fu. A large part of the relevant material is contained in translations of the Bible, and some of the significant manuscripts have been edited and published by Paper: the Vatican Judeo-Persian Pentateuch (1964–68), the Ms. HUC 2193 (1972b), a Judeo-Persian Pentateuch in the Ben Zvi Institute (1972a), sample Bible texts (1968), a further treatment of the Bible in Judeo-Persian (1973a), Ecclesiastes (1973c) and Job (1976). Paper has compared Yiddish and Persian as two examples of Indo-European-Semitic contact (1958) and has also discussed the state of and the need for research in the field (1973b). The outstanding example of classical Persian written in Hebrew characters is the poetry of Shahin Shirazi of the fourteenth century. His masterwork, *Shahin Torah*, is an epic that tells the stories of Scripture with midrashic embellishments, in imitation of the national epic poet of Iran, Ferdowsi (tenth century). Paper (1982) has also written on Judeo-Persian proverbs.

Different Judeo-Persian dialects

Judeo-Persian is composed of various dialects: 1) Standard Classical Persian written in the Hebrew alphabet (*Shahin*), 2) Standard Persian with an admixture of Hebrew-Aramaic loanwords and loan adaptations, i.e., Bible translations, and 3) various spoken dialects used in Iran, Afghanistan, and Central Asia. Included in the last category is Bokharan, which can be called Judeo-Tajik. In Daghestan the spoken dialect is Judeo-Tat. Paper (1978b) feels that while some research in this area has been done in Israel, more is needed.

Paper (1978b: 109) also gives some examples of the way in which Hebrew and Aramaic words were adapted for Judeo-Persian. For example, Hebrew forms were integrated morphologically with Persian suffixes or plural indicators. This pattern is similar to the pattern followed in the Persian integration of Arabic elements. Another category of adaptation is the use of an existing Arabic word as the model for a cognate Hebrew word, even though there is no semantic relationship between them, e.g., Hebrew *ḥag* 'festival' translated by Arabic *haj* 'pilgrimage.'

Judeo-Persian has been described by Lazard (1971) in *EJ*, as well as its dialectology, which he described earlier (1968). Recently he has published a note on the jargon of Iranian Jews (1978). Also active in this field is Asmussen, whose collection of Jewish-Persian texts (1968) and his other studies (1970, 1973) are noteworthy. Fischel (1971) surveys Judeo-Persian literature and includes a useful bibliography.

Melamed (1979) notes that, in addition to the spoken language, one source for the Hebrew elements in Judeo-Persian is Persian-language midrashim on the Torah. In this case, Hebrew words underwent changes of gender and meaning.

Loterāʾi, a Judeo-Persian dialect

Yarshater (1977) has described the hybrid language of Persian Jews, called *Loterāʾi*, a language designed to ensure privacy from non-Jews. Much of its lexicon is Hebrew or Aramaic. Nouns, verb bases, and some prepositions are Semitic, while verbal endings, modal prefixes, suffix pronouns, most particles, and sentence structures are Iranian. Thus we find the followings usages: [even] 'stone,' [melaxa] 'work,' [punim] 'face,' [mayera] 'quickly' (= *mᵉhērāh*), and [hebel] 'bad' (= *hebel* 'vanity'). *Zargari* is used by goldsmiths and is unintelligible to non-Jews. Earlier, Garbell (1947) also studied the pronunciation of Hebrew consonants by Iranian Jews.

Further studies

A number of studies on this topic appeared in *Irano-Judaica* (Jerusalem: The Ben-Zvi Institute, 1982). Paper (1982), for instance, published a Judeo-Persian version of the book of Proverbs, from a manuscript in the Jewish Theological Seminary in New York (Elkan Adler collection, B 46 = Lutski 433); Mainz (1982) published a Judeo-Persian version of the book of Daniel, from a manuscript in the Bibliothèque National in Paris (Ms. 129); A. Netzer (1982) has published an Isfahani folk-song, with a brief survey of the phonology and morphology of the dialect, *Jidi*; Souroudi (1982) has published a Judeo-Persian wedding song; and S. Shaked (1982) has published fragments of two Karaite commentaries on Daniel in Judeo-Arabic. Now a major bibliographical tool by A. Netzer (1985) gives a bibliography of Judeo-Persian, lists manuscripts and discusses the phonology of the various dialects.

JUDEZMO

Recent surveys of the studies being done in Judezmo have been made by Lida, Bunis, and Jochnowitz, all of which are included in the collection of papers on Jewish languages edited by

Nomenclature: Judezmo and Ladino

Paper (1978a). While the name "Ladino" is widely used for Judezmo, there is some opinion that it is inappropriate. Lida (1978) traces the semantics of the word, various stages of meaning, including "a Moor who knew Latin" (thirteenth century), "a cultured artistic language closer to Latin than the spoken vernacular" (fifteenth century), then to "astute, clever, wise" and "cunning, shrewd, wily" (sixteenth century) and prefers to use "Judeo-Spanish." Bunis (1978) also discusses the problematics of "Ladino," noting that among Sephardic Jews the term "Ladino" is restricted to the semi-archaic, semi-artificial and stylized languages used to translate sacred texts, something like Yiddish *ḥumesh-ṭayṭsh.* The terms "Judeo-Spanish" and "Spanyol" are also inadequate, because these were imposed on the native speakers by well-meaning Spanish scholars who believed that they had rediscovered their countrymen, long after their exile from Spain. Native speakers called their language "Judezmo," that is, "Jewish," and Bunis prefers this term for scientific work. Lazar (1971), however, feels that "Ladino" is appropriate for the spoken dialects and for the literary language.

Ladino as calque

Sephiha (1981) also distinguishes between Judezmo or Espagnol, which he considers to be the language of a particular locale, and Ladino, which is a calque, used by the Spanish Jews to translate Hebrew texts. Ladino reflects in its structure and vocabulary the original Hebrew. Bible translations in Ladino can be distinguished from Judezmo and Spanish. An example of close adherence to the original Hebrew, including use of the particle *ʾēṯ*, is: *En prençipio kir.o el Dio a los çielos i a la tiēra*, 'in the beginning God created the heavens and the earth.' In a Judezmo translation prepared by missionaries in 1873 the syntax is different: *en el prençipio kri.o el Dio loş çieloş i la tiera* (see also Sephiha 1975c, 1978b). Sephiha has written extensively on calques in Ladino (1972a, 1972b, 1973a, 1974, 1975a, 1975b, 1975d, 1976a, 1977a, 1977b, 1977c, 1978c, 1980a, 1980b, 1981, 1982).

Basic resources

Lida (1975, 1978) discusses some of the basic problems and research areas, among them: determining what is, prior to 1492, Judeo-Spanish literature; Spanish archaisms in Judezmo; the treatment of oral literature; and the question of Hispanic or Hebraic origin of proverbs. Basic research tools, cited by Jochnowitz (1978: 66) are: a dictionary, *Diccionario Ladino-Hebreo*, in preparation at the Ben Zvi Institute in Jerusalem; the *Tesoro Lexicografico Judeo-Espagnol*, to be published by the Instituto Arias Montano; M. Studemund's *Bibliographie zum Judenspanischen* (1975); a research bibliography compiled by Marius Sala, to be published by

Mouton. The Hebrew University, Harvard University, and Yeshiva University are engaged in bibliographical research. Bunis (1981b) has compiled a research bibliography for Sephardic studies. A dictionary has also been compiled by Nahama (1977). A volume edited by Benabu and Sermoneta (1985) includes studies in Judeo-Spanish and other Judeo Romance languages.

Social position of Judezmo

A. Levi (1981) discusses the position of Ladino (his term; we shall use "Judeo-Spanish") and literature in that language (he does not observe the distinction made by Sephiha 1981 and Bunis 1978). According to him, Hebrew occupied the prestigious sacred realm, while Judeo-Spanish was the language of conversation and business. Judeo-Spanish was set in various language setting and borrowed many foreign words: Turkish, Greek, and Arabic. Only Hebrew, however, and never Judeo-Spanish served as the language of instruction in school. Judeo-Spanish is, consequently, poorer in written literature and richer in oral folklore. Levi traces the history of written literature in Judeo-Spanish. Between 1492 and 1730, there were partial translations of the Bible and the Code of Jewish Law (*Shulḥan ʿarukh*), but by the beginning of the eighteenth century there was an increase in translated religious works. By the latter part of the nineteenth century Judeo-Spanish newspapers were flourishing. But subsequent historical events brought about a change: the modernization of the Turkish empire, the destruction of Balkan Jewish communities by the Nazis, and the emigration of Sephardic Jews to Israel. Now only two Judeo-Spanish newspapers remain: *Shalom* in Constantinople and *La Luz* in Tel Aviv.

Judezmo in different areas

Some basic surveys of Ladino and Judezmo include: Sala (1976), Moskona (1971, 1979), Lazar (1971), Gold (1977b), Wexler (1977) on the position of Judezmo within Ibero-Romance, S. Marcus (1965), Bentes (1981) and Bunis (1981, doctoral dissertation). This last work analyzes the Hebrew and Aramaic components of Judezmo (Bunis prefers this term over "Judeo-Spanish"). A similar interest is shown by the study of Benvenisti (1985). The Judezmo of specific areas has been analyzed in the following studies: Sala (1971), Bucharest; Revah (1970), the Balkans; Stankiewitz (1964) on Balkan and Slavic elements in Yugoslavian Judezmo; Sephiha (1973b), Turkey; Berger (1971–78), proverbs from Sarajevo and Hungarian parallels; Bentolila (1985) on the Hebrew component of Moroccan Judeo-Spanish, also called *hakitia*. On Sephardic music and ballads, we can cite the study of I. Katz (1980), which has bibliographical information; the collections of Larrea Palacín (1952, 1954); Algazi (1958); I. Levy (1959); Armistead (1982) on ballad research; Armistead and Silverman

(1971a, 1971b, 1981); their study on Christian elements in the *romancero* (1965); and a critical bibliography, 1970–75, by Armistead and Carracedo (1978). The linguistic features of the Judeo-Spanish romances are appraised by Weich-Shahak (1985).

A doctoral dissertation by Hirsch (1951) describes a Jewish-Spanish dialect spoken by a Sephardic family in New York. The entire state of research in Judezmo in America has been reviewed by Reider (1978), who provides a bibliography, including the studies of Besso (1951, 1952, 1963). Besso (1980) has compiled a bibliography of 145 items on Jewish-Spanish proverbs. Problems of writing and transliteration of Judezmo are discussed by Halio-Torres (1980).

Schwarzwald (1981c) cites evidence for a general rule among eastern Sephardic communities (primarily Salonica) of treating *ᶜayin* as ∅ or *alef* when reading the Bible (not so, however, among old families in Jerusalem or Safed) and pronouncing it as [x] in prayers and fused words, e.g., [yodeax lašon] (*yôdēᶜa lāšôn*) 'one who knows the language,' i.e., a non-Jew who understands Judeo-Spanish; [rašax] (*rāšāᶜ*) 'wicked'; [yeṣer arax] (*yēṣer hāraᶜ*) 'the evil inclination.' This rule, however applies only to the occurrence of *ᶜayin* in closed syllables. Schwarzwald (1982a) discusses the methods of fusing Hebrew words into Judeo-Spanish (her preferred term) and the way words acquired expanded meanings. She assesses the quantity of Hebrew words in Judeo-Spanish (1981–82a) and discusses Hebrew in Judeo-Spanish as a means of concealment (1981–82b). She treats the question of the morphology of Hebrew words in Judeo-Spanish (1985a) and the fusion of the Hebrew–Aramaic component (1985b). Surveying different translations of *Pirkei Avot* (1986) she finds evidence of different dialects.

T. K. Harris (1979, doctoral dissertation) discusses the prognosis for Judeo-Spanish, its present status, survival, and decline in the light of the general study of language death. Malinowski (1979, doctoral dissertation) analyzes contemporary Judeo-Spanish in Israel, basing his work on oral and written sources.

Judezmo of Portuguese Marranos

Szajkowski (1964b) raises the issue of a distinctive Judezmo of the Portuguese Marranos. In contrast to Cecil Roth, who claimed that Marranos assigned a higher prestige to Portuguese while they themselves spoke Spanish, Szajkowski maintains that it is often difficult to establish a dividing line between the two tongues. The Marranos of Saint-Esprit-les-Bayonne pronounced their Spanish words differently from those in Bordeaux. In the Bayonne synagogue some songs were sung in Basque. In summary, Szajkowski concludes that the linguistic monuments of the Sephardim in these areas are too unreliable to answer the question of a distinctive speech. Now, however, Wexler (1985) has contributed a detailed study of various forms of Judeo-Portugese, including Peninsular Judeo-Portugese, Marrano-Portugese, and the influence of the latter upon other languages, such as South-American Creole languages.

JUDEO-ITALIAN AND JUDEO-FRENCH

Judeo-Italian dialects

Jochnowitz (1978) describes the current study being done in Judeo-Italian (*Italkian*), Judeo-Provencal, and Judeo-French. The pronunciation of Hebrew by Italian speakers has been described by E. Artom (1947). In Leghorn the dialect is called *bagito* [bažíto], while in Ferara it is referred to as *ghettaiolo*. Modern Judeo-Italian often adds Italian prefixes and suffixes to Hebrew and Aramaic roots and retains the voiceless fricative [x], e.g., [šaxtare] 'to slaughter,' [paxadoso] 'timid.' The velar nasal consonant is retained in the initial position, as in [ŋarel] 'non-Jew.' Other features appear in various dialects from other geographic areas and a good deal of diversity exists between the dialects spoken in different cities. The earliest texts have been described by Alan Freedman in his edition of Italian texts in Hebrew characters (1972). The immediate tasks of research are the gathering of language examples from living speakers and the study of linguistic geography.

Jochnowitz (1974) has also studied derivations from Hebrew and Romance in Judeo-Italian. Cuomo (1974, doctoral dissertation) sees in the vulgar glosses in the *ʿArukh* of Rabbi Nathan ben Yehiel of Rome an expression of the particularism of the earlier period of the Middle Ages as opposed to the *koine* which characterized the later Jewish culture in southern Italy. Her study of the glosses in the Parma manuscript of the Mishnah, De Rossi 138 (1977, summarized in Sarfatti 1981), shows that they reflect the dialect of Salento in southern Italy and that the manuscript dates from the eleventh century. Sermoneta (1971) has written a general survey of Judeo-Italian, and a study (1985) of bilingual prose and poetry of Italian Jews; and Crown (1976–77), Sermoneta (1978), and M. Artom (1980) discuss Hebrew transcriptions of Italian.

Hebrew words in Italian

An interesting source of Hebrew words is literary works from medieval and early modern Italy. Hebrew words from these sources reflect the contact of non-Jews with Jews in the ghettos, especially those associated with money-lending, and reveal a satirical and mocking attitude toward them. Such Hebrew-derived words may have been distorted in the transmission. In addition, then, to *Amen*, *Osanna*, *Alleluia*, *Messiah* (words from the sphere of religion) there are other Hebrew words, such as *Jochodimmi* (*Y^{e}hûdîm*) 'Jews,' *tavarre* (*dāḇār*) 'a thing,' *bassare* (*bāśār*) 'meat,' *Merdochai* (*Morḏ^{e}ḵai*), *Baruchaba* (*bārûḵ ha-bāʾ*) 'blessed is he who comes.' Mordecai was distorted into various forms, in addition to *Merdochai*, and appeared as *Menacai* and *Smerdacai*. From the sphere of money-lending there is *moskon* (*maškôn*) 'pledge, surety.' From the present-day Venetian dialect come the phrases *zucca santa*, *suca baruca* 'holy squash, blessed squash,' the last word deriving from *bārûḵ* or *b^{e}rûḵāh* 'blessed.' This information is presented in a study by Fortis (1977–78).

Fortis and Zolli (1979) have studied the Judeo-Venetian dialect, comparing it with other Judeo-Italian dialects from the point of view of phonology, morphology and etymology. M. Bar-Asher (1980b) studies the tradition of Mishnaic Hebrew in fourteenth-century Italy, based unique morphological structures in the Paris manuscript 328–29. The bibliography of Luzzatto and Moldavi (1982) contains entries on linguistics.

Judeo-French dialects

The department (governmental region) of Vaucluse in southern France corresponds generally to the old area called the Comtat-Venaissin. The dialect was described by Szajkowski (1948). It is also called "Judeo-Provencal," but it is distinct from the dialect spoken by the Jews of Nice. Some of its early literature is listed by Jochnowitz (1978), who also discusses the phonology. Voiced intervocalic fricatives either unvoice (*juge* > *chuche*), become stops (*travalha* > *trabalha*), or change in other ways. The Hebrew letters *s*, *ś*, *t* are all realized as [f], suggesting that there was an early θ stage. In distinction to this dialect, Judeo-French is called "Zarphatic." The earliest texts are the glosses of Menachem bar Helbo and Pseudo-Gershom from the eleventh century. Bilingual Hebrew-Zarphatic songs for weddings have been described by Blondheim (*REJ* 82 [1926] 379–93) (Jochnowitz 1978: 69–71).

French influence upon Rashi

Banitt (1968a) has demonstrated French influence on Rashi's biblical commentary. The semantic range of the French word used to translate a Hebrew word makes possible another, extended meaning, which is then translated into Hebrew and offered as one of several interpretations of a word. French influence extends to the change of gender of Hebrew nouns. The particle *še* is used widely, due to the influence of French *que*. There are loan translations, such as *šaʾal ʾel* 'asked of' < *demander à*, and *ṭaʿan ʾeṯ*), Hebrew *ʾāz* 'then' is used in the sense of *ʾim* 'if' < alors, *ʾaḥar* 'after' for *l*^{e}*p̱î* 'because' < après, and *ʾaḥărê ʾăšer* 'after that' for *kēwān* 'since.' The implication is that the Bible was studied by a translation method.

Sarfatti (1972–73) maintains that Rashi used French words for something more than mere clarification of the Hebrew, intending also to show that certain linguistic features were common to both languages, e.g., verbs of complaint are reflexive; a collective noun is formed from the singular; there are similar extensions of meaning, e.g., 'hear' > 'understand'; denominative verbs can be privative; and the infinite absolute corresponds to the French participle or *gérondif.* Rashi as exegete has been treated by Pereira-Mendoza (1940), Shereshevsky (1957), and by Y. Avinery in his encyclopedia, *Hekhal Rashi* (1940ff.). The glosses were earlier studied by Darmesteter (1909), and more recent work on the subject of glosses has been done by Banitt (1968b = 1969, 1972, 1986). Melamed (1975, 1:357–448) provides comprehensive listing of Rashi's various exegetical methods and grammatical ideas, including the Old French glosses.

Rashi's exegetical methods

R. Levy (1964) has produced a very useful and thorough study of the language used by the French Jews in the Middle Ages, a work reviewed by Kukenheim (1967), who, there and elsewhere (1963), has rejected the idea that there ever existed a distinctive Judeo-French which could be compared to Yiddish. Bibliographical material on Jews in France has been assembled by Blumenkranz (1974, with M. Levy), and the printed works of medieval authors in France are catalogued by Blumenkranz (1975, with Dahan and Kerner). The article by Amzalak in *EJ* (1971) is a survey of the general field of Judeo-French.

Divergent views on status of Judeo-French

Jochnowitz (1978: 71) discusses the various views of Blondheim, Max Weinreich, and Banitt on the reality of Jewish dialects in the Middle Ages and their interrelation. Banitt (*RLR* 27 [1963] 245–94), like Kukenheim (1963, 1967), denies that there was a French-Jewish speech, arguing that words found in texts in support of such a speech may have been invented for the sake of translation. Blondheim and Weinreich, however, maintain that there was a common origin for the various dialects of Judeo-Romance. Agus (1974) has also expressed the view that *laʿaz*, spoken by the Jews in the Middle Ages, was a Judeo-Latin dialect. One piece of evidence for a common origin going back to the Roman Empire is the word *meltare*, *meldar*, Judeo-French *melder*, *miauder*, and *mader*, with meanings in various localities that include 'teach, study, read'; this word had its origin in Septuagint *meletaō* for Hebrew *hāgāh* 'to meditate.' It is not of Hebrew origin and yet appears in all the dialects. A brief article on the Judeo-Greek dialect has been written by Dalven (1971, in *EJ*). Diament (1979) discusses the possibility that the language of the troubadours reveals an underlying Hebrew semantic-syntactic structure.

HEBREW IN SPAIN

Phonology of Hebrew in medieval Spain

An important study by Garbell (1954) presents data concerning the pronunciation of Hebrew in medieval Spain, both Christian and Moslem. For example, *q* was represented in Moorish Spain by the corresponding Arabic letter, but in Christian Spain by a sound midway between unvoiced [k] and voiced [g]. In Castille, Portugal, and Catalonia, final *m* was realized as [n], e.g., [Abran, Abrahen] (Abraham). Throughout the peninsula *r* was a voiced alveolar consonant. The consonant *ṣ* was realized in Christian Spain and Catalonia as [z], e.g., the name [Zag] (*Yiṣḥāq*, Isaac). In Moorish Spain the final *t* was realized as [th], but in Christian Spain it was realized in various ways, [th, t, d, s, z], e.g., [vacasot] 'requests' (*baqqāšô<u>t</u>*), [Sabad] 'Sabbath,' [besdin] 'court' (*bē<u>t</u> dîn*), [malçinuç] 'slander' (*malšinû<u>t</u>*), and [lelezmuroz] 'a night of watching,' i.e., the first night of Passover, (*lēl ʾašmûrô<u>t</u>, lēl šimmûrîm*). In Christian Spain the consonant *š* was realized [s], and *b* after *l* was spirantized. Final consonants could be dropped. These and other phenomena are illustrated by the following examples: [malvise] 'those who clothe' (*malbîšê*), [Sento(th)] 'good name,' used as a personal name (Shem Tov), [Yago] (Yaʿaqov) and [tisabaf] 'the ninth day of Av' (*tishʿah beʾav*).

A Jewish Basque bibliography has been published in *JLR* 1 (1981): 127–32 and *JLR* 2 (1982): 95–97. Zimmels (1958), in his general study of the differences between Ashkenazim and Sephardim, includes many references of interest regarding pronunciation, grammar, and script (1958: 82–98).

HEBREW IN THE ASHKENAZIC MILIEU

Medieval Ashkenazic pronunciation of Hebrew

Yalon (1937b, 1942a, 1942b) established that Sephardic pronunciation was used in France in the eleventh century, the period of the commentator Rashi. Kimchi, in his commentary on Judg 12:6, the famous shibboleth incident, informs us that the French Jews pronounce *š* as an aspirated *<u>t</u>*, that is, as [th], and speculates that this raising of the tongue to the upper teeth may have been due to climactic conditions. Gumpertz (1942–43) has reconstructed Hebrew pronunciation in medieval France. On the basis of transcriptions in a French translation of Ibn Ezra's *Reshit ḥokhmah* from 1273, and of the Latin transcription of the disputation involving Rabbi Yehiel of Paris in 1240, the following facts can be noted: [x] represented *s*, e.g., [hameoraxa] for *hame'ōrāsāh* 'the one who is betrothed'; *š* was pronounced as [s], e.g., [hamforas] for *hamepôrāš* 'special, clearly expressed' (used to refer to the Tetragrammaton); *y* was palatalized and realized as [g], e.g., [gessivah] for *yešîḇāh* 'house of study'; and *d* without *dagesh* was pronounced as [z], e.g., [senhezerim] for *Sanhedrin*. Gumpertz's study (1942–43) reappears in his collected essays, and the pronunciation of *y* and *š* is dealt with there at greater length (1953: 1–86). Habermann (1975) also discusses medieval German Hebrew.

Transliteration and vocalization as evidence for medieval Ashkenazic Hebrew

Merchaviah (1964–65) has observed the following features in the transliteration of Hebrew in a thirteenth-century Latin manuscript: the pronunciation is Sephardic, final vowels are dropped off because of French influence, the letter *z* can represent Hebrew *z*, *ṣ*, *d*, *s*, *š*, and the *š* is not consistently transliterated. Beit-Arié, in a masters thesis (1964) and in an article (1964–65), notes that the vocalization of the *Worms Maḥzor* resembles that of the Kaufmann manuscript of the Mishnah, demonstrating again that the "Sephardic" pronunciation was current in Germany until the fourteenth or fifteenth century.

Tiberian and non-Tiberian vocalizations

The work of Eldar (1974–75, 1976, 1977, 1978) on the vocalization of Ashkenazic *maḥzorim* of the twelfth and thirteenth centuries leads to the following description of the linguistic situation of Ashkenazic Jewry. There were three types of Tiberian vocalization in use: 1) the "orthodox" type, rather close to the Tiberian vocalization of the Bible; 2) the "popular" type, in which Tiberian graphemes were used, but with considerable deviation from the norm, reflecting local pronunciation ("our vocalization"); and 3) the "average" type, somewhere in between types 1 and 2 in its adherence to Tiberian norms and variation from them due to local pronunciations. There was also a modified form of the Palestinian-Tiberian vocalization.

When Ashkenazic Jewry felt the need for a vocalization system, around the middle of the twelfth century, both the Tiberian and the Palestinian-Tiberian systems were available. The latter corresponded to the vowel system of Ashkenazic Jews, called "Southwest" by M. Weinreich (1954) and "Sephardic" by I. Eldar

(1974–75), but the high status of the Tiberian system made it a competitor to the Palestinian-Tiberian. The conflict between the two lasted for about a hundred years. The Tiberian system prevailed for two reasons: the influence of Sephardic scholars and the changes in Hebrew pronunciation toward the "Ashkenazic." These changes were due to the influence of Jewish-German and French, the spoken languages, and included diphthongization of *ḥolem* and *shureq*, the shift from *qamets gadol* to *ḥolem*, and the pronunciation of *š* as [s].

A classic source on the different vocalization systems is the statement in the commentary on *Abot* included in *Maḥzor Viṭri* (twelfth century, France; ed. S. Hurwitz [Berlin, 1893], 462): "therefore Tiberian vocalization does not resemble our vocalization, and neither of them resembles Palestinian vocalization." Kahle, Yellin, and Klar have identified "our vocalization" with the Babylonian supralinear; Allony (1963–64; 1971–72: 368) considered it to be Palestinian-Tiberian. Eldar (1974–75: 210–11; 1978: xx–xxiii) identifies "Palestinian" with the Palestinian-Tiberian and "our vocalization" with a local French pronunciation (Ms. Sassoon 535; the Haggadah of *Maḥzor Viṭri*).

Hebrew of responsa: evidence of German and Judeo-German influence

Linguistic interference in the Hebrew of medieval responsa is documented by Heilprin (1946–47) and Kahana (1946–47). Heilprin shows that *kippāh* 'vaulted ceiling' also means 'wine cellar,' from German *Gewölbe*; that Hebrew *ʾôrēaḥ* 'guest' means 'traveling merchant' and *bᵉriḥāh* 'flight' has the extended meaning of 'bankruptcy.' The sources of these developments are varied, some reflecting German influence and others the influence of Talmudic and pietistic texts. Kahana shows that *ḥāṯaḵ* 'cut' is used for 'deduct,' influenced by Arabic *qaṭaʿa* 'cut, deduct,' and that *hilbîš ʾôṯām hammāʿôṯ* 'invested the money with them' (lit. 'he dressed them with the money') reflects the same development as 'invest' from the Latin or is a calque. Other examples are: *maʾămār* 'statement' in the sense of 'decree'; *diglạn* 'flag-bearer' for 'office,' from German *Fähnrich*; and *sᵉṯiyyaṯ heʿāšān* 'the drinking of smoke,' based on Arabic *ṯaraba* 'drink, smoke.' Schapira (1955–56) has studied the sources of words for whiskey and alcohol, and in several studied (1959–60, 1961–62, 1962–64) discusses chemical and technical terms in traditional sources. P. Doron (1964, masters thesis) studies terms for realia in seventeenth and eighteenth century responsa. Ratzhaby (1981–82) further considers the linguistic aspects of the responsa literature. Kaddari (1984, 1985a) surveys the use of *mammāš* 'really' and *mikkol māqôm* 'nevertheless, however' in this literature as instances of possible Yiddish influence on Hebrew.

Rabin (1968a) has dealt with the Hebrew of *Sefer ḥasidim*; Azar (1966) deals with the verb and Kogut (1968) with conditional sentences, both in masters theses also dealing with *Sefer ḥasidim*. Kogut (1980, 1984a, 1984b) finds in *Sefer ḥasidim* many expressions which are commonly thought to have originated in modern Hebrew. E. Goldenberg (1971) observes the following Germanic influences on Hebrew: *raq* 'only, but' < German *nur*, and *ᶜāśāh ᶜăḇērāh* 'sinned,' as against Mishnaic Hebrew *ᶜāḇar ᶜăḇērāh*. This is due to German constructions with *machen*. Simonsohn (1974) discusses the Hebrew revival among early medieval Jews, Agus (1974) treats the languages spoken by Askhenazic Jews in the High Middle Ages, and Habermann (1975) gives examples from medieval Germany. Noble (1958–59) has documented translation loanwords from Yiddish in rabbinic Hebrew. S. Reif's study of Shabbethai Sofer includes material on variant traditions of vocalization in the sixteenth and seventeenth centuries (1979: 29–38). A masters thesis by Ring (1971) illustrates linguistic innovations in the record books of the Council of the Four Lands, and a masters thesis by K. Katz (1968) treats the phonology of the reading of the Mishnah by Lithuanian Jews.

Early evidence of the Ashkenazic pronunciation

Some early evidence of Ashkenazic Hebrew pronunciation is evaluated in Altbauer's study (1977b) of Hebrew elements in Cyrillian transcription from the first half of the sixteenth century. These were transcribed by the Byelorussian scholar, Francisk Skorina (1485–1540). It is clear that certain features of Ashkenazic pronunciation are present, the *qamets* realized as [o] e.g., *orets* 'land,' and *ṯ* realized as [s], e.g., *umibes* 'and from the house of.' However, Altbauer concludes that Skorina did not really know Hebrew and that he was influenced by earlier materials from which he copied, among them the transcriptions of Origen and Jerome. Thus, not all his transcriptions have value in reconstructing phonology. For example, one finds alongside *Breshis* 'Genesis' the form *Bresshif*. The last consonant is Cyrillic Ф, the direct continuant of Greek φ. Skorina's transcription contains palatalized consonants and an unlikely, unmasoretic realization of *t* as [s], e.g., *umimoljadesekho* 'and from your birthplace.' Since the Cyrillic alphabet can express [š] by Ш instead of [s], which Latin and Greek could not, we find *Breshis* 'Genesis' and *Moshe* 'Moses.' However, we also find forms like *sira sirim* 'the Song of Songs' (*šîr haššîrîm*). It might be thought that this is evidence of the pronunciation of *š* as [s] in parts of Lithuania (see U. Weinreich, "Sabesdiker losn," in *Word* 8 [1952] 360–77). This possibility is ruled out by Altbauer, however, since Skorina was influenced by

Jerome, who transliterated *sir assirim* for 'Song of Songs.' Actually it is in material of Czech origin that we find the first attestations of Ashkenazic pronunciation in Slavic sources.

THE STUDY OF YIDDISH AND ITS RELATIONSHIP TO HEBREW

Basic resources on Yiddish

Current surveys of the situation in Yiddish studies, as well as important bibliographies, may be found in works by Althaus (1972), Shmeruk (1978), U. Weinreich (1971), Herzog (1978), and Prager (1974). It is impossible to list here all the relevant bibliographical entries in the field. A bibliography of Yiddish language and folklore was compiled by U. and B. Weinreich (1959), covering the period up to 1958. The subsequent items are available in the proceedings of the Modern Language Association. Recently, three important bibliographical contributions have appeared: Bratkowsky (1981), a comprehensive multilingual bibliography of 2,000 items published between 1959–73; Bunis (1981a), a classified bilingual index to Yiddish serials and collections, 1913–58; and Prager (1982), an annotated bibliography of Yiddish literary and linguistic periodicals. The survey article by J. A. Fishman (1981b) on the sociology of Yiddish is important for the text as well as the bibliography, and the volume *Never Say Die*, edited by Fishman (1981a), is a collection of Yiddish and English articles, also on the sociology of Yiddish. Articles in the field of Yiddish studies are found in the periodicals *Yiddish shprakh*, *Zukunft*, and *Yivo Bleter*.

The studies of M. and U. Weinreich

M. Weinreich has made a major contribution in his four-volume history of the Yiddish language (1973, Yiddish; translated by S. Noble with J. A. Fishman, 1980). This work is the culmination of M. Weinreich's numerous and influential publications, including the following: 1931, 1936, 1938, 1953, 1954, 1954–55, 1956a, 1956b, 1958, 1959a, 1959b, 1960, 1963–64, 1967). His distinguished son, Uriel Weinreich, contributed further to the field with his significant research, which includes the following publications: 1954b, 1956, 1959–61, 1961–62, 1964, 1969, as well as his textbook, *College Yiddish* (1949), and his dictionary (1968).

Additional resources

Additional important material is collected in the four volumes of *FY* (vol. 1, ed. by U. Weinreich, 1954a; vol. 2, idem, 1965; vol. 3, edited by M. Herzog, W. Ravid, and U. Weinreich, 1969; and vol. 4, edited by M. Herzog, B. Kirshenblatt-Gimblett, D. Meron, and R. Wisse, 1980) and also in *For Max Weinreich on His Seventieth Birthday* (London/The Hague, 1964). The *Great Dic-*

tionary of the Yiddish Language, edited from vols. 1 to 4 by the late Yudel Mark, is now under the direction of M. I. Herzog, assisted by M. Schaechter and, in Jerusalem, by W. Moskovitch and M. Wolf. There are also two important volumes by Shmeruk (1978, 1981) which stress literary-linguistic relationships. S. Wolf (1962) has compiled a dictionary, and there are surveys by S. Birnbaum, a brief one (1974) and a detailed survey and grammar (1979). The latter study (1979: 3–189) surveys developments in dialect, the pronunciation of Hebrew as witnessed by Yiddish, and provides examples of the various dialects.

M. Weinreich's magnum opus (1973, 2.386–96) divided the history of Yiddish into periods: two phases of earliest Yiddish, up to 1250; Old Yiddish (1250–1500); Middle Yiddish (1500–1700); and Modern Yiddish (1700 to the present). M. Weinreich also stressed that the major influence on Yiddish was the traditional Jewish way of life, *derekh hashas* (1953, 1967).

Views on the evolution of the language map

Dominating the field is M. Weinreich's view that the far-reaching phonological correspondences in Yiddish are due to a successive series of *Stammbaum* splits. His view was that a system of protovowels was subjected to various processes of lengthening, diphthongization, etc. Herzog (1978), however, suggests that correspondences on the language map of Yiddish are the result of successive convergent developments. Under favorable conditions of communication, the persistence of dialect boundaries—not their elimination—is unusual enough to require explanation.

Earliest evidence of Yiddish

The earliest evidences of Yiddish are names on tombstones and in martyrologies from 1096, as well as a rhymed couplet inserted in a Hebrew prayerbook from Worms dating from 1272 (Herzog 1978). The earliest Yiddish literature is surveyed by Shmeruk (1978: 9–71) in terms of its social importance relative to Hebrew. Yiddish was able to occupy a place in areas in which tradition had not already enthroned Hebrew or for people who did not study Hebrew and Talmud, for example, women. Thus, there were popular hymns written in both Hebrew and Yiddish, and others, for special occasions, in Yiddish. The movement to write manuals of Jewish law in Yiddish was resisted by some, but it did bear fruit. Romances current in the non-Jewish world were translated into Yiddish, with some modification of objectionable content. There were voices, however, that protested against the secular and non-religious nature of the material.

Shmeruk (1978: 9–10) also cites the rhyme already alluded to in Herzog's work. It appears in the spaces of heading letters in the *Worms Maḥzor*, a symbolic picture of the position of Yiddish at that time. It reads: *gut tag/ihm btage/s ʾvayr dies maḥzor in bēṯ hakk^{e}neseṯ trage*, 'a good day will shine upon him who carries this *maḥzor* to the synagogue.' The dating of the *Maḥzor* to 1272 is based on Ernst Roth, ed., *Die alte Synagoge zu Worms* (Frankfurt aM, 1961) 217–26. There are plans to publish a limited facsimile edition of the *Worms Maḥzor* (Cyelar Publishing Co., London, and the Jewish National and University Library, Jerusalem), with a commentary volume including articles on liturgy by E. Fleischer, on linguistics by I. Eldar, and Yiddish linguistics by Jacob Allerhand. M. Goldwasser (1973) discusses the sixteenth century text, *Azhoras noshim*. Gealia (1980) has written on the oldest Yiddish biblical glosses, and Turniansky discusses bilingualism in Ashkenazic society (1980).

Studies and editions: medieval Yiddish compositions

Fuks (1954) writes about a Yiddish manuscript from the University Library of Cambridge, originally in the Cairo Geniza, which he considers to be the oldest extant Yiddish manuscript. It contains the epic poems *Moses*, *Paradise*, the *Patriarch Abraham*, *Pious Joseph*, the *Duke Horant*, and the *Fable of a Dying Lion*. It also includes a list of pentateuchal sections and a glossary of stones on the breastplate of the High Priest. The manuscript was published by Fuks (1957), who maintains that it contains material with a *terminus ad quem* of 1382 and that the manuscript is evidence of the existence of a Yiddish-speaking group in Egypt in the fourteenth century. This manuscript is discussed by Shmeruk (1978: 28–39), with attention to the internal and external forces operating in literature of this type, in which external material is translated and slightly modified so as not to offend Jewish religious sensibilities. M. Weinreich (1960) has written on old Yiddish poetry. Giniger (1954b) has a brief article on the story of *Duke Horant*, Althaus (1971) has produced a critical edition of the *Fable of the Lion*, and Dreesen (1971) and Matenko and Sloan (1968) have treated the sixteenth century epic, *ʿAqedat Yitshaq* (*The Binding of Isaac*). Sadan (1965b) has demonstrated the dependence of the *Paradise* epic on midrashic material, showing its inspiration to be internal, not external. A doctoral dissertation by J. A. Howard (1972) deals with problems of old Yiddish literature. An old Yiddish midrash to *Ethics of the Fathers* has been published by Maitlis (1979).

Shmeruk (1981: 89–104) discusses at length the *Bovo Bukh* of Elijah Levità (Eliyahu Bachur, 1468/69–1549), and a doctoral dissertation by J. C. Smith (1968) also deals with this subject. Levità's use of the Italian *ottava rima* is discussed by Shmeruk (1978: 100–101) in light of the research of Hrushovski (1964).

There were other early documents as well. A study by Shazar (1929, reprinted 1971) shows that religious court documents which recorded oral testimony are valuable as evidence for early Yiddish. S. Birnbaum (1965) cites examples of Yiddish from eight centuries. Yiddish poems from the Geniza are treated in a doctoral dissertation by E. Katz (1963).

Relationships of German and Yiddish

Opinions are divided on the relationship of Yiddish and German. M. Weinreich (1954–55) held that the Jews retreated from the Roman empire under the pressure of the invading Germanic tribes and did not return until four hundred years later. Thus, they played no part in the development of the German language. Marchand (1965), however, holds that Jewish settlement in Germany was unbroken during this period and that German and Yiddish development should be considered together. Bin–Nun (1973) discusses the relationships of Yiddish and Germanic dialects.

Which Hebrew dialect entered Yiddish?

The early history of Yiddish casts light on Hebrew phonetics during the same period, as demonstrated in studied by M. Weinreich (1954, 1963–64), U. Weinreich (159–61, 1961–62), and Altbauer (1968). M. Weinreich (1954) distinguished between "whole Hebrew," that is, liturgical and learned Hebrew which has been affected by the vernacular, and "merged Hebrew," which has been absorbed into Yiddish and has surrendered to the general phonologic and morphological system as a whole. He distinguished three basic systems of vowels: 1) Eastern (Babylonian): *i, e, ē, o, ō, u* 2) Northwest (Tiberian): *i, e, ē, a, o, ō, u*; and 3) Southwest (South Palestinian): *i, e, a, ō, u* (but now see Revell 1970b). The present Ashkenazi pronunciation is based on the northwest system, but at an earlier period, the southwest, that is, the "Sephardic," prevailed. Thus certain words entered Hebrew with Sephardic pronunciation, e.g., [yam] 'ocean' (not *yām*) and [xaver] 'friend' (not *ḥāḇēr*; Waldman 1975a: 1305–6). These questions are treated in greater depth in M. Weinreich (1963–64) and U. Weinreich (1959–61, 1961–62).

The Hebrew component of Yiddish

Mark (1954), in a preliminary report, found that hebraisms constituted no more than 5.38% of Yiddish vocabulary. This surprisingly low figure, contrasted with earlier estimates of 10 to 20%, reflects the fact that a different method of tabulation was used; earlier, only words with lexical content were counted and connecting words were overlooked. The results also vary with the type of text, since more Hebrew was used in Hasidic and folk tales. Poetry after World War II has more hebraisms, due to the poets' search for more refined and abstruse words. Mark (1958) surveys numerous words and expressions that were created in the Yiddish environment, some of which are new Hebrew words formed according to the rules of Hebrew word-formation while others are Hebrew-sounding words which are purely Yiddish in origin. Examples of the first category are: *qabṣān* 'beggar,' *šadḵān* 'marriage-broker,' *hanhālāh* 'leadership, management' (now used in modern Hebrew). Examples of the second category are: *baᶜal dabrān* 'talker,' *baᶜal mᵉḥabbēr* 'author,' and many combinations with *baᶜal*, used in a manner inconsistent with Hebrew usage. Unger (1968) also surveys the incorporation of Hebrew words into folk literature, in this case, the genre of wonder tales.

Herzog (1965a: 271) has taken issue with the commonly held view that every Hebrew word is potentially a Yiddish word. Based on a study of M. Weinreich, he notes that there is an unpredictable diversity in phonological and grammatical forms. The variability of Hebrew words conforms to common geographical distribution patterns and is not related to the origin of the words; e.g., *tōmid* 'always' < Hebrew *tāmíd*, in Poland a southern isogloss (see *ibid.*, fig. 3:38). Noble (1958) notes the influence of the vernacular on the Hebrew language of the Jews in the form of loanwords and loan translations. The process of borrowing was set into motion by dynamic changes, such as the dislocation of Jewish life in the wake of the Crusades. In another study (1964) Noble surveys hebraisms in the Yiddish of seventeenth-century Ashkenaz (primarily Bohemia), showing that almost one-half of the words were of Hebrew-Aramaic origin. The terminology of kinship is almost entirely derived from this source, and the technical language of business is heavily influenced. The evidence shows that among men the proportion of words derived from Hebrew or Aramaic was greater, but in Eastern Ashkenaz (Poland, Russia) the incidence of vocabulary of Hebrew origin was not as frequent. A recent study by Matisoff (1979) treats psycho-ostensive expressions in Yiddish: expressions of blessing, curse, hope, and fear. These are described and classified in terms of their syntax. Szulmajster (1980) studies linguistic structures in Yiddish popular songs, with a focus on the Slavic, non-Germanic elements.

Socio-linguistics of the Hebrew component

King (1980) studies the problem of final devoicing in Yiddish and its various dialects, revising and updating an early suggestion by Edward Sapir and Max Weinreich. The initial cause of the loss of final devoicing in Yiddish is related to the loss of final *-e*. This change took place in Yiddish between 1400 and 1500. With apocope, final devoicing became opaque and finally was lost altogether. Wexler (1980) is concerned with the problem of the adaptation of Semitic verbal material by a non-Semitic language.

He compares Turkish with germanic and slavicized Yiddish. His conclusions are that Arabic verbal nouns are productively borrowed by Turkish, while Yiddish makes scant use of Hebrew verbal nouns in periphrastic constructions. Both Yiddish and Turkish tend to borrow only one form of the Semitic participle rather than active-passive pairs.

Yiddish and Turkish compared

Much work has been done on the various dialects of Yiddish evident on the linguistic map. Birnbaum (1954) has provided evidence that Eastern Yiddish is based on two German dialects, the Thuringian Upper Saxonian dialect of the Central German group, and the Bavarian-Austrian dialect of the Upper German group. Yiddish derived the shortening of vowels from the first group, e.g., *lozn* 'to let,' Middle High German *lâzen*) and mutated forms such as *glaiben* 'believe' (Middle High German *gelöuben*). From the second group it derived the *l*-diminutive, e.g., *baiml* 'a little tree' and the insertion of *d* between *n* and *l*, e.g., *ḥazendl* 'a little cantor.' Birnbaum provides a full list of features and suggests that Jewish emigrants to Poland came from both areas. Joffe (1954) dates the formation of the Polish-Ukrainian dialect to the fourth decade of the eighteenth century. In various studies, Guggenheim-Grünberg (1954, 1958, 1961, 1964, 1965, 1969, 1973, 1976, 1980) has studied western Yiddish dialects. Alsatian proverbs are collected in A. Zivy, ed. (1966). Beem (1954) traces the development and demise of Yiddish in Holland, also publishing lists of the surviving Yiddish words and proverbs in the speech of Dutch Jews (1959, 1974). Devries (1961) examines the Hebrew element in Netherlands Yiddish, while Hutterer (1969) deals with theoretical problems of Western Yiddish. Althaus (1973) applies comparative dialectology to Western Yiddish and German.

Various Yiddish dialects

Other area studies include: Beranek (1958) on Pinsk Yiddish and (1965) an atlas of Western Yiddish; Herzog (1964, 1965a) on Polish Yiddish and dialect boundaries; J. Jofen's *The Linguistic Atlas of Eastern European Yiddish* (New York, 1964; reviewed by Herzog, 1965b) and her doctoral dissertation (1953) on the dialectic makeup of East European Yiddish. Yiddish in Canada is treated by Thiessen (1973), and F. Manfred Klarberg (1970) has done a study of the Yiddish of Australia.

The Arabic element in the Yiddish of the old Yishuv in Palestine is treated in a volume by Kosover (1966), and the position of Yiddish in Israel is surveyed by J. and D. Fishman (1974, 1978). Gris discusses the Yiddish elements in "Ivrit" (1968), and Blanc (1965) examines Yiddish influences in Israeli Hebrew. Studies on Jewish-Slavic language contact include Wexler (1964),

Yiddish contact with other languages

Altbauer (1972, 1977a), Gold (1978c), and Gold and Orenstein (1976). A doctoral dissertation by Bratkowsky (1974) is concerned with bilingual dialectology.

Noble, in his doctoral dissertation (1940), dealt with the survival of Middle High and Early High German in Judeo-German Bible translations. Shmeruk (1979) has published Yiddish plays on biblical themes from the period of 1697–1750. Copeland and Susskind (1976) have studied the dialect of a later play, Joseph Herz's *Esther*, which first appeared in 1828 and was reissued in 1858. The play, written for a generation of German Jews in transition, undergoing the struggle for acceptance into German society, reflects the linguistic aspect of that ambivalent situation. The commentary by Copeland and Susskind is a most informative study of phonological, lexical, and sociological factors in language. Herz created an inauthentic dialect for humorous effect. High German is used when Herz is serious. Esther speaks to Jews in Yiddish and to the king in German, but the king always speaks in High German. In the notes it is explained that hebraisms may have been used for euphemisms but that Slavic languages were the source of vulgarisms. A Hebrew word used in Yiddish would also tend to have a strong emotional effect.

Socio-linguistic factors

Volumes 2 and 3 of *The Field of Yiddish* are replete with dialect and geographical studies. Leibel (1965) treats Ashkenazic stress, M. Weinreich (1965) discusses the dynamic of dialect formation, Trost (1965) treats Yiddish in Bohemia and Moravia, Garvin (1965) studies the dialect geography of Hungarian Yiddish, Hutterer (1965) the phonology of Budapest Yiddish, Lowenstein (1969) reports on linguistic mapping investigations among German Jews, Zuckerman (1969) explores Alsatian Yiddish, Herzog (1969) Ukrainian Yiddish, U. Weinreich (1969) Belorussian Yiddish, M. Wolf (1969) the geography of case and gender variations in Yiddish, and Green (1969) the accentual variants in the Slavic component of Yiddish.

Recent studies in Yiddish linguistics

The collection of studies, *The Field of Yiddish* 4 (1980), contains a number of studies in Yiddish linguistics. Waletzky (1980) treats contextual stress in Yiddish, discussing the relation "topic-of the sentence," which is the analog in surface structure of the relation "subject-of the sentence" in deep structure. The notion of "topicalized sentence" is, in his opinion, a general one, applicable to sentences of discourse, matrix sentences, and imbedded sentences (relative clauses).

Herzog (1978) writes on the history of the advocacy of Yiddish and philological study, dealing with the history of the study of

Yiddish, including in his survey the efforts of Christian humanists, missionaries, and even police officials, who saw Yiddish as a key to the language of the German underworld. Gininger (1954a) has evaluated the achievements and shortcomings of the Yiddish and Romanian linguist, Lazare M. Sainean (1859–1934). D. Katz (1980a) briefly discusses Ber Borochov, a pioneer of Yiddish linguistics. There is more on Borochov in the essay by Prager (1974; reprinted in J. A. Fishman, ed., 1981a, see 533–34), as well as a general survey of the position of Yiddish in the university and the current state of academic Yiddish studies. Goldsmith (1975) discusses the relationship of Zhitlovsky to American Jews, and in his book (1976) presents the biographies and ideological development of several leading Yiddishists of the early twentieth century. The historical study of Mieses (1915) has been reissued (1979).

The Tshernovits conference and the prestige of Yiddish

The Tshernovits conference, so important in the organization of advocates of Yiddish and for stimulating a Hebraist counter-reaction, is discussed in Goldsmith's book (1976). J. A. Fishman has treated the role of the conference from the point of view of sociolinguistics (1980a, reprinted in J. A. Fishman, ed., 1981a: 369–94). Fishman pays careful attention to the planning of the conference, the reasons for holding it in Tshernovits and the individuals who were present. The reactions of American and Eastern European Yiddishists, as well as the response of Hebraists, are recorded in depth. The goal of the conference was to raise the social prestige and function of Yiddish from a traditional, utilitarian function or a means of educating the masses to that of the major or sole means of expression. The relationship of Yiddish to Hebrew, as utilitarian tongue to "sacred tongue" (*lošn qoydeš*) and ideal of the Zionist Hebraists, was undergoing change. Fishman takes this into account and also evaluates the success of the conference.

Socio-linguistics and vowel change

In the area of Yiddish sociolinguistics, there are a number of significant studies. Schaechter (1977) surveys the approach of four schools of thought in Yiddish language-planning. D. Katz (1980b) traces certain vowel changes and their acceptance from a sociolinguistic point of view. He traces the developments of Proto-Yiddish vowels 22 (*ē*) and 25 (ε) in the Great Yiddish Vowel Shift. The main concern of the study is the use of these vowels in Hebrew-derived segolates, such as *melek̲* 'king' and *keleb̲* 'dog.' The variation has followed the phonemic history of each variety of Yiddish where Protovowels 22 and 25 have not merged. In the modern language segolates appear here as vowel 22 survivals and there as vowel 25 innovations.

Institutions concerned with the survival and development of Yiddish have been treated in a number of studies. B. Z. Goldberg (1970) surveys the growth and function of the Yiddish press. Clurman (1968) briefly discusses the Jewish theater, and a book by Nahma Sandrow surveys its development in various countries (*Vagabond Stars*, New York: Harper and Row, Jewish Publication Society, 1977). Neither study treats linguistic matters. A study by Gold (1980) traces Spanish, Portuguese, and Hebrew names for Yiddish.

Works edited and authored by J. A. Fishman in Yiddish socio-linguistics

The collection of articles in Yiddish and English by J. A. Fishman, editor (*Never Say Die*, 1981a) is a major contribution to Yiddish sociolinguistics. As noted above, the introductory essay by Fishman (1981b) is a major contribution. Fishman notes the ambivalent attitude toward Yiddish in various groups and the resultant defensiveness that has stimulated scholarship and education. He cites the views of writers like M. Weinreich (1953), followed by other writers, among them Landis (1964) and Susholtz (1976), who see in Yiddish the embodiment of essential Jewish humanistic values. Fishman discusses the literature on the ambivalent attitude toward Yiddish of various branches of Jewish orthodoxy and the changes wrought by the Enlightenment (*haskalah*; Yiddish: *haskoleh*) in attitudes toward Hebrew and Yiddish. His essay is organized to parallel the divisions of the book and the articles collected within it. In this way it surveys 1) sociohistorical perspectives on Yiddish; 2) the attitudes of Orthodoxy; 3) modernization movements; 4) significant historic moments, such as the Tshernovits conference; 5) formal institutions, such as theater and press; 6) shifts in populations using Yiddish as a language; and 7) linguistic planning and the setting of norms. In the last section Fishman surveys the history of Yiddish linguistics and the literature which discusses Yiddish affinity with or differentiation from Hebrew and German. Fishman maintains that there is a dearth of research on conversational Yiddish.

The following is a partial list of articles found in Fishman's book; an article by Poll (1965; reprinted Fishman, ed., 1981a: 197–218), who studies the spectrum of Hungarian-Jewish attitudes toward Yiddish and Hebrew (another study on orthodox attitudes toward both languages is Poll, 1980); Heilman (1981, 1983: 161–200) on language shift and identification in Talmudic study-groups, with attention to intonation and musicality; Szajkowski's study (1964a; reprinted in Fishman, ed., 1981a: 565–89) of the different attitudes among German Jews and Gentiles and Eastern-European Jews to Yiddish and its relationship to German during the First World War; Hudson-Edwards (1981) on the knowledge, use, and evaluation of Hebrew and Yiddish by American college students (his doctoral dissertation 1977 is also in the area of language identification); Schaechter (1969; reprinted in Fishman, ed., 1981a: 671–97), who shows that German usage continues to play a role as a hidden standard in written Yiddish, despite efforts to eliminate *daytshmerish* (German normative influence); Erlich (1973, reprinted in Fishman, ed., 1981a: 699–708) on political/linguistic influences on the standardization of Soviet Yiddish; Jochnowitz (1968, reprinted in Fishman, ed., 1981a: 721–37) on bilingualism and dialect mixture among Lubavitch Hasidic children. The final study in the book, by Fishman (1981c), considers Yiddish linguistic study as a contribution to general linguistics. Another study by Fishman (1980b) deals with attitudes toward Yiddish in the wake of the holocaust. Blumental (1981) has compiled a dictionary of words and phrases current during the holocaust period, many of which originated in German, the Slavic languages, and in Biblical and Rabbinic Hebrew, often with a deep imprint of irony and bitterness and with a motivation to conceal.

The place of Yiddish and Hebrew in Hasidism

The status of Yiddish vis à vis Hebrew in Hasidism is discussed at length by Shmeruk (1978: 198–234). Hebrew remained the primary vehicle for the philosophical-mystical interpretations of the Torah by the Hasidic leaders. Yiddish, however, was the language of the composition and transmission of tales concerning the Baal Shem Tov, but the first printings were in Hebrew. Yiddish translations followed, based on printed editions or unpublished Hebrew manuscripts. Some leaders were concerned that the Yiddish popularization of Hasidic teachings would lead to distortion. Nachman of Bratzlav composed his tales in Yiddish, but they were published simultaneously in Hebrew and Yiddish, with both languages on the same page. Shmeruk (1981: 119–39) discusses the relationship between *The Praises of the Besht* and tales concerning the earlier (fictional) figure, Rabbi Adam. An earlier article by Shmeruk on this subject appeared in *Zion*, 23/1–2 (1963) 101–5.

It is evident from the Hebrew of *The Praises of the Besht* that Yiddish influenced it, e.g., *biqqēš R. Adam . . . ʾeṯ haqqēsār ʿal s*^{e}*ʿûḏāh*, 'Rabbi Adam invited the emperor for a meal,' *higbîlû z*^{e}*mān ʿalʾ ēzeh yôm šeyāḇōʾ*, 'they set a time for which day he should come,' *w*^{e}*ṣiwwāh ʿal lip̱nê histalqûṯô liśśāʾ ʾiššāh*, 'he commanded before his death that (I) take a wife' (Y. Dan, *Hanovellah haḥasidit* [Jerusalem 1965] 25, 27). The various occurrences of *ʿal* 'on, upon' reflect Yiddish *oif*.

Further examination of Dan's collection of stories shows that this stylistic feature is not present in all examples. The various levels of Hasidic Hebrew deserve further study. One topic in need of investigation is the use of *waw*-consecutive and Hebrew words in unique ways, e.g., *ûmāṣāʾ ʾeṯ hāʿîr hepqēr bayyahăḏûṯ*, 'he found the city chaotic as relates to Judaism.' The Yiddishisms of the first example (*ʿal* < *oif*) are not present in this example (Dan, *Hanovellah hahasidit*, "The Miracle of the Grandfather from Shpole," 83ff.).

A masters thesis by Heckelman (1974) deals with the language of the Hasidim as reflected in the satirical *Megalleh ṭmirin* by Perl, and a masters thesis by Greenzweig (1973) treats the linguistic aspects of the *Praises of the Besht*.

KARAITE HEBREW AND FRINGE PHENOMENA

Karaite Hebrew

Federbush (1967: 54–61) has collected interesting general information about the attitude of the Karaites toward Hebrew. Allony (1964b) has published a list of grammatical terms used by Karaites, dating from the eighth century, while Musaev (1964) describes the language of the Karaites of Troki and Galicia. There is a general survey by E. Goldenberg (1971: 1634–35), and Altbauer (1956–58) has also made a contribution to the study of Lithuanian Karaite Hebrew.

A. Loewenstamm (1977–78) has published a preliminary study of Karaite Hebrew, based on the *Historical Dictionary* being prepared in Jerusalem. Although the founder of the Karaite sect, Anan ben David, compiled his book of commandments in Aramaic (end of eighth century), Karaites began to write Hebrew as early as the beginning of the ninth century. There are extant original Hebrew works and translations from the Arabic. The first group is comprised of the book of the laws of Benjamin Al-Nahawendi, a commentary on the Twelve Prophets by Daniel Al-Kumisi, the *Book of the Wars of The Lord* of Suliman ben Yeruhim, and various poems and Geniza fragments. The second group includes six major works: the book of the commandments of Levi ben Yefet; the book *Maḥkimat peti*; *Sefer haneʿimot* of Joseph the Seer; *Sefer hayashar* and *Bereshit rabbah*, both by Yeshua ben Yehudah; and part of *Otsar Neḥmad* of Toviah ben Moshe (Maman, 1979).

Karaitic language was not used in the same way by all speakers, and one finds various styles. The language of Benjamin Al-Nahawendi is less influenced by Arabic, while Daniel Al-Kumisi, writing a half-century after him, is replete with borrowed words and translation loans. Some of the Arabisms can be listed: *hēnāh* 'here,' *mîn daʿtî* 'according to my opinion,' *lōʾ yiḵšar* 'it is not possible,' *ʾamtah* 'truth' (in place of *ʾemet̲*). All of these go back to Arabic models and occur in the original Hebrew literature. There are more Arabisms in the translations, e.g., *haḥēp̄eṣ b-* 'the intention is,' *gālûy* 'the iiteral meaning,' *ʿôb̲ēr* 'permission.' Loewenstamm points out that similar Arabisms occur in Rabbanite literature in the Middle Ages. Karaites consulted Rabbanite literature and formed their noun in the patterns of Mishnaic Hebrew. Rabbanite scholars consulted Karaite works. There are cases where Karaites studied the works of their own predecessors in Rabbanite copies.

Karaite writers made their contribution to the enrichment of the Hebrew lexicon, especially through the re-patterning of Hebrew roots already known, e.g., *nôhar* 'light' (*nhr* 'shine'); *maqrîṣ u-mark̲îl* 'slanders' (cf. *qōrēṣ*, Prov 6:13 and *ăk̲alû qarṣêhôn,* Dan 3:8; *rāk̲îl*, Lev 19:16); *qeneṣ* 'argument, pretext' (*qinṣê lᵉmillîn*, Job 18:2), also used by the Karaites in the sense of 'proof'); *pûgāh* 'doubt'; and the root *zlʿ* for Hebrew *blʿ* 'swallow.' Rabbinic Hebrew *hēn* 'yes' was limited by the Karaite writers to the sense 'positive commandments, in contrast with *lawwîn* 'negative commandments.' The patterns from Mishnaic Hebrew for nouns, such as *qeṭel*, *qiṭlôn*, *qaṭlûṯ*, *qiṭṭûl*, and *qᵉṭîlāh* were used by Karaite writers. The lexical aspects of *Eshkol hakofer* by the Karaite Judah Hadassi are the subject of a masters thesis by N. Netzer (1969).

Some of the problems of the bi- and trilingualism of Byzantine Karaites involving borrowings and loan translations are treated in the historical study of Zvi Ankori, *Karaites in Byzantium, the formative years, 970–1100* (Columbia University Press, 1957) 415–31. Both Arabic and Greek affected the Hebrew of these writers.

David Hareʾuveni's Hebrew

An early study by Aescoly (1932–33) on the language of David Hareʾuven is inconclusive regarding the source of interferences and barbarisms in his Hebrew. Several European languages and Yiddish are considered.

5

MEDIEVAL GRAMMARIANS AND POETS

LANGUAGE CONSCIOUSNESS

Defining the period

It yet remains for consensus to be reached on the definition of the medieval period. Bendavid (1985) sees four periods: 1) the thousand years until the Common Era, with the biblical paradigm preferred; 2) until 950 C.E., with the mishnaic paradigm dominant; 3) the following nine hundred years with great diversity and no norm; and 4) from the mid-nineteenth century until the present, a very eclectic period. Téné (1985, 1986) sees 1) an ancient Hebrew period with Hebrew dominant; 2) a medieval period, from 250 B.C.E. to 1900, divided into five subdivisions, based upon different centers, with one or the other language (Aramaic, Arabic, Italian, Provencal, Yiddish, etc.) as the counterpart to Hebrew in a diglossia, and 3) the modern period, from 1900. On the other hand, Rabin (1985b) and Pagis (1986) eschew such divisions. The different Jewish centers adopted their own attitudes to the language consolidation termed Mishnaic Hebrew (Rabin) and each one developed in its own way, so that there must be a pluralistic periodization of the stages of the Hebrew language (Pagis). Clearly, more than linguistic factors are operating. There are ideological, sociological and historic factors to be considered.

We must proceed without an agreed upon definition of the medieval period. One possibility is to begin with the advent of Arabic influence. On the other hand, *Sefer Yetsirah* and commentaries upon it stimulated grammatical study, and that book has been dated to the sixth century. At any rate, it seems that we should include Masoretic activity in our medieval period. Parts of

Massekhet Soferim have been dated to the sixth century—although the beginnings of this work lie in the talmudic or even mishnaic period.

The medieval period was characterized by the development of a self-consciousness about the Hebrew language. Rudimentary historical speculations from that period deal with the differences between Biblical and Mishnaic Hebrew and with the affinities between Hebrew, Aramaic, and Arabic. The mystical book, *Sefer yetsirah*, *The Book of Creation*, presents a rudimentary grammatical theory mixed with mystical-philosophical elements. The consonants are classified according to their points of articulation and are traced back to three '*matres*'—*alef*, *mem*, and *shin*. The consonants *b*, *g*, *d*, *k*, *p*, *r*, *t* are defined as being capable of doubling (Bacher 1895: 20–23; Har Zahav 1951: 1.168; *Kuzari* IV:25). Allony (1973b) discusses the anagrammatic system of lexicography in *Sefer yetsirah*.

Sefer yetsirah and grammatical speculation

Allony (1969a: 30; 1974–75) finds direct Arabic influence upon *Sefer Yetsirah* and its linguistic theory to be considerable. He also notes the indirect influence of *Šuʿubiyah*, the reaction against *ʿArabiyah*, the latter being the term used to describe the supreme value placed by the Arabs upon their language and culture (Allony 1974–75: 239, n 35, with bibliographical references).

The position of *ʿArabiyah* is that Arabic is the richest and most precise language, it is the medium of the revelation of the Koran to Mohammed through the angel Gabriel, it is the language of angelic praise of God, and Arabic, of all the languages of the world, is most suited to express all human emotions. The reaction of Jews to this view was that Hebrew is the chosen tongue, that it is holy, and that it is capable of expressing all emotions. Many Jews were influenced by the Arabs' view of their language and felt a sense of inferiority about their own tongue or a need to enrich it through coinage of new words. Moses ibn Ezra was rejected by Jacob ben Elazar for his views on Arabic. Jacob, along with Judah Al-Harizi and Nahum ben Jacob of Fez (1165–1244), was an ardent defender of the supremacy of Hebrew (Allony 1973–74b; 1977: 6–10).

Arabic influence

Some characteristic speculations from this era are those of Judah Halevi, who maintained that Hebrew, the language in which God spoke to man and, therefore, the most perfect of languages, suffered a decline parallel to that of the Jewish people politically. Abraham, he believed, as bilingual, speaking Aramaic as his secular tongue and Hebrew as a sacred language (*Kuzari* II:68; grammatical theory is presented in II:78–80). Halevi praises Mishnaic Hebrew, which was belittled by Karaites, pointing out that it has

Hebrew in competition with Arabic

many characteristics not present in Biblical Hebrew and that only one who is ignorant will despise it (*Kuzari* III:67). This last comment reveals the existence of a controversy over the mishnaic phase of Hebrew and a questioning of its esthetic value and its usefulness as a tool for biblical exegesis (Waldman 1975a: 1307–8).

Ibn Janah's introduction to his *Sefer hariqmah* (Wilensky, Téné, Ben-Hayyim 1964: 19–20) reveals the same situation. He notes the objections to Mishnaic Hebrew on the grounds that it contains many foreign words and that its morphology differs from Biblical Hebrew and replies that these changes occur in a natural way when speakers, through repetition, simplify the forms they use. The introduction praises the level of grammatical knowledge among the talmudic rabbis and makes note of the gaonic contribution to the understanding of rare biblical words by the use of Mishnaic Hebrew. He defends the mishnaic creation of new verbs, such as *trm* 'give a heave-offering' and *hiṯrîᶜa* 'sound the shofar,' even though the initial letter *t* was considered part of the root when it was originally the indicator of a nominal form. Maimonides (Commentary on *m. Ter.* 1:1) defends the use of *trm* against the critics. He maintains that language goes back to actual speech and that the scholars quoted in the Mishnah lived in the Holy Land, speaking Hebrew and using such forms. They are, therefore, legitimate, and no one may find fault with Mishnaic Hebrew on the grounds that it is corrupt and lacks elegance.

Medieval defenses of Mishnaic innovation

Ibn Ezra, in his *Safah berurah*, compares Hebrew, Aramaic, and Arabic (Wilensky 1978: 46–82, discussion and text). He rejects a prevailing notion that the "natural" language is Aramaic. Hebrew, he claims, is primary, although all languages, Hebrew, Arabic, and Aramaic, are one. Aramaic, he believes, is inferior to the other two, because it does not form a construct except by means of the particle *dî* (cf. also Weil 1968: 1–11).

The use of Arabic to elucidate Hebrew

The dispute between those who felt that Arabic could be enlisted for the exegesis of Hebrew and those who were opposed is alluded to in Wechter's study of Ibn Barun (1964: 4–5; cf. Bacher 1895: 63–95, Judah ibn Kuraish contrasted with Menachem ben Saruk). The principles governing lexical similarities between the two languages, as seen by Ibn Barun, are treated by Wechter, including the erroneous assumption of identity between Hebrew *g* and Arabic *ǵ*, Hebrew *ḵ* and Arabic *ẖ* (Wechter 1964: 57–60). Additions to Ibn Barun's book on comparisons were published by D. Becker (1980). Halkin (1963) has made a thorough study of the medieval Jewish attitude to language and the position of Hebrew. Belief in the divine origin and primacy of Hebrew was not limited to the Jews. On the contrary, it was maintained by scholars throughout the Middle Ages and into the eighteenth century (J. Waterman, *Perspectives in Linguistics* [University of Chicago, 1963] 11–15).

Ibn Ezra's rejection of the language of the *payyeṭanim* is strongly expressed in *Safah berurah* (Wilensky 1978: 72) and in his commentary to Qoh 5:1. In the first source he scores the poets who departed from biblical usage and created difficult words, such as *taḥan* in place of *t^eḥînāh* 'plaint,' and in the second he bitterly criticizes Eleazer Qallir for deliberate obscurity and abandonment of biblical standards of vocabulary and syntax.

A plea for simplicity and clarity

Carlos del Valle Rodriguez (1981) has written a history of the development of the distinctively Spanish school of grammar in the tenth and eleventh centuries, a new school of thought which followed a period of dependency upon Tiberian Masoretes and grammarians. Rodriguez has also compiled a bibliography of language study in Spain (1976). The history, which is reviewed by Allony (1981), deals with the following topics: personalities, polemics, linguistic theory, and translations into Spanish of selected documents. While the history is indebted to Bacher (1895) and Yellin (1945), it has a much wider scope and makes use of recent publications of Geniza material as well as literature published in Modern Hebrew. Now, Eldar and Morag (1986) have collected various articles on linguistic theory in the Middle Ages.

Various resources

MEDIEVAL GRAMMARIANS

General studies of medieval grammar and grammarians include: W. Bacher, *Die Anfänge der hebräischen Grammatik* (Leipzig, 1895), reprinted in 1970 in Hebrew translation; Hirschfeld (1926); Federbush (1967: 73–112); Har Zahav (1951–56: 1.164–258); Chomsky (1945, 1957: 117–38; 1967: 158–91); Mierowsky (n.d.); Weil (1968); Yellin (1945); and Barr (1968: 60–175). Several articles in the *EJ* have enriched the discussion, among them: Ornan (1971a) on grammar; E. Goldenberg (1971) on the medieval period of Hebrew; and Barr (1971), a history of medieval linguistic concepts. I. Bendavid (1974–75) surveys the treatment of verbal stems by medieval and modern grammarians. A collection of sources has been compiled by Ben-Hayyim (1961). The collected essays of Klar (1954) contain much material on grammarians and the pronunciation of Hebrew. There are two essays which particularly stand out in this work, one dealing with methods of vocabulary extension

Various resources

(1947a) and one which is an introduction to *Sefer hashoham* (1947b).

Medieval definitions of "high" and "low" vowels

M. H. Segal has collected much material on phonetics (1928). Garbell (1950–51) discusses various methods of classifying the vowels and includes in her work a study of *Diqduqe haṭeʿamim* (cf. Dotan 1967), Dunash ibn Tamim's commentary on *Sefer yetsirah*, Jonah ibn Janah, and Judah Halevi. Medieval phonetic terminology was based on positions of the tongue and lower jaw and was influenced by similar classifications among Arab grammarians, e.g., *ō* and *ū* as "high," *ā*, *a*, and *e* as "stationary," and *e*, *i* as "low" (*Diqduqe haṭeʿamim*). Other authors who have written in this area are Morag (1962a), Ben-Hayyim (1952–53a), M. H. Segal (1928: 92–144) and Dotan (1951, masters thesis; 1954, 1974). Dotan's 1974 study relates the terms *milʿel* and *milraʿ* 'above' and 'below' to contemporary theories which ranked the vowels from high to low. Now Eldar (1981b) has presented a chapter from *Hidāyat al-qāri* (first half of the eleventh century) which presents six points of articulation for the consonants (see the discussion in the chapter on Masorah). Morag (1979b) traces the development of the term *muṣawwitāt* 'sonorant' and 'long vowel.' Eldar (1983) surveys the Arabic and Jewish theories of the threefold, physiologically-based articulation of the vowels. Abramson (1983–84) discusses aspects of the *ʿArukh* and (1985a) of a Talmud dictionary of Samuel ben Hofni.

Karaite grammarians

Skoss (1928: 4–35) surveys the pertinent facts about the early Karaite grammarians, ʾAbu Yaʿqub Joseph ben Nun, Abuʾl Faraj Harun ben Al-Faraj, and ʿAli ben Suleiman, in the introduction to his edition of the Genesis commentary of ʿAli ben Suleiman. ʿAli ben Suleiman, in his *Egron*, shows himself to be a consistent follower of the biliteral theory of David ben Abraham, even accepting uniliteral roots, although he was familiar with Hayyuj's triliteral theory. He freely uses mishnaic and talmudic words, transposes root letters, and even alters them completely, equating, for example, *wayyimṭāḥēm* 'he stretched them' (Isa 40:22) with *wayyinṭāʿēm* 'he planted them.' Rare words are listed alphabetically, not under the initial presumed root letter but under the preformative.

Skoss also produced a major study on the Karaite grammarian David ben Abraham, who flourished in the tenth century (1936, 1945). His *Egron* demonstrates a great dependence on Arab grammarians, with some measure of independence in terminology. David ben Abraham applied the method of interchange of letters, or metathesis. He also compared biblical words with Arabic,

Aramaic, and Mishnaic Hebrew words. He considered the imperative to be the basic form of the verb, a view held by other Karaite grammarians, and recognized uniliteral and biliteral roots, counting as radicals those letters which remain in all inflections.

Saadiah studies

Saadiah Gaon (892–942) has been studied by several writers (Bacher 1895: 38–62; Skoss 1955; Allony 1969a, 1969b; 1986, collected studies on Saadiah; Ben-Hayyim 1952–53a). Skoss (1955: 64) presents Saadiah as a pioneer in Hebrew grammar, greatly influenced by the Masorah. Thus Saadiah can group together forms like *šibbar* 'broke,' *hiṣṣîl* 'saved,' and *hikkāh* 'smote' because all three have a *dagesh* in the middle radical and their participial stems all begin with a preformative *mem*. Saadiah fails, however, to recognize the differences in their roots. A major work by Allony (1969a) is the edition of Saadiah's *Egron*. This work was designed to fulfill several needs: to be a reference book for poets, to revive the biblical language and assure elegance of expression, to prevent the lapse of usage of Hebrew, to provide information about the laws of the Torah and to contend against the Karaites. Saadiah's idea of "elegant expression" included the practice of developing new forms from current roots through a widespread use of analogy: thus *gišmôn* and *gišmāh* from *gešem* 'rain'; *ᵓăhab̲* from *ᵓahăb̲āh* 'love'; the favoring of the feminine form, e.g., *ᶜeštōnet̲* 'thought,' based on the plural *ᶜeštōnôt̲* 'thoughts'; *ᶜilgāt̲ām* 'their confused tongue' (Zulay 1964: 31–40). He is influenced in this by the earlier *payyeṭanim*.

Allony's work, which contains much historical and bibliographical material, has been reviewed by Téné (1971–72) and by E. Goldenberg (1972–74). Goldenberg takes issue with some of the conclusions and methodology of Allony, differing with him, for example, on the view that Saadiah was the "father of Spanish poetry." Goldenberg contends that Saadiah's method of creating new words was abandoned by the later poets, and that he deserved this title only in the sense that he tied poetic expression to precise grammatical knowledge and to the ideal of "elegant expression." The grammar and the concept of style were later given different content. While Allony classes the *Egron* as an anagrammatic dictionary, Goldenberg argues that this term can only apply to a grouping together of roots that have only letters, not meaning, in common. The *Egron*, however, joins roots which are perceived as being organically related. Saadiah's concept was that the *y*ᵉ*sôd* 'foundation' meant a basic, unconjugated or undeclined form. He saw the development of a verb from its base form to the expanded forms of the paradigm as analogous to the expansion of basic forms in the creation of new verbs, e.g., *ysd* 'lay a foundation' > *sdsd*, or the development of *taḥan* from *t^eḥinnāh* 'supplication.' Goldenberg (1971) doubts that Saadiah shared the biradical theory, basing her conclusion on the fact that a form like *ᶜāś* 'did' instead of *ᶜāśāh*, suggesting a biradical theory, is limited to the *qaṭal* form. Instead of reflecting a departure from the triradical theory, it may be a secondary form or a sort of poetic license. Allony (1973–74a) argues vigorously against this, supplying a great deal of evidence for the history of the multi-radical (as against tri-radical) verb theory. He finds it in rabbinic literature, in Arabic grammatical theory, and in the writings of David ben Abraham Alfasi (890–950), who was the first to articulate the theory. Saadiah and Menahem ben Saruq after him maintained the multi-radical theory.

Revell (1974b) reviews Allony (1969a), calling attention to one aspect of the *Egron*, the use of the biblical accents in the text. Some of these accents, moreover, are not Tiberian. The use of the accents by Saadiah aroused strong resentment, and he was accused by some of posing as a prophet. Revell proposes that Saadiah was attempting to imitate biblical language and style. He regarded Mishnaic Hebrew as an extension of Biblical but definitely as second class, fitted for worldly rather than heavenly use. Disagreeing with Allony, Revell argues that Saadiah did not aim to restore Hebrew speech, although it is true that some Hebrew was spoken at that time (*Egron*, Allony 1969a: 72, 391; Allony 1967–68).

One feature of Saadiah's grammatical theory is connected with the accents as he used them. All prefixes and suffixes are treated as inflections of a noun or verb form (Skoss 1955: 11–18) on the same level as a pronomial element in a verb; they are not additions to the word. Nouns are quoted in the dictionary with the preposition attached. Revell suggests that Saadiah regarded a word in the biblical text marked by a single accent as a single word.

Eytan (1967) surveys some examples of Saadiah's biblical lexicography. Saadiah's Hebrew conjugation table, modeled after the work of Arab grammarians, is analyzed by E. Goldenberg (1978–79). Eldar (1981a) deals with two genizah fragments that present an abridgement of Saadiah's views on vowel and pausal-form changes. Other non-biblical texts written with accents have been published by Allony (1973a).

A Geniza fragment from Saadiah's school

Dotan (1981) has published a Geniza fragment, Taylor-Schechter AS 141.1, which consists of three fragmentary leaves of an *Egron*, a listing of lexical items. This manuscript, in turn, is part of T–S D.1.19, which Allony (1969a) considered to be a part of the *Egron* authored by Saadiah. Dotan (1981) argues that this section cannot be by the hand of Saadiah because of the difference in grammatical theory. Saadiah posited the incompatibility of certain consonants, among them *ṭ* and *d*, yet T–S AS 141.1 specifically lists the name of the Temple gate, *Ṭādî* (*ṭdy*) as a legitimate example. There are other differences in the arrangement of the lexical items. Moreover, while there are some Arabic translations in Saadiah's *Egron*, there are none in the new fragment. Dotan, after presenting the text with annotations, concludes that the author may have been a grammarian who belonged to Saadiah's school and lived not long after him.

Dunash ibn Labrat

Sáenz-Badillos (1982) discusses the language of Dunash ibn Labrat on the basis of the critical edition of the *Teshuvot*, which he has edited (University of Granada, 1980). Dunash wrote in a late, not archaic biblical language. Rabbinic Hebrew is not a heavy influence upon his style, except for the use of the tenses. He expresses present time through the use of the active participle. Arabic is a major influence on his style.

Menahem and Judah Hayyuj

G. Goldenberg (1980) gives a historical survey of the different conceptions of the Hebrew root held by the medieval grammarians. He observes that the principle of triliterality was held by Menahem ben Saruq, prior to Judah Hayyuj. The innovation of Hayyuj was his idea of the quiescent letter. The grammarians did not have a unified terminology for designating the quiescent letter, and their different terms were varying translations of Arabic *sakin layyin*. There also was no agreement on the meaning of "root," some regarding it as "basic etymon" and others as the minimal unit representing the lexeme in the paradigm. Sáenz-Badillos (1986) discusses a new critical edition of *Mahberet Menaḥem*.

Maimonides

The linguistic conceptions of Maimonides, especially his method of hebraizing the talmudic Aramaic citations which were the legal sources for his code of law, the *Yad haḥazaqah*, are treated in a brief article by Zeidman (1956) and in a monograph by Ashkenazi (1964–65). A doctoral dissertation by Fink (1980) analyzes the Hebrew grammar of Maimonides in terms of orthography, morphology, and syntax, with attention to non-Hebrew influences. The masterful study by Twersky on the code of Maimonides contains a richly annotated chapter on Maimonides' style and attitude toward language (1980: 324–55). Arabic influences upon Maimonides' elegant Hebrew, modeled in part after the Mishnah, are discussed briefly in the preface to P. Birnbaum's abridged edition of the *Mishneh Torah* (New York, 1944: xxvi–xliv), e.g., *šᵉyēš šām máṣûy riʾšôn* '(to know) that there exists a first cause' (cf. Chomsky

1967: 196, 201–2). Arabic influences on the style of Abraham ibn Daud are discussed briefly in the edition of *Sefer haqabbalah* by G. Cohen (Philadelphia [1967] 305–7). The traditional grammar of the Yemenite Jews, the *Tijan*, has been surveyed by Kor (1979, masters thesis).

Rashi and other exegetes

Hebrew grammar, as found in the works of biblical exegetes, has been dealt with in various studies. Melamed (1975) has collected all the relevant sources illustrating the exegetical methods of the rabbis, the Targumim, Rashi, Abraham ibn Ezra, David Kimchi, and Ramban. Rashi as exegete and grammarian has been studied by Pereira-Mendoza (1940), Florsheim (1973–74), Shereshevsky (1957, doctoral dissertation; 1981, book), Y. Avinery (*Hekhal Rashi*, 1940ff.), Englander (1937–38, 1942–43), Zimrani (1938, masters thesis dealing with the lexicon), Darmesteter (1909), Banitt (1968b–69, 1972), Sarfatti (1972–73; the last three authors dealing with the glosses), Barzel (1973, masters thesis dealing with semantic changes in Rashi's use of earlier sources) and Moreshet (1977–78, showing how tradition influenced Rashi's exegetical choices in ambiguous words). Moreshet's article (nn 1 and 2) provides bibliographical material. See also the article by I. Garbell in *EIv* 13.37–38 dealing with Rashi's innovations and the article by M. Z. Kaddari in *EJ* 13.1566.

Judah ibn Balaam

The various methods used by Judah ibn Balaam (second half of the eleventh century) in the elucidation of *hapax legomena* are discussed by Perez (1981). These approaches are ranked according to priority: the use of traditional literature (i.e., Rabbinic Hebrew); appealing to Aramaic material; the use of Arabic; a resource; and, finally, permutation and metathesis of letters. If none of these yielded results, the context would be decisive in determining meaning. This ranking shows that in ibn Balaam's day the use of Rabbinic Hebrew met with no resistance, the use of Aramaic met with some, but Arabic was vigorously opposed. Téné (1983), however, describes how grammarians of the tenth and eleventh centuries naturally associated Hebrew and Arabic for the elucidation of the former.

Moses ben Nachman (Ramban) has been studied by Hoter-Yishai (1944, masters thesis) and Moreshet (1966, masters thesis; 1966–67a). The main features of the exegetical activity of Samuel ben Meir (Rashbam), the grandson of Rashi, have been outlined by H. R. Rabinovitz (1975–76). The biblical lexicon of Abraham ibn Ezra was studied by H. Zeliger (1940, masters thesis).

David Kimchi's *Mikhlol* was translated and rearranged along the lines of modern grammars by Chomsky (1952). His notes are a rich source of comparative and historical material. A desideratum would be the updating of these notes, using material published since the study appeared. The Kimchis, as is known, were responsible for a number of developments in Hebrew grammar, among them the distinction between long and short vowels, based on Latin grammar (Har Zahav 1951–56: 1.207; A. Bendavid 1957–58b), and the rule that every *shewa* following a long vowel must be vocalic. As shown by Chomsky (1952: 31–32; 1967: 178; 1971b), this view derived from a misunderstanding of the function of the *meteg* under the letter with the long vowel. It was erroneously assumed that its function was to close the syllable. Earlier grammarians, however, had regarded the *shewa* in this position as silent (Yalon 1937a).

The Kimchis

Eldar (1978–79a) discusses the authorship and historical antecedents of an important work of Ashkenazic grammatical study, the *Shimshoni* of Rabbi Shimshon Hanaqdan of the thirteenth century. Ashkenazic grammarians have not, to date, received adequate scholarly attention.

An Ashkenazic grammarian

Individual grammarians who have been discussed in articles and monographs, apart from the above-mentioned general surveys of Bacher (1895), Har Zahav (1951–56: 1.164–258), E. Goldenberg (1971), and Barr (1968: 60–175; 1971), include the following:

Saadiah Gaon: Skoss (1955), Allony (1969a, 1973–74a); Ben-Hayyim (1952–53a; D. Téné (1971–72); E. Goldenberg (1967, masters thesis; 1972–74); Revell (1974b); Eytan (1967); Dotan (1981).

Guide to studies on individual grammarians

Dunash ibn Labrat: Wilensky (1978: 7–12); Sáenz-Badillos (1982).

Judah Hayyuj: Allony (1962–63); Abramson (1978), publishing sections from *Kitab al-nataf* on 2 Samuel with critical and historical treatment; Wilensky (1978: 13–18); Eldar (1978–79c).

Judah ibn Quraish: Goodstein (1960, doctoral dissertation), an edition of the *Risala*, comparing Hebrew, Aramaic, and Arabic.

Jonah ibn Janah: Wilensky (1978: 19–26; 32–34). *Sefer hariqmah*, originally edited by Wilensky in 1939, has been further edited by D. Téné and Ben-Hayyim (1964). D. Téné (1956, masters thesis) deals with the treatment of syntax of *Kitab al-tanqiah*. Coffin (1968, doctoral dissertation) made a detailed study of terminology and linguistic philosophy; David Freedman (1980, doctoral dissertation).

Judah ibn Balaam: Abramson (1976); Allony (1975–76); Perez (1981).

Levi ibn Altabban: A. Bendavid (1957–58a); Pagis (1962–64).

Isaac ibn Barun: Wechter (1964); D. Becker (1980).

Abraham ibn Ezra: Bacher (1881, translated into Hebrew 1931); Prijs (1950, 1973); Ben-Hayyim (1951); Eytan (1974–75); I. Levin (1970); Valle Rodriguez (1977).

Abraham bar Hiyyah: Rabin (1945).

Solomon Almoly: *Berggrün* (1946); Yalon (1962–64); Morag (1982).

Eli ben Yehudah Hanazir: Allony (1969–70).

Joseph ibn Kaspi: Mesch (1975).

Abraham ben Azriel: Fruchtman (-Agmon) (1973, masters thesis).

Abraham Balmat: Gevaryahu (1954, masters thesis).

Joseph Kimchi: Gil (1973–75).

Moses Kimchi: Sermonetta (1967).

David Kimchi: J. Lipschutz (1931, masters thesis); Chomsky (1952); A. Bendavid (1957–58b); Moshe Amit (1950, masters thesis), comparing the biblical commentaries and *Sefer hashoroshim*; S. C. Reif (1973); Talmadge (1975), dealing with Kimchi as a Bible commentator.

Profiat Duran: E. Goldwasser (1957, masters thesis).

Tanchum ben Joseph Yerushalmi: B. Toledano (1961); Shay (Gershter: 1967, masters thesis; 1976, doctoral dissertation).

Elijah Levità: Berggrün (1948–49); Weil (1963a, 1964); Yalon (1962–64); Medan (1971).

The above listing is not exhaustive. It appears that, at the present time, there are numerous studies of individual grammarians, but a synthesis and comprehensive history of the development of grammatical theory and of Hebrew language in the Middle Ages has not yet been produced. Kogut (1970–71) has written a survey article dealing with the state of research into medieval Hebrew.

It is important to note in this connection that work in the area of dialect and medieval studies has been done in Russia by Hayim Sheynin (I. Axelrod-Rubin 1984: 289–90). This includes a grammar of Ladino in Russian and a dissertation on the poetry of Joseph ben Tanchum Hayerushalmi, neither of which were allowed to be published. Axelrod-Rubin's article was completed in 1978, and Sheynin left the Soviet Union prior to that date. Under different conditions the fruits of his efforts are now being published; see now *Community and Culture* (Philadelphia, 1987) Hebrew section, 45–52, ed. N. Waldman.

While it may be a matter of debate whether Spinoza belongs to the medieval period or to the beginning of the modern period, we conclude this section with a summary of a study by Kaye (1980) on Spinoza as a linguist. Kaye notes that the linguistic aspect of Spinoza's work has largely been overlooked, yet there are many insights in his *Compendium* which parallel modern linguistics. Spinoza discussed what in modern parlance is called *Ablaut* or apophony, phonotactics, and morphophonemics. Spinoza regarded the Masoretes as having intervened in the regularization process of archaic forms, as in the 2 f.s. *-t* instead of *-ti*. Kaye attributes to Spinoza a kind of "deep structure" concept, in that Spinoza thought that all Hebrew words, with the exception of interjections and conjunctions, have the force and property of nouns. Kaye summarizes the views of modern grammars on the question of the primacy of noun or verb. Spinoza's theory on the currently unsettled problem of tense versus aspect in the verb system was that the Hebrew tense system was divided between past and non-past (present-future). In Spinoza's view, the ancient Hebrews "viewed time to be like a line consisting of many points each of which they considered the end of one part and the beginning of another." Spinoza was influenced by the Cartesian perspective that the grammar of a language is a theory of that language, the purpose of which is to account for an infinite number of possible grammatical sentences not confined to the ones actually found in the corpus (Kaye 1980: 120). Z. Levi (1979) has also written on the problem of normativism in the *Compendium* of Spinoza. Christian Hebraists of the Renaissance and Reformation have been discussed by Willi (1974), while Katchen (1979) traces the contact of Christian Hebraists and Dutch rabbis in the study of *Mishneh Torah* of Maimonides. Christian Hebraism in seventeenth-century England, as reflected in John Lightfoot, has been studied in a dissertation by Schertz (1977). Jones (1983) presents the history of Hebrew in Tudor England.

Spinoza as linguist

Christian Hebraists

SPECIAL TOPICS

A limited amount of research has been done on the Hebrew of the mystical literature. Of special note are the works of Zelikovitz (1953, masters thesis) on *Hekhalot* and Libes (1977, doctoral dissertation) on the lexicon of the Zohar.

Sermoneta (1969) has published a new edition of a thirteenth-century Hebrew dictionary of philosophy, and Y. Joel (1971, doctoral dissertation) has treated the syntax of Levi ben Gershom's

Milhamot hashem. Meltzer (1972) discusses the linguistic innovations of Asaf the Physician (see *JE* 2.162–63).

Mathematical terminology during the Middle Ages has been treated at length by Sarfatti in his masters thesis (1957), another study (1958–60), his doctoral dissertation (1963) and a book based on the dissertation (1968a).

Shay (Gershter; 1980) discusses briefly the various types of dictionaries that were compiled in the Middle Ages for various purposes and describes an anonymous dictionary of which nine manuscript pages were discovered in the National Library in Jerusalem. The dictionary is unique in that it organizes its material around semantic fields. Its interpretations are based on the Mishnah commentary of Maimonides, and its provenance may be North Africa, but the author may have been Yemenite.

POETRY

The post-talmudic and medieval poetry of the Jews, religious and secular, is of significant value in determining the state of the Hebrew language in various periods. Kahle (1959: 34–38, 167) argued for the loss of gutturals and the primacy of the *-āḵ* form in the 2 m.s., in part on the basis of manuscripts of Hebrew poetry from Palestine.

Basic resources

It is impossible to give a full bibliography here, but we list the following historical surveys of the field of medieval poetry: Yellin (1940) on Spanish poetry, reissued with an important, updated bibliography by Pagis (1972); the survey by Spiegel in L. Finkelstein, ed., *The Jews* (Philadelphia, 1949) 2.528–66; a historical survey by Habermann (1970, 1972a) and a collection of articles by the same author, rich in bibliographical information (1972b); a history of the beginnings of *piyyuṭ* by A. Mirsky (1965).

A major source is the series *Studies of the Research Institute for Hebrew Poetry* (Berlin, 1933ff., resumed in Israel after the war). Studies on meter, rhyme, and form include those by Mirsky (1956–57, 1958a=1968, 1968–69) and by Bacon (1968). Mirsky (1958a) finds the origin of structures in early *piyyuṭ* in the forms of midrashic presentation, which also had metrical aspects. Fleischer (1976) has thoroughly studied the different genres of liturgical poetry and their *Sitz im Leben*.

Various lexical studies

Lexical studies, treating the language of the poets in general and with attention to the influence of Mishnaic Hebrew, include:

Medan (1950–51); A. Mirsky (1952–53); Y. Ratzhaby (1966–69, 1971–72, 1972–73a, 1972–73b); Allony (1959, 1960, 1966, 1968), with useful bibliographies; Berggrün (1967–68); Tobi (1972–73, 1975); Abramson (1965). Abramson demonstrates how earlier poetry was often quoted without identification of the source. Y. Yahalom (1974) studies the syntax of the ancient *piyyuṭ*.

Selected list of poetic materials

Earlier compilations of medieval poetry include: *Anthologia Hebraica* by H. Brody and M. Wiener (Leipzig, 1922); Israel Davidson, *Selected Religious Poems of Solomon ibn Gabirol*, translated by Israel Zangwill (Philadelphia, 1923); H. Brody, *Selected Poems of Judah Halevi*, translated by Nina Salaman (Philadelphia, 1924); and H. Brody, *Selected Poems of Moses ibn Ezra*, translated by Solomon Solis-Cohen (Philadelphia, 1934). The *Diwan* of Judah Halevi was published by H. Brody in four volumes (Berlin, 1894–1930); see also S. Bernstein, *Jehuda Halevi, Selected Liturgical and Secular Poems* (Hebrew; New York, 1944), and the edition of Ibn Gabirol's poetry in three volumes by Bialik and Ravnitsky (Berlin-Jerusalem, 1924–32).

More recent collections of medieval poetry include: J. Schirman's anthology of poetry from Spain and Provence (1954–56); anthologies by A. Mirsky (1958b, 1958–59); new poems from the Geniza, edited by Jarden (1967); Geniza fragments published by Katsh (1964); and the masterful edition of new materials from the Geniza, edited with rich bibliography, by Schirmann (1965). His study on post-biblical Hebrew poetry (1967) and his collected studies (1979) should be noted.

In addition, there are materials which were collected for a seminar by Fleischer (1971), a short collection of Yemenite poetry by Ratzhaby (1968), late poetry from Italy collected by Pagis (1974–75), another study by Pagis on developments in secular poetry (1976c) and *piyyuṭim* for special Sabbaths collected by Loewinger and Yahalom (1973). These listings and the ones which follow are incomplete, and the student is referred to the bibliographies of Pagis (1972) and Schirmann, the latter appearing regularly in *KS* until his death, and to the relevant articles in *EJ*.

Individual poets whose works have been published or studied include:

Eleazar Qilar and *Eleazar Qallir*: S. Elitsur (1981).

Yose ben Yose: Mirsky (1974, 1977a).

Guide to studies on individual poets

Yannai: Zulay (1936, 1938, 1946); Y. Yahalom (1974); Z. M. Rabinowitz (1965, 1977); Spiegel (1958); Mirkin (1968).

Hewdata: Y. Yahalom (1966, masters thesis; 1969–70, 1974).

Dunash ibn Labrat: Allony (1947a, 1947b, 1951).

Saadiah Gaon: Zulay (1964).

Hai Gaon: Fleischer (1977).

Samuel Hanagid (or *ibn Nagrela*): Ish-Shalom (1949, masters thesis); Stiasny (1971, masters thesis); I. Levin (1973b); Yellin (1939); Abramson (1947, 1953); Habermann (1947); Jarden (1966); L. Weinberger (1973).

Eliyah bar Shemaᶜyah: David (1977).

Amitay ben Shefatyah: David (1975).

Shelomoh Habavli: Fleischer (1973).

Isaac bar Levi ibn Mar Shaᵓul: Fleischer (1983).

Solomon ibn Gabirol: Jarden (1967–75, on the language; 1971, 1973, 1975, 1976, editions of the poems); Pagis 1978 (a Hebrew-Spanish edition of selected poems); Brody and Schirmann (1974).

Shimon Biribi Migas: Y. Yahalom (1980a).

Moses ibn Ezra: Bernstein (1957); Halkin (1972–73, 1975); Pagis (1970); Y. Ratzhaby (1958–59).

Abraham ibn Ezra: I. Levin (1970, 1975).

Isaac ibn Ezra: Schmeltzer (1981).

Isaac ben Israel (Babylonian, thirteenth century): Tobi (1977).

Shem Tov ben Yitshaq Ardutiel: Nini and Fruchtman (1980).

Emanuel of Rome: Jarden (1954, doctoral dissertation; 1949–50).

David ben Aharon Hasin: Hazan (1984).

Meir bar Isaac: Lavin (1984, doctoral dissertation).

Abraham bar Jacob of Regensburg: Z. Malachi (1977b).

Shalem Shabazzi: Ratzhaby (1971, 1974); Rabi̡ (Rabeeya, 1977); Yeshᶜayahu (1975); Seri and Tobi (1976).

Saᶜadyah ben Abraham al-Bashiri (Yemenite, seventeenth century): M. Caspi (1981).

Jacob Frances (seventeenth-century Italian poet who denounced Shabbetai Tsvi in his compositions): P. Naveh (1969).

Spanish and Yemenite poetry

Tobi (1975) and Caspi (1975) discuss the influence of Spanish-Hebrew poetry upon Yemenite creativity. Poetry in Yemen was influenced by the early Palestinian *piyyuṭ* and by Babylonian models, but Spanish poetry was such a dominant force that Tobi considers the entire poetic output from the twelfth century onward to be an offshoot of it. Unique to Yemenite poetry is the custom of beginning a festive occasion with a *nashid*, a form in which the same melody is repeated from verse to verse and is more sparsely represented in the *diwan*-s. There is a richer repertoire in the *shirah* which follows the *nashid*. Rabi (1977) presents an unpublished *nashid* of Shabazzi (1977), and Yeshᶜayahu (1975) discusses themes of national redemption in his poetry. Ratzhaby (1984–85) publishes thirteen new Yemenite poems, and Lasery (1987) has collected the popular poetry of Moroccan Jews. M. Caspi (1982) has published the *Maranot piyyuṭim* of the Yemenites.

Pagis (1970) studies the history of poetic theory in Spanish poetry. Taking Moses ibn Ezra as the typical representative of the Golden Age, Pagis studies his poetry and that of others of the period in terms of genre, poetic theory, and language. As observed by Abramson (1965), there was much borrowing and reworking of material from other authors and from other genres of literature. The acceptability of a poet's work was determined by the way the poet handled his material, not the originality of his conception. Pagis deals with several genres: the songs of praise to a patron, poems of love, wine, lament, and religious meditation. He points out that earlier scholars erred in attempting to derive biographical information from a poet's work in a specific genre. The study treats the epistolary form, letter-poems, and word play, going further than earlier researchers. Imagery was seen, not as an integral part of, but as an ornamental addition to speech. Fleischer (1986) discusses medieval research in poetry. Mashia (1972), in a doctoral dissertation, reexamines the terminology of rhetoric, *badiᶜ*, and *ᶜruḍ*, earlier misunderstood by translators. The sixteen meters are compared to Arabic models.

Medieval poetic theory

Pagis (1976b, 1979) surveys trends in the study of medieval Hebrew literature from the nineteenth century to the present. He notes that the nomenclature "medieval" is problematic, as the term can cover a millennium or more. In another study (1986) Pagis argues that different Jewish cultural centers developed at their own pace. No standard periodization is possible and we must accept a pluralistic periodization. Davidson's *Thesaurus* spans a period from the canonization of the Bible to the beginning of the Enlightenment, in the late eighteenth century. The alternatives "post-biblical" or "pre-modern" pose other problems. The study of texts has made rapid strides, especially because of Geniza manuscripts. The Institute for Research of Hebrew Poetry was founded by Shocken in Berlin and was later transferred to Jerusalem, though it is now defunct. The institute published seven volumes of texts in its *Studies* series. In the late 1950s a microfilm center was founded at the National Library in Jerusalem. A Research Institute of the Piyyut in the Geniza, sponsored by the Israel Academy of Sciences and Humanities, is now headed by Ezra Fleischer. Halkin (1975) has published the text of the original of Moses ibn Ezra's *Kitab al-mukhadara wal-mudhakara* with an accurate Hebrew translation, and a doctoral dissertation by J. Dana (1977) treats its

Current research

poetical theory. Ibn Ezra's *Treatise on Metaphorical and Literal Language* remains available only in manuscript form.

In the area of literary history and historiography, Pagis points out that scholars were misled either by the evaluations of the medievals or by subjective norms against which they judged various bodies of poetry. For some, Andalusian poetry became the norm, and poetry was regarded as either ascending to Alharizi or declining from the standard of his work. Italian poetry was judged against Spanish to its detriment, while in reality the Italian school showed great growth and dynamism. Pagis observes the pitfalls in the parallel study of poetic traditions and attempts to discover literary sources.

Biased judgments

In the area of literary analysis, Zulay (1938) compared the Kaliric and Saadianic styles from a philological standpoint. Mirsky (1958a) traced formal prototypes common to the midrash and the ancient *piyyuṭ*, and Fleischer (1976) has traced genres and forms in the light of the liturgical function of *piyyuṭ* in various rites and periods. More needs to be done in this field. Elucidation of individual styles remains a desideratum. Pagis (1976a) has surveyed various theories of poetics held by medieval Hebrew poets.

Unique features in South Yemenite poetry

Linguistic traditions diverging from the Tiberian are attested in South Yemenite poetry, where *ḥolem* and *tsere* are rhymed. In addition, *segol* and *pataḥ*, undistinguished in the Babylonian tradition, are also rhymed (Ratzhaby 1968: 28, Morag 1963: 92–99, 119–20). Ratzhaby also gives examples of Aramaic and Arabic words which are used in poetry but treated as though they were Hebrew and identifies new verb coinages based on unusual nominal forms. Arabic influence on Hebrew poets in the irreverent use of sacred texts is illustrated by Ratzhaby (1970). Hebrew poets' usage of such texts, however, shows less heresy and none of the pornography. A. Citron (1965) has also studied the love element in medieval Hebrew poetry.

The linguistic situation revealed by early poetry: Yose ben Yose and Yannai

The linguistic situation recoverable from early poetry has been described by several authors. A. Mirsky (1977a: 70–74) demonstrates the prevalence of Biblical Hebrew in the poetry of Yose ben Yose, with the clear additional presence of Mishnaic Hebrew patterns. There are unusual word forms and uses, e.g., *ʾeder* 'praise,' *ṭerem* 'in the past,' and Hebrew words clearly influenced by the Targum, e.g., *rîhûq* 'abomination,' *yāqrû* 'honored.' Z. Rabinowitz (1965), in his study of *halakhah* and *aggadah* in the poetry of Yannai, points out the elements of Mishnaic Hebrew that are dominant. Where Yose ben Yose favored the *yifʿal* and the *waw*-consecutive, Yannai preferred the present participle ending in *-îm* (impersonal) and avoided the *waw*-consecutive, except where required by the acrostic form of the poem. Gutturals are attenuated, and homophonic rhymes such as *ᶜayin* 'eye' and *ᵓayin* 'there is not' are used. Vocalization follows the later Ben Naphtali method, e.g., *waw-copula* + initial *yod* = *wi-*. New patternings follow Mishnaic Hebrew and go beyond it, e.g., *mašpîr* 'perfects,' *ᵓiwwûy* 'desire.' Verbs of I *y*, I *n*, and III *h* classes are treated as II *w*, e.g., *ᶜāṣû* for *yaᶜăṣû* 'they advised.'

Zulay (1936: 244–48) has also documented features in the poetry of Yannai, such as the rhyming of *ᶜaḇdāḵ* 'your servant' (m.) with *dāḵ* 'humble,' and rhymes between *ᶜayin*, *ᵓalef*, *he* and *ḥet*, *ḥolem* and *shureq*. Moreover, there is rhyming between the aspirated and plosive forms of *b* and *k*, that is, where the traditional grammar indicates they should occur. This suggests that the realization of these phonemes did not follow masoretic rules. Y. Yahalom (1974, doctoral dissertation) has studied the syntax of ancient *piyyuṭ*, including that of Yannai.

Internal passives in early *piyyuṭ*

Y. Yahalom (1980b) surveys the complex situation of the internal passives, *Puᶜal* and *Hufᶜal*, in mishnaic and early *piyyuṭim* (before the Arab conquest). These verbal themes appear in the early poetry, but not in a passive sense, which Mishnaic Hebrew prefers to express by forms with consonantal affixes, *Nifᶜal* and *Hitpaᶜel*. Both in the *piyyuṭ* and in Mishnaic Hebrew the internal passive expresses an active mode, what the biblical *Qal* had earlier expressed. The internal passive in the *piyyuṭ* expresses action by an indefinite subject, e.g., *ḥuppāzû lāsēᵓṯ* 'they hastened to leave.' The internal passive can occur in a string of actives, suggesting that it, too, has an active sense, e.g., *tāᶜînû . . . šāgagnû . . . ruḥaqnû . . . qilqalnû*, 'we have strayed . . . erred . . . become distant . . . corrupted.' The composers of *piyyuṭ* were not content to use stylized biblical forms of the internal passive. They also made creative use of the *Nitpaᶜel* form in verbs of haste, e.g., *ṭāᶜan luḥôṯ wᵉniṯmahār* 'he (Moses) carried the tablets and hastened' and *zeh yittᵉnû wᵉlōᵓ yiṯmattᵉnû* 'this they shall give and not delay.'

Shelomoh Habavli

In Fleischer's study of the poems of Shelomoh Habavli (1973), a poet of Oriental origin who flourished in Italy in the tenth century, interesting aspects of Mishnaic Hebrew are clearly demonstrated. The poet tended toward the noun stems *piᶜul*, *pᵉᶜîlāh*, *paᶜălān*, and *pôᶜălān*, e.g., *ᵓiwwûy* 'desire,' *gᵉḏîlāh* 'a plant,' and *mîṭāh* 'tottering.' He also used forms such as *nagḥān* 'a gorer' and *rôḏyān* 'one who dominates.' He preferred the *Hifᶜil* and the use of the *Piᶜel* in the sense of the *Hifᶜil*. I *n* verbs are treated as though they were II *w* or II *y*, e.g., *tattî* for *naṯattî* 'I gave.' Verbal prefixes are treated as though they were part of the root, thus creating new roots, e.g., *ymn* from *mnh* 'appoint,' under the influence of *way-*y^{e}*man* 'and he (the Lord) appointed' (Jonah 2:1), and *yḥṣ*, as in l^{e}*hiṯyaḥăṣāh* 'divided in half,' from *ḥṣh*, influenced by *wayyaḥaṣ* 'and he divided' (Gen 32:8). Verbs of the II *w* class were treated as though they were III *y*, e.g., *diṣṣûy* (from *dwṣ*) w^{e}*riṣṣûy* 'joy and reconciliation.' More than other *payyeṭanim*, Shelomoh Habavli loved word inversions, e.g., *ʾăhaḇ* for *ʾahăḇāh* 'love,' and the use of the definite article as a relative pronoun before a verb, e.g., *ha-hôrîḏ*, instead of *ʾăšer hôrîḏ* 'who brought down.' There is some earlier evidence of this last usage, cf. biblical *hehāl*^{e}*ḵû ʿimmô* 'who went with him' (Josh 10:24; G–K 447, §138i). Rabin (1970a: 325) notes that the listing of the various changes does not explain how they came about, and a diachronic study is needed. Perhaps a desire to demonstrate that Hebrew could compete with the rich lexical resources of Arabic stimulated the desire to press into service *hapax legomena* and to transfer roots into new patterns (Zulay 1964: 19–20, 33–38). As observed above in the discussion on Saadiah, there is some debate on the continuity between the poetic and grammatical theory of Saadiah and the later Spanish poets, Zulay and Allony arguing for continuity and E. Goldenberg (1971: 1610–21) concluding that Saadiah's theories were later abandoned. Cnaani (1960) has compared some of the medieval coinages with similar constructions innovated independently by Modern Hebrew writers.

Debate on continuity between Saadiah and the Spanish school

Starting with the writing of Dunash ibn Labraṭ (c. 920–990), Hebrew poetry, not without opposition, was adapted to Arabic quantitative meter based on various groupings of long syllables before and after a juncture of a short and a long syllable. In Hebrew, the vocalic *shewa* (here represented as Sh_v and the silent *shewa* as Sh_s) was treated as the equivalent of the Arabic short vowel. Hebrew grammarians prior to the Kimchis did not distinguish between long and short vowels. The union of the consonant bearing Sh_v and the consonant bearing the vowel (CV) was called *yāṯēḏ* 'tent peg' (◡—). The treatment of Sh_v as a vowel had a basis in actual speech (Allony 1951: 52–59; Morag 1963: 135–91). The characteristic patterns of Hebrew poetry are elucidated by Yellin (1940: 47–53), Allony (1951: 70–100), and Habermann (1970: 265–72).

The adoption of Arabic meter

In order to accommodate Hebrew to this metric scheme, Dunash and his followers arbitrarily transmuted Sh_v and Sh_s into one another, one example of which is *š*^{e}*ḇû w*^{e}*nûḥû* 'sit and rest,' scansioned as *š*^{e}*-buw nû-ḥû*, which makes a pattern ◡——— in which

$Sh_v > Sh_s$. Another example, of the opposite process, is *ʾôr ʿaṭîṯā* 'you wrapped yourself in light,' scansioned as *ʾô-rᵉ ʿā-ṭî-ṯā*, a – ⏑– – – pattern, in which $Sh_s > Sh_v$. Closed syllables could be treated during this period as open ones by considering the final consonant as belonging to the following syllable. The syllable, however, was not thought of as actually open. In the theory of Hayyuj, every long vowel was thought to be closed by a written or unwritten quiescent letter, *ʾ*, *w*, or *y* (Chomsky 1952: 31, 33; Barr 1971: 1369–70; Judah Halevi, *Kuzari* II:78, 80). Halevi denounces the treatment of Sh_v as Sh_s in Spanish poetry (*Kuzari* II:78) and is guilty of doing the same himself, e.g, *dôrᵉšê šᵉlômēḵ* 'those who seek thy peace,' treated as *dôr-šê šᵉlômēḵ* (Hirschfeld 1927: 304, n 46). Of course, it might be countered that prior to the Kimchis the *shewa* following a *ḥolem* was not regarded as necessarily Sh_v (Chomsky 1952: 31–32; 1967: 178; 1971b; Waldman 1975a: 1310–11).

Dialectic factors in the adaptation of Arabic meter

It is possible that these alterations were not as arbitrary as they seemed, but rather had a basis in linguistic traditions, such as the Babylonian, which were prevalent in Spain (Y. Yahalom 1982: 44–45). Compare Babylonian *yisōḏ* 'foundation' (Tiberian *yᵉsôḏ*) and *haysōḏ*, (Tiberian *hayyᵉsôḏ*). In the first case there is an initial vowel instead of Sh_v; in the second the *yod* is silenced. With initial *he* in the *Nifʿal*, Babylonian has *nihras* 'destroyed' and *nihpaḵ* 'overthrown' (Tiberian *nehᵉras*, *nehᵉpaḵ*; Yeivin 1973a: 37–38, 87). Yemenite tradition also parallels some of the changes, e.g., Tiberian *upiryô* 'and its fruit' is realized as [weferyo] (Morag 1963: 86; Waldman 1975a: 310–11).

E. Goldenberg (1983) discusses the problem of grammatical deviations forced by meter and possible justifications for them. Ibn Ganah, following Arab grammarians, permitted such changes under certain conditions, one of which was the 'return to an original form.' This would permit $Sh_v > Sh_s$ if it were originally silent or treating vowels with *ḥaṭaf* as if full vowels.

Mixed dialectic features have been observed by Tobi (1972–73) in Spanish Hebrew poetry. Disagreeing with Y. Ratzhaby (1971–72), who maintains that the Spanish poets treated words from Mishnaic Hebrew in their Babylonian pronunciation, Tobi finds Tiberian, Palestinian, and Babylonian dialectic features, used as meter and rhyme require. A feature which does go back to the Yemenite and Babylonian tradition is the relative pronoun *š-*, usually vocalized *še-* in Tiberian (with an exception in Qoh 3:18) but with a Sh_v in the poetry of Samuel Hanagid. He is not consistent in this usage, however. Dialect variations found in

Spanish poetry include *m^{e}mônôṯ/māmônôṯ* 'funds,' *map̱tēḥôṯ/map̱t^{e}ḥôṯ* 'keys,' *qālēp̱/q^{e}lāp̱* 'parchment,' *l^{e}ḵēn/lāḵēn* 'therefore,' *ṭallēṯ/ṭallîṯ* 'garment, prayer shawl,' *sômeʾ/sūmāʾ* 'blind person,' and *ʾēnô/ʾēnû* 'he is not.'

Opposition to Arabic meter

Abramson (1965: 14) comments on the views of the students of Menahem ben Saruk and their opposition to the innovations of Dunash, who confused the two kinds of *shewa*s for metric purposes. Saruk's school was primarily opposed to violations of standard grammar and the artificial distinction between long and short syllables in the Arabic manner (Y. Yahalom 1982: 61). His students had no objection to meter or theme of Arabic origin *per se*. With the acquisition of greater knowledge, the glaring grammatical violations tended to disappear. The challenge to Dunash's innovations posed by Menahem's students was published in 1855 by Filipowski as *Sefer teshuvot Dunash ben Labrat*, reprinted in 1967. Allony (1947a, 1951, 1965) has analyzed the language of Dunash.

Debate over the origin of meter

Fleischer (1983a), in his study of Isaac bar Levi ibn Mar Shaʾul, discusses the syllabic system which allowed each line an exact number of syllables with no differentiation between short and long, similar to Arabic quantitative meter. The syllabic system was used for secular poetry and not limited to *piyyuṭ*, as originally thought. Fleischer considers it to have had a Romance origin. Yahalom (1982), however, believes that it was Arabic in origin, predating quantitative meter. The themes of poetry or parables written in this meter imply that it had an eastern origin. Saʿid ben Babshad, with whom this meter is associated, had a Persian name, and his sayings can only be scanned by assuming a Babylonian pronunciation. Babylonian Hebrew had few *ḥaṭafim*, allowing no equivalent for the Arabic short vowel. Only in Spain could Dunash, well versed in Arabic meter, apply it to Hebrew, because Spanish Hebrew had more *ḥaṭafim* to serve as the short vowel.

Further studies

Fleischer (1983b) discusses the poetry of the Gerona school, concentrating on Moses ben Nachman (Nachmanides) and Meshullam ben Shlomo da Piera. In Christian Spain the *Sitz im Leben* of Andalusian poetry vanished, and Hebrew poetry changed in its social context, themes, and seriousness. Meshullam da Piera was unique, writing entirely in non-biblical language. Nachmanides, developing new themes, used the classical motifs ironically. Only two of the classical ten meters were used in Christian Spain.

The jubilee volume in honor of A. M. Habermann, edited by Z. Malachi (1977a), contains important studies on various aspects of medieval poetry. There is a bibliography of A. M. Habermann, compiled by Z. Malachi. The volume contains: poems in honor of the wedding day of Moses Hayyim Luzzatto, edited by Benayahu; a study by Tobi (1977) on the thirteenth-century Babylonian poet, Isaac ben Israel; two *piyyuṭim* of Moses ibn Ezra, published by Itzhaki; a study by A. Mirsky on the significance of rhyme in liturgical *muwaššaḥat* (1977b); a study by Fleischer (1977) on the poetry of Hai Gaon; a study of rhyming animal fables by Abraham bar Jacob of Regensburg by Z. Malachi (1977b), and a newly discovered *qerova* to Deut 32:1 by the poet Yannai, published by Z. M. Rabinowitz (1977). The collected studies in liturgy and synagogue poetry of D. Goldschmidt have been published (1980). The synagogue poetry of Greece, Anatolia, and the Balkans has been published by L. Weinberger (1975) and that of Bulgaria by the same editor (1983).

6

MODERN AND CONTEMPORARY HEBREW

DEFINITION OF THE MODERN PERIOD

It is generally agreed that, following the medieval period of the Hebrew language, there came a modern period of revival; but there is no agreement on when it began and by what criteria it is to be defined. Har Zahav (1951–56: 1.88–135) designated the periods according to the analogy of the childhood, youth, maturity, and old age of a human being. If this analogy is followed, the period of revival of Hebrew came after all these eras, almost miraculously. One senses in this description the influence of Nachman Krochmal (1785–1840) who, following Giambattista Vico, posited the existence of three phases in the life of every people; the regeneration of the Jewish people after the third phase, destruction, is exceptional. Har Zahav considers the period of revival to have begun with Moses Hayyim Luzzatto (1707–1740), an Italian Hebrew poet and mystic who wrote allegorical drama in a biblical style and whose novelty was rejection of the mixed Aramaic-Hebrew rabbinic style.

Different definitions of the modern period

M. H. Segal (1936: 1) also holds that the period of revival followed the prehistorical, biblical, and mishnaic periods, and one which he called the period of exile. He admits that the boundaries of these periods cannot be clearly defined. Chomsky (1967: 206–11) posits a transitional period between the Golden Age in Spain and the revival of Hebrew speech in Palestine. This transition includes both medieval and early modern Italian Hebrew literature and the German Haskalah of Mendelssohn and Wessely. In this description, Luzzatto broke with the restrictions of Spanish meter and returned to the simplicity and grandeur of biblical idiom, while at the same time drawing on the resources of Italian humanism. The transitional period was characterized by struggles to expand the narrow liturgical language used previously and to enrich the descriptive and expressive capacities of the Hebrew language. Biblical Hebrew became the basis of a new medium, without, however, rejecting rabbinic idiom. The struggle for language expansion, an interest in secular themes, and use of biblical idiom were especially characteristic of the German Haskalah movement and its followers, but, in the view of Chomsky and others, Luzzatto and his Italian followers can be included in this period.

Additional reflections on the problem of periodization in general have been presented by Ben-Hayyim (1983b) and Rabin (1983b). Rabin notes the difficulties in periodization, due to the varying evidence presented by different language registers and diglossia. Ben-Hayyim observes that medieval writers saw Biblical Hebrew and Mishnaic Hebrew as a unity in terms of grammar, the only differences being in lexicography. To them, *lāšôn qôdeš* also included Mishnaic Hebrew.

The linguistic question cannot be separated from the search for definitions of boundary in the history of literature. The various views on when Modern Hebrew literature had its start are summarized by Shaʾanan in his history of Modern Hebrew literature. Both Joseph Klausner and Fischel Lachover maintained that Modern Hebrew literature begins with the advent of secular themes, thus differentiating it from the essentially religious Middle Ages. Klausner saw this secularism in Wesseley at the end of the eighteenth century, while Lachover saw it in Moses Hayyim Luzzatto. To Lachover, Luzzatto was the harbinger of a new age, while to Klausner he represented the culmination of a waning medieval period. The poet Bialik is actually responsible for the glowing view of Luzzatto's role. In his essay "The Young Man from Padua," he hails Luzzatto as the initiator of three trends in nineteenth-century Jewish life: the liberation of Hebrew literature, the founding of the ethical (*musar*) movement, and the stimulation of the mystical search which was expressed so fully in Hasidism (E. Silberschlag, *From Renaissance to Renaissance*, 1 [New York, 1973] vii–viii). Kurzweill, who greatly emphasized the secular revolution of Hebrew literature which opposed the traditional religious world view, denies Luzzatto the role of innovator. He notes that secularism had different meanings for Luzzatto and Wessely (*Sifrutenu haḥadashah—hemshekh o mahpekhah?* [Tel Aviv, 1969] 16–17). Barzilay (1970) sees the Renaissance writers as essentially looking backward, not forward.

Other authors define the period not in terms of ideology, that is secularism and humanism, but in terms of its relationship to major events in Jewish history. Dov Sadan (*ʿAl sifrutenu hahadashah* [Jerusalem, 1950], introductory essay) places the origin of Modern Hebrew literature in the creativity which emerged between two cataclysms, the persecutions of 1648 and the holocaust under the Nazis. This period would include Hasidic literature, which is contemporaneous with Modern Hebrew literature but is not at all secular (A. Shaʾanan, *Hasifrut haʿivrit haḥadashah lizramehah* [Tel Aviv, 1962], 1.13–19). Shaʾanan himself, following Klausner, opts for dating the beginning of the new period in the wake of the French Revolution. Silberschlag (op. cit.) rejects secularism as the criterion; he dates the beginning of the modern period to 1492, the year of the expulsion from Spain. In one chapter he includes humanists and mystics, in a second, mystical apocalyptic writers—Luzzatto is included here—and in the third chapter he discusses Mendelssohn and Wessely. More recent discussion (see the beginning of ch. 5) has not resolved the problem, which is one of linguistic, ideological and historical criteria being selectively or collectively applied. In the opinions of Bendavid (1985) and Téné (1985, 1986) the end of the Middle Ages and the beginning of the modern period is 1850 and 1900, respectively. Rabin (1985b) and Pagis (1986) argue that different Jewish centers developed in their own way and that periodization cannot be uniform and rigid.

These considerations and the fact that there is no agreement on period boundaries complicate the linguistic question. In fact, our chapter division here follows Klausner.

The German Haskalah was most self-conscious in its aspiration toward European values and language expansion. However, we must raise the question of Hasidic Hebrew, which is roughly contemporary with Haskalah. We have examined Hasidic Hebrew in the section on dialects, observing that it contains Yiddishisms. These categories are not final, however. As noted above, Hasidic literature should be studied in terms of the various types of Hebrew in it, that which is Yiddish-influenced as well as that which is not, and also, in terms of the new terminology it created for its own spiritual concerns. The issues summarized above demonstrate that even periods which emerge with significant self-consciousness and ideological self-proclamation may actually be indebted to earlier periods more than their protagonists recognize. We also include in this section discussion of contemporaries whose ideologies diverged from those of the Haskalah writers.

HASKALAH WRITERS AND HEBREW

General descriptions of the literary and ideological preoccupations of the period can be found in the histories of Hebrew literature, Ben Or (Urinovsky; Tel Aviv, 1946, vol. 1), Shaᵓanan (Tel Aviv, 1961, vol. 1), Silberschlag, and Waxman.

Lexical innovations and different styles among Haskalah writers

There has been a general tendency to scorn the coinages of the Haskalah writers as being on the naïve level of *dilûg-rab̲* 'great leap,' an imaginary derivation in modern Hebrew for 'telegraph' (Y. Avinery 1946: 135–36). Such coinages, however, were not taken seriously even in their own times. Several studies have shown that the lexical innovations of Haskalah writers must be considered as serious contributions. Cnaani (1932–33a) and Porath (1935–36) have written on the creation of new words. Noah Schapira has surveyed historically the various attempts to translate scientific and technical terms (1959–60, 1962–64). Yitzhaki (1970–71) has presented in detail the views of leading Haskalah writers on the creation of new words, the valence to be assigned to Biblical or Mishnaic Hebrew, and the preference for Sephardic as against Ashkenazic pronunciation. The following writers are treated by Yitzhaki: Wessely, Keslin, Satanov, Levisohn, Samuel David Luzzatto, and Schulbaum. These writers did not reject the mishnaic language but saw in it a valuable resource and a natural continuation of Biblical Hebrew. Shachevitz (1966–67) has studied stylistic levels in the journal *Hameᵓassef*: rabbinic, Tibbonite, "maskilic," and synthetic.

Attitudes to the Hebrew language

The attitudes toward the Hebrew language of Haskalah writers such as Wessely, Satanov, Schnaber, and Ben Zeᵓev are described by Pelli (1972, 1979: 73–90). The Maskilim saw the Hebrew language as a means to aid the revival of the Jewish people; thus it was both a means to an end as well as an end in itself. The early Maskilim were painfully aware of the deterioration of the language. They attributed this to the conditions of exile and to the baneful influence of Yiddish ("jargon"), as well as to pilpulistic talmudic study. The Maskilim, however, believed that Hebrew was the mother of all languages and that the presence of foreign words was not a stigma. Schnaber, for example, considered the three-tense system a sign of superiority.

Secularization of Hebrew

Secularization is evident in the different meanings the Maskilim gave to the term *lᵉšôn haqqôdeš*. Mendelssohn based his contention that Hebrew is the "holy tongue" on the fact that the Bible was written in it and that it was the language in which God had spoken to the prophets. Wessely took *qôdeš* in the sense of 'different, distinguished.' Another writer separated *lāšôn* from *qôdeš*, maintaining that Hebrew is the tongue in which the Torah was written. This, according to Pelli, is evidence of a growing secular attitude to the language. The Maskilim believed in the possibility and desirability of the revival of the language. Schnaber referred to it as *l*^{e}*šôn haqqôdeš haḥădāšāh* 'the new holy tongue.' Shochet (1985) discusses the attitudes of the leading Russian Maskilim to the Hebrew language.

Barzilay (1979) distinguishes between the Italian Hebraists—Yehudah Messer Leon, Samuel Archivolti, Leon of Modena, Menahem Lonzano, and Moshe Hayyim Luzzatto—and the writers of the German Haskalah with regard to their attitude toward language. The former were purists who rejected the mixing of Hebrew and Aramaic and the excesses of the *piyyuṭ*. They were satisfied that Biblical and Mishnaic Hebrew were adequate vehicles for expressing all aspects of the natural world.

Attitudes toward Yiddish, Biblical, and Mishnaic Hebrew

The Maskilim had a different perspective. Gumpel Schnaber lamented the inadequacy of Hebrew. Shlomo Pappenheim advocated the legitimizing of Mishnaic Hebrew and its use as a source for expanded vocabulary. Isaac Satanov demanded the expansion of the Hebrew vocabulary and stated that only the political restoration of the people to Zion would enrich the language. While Wessely limited the use of Hebrew to religious matters, Ben Ze$^{\supset}$ev considered it appropriate for the expression of all aspects of life, including popular proverbs. Menahem Mendel Lefin is thought to have been first to introduce Mishnaic Hebrew into Modern Hebrew literature (Barzilay 1979: 13) and to have coined words that have survived into Modern Hebrew: *b*^{e}*ḥîlāh* 'nausea,' *ḥôqen* 'enema,' and *ši*^{c}*ul* 'cough.' The Maskilim were both purist and expansionist in their attitude toward the Hebrew language. The reverse side of their admiration for Hebrew was their rejection of Yiddish as a "jargon." Shmeruk (1978: 235–60) discusses the anti-Hasidic satire written by Haskalah writers in Yiddish. They used Yiddish to reach the masses, but would not permit their own names to be attached to such works for fear of ridicule by other Haskalah writers. Habermann (1980) denies that Joseph Perl wrote compositions in Yiddish, while Werses (1980) affirms that he translated Fielding's *Tom Jones* into Yiddish. Miron (1973: 1–66, 1980) also discusses the use of Yiddish and the ambivalent attitude of Haskalah writers.

Some studies of individual writers and their contributions are listed here. Shachevitz (1967–68) has treated lexical elements as dominant stylistic characteristics in the prose of Wessely, and a masters thesis by Potchinsky (1943) has dealt with his linguistic methods. Carmiel (1964–65; doctoral dissertation) has examined the post-biblical vocabulary of Abraham Mapu's fiction. Berakha Fischler (1983) illustrates how Mapu altered talmudic quotations in *ᶜAyyiṭ tsavuᶜa* to adjust them to the then prevailing biblical stylistic model. Levenson (1972; doctoral dissertation) has elucidated many of the subtleties of Mendelssohn's exegesis of the Bible contained in his *Sefer netivot hashalom* (Berlin, 1780–83), which embraces his German translation of the Pentateuch, a Hebrew commentary, and a masoretic study, the *Tiqqun sofrim*. The stylistic features which Mendelssohn identified include the use of the masoretic accents to define an "enclosed expression," the use of *kelal ufrat* 'general and specific,' and the finer nuances of tense, indicating pluperfect and future-perfect. Y. L. Gordon's approach to new coinages is described in a brief article by R. Weiss (1962–63) and more recently by R. Sivan (1979–80a). Kutscher (1982: 183–92) surveys the forces operating upon the Maskilim. He notes the research of Karu, who discovered many words currently in use which were common in the Hebrew weekly *Hatsfirah* in 1881. These include *daᶜaṯ qāhāl* 'public opinion,' *ḥašmal* 'electricity,' *môqēš* 'mine,' *mašber* 'crisis,' *mišpāṭ qādûm* 'prejudice, and *tappûḥê zāhāḇ* 'oranges.' Kutscher also discusses the significance of Mendele's integration of biblical and mishnaic style. Rabin's treatment of this phenomenon (1979f.) is referred to below. The vocabulary of Modern Hebrew literature between 1750 and 1920 is analyzed by Mirkin (1980) in terms of its lexicographical, stylistic, and grammatical aspects.

Studies of individual writers

The work of Samuel David Luzzatto (1800–1865) on the Hebrew language was earlier studied in a masters thesis by Kashtan (1949) and more recently by Kaddari (1969a) in a comprehensive article. Luzzatto dealt with many areas, including phonology, morphology, history, stylistics, and language policy. He anticipated the modern concept of semantic fields and applied morphological oppositions in establishing meanings in specific contexts.

Samuel David Luzzatto

Weissblüth (1983) has described Rabbi Nachman Krochmal's language, as it appears in his classic *Moreh nevukhe hazman*. The variety of language usages and linguistic structures, stemming from different chronological layers, are classified. Many phrases coined by Krochmal are still part of current usage.

The biblical commentator Meir Leib ben Yechiel Mikhael Malbim (1809–79) was a contemporary of the Haskalah writers, although ideologically he was not one of them. The propriety of

The Malbim, biblical commentator

him in this chapter depends on whether ideological or chronological criteria are chosen for defining the modern period. While we have accepted Klausner's dating of the modern period from the Haskalah, we also recognize the validity of Sadan's inclusion of different kinds of Hebrew writing based on different ideologies. A masters thesis by Atlas (1946) deals with the Malbim, and Kaddari (1963–64) has described his principles of syntax and semantics as applied to biblical exegesis.

LANGUAGE PLANNING AND THE REVIVAL OF HEBREW SPEECH

Early efforts at revival of Hebrew speech

Parfitt (1972) has described the situation of spoken Hebrew in Palestine in the nineteenth century, and reactions to his ideas are found in works by Ber (1974–75) and Rabin (1974–75b). The innovations in agricultural terminology of the Bilu pioneers in the 1880s are the subject of a masters thesis by Adar (1965). General information on this early period is provided in Y. Avinery (1946), Chomsky (1962; 1967: 212–34, 254–74), W. Weinberg (1966), Rosén (1956a: 138–242), and Eytan (1971). The efforts of devoted school teachers who labored to spread Hebrew speech are described in J. Fellman's study on Ben Yehudah (1973a: 11–17, 94–111). A book by Haramati (1979) deals in depth with the role of the teachers in the revival of Hebrew speech between 1882 and 1914.

Competing dialects

Competing dialects existed in the early period. Bar-Adon (1973b, 1975) has described the rise and fall of the Galilean dialect by interviewing older residents of Galilee as well as consulting other sources of information. Humorous references to this dialect as are found in Agnon's story *ʿAd hēnāh*. The idyll of David Shimoni (Shimonovitz), "The War of Judah and Galilee," as well as other modern stage plays, do not give a full picture. Teachers, such as Yitshak Epstein and Simchah Wilkowitz, sought to imitate the dialect of Hebrew spoken by the Sephardic residents of Upper Galilee, South Syria, and Lebanon. Guided by their own linguistic theories, they tried to realize the *bet* as plosive in all situations and to realize the gutturals as in Arabic. Thus, /ḥ/ was to be realized as [ḥ] and not as [x]. Bar-Adon has summarized his conclusions briefly in his study of Agnon's attitudes toward the rise of Modern Hebrew (1977: 29–31). The role of the Second Aliyah in general in language renewal is assessed by Bar-Adon (1986).

Haramati (1976, 1978) examines the activities and views of the three predecessors of Eliezer ben Yehudah: Joseph Halevi, Barukh

Mitrani, and Nissim Behar. Haramati denies Ben Yehudah the credit for innovating the *methode naturelle* (*ʿIvrit beʿivrit*). It was heralded by Behar and further developed by David Yellin and Yitshak Epstein in two different versions. Haramati stresses that the contributions of the Sephardic Jews to the renaissance of Hebrew must not be overlooked.

Predecessors of Ben Yehudah

The efforts of Eliezer ben Yehudah in the revival of Hebrew speech, the creation of the great dictionary, and the direction of language policy have been studied in numerous monographs and articles. Some are enumerated in Rabin (1970a: 328, and n 136). Sivan (1960–61, 1969, 1970, 1972–73, 1976, 1978) deals with different aspects of Ben Yehudah's work. The last work (1978) is an anthology of some of his major articles and includes bibliographical material (1978: 32–33) and a biographical essay. Here Sivan contrasts some of Ben Yehudah's coinages with current usage. Other writers on the subject include Neʾeman (1973–74) and J. Fellman, who has concentrated on the sociolinguistic aspect of Ben Yehudah's work in various studies (1971, a doctoral dissertation; 1973a, 1973b, 1975b).

Eliezer ben Yehudah: evaluations

Fellman recognizes seven steps in Ben Yehudah's activity: the establishment of the first Hebrew-speaking household, the call to Diaspora Jewry and to the local population, the establishment of Hebrew-speaking societies, the institutionalizing of Hebrew in the schools, the use of newspapers which he himself edited (see G. Kressel, תולדות העיתונות העברית בארץ ישראל [Jerusalem, 1964]), the compilation of the great *Thesaurus*, and the founding of the Language Council. Ben Yehudah discovered that the Sephardic and Ashkenazic communities in Palestine could communicate with each other only in Hebrew and that rudimentary conversational Hebrew already existed, with many Sephardim being able to use it with ease.

Evaluations of the significance of Ben Yehudah and his impact upon the revival of Hebrew differ. He is given great credit for his single-handed achievement with the dictionary, given the then-current state of language development and scholarship (Sivan 1969). On the other hand, Fellman (1973a) comes to the conclusion that Ben Yehudah was not a prime mover but peripheral in the revival of Hebrew. The weaknesses of his work, as presented by Fellman, are that the early Language Council viewed language in laymen's terms, solely in terms of vocabulary with no attention to structure; the unscientific nature of the dictionary; and the fact that Ben Yehudah, living in Jerusalem, was not where the action was. The primary impetus came from the teachers in the agricultural

The early Language Council

settlements and the other settlers, while Ben Yehudah was in Jerusalem, an area of great religious conservatism and hostility to the secularization of Hebrew.

The "Battle of the Languages"

During the great "Battle of the Languages," when students and teachers in 1913–14 struggled to establish Hebrew as the language of science instruction at the Haifa Technion, Ben Yehudah, contends Fellman, was relatively silent. He was preoccupied with his dictionary, which was being supported by German-Jewish money. However, in fairness to Ben Yehudah, his home was the planning center for strategy, and he did write and speak forcefully to the German-Jewish representatives who opposed Hebrew in the science program of the Technion. A comparison with Herzl may not be out of order. He, too, was at the center of much controversy and was not the only Zionist, yet his charisma and the agencies he fathered carried on the effort, apart from the acceptance of specific proposals. Many of Ben Yehudah's neologisms are still used today. Unfortunately, Fellman (1973a) does not cite them in Hebrew, but his bibliography is most useful.

Applicability of terms: monolingualism, bilingualism, and diglossia

Wexler (1975) has reacted to Fellman's study (1973a) and has challenged his use of the term diglossia to describe the peculiar situation of Hebrew on the eve of the revival, alive in letters but largely unspoken. He proposes that the situation be characterized as incipient bilingualism, aiming to attain functional oral bilingualism, or as incipient bilingualism, to be superseded immediately by monolingualism (with diglossia). Other European languages were in a different position. In their case, the problem was to ascribe new written functions to what was primarily a spoken language. Belorussian, Ukrainian, and Czech, as described by Wexler, aspired to the creation of diglossia anew, usually with the rejection or downgrading of bilingualism. German and Russian aimed at a redefinition of the diglossia relationship. Hebrew, however, aspired to the creation of functional bilingualism as preliminary to a redefinition of diglossia.

Various norms in Ben Yehudah's time

In Wexler's view, there still remain several areas to be investigated: the early Hebrew dialects spoken in Palestine and abroad (but see Parfitt 1972 and Bar-Adon 1973b, 1975), the spread of the rural and Jerusalem dialect norms to Europe and influences in the opposite direction, the differential impact of Arabic and European languages on the dialects of early modern Hebrew, and the difference between the norms that existed at that time, e.g., Lithuania, Odessa, and Jerusalem. The reaction, often hostile, of the diaspora Hebrew writers to the new words and less traditional syntax of the "Jerusalem style" is described by Sivan (1976, 1979–80b). Arel

(1978) studies the revival of Hebrew in the light of linguistics, and S. Shur (1977, 1979) discusses it in its socio-political context.

Further contributions to the evaluation of Ben Yehuda's role in the revival of Hebrew are to be found in the papers of the Oxford symposium of 1979 (Silberschlag, ed., 1981). G. Mandel (1981) argues that Ben Yehuda's essay, *Sheʾelah nikhbadah* (1879), devoted only nine words to the question of the revival of Hebrew speech. At that point his thought was similar to that of Smolenskin, namely, that Hebrew would serve as a connector between the various Jewish communities, as it actually did in Jerusalem. A few months later he advanced to the idea that the revival of speech was essential to national revival. At first, then, he accepted diglossia, later rejecting it. Parfitt and Turčanová (1981) compare Ben Yehudah with L'udovit Štúr, the creator of the Slovak literary language. The common elements, according to these writers, are that neither man initiated the idea of a language revival but carried on what was already in progress. Ben Yehudah merely carried on what already existed, the use of Hebrew for communication between the Jewish communities.

Ben Yehudah compared with innovators in other languages

Rabin (1979f) discusses the revival of Hebrew in sociolinguistic terms. He rejects the negative view of Ben Yehuda's contribution expressed by Parfitt (1972). The "revival" of a language has different meanings in different contexts; contrast the expansion of an already-existing literary language which is also spoken with the establishment of full verbal communication in a language that lives as a literary language. Ben Yehuda stressed the second aspect. He accepted the current European nationalistic view that a "living" language is one that is spoken. The limited use of Hebrew that existed in the Yishuv in Palestine could not have been unknown to Ben Yehudah, but to him that was not enough to characterize it as a "living language." In a later study, Rabin (1983d) traces Ben Yehudah's development until he arrived at this position.

Sociolinguistic factors

Rabin further treats the tension between the language as viewed linguistically and as viewed sociologically. Terminology must be developed to distinguish between the language that has been revived, modern Israeli Hebrew, and the language of the literary sources which it was the intention to revive. Here lies the problem of normativism and actual usage. Not until the 1950s, due to the work of H. B. Rosén and Haim Blanc, was the notion accepted among Hebrew linguists that actual usage deserves scientific treatment and is something more than a collection of errors deviating from the classical norm. However, as the classical norms when applied to the current language become more confused, the

Modern Hebrew is not classical Hebrew revived

common impression that the revived language is the classical language revived, weakens. The socially useful fiction that Classical Hebrew lives again is shown to be just a fiction.

The role of Mendele

Rabin elaborates upon the important development in 1886, the serializing of Mendele's story, "*Beseter raᶜam*," in the newspaper *Hayom*, which was published in St. Petersburg. Mendele created a style that synthesized biblical and mishnaic elements. He was not the first to do so—Hasidic literature and some Maskilim had done so before—but Mendele made this synthesis, with its expanded capacities of expression, more widely available. Sivan (1982) also deals with sociological factors in the revival of Hebrew, attaching great importance to the vitality of religion at that time. Izreᵓel (1986) also deals with the revival of Hebrew.

Conflicting contemporary attitudes to Ben Yehudah and new coinages

The struggles between various normativist views and the emerging contemporary Hebrew language in Palestine are documented in the proceedings of the Language Committee and its successor, The Academy of the Hebrew Language (Rabin 1970a: 329, n 329; 1973c: 55–62). Eisenstadt (1967) has much interesting information on personalities and institutions. Some of the pertinent documents are anthologized in *Leqeṭ teᶜudot* (Sivan and Kressel 1970) and in Saulson (1979), which is a translation with critical and evaluative conclusion (see the discussion below). In this book one can find the views of Ahad Ha-Am, Joseph Klausner, Bialik, Yellin, and others. Ahad Ha-Am, for example, did not support the conscious coining of new words for their own sake. He maintained that advancing the intellectual content of Hebrew expression would in itself guarantee the development of new words. In his own writing he preferred foreign forms for abstract concepts (e.g., *qûltûrāᵓ*). In the "battle of the languages" at the Haifa Technion it was Ahad Ha-Am's theory that sciences could not be taught in Hebrew, given its stage of development at that time. Simon Bernstein rejected entirely the concept of spoken Hebrew. This historical period and Ben Yehudah's role are summarized in Rabin (1973c: 47–54).

S. Y. Agnon's views on Ben Yehudah

Bar-Adon's studies (1972–73, 1977a) on S. Y. Agnon's attitude toward the development of Modern Hebrew are based on the writer's stories and taped interviews. These studies, especially the later one (1977a), give a fresh view of the debates and clashes of personalities which occurred in the earlier part of the century. Like Bialik and Joseph Hayyim Brenner, Agnon regarded the new coinages of Ben Yehudah and his family (his wife, Hemda, and his son, Ittamar) as artificial and removed from organic contact with the Jewish sources. In several places in Agnon's stories, down to the posthumously published novel, *Shirah*, there are ironic and humorous references to self-appointed language innovators, a transparent criticism of the Ben Yehudah approach. There were more than just linguistic considerations operating here, however. Attitudes toward the religious heritage and to Zionism were also involved. Ben Yehudah was not religiously observant, and he favored the controversial Uganda proposal. The view, advanced by Menahem Ussishkin, that Ben Yehudah was the "father of spoken Hebrew," irritated both Agnon and Bialik. They rejected the claim, since Hebrew was spoken by Ashkenazim and Sephardim in Palestine before Ben Yehudah's arrival.

Ben Yehudah's use of Arabic in new coinages

Ben Yehudah's approach to the creation of new words has been described by R. Weiss (1960–61, 1961–62) and Sivan (1960–61; 1969; 1972–73; 1978: 26–33). In a lecture before the Language Committee (*Proceedings*, 1912; cited in Sivan 1978: 213–27) Ben Yehudah urged the Language Committee to adopt roots found in Arabic, after proper selection, as *bona fide* Hebrew roots. He also proposed creating new roots *ex nihilo*, wherever needed, but his suggestions were not accepted. Although some Arabic words have entered Modern Hebrew, e.g., *ʾadîḇ* 'generous,' *ṣabbār* 'cactus,' *rašmî* 'official,' *timrôn* 'maneuver,' and more have entered slang, the quantity of such adoptions is nowhere near the proportion envisioned by Ben Yehudah. Shunarry (1976) traces the development of Ben Yehudah's views on Arabic and the reaction of his contemporaries. Other treatments of this aspect of language-creation are found in works by Y. Avinery (1946: 81–88), Rosén (1956a: 75–77), Piamenta (1960–61), and J. Fellman (1973a: 59–60, 65). Blanc (1954–55) has examined the Arabic element in Modern Hebrew.

Simple coinages and European roots

Ben Yehudah sought to avoid compounds and preferred to substitute simple coinages instead, e.g., *miṭriyyāh* 'umbrella' instead of *maḥseh mi-māṭār* 'protection from rain' and *ʿîriyyāh* 'city hall' in place of *bēṯ môʿeṣeṯ hā-ʿîr* 'seat of the city council.' An essay, published in the Nahum Sokolow *Festschrift* in 1904 (Sivan 1978: 186–200) demonstrates Ben Yehudah's approach to words made up of several elements that have been fused. Ben Yehudah accepted European roots, such as *bubbāh* 'doll,' *sabbôn* 'soap,' *miḇrešeṯ* 'brush,' but on the other hand, he replaced European words then current with Hebrew ones, e.g., *miḇrāq* for *ṭelegrammāh*, *ḥaydaq* for *baqṭeriyāh*, *ʾôp̱nāh* for *môdāh* 'fashion.' In a series of articles, Mirkin (1972–73, 1974–75) discusses the development of Ben Yehudah's dictionary. Sagi (1976), in a masters thesis, compares the journalism of Ben Yehudah with contemporary practice in regard to the order of subject and predicate.

The son of Eliezer ben Yehudah, Ittamar ben Avi (an acronym for his father's name which also means "my father") was also noteworthy as a coiner of new words. Some of his contributions are described by R. Weiss (1961–62) and Ben Sira (1971–73), e.g., *riʾyen* 'interviewed' and *ʿaḵšāwî* 'contemporary, current.' His writing style was much influenced by French, and its emotionalism, like his father's, evoked opposition. He was also associated with an attempt to adapt the Latin alphabet for the printing of Hebrew (Federbush 1967: 86; W. Weinberg 1971: 106–18).

Other language innovators

R. Weiss (1982) surveys the linguistic innovations of Y. L. Gordon, Zev Yaʿavets, Ben Yehudah and his son, Klausner, Bialik, Persky, Agnon, Moshe Sharett, and Shlonsky, and discusses other issues in contemporary Hebrew usage.

The approach of Moshe Schulbaum (1830–1918) to these problems has been contrasted with that of Ben Yehudah by Cnaani (1932–33b) and Tannenblatt (1963–64). Schulbaum, too, was greatly concerned with enriching the lexical stock of Modern Hebrew. He rejected the Arabic component and urged the translation of Aramaic phrases into Hebrew. This idea did not win acceptance because of the great influence of traditional talmudic studies and the mixed Hebrew-Aramaic style of the rabbinic leaders. Schulbaum did not accept the idea that there was a sister-relationship between Hebrew and Arabic. He wrote: "The ruin of Hebrew will not be built up from Arab booty" (Tannenblatt 1963–64: 230).

There were, however, some artificial elements in Schulbaum's approach—for example, his belief that new roots can be created by changes of consonants and metathesis. Despite his insistence on authentic native sources for new words, he entered words like *ʾăṭalgrēp̱* 'I will telegraph' and *pilsēp̱* 'he philosophized' into his dictionary. He demanded that words be useful and esthetic and urged that a "high court" be set up to be responsible for creating new words. Others who also wanted such a body are referred to in the writings of Ben Yehudah (Shunarry 1976). Other innovators' ideas have also been examined in brief articles: Joseph Klausner by R. Weiss (1973–74) and David Yellin by I. Zeidman (1963–64). Haramati (1981–82) evaluates the roles of Yitshaq Epstein and (1982–83) Israel Hayim Tevyov in the revival of Hebrew.

An attempt to direct language development, guided by a quasi-public or official agency, was made by Ben Yehudah and his contemporaries. Various studies have dealt with the problems and the results of the language planning of the Language Committee and the Academy of the Hebrew Language. The efforts of these organizations has been analyzed and compared with the efforts of parallel bodies in other countries in which language modernization is an issue. Sivan (1964; doctoral dissertation) researches goals and verbal patterns in the reviving of the Hebrew language. Noun patterns employed by the Academy are discussed by Ben-Asher (1960). Shanbal (1977; masters thesis) studies language problems as reflected in the newspapers between 1900 and 1948. J. Fellman (1974) surveys the history, structure, and function of the Academy.

The Academy of the Hebrew language and parallel institutions

From an early period the language reformers in Israel watched carefully the efforts of other nations. Klausner, for example, in an essay written in 1929 (in collected essays 1957: 45–47), makes reference to the Modern Greek innovators. On a more scientific basis, there are several studies which treat the question comparatively. H. Shahade (1971–72) has compared the work of the Language Academy with similar developments in Syria, carried out under the guidance of the corresponding Arabic academy. Nahir (1974a) has written about the Academy of the Hebrew Language at length, comparing its work with that of parallel institutions, such as the French Academy, the Gaelic League, and similar bodies in Turkey and Malaysia. These various language bodies share common aims with respect to language: purification, revival, reform, standardization, and lexical modernization. Nahir identifies these phases in the work of the Hebrew Language Academy. Nahir (1974b) has also studied the method used by the Academy in accepting lexical work. Arel (1981) compares Hebrew and Norwegian in questions of language norms and status. Very useful for comparative purposes is the selected bibliography of the language problems of developing nations compiled by Bar-Adon (1973a).

The renaissance of Hebrew and Arabic compared

A monograph by Blau (1976b; translation, 1981) compares the renaissance of Hebrew and Arabic. Both languages are heavily influenced by their classical traditions, and there are many parallels in their progress toward modernization. Both languages have remained rather static in morphology and spelling, and the greatest developments have been in the area of phraseology. Both Hebrew and Arabic language academies stress simpler constructions, but both have also been influenced by European literary usage. Thus one may find in Hebrew the indirect influence of the New Testament, e.g., *ṭ*^{e}*ḇîlaṯ ʾēš* 'baptism of fire,' a phrase mediated by general European influence. Similar phenomena occur in Arabic. The process of secularizing a classical, religious language has gone much further in Hebrew than in Arabic, due to the non-religious sentiment dominant in Israel, while secularization is inhibited by the more traditional Arab society.

Socio-linguistic responses to new words

There are several studies on the sociolinguistics involved in the acceptance by various segments of Israeli society of the innovations of the Language Academy. We have already referred to a study by Nahir (1974b). In *Linguistics* 120 (1974) a number of articles on this question appeared: introductory remarks by J. A. Fishman; a survey of literature on sociolinguistic problems in Israel by Rosenbaum, Nadel, and J. Fellman (1974); Allony-Fainberg (1974) on the knowledge, usage of, and attitudes toward official Hebrew terms for parts of the car; J. Hofman (1974a) on chemists and (1974b) and psychologists in Israel; and Seckbach (1974) on Israeli teachers. Fisherman (1972) discusses police attitudes toward official Hebrew, and a doctoral dissertation by Allony-Fainberg (1977) examines linguistic, social-demographic factors, and the prospects for acceptance of officially-coined Hebrew terms. Ben-Hayyim (1978a) has written an evaluation of the work of the Language Academy during its twenty-five years of existence.

Sociolinguistic evaluation of the Hebrew Language Academy

Saulson (1979: 161–97) adds an evaluative conclusion to his translation of Sivan and Kressel's collection (1970) of documents on language planning in Israel. He evaluates language planning in terms of pre-specified criteria. Establishing criteria is a complex problem which gives rise to further problems, such as: the proper balance between clarity, redundancy, and economy, and determining an expedient relationship between tradition and ideal which also takes into account historical factors. But Hebrew, he feels, was the product of a political philosophy. There were both "push" and "pull" factors, the "push" being the rejection of medievalisms or "diasporisms" and the "pull," a tendency toward conservatism. Both vectors have been weakened. There are now multiple Hebrew-language-speaking communities which are no longer co-extensive. There has been a shift from a value-oriented language situation to one where function dominates. In addition to the factors which contributed to the rise of multiple-language communities, such as technical specialization and slang, there is the factor of continued immigration. Language training for immigrants is short-term and is oriented toward mastering "understandable" communication while being integrated into the labor market.

Certain anomalies have been noted. The general language community is more purist than the Academy, demanding Hebrew words to replace foreign ones (Kornblueth and Aynor 1974: 44). The older generation is more ideological about Hebrew though speaking it less exclusively, while the younger generation is far less ideological while exclusively Hebrew-speaking. In both cases, the motivations are compensatory and tend toward the preservation of national integrity in the midst of technological revolution.

The role of "language managers"

Saulson, following H. B. Rosén, is critical of the conservatism of language managers and of their lack of concern for the general community. They are self-assured and convinced that everyone, including the uneducated and the immigrants, should make the same effort to learn Hebrew which they made. There is a tendency to protect established "good" usage from continual change, but these usages are based, not on classical Hebrew, but on the Hebrew of the language managers themselves (Rosén 1969c: 97). The weaknesses of the planning of the language managers are related to normativism and insufficient consideration of the participation of other groups in the population.

In a democratic society, language planning must be mediated through various interest groups in the society. Without their cooperation, there can be no success. These groups include writers, educators, journalists, proofreaders, and printing-room supervisors. They tend to be attached emotionally to earlier spelling forms. A notable exception in the area of language planning is the word-coining department of the Israel Defense Forces. Its work proceeds more rapidly and many words gain wide acceptance. This is due to the representative quality of the Army in its relationship to Israeli society.

In conclusion, Saulson states: "The predominantly normative linguistic rationale maintained by the managers does not mesh with the realities on which language planning authority rests in Israeli society" (Saulson 1979: 193–94). The orthoepists, the language managers, have created, not Modern Hebrew but "Academese" Hebrew. This, claims Saulson (1979: 196) "infects" the literary language of the sources by declassicizing them and projecting the modern content back upon classical Hebrew. There are different linguistic analyses of the possibility of maintaining an unmixed Modern Hebrew. Rosén (Rabin 1970a: 332) has claimed that the non-orthoepic strategy is the only valid one, that Israeli Hebrew should be accepted as the standard and the attempt to impose classical rules upon the modern language be discarded. Saulson suggests that minor changes be introduced, but that several alternate solutions be allowed to coexist indefinitely so that they can be evaluated.

FORCES ACTING ON CONTEMPORARY HEBREW FROM WITHIN AND WITHOUT

Contemporary Hebrew: continuity or break?

The problem which occupies the research considered here is whether contemporary Hebrew is a continuation of the earlier levels of the language or a radical break with the past. Tied in with this question is the problem of foreign influence on contemporary Hebrew, many of whose speakers are at least bilingual. Many new coinages have been modeled on European idioms and words.

Contemporary Hebrew reflects outside influences

There are some extreme views. Katzenelson (1960: 63–76) claims that contemporary Hebrew is nothing but Yiddish and other European languages garbed in Hebrew words and makes a plea for Jews to return to Yiddish. Wexler (1981: 107) considers Israeli Hebrew to be a non-Jewish language acquiring numerous Jewish features. Shaffer (1972) argues that Ben Yehudah did not revive Hebrew, since British consuls reported that it was spoken before his time, and that contemporary Hebrew is a continuation of Aramaic, not of Biblical Hebrew.

Apart from such views, there is a significant amount of study which has been done on foreign influences upon contemporary Hebrew. Blau (1978a) sees Hebrew as drawing from several historical levels and also as being deeply influenced in phraseology and syntax by Standard Average European. Rabin (1968–69) deals with loan translations and Altbauer (1964) with new negation constructions. Blanc (1965) demonstrates Yiddish influences, e.g., *nāṯan ṣ*$^{e c}$*āqāh/d*^{e}*p̱îqāh* < *er hot gegeben a geshrey/a klap* 'he gave a shout/a blow' and the aspective modification, *yāšaḇ* 'he sat' *hiṯyaššēḇ* 'he settled down' < *er hot sikh avekgesetst*. Moskovich and Guri (1982) also discuss Yiddish influence on contemporary Hebrew in phraseology and in adding new meanings to existing Hebrew words. Schmeltz and Bachi (1972–73, 1974) have appraised the effects of several conditions upon the speakers of Israeli Hebrew: age at immigration, length of stay in Israel, current age, sex, educational attainment, country of birth, labor force status, and residence. These variables may include the effects of mother-tongue interference, although the authors do not identify this as a separate variable. A masters thesis by Weller (1971) deals with the effect of mother-tongue interference on language learning. Other studies have been made on mother-tongue interference by Levenston (1971); Harkavy (1972–73) on Georgian Jews; Gumpertz (1953: 19–33) on German Jews; and D. Doron (1964), a masters thesis, on the Hebrew of Arabic speakers, based on the *bagrut* examination. A. Shivtiel (1971; masters thesis) studies the influence of the Arabic language upon the writing of Hebrew during the period of the revival. Vidislavsky (1980; masters thesis) studies syntactic and lexical factors in the spoken language of students of eastern and western origin. Bentolila (1984) surveys the Hebrew pronunciations of a Moroccan Jewish community in the Negev as an instance of phonology related to sociolinguistics.

Outside influence on morphology

A number of studies in morphology by Masson (1973, 1976b) demonstrate the influence of other languages. The first study discusses the suffix *-nîq*, which indicates the member of a class—political, military, social, or other—e.g., *qibbûṣnîq* 'member of a kubbutz,' *garağnîq* 'one who works in a garage,' and *k*^{e}*lûmnîq* 'a nobody.' These suffixes could conceivably derive from Yiddish, Russian, or Polish, but Masson concludes that Yiddish is the source. The second study (1976b) deals with the *CaCiC* form of the verbal adjective in Hebrew, *qārîʾ* 'readable,' *pāgîʿa* 'vulnerable.' It is possible that a precedent for this existed in Classical Hebrew; thus *nāḇiʾ* 'prophet' was not only one who was called but one who had the faculty of prophesying. However, European influence is clearly apparent here, for the early settlers needed a Hebrew form to parallel expressions such as German *sichtbar*, English *visible*, or Russian *vidimyi*.

Conflicting normativist views

The struggle between normativists and those who maintain that Israeli Hebrew is subject to its own rules is described by Rabin (1970a: 329–44). The theoretical basis of this dichotomy in terms of sociolinguistics is discussed by Rabin in a later study (1979f.: 138–40). Ben-Asher (1969) compares the views of a selected group of normativist grammarians, including Har Zahav, Avinery, Peretz, and Ornan. Innovations in Israeli Hebrew are described by Chomsky (1967: 212–34), W. Weinberg (1966, 1974), and Kutscher (1982: 243–69).

Rosén (1956a, 1957, 1961, 1962, 1976) has taken the position that Israeli Hebrew is free of the rules which operated on earlier levels and that these earlier levels, often hopelessly mixed, should not set norms for contemporary Hebrew. The fact that Hebrew is heir to many layers of language history, all accessible in well-studied classical sources (Bible, Mishnah, Siddur, medieval poetry and prose), accounts for the battle of styles, the extra-linguistic, ideological positions taken in favor of the biblical or mishnaic style. Rabin (1970a: 330–31) has described this situation, referring to the views of Klausner, Har Zahav, and Bendavid. The development of Bendavid's thinking is reflected in the change of title between his earlier work (1951), *Biblical Hebrew or Mishnaic Hebrew?* (*H*), and the revised version (1967, 1971), *Biblical Hebrew and Mishnaic Hebrew* (*H*). An attempt to arrive at a synthesis is outlined in Bendavid (1967: 239–329).

New coinages on the basis of obscure, rare words

Literary (as opposed to organic) continuity may explain why some biblical *hapax legomena*, whose precise meanings are subject to doubt, have been taken into the common vocabulary. A doctoral dissertation by Chaim (H. R.) Cohen (1975) interprets these words in light of Akkadian and Ugaritic and semantic parallels. Examples of *hapax legomena* used in modern Hebrew are *tôṯāḥ* 'cannon' (cf. Job 41:21), *paʿnēaḥ* 'decode' (from *ṣop̱naṯ paʿnēaḥ*, Gen 41:45; BDB 861), *ʾôḇeḵ* 'dust-laden air' (from *hiṯʾabēḵ*, Isa 9:17; BDB 5). In some of these cases there is a discontinuity between the basic meaning in the biblical text and the traditional rabbinic and medieval understanding. However, beginning with the post-biblical period, the relationship of meanings is continuous. We might compare, for example, *ʾărešeṯ* 'expression, utterance,' *ʾărešet pānîm* 'facial expression,' based on Ps 21:3. Fundamentally, *ʾrš* is cognate with Akkadian *erēšu* and Ugaritic *ʾrš* 'desire' (Dahood 1965: 131). However, the Targum, Rashi, Kimchi, and Ibn Ezra all agree that it means "utterance," the meaning it has in the prayer of the Jewish New Year after the sounding of the shofar. Adini (1975–76, 1979–80) follows the development of *pirḥāḥ* (Job 30:12) from medieval to modern times. There are modern cases of ingenious adaptation of words to senses not intended in the Bible but suggested by midrashic interpretation, many of these attributable to Ben Yehudah, e.g., *balšān* 'linguist,' *balšānûṯ* 'linguistics.' This word is based on a play on the name *Morḏ^{e}ḵay Bilšān* (Ezra 2:2) understood midrashically as *baʿal l^{e}šônôṯ* 'master of languages' (*t.b. Men.* 65a; Waldman 1975a: 1313–14). Perhaps the root *blš* 'search' was also involved. Fuchs (*Leš* 41 [1976–77] 75) connects *bilšān* with Akkadian *bēl lišāni*, 'one who is master of a language,' an ironic confirmation of a midrashic play.

Joseph Klausner's contribution evaluated

The views of J. Klausner on several problems—archaisms, biblical and mishnaic forms, and aramaisms—are presented in his collected essays (1957). Klausner objected to linguistic anarchy in an essay published in 1925 (1957: 57–71), complaining loudly that both purists and non-traditionalists were guilty of arbitrariness. At that time, the Greek-derived word *p^{e}santēr* 'piano' (see Dan 3:5) was rejected by some in favor of *makkûšîṯ*, which contained the idea of percussion or striking. The commonly accepted word *gap̱rûr* 'match' was rejected by some for *ṣittāh* or *madlîq*. In 1935 (1957: 72–78) Klausner argued against letting Hebrew become a graveyard of archaic forms. In general he favored the later mishnaic forms over the more archaic biblical, seeing in them a natural historical development. In 1934 (1957: 84–90) he argued against the misuse of talmudic and biblical words which were not fully understood. In 1949 (1957: 163–68) he tried to persuade the public that Hebrew had no need for aramaisms, which have only a snob appeal. Thus, he sought to replace *šēn tôṯeḇeṯ* 'false tooth' by *šēn tôšeḇeṯ*, the corresponding Hebrew form, and *ᶜayyēn leᶜēyl* 'see above' by *ᶜayyēn lemaᶜălāh*. However, planned-language logic and language reality do not always correspond. It is a fact that Aramaic serves as a major source for words, especially when semantic differentiation is needed, e.g., *māqôm* 'place,' *ʾăṯar* 'site,' (vb.) *leʾattēr* 'to locate.' An article by R. Weiss (1973–74) evaluates Klausner as a language innovator.

The influence of the biblical lexicon

Radday notes, in his survey (1970–71) of Hebrew frequency lists, that Modern Hebrew relies heavily on lexical units originating in the Bible. In the frequency list of Rieger (dating from 1935) a mere 197 words out of 1000 are not in the Bible, and in the list of Balgur (from 1968), only 140 are not in the Bible. These lists identify basic roots, not patterns or syntactic usage. Despite the lexicon, it cannot be assumed that contemporary Hebrew bears a close resemblance to Biblical Hebrew apart from the use of formal expressions. Some of the differences between the two levels are described by D. Gutman (1970). A masters thesis by Hatab (1977) analyzes the broadening of choices in the use of verbs from Biblical Hebrew in contemporary Hebrew.

Drawing upon many strata

The peculiar historical and literary relationship between Modern Hebrew and Classical Hebrew also accounts for the emergence of forms based on incorrectly transmitted texts. Tur-Sinai (1954–59, *Halashon*, 363–92) has collected many examples of these, e.g., *melasṭēm* 'robs,' thought to be derived from **lîsṭîm* but actually coming from Greek *lēstēs* "robber.' In this case the final *mem* and the *samekh* were confused. The development of current expressions through syntactical restructuring of classical literary material has been described in detail in studies by Jarden (1956), Moreshet (1966–67b), and R. Landau (1967, 1970, 1971). Kutscher (1961) has traced many contemporary words to early Hebrew, Aramaic, or Akkadian origins. In his history of the Hebrew language (1982, edited posthumously by his son, Raphael Kutscher)

The influence of mysticism and medieval philosophy

there is much material which shows how Hebrew has drawn upon its different historical strata, upon various fused-Hebrew dialects (for example, Yiddish and Judeo-Spanish) and foreign languages (1982: 193–225). Kaddari, in a book (1970a) and in a series of articles in *LLA*, has traced the history of expressions that go back to kabbalah and medieval philosophy. For example, *šiddûd maᶜărāḵôṯ* 'radical change, a shakeup' (often pronounced as [siddud maᶜăraxot]) derives from philosophical writings, in which the name *Šadday* 'Almighty' is explained as 'the one who robs/overpowers the ranks of the heavenly hosts,' that is, who governs Israel directly, overruling the domination of stars and constellations (see Nachmanides on Gen 16:1, quoting Abraham Ibn Ezra, who in turn, cites Samuel Hanagid). A full discussion of this idiom occurs in Kaddari (1970a: 40–42). Another instance is *ᵓênennî bᵉqaw habbᵉrîᵓûṯ* 'I am not well,' lit., 'I am not in the line of health,' derived from cheiromantic terminology (G. Scholem, *Kabbalah* [Jerusalem, 1974], 319). Nir (1975) has also treated the survival of obsolete expressions. A. Bendavid, in a series of articles in *LLA*, has traced the Hebrew expressions currently used in connection with the festivals back to their origins (1971–72a, 1971–72b, 1972–73, 1973–74a, 1973–74b, 1973–74c, 1975–76, 1976–77a). The secularization of words from the realm of the sacred is analyzed by Gan (1961–62) and Yannai (1978, 1980). A doctoral dissertation by D. Shalom (1979) studies the Aramaic component in modern Hebrew.

Hebrew study in the Soviet Union

The fate of Hebrew in the Soviet Union is described by Gilboa (1982) in terms of historical and political factors. I. Axelrod-Rubin (1984) discusses in great detail the role of Jews in Oriental and Semitic studies in the Soviet Union, up to the present. Of special interest for this volume is her description of the role of scholars in Hebrew and Semitic studies (1984: 277–90). These include B. Grande, J. B. Grundfest, A. B. Dolgopolsky, I. N. Vinnikov, and M. L. Geltser in comparative Semitics; Joseph Amusin on the Dead Sea Scrolls; Hayim Sheynin in medieval studies; and Leyb K. Vilster in Samaritan studies.

PHONOLOGY OF CONTEMPORARY HEBREW

For the sake of clarification, the term "contemporary Hebrew" is meant in this work to refer to current Israeli Hebrew. All studies cited hereafter are concerned with the living language. A new bibliography edited by Fischler (1984) lists 951 items published in Israel on contemporary Hebrew.

Various studies on contemporary Hebrew phonology

A number of articles and studies have attempted to describe the phonology of Israeli Hebrew. Patai's article (1953) is not considered significant. Weiman (1950) contributed a pioneering work which has been reviewed critically by Rabin (1970a: 333), Goshen-Gottstein (1950), Rosén (1955–56), and Ben-Hayyim (1954–55). Ornan (1973a) has edited a convenient anthology of articles on contemporary Hebrew phonology.

Enoch and Kaplan (1968–69) discuss the physical nature of accent. D. Téné (1962) has measured the length of vowels by means of the cimograph. His findings include: the average length of a pretonic vowel is about half of a tonic vowel; these contrasts are independent of vowel quality and consonant environment; the accented vowel on an open syllable is longer by 5% than an accented vowel in a closed syllable; and a syllable ending in a voiced consonant tends to be longer than one ending in an unvoiced consonant. Téné used two subjects in this study, and it is possible that a broader sample would modify the conclusions. The consonantal phonemes in Israeli Hebrew are analyzed by J. Fellman (1974–75).

Semiloff-Zelasko (1973) has studied vowel reduction and loss in contemporary Hebrew fast speech and (1975) has also discussed the acoustics and perception of *alef* and *ᶜayin*. Research on sound frequency has been done by Peladah (1958–59) and Radday and Schor (1976). The study by Radday and Schor compares the frequency of consonants in Biblical and Israeli Hebrew. The statistically significant changes are the decrease by one-half in the frequency of *alef* due to the greater frequency of *ʾāmar* 'said' in Biblical Hebrew, and the increase in *samekh*, *ṭet*, *gimmel*, and *qof*, which can be explained by the presence of a greater number of foreign loanwords. The purpose of the research was to quantify the affinity between the two strata of the language, and the conclusion was that the resulting coefficient of contingency is approximately 0.200. Analogous calculations have determined the affinity between Dutch and German to be 0.222, meaning that a speaker of Biblical Hebrew would be as capable or incapable of understanding Israeli Hebrew as a modern Dutchman is of understanding German. Strictly speaking, this study covers more than phonology, as the measure of the frequency of consonants reflects.

A general description of the phonology by Téné (1969: 52–54) distinguishes between two varieties of speech: one in which the pharynx is used and one in which it is not. The first variety uses both pharyngeal, unvoiced *ḥ* and pharyngeal, voiced ᶜ (both are fricatives). It also distinguishes between [ḥ] and [x], the palatal and velar fricatives. Thus [maḥar] 'tomorrow' and [maxar] (*māḵar*) 'sold' are distinguished in articulation. These distinctions are not present in the second variety of speech, in which orthographic *ḵ* and *ḥ* are both realized as [x]. The first variety, then, distinguishes between [hu me^{c}ir oto] (*hûʾ me^{c}ir ʾôṯô*) 'he wakes him up' and [hu meir oto] (*hûʾ meʾîr ʾôṯô*) 'he sheds light on him,' whereas the second realizes both as [hu meiR oto], leading to ambiguity. The first variety is "arabized" Israeli speech, used by speakers whose parents spoke Arabic or Judezmo, while the second is "Ashkenazoid," spoken by children of immigrants from Central or Eastern Europe where Yiddish was spoken. Both varieties demonstrate the interference of either Arabic or Yiddish.

Ashkenazic and oriental pronunciations

There has been some discussion of the relationship of sociology to phonology. Blanc (1956–57, 1964a) has collected texts of transcribed Israeli speech. He distinguishes between "Ashkenoid" and "Arabized" Israeli speech. Although these two varieties are set off from each other by phonic, phonemic, grammatical, and lexical differences, he feels that the similarities outweigh the differences and prefers to use the comprehensive term "General Israeli." He describes the vowel system as being a typical "2×2×1" system, e.g.,

/i/		/u/
/e/		/o/
	/a/	

There are variants in the realization of these phonemes.

The consonants are arranged in a "4×4" obstruent system, e.g.,

/p/	/f/	/t/	/s/	/č/	/š/	/k/	/x/
/b/	/v/	/d/	/z/	/ǧ/	/ž/	/g/	/r/

There are two nasal continuants, /m/ and /n/, one lateral /l/, and a semi-consonant, /y/. Some speakers have an apically trilled /r/ which pairs off with /l/ rather than with /x/. This is the rule in Arabized Israeli, which also includes two additional obstruents, /ḥ/ and /^{c}/. J. Fellman (1974–75) follows Blanc (1964a: 136) in describing the consonantal system.

Chayen (1969, doctoral dissertation; 1971–72, 1972, 1973) has described the phonology of Israeli Hebrew, aiming at identifying an "accepted pronunciation" which is independent of local and community dialects. A further study in phonology is by Chayen (1986). Morag (1972–73) dissents from Chayen's description, arguing that a distinction must be maintained between "General Israeli" and "Oriental Israeli." The distinguishing features of the latter, as noted, are pharyngeal /ḥ/ and /^{c}/ and forward /r/. In Morag's opinion, this difference in the realization of some consonants affects the vowel system as well. "General Israeli" has six vowels:

/i/	/u/
/e/	/o/
/a/	/ɑ/

while "Oriental Israel" has only five:

/i/		/u/
/e/		/o/
	/a/	

The difference is due to the presence of the pharyngeals. Ornan (1973b: 335) observes that no class distinctions can be attached to the "Ashkenazoid" and "Arabized" pronunciations, since both are present in the same sociological or occupational groups.

A reexamination of this entire question has been undertaken by Devens in her doctoral dissertation (1978) and in an article (1980). A group of speakers of Oriental Israeli Hebrew (OIH) and General Israeli Hebrew (GIH) were studied, using transcriptions, spectrograms, and palatograms. The subject of intonation in OIH has not been studied systematically, but it promises fruitful results. There is a greater 'singing' quality in OIH. Some tentative results are presented (1980: 33–34). The conclusion is that OIH, despite official advocacy and its use by radio announcers, is headed for extinction in the educated levels of society. The movement is unilateral, from OIH to GIH. An originally geographically-based speech variety is turning into a socio-economically defined one. Devens (1983) has observed the occurrence of interdental variants of the denti-alveolar consonants [t], [d], [n], [l], [s], and [z]. These are variants, not allophones, and seem to depend on the presence of front vowels. No differentia by age or origin can be ascertained.

Influence of phonetics upon other areas of language

Phonetic changes in Israeli Hebrew have exerted influence on the rest of the system. Rosén (1956a: 112–15) has attempted to describe these. For example, with the adoption of the Sephardic pronunciation and the identical realization of the entities transcribed as *a* and *ā*, there is no way to distinguish between present *nilḥām* 'fights' and past *nilḥam* 'fought.' Rosén maintains that the differentiation is effected through the use of an auxiliary verb, thus *hāyāh nilḥām* 'was fighting' eliminates any ambiguity. Following Rosén, Fischler (1976) holds that the only way to distinguish between present *gārā́h* 'she resides' and past *gā́rāh* 'she resided' is not through the accent but through suppletion, by the addition of the verb 'to be,' e.g., *hāy^{e}ṯāh gā́rāh* 'she resided.' However, Rosén's view is vigorously disputed by Ben-Hayyim (1954–55). Rosén claims that the traditional rules relating the plosive and fricative articulations of the /bgdkpt/ phonemes to the length of the preceding vowel are inoperative, e.g., long vowel + aspirated consonant / short vowel + geminated consonants, *dāḇār* 'word,' *dabbēr* 'speak.' This is the result of the coalescence of *a* and *ā*. Whereas in the past [b,v], [t,x], and [p,f] were positional variants of the same phonemes, they have now become different phonemes in Israeli Hebrew, and a clear rule cannot be formulated. Rosén (1956a: 125–26) also rejects the traditional rules for the vocalization of the definite article, *ha-*, *he-*, or *hā*, in various contexts for Israeli Hebrew. He claims that the Masoretes mainly transcribed phonetically allophonic variants which were realized differently in different contexts but which were not in phonemic opposition.

Changes in articulation of vowels

Barkai (1972; doctoral dissertation) describes developments in Israeli phonology. He observes that there is a lowering of front vowels in the environment of a back consonant, provided that these vowels are either in a prefix or epenthesized. Non-prefix base vowels are not affected. Prefixed and epenthesized vowels carry tertiary stress. Two pharyngeal continuants, /ᶜ/ and /ḥ/, must continue to be recognized, although historical /ᶜ/ has been replaced by /ᵓ/, and underlying /ḥ/ is absolutely neutralized as /x/. Regarding spirantization, the language is seen to be in a process of change. The former rules are being replaced as dependence on morphology increase. There are also differences between adult and child interpretations of spirantization. A recently added rule describes the dissimilation of a stop to a fricative after another stop. This rule describes adult speech, although the speech of children is usually different in this regard.

Further studies in phonology

Bolozky (1972), in his dissertation on categorial limitations on rules in the phonology of Modern Hebrew, notes that it is natural for morphophonemic rules to be restricted to grammatical categories. It is incorrect to extend these categorial rules to the whole grammar, even if it appears that "they work." He illustrates a constraint that used to be general but has recently been limited to the verb system. Barkai (1978a) discusses the theoretical implications of consonant sequence constraints in Israeli Hebrew. Barkai and Horvarth (1978) compare Hebrew, Russian, and Hungarian evidence on voicing assimilation and the sonority hierarchy.

Phonemic status and rules of articulation of /bkp/

We have noted Rosén's observation (1956a: 112–15) that in Israeli Hebrew allophones such as [b/v], [k/x], and [p/f] have achieved phonemic distinction. Ornan (1973b) surveys the currently accepted view that /b/, /v/, /k/, /x/, /p/, and /f/ are distinctive phonemes (Blanc 1964). In some situations these sounds alternate in different forms of the same word, e.g., [baxa] 'cried' : [yivke] 'will cry.' In other situations there is no change, e.g., [rakav] 'rotted' : [yirkav] 'will rot'; contrast [raxav] 'rode' : [yirkav] 'will ride.' (The description is one of articulation. The accepted transliteration shows the historical distinction, *rāqab̲:yirqab̲*, *rāk̲ab̲: yirkab̲*). One solution to the problem has been the concept of "morphophonemic alternants" (Harris 1941; Weiman 1950), according to which the distinctive phonemes become identical in parts of the paradigm. Another concept invoked to account for these phenomena is that of "compound roots" which are contrasted with "simple roots." In a "compound root" one or more of the consonants alternates with another, a complement, e.g., [p/f-t-x] 'open' and [r-x/k-v] 'ride, travel.' Ornan's goal, however, is to describe a simpler and more inclusive set of rules for the phenomena.

Proceeding in several steps, Ornan formulates several rules. When there is consonant doubling at the end of a word, with nothing following, an epenthetic vowel is added, usually *e*, e.g., *yaldî* 'my child,' but **yald > yeled* 'child.' The phonemes /b/, /k/, and /p/ are articulated as fricatives when they are the second of a cluster which opens a syllable, e.g., [bevakaša] 'please' (*b^{e}b̲aq-qāšāh*), or when they follow a vowel, provided that the same phoneme does not occur again, or in other words, it is not doubled, e.g., [dov] 'bear' compared to [dubbim] 'bears.' The main conclusion of this complex analysis is that the plosive and fricative articulations of [b/v], [k/x], [p/f], do not represent separate phonemes. Further on in the study, Ornan raises the theoretical possibility that the deep structure of Israeli Hebrew reflects a diachronic situation and development, even if the surface structure does not seem to. This view challenges in its implications the insistence of Rosén (1956a, 1957) that Israeli Hebrew is completely independent of the rules that operated on earlier levels. Ornan's approach to the diachronic relevance of a synchronic analysis parallels his earlier work on the rules operative in Masoretic Hebrew (1964b). Ornan also develops his argument elsewhere (1975). J. Fellman (1978b) accepts Ornan's description and states that the morphophonemic system usually parallels the unpointed consonantal writing system.

Schwarzwald (1975–76) traces the history of the treatment of /bgdkpt/ in the various stages of Hebrew and outlines the various theories behind explanations of the rules of doubling. While in Biblical Hebrew the laws for the articulation of these phonemes were rigid, they were weakened in Rabbinic Hebrew, and in Modern Israeli Hebrew the laws are even less applicable. Whether one applies the method of minimal opposition or analyzes in terms of morphophonemic change, the rules for /bkp/ are restricted to limited contexts and are not productive. Schwarzwald's conclusion is that the distinctions will ultimately disappear in Modern Hebrew except for formalized discourse.

Accounting for exceptions to the normative rules of /bkp/

Efratt (1980) also examines the status of the dual articulation of /bkp/ in contemporary Hebrew, when they are in initial position and follow an attached particle. The rules which emerge are: 1) foreign words are articulated as without the particle, e.g., [bepolitika], [befilosofya]; 2) when the particle is *še-* or has *a* as its vowel or *m* as its consonant, the articulation is plosive, e.g., [babdika] 'in the examination' and [šepaxot] 'that it is less'; 3) when the particle has *b*, *k*, *l*, *v*, and the vowel is not *a*, or the particle is *u* 'and,' and the combination of particle and word forms a recognized lexical entity, the articulation is fricative, e.g., [bixlal] 'in general'; 4) when there are two particles of the type in rule 3, and the combination is not a recognized separate lexical entity, the articulation is plosive, e.g., [ubeᵓezo] 'and in which,' [ubederex] 'and in a manner'; 5) when the conditions of rule 4 are not operative, and the particle is as in rule 3, a grammar-conscious speaker will give a fricative articulation, e.g., [ufratim] 'and details'; 6) words of great frequency, preceded by particles as in rule 3, are articulated either in a fricative or plosive manner, in free alternation, e.g., [lekol], [lexol] 'to all.'

Semantic transparency

Fischler (1975) earlier discussed a number of cases in Israeli Hebrew in which the traditional rules of spirant and plosive articulations of / bkp / are not observed. The motivating principle is the preservation of the basic form. Semantic transparency plays a role, e.g., [lekaxev] 'to star' (in the theater), [leraxel] 'to gossip' from [rexilut] 'gossip.' Some of these exceptions are caused by word-borrowing, e.g., [flirtet] 'flirted' (see above, Yannai 1973–74).

Storm (1974; doctoral dissertation) described Israeli phonology in terms of generative grammar. The system of rules, she holds, is adequate, and Hebrew does not require two phonetic systems. All four guttural consonants are required, and fricative consonants are more basic than the plosive. There is a greater extension of epenthesis, paralleling earlier historical changes.

Sociolinguistic factors and /bkp/ realization

Schwarzwald (1981b) describes an empirical study in Israeli schools to determine whether the / bkp / rule is naturally phonological or normative. The results showed that / bkp / were pronounced better as first radical than as second; there were fewer errors in the familiar words; disadvantaged children made more mistakes; and performance was improved by age, especially in the pronunciation of the second radical. These results support the normative assumption. The rarely used passive forms, *Puᶜal* and *Hufᶜal*, were pronounced with more errors than other verbal patterns. The future tense, not as frequently used, also had a greater rate of mistakes (English abstract, vii–ix).

Laufer (1976–77) deals with the general problem of describing a vowel system, and his work has relevance for the Hebrew situation as well. Auditory description of vowels is based on comparison of a vowel sound with a known vowel, e.g., the vowel [æ] with "cat." One problem with this comparative method is that there are different dialects and different realizations of the /a/ in "cat." Another method differentiates by means of points of articulation, e.g., the contact of the top of the tongue with the palate. The well-known trapezoidal diagram of the vowels is based upon this system. Laufer shows, however, that this system is inadequate for giving instructions regarding the articulation of a vowel. X-rays show that the position of the tongue is not always crucial and that the same vowel can be articulated with the tongue on various positions, at least, not where the theoretical trapezoid would have them. The problem is very much a matter of idiolect.

Physiological bases for vowel articulation

The idea was already expressed in 1928 by G. O. Russel: "Phoneticians are thinking in terms of acoustic fact, and using physiological fantasy to express the idea." Laufer concludes that a person's ability to distinguish vowels is acoustic and that the terms of articulation are no more than signs indicating relative position. Research is continuing in the matter of the relationship between the perceived vowel and the acoustic facts. In a further study (1983) Laufer describes a methodology of using the spectrograph to correct acoustic impressions of the phonetic system.

Laufer's doctoral dissertation (1972) is entitled *Synthesis by Rule of a Hebrew Idiolect*. In his writings (1975, 1975–76) he proposes a program for the mechanical synthesis of Hebrew speech, of which he has produced recorded specimens. Laufer and Condax (1981) conclude that in Hebrew, Arabic, and other languages the epiglottis is an independent and acoustically significant articulator.

Mechanical synthesis of Hebrew speech

A dissertation by Ben Tur (1978) explores the relationship of a knowledge of orthography to linguistic knowledge. She concludes that exposure to orthography may lead to a reformulation of phonetic rules because there is extra information observable in the printed word, information which is not observable in completely oral data. Orthographic representation plays an important role in identifying and distinguishing between morphemes and may lead to the establishment of phonemic contrasts. Shtal (1972,

Role of orthography in recognizing morphemes

doctoral dissertation; 1978, book) contrasts the Hebrew written by children of Ashkenazic parents with Hebrew written by children of Sephardic origin and draws conclusions for emotional therapy for disturbed children.

The glottal stop

A study by Farrar and Hayon (1980) attempts to identify the clues which facilitate the perception of the glottal stop. It is known (Semiloff-Zelasko 1975) that native speakers, hearing words pronounced in isolation, perceive a glottal stop when there is none. The experiment, using a synthesizer and spectrum analyzer, concluded that there are two clues which enable native speakers to perceive a glottal stop. The first is the actual glottal stop itself or laryngealization (squeaky voice). The second is syllabification. The role of consonant length is unclear and requires further study.

MORPHOLOGY AND MEANING IN CONTEMPORARY HEBREW

We cannot undertake to list Hebrew grammars in this section. They are listed in Bulletin #9 of the Council on the Teaching of Hebrew (Lidovsky and Uval 1979). Rather than descriptions of standard grammar, listed here are studies on innovations in Israeli Hebrew and synchronic descriptions. The grammars of Rosén (1962, 1976[2]) accept as new norms the innovations of Israeli Hebrew, contrary to the views of traditional normativists.

Studies in morphological innovations

Some recent studies dealing with innovations in morphology are described briefly by Rabin (1970a: 334–35). Mirkin (1957–58) discusses new suffixes. The replacement of the imperative by forms of the future is described by Rosén (1956a: 216–18) and Bar-Adon (1964, 1966). Hanele (1971; masters thesis) analyzes new forms of nouns and adjectives and their relationship to traditional patterns. F. Werner (1982) also discusses different methods of forming words. He distinguishes between primary roots which have a general meaning and generate many words (*šāmar* 'guarded') and secondary roots, which are restricted but generate a specific range of meanings (*ʾîš* 'man,' *ʾiyyēš* 'manned').

Developments in journalistic Hebrew

Sivan (1964), comparing a corpus of material from a Hebrew weekly of 1880 with samples of journalism from 1961, notes that verbs in the *Piʿel*, *Puʿal*, and *Hitpaʿel* stems are more prolific in generating verbs from existing roots in the later sample than they were in earlier periods. He attributes this to the greater clarity or meaningfulness of these forms. They are spelled *plene*, thus avoiding the ambiguity of the *Qal* when written without vowels. The problem of ambiguity in the unpointed Hebrew spelling is studied by Pines (1975). An unpointed Hebrew form is potentially identifiable as several different parts of speech. Most decoding of ambiguities is carried out on the syntactic level, and there are several devices, e.g., the definite article, *ha-*, the relative pronoun, *ha-*, the question indicator, *hă-*, and the relative pronoun, *še-*, which are examined with regard to their functions in ambiguous contexts. A doctoral dissertation by Allon (1984) also deals with the decoding processes in reading unvocalized Hebrew.

Decoding of ambiguities

Masson has dealt with various aspects of morphology. We have already noted his study on the suffix *-nîq* (1973) and his view that Yiddish is the main external influence, as well as his study of the *CaCiC* form (*qārîʾ* 'readable,' *pāgîᶜa* 'vulnerable') (1976b), and the felt need to find an existing Hebrew form to express ideas present in European languages. In addition, one should note his studies on diminutives (1974), the development of chemical terms (1975), and the selective use of classical patterns in Israeli Hebrew (1976a). Masson's doctoral dissertation (1976c) deals with the various patterns of neologisms in Israeli Hebrew.

Masson's studies

Yannai (1970, 1973–74) has studied augmented roots in Hebrew, observing that four- and five-radical verbs make up 44.4% of the verbs in Modern Hebrew compared to the 2% in Biblical Hebrew. One-fourth of these are loanwords, and the intermediary role between the original tri-radical forms and the multi-radical forms was played by nouns. The verbs are conjugated according to the *Piᶜel*, *Puᶜal*, and *Hitpaᶜel* stems. Yannai does not accept the view of Har Zahav, that a *Peᶜalᶜal* stem should be recognized.

Augmented roots

Mirkin (1967–68) studied the widespread formation of "intensive" passive participles from non-verbal bases. The pioneer work of Shapiro and Choueka describes computer analysis of Hebrew morphology (1962–64). Rosén (1976) observes that there is disagreement about which forms in the verbal system underlie and "motivate" other verbal forms. If for the purpose of teaching some forms are considered *formes motivantes* while others are *formes motiveés*, it is merely a question of convenience and has no relation to actual language structure.

Ben-Asher (1976a) establishes that the *nomen actionis* and the infinitive in Biblical Hebrew are accepted by most grammarians as identical in function and interchangeable, but in Israeli Hebrew they are clearly distinguished. As subjects of the sentence, they may be interchanged, but there is usually a change in word order, e.g., *hakkᵉnîsāh lammilḥāmāh hāyᵉṯāh mišgeh* 'entry into the war was a mistake' (*nomen actionis*), but *hāyāh zeh mišgeh lᵉhikkānēs*

The *nomen actionis* and infinitive are distinct in contemporary Hebrew *lammilḥāmāh* 'it was a mistake to enter the war' (infinitive). As predicates, they are more interchangeable but still distinguished. When they are used as objects, there are cases in which interchange is possible and others where it is not, especially when the *nomen actionis* has a personal suffix, e.g., *huᵓ hiḵrîz ᶜal tᵉmîḵāṯô bᵉhesdēr mᵉdînî* 'he announced his support of a political arrangement.'

A re-definition of *millôṯ yaḥas*, "prepositions"

A study of the function and origin of prepositions in contemporary Hebrew has been made by Ben-Asher (1973–74), who surveys the views in the various normative grammars and concludes that the Hebrew term for "prepositions," *millôṯ yaḥas*, a translation of German *Verhältniswörter*, is inadequate. This term signifies only that prepositions mark a relationship between two words. He seeks to formulate a definition based on linguistic considerations, taking into account morphological, semantic, and syntactic factors. It is his view, following Brockelmann, that prepositions are related to the noun-class. Through combination with the particle *še-*, certain prepositions have become conjunctions, introducing subordinate clauses, e.g, *lamrôṯ še-* 'because,' *biglal še-* 'because.'

Possession and construct state

Rosén's view that *ḥăḇērî* 'my friend' signifies inalienable possession while *heḥābēr šelî* denotes alienable possession is contested by Ornan (1968b). Azar (1976a) has studied the three possessive constructions in the daily newspapers, 1) joined (*bēṯ hāᵓîš*), 2) separated (*habbayiṯ šel hāᵓîš*), and 3) double (*bēṯô šel hāᵓîš*). The tendency is to prefer the double form if the construct noun is a single word and the separated form if it is two or more words. Both the double and the joined forms are used to indicate possession. Other types of construct use the separated form, e.g., *hammᵉṣîᵓûṯ šel hāᶜîr hayyiśrᵉᵓēlîṯ* 'the reality of the Israeli city.' If the construct state expresses relationship, the double construction is used, e.g., *ᵓāḇîw šel Šᵉlōmōh* 'Solomon's father.' Seikevicz (1979; doctoral dissertation) studies this problem in the light of sociolinguistics. The dissertation surveys the normative grammarians on the topic and establishes that *šel* is used for possession while the construct state is the primary means of combining two nouns for purposes other than possession. Also, nouns in the construct state show a deviation from the meaning they have when apart. The dissertation also discusses the feeling of inadequacy that speakers of Hebrew have in finding ways to express the various relationships and deals with some of the language problems of Israeli society.

A new jussive construction

A new jussive construction in contemporary Hebrew is noted by Rabin (1957–58a), *šetāḇōᵓ* 'come,' which is not to be regarded as an ellipsis of *ᵓănî rṣeh šetāḇōᵓ* 'I want you to come.' Rabin claims that the new jussive, acting as an imperative, is realized [šetavo], while the subjunctive or relative is realized [štavo]. Bar Adon (1966) objects, observing that there is no apparent differentiation in the realizations of either usage. We may also compare the transcriptions of Blanc (1964) in which no difference is recorded. New jussives are exemplified by [šenazuz kvar mikan] 'let's move from here already' and imperative by [štamut] 'drop dead' and [štistalek mikan] 'get out of here.'

New expressions of the negative

Innovations in the expression of the negative are discussed by Rabin in the same study (1957–58a). Under the influence of foreign constructions with *in-*, *un-*, *non-*, innovative forms like *ʾî mᵉsîrāh* 'non-delivery' and *ʾî-ḥuqqî* 'illegal' have developed. Perhaps, for reasons of linguistic purism, forms with *loʾ* 'not' were rejected, in the same way that purists reject the universally used *lōʾ* before uninflected forms of the verb in the present tense and prefer instead *ʾēn*, eg., *ʾēnî hôlēk* instead of the very common *ʾănî lōʾ hôlēḵ* 'I am not going.'

Some of the observations of Rabin need further study. Constructions with the bound element *ʾî* are frequent, indicating its productivity, e.g., *ʾî -nôḥiyûṯ* 'discomfort.' *ʾî-śᵉḇîʿaṯ-rāṣôn* 'dissatisfaction.' However, there still remains the problem of defining the usage of combinations with *ḥōser-* 'lack of,' e.g., *ḥōser ʾirgûn* and *ʾî-sēder* 'disorganization,' *ʾî-šeqeṭ* and *ḥōser mānôaḥ* 'disquiet.' With adjectives, the question to be investigated is whether *ʾî-ḥuqqî* or a simple negative *lōʾ ḥuqqî* 'illegal' is more prevalent. For example, is 'inorganic' rendered *ʾî-organî* or *lōʾ ʾorganî*? Both are given in dictionaries but the facts of actual usage must be established. Further study on the combination of *ʾî* and *nomen-actionis* can be found in Mirkin's article (1961–62).

A study by R. Landau (1971) treats formative fragmentation as a means of attaining distinction in meaning. This article takes note of ambiguous semantic differentiation between alternate forms, e.g., *hinniaḥ* and *hēniaḥ* 'lay down,' and the lack of agreement among normativists and lexicographers. Schwarzwald (1973a, 1973b, 1973–74), dealing with verbal root patterns and morpheme structure, has sought to formulate more inclusive rules than those based traditionally on the primacy of an abstraction, the triliteral root without its vowels, and morphological development. Bar-Lev (1979) discusses the ordering of Hebrew morphological processes.

Bolozky (1979) believes that the new imperatives of contemporary Hebrew derived from corresponding future forms used imperatively. There is thus an intermediate form: [tekabel > tkabel; kabel] 'receive,' [telamdi > tlamdi; lamdi] 'teach' (f.s.). Rhythmic factors are important here too. In Hebrew, the imperative is always utterance-initial and two adjacent stresses do not occur as a result of this intermediate shortening process. It is possible, therefore, to plot a derivation [tisgór ʾet haxalón > tsgór ta xalón] 'close the window.' The second person future, on the other hand, is not normally utterance-initial, and if there is to be shortening there will be the unwanted result of adjacent stresses. Thus one finds [matáy tisgór ʾet haxalón] and not [matáy tsgór taxalón] 'when will you close the window?'.

New imperatives and future forms

Bolozky (1980) studies paradigm coherence in contemporary Hebrew in the light of general study of the phenomenon in generative phonology. Data from contemporary Hebrew supports the principle of paradigm coherence and the claim that inflection tends to minimize allomorphy while derivation preserves it. One may speak of a continuum on which syntactic and morphological relations are strongest in a tense paradigm, less strong in the verbal conjugation as a whole, weaker between a verbal conjugation and its infinitive, and weaker still between a verbal conjugation and its passive verbal counterpart. The likelihood of analogy depends on the strength of the inter- or intra-paradigmatic relationship between alternating forms. The evidence indicates that speakers tend to level with the unmarked base form. If not, other factors, such as the nature of opacity and the avoidance of semantic opacity ought to be considered.

Paradigm coherence

Even-Shoshan (1979) surveys the new *binyānim* 'stems' of the verb in Israeli Hebrew. These include *Tifᶜel* which corresponds to the fifth Arabic stem, *tafᶜala*, a most productive stem; *Mifᶜel*, as in *misḥēr* 'marketed, merchandized'; *Piᶜlēl* as in *girdēḏ* 'scratched lightly'; *Piᶜlēn*, as in *ᶜiṣbēn* 'made nervous'; *Ifᶜel*, as in *ʾiḵzēḇ* 'disappointed'; and *Hitpāᶜēl* (not *Hitpaᶜel*), as in *hiṯḥāḇēr* 'be a friend' (see Fischler 1975: 89). The latter form is the reflexive of the *Qal*, not of the *Piᶜel*. Many of these forms are denominatives, and they have been adumbrated in earlier stages of Hebrew letters. They have, however, received a major new impetus in contemporary Hebrew.

Studies on *binyanim*, "stems": innovation and function

Ariel has studied the *binyanim* a number of times (1961, doctoral dissertation; 1972, 1973a, 1973b). The last study maintains that any adequate description of the *binyanim* must distinguish between 1) *binyanim* contrasting in meaning in the same lexical and semantic environments (Aktionsart) and 2) *binyanim* which are associated with different though related syntactic patterns in the same lexical and semantic environments. Ornan (1980) also discusses the *binyanim*. Ornan (1983b) suggests a model for relating roots and patterns, identifying the root of different patterns and identical patterns of different roots, a model which aids in analysis and interpretation. Ornan equates *mishqal* and *binyan* in this study.

Establishing rules for different feminine noun endings

Podolsky (1981) offers a generalization on the feminine counterparts of masculine nouns ending in *-î*. Masculine nouns with stress on the ultima (*milra*^{c}) and with accent changes in the paradigm have a feminine form ending in *-iyyāh* when reference is made to a woman (*rûsiyyāh* 'a Russian woman') and a feminine form ending in *-îṯ* when reference is made to a city or language (*rûsîṯ* 'the Russian language'). Masculine nouns which have stress on the penult (*mil*^{c}*el*) have a feminine counterpart ending in *-îṯ* for both categories. Schwarzwald (1981a) notes that there are some exceptions to the first part of the rule, and offers an explanation which is lexico-semantic rather than morphophonemic. Her conclusions are: 1) masculine nouns in *-î* generally have as their feminine counterpart *-ṯ* (this includes designations of religion or nationality); 2) certain exceptional masculine nouns which are ultimate-accented, have as the feminine *-iyyāh*, e.g., *ʾăniyyāh* 'poor woman'; 3) in certain nouns designating national or religious origin, *-iyyāh* designates a noun, e.g., *ṣorp̱atiyyāh* 'a French woman,' while *-îṯ* designates an adjective, 'French' (language, word, etc.). The difference is lexical, not accent-related, as Podolsky claimed.

SYNTAX IN CONTEMPORARY HEBREW

Various studies in syntax

There are a number of studies which trace new developments in various aspects of syntax in contemporary Hebrew. Some of the recent work is reviewed by Rabin (1970a: 336–37). Rosén (1956a, 1957, 1967) deals with various innovations in Israeli syntax, a major one being the periodic sentence. It is not present in Biblical Hebrew and was introduced incipiently only into Mishnaic (Rosén 1956a: 128–33). Kaddari (1964–65a) has classified adjectival compounds, a new phenomenon in Hebrew, showing the influence of European languages. The endocentric compound is characterized by a relationship between the first component and other parts of speech identical to that of the entire compound. The exocentric compound differs in that the relationship of the first element to the rest of the parts of speech is different from that of the compound as a whole.

Mordechai Amit (1976–77) establishes that in a contemporary Hebrew sentence, the order of qualifiers depends on length; the shortest qualifier comes first. Where there are exceptions, a long adverb of time will precede a short adverb of place. If one of the two adverbs is the result of an imbedded sentence, it comes last.

Ariel and Katriel (1977) give a syntactic-semantic analysis of the range-indicators, *gam* 'also,' *raq* 'only,' *ʾap̄îlû* 'even,' and *dawqāʾ* 'only so, exactly' in contemporary Hebrew. A sentence containing a range-indicator makes implicit reference to that portion of the field of reference of the predicate which is not explicitly mentioned in it. A masters thesis by Ben-Asher (1964) deals with conditional sentences, and a masters thesis by Maschler (1966) deals with methods of expressing modality. Barri (1978) challenges traditional grammar in seeking a definition of the relationship between the noun and the adjective. S. Bahat (1964), in a masters thesis, treats dependent clauses in contemporary Hebrew, and T. Vardy (1967, masters thesis) deals with the concessive clause. Selinker (1970) discusses basic clause types in contemporary Hebrew. Peretz (1961–62) deals with methods of expressing emphasis and (1967) with the relative clause. R. Pines (1975) discusses syntactic ambiguity. Moreshet (1983) shows that in Biblical Hebrew and Mishnaic Hebrew a predicate preceding a compound subject is singular, but in contemporary Hebrew, logic prevails over grammar, and the predicate is plural.

Ornan's studies on syntax

Important contributions have been made by Ornan in the area of syntactic studies: on mechanical-syntactic analysis and the teaching of syntax (1958–59); on the parts of speech (1960–61); on structural analysis of literary imagery (1961–62); on contemporary Hebrew syntax (1965b; based on lecture notes); on the pronouns *kāzeh* and *kāzōʾṯ* 'like this, such' (1967–68a); on the compound nominal clause (1967–68b); on the simple sentence in modern Hebrew (1968a); a transformational-grammatical study of the coordinating conjunction with a sentence (1970–71); an attempt to formulate rules for the generation of all the forms of the *beynoni* 'present' independent of the *binyan* 'stem' (1971c); and a description of transformational grammar (1971–72).

E. Rubinstein's studies in syntax

Work in the area of syntax by E. Rubinstein includes the following studies: a masters thesis on the compound nominal clause (1964); a doctoral dissertation on the nominal sentence (1968a; book form, 1968b); on the positions of sentence and verb modifiers (1970–71); on the complex sentence and methods of teaching it (1971b); on the development of *lip̄nê* 'before' + nominal phrase, from an indicator of place to one of cause (1975–76); and a study of the tension between semantic and syntactic valence (1978–79).

Rubinstein's study of categorical shifts in adjectival constructions (1975a) is based on colloquialisms as reproduced in fiction. It demonstrates that words whose meanings have undergone change from the historical classical level can enter syntactic constructions in which they previously could not have appeared, e.g., adjectives as adverbs—modifiers of other adjectives, as in *ʾabbāʾ šelî hāyāh nôrāʾ miskēn* 'my father was very miserable,' *ʾănî rôʾeh iššah ʾaḥat kāḵāh neḥmāḏāh* 'I see a really nice woman,' and *ʾănî rôʾeh ʾeḥāḏ šebāʾ, kāzeh ʿāgôl, šāmēn* 'I see someone coming, very round, fat.' The emphasizing words have acquired new meanings and syntactic relationships, enabling them to be used for adjectival intensification, e.g., *hûʾ meʾōḏ ṭanq* 'he is very strong (lit. a tank).' Rubinstein makes no normative judgments on this phenomenon.

Further studies in syntax

Other studies in the area of syntax include: general surveys by W. Weinberg (1966) and Chomsky (1958–59, 1962); Ariel (1961, 1972, 1973a, 1973b) on verb stems and conjugations, semantic and syntactic studies; Azar (1971–72) on verbs governing prepositional phrases; Ben-Asher on syntax in general. Sadka (1978) examines the construction *yēš lîʾeṯ* . . . 'I have . . . ,' where the accusative indicator, *ʾeṯ*, is used contrary to classical usage. A. Zilkha (1970, doctoral dissertation) treats negation in Hebrew and (1976) contradictions in deep structure. Atias (1981, doctoral dissertation) studies adjective order in Israeli Hebrew.

Zeldis (1973) classifies container verbs in his doctoral dissertation, establishing that some unambiguously belong in this category, e.g., *ḥāšaḇ* 'thought,' *sippēr* 'told,' while others are definitely not, e.g., *lāḥaš* 'whispered.' Another group is ambiguous, e.g., *hiḵrîz* 'announced, proclaimed,' *ʾāhaḇ* 'loved.' Bar-Hillel (1956–57) offers some methodological considerations on morphological studies in a critique of Rosén (1956a). His study on sentence structure (1960–61) and his *Aspects of Language* (1970) deserve mention.

New compounds influenced by European languages

Rosén (1969b, a Hebrew version of a paper delivered in French, which appeared in *GLECS* 10:126–35) describes some categories of compounds in Israeli Hebrew that are unparalleled in Semitic languages but bear the imprint of modern European languages, e.g., constructs like *marḥîq-leḵeṯ* 'far-reaching,' *ṭôḇ-lēḇ* 'good-hearted,' and compounds with *ben*, *baṯ* (lit. 'son of, daughter of') such as *ben ḥāmēš šānîm* 'five years old.' He relates this to foreign influence, as in German *fünfjahrig*, but it must be noted that there are Mishnaic Hebrew antecedents, e.g., *hărê ʾănî keḇen šiḇʿîm šānāh* 'I am like one that is seventy years old' (*m. Ber.* 1:5). It has been pointed out by Haneman (1980b), however, that *ben x šānîm* in Mishnaic Hebrew means 'one who has completed X−1 years and is now in his X-year,' while in contemporary Hebrew it means 'one who has completed X years and is in his X+1 year.' Rosén also sees compounds with *ḥăsar*, e.g., *ḥăsar hăḇānāh* 'without understanding,' as based on foreign influence. Mishnaic Hebrew *m^eḥussar kappārāh* 'requiring (lit. lacking) atonement' (*m. Ker.* 2:1) is similar but not identical. Schwarzwald (1978–79a) discusses whether the predicate will be singular or plural in sentences expressing alternatives. The tendency in Biblical Hebrew is to have a singular predicate, while contemporary Hebrew and Mishnaic Hebrew tend to have a plural predicate (compare Moreshet 1983).

Azar (1981b) studies the three contrastive morphemes, *ʾelāʾ*, *ʾelāʾ še-*, and *ʾăḇāl*, in contemporary Hebrew. He concludes that the three are mutually exclusive, expressing three different types of "contrastiveness." The first, *ʾelaʾ*, used in the construction Negation $- S_1 +$ *ʾelāʾ* $+ S_2$, is used to assert something (S_2) opposed to another assertion (S_1), the denial of which serves as a reason for the assertion S_2. The second, *ʾelaʾ še-*, in the construction $S_1 +$ *ʾelaʾ še-* $+ S_2$, is used when S_1 raises an implicit question to the hearer, of which S_2 serves as a reply. The third, *ʾăḇāl*, used in the construction $S_1 +$ *ʾăḇāl* $+ S_2$ or at the beginning of a sentence, is used when the speaker wishes to say something directly or indirectly contrastive to what has been said or to the consequence of what has been said by the speaker himself or by another speaker. The differences between *ʾăḇāl* and *ʾelāʾ* have been studied earlier by Dascal and Katriel (1977). Glinert (1982a) deals with various types of counterfactual sentences in contemporary Hebrew on the basis of transformational analysis and shows (1982b) that the second in a pair of reciprocal pronouns is felt to be in the plural, e.g., *ʾeḥāḏ laššēnî, zeh lāzeh* 'one to the other.' Rosén (1982) treats the question of sentence order, which he believes varies with needs of expression and stylistic register. He rejects the fixed formulations of normativists, consistency with his long-held views on the independence of contemporary Hebrew from earlier norms.

A dissertation by Kopelovitch (1982) analyzes modality. Her conclusion is that modal expressions do not constitute a syntactic class and that the question of modality must be considered in terms of three bipolar oppositions: 1) personal-impersonal, 2) modality-modulation, and 3) subjective-objective. Aphek and Kahaneman (1984–85) study new functions for the preposition *ʿal*. Bolozky (1984) discusses subject pronouns in colloquial Hebrew. E. Doron (1984, doctoral dissertation) treats the verbless predicate in Hebrew. Schwarzwald (1984) analyzes prefixed particles in terms of markedness relations. Kopelovich(-Hanash) (1984) studies the functions of *ʾăḇāl* and *ʾelaʾ*.

GENERATIVE-TRANSFORMATIONAL GRAMMAR

Generative-transformational grammar has made its mark on the recent study of the Hebrew language. Battle (1969, 1971) and Greenstein (1974) have applied it to the study of biblical poetry. Other authors who have used generative-transformational grammar in their study of Biblical Hebrew include E. Rubinstein (1975–76, 1977) and Kaddari in his collection of studies (1976).

However, some traditional, historically overlooked linguists have been critical. An initial survey by Blau (1971a), for example, demonstrated little enthusiasm for the method, and Ornan (1970–71), in the course of an article on coordinating conjunctions, felt a need to explain the method to his readers. Blau has repeatedly criticized the transformational approach (1971–72b; 1978–79a, a review of Kaddari 1976; Cole, ed., 1976a; Azar 1977a). Nevertheless, the method continues to be widely applied. Daniel Cohen (1973–74) used it to reach conclusions different from Ornan (1970–71). Sadka (1976–77) suggested a revision of terminology and a different conclusion in the analysis of the coordinated clauses. Ornan (1971–72) devoted a whole fascicle of *LLA*, the popular journal of language studies, to the transformational approach. Now, Chayen and Dror (1976) have co-authored in Hebrew an introduction to Hebrew transformational grammar, with an appendix by Y. Bar-Hillel. The study was reviewed by R. Berman (Aronson) (1976–77).

Criticism and application of transformational grammar

It is interesting to note that Noam Chomsky's first attempt to propose an explanatory theory in linguistics was an undergraduate thesis at the University of Pennsylvania in the late 1940s, entitled *Morphophonemics of Modern Hebrew*, later expanded to a masters thesis with the same title in 1951. The method he used was a rudimentary generative phonology and generative syntax. The interest and suggestions of Yehoshua Bar-Hillel were instrumental in the further development of the theory first set out in these productions (Noam Chomsky, *Language and Responsibility*, based on conversations with Mitsou Ronat [New York, 1977] 111–12, 130).

A number of recent doctoral dissertations make use of the transformational approach; Berman (Aronson) (1973) on gerunds;

Recent studies using transformational grammar

Glinert (1974) on peripheral categories; Malisdorf (1975) on sentential components in Hebrew; Sadka (1974) on verbal supplements; and J. A. Reif (1968) on construct-state nominalizations. Reif's study derives construct-state nominalizations from one or two kernel sentences. In the more complex instance, one sentence has been nominalized and imbedded in the other. Three basic sentence types are isolated: 1) N(oun) V(erb), 2) NVN, and 3) NVP(reposition). A new conclusion is that P is to be considered a lexical category, not a closed part of the grammatical structure. The doctoral dissertation by Dubrow (1973) is a generative-transformational contrastive analysis of English and Hebrew. It deals with selected structures which are difficult for the Hebrew-speaking learner of English.

Other studies using this approach include Kaddari (1977–78), who treats biblical *mn*^{c} 'prevent,' showing that ambiguities on the surface level are clarified, not only by the deep structure, but also by parallelism. E. Rubinstein (1970–71), in a study of sentence and verb modifiers, concludes that the modifier for the entire sentence may come at the beginning, end, or middle, between subject and predicate, whereas the modifier which is part of the verb is found after the verb in a normal nonemphatic sentence. Kasher (1969; 1971, doctoral dissertation; 1974, 1976) applies transformational grammar to Hebrew syntax. Shapiro and Choueka (1962–64) have dealt with the problem of mechanical analysis of Hebrew morphology, considering the question of recognition grammar which can guide the reader formally in reconstructing the derivational tree of a given word.

Hayon (1969, 1971a, 1971b) applies the method to relative clauses and other syntactic structures which are derived from underlying relative clauses. There are two classes, relative clauses with verbal predicates and relative clauses with non-verbal predicates. Hayon observes that the so-called copula is not generated by the base rules of the Hebrew grammar but by the transformation. Morgenbrod and Serifi (1976) have written on computer-analyzed aspects of Hebrew verbs. Givon (1973) has studied complex noun-phrases, word order, and resumptive pronouns in Hebrew. Many studies in this area appear in *Hebrew Computational Linguistics* (in Hebrew: בלשנות עברית חפ״שית) which is published by Bar-Ilan University. This journal also carries a review of recent literature in Hebrew linguistics.

A recent collection of papers on the generative study of Hebrew syntax and semantics has been edited by P. Cole (1976a). The collection advances the field considerably and brings to the fore a whole group of young scholars. Moshe Azar (1976b) treats the emphatic sentence; Gad Ben Horin (1976) surveys aspects of syntactic pre-posing; Berman (1976) treats derived and deriving nominals; Berman and Grosu deal with aspects of the copula (1976); Cole, the editor (1976a), also gives an overview of the generative study of contemporary Hebrew syntax and semantics (1976b) as well as studying a causal construction (1976c) and (1976d) discussing an apparent asymmetry in the formation of relative clauses. Talmy Givón (1976a) treats the VS word order; Yael Ziv (1976) offers a reanalysis of grammatical terms in Hebrew possessive constructions, revising earlier views, such as those in J. A. Reif (1968); and L. Glinert (1976) treats *ᶜôḏ*, a pseudo-quantifier. Glinert also has published other studies (1977, 1982a, 1982b). Goshen-Gottstein (1980) challenges the adequacy of transformational analysis to analyze the syntagma of: verbal noun + plus nomen rectum + object marker + post nominal object, e.g., *hakkāraṯ hammôrîm ʾeṯ hattalmîḏîm* 'the teachers' recognition of the student.' Choueka (1966) has written on computers and grammar as have Ornan (1985c), Daniel Cohen (1986), Efratt (1986), and Knisbacher (1986).

DISCOURSE ANALYSIS

A group of studies on discourse analysis, edited by Blum-Kulka, Tobin, and Nir, has appeared in 1981 with an introduction by Chaim Rabin. Rabin cites Zellig Harris (*Language* [1952] 28.1–30) as the source of the idea that linguistic analysis must be applied to a unit greater than the sentence. Interest in this field did not become marked, however, until the 1970s. Rabin discusses various definitions of the unit of discourse and calls attention to the significant role of sociolinguistics in discourse analysis. An essay by Walters (1981) surveys the current state of the study of contextual factors in language use, citing the relevant literature and noting the possibilities of this discipline for the study of bilinguals and bilingual children.

Discourse analysis: a unit greater than the sentence

Olshtain (1981) sets up a model of the relationship between a piece of writing and the aims and perceptions of the author and the reader. Reading competence is discussed in terms of the strategies a reader must acquire in relation to the structure of a text. Nir (1981a) treats primary and secondary newspaper headlines as discourse units. He takes note of the presuppositions made by the newspaper writer of the reader's ground information and the general assumptions they share. He also treats the different ways the first and the second headline divide up significant information. A further study in this area is by Nir (1986). Weitzman (1981) also deals with newspaper communication. He analyzes newspaper articles in terms of 1) varying levels of old and new information, 2) explicitness versus implicitness, and 3) the relation between reporting events and expressing attitudes.

Blum-Kulka (1981) compares native speakers and language-learners and their differing abilities to devise alternative communication strategies in order to achieve their goals. She concludes that these differences are related to varying language competencies and to different cultural backgrounds. Berman (Aronson) (1981) analyzes the invented narrations and retold stories of a six-year-old child (her daughter). The child is seen to be clearly aware of two different stylistic registers—an "oral" and a "literate" discourse style. The child's use of various devices for indicating segmentation are evaluated. A masters thesis by Chernofsky (1980) studies syntactic development in the conversation of three- and four-year-olds.

Tobin (1981) deals with specific macro-stylistic phenomena (e.g., the historical present) in Hebrew texts by Agnon, Lubetkin, and Alterman. He compares the Hebrew original and the English translation with the objective of developing data helpful in the process of literary translation. Giora (1981b) observes that similar content is expressed in differently ordered sentences at different points in the text. The aim of the study is to determine what in the word-order is derivable from the position of the sentence in the text and what the functions of the different word orders in the discourse are.

Ziv (1981) deals with existential sentences in modern colloquial Hebrew which apparently contradict the universal rule requiring them to be indefinite. An example of the rule is: *yēš baḥeder ḥāṯûl qāṭān* 'there is a small cat in the room' (indefinite) and *heḥāṯûl haqqāṭān nimṣāʾ/yešnô baḥeder* 'the small cat is in the room' (definite). Excluded are: **yēš heḥāṯûl haqqāṭān baḥeder* and **yēš baḥeder heḥāṯûl haqqāṭān*. However, modern colloquial Hebrew permits the following: *yēš ʾeṯ hassēp̱er hazzeh bassip̱riyyāh hallᵉʾûmîṯ* 'this book is in the National Library.' A solution to the problem is offered which considers the sentence type to be a blend of some morpho-syntactic characteristics of existentials, on the one hand, and of certain prosodic and discourse functional properties of locative sentences, on the other. Abadi (1979) has studied various stylistic devices which bind together a supra-sentential text unit. The corpus she examines is the essays of Eliezer Steinman. Abadi (1986) discusses bonding and subordination in linguistic units larger than the sentence.

LEXICOGRAPHY

Some developments in lexicography have been described by Rabin (1970a: 328, 337–39). Ben Yehudah's *Thesaurus totius hebraitatis*, based on sources from all periods, was continued after his death by others. The sixteen volumes appeared between 1908 and 1958, first in Berlin and later in Jerusalem. It is impossible to give here a complete listing of dictionaries, as these generally undergo revision and multiple printings. The various dictionaries of Even-Shoshan and *Otsar halashon haᶜivrit* (Jerusalem, 1962ff.) by Cnaani are noteworthy. Another useful tool is the annotated bibliography of dictionaries published in Israel and abroad since 1948, compiled for the Council on the Teaching of Hebrew by E. Weinberg and H. Polani (Jerusalem, 1975). An introduction to the dictionary by Goshen-Gottstein, based on texts from the 1880s and onward, has been published by Shocken (1969a).

Major dictionaries

The Academy of the Hebrew Language has undertaken the task of compiling a *Historical Dictionary of the Hebrew Language* with Z. Ben-Hayyim as editor. This dictionary proposes to set forth the history of every word in the Hebrew language—etymology and meanings, use and combinations—for the various periods of the language. During the early years of the project (1959–63), basic principles and tools were established. A *Sefer hamqorot* (Book of Sources) was compiled, which contained literary items composed from the end of the biblical period to the end of the gaonic era, 1050 C.E. (Jerusalem 1963, 1970^2). A modern list of sources has been published (part I; Jerusalem, 1977), containing sources from 1860–1920.

The material for the dictionary is being assembled in a permanent archive, with the aid of the computer. The archive includes 1) an alphabetic listing of quotations and 2) a listing according to frequency and structure. From this permanent base the dictionary will be compiled. Three sections are now functioning: 1) the ancient literature section, 2) the Modern Hebrew section, and 3) the computation section, involving the preparation of the material assembled in sections 1 and 2 for entry into the computer. The *Book of Ben Sira* (Jerusalem, 1973) has been published, as well as a sample section illustrating the root *ᶜrb*. This

Procedure for the *Historical Dictionary* and initial results comprises vol. 46/3–4 of *Leš* (1982), and the present description is taken from the English summary in that source. Numerous articles in *Leš* have appeared under the general title *Min haᶜavodah bamillon hahistori*. These are not items from the dictionary itself but represent research by the members of the staff. Some of the technical problems are discussed in *Leš* 42 (1977–78) by Abramson (9–16), Ben-Hayyim (17–24), Mishor (25–36), A. Loewenstamm (37–50) and anonymously (51–59). Ben-Hayyim described the overall plan in *Leš* 46.165–73. A masters thesis by Almagor (1973) discusses the use of mechanical aids in lexicography.

Continuing lexical studies

Important lexical studies appear in the pages of *LLA*, noteworthy among them the continuing column of R. Sivan, *Meḥayye hamillim*; R. Mirkin's series *Lehashlamat heḥaser bamillonim*; Dov Sadan's studies on the history of words and phrases (compare his book, 1956); M. Kaddari's series of studies on phrases originating in medieval philosophical and kabbalistic literature, later collected in a book (1970a). There is another series in *LLA* by I. Hurwitz, *Meᵓadam weᶜad tolaᶜat* (*From man to worm*), proverbs based on animal life (*LLA* 19/5 [1968]-23/5 [1972]). Foreign words in Modern Hebrew are discussed by M. Eshel (no date).

A. Gordon (doctoral dissertation, 1983) proposes a model of the lexicon that accounts for gaps in which the source of derived words is absent. The base, an abstract, should be abstracted from the common material in the related words. The base is specified only once, and for words derived from the base only the material unique to a specific word is listed.

Children's speech, slang, and special vocabularies

There are a number of studies dealing with special vocabularies. Bar-Adon (1966–67, 1968, 1971, 1977b) has studied the spoken Hebrew of children (see Rabin 1970a: 338, n 211). His last study (1977b) discusses the role of children's language in making Hebrew a mother tongue. Zeidner (1978) deals with the psycholinguistic aspects of children's speech. R. Scholes and P. F. Grossman (1976) have written on utterance imitation by Hebrew-speaking children. Peres–Walden (1982, doctoral dissertation) studies children's perceptions and constructions of word formation. Shamosh (1971) has written on words with special meaning in the kibbutz. Writings on Israeli slang include the work of M. Fraenkel (1949), Sappan (1961a, 1963, 1972^2), Shalev (1973–74), Kornblueth, and Aynor (1974), and the dictionary of Ben Amotz and N. Ben Yehudah (1971, 1982). The special vocabulary of sailors and fishermen has been studied by Altbauer (1953–54) and Morag and Sappan (1966–67). Diplomatic Hebrew is the subject of two dictionaries by Marwick (1957, 1980).

SEMANTICS

Initial steps in the study of semantics in contemporary Israeli Hebrew are surveyed by Rabin (1970a: 339). Altbauer (1957–58) has discussed shifts in meaning, while formal differentiation as a result of semantic development is surveyed by Ben-Asher (1966–67b). Gan (1961–62) and Yannai (1978, 1980) discuss the secularization of words from the sacred sphere, e.g., *tôrat̠ Marqs* 'the teaching of Marx,' *mišnat̠ hāʾălîmût̠* 'the doctrine of violence,' and *m^ek̠ahēn* 'serves (as mayor, etc.).' Peretz (1963–64) treats abstract-concrete metonomy, and Téné (1967–68) discusses content structure in the Hebrew root. A survey by Kaddari (1975) covers literature up to that point on semantics, polysemy, onomastics, and stylistics.

Recent studies in semantics

Two books on semantics in contemporary Hebrew have appeared, Nir (1978) and Sarfatti (1978). Both books are reviewed by Rabin (1978–79). The importance of these books for the relatively new discipline of Hebrew semantics, as pointed out by Rabin, is that specific examples from the language in which a reader has experience and intuition give life to the theoretical discussion. Sarfatti combines a synchronic-diachronic approach and gives attention, not only to general phenomena, but also to specifically, historically Hebrew ones. Nir devotes less attention to historical-semantic shifts but concentrates more on synchronic-structural aspects. He has sections on ambivalence, emotional-psychological elements, idioms, and semantic components.

R. Landau (1972) has written a doctoral dissertation on polysemy in contemporary Hebrew. In a later study (1975b) she investigates types of selectional sets and their relationship to meaning. Selectional sets can be syntactic or semantic. The first class permits a wider freedom of choice, and the syntax conditions the meaning of the verb. The semantic selectional set can be further subdivided into categorial sets, e.g., 1) *nāśāʾ* 'carried' + inanimate objects/humans + adverbial phrase; 2) collocations in which the elements have a common semantic component, such as *nāśāʾ ʿênāw/pānāw/rōʾšô/yādô/qôlô* 'he raised his eyes/face/head/hand/voice'; 3) collocations in which the items relate to a specific domain, as in *nāśāʾ bāʿôl / bam^eśîmāh /bāʾaḥ^arāyût̠ / bahôṣāʾôt̠* 'he bore the yoke/the assignment/the responsibility/the expenses'; and 4) fixed expressions with no freedom for substitution, as in *nāśāʾ w^enāt̠an* 'did business.' A clear understanding of these levels of semantic dependency is essential to the proper learning of a foreign language. In another study (1976), Landau goes further

Polysemy and selectional sets

into the question of collocations, that is, the joining of a specified lexical entry and a restricted set of items. "Monomial" collocations are those in which a lexical entry is limited to a single item, e.g., *ʿāṣam ʿēnāw* 'shut his eyes,' *ʾāṭam ʾoznāw* 'stopped his ears.' "Polynomial" collocations are exemplified by numbers 2 and 3 above. The collocations occupy a position intermediate between completely free choice and petrified expression, being the first step in the breakdown of the latter. Collocations of class 2 above (in which the items have a common semantic component) have a higher degree of constancy than those in which the items relate to a specific domain (no. 3). A further study by Landau (1976–77) deals with the degree of collocativity between different stems and inflections of the Hebrew verb.

Linguistic transparency

Recently, research has been done in the areas of popular etymology and linguistic transparency. Nir (1976) distinguishes between "linguistic transparency," which includes the morphological component, e.g., *zammēr* 'sing' > *zammār* 'singer' and the semantic, e.g., *regel* 'foot' > *regel haššulḥān* 'the foot of the table,' and "psycholinguistic" transparency. The latter is subjective, whereas the first is objective, belonging to the realm of *langue*. Words can be motivated from a linguistic point of view and yet be opaque subjectively, e.g., *t^erîs* 'shield,' limited by synechdoche to 'shutter' (against the sun). There is an opposite situation in which no objective relationship exists, yet a transparency is subjectively assumed, that is, "pseudo-motivation" or "popular etymology," e.g., *tôḵen* 'content,' erroneously derived from *tôḵ* 'inside' but really based on biblical *tkn* 'measure.' Nir relates this analysis to problems of language teaching. Barkai (1978b) deals with two cases of semantic transparency. Nahir (1978) studies the relationship between normativism and educated speech.

Popular etymologies

In a number of studies Sarfatti (1971–72, 1974–75, 1975–76) enumerates various processes which operate in the creation of popular etymologies. His material is on several levels, and some of his examples are really "learned" popular etymologies. Factors which are operative include: the similarities perceived to exist with other words; an attempt to bring the form of an utterance closer to its perceived meaning, that is, to increase semantic transparency; the unfamiliarity of speakers with classical sources; and the loss of phonemes and their assimilation to others. Among Sarfatti's examples are *ʿaḇṭîṭ* 'thick clay,' in Biblical Hebrew 'pledge,' but popularly perceived to derive from *ʿāḇ* 'thick' and *ṭîṭ* 'clay'; *purqān* 'relief from a burden,' but in Aramaic 'salvation,' the modern use based on Hebrew *prq* 'unload'; *ʾabbûḇ* 'musical instrument, pipe'

(Akkadian *embubu*), now adapted for 'oboe'; *ʾaššāp̱* 'magician' (Akkadian *āšipu*), adapted for the similar-sounding 'chef'; *massēḵāh*, in Biblical Hebrew 'molten image,' now used for 'mask,' because of the external similarity; and *yôḇēl* 'jubilee' in Biblical Hebrew, now used for 'anniversary, festival,' influenced by German *Jubel.* Nir (1979b) treats the semantic structure of compound nouns in contemporary Hebrew. Finally, it should be noted that a dictionary by Rabin and Raday (1974) is organized on the basis of semantic fields, rather than on the alphabet.

Verbal nouns: the infinitive, the gerund, and the derived nominal

Berman (Aronson) has treated the verbal noun in a doctoral dissertation (1973) and in an article (1974–75). She distinguishes three categories, 1) the infinitive, the absolute form + the prefix *l*-, 2) the gerund, which is the absolute form without prefix *l*- but can occur with personal endings, and 3) the action-noun or "derived nominal" which is derived from a verb and expresses action or condition. The article (1974–75) is mainly concerned with exploring the similarities and differences between the last two categories. The gerund partly overlaps the category of "factive," while the action noun partly coincides with the "action (derived) nominal," terms first used by Robert Lees (*The Grammar of English Nominalizations* [Bloomington, 1960]). The article concludes that the action noun is more free than the gerund, because the action noun can appear with or without its deep subject, but the gerund requires a specific subject. Furthermore, the action noun participates in constructs more readily than the gerund, which, for example, is acceptable in *bôʾ harôp̱ēʾ* 'the coming of the doctor' and *bôʾô šel harôp̱ēʾ* 'the doctor's coming' (double possessive), but excluded in **bôʾ šel harôp̱ēʾ*, in which the two elements, *nomen regens* and *nomen rectum*, are separated. The action noun can also occur in adverbial phrases which modify either the entire sentence or any one of its elements—subject, predicate, object—but the gerund, on the other hand, can participate in such phrases only when they have an adverbial function related to the entire sentence. In general, the action noun can potentially replace the gerund under any circumstance, but the reverse is not true. The action noun, while traceable to a verb, is less regular and predictable in that relationship than is the gerund.

Relationships between verb roots and patterns

Berman (1975a) discusses the methods of representing verb forms as a relationship between two elements: the consonantal root and the morphological pattern (*binyan*). There are three approaches: 1) total regularity—the root is the basic lexical element, the conjugations obligatory additives, each with a fixed semantic content and syntactic function, 2) total anomaly or irregularity—the basic element being made up of root plus conjugation, and 3) lexical redundancy—the basic lexical element as root plus conjugation. The last view is endorsed by Berman for having the advantage of recognizing that each root is realized in one conjugation or another as a "base form" and that each conjugation has predictable regularities.

Heḥ^e^lî ᵓôṯî

Berman (1979a) examines the differences between predicates expressed through the *binyan* system and otherwise, e.g., *hamma^c^ăśeh heḥ^e^lî ᵓôṯî* and *hamma^c^ăśeh ^c^āśāh ᵓôṯî ḥôleh* 'the deed sickened me/made me sick.' Contemporary Hebrew seems to prefer a periphrastic, analytic form in place of the older, more normative word morphology for expressing notions such as causative, inchoative, reflexive, and reciprocal. The use of these forms expresses a specific semantic difference, related to a greater sense of involvement or "incorporatedness" in the action by the speaker. These forms may also be due to foreign influence. Berman has also written (1979b) on passives, middle voice, and impersonals, (1979c) on subjectless constructions, and (1978) a book on Modern Hebrew structure.

Auxiliary verbs

Berman (1980a) deals with the category of auxiliary in Modern Hebrew. Her study is limited to auxiliary verbs rather than to the general category of auxiliary in grammar theory. Hebrew grammarians refer to *pô^c^al ^c^ēzer* 'helping verb,' and *nāśûᵓ murḥāḇ* 'extended predicate.' The first verb is finite, and the second infinitive. Such constructions can express modality, e.g., *hûᵓ ^c^ālûl l^e^hapsîḏ* 'he is bound to lose'; process-aspectual, e.g., *hēm ^c^ômdîm l^e^haggî^c^a* 'they are about to arrive'; habitual-aspectual, e.g., *ᵓănaḥnû nohăgîm l^e^hazmîn ᵓôṯô* 'we customarily invite him.' It is Berman's conclusion that Hebrew uses auxiliary verbs in a restricted manner, primarily forms of *hāyāh* 'be', to express inchoativeness, e.g., *happ^e^rî hāyāh bāšēl* 'the fruit was ripe.' This limited use of auxiliary verbs is due to other features of the language, such as an abundance of and preference for verbs with specific lexical content. Hebrew, preferring verb-initial, predicate + complement type constructions, is provided with a major device for expressing modality by means other than auxiliary-type verbs.

Studies in emotive verbs

E. Rubinstein (1980a) treats verbs which express an emotional state and occur in the syntactic context of one or two noun phrases. Semantic analysis of sentences containing emotive verbs indicates that the noun-phrase complementing such verbs is the realization of a non-volitional cause, e.g., *Dāvîḏ śāmaḥ ^c^al hassēp̱er* 'David was happy about the book,' going back to a deep structure *David śāmaḥ ^c^al ᵓăšer yēš lô sēp̱er* 'David was happy because he had the book.' On the other hand, the noun-phrase which complements verbs such as *sālaḥ* 'forgave,' *dāʾag* 'worried' results from the raising transformation applied to a potential sentential component, which is then deleted. A further study by Rubinstein (1983) is concerned with the analysis of the relationship between certain verbs, such as *sāp̱ar* 'counted,' *hēḇîn* 'understood,' *ḥāšaḏ* 'suspected,' and *heʾĕšîm* 'blamed' and their noun-phrase complement. The proper analysis of the relationship is essential to the understanding of the meaning of the verb and should influence lexicography.

PROBLEMS OF TRANSLATION

The problems of translation from English to Hebrew and from Hebrew to English are dealt with in several studies. These have theoretical interest as well as practical application, being useful in developing teaching strategies. Dubrow, in a doctoral dissertation (1973), has made a generative-transformational contrastive analysis of English and Hebrew for selected structures that are difficult for Hebrew-speaking learners of English. S. Blum-Kulka (1976) discusses situations in which Israeli translators of American fiction fail to reproduce the different stylistic levels of the original because they adhere too closely to the spoken level of Israeli Hebrew.

Studies in translation problems

Dagut (1972, doctoral dissertation; 1978, 1981) discusses the semantic voids, that is the "holes" in the semantic maps of two different languages, which are problems for the translator. The voids are caused by differing cultural experiences. Sometimes then, a word or concept exists in the source language, but the same does not exist in the target language (Dagut 1976). Dagut (1981) observes that cultural void poses greater problems in translation, forcing roundabout and cumbersome translations, while lexical void can be overcome by lexical items in the target language.

Semantic and cultural voids

Toury (1977) describes the norms of translation operating from 1930 to 1945 in Hebrew translations from English and German literature. He considers the crystallization of these norms and the factors governing this crystallization and also compares these translation norms with others operating in original Hebrew literature and in other categories of writing translated into Hebrew during that period. In a brief study (1981) Toury summarizes his views. He holds that several equivalencies are possible in the relationship between the original and the translation. The decision

Shifting cultural norms and translation

which determines which of these possible equivalencies will be selected depends on cultural and social norms operating in that time period. There is need to devise a descriptive and interpretive theory to account for preferred translations. Azar (1981c) deals with the translation of metaphor and concludes that a "pure metaphor," that is, one which breaks established language rules and establishes a new symbolism, is easier to translate than an "impure metaphor." The latter is encrusted with cultural and linguistic history and makes finding of an equivalent more difficult. Amit-Kochavi (1981) compares the translations of Judah Halevi's Kuzari by Ibn Tibbon (medieval) and by Even-Shemuel (modern). The differences are related to cultural factors and to the aims of the translator.

Hebrew and English structure compared

Levenston (1976) analyzes translations of English prose into Hebrew and concludes that Hebrew prefers lexical repetition, while English favors grammatical anaphors. Hebrew sentence structure requires more semantic interpretation. That is, an English sentence will be more abstract, ambiguous, or metaphorical, while Hebrew prefers concretion and specificity. For example, English "the fifteenth century saw an outburst of commercial activity" is rendered in Hebrew "in the fifteenth century we are witnesses to an outburst of commercial activity" or again, " . . . the pain and agitation of the Industrial Revolution" is rendered in Hebrew "the pain and agitation which accompanied the Industrial Revolution." English sentences tend toward the periodic form, and they are "top-heavy" in comparison with Hebrew.

Levenston (1966), in his doctoral dissertation, did a "scale and category" description of the syntax of Israeli Hebrew, with special reference to English-Hebrew translation equivalence. Sirat (1976) examines the problem of translation in terms of the different stylistic registers existing in Hebrew. A doctoral dissertation by Even-Zohar (1971) and a further study (1972) also deal with the subject of literary translation. R. Nir (1983) deals with aspects of translation to Hebrew in imported television films. A doctoral dissertation by Ungar (1984) seeks to establish a syntactic and semantic model for the analysis of relative clauses in both English and Hebrew.

More studies in applied linguistics appear in *Applied Linguistics and the Teaching of Hebrew*, *Min Hasadna* 3–4, edited by Rabin (1977e). It includes studies by S. Blum-Kulka, M. Chayen, E. Levenston, R. Nir, and C. Rabin. The Israel Association for Applied Linguistics has been publishing *Balshanut Shimushit* (*Applied Linguistics*) twice yearly since 1977. In the area of applied linguistics, a doctoral dissertation by Donag-Kinrot (1978) deals with norms and reality in connection with the language of school children (see also *LLA* 26 [1975], 261–67, 277–86). Regev (1979, doctoral dissertation), Sarel (1984, doctoral dissertation) and Parks (1979, doctoral dissertation) deal with the application of linguistics to problems of teaching.

LITERARY AND JOURNALISTIC STYLE

Linguistic studies on individual writers

A good number of studies and dissertations deal with the linguistic aspects of the work of Hebrew poets and writers of fiction. Ornan (1964a, doctoral dissertation; 1965a, book) treats the nominal phrase in the prose of Chaim Nachman Bialik. Two masters theses, by Nathan Schapira (1974) and Shashar (1963), deal with Yiddish and Aramaic, respectively. E. Kagan has contributed several studies on metrics, among them one on the poetry of Shlonsky (1963–64), one on the use of the *shewa mobile* in contemporary poetry (1966–67), a study on metrics and cadences (1968–69), a study on the change from Ashkenazic to Sephardic pronunciation in the poetry of Jacob Cahan (1971–72), and a study of patterns in free accentual verse (1976). Kremer (1974–75) has treated the language of Jacob Klatzkin and Dov Sadan.

A masters thesis by Shahadeh (1969) examines the breakup of construct states in the prose of Aharon Meged, and Nir (1979a) discusses lexical innovations in that writer's work. Sadan (1979) has devoted a study to the language of the poet Shimshon Meltzer. The noted writer Agnon, whose rabbinic and midrashic style is unique in the modern period, has been treated in a number of studies: Rabin (1957–58b, 1958–59); Mansour (1965, doctoral dissertation; book, 1968); Bar-Adon (1972–73, 1977a) on Agnon's role in and attitude toward the revival of Modern Hebrew (discussed above); Kaddari (1972a) on ergative verbs in the novel *Shirah* and a book (1980a) on stylistic features in Agnon; Bronznick (1978) on lexical innovations; and Donag-Kinrot (1969, masters thesis) on Agnon's corrections to "And the Crooked Shall Become Straight." Landau (1980a) discusses the biblical style in "Bidmi yamehah," a story by Agnon. Aphek and Tobin (1984) treat the untranslatability of metaphor and polysemy in Agnon and modern Hebrew.

B. Sasson (1946, masters thesis) deals with lexical innovations in the poetry of Shlonsky. These are also classified by Cnaani (1978–79). Lexical innovations in the poetry of Uri Zvi Greenberg are treated by Y. Bahat (1974–75), and Hrushovski (1968) deals with metrical innovations. Goldin (1954, masters thesis) studies the language of Alterman. Hazzaz's attempt to recreate a primitive Biblical Hebrew in his story *Ḥatan damim* ("Bridegroom of Blood") is discussed in a masters thesis by Y. Greenberg (1973). Behar (1972), in a masters thesis, treats Shamir's use of rabbinic Hebrew in his novel *King of Flesh and Blood.*

Linguistic study of earlier writers

Studies on earlier writers include a masters thesis by Putchinsky (1943) dealing with the Hebrew of Wessely, and a masters thesis by Shavit (1973) on the use of the biblical tenses in the writing of David Frischmann. Other masters theses in this area include: Spak (1975) on methods of translating Shalom Aleichem" by Berkovitz and Brenner; Sagi (1976) on Eliezer ben Yehudah's method of inverting subject and predicate in his writing. Hrushovski (1964) has contributed an important study on the role of Elijah Levità in introducing accented meter into Yiddish and Hebrew poetry, while Mirkin (1978a; 1978b; 1979, doctoral dissertation) studies developments in the style of Mendele Mokher Sefarim. Y. Wertheimer (1968, masters thesis) studies the language of the writer, Joseph Rivlin (see, for example, Rivlin 1939, 1956–57, 1959). In her doctoral dissertation (1983) she surveys the language of Moses Leib Lilienblum. Berakha Fischler (1983) examines Abraham Mapu's treatment of talmudic language.

Revision of semantic perceptions in the process of reading

A significant work by Perry (1976) deals with semantic dynamic in poetry and is based on the work of Hrushovski (1965, 1968). The theory is applied to the poetry of Bialik. Perry begins with the assumption that literature is a temporal art which is seen in two aspects: a) the literary text, a continuum of signs whose realization is a process, and b) the reconstructed level, e.g., plot, ideas, which may be organized in patterns of succession. There are two vantage points from which the text continuum can be described: a) the movement of the reader along the continuum, which is a step by step description of the process of semantic integration, and b) the principles of material distribution in the work—generalizations about principles of order and positional relations. The reader begins to construct a system of hypotheses which explain or relate details he has read. As the reading process goes on, these hypotheses are revised and reformulated, and gaps are perceived and filled in. A major part of Perry's work deals with the nature of this gap-filling. The first stage of the reading process affects all the subsequent ones, because the reader expects coherence and consistency. In Bialik's poetry the technique of the inverted poem is very frequent. The major pattern in the hierarchy of semantic patterns in the first part of the poem is replaced. The retrospective consideration of the details which takes place after the replacement/inversion causes a richer perception.

A masters thesis by Bar-Daroma (1981) surveys the language of the newspaper *Haʾarets* in the 1920's. Nir (1977, 1986) discusses clarity and ambiguity in journalistic Hebrew. The rhetoric of news presentation on the Israel radio is the subject of a study by I. Roeh (1982).

Journalistic Hebrew

The following dissertations and theses have been completed: Ilani (1977, masters thesis; see also 1982) on the broadening of categories of choice in contemporary Hebrew; Hatab (1977, masters thesis) on the various uses of situation-describers and their contribution to the solution of the problem of ambivalence.

BIBLIOGRAPHY

Aartun, K.

1974 Notizen zur hebräischen Nominalmorphologie. *BiOr* 31.38–39.

1975 Über die Grundstruktur der Nominalbildungen vom Typus *qaṭṭāl*/*qaṭṭōl* im Althebräischen. *JNSL* 4.1–8.

Ababneh, J. N. A.

1978 *The morphophonemics of pluralization in Biblical Hebrew and Classical Arabic.* Doctoral dissertation, University of Utah.

Abadi, A.

1979 עיונים בתחביר הטקסט. *Leš* 44.138–58.

1983 כמה תכונות של לכידות בשיח העברית הכתובה. Doctoral dissertation, Hebrew University.

1986 איחוי ושעבוד מעבר לגבולות המשפט. *WCJS* 9, Division D., 93–100.

Aberbach, M. and Grossfeld, B.

1982 *Targum Onkelos to Genesis.* New York and Denver, Ktav and Center for Judaic Studies, University of Denver.

Abramson, G.

1971–72 Colloquialisms in the Old Testament. *Semitics* 2.1–16.

Abramson, S.

1947 שמואל הנגיד .בן משלי. Tel Aviv.

1953 בן קהלת. Tel Aviv.

1956–57 מלשון חכמים. *Leš* 21.94–103.

1965 בלשון קודמים .מחקר בשירת ישראל. Jerusalem, The Schocken Institute of the Jewish Theological Seminary of America.

1971–74 לחקר הערוך. *Leš* 36.122–49; 37.26–42, 253–69; 38.91–117.

1974 על לשון עברי שבבבלי. *Archive of the new dictionary of rabbinical literature*, vol. 2, ed. by M. Z. Kaddari, 9–15, Ramat Gan.

1976 יהודה אבן בלעם, שלשה ספרים. Jerusalem, Kiryath Sepher.

1976–77a מן כתאב אלחאוי (ספר המאסף) לרב האי גאון. *Leš* 41.108–16.

1976–77b אינו דין, אינו בדין, בדין, דין הוא. *LLA* 28/10.275–79.

1978 מן כתאב אלנתף לרב יהודה חיוג׳ לשמואל ב׳. *Leš* 42.203–36; 43.29–51.

1978–79 מקור ושם הפועל. *Leš* 43.211–16.

1979 פרקים שנוגעים לר״י חיוג׳ ולרבי יונה בן ג׳נאח. *Leš* 43.260–70.

1983 במקראות, בחז״ל ובפיוטות. *ML*, 1–12.
1983–84 ספר ה״ערוך״ לרב נתן ב״ר יחיאל מרומא. *Sinai* 95.27–42.
1985a מילון לתלמוד לרב שמואל בן חפני. *Sefer Avraham Even-Shoshan*, ed. B. Z. Luria, 13–65, 293–94. Jerusalem.
1985b מחקרים בלשון, על לשון מקרא בלשון חז״ל, ed. M. Bar-Asher, 211–42. Jerusalem, Department of Hebrew Language, Hebrew University.

Ackroyd, P. R.
1950–51 The Hebrew root *bʾš*. *JTS* n.s. 1.31–36.

Adams, W. J.
1984 Diachronic development of narrative and exhortation discourse structures in Hebrew epigraphical sources. *SBLSP* 23.75–91.

Adar, H.
1965 חידושים בלשון החקלאות בתקופת הביל״ויים. Masters thesis, Hebrew University.

Adini, U.
1975–76 למקורו ולמהותו של ׳פרחח׳. *Leš* 40.92–94.
1979–80 A biblical *hapax-legomenon* in modern Hebrew. *HS* 20–21. 12–16.

Aescoly, D.
1932–33 לשונו של דוד הראובני. *Leš* 5.142–51.

Agus, I. A.
1974 The languages spoken by Ashkenazic Jews in the High Middle Ages. *Joshua Finkel Festschrift*, 19–28. New York.

Aharoni, A.
1981 Arad inscriptions. Jerusalem, Israel Exploration Society.

Ahuviah, A.
1974–75 והנה ״ישב״ ו״שוב״ כמו ״יטב״ ו״טוב״. *Leš* 39.21–36.
1976–77 ביטויים מן השדה הסימנטי של הבריתות בלשונו של ישעיה השני. *BM* 23.370–74.

Aistleitner, J.
1965 *Wörterbuch über der ugaritischen Sprache*. Berlin.

Albeck, H.
1959 מבוא למשנה. Jerusalem, Dvir.

Albright, W. F.
1947 The Phoenician inscriptions of the tenth century B.C. from Byblus. *JAOS* 67.153–60.
1950 Alphabetic origins and the Idrimi statue. *BASOR* 118.11–20.
1964 The Beth Shemesh tablet in alphabetic cuneiform. *BASOR* 173.51–53.
1966 *The Proto-Sinaitic inscriptions and their decipherment*. Harvard theological studies 22. Cambridge.

Algazi, L.
1958 *Chants sèphardis.* London.
Allchin, N. E.
1972 *A critical and lexical study of the root ᵓ-M-N in the Hebrew Old Testament.* Masters thesis, University of Melbourne.
Allon, E.
1984 דרכי הקריאה של העברית הכתובה הבלתי מנוקדת. Doctoral dissertation, Tel Aviv University.
Allony, N.
1947a מלשונו של דונש אבן לבראט *Leš* 15.161–72.
1947b דונש בן לבראט, שירים. Jerusalem, Mossad Havav Kook.
1951 תורת המשקלים של דונש, יהודה הלוי ואברהם אבן עזרא. Jerusalem.
1957 מחקרים בספרות ימי־הבינים. Jerusalem. Kiryath Sepher.
1958–59 פסיקתא דרב כהנא בניקוד ארץ ישראל. *Leš* 23.57–71 (with A. Díez-Macho).
1959 משירת ספרד ולשונה, 1. *Sinai* 44.152–69.
1960 משירת ספרד ולשונה, 2. אוצר יהודי ספרד 3.15–49.
1961 השקפות קראיות במחברת מנחם. אוצר יהודי ספרד 5.21–54.
1962–63 קטע חדש מספר הקרחה לר׳ יהודה חיוג׳. *BM* 16.90–105.
1963–64 איזהו "הניקוד שלנו" ב"מחזור ויטרי"? *BM* 17.135–45.
1964a ספר הקולות (כתאב אלמצותאת) למשה בן אשר. *Sefer Segal*, 272–91. Jerusalem.
1964b רשימת מונחים מהמאה השמינית (תכנית למודים והשכלה קראית עתיקה). *Korngren memorial volume*, 324–63. Jerusalem.
1964c משירת ספרד ולשונה. *Sinai* 55.236–62.
1965 הקדמת דונש לתשובותיו למחברת מנחם. *BM* 22.45–63.
1966 משירת ספרד ולשונה 4. *Sinai* 58.127–42.
1967–68 קבוצת העשר בלשון הדבור במאה העשירית. *Leš* 32.153–72.
1968 משירת ספרד ולשונה 5. *Sinai* 64.12–35.
1969a האגרון, כתאב אצול אלעבראני מאת רב סעדיה גאון. Jerusalem. Academy of the Hebrew Language.
1969b ספר הניקוד לרב סעדיה גאון. *BM* 40.19–67.
1969–70 עלי בן יהודה הנזיר וחבורו "יסודות הלשון העברית". *Leš* 34.75–105, 187–209.
1970–71 חמש מאות מלים בלשון הדבור במאה העשירית. *BM* 16(44).85–106.
1971–72 Review of Díez-Macho 1971 (H̱). *BM* 17(50).365–72.
1972 A new introduction to Bible and Hebrew linguistics (on Díez-Macho 1971). *JQR* 63.145–67.
1973a קטעי גניזה של משנה, תלמוד ומדרש מנוקדים בניקוד ארץ־ישראלי Jerusalem.
1973b השיטה האנאגרמטית של המילונות העברית ב"ספר יצירה". *WCJS* 5, 4.127–29. Jerusalem.

1973–74a ההיתה שיטת שרשים רב־גונית או לא? *BM* 19(57).202–24.
1973–74b תגובת ר׳ משה אבן עזרא ל׳ערבייה׳ בספר הדיונים והשיחות (שירת ישראל). *Tarbiz* 42.97–112.
1974–75 תורת הבלשנות הטברנית ודקדוק המסורה. *BM* 20(61).231–65 (review of Dotan 1967).
1975–76 Review of Abramson 1976 (*H*). *BM* 21(67).602–8.
1976 משירת רשב״ג ולשונו. *HUCA* 47.1–104 + 17 plates.
1977 יעקב בן אלעזר כתאב אלכאמל. The American Academy for Jewish Research, Monograph series 1. Jerusalem.
1981 שלושה ספרי בלשנות בשלוש ארצות. *Leš* 45.299–306.
1982 יסודות הבלשנות הטברנית (1100–650). *WCJS* 8, Division D, Hebrew section, 25–30. Jerusalem.
1983 ספר הקולות (כתאב אלמצותאת) למשה בן אשר. *Leš* 47.85–124.
1986 מחקרי לשון וספרות א; פרקי רב סעדיה גאון. Jerusalem, The Ben-Zvi Institute (Collected studies).

Allony, N., and Yeivin, I.
1985 מספרות הקולות. *Leš* 48–49.85–118.

Allony-Fainberg, Y.
1974 Official Hebrew terms for parts of the car: a study of knowledge, usage and attitudes. *Linguistics* 120.67–94.
1977 גורמים לשוניים וסוציו־דמוגרפיים וסיכויי התקבלות מונחים עבריים חדשים. Doctoral dissertation, Hebrew University.

Almagor (Rimmon), R.
1973 הצירוף המילוני—דרך מיכנית למיונו. Masters thesis, Hebrew University.

Altbauer, M.
1953–54 מלשון דייגי ישראל. *LLA* 5/3-4(45-46).26–32.
1954–55 מגבול אל גבול. *LLA* 6(53).14–17.
1955–56 על יסודות תחבירריים זרים בלשון ימינו. *LLA* 7(65).3–7.
1956–58 על העברית שבפי קראי ליטא ועל היסודות העבריים שבלשונם. *Leš* 21.117–26; 22.258–65.
1957–58 גלגולי משמעות. *LLA* no. 84.
1964 New negation constructions in Modern Hebrew. *For Max Weinreich on his seventieth birthday*, 1–5. The Hague, Mouton.
1968 מחקר המסורת העברית האשכנזית וזיקתו לדיאלקטולוגיה של היידיש. *WCJS* 4, 2.455.
1972 Achievements and tasks in the field of Jewish-Slavic language contact studies. Paper delivered to the International conference on Jews and Slavs, held at the Russian and East European Center of the University of California, Los Angeles.
1977a מחקרים בלשון. Vol. 1. Jerusalem (collected studies).
1977b יסודות של עברית אשכנזית בתעתיק קירילי מהמחצית הראשונה של המאה הט״ז. *Sefer Dov Sadan*, 55–65. Jerusalem.

1983 מאת י׳ היתה זאת היא נפלאת בעינינו (תה׳ קיח, כג) על משמעות הסתמיות בכינוי הרומז בעברית ודרכי תרגומה בלועזית. *ML* 57–66.

Althaus, H. P.

1971 *Die Cambridger Löwenfabel von 1382: Untersuchung und Edition eines defektiven Text*. Berlin/New York, Walter de Gruyter.

1972 Yiddish, in *Current Trends in linguistics*, 9: Linguistics in western Europe, ed. by T. A. Sebeok, 1347–82. The Hague, Mouton.

1973 Western Yiddish and German dialects. *WCJS* 5, 4.1–15.

Ambar, O.

1980 עיון סמנטי בפעלים במבנה התחבירי צ״ש + פועל + צ״ש$_2$ + ומקור. Masters thesis, Tel Aviv University.

Amit, Mordechai

1976–77 סדר התאורים במשפט. *Leš* 41.44–47.

Amit, Moshe

1950 השוואה בין שיטתו הבלשנית של רד״ק בספר השרשים לבין שיטתו בחיבוריו הפרשניים. Masters thesis, Hebrew University.

Amitay, S.

1949 מדרשי השמות במקרא מהצד הלשוני. Masters thesis, Hebrew University.

Amit-Kochavi, H.

1981 היבטים אחדים של שני תרגומים. לקטע מתוך ספר ״הכוזרי״ לרבי יהודה הלוי. עיונים בבלשנות ובסמיוטיקה, 83–96. Jerusalem.

Amzalak, M. B.

1971 Judeo-French. *EJ* 10.423–25.

Andersen, F. I.

1966 Moabite syntax. *Orientalia* 35.81–120.

1970a *The Hebrew verbless clause in the Pentateuch*. JBL monograph series 14. Nashville/New York, Abingdon.

1970b Biconsonantal by-forms of weak Hebrew roots. *ZAW* 82.270–75.

1971 Passive and ergative in Hebrew. *Near Eastern studies in honor of W. F. Albright*, ed. H. Goedicke, 1–15. Baltimore/London, Johns Hopkins.

1974 *The sentence in Biblical Hebrew*. Janua linguarum, Series practica 231. The Hague, Mouton.

Andersen, F. I. and Forbes, A. D.

1986 *Spelling in the Hebrew Bible*. Leiden, Brill.

Aphek, E. and Kahaneman, I.

1984–85 מגמות חדשות בתפקודה של המילית על בעברית הישראלית. *LLA* 36/2 (352).47–61; 36/3–4 (353–54).84–98; 36/8–10 (358–360).205–15.

Aphek, E. and Tobin, Y.
1984 The place of "place" in a text from Agnon; on the untranslatability of metaphor and polysemy in Modern Hebrew. *Babel* 30.148–58.

Arel, E.
1978 המעשה החינוכי. תחיית העברית מנקודת הראות של מדעי הלשון 291–307.
1981 הקבלות בין העברית והנורבגית בקונפלוקט מסביב לנורמאטיביות ולסטאטוס בחינוך. עיונים בבלשנות ובסמיוטיקה, 20–22. Jerusalem.

Arend, M.
1960 תפיסתם הבלשנית של חז"ל כפי שהיא משתקפת בדרשותיהם במדרש בראשית רבה. Masters thesis, Hebrew University.

Ariel, S.
1961 *The verb stems and conjugations in colloquial Israeli Hebrew: a syntactic and semantic study.* Doctoral dissertation, University of London.
1972 The function of the conjugations in colloquial Israeli Hebrew. *BSOAS* 35.514–30.
1973a The system of stem-forms in colloquial Israeli Hebrew. *TPS* 1971, 192–271.
1973b The functions of the *BINYANIM* in Modern Hebrew. *WCJS* 5, 4.17–30. Jerusalem.

Ariel, S. and Katriel, T.
1977 Range indications in colloquial Israeli Hebrew: a semantic-syntactic analysis. *HAR* 1.29–51.

Aristar, A. M. R.
1979 The II *wy* verbs and the vowel system of Proto-West Semitic. *AAL* 6/6.

Armistead, S.
1977 *El romancero judeo-español en el Archivo Menendez Pidal*, 3 vols. Madrid, Catedra-Seminario Menendez Pidal (includes the collection of Manrique de Lara, 1863–1929).
1982 New perspectives in Judeo-Spanish ballad research, in I. Ben-Ami, ed., *The Sephardi and Oriental Jewish heritage*, 225–235. Jerusalem, Magnes Press.

Armistead, S. and Carracedo, L. et al.
1978 Bibliotheca Sefardica. *E Sef* 1.213–312 (critical bibliography, 1970–75).

Armistead, S. and Silverman, J. H.
1965 Christian elements and de-Christianization in the Sephardic romancero. *Collected studies in honor of Americo Castro's eightieth year*, ed. by M. P. Hornik, 21–38. Oxford, Lincombe Lodge Research Library.

1971a *The Judeo-Spanish ballad chapbooks of Yacob Abraham Yona.* Berkeley.

1971b *Jewish-Spanish ballads from Bosnia*, with B. Šljivić-Šimšić. Philadelphia.

1981 eds. *Judeo-Spanish ballads from New York, collected by Maír José Benardete.* Berkeley, Los Angeles, London, University of California.

Aro, J.

1964 *Die Vocalisierung des Grundstammes im semitischen Verbum.* Studia Orientalia, Societas Orientalis Fennica 31. Helsinki.

Artom, E.

1947 מבטא עברית אצל יהודי איטליה. *Leš* 15.52–61.

Artom, M.

1980 הערות על חקר התעתיק של מלים איטלקיות באותיות עבריות. *Leš* 42.310–13.

Ashkenazi, S.

1964–65 הרמב"ם המתרגם מלשון התלמוד המשנה. *LLA* 16/6 (158).

1965–66 מילונות עברית כיצד? הערות על "המלון החדש". *Leš* 31.123–27.

Asif, S.

1975 פסוקי הזמן הבו־זמניים הנבנים באמצעות שם פועל ("בעשות, כעשות") בחומש ובתרגומיו לארמית. Masters thesis, Hebrew University.

Asmussen, J. P.

1968 *Jewish-Persian texts: introduction, selections and glossary.* Wiesbaden.

1970 *Studier Jødisk-Persisk Litteratur.* Copenhagen.

1973 *Studies in Judeo-Persian literature.* Studia post-biblica 25. Leiden.

Asmussen, J. P. and Paper, H.

1977 *The Song of Songs in Judeo-Persian.* Copenhagen, Det Kongelige Danske Videnskabernes Selskab, Historisk-filosofiske Skrifter 9:2.

Atias, T.

1981 *Adjective order in Israeli Hebrew.* Masters thesis, Tel Aviv University.

Atlas, Y.

1946 ידיעותיו והשקפותיו הבלשניות של המלבי"ם על פי פירושו לתורה. Masters thesis, Hebrew University.

Attal, R.

1973 *Les Juifs d'Afrique du Nord: bibliographie.* Jerusalem: The Ben-Zvi Institute.

1984 *Les Juifs de Grèce de l'expulsion d'Espagne à nos jours.* Leiden: Brill.

Aufrecht, W.

1975 *A synoptic concordance of Aramaic inscriptions* (according to H. Donner and W. Röllig). Missoula, MT, Scholars Press.

Austel, H. J.

1969 *Prepositional and non-prepositional complements with verbs of motion in Biblical Hebrew.* Doctoral dissertation, UCLA. Ann Arbor, University Microfilms.

Avigad, N. and Yadin, Y.

1956 *A Genesis apocryphon.* Jerusalem.

Avinery, I.

1968 היסודות הערביים בניב הארמי של יהודי זאכו. Masters thesis, Hebrew University.

1974 סיפור בניב הארמי של יהודי זאכו. *H. Yalon memorial volume,* Bar-Ilan departmental researches 2, 8–16. Jerusalem.

1977 A folk tale in the neo-Aramaic dialect of the Jews of Zakho. *JAOS* 98.92–96.

1979 היסודות הארמיים בספרות ממנדלי ועד קום המדינה. ספר שלום סיון, ed. by A. Even-Shoshan *et al.*, 73–92. Jerusalem, Kiryath Sepher.

Avinery, Y.

1940 היכל רש״י. 5 vols. Tel Aviv (1979, revised edition, vol. 1. Jerusalem, Mossad Harav Kook).

1946 כבושי העברית בדורנו. Merchaviah.

1955–56 שבילי סמיכות. *LLA* 6/7 (59).

1964a יד הלשון. Tel Aviv.

1964b כתיב וכתב. Tel Aviv.

1976 היכל המשקלים. Tel Aviv.

Avisar, S.

1973 La vexata quaestio dell'affinita tra l'ebraico e il latino. *RMI* 39.103–13.

1978 *Du française à l'hébreu: la méthode du thème et stylistique comparée.* Strasbourg, Institute d'Études Hebraïques de l'Université de Strasbourg: Jerusalem, Kiryath Sepher.

Avishur, Y.

1971–72 Pairs of synonymous words in the construct state and in appositional hendiadys in Biblical Hebrew. *Semitica* 2.17–81.

1973 דרכי החזרה במספרי השלמות (3, 7, 10) במקרא ובספרות השמית הקדומה. *Beʾer Sheva* 1.1–55.

1974 צמדי מלים במקרא ומקביליהם בשפות השמיות של המזרח הקדמון. Doctoral dissertation, Hebrew University.

1975 Word pairs common to Phoenician and Biblical Hebrew. *UF* 7.13–47.

1975–76a זוגות מלים נרדפות מן המקרא המצומדים כסמכויות בפיוט הקדום. *BM* 21(66).412–57.

1975–76b שקיעים מספרות פיניקיה במשלי ג׳. שנתון, an annual for biblical and near eastern research, 1.13–25.

1976 Studies of stylistic features common to the Phoenician inscriptions and the Bible. *UF* 8.1–22.

1976–77 על הצירופים מסוג ״בין ידיים״ במקרא ומקביליהם בשפות השמיות. *BM* 22(69).199–208.

1977a סמכויות הנרדפים במליצה המקראית. Jerusalem, Kiryath Sepher.

1977b מלים וצירופים במקרא לאור מקביליהם באכדית. שנתון, an annual for biblical and near eastern studies 2.11–19.

1978–79 לא שמת להם רחמים׳—בין דפוסי סגנון לתרגום בבואה מאכדית. שנתון, an annual for biblical and ancient near eastern studies, 5-6.91–99.

1979a כתובות פניקיות והמקרא, 2 vols. Jerusalem.

1979b צמדי בטויים משותפים לספרות המקראית הכנענית. ספר שלום סיון, ed. by A. Even-Shoshan *et al.*, 141–62. Jerusalem, Kiryath Sepher.

1979c הספרות העממית של יהודי בבל בערבית־יהודית. פעמים 3.83–90.

1980a ״וכליותי אשתונן״—למשמעות הפועל שנ״ן בעברית ובאוגריתית. *Leš* 44.263–67.

1980b Expressions of the type *byn ydym* in the Bible and Semitic languages. *UF* 12.125–34.

1981 רום (רמם)—בנה באוגריתית ובמקרא (ולהפריח—לבנות במקרא ובתוספתא). *Leš* 45.270–79.

1984 *Stylistic studies of word-pairs in biblical and ancient Semitic literatures*, AOAT 210. Kevelaer, Verlag Butzon and Bercker.

1985 על סדר המלים בצמדים המקראיים והאוגריתיים. *Sefer Avraham Even-Shoshan*, ed. B. Z. Luria, Jerusalem, 335–51.

Avistar, A.

1979 The II *wy* verbs and the vowel system of Proto-West Semitic. *AAL* 6/6.

Avizemer, S.

1983 ייחודה של יהדות תימן בתחום הלשון העברית ותרבותה. סעי יונה, 327–35.

Azar, M.

1966 הפועל בספר חסידים—בחינה־סימנטית. Masters thesis, Hebrew University.

1970 *Analyse morphologique automatique du texte hébreu de la Bible*. Nancy, Centre du Recherche et d'Application Linguistique de la Faculté des Lettres et des Sciences Humanines.

1971–72 סימני הצרכה, מלות הדרכה והיחידות המילוניות של הפועל. *Leš* 36.220–27, 282–86.

1976a הסמיכות הפרודה והסמיכות הכפולה בעיתונות היומית. חקר ועיון, 9–24. University of Haifa.

1976b The emphatic sentence in Modern Hebrew, in P. Cole, ed., *Studies in Modern Hebrew syntax and semantics*, 209–29. Amsterdam.

1977a שטח ועומק בתחביר. University of Haifa.

1977b צרוף היחס כלוואי במקרא. *WCJS* 6, 1.43–54.

1977c על "הסומך נודד" במקרא. *Leš* 41.180–90.

1978 המטפורה הסימנטית, הרטורית והסימבולית. *LLA* 29.259–68.

1981a לשונות התחייבות במקרא ובמשנה. Haifa, Pinat Hasefer.

1981b אבל, אלא ואלא ש—בעברית של ימינו. *Leš* 45.133–48.

1981c המטאפורה והתנאים לתרגומה המילולי. עיונים בבלשנות ובסמיוטיקה, 63–70. Jerusalem.

1982 "אלא" במשנה—בחינה תחבירית־סימאנטית פרגמטית. *WCJS* 8, Division D, Hebrew section, 11–14. Jerusalem.

1985 התחביר ואחדות הלשון העברית. מחקרים בלשון, ed. M. Bar-Asher, 157–61. Jerusalem, Department of Hebrew Language, Hebrew University.

Babalikshvili, N.

1979 המבטא העברי של יהודי גרוזיה. *Leš* 44.66–90.

Bach, D.

1978 Rite et parole dans l'ancient Testament. *VT* 28.10–19.

Bacher, W.

1882 *Abraham ibn Esra als Grammatiker*. Strasbourg, Trübner (translated by A. Z. Rabinowitz, Tel Aviv, 1931).

1885 *Leben und Werke des Abulwalid Merwan ibn Ganah*. Leipzig, O. Schultze.

1892 *Die hebräische Sprachwissenschaft vom zehnten bis zum sechsten Jahrhundert, mit einem einleitenden Abschnitt über die Masora*. Leipzig.

1895 *Die Anfänge der hebräischen Grammatik*. Leipzig (reprinted in Hebrew translation, Jerusalem, 1970). Bacher 1892 and 1895 reprinted 1974, with bibliography by Ludwig Blau, supplemented by D. Friedman and with an introductory article by J. Fellman, "Wilhelm Bacher, pioneer in the history of Hebrew linguistics," Theory and history of linguistic science III, 4. Amsterdam, John Benjamins.

1903 *Aus dem Wörterbuch Tanchum Jerushalmis*. Strasbourg (for full bibliography, see also *JE* 2.422).

Bacon, Y.

1968 פרקים בהתפתחות המשקל של השירה העברית. Tel Aviv University, Mif^{c}al hashikhpul.

Bahat, S.

1964 משפטי הזיקה בעברית החדשה. Masters thesis, Hebrew University.

n.d. למה ומדוע. Jerusalem, Rubinstein (based on Kol Yisrael program dealing with language).

Bahat, Y.

1974–75 החינוך. אורי צבי גרינברג: בינו ובין שימושי לשון וחידושי לשון 4-5.290–93.

1975 שיטתו של אבא בנדויד בתיקוני לשון. Masters thesis, Hebrew University.

Bailey, H. W.

1982 Adversaria Iranica. *Irano-Judaica*, ed. by Saul Shaked, 1–3. Jerusalem, The Ben-Zvi Institute.

Baker, D.

1980 Further examples of the *waw explicativum*. *VT* 30.129–36.

Baldacci, M.

1978 The Ammonite text from Tell Siran and Northwest Semitic philology. *VT* 31.363–68.

Balentine, S. E.

1980 A description of the semantic field of Hebrew words for 'hide'. *VT* 30.137–53.

Baltzer, K.

1971 *The covenant formulary.* Oxford, Blackwell (originally published as *Das Bundesformular*, Neukirchen, 1960).

Bandstra, B. L.

1982 *The syntax of particle* ky *in Biblical Hebrew and Ugaritic.* Doctoral dissertation, Yale. Ann Arbor, University Microfilms.

Bange, L. A.

1971 *A study of the use of vowel letters in alphabetic consonantal writing.* Munich (Inaugural dissertation, Oxford, 1961–62).

Banitt, M.

1961 Fragments d'un glossaire judéo-français du moyen âge. *REJ* 120.259–96.

1963 Une langue fantome: le judéo-français. *RLR* 27.245–94.

1968a פירוש רש״י למקרא ולעז־העולם. Benjamin De Vries memorial volume, 252–67. Jerusalem.

1968b L'étude des glossaires bibliques des juifs de France au moyen âge—methode et application. *PIASH* 2, Jerusalem (Also published in Hebrew in the Proceedings of the Academy, 1969, 135–49).

1971a Judeo-French. *EJ* 10.432–35.

1971b *Laᶜaz. EJ* 10.1313–15.

1972 *Le glossaire de Bâle*, vol. 1–2. Jerusalem, Academie nationale des sciences et des lettres d'Israel.

1986 הלעזים בפירוש רש״י ובספרי הפתרונות. *Teᶜudah* 4, ed. M. A. Friedman and M. Gil, 143–68. Tel Aviv University.

Bar-Adon, A.

1959 לשונם המדוברת של הילדים בישראל. Doctoral dissertation, Hebrew University.

1964 Analogy and analogic change as reflected in contemporary Hebrew. *PICL* 9, 758–64. The Hague, Mouton.

1965 The evolution of Modern Hebrew, in *Acculturation and integration: a symposium by American, Israeli and African experts*, ed. by J. L. Teller. New York, American Histadrut Cultural Exchange Institute.

1966 New imperative and jussive formations in contemporary Hebrew. *JAOS* 86.410–13.

1966–67 עיונים באוצר המלים של ילדי ישראל. *LLA* 18/2 (174).

1968 סדר מלים ומבנה תחבירי בלשון הילדים בעברית. *WCJS* 4, 2.123–28 (English summary 188).

1971 Primary syntactic structures in Hebrew child language, in Bar Adon and W. Leopold, eds., *Child language—a book of readings*, 433–72. Englewood Cliffs, NJ, Prentice-Hall.

1972–73 S. Y. Agnon and the revival of Modern Hebrew. *TSLL* 14.147–75.

1973a Language problems of developing nations, a selected bibliography. *HCL* 7.89–180.

1973b The rise and decline of an upper-Galilee dialect. *Language planning, current issues and research*, ed. by Joan Rubin and Roger Shoy. Washington, DC, Georgetown University Press.

1975 *The rise and fall of a dialect: a study in the revival of Modern Hebrew*. Janua linguarum, Series practica 197. The Hague, Paris, Mouton.

1977a עגנון ותחיית הלשון העברית. Jerusalem.

1977b On the nationalization of modern Hebrew and the role of children in this process, in *Studies in descriptive and historical linguistics*, Festschrift for Winfred D. Lehmann, ed. by P. J. Hopper, 487–98. Amsterdam, John Benjamins.

1980 על תחיית הלשון באספקלריה של עגנון. *WCJS* 6, Division D, 15–28. Jerusalem.

1982 בין לשון־חכמים ללשון־ילדים בהתפתחותה. *WCJS* 8, Division D, 31–37. Jerusalem.

1986 על תרומתה של העלייה השנייה לתחיית הלשון העברית—דימוי ומציאות. *WCJS* 9, Division D, 63–70. Jerusalem.

Bar-Asher, Moshe.

1968 פרקים בדקדוק המשנה על פי כתב יד פארמה ב׳ (פה דה־רוסי 497) לסדר טהרות. Masters thesis, Hebrew University.

1972 קובץ מאמרים בלשון חז״ל. Jerusalem, Hebrew University, Faculty of Humanities, Department of Hebrew Language.
1976 על מסורותם הלשונית של בני עדות המזרח והספרדים בסידור התפילה. *LLA* 27/10 (170).271–82.
1976–77 צורות נדירות בלשון התנאים. *Leš* 41.83–102.
1977–78 על היסודות העבריים בעברית המדוברת של יהודי מרוקו. *Leš* 42.163–89.
1978 *M.A. and doctoral theses on Hebrew and Aramaic submitted in Israeli universities* (1938–1977). Brochure no. 5. Jerusalem, Council on the Teaching of Hebrew.
1980a קובץ מאמרים בלשון חז״ל, part 2. Jerusalem, Hebrew University, Faculty of Humanities, Department of Hebrew Language.
1980b פרקים במסורת לשון חכמים של יהודי איטליה על פי כתב יד מפאריס 328–329. מפעל מסורות הלשון של עדות ישראל 13. Jerusalem, Hebrew University.
1981 כתיבים שלא הובנו. *Leš* 45.85–92.
1983 נשכחות בלשון התנאים בין הסופר לנקדן של כתב־יד קויפמן של המשנה (בירור ראשון). *ML* 83–110.
1983–84 הטיפוסים השונים של לשון המשנה. *Tarbiz* 53.187–220.
1984a *Massorot* 1 (editor). Jerusalem, Hebrew University.
1984b על משוגות הניקוד בכתב יד קאופמן של המשנה. *Massorot* 1.1–17.
1984–85 היסוד העברי בשַׂרח של יהודי מרוקו. *Leš* 49.227–52.
1985a מחקרים בלשון (editor). Jerusalem, Department of Hebrew Language, Hebrew University.
1985b אחדותה ההיסטורית של הלשון העברית וחלוקתה לתקופות—כיצד?. מחקרים בלשון, ed. M. Bar-Asher, 3–25. Jerusalem, Department of Hebrew Language, Hebrew University.
1986 מחקרים במדעי היהדות (editor). Jerusalem.

Bar-Daroma, M.
1981 העיתונות של שנות ה־20 עפ״י ״הארץ״. Masters thesis, Tel Aviv University.

Bar-Hillel, Y.
1949 תורת הקטגוריות התחביריות. Doctoral dissertation, Hebrew University.
1956–57 Review of Rosén 1956a (*H*). *Leš* 21.127–38.
1960–61 סיבוכו של פסוק מהו? *Leš* 25.150–64.
1970 *Aspects of Language*. Jerusalem.

Barkai, M.
1972 *Problems in the phonology of Israeli Hebrew*. Doctoral dissertation, University of Illinois at Urbana-Champaign. Ann Arbor, University Microfilms.

1975 On phonological representation, rules and opacity. *Lingua* 37.363–76.
1978a Theoretical implications of consonant sequence constraints in Israeli Hebrew. *AAL* 6.1–13.
1978b Phonological opacity versus semantic transparency: two cases from Israeli Hebrew. *Lingua* 44.363–78.
1980 Aphasic evidence for lexical and phonological representations. *AAL* 7/6.

Barkai, M. and Horvarth, J.
1978 Voicing assimilation and the sonority hierarchy: evidence from Russian, Hebrew and Hungarian. *Linguistics* 212.77–88.

Bar-Lev, Z.
1977 Natural-abstract Hebrew phonology. *FoL* 11.259–72.
1978 Hebrew intraphonemics. *Linguistics* 212.57–68.
1979 The ordering of Hebrew morphological processes. *AAL* 6.15–22.

Bar-Magen, M.
1977–78 על החריגים בסיומת "ן" במקרא. *BM* 23(74).363–69.
1980 המלה "נא" במקרא. *BM* 25(81).163–71.

Barnes, O.
1965 *A new approach to the problem of Hebrew tenses and its solution without recourse to* waw-*consecutive.* Oxford.

Barnett, R. D.
1982 A legacy of the captivity—a note on the paleo-Hebrew and neo-Hebrew script. *EI* 16.1*–6*.

Bar-Nir, P.
1976 תחליפי משפט בלשון המקרא על פי ספרי התורה ונביאים ראשונים. Masters thesis, Tel Aviv University.

Barr, J.
1961 *The semantics of biblical language.* Oxford.
1967 St. Jerome and the sounds of Hebrew. *JSS* 12.1–36.
1968 *Comparative philology and the text of the Old Testament.* Oxford.
1969 The ancient Semitic languages, the conflict between philology and linguistics. *TPS*, 37–55.
1970 Which language did Jesus speak? *BJRL* 53.9–29.
1971 Linguistic literature. *EJ* 16.1352–1401.
1972 Semantics and biblical theology, a contribution to the discussion. *VT* supplement, 22.11–19.
1974 Etymology and the Old Testament, *OTS* 19.1–28. Leiden.
1979 Semitic philology and the interpretation of the Old Testament, in G. W. Andersen, ed., *Tradition and Interpretation*, 31–64. Oxford.

Barri, N.
1978 שם־תואר מועצם ושם עצם מותאר בעברית חדשה מדוברת. *Leš* 42.252–72.
1979 הרכב מכח הטעמה. *LLA* 30.58–59.
1980 בין יוונית לעברית. מחברות לספרות, חברה וביקורת 6.40–41.
Barth, J.
1894 *Nominalbildung in den semitischen Sprachen.* Berlin.
Barth, L.
1973 *An analysis of Vatican 30.* Cincinnati/New York, Hebrew Union College—Jewish Institute of Religion.
Barthélemy, D. and Rickenbacher, O.
1973 *Konkordanz zum hebräischen Sirach.* Göttingen.
Baruch, Y.
1969–70 סדר נושא ונשוא במשפטים הפותחים במלות אשר, כאשר־שֶׁ, כְּשֶׁ, מִשֶּׁ, לְכְשֶׁ (מחתימת המשנה עד סוף תקופת הגאונים). *LLA* 21.13–27.
Bar-Yosef, A.
1981 מבוא לתולדות הלשון העברית. Tel Aviv, Or Am.
Barzel, R.
1973 שינויים סימנטיים שחלו בלשונו של רש״י לעומת לשון המקורות על פי לשונו בפרושו לתורה. Masters thesis, Hebrew University.
Barzilay, I.
1979 From purism to expansionism: a chapter in the early history of modern Hebrew. *JANES* 11.3–15.
Battle, J.
1969 *Syntactic structures in the masoretic Hebrew text of the Psalms.* Doctoral dissertation, University of Texas at Austin. Ann Arbor, University Microfilms.
1971 Transformational concepts in the Hebrew text of the Psalms. Papers given at the fifth Kansas conference on linguistics, ed. F. Ingemann, 8–16. University of Kansas.
Batto, B.
1971 DINGIR.IŠ.ḪI and spirantization in Hebrew. *JSS* 16.33–34.
Bauer, H. and Leander, P.
1922 *Historische Grammatik der hebräischen Sprache des alten Testaments.* Halle, M. Niemeyer.
1927 *Grammatik des biblisch-aramäischen.* Halle.
Baumgarten, I.
1951 אוצר לשון הפתגמים אשר במקרא מחוץ לספר משלי. Masters thesis, Hebrew University.
Bean, A. F.
1976 *A phenomonological study of the* hithpaᶜel *verbal stem in the Hebrew Old Testament.* Doctoral dissertation, The

Southern Baptist Theological Seminary. Ann Arbor, University Microfilms.
Becker, D.
1970 שם הפועל בתחביר העברית של ימינו + ל. Masters thesis, Tel Aviv University.
1977 ה״רסאלה״ של יהודה בן קוריש. Doctoral dissertation, Tel Aviv University.
1980 השלמות לכתאב אלמואזנה (= ספר ההשואה ליצחק בן ברון). *Leš* 44.293–98.
1984 ה׳ רסאלה׳ של יהודה בן קוריש: מהד׳ ביקורתית. Tel Aviv University.
Becker, J.
1973 Einige Hyperbata im alten Testament. *BZ* 17.257–63.
Beem, H.
1954 Yiddish in Holland: linguistic and sociolinguistic notes. *FY* 1, ed. by U. Weinreich, 122–33. New York.
1959/1970[2] *Jerosche. Jiddische speekworden en Zegswijzen. uit hed Nederlandse taalgebied.* Assen, Van Gorcum.
1967/1975[2] *Resten van een Tal. Woordenboekje van het Nederlandse Jiddische.* Assen and Amsterdam, Van Gorcum.
1974 *Uit mokum den die mediene. Joodse woorden en Nederlandse omgeving.* Assen, Van Gorcum.
Beer, G.
1929 *Faksimile-Ausgabe des Mischnakodex Kaufman* A 50. The Hague (reprinted Jerusalem, 1968).
Beer, G. and Meyer, R.
1952 *Hebräische Grammatik.* Berlin.
Beeston, A. F. L.
1979 Hebrew *šibbōleṯ* and *šōḇel*. *JSS* 24.175–79.
Behar, D.
1972 לשון חז״ל כפי שהיא נראית בעיני סופר בן זמננו על פי ״מלך בשר ודם״ למשה שמיר. Masters thesis, Hebrew University.
Beit-Arié, M.
1964 ניקודו של מחזור ק״ק וורמייזה. Masters thesis, Hebrew University.
1964–65 ניקודו של מחזור ק״ק וורמייזה. *Leš* 29.27–46, 80–102.
1979 שיחון עברי־לאטיני מן המאה העשירית. *Tarbiz* 48.274–302.
1981 *Hebrew codicology: tentative typology of technical processes employed in Hebrew dated medieval manuscripts.* Jerusalem, Israel Academy of Science and Humanities.
1982 דף נוסף לכתר ארם צובא. *Tarbiz* 51.171–74.
Bekkum, W. Jac. van
1983a Observations on stem formations (binyanim) in Rabbinical Hebrew. *OLP* 14.167–98.

1983b The origins of the infinitive in Rabbinical Hebrew. *JSS* 28.247–72.

Beld, S. G., Hallo, W. W. and Michaelowski, P.

1984 *The Tablets of Ebla, Concordance and Bibliography*. Winona Lake, Eisenbrauns.

Benabu, I. and Sermoneta, J. (G).

1985 *Judeo-Romance languages*. Jerusalem.

Ben-Ami, I.

1970 אלף ואחד פתגמים יהודיים ממרוקו. Folklore research center studies 1, ed. by Dov Noy and I. Ben-Ami, 35–148. Jerusalem.

Ben Amotz, D. and Ben Yehuda, N.

1972/1982 מלון עולמי לעברית מדוברת. Jerusalem, Levin-Epstein.

Ben-Asher, Mordechai.

1960 ניצול המשקלים בחידושי האקדמיה ללשון. בשער 3.38–46.

1964 משפטי התנאי בעברית החדשה הבינונית. Masters thesis, Hebrew University.

1966–67a על שם הפעולה העברי. *LLA* 18.105–12.

1966–67b התפתחויות לשוניות. *LLA* 18.236–43.

1968 היווצרות הדקדוק הנורמטיבי בעברית החדשה. Doctoral dissertation, Hebrew University.

1969 התגבשות הדקדוק הנורמטיבי בעברית החדשה. Hakkibutz Hameuchad.

1970–71 להבחנה בין מושא עקיף ותיאור־פועל. מעלות 2.28–36.

1972 בנייני הפועל—עניין לדקדוק או למילון? האוניברסיטה 17/2.31–34.

1973 עיונים בתחביר העברית החדשה. Hakkibutz Hameuchad.

1973–74 על מלות היחס בעברית החדשה. *Leš* 38.385–93.

1975–76 Review of Boyle 1973 (*H*). *Leš* 40.263–68.

1976a שמושי המקור ושם הפעולה בלשון המקרא לעומת לשון ימינו. *Chaim Rabin volume*, ed. by B. Fischler and R. Nir, 23–35. Jerusalem.

1976b חקר ועיון, מלים בעלות סיומת זכר וסיומת נקבה במקרא ובעברית 61–76. University of Haifa.

1978 Causative *Hifᶜil* verbs with double objects in biblical Hebrew. *HAR* 2.11–19.

1982² דקדון העברית, a translation of the 28th edition of the Gesenius-Kautzsch *Hebräischer Grammatik* by G. Bergsträsser. Jerusalem, Magnes Press (with corrections by J. Blau; first edition 1972).

Bendavid, A.

1940 משפט הזיקה בעברית. Masters thesis, Hebrew University.

1951 לשון המקרא או לשון חכמים?. Tel Aviv, Maḥbarot lesifrut.

1957 על מה נחלקו בן אשר ובן נפתלי?. *Tarbiz* 26.384–409.

1957–58a מקורות לפעולתו של לוי אלתבאן במחקר הלשון. *Leš* 22.7–35.

1957–58b מניין החלוקה לתניעות גדולות וקטנות?. *Leš* 22.110–36.
1957–58c Review of Murtonen 1958 (*H*). *KS* 33.482–91.
1967 לשון מקרא ולשון חכמים, 1. Tel Aviv, Dvir.
1971 לשון מקרא ולשון חכמים, 2. Tel Aviv, Dvir.
1971–72a על ספרי עתיקות. *Leš* 23/7-8 (227–28).203–8; 23/9 (229).242–48.
1971–72b לשון כסה ועשור. *LLA* 23/10 (230).
1972–73 לשון למועד, שיחה בענייני לשון לקראת הפסח. *LLA* 24/7 (237).183–99.
1973–74a עוד לשון למועד (חג חסוכות). *LLA* 25/1 (241).3–13.
1973–74b לשונות למועדים, ט"ו שבט ופורים. *LLA* 25/6 (246).
1973–74c לשונות חג השבועות. *LLA* 25/8 (248).199–212.
1975–76 לשונותיה של חנוכה. *LLA* 26/2 (252).
1976–77a לשונות שלש הרגלים. *LLA* 28/4 (274–75).
1976–77b הידעת מאין הביטוי?. *LLA* 28/7-8 (276–78).
1985 תקופות הדיבור העברי ותקופות העברית הכתובה. מחקרים בלשון, ed. M. Bar-Asher, 163–73. Jerusalem, Department of Hebrew Language, Hebrew University.

Bendavid, I.
1974–75 משקל, בנין, תבנית. *Leš* 39.123–32, 296–307.
1981 אֶתְרֹג, אֶתְרֻגִּים וכיוצא בו שמות מן החלוּמים. *Leš* 46.76–79.
1982 תנועת *ā* בשמות־פעולה. *Leš* 46.143–49.
1985 שני עניינים מלשון חכמים. *Sefer Avraham Even-Shoshan*, ed. B. Z. Luria, 315–23. Jerusalem.

Ben-Hayyim, Z.
1948 תרגומים נשכחים ומתמיהים. *Leš* 16.156–63, 228.
1951 Review of Prijs 1950 (*H*). *Leš* 17.241–47.
1952–53a תורת התנועות לרב סעדיה גאון. *Leš* 18.89–96.
1952–53b לשון עתיקה במציאות חדשה, שיחות על בעיות בלשון העברית החיה. *LLA* 4/3-5, 8-9 (35–37, 40–41).
1953 צורת הכנויים החבורים, ־ךְ, ־תָ, ־הָ, וכו׳. *Sefer Asaf*, 66–99. Jerusalem, 1954. Studies in the traditions of the Hebrew language. Madrid-Barcelona.
1954–55 לתיאורה של העברית כפי שהיא מדוברת. *Tarbiz* 24.337–42.
1956–57 כללי השוא לר׳ יהודה חיוג׳. *Leš* 20.135–38.
1957–77 עברית וארמית נוסח שומרון. The Academy of the Hebrew Language, Texts and studies 1, 2, 3, 6; vols. 1–2, 1957; 3/1, 1961; 3/2, 1967; 4, 5, 1977.
1957–58 מסורת השומרונים וזיקתה למסורת הלשון של מגילות ים המלח וללשון חז"ל. *Leš* 22.223–45.
1958 Traditions in the Hebrew language, with special reference to the Dead Sea scrolls. Aspects of the Dead Sea scrolls, *SH* 4, ed. by C. Rabin and Y. Yadin, 200–14. Jerusalem.

1958–59 בין עברית לעברית. *LLA* 20.252–56.
1961 לקט מקורות לתולדות הדקדוק העברי. Jerusalem.
1963 בדבר מקוריותה של הטעמת מלעיל בעברית. H. Yalon Jubilee volume, ed. by S. Lieberman, E. Y. Kutscher, and S. Esh, 150–60. Jerusalem.
1967 Observations on the Hebrew and Aramaic lexicon from the Samaritan tradition. *Hebräische Wortforschung*, W. Baumgartner Festschrift, VT Supplements 16, 12–24. Leiden.
1967–68/1977–78 Bibliography of Z. Ben Hayyim, compiled by R. Mirkin, *Leš* 32.1–13, 42.4–8.
1968 דרך חדשה במילונאות. *WCJS* 4, 2.247–32.
1969 The contribution of the Samaritan inheritance to research into the history of Hebrew. *PIASH* 3. Jerusalem.
1970a עיונים בארמית של ארץ ישראל. *J. Schirmann volume*, 39–68. Jerusalem.
1970b ערכי מלים. *S. Yeivin volume*, 426–39. Jerusalem.
1974 ערכי מלים ב. *H. Yalon memorial volume*, Bar-Ilan Departmental researches 2, 46–58.
1977 ״זמני״ הפועל בלשון המקרא ומסורת השומרונים בהם. *Sefer Dov Sadan*, 66–86. Jerusalem.
1978a האקדמיה ללשון העברית בפעולתה. כ״ה שנים לייסודה, סיכומים וסיכויים. *LLA* 29.225–56.
1978b הרהורים על מערכת התנועות בעברית. *Studies in Bible and the ancient Near East presented to Samuel E. Loewenstamm on his seventieth birthday*, 2.83–99. Jerusalem.
1979 Mono- and bi-syllabic middle guttural nouns in Samaritan Hebrew. *JANES* 11.19–29.
1980 השורש ערב—הכלול בו והנלוה עמו. *Leš* 44.85–99.
1983 Bibliography of Z. Ben-Hayyim, compiled by R. Mirkin. *ML* י״ג to כ״ז. Selected surveys and evaluations of Z. Ben-Hayyim, compiled by M. Bar-Asher, *ML* כ״ט to ל״ב.
1985a האומנם נסתר במקום מדבר?. *Sefer Avraham Even-Shoshan*, ed. B. Z. Luria, 93–98. Jerusalem.
1985b האחדות ההיסטורית של הלשון העברית וחלוקתה לתקופות—כיצד?. מחקרים בלשון, ed. M. Bar-Asher, 3–25. Jerusalem. Department of Hebrew Language, Hebrew University.

Ben Horin, G.
1976 Aspects of syntactic preposing in spoken Hebrew, in P. Cole, ed., *Studies in modern Hebrew syntax and semantics*, 193–207. Amsterdam.

Ben Horin, G. and Bolozky, S.
1972 Hebrew *b k p*, rule opacity or data opacity. *HCL* 5.24–35. (English section).

Bennet, R.
1975 Wisdom motifs in Psalm 14–15—*nāḇāl* and *ʿēṣāh*. *BASOR* 220.15–21.

Benoliel, J.
1977 *Dialecto judeo-hispano-marroqui*. Madrid (appeared originally between 1926–1928 in Boletin de la Real Academie de la langue Espanola).

Ben Shahar, R.
1974 עיונים בתרגום ״מחכים לגודו״ לסמואל בקט. Masters thesis, Hebrew University.

Ben Sira, A.
1971–73 איתמר בן אב״י—לוחם ומחדש. *LLA* 23/9 (229).231–36 (1971); *ibid.*, 24/1 (271).8–16, 24/5 (235).124–28, 24/8 (238).233–40, 24/9 (239).256–60 (1972–73); *ibid.*, 25/1 (241).22–26 (1973).

Bentes, A. R.
1981 *Os Sefardim e a hakitía*. Rio de Janeiro.

Bentolila, Y.
1973 לשון כה״י 138 בספריית בית המדרש לרבנים בניו יורק (כ״י דיינארד; משנה: חלקים מהסדרים מועד ונשים). Masters thesis, Hebrew University.
1984 מבטאי העברית המשמשת במושב של יוצאי מרוקו בנגב: פרק בפונולוגיה חברתית. Jerusalem, Hebrew University (revised version of author's dissertation; see *KS* 59, no. 1527).
1985 Le composant hébraïque dans le judeo-espagnol marocain. *Judeo-Romance languages*, ed. I. Benabu and J. (G). Sermoneta, 27–40. Jerusalem.

Ben Tur, E.
1978 *Some effects of orthography on the linguistic knowledge of modern Hebrew speakers*. Doctoral dissertation, University of Illinois at Urbana-Champaign. Ann Arbor, University Microfilms.

Benvenisti, D.
1985 המלים העבריות בשפה היהודית-ספרדית. *Sefer Avraham Even-Shoshan*, ed. B. Z. Luria, 99–138. Jerusalem.

Ben Yaacov, A., Semah, D. and Tobi, J.
1970 שירה ופיוט של יהודי בבל בדורות האחרונים. Jerusalem, Makon Ben Zvi, Hebrew University.

Ben Yehudah, B.
1974–75 לקצב הטונלי במקרא. *BM* 20(61).180–86.

Ber, N.
1974–75 הדבור בארץ ישראל במאה שעברה לפני אליעזר בן יהודה. *LLA* 26.195–203.

Beranek, F. J.
1936 Yiddish in tshekhoslovakay. *Yivo-bleter* 9.63–75.

1957 Jiddisch, in *Deutsche Philologie im Aufriss*, 1.1955–98. Berlin, Erich Schmidt.
1958 *Das Pinsker Jiddisch und seine Stellung in Gesamtjiddischen Sprachraum*. Berlin, de Gruyter.
1961 Die frankische Landschaft des Jiddischen. *JFL* 21.267–303.
1965 *Westjiddischer Sprachatlas*. Marburg, Elwert.

Berger, I.
1977–78 Sjarajevói ladino közmondások, szólások és magyar megfelelóik (Ladino proverbs and sayings of the Jews of Sarajevo and their Hungarian parallels). Évkönyv, 49–55.

Bergey, R.
1983 *The book of Esther—its place in the linguistic milieu of post-exilic biblical Hebrew prose: a study in late biblical Hebrew*. Doctoral dissertation, Dropsie College. Ann Arbor, University Microfilms.

Berggrün, N.
1932 בינוני עם כנויי הגוף. *Leš* 4.173–77.
1946 ר׳ שלמה אלמולי הליכות שוא. *Leš* 14.214–19.
1948–49 כלל ה׳ של ר׳ אליהו בחור—פרק בתולדות הדקדוק העברי. *Leš* 16.169–79.
1949–50 עניינים לכסיקליים בלשון חכמים. *Leš* 17.3–11.
1962–63 ממנוֹ בגוף נסתר. *Leš* 27.40–43.
1967–68 בירורי לשון. *LLA* 19.156–62.
1969–70 לשון הדיבור היהודית בגולה כמקור לחקר העברית. *Leš* 34.165–71.
1972–73 ברירה, באין ברירה, בדלית ברירה, עיון לקסיקלי. *Leš* 37.21–22.
1974 בירורים בלשון חכמים. H. Yalon memorial volume, Bar-Ilan departmental researches 2, 59–63. Jerusalem.
1975–76 בירורים בלשון: א. ״אי״ השלילה ב. הפילולוגיה בלשון חכמים. *Leš* 40.163–66.

Bergsträsser, G.
1928 *Einführung in die semitischen Sprachen*. Munich (Engl. tr. by P. Daniels, *Introduction to the Semitic Languages*, Winona Lake, IN, Eisenbrauns, 1983).

Berlin, A.
1977 Shared rhetorical features in biblical and Sumerian literature. *JANES* 10.35–42.
1978 Psalm 118:24. *JBL* 96.567–68.
1979 Grammatical aspects of biblical parallelism. *HUCA* 50.17–43.
1985 *The dynamics of biblical parallelism*. Indiana University Press.

Berlin, C.
1971 *Index to Festschriften in Jewish studies*. Cambridge/New York, Harvard College Library and Ktav.

Berman (Aronson), R.

1969 The predictability of vowel patterns in the Hebrew verb. *Glossa* 3.127–45.

1973 השמות הפעליים בעברית החדשה. Doctoral dissertation, Hebrew University.

1974–75 הפעולה ושם הפועל בעברית החדשה. *Leš* 39.99–122, 217–35.

1975a רישומם המילוני של פעלים, שורשים ובניינים. *Rosen memorial volume*, ed. by U. Ornan and B. Fischler, 25–36. Jerusalem, Council on the Teaching of Hebrew.

1975b Morphological realization of syntactic processes in the *binyan* system (Hebrew). *HCL* 9.25–39.

1976 On derived and deriving nominals in modern Hebrew, in P. Cole, ed., *Studies in modern syntax and semantics*, 57–98. Amsterdam.

1976–77 Review of Chayen and Dror (*H*). *Leš* 41.61–70.

1978 *Modern Hebrew structure.* Tel Aviv, University publishing projects.

1978–79 Review of Sadka (n.d.), תחביר המשפט לאור תיאוריות חדשות. *Leš* 43.224–28.

1979a Lexical decomposition and lexical unity in the expression of derived verbal categories in Modern Hebrew. *AAL* 6/3.1–26.

1979b *Form and function: passives, middles and impersonals in Modern Hebrew.* Berkeley Linguistic Society, vol. 5.

1979c The case on an (S)VO language: subjectless constructions in Modern Hebrew. Paper delivered at the Linguistic Society of America's summer meeting, Salzburg, August 1979 (see also *Language* 56[1980].759–76).

1979d The re-emergence of a bi-lingual: case study of a Hebrew-English speaking child. Working papers in bilingualism 19.157–79.

1979e Repetition as a feature of Modern Hebrew grammar and discourse. Paper read at the 12th conference of European Linguistic Society, Hebrew University, Jerusalem, August 1979.

1980a On the category of auxiliary in Modern Hebrew. *HAR* 4.15–37.

1980b Acquisition of Hebrew as a native tongue, Paper prepared for Berkeley Conference on Cross Linguistic Study of Language Acquisition, November, 1980 (to appear in Slobin, D., ed., *Cross-linguistic study of language acquisition*, Hillsdale, NJ, Lawrence Erlbaum).

1981 על דרכי השיח בגיל צעיר: עיון בסיפוריה של ילדה בת שש. עיונים בדרכי השיח, ed. by S. Blum-Kulka, Y. Tobin and R. Nir, 177–212. Jerusalem.

1982a On the nature of "oblique" objects in bitransitive constructions. *Lingua* 56.101–25.
1982b Verb pattern alternations: the interface of morphology syntax and semantics in Hebrew child language. *JCL* 9.169–91.

Berman, R. and Dromi, E.
1981 A morphemic measure of early language development: data from Modern Hebrew. *JCL* 9.403–24.

Berman, R. and Grosu, A.
1976 Aspects of the copula in Modern Hebrew, in P. Cole, ed., *Studies in Modern Hebrew syntax and semantics*, 265–85. Amsterdam.

Bernstein, S.
1932 דיואן, לר׳ עמנואל בן דוד פרנשיס. Tel Aviv.
1938–39 משירי ישראל באיטליה. Jerusalem, Darom.
1942 דיואן, *The divan of Salomo ben Meshullam Dapiera.* New York.
1957 משה אבן עזרא, שירי קודש. Tel Aviv.

Besso, H. V.
1951 Judeo-Spanish in the United States. *Hispania* 34.89–90.
1952 Bibliograffa sobre el judeo-español. *BHi* 34.412–22.
1963 Situation actual del judeo-español. *Arbor* 55.155–72.
1980 Judeo-Spanish proverbs: an analysis and bibliography. *Studies in Sephardic culture, the David N. Barocas memorial volume*, ed. by M. D. Angel, 21–55. New York, Sepher-Hermon.

Beyer, K.
1962 *Semitische Syntax im neuen Testament.* Gö7ttingen.
1969 *Althebräische Grammatik, Laut- und Formlehre.* Göttingen.
1984 *Die aramäischen Texte vom Toten Meer.* Göttingen.
1986 The pronunciation of Galilean Aramaic according to Geniza Fragments with Palestinian and Tiberian pointing. *WCJS* 9, Division D, English section, 17–22. Jerusalem.

Bibliographie Linguistique
1952– Published by the Permanent International Committee of Linguists under the auspices of the International Council for Philosophy and Humanistic Studies. Utrecht-Antwerp, Spectrum (from 1980, published by Martinus Nijhoff, The Hague, Boston, London).

Bicknell, B. J.
1984 *Passives in biblical Hebrew.* Doctoral dissertation, University of Michigan. Ann Arbor, University Microfilms.

Bin-Nun, Y.
1973 Yiddish und die deutsche Mundarten. Unter besonderer Berücksichtigung des ostgalizischen Jiddisch. Tübingen, Niemeyer.

Biran, A.

1977 המשפט השמני בספרי נביאים ראשונים. Masters thesis, Tel Aviv University.

Birkeland, H.

1940 *Akzent und Vokalismus im Althebräischen.* Oslo.

1949 *Spraak og Religion his Joeder og Arabere.* Oslo.

1954 *The language of Jesus.* Oslo.

1955 Some linguistic remarks on the Dead Sea scrolls. *Interpretations ad Vetus Testamentum pertinentes, S. Mowinkel volume,* 24–35. Oslo.

Birnbaum, G.

1984–85 אותיות בכ״ל של מנקד כ״י קאופמן. *Leš* 49–50.269–83.

1986 יידוע השם בלשון המשנה. *WCJS* 9, Division D, 39–43. Jerusalem.

Birnbaum, S.

1918 *Praktische Grammatik der jiddischen Sprache.* Vienna, A. Hartleben.

1922 *Das hebräische und aramäische Element in der jiddischen Sprache.* Leipzig, Gustav Engel.

1932a *Yidish verterbikhl.* Lodz, Beys Yankev.

1932b Jiddisch. *EJ*, B-9. cols. 112–27.

1943 Yiddish, *UJE* 10.598–601.

1944 Jewish languages. *Essays in honour of Dr. J. H. Hertz*, ed. by Isidore Epstein et al., 51–67. London, Goldston.

1954 Two problems of Yiddish linguistics. *FY* 1.63–72.

1965 Specimens of Yiddish from eight centuries. *FY* 2.1–33.

1971a Hebrew scripts. *EJ* 1.689–743.

1971b/1972 *The Hebrew scripts*, 2 vols. Leiden, Brill.

1971c Jewish languages, *EJ* 10.66–69.

1974 *Die jiddische Sprache: ein kurzer Überblick und Texte aus acht Jahrhunderten.* Hamburg.

1979 *Yiddish; a survey and a grammar.* Toronto, University of Toronto Press.

Black, M.

1954^2/1967^3 *An Aramaic approach to the Gospels and Acts.* Oxford.

1956 Die Erforschung der Muttersprach Jesu. *TLZ* 81.653–68.

1965 Second thoughts IX: The Semitic element in the New Testament. *ET* 77.20–23.

1968 Aramaic studies and the language of Jesus. *In memorium Paul Kahle, BZAW* 103.17–28.

Blake, F. R.

1917 Studies in Semitic grammar. *JAOS* 35.375–85.

1942 Studies in Semitic grammar II. *JAOS* 62.109–18.

1950 The apparent interchange between *a* and *i* in Hebrew. *JNES* 9.76–83.
1951a *A re-survey of Hebrew tenses.* Rome.
1951b Pre-tonic vowels in Hebrew. *JNES* 10.243–55.

Blanc, H.
1954–55 ליסוד הערבי בדבור הישראלי. *LLA* 6/1(53).6–14; 6/2–3(54–55).27–32; 6/4(56).20–26.
1956–57 קטע של דבור עברי ישראלי. *Leš* 21.33–39.
1956 A note on Israeli Hebrew 'psycho-phonetics'. *Word* 12.106–13.
1957 Hebrew in Israel: trends and problems. *MEJ* 11.397–409.
1960 *Intensive spoken Israeli Hebrew*, course with 114 pre-recorded tapes. Washington, DC.
1964a Israeli Hebrew texts. *Studies in Egyptology and linguistics in honor of H. J. Polotsky*, ed. by H. Blanc, 132–52. Jerusalem.
1964b *Communal dialects in Baghdad*, Harvard Middle Eastern monograph series, 10. Cambridge, MA.
1964c Notes on the literary idiom of Baghdadi Jews. *For Max Weinreich on his 70th birthday*, 18–30. The Hague, Mouton.
1965 Some Yiddish influences in Israeli Hebrew. *FY* 2.185–201.
1968 The Israeli koine as an emergent national standard. *Language problems of developing nations*, ed. by J. A. Fishman *et al.*, 237–51. New York.
1973 Israeli Hebrew in perspective. *Ariel* 32.93–104.
1979 הערבית־היהודית בימינו. פעמים 1.45–49.

Blau, J.
1956–57 "או שֶ־" בלשון חכמים. *Leš* 21.7–14.
1957 Über die *t*-Form des *Hifᶜil* im Bibelhebräisch. *VT* 7.385–88.
1957–58 על היסודות העבריים בטקסטים ערביים יהודיים מימי הביניים. *Leš* 22.183–96.
1960–61a הזוגי ורקעו הלשוני בערבית יהודית. *Tarbiz* 30.130–38.
1960–61b Review of books in linguistics (*H*). *Leš* 25.96–110.
1961/1980[2] (revised) דקדוק הערבית־יהודית של ימי הביניים. Jerusalem, Magnes Press.
1961–62 ערבית במאות הראשונות של האיסלאם. *Leš* 26.281–84 (review article on Goitein 1962).
1965a *The emergence and linguistic background of Judaeo-Arabic: a study of the origins of Middle Arabic.* London, Oxford University Press (reprinted 1981, Leiden, Brill).
תורת ההגה והצורות, based on the lectures of J. Blau, transcribed by J. Shaked. Mifᶜal hashikhpul, Student Association, University of Tel Aviv.
1966 יסודות התחביר. Jerusalem.

1966–67 Review of R. Meyer, *Hebräisches Grammatik*, Berlin 1966. *Leš* 31.318–20 (*H*).

1968a Some difficulties in the reconstruction of "Proto-Hebrew' and 'Proto-Canaanite.'" *BZAW* 103.29–43.

1968b Review of Bendavid 1967 (*H*). *KS* 44.29–35.

1968c דקדוק עברי שיטתי, 2 vols. Jerusalem.

1968d יסודות עבריים וכתב עברי בערבית־היהודית של ימי הביניים. *WCJS* 4, 2.107–8.

1968e Judaeo-Arabic in its linguistic setting. *AAJR* 36.1–12.

1969 Some problems of the formation of the old Semitic languages in the light of Arabic dialects. *PICSS*, 38–44. Jerusalem.

1970a הערות לגלגולי ההטעמה בעברית הקדומה. J. Schirmann volume, ed. by S. Abramson and A. Mirsky, 27–38. Jerusalem.

1970b *On pseudo-corrections in some Semitic languages*. The Israel Academy of Sciences and Humanities. Jerusalem.

1970c בעיות בהיסטוריה של הלשון העברית. In memory of Gedaliahu Alon, מחקרים בתולדות ישראל ובלשון העברית. 9–23. Hakkibutz hameuchad.

1970–71 Review of I. J. Gelb 1969 (*H*). *Leš* 34.303–7.

1971a על הדקדוק הטראנספורמאטיבי. *LLA* 22.47–57.

1971b Hebrew language: biblical. *EJ* 16.1568–83.

1971c Studies in Hebrew verb formulation. *HUCA* 42.133–58.

1971d על חזרת הנשוא במקרא. המקרא ותולדות ישראל, *Studies in Bible and Jewish history dedicated to the memory of Jacob Liver*, ed. by B. Uffenheimer, 234–40. Tel Aviv University.

1971–72a Revew of Beyer 1969 (*H*). *KS* 47.642–46.

1971–72b Review of Ornan 1970–71 (*H*). *Leš* 36.317–19.

1972a Marginalia Semitica 2. *IOS* 2.57–82. Jerusalem.

1972b תורת ההגה והצורות. Hakkibutz Hameuchad.

1972–73 Review of Andersen 1970a (*H*). *Leš* 37.69–74.

1973a Der Übergang der bibelhebräischen Verba *w*(*y*) von *Qal* im *Hifᶜil* im Lichte des Ugaritischen. *UF* 5.275–77.

1973b דין וחשבון על המחקר הבלשני בערבית הבינונית בכלל ובערבית־היהודית בפרט. *WCJS* 5, 151–57. Jerusalem.

1973–74a Review of W. Eisenbeis 1969 (*H*). *Leš* 38.228–30.

1973–74b Review of R. Meyer 1969 (*H*). *Leš* 38.303–6.

1974a עיונים בתורת הכינויים (כולל את היידוע) בלשונות שמיות. *Henoch Yalon memorial volume*, Bar-Ilan departmental researches, 2, 17–45. Jerusalem.

1974b Classical Arabic, middle Arabic, middle Arabic literary standard, neo-Arabic, Judaeo-Arabic and related terms. *Joshua Finkel Festschrift*, ed. by S. B. Hoenig and L. Stitskin, 37–40. New York.

1975 על בעיות בתחום ההטעמה בעברית הקדומה. *Sefer Kurzweill*, ed. by M. Z. Kaddari, A. Saltzman and M. Schwarcz, 62–73. Tel Aviv/Ramat Gan.

1976a *A grammar of Biblical Hebrew*. Wiesbaden, Harrassowitz.

1976b תחיית העברית ותחיית הערבית הספרותית. Academy of the Hebrew Language, Texts and studies 9. Jerusalem.

1977a An adverbial construction in Hebrew and Aramaic. *PIASH* 6, 1. Jerusalem.

1977b 'Weak' phonetic change and the Hebrew *śîn*. *HAR* 1.67–119.

1977c זוטות מתחום משפטי הזיקה בעברית המקראית. שנתון, an annual for biblical and ancient near eastern studies, 2.50–53.

1978a The historic periods of the Hebrew language, in Jewish languages: theme and variation, ed. by Herbert Paper, 1–13. Cambridge, MA, Association for Jewish Studies.

1978b Medieval Judeo-Arabic, *ibid.*, 121–22.

1978c כינויי נסתר ונסתרת ב־נ׳ ובלעדיה בעברית המקרא. *EI* 14.125–31.

1978d Hebrew and Northwest Semitic: reflections on the classification of the Semitic languages. *HAR* 2.21–44.

1978e על הסביל הסתמי במקרא. *Studies in Bible and the ancient Near East presented to Samuel E. Loewenstamm on his seventieth birthday*, 2.85–94.

1978–79a שלשה מחקרים גנראטיביים מתחום העברית. Review of Kaddari 1976; Cole, ed., 1976a; and Azar 1977a (*H*). *Leš* 43.148–56.

1978–79b בין לשון המקרא לערבית יהודית. שנתון, an annual for biblical and near eastern studies, 3.198–203.

1979a Non-phonetic conditioning of sound change and biblical Hebrew. *HAR* 3.7–15.

1979b Redundant pronominal suffixes denoting intrinsic possession. *JANES* 11.31–37.

1980a על גלגוליה של החלשת הגרוניות כתופעה חיה. *Leš* 45.32–39.

1980b The parallel development of the feminine ending *-at* in Semitic languages. *HUCA* 51.17–28.

1980c כיצד עשויה השוואת התהיליכים הלשוניים שבערבית הספרותית החדשה לסייע להבנת העברית החדשה? *WCJS* 6, Division D, 11–13.

1981a *The renaissance of Modern Hebrew and Modern Standard Arabic*. University of California publications, Near Eastern studies 18. Berkeley, Los Angeles, London, University of California Press.

1981b קווים דיאלקטיים בבליים בערבית־יהודית של ימי הביניים in S. Moreh, ed., מחקרים בתולדות יהודי עיראק ובתרבותם, 31–33. Tel Aviv, Center for the Heritage of Iraqi Jewry.

1982a On polyphony in biblical Hebrew. *PIASH* 6, 2. Jerusalem.
1982b Remarks on the development of some pronomial suffixes in Hebrew. *HAR* 6.61–67.
1982c משפטים בלתי־מקושרים הפותחים בשם עצם והמוצרכים על ידי מלת־יחס. *Te^cudah* 2, Bible studies Y. M. Grintz in memoriam, ed. B. Uffenheimer, 277–85. Tel Aviv University.
1983a לבירורן של מקבילות ערביות לאוצר המלים המקראי. *ML* 67–82.
1983b האם צורות נסתרת מעין הָיָת שבלשון חכמים צורות קדומות הן? *Leš* 47.158–59.
1983c לשון המקרא בזיקתה לערבית–בתשומת לב מיוחדת לערבית הבתר־קלאסית. *WCJS* 8, Bible and Hebrew Language, 63–68.
1984–85 Review of Janssens 1982. *Leš* 48–49.76–80.
1985a הערות לאופיה רב־השכבות של העברית החדשה. *Sefer Avraham Even-Shoshan*, ed. B. Z. Luria, 87–92.
1985b מחקרים בלשון העברית המשוערבת והשפעת הערבית הבינונית, ed. M. Bar-Asher, 243–50. Jerusalem, Department of Hebrew Language, Hebrew University.
1986a המסמנות התנועות בניקוד הטברני הבדלים כמותיים? *Te^cudah* 4, ed. M. A. Friedman and M. Gil, 137–41. Tel Aviv University.
1986b על הכרונולוגיה של חוק פיליפי. *WCJS* 9, Division D, 39–43. Jerusalem.

Bloch, A.
1963 Zu Nachweisbarkeit einer hebräischen Entsprechung des akkadischen Verbalform *iparras*. *ZDMG* 113.41–50.

Block, D. I.
1982 *The foundation of national identity: a study in ancient Northwest Semitic perceptions.* Doctoral dissertation, University of Liverpool. Ann Arbor, University Microfilms.

Blodgett, T.
1981 *Phonological similarities in Germanic and Hebrew.* Doctoral dissertation, University of Utah. Ann Arbor, MI.

Blommerde, A. C. M.
1969 *Northwest Semitic and Job.* Rome, Pontifical Biblical Institute.

Bloomberg, J. I.
1980 *Arabic legal terms in Maimonides.* Doctoral dissertation, Yale University. Ann Arbor, University Microfilms.

Blum, A.
1945 מלים לועזיות—יווניות ורומיות—בתלמוד לפי ספרות הגאונים, פרש״י וגדולי המפרשים. Masters thesis, Hebrew University.

Blum, B. L.
1972 *L'ancient hébreu et l'hébreu israelien.* Jerusalem, Mitu Grosu.

Blum-Kulka, S.
1970/1972[2] *Bulletin no. 2*, an annotated bibliography of Hebrew textbooks for youth and adults, published since 1948 in Israel and abroad. Jerusalem, Council on the Teaching of Hebrew.
1973 "עברית קלה" כאמצעי להוראת עברית למבוגרים. Doctoral dissertation, Hebrew University.
1976 מבעיות התרגום הספרותי לעברית. *C. Rabin jubilee volume*, ed. by B. Fischler and R. Nir, 9–22. Jerusalem.
1981 ביצוע פעולות דיבור בלשון שניה in עיונים בחקר השיח, ed. by S. Blum-Kulka, Y. Tobin, and R. Nir, 147–75. Jerusalem, Akademon.

Blumenkranz, B.
1974 *Bibliographie des juifs en France* (with Monique Levy). Toulouse.
1975 *Auteurs juifs en France médiévale: leur oeuvre imprimée* (with G. Dahan and S. Kerner, edited by E. Privat). Toulouse.

Blumental, N.
1981 ווערטער און ווערטלעך פֿין דער חורבן־תקופה. Tel Aviv, I. L. Peretz Publishing House.

Boadt, L.
1975 The A:B:B:A chiasm of identical roots in Ezekiel. *VT* 25.693–99.

Bobzin, H.
1963 Überlegungen zum althebräischen 'Tempus' System. *WO* 7.141–53 (review article on Siedl 1971).
1974 *Die 'Tempora' im Hiobdialog.* Doctoral dissertation, Marburg, Lohn.

Bolozky, S.
1972 *Categorical limitations on rules in the phonology of Modern Hebrew.* Doctoral dissertation, University of Illinois at Urbana-Champaign. Ann Arbor, University Microfilms.
1978 Word formation strategies in the Hebrew verb system. *AAL* 5.1–26.
1979 On the new imperative in colloquial Hebrew. *HAR* 3.17–24.
1980 Paradigm coherence: evidence from Modern Hebrew. *AAL* 7/4.1–24.
1981 A note on frequency in phonetic change. *HAR* 5.15–19.
1984 Subject pronouns in colloquial Hebrew. *HS* 25.126–30.

Boman, T.
1968 *Hebrew thought compared with Greek.* New York.

Borer, H. and Aoun, Y., eds.
1981 *Theoretical issues in the grammar of Semitic language.* M.I.T. working papers in linguistics, vol. 3. Cambridge, MA.

Bornemann, R.

1970 *Verbal parallelism in Ugaritic and biblical poetry.* Doctoral dissertation, Dropsie College.

Borochovsky, E.

1981 גלגולים מקדימים והצרכת הפועל—עיון תחבירי וסימנטי בפעלים מן העברית החדשה. Masters thesis, Tel Aviv University.

Botterweck, G. J.

1952 *Der Triliteralismus in Semitischen.* Bonn.

Botterweck, G. J. and Ringren, H.

1973ff. *Theologische Wörterbuch zum alten Testament.* Stuttgart (Fascicles, 1970ff.; English translation, Grand Rapids, MI, Eerdmans, 1974ff.).

Boucher, P.

1950 חיקוי הקול בשמית צפונית. Doctoral dissertation, Hebrew University.

Bowker, J.

1969 *The Targums and rabbinic literature.* Cambridge.

Bowman, J.

1959 The importance of Samaritan researches. *ALUOS* 1.43–54.

Boyarin, D., ed.

1976a *Targum, Onkelos, a collection of fragments in the library of the Jewish Theological Seminary of America*, 4 vols. New York.

1976b עיונים בארמית בבלית. *Leš* 40.172–77.

1978 On the history of the Babylonian Jewish Aramaic reading traditions: the reflexes of *a and *ā. *JNES* 37.141–60.

1980–81 ללקסיקון התלמודי I. *Tarbiz* 50.164–92.

1982 Review of Sabar 1976. *Maarav* 3.99–114.

1982–83 ללקסיקון התלמודי II. *Teᶜudah* 3, 113–19.

1986 ללקסיקון התלמודי III. *Teᶜudah* 4, ed. M. A. Friedman and M. Gil, 115–27. Tel Aviv University.

Boyle, M. L.

1969 *Infix-*t *forms in Bible and Hebrew.* Doctoral dissertation, Boston University. Ann Arbor, University Microfilms, 1973.

Branden, A., Van Den.

1962 L'origine des alphabets protosinaïtique, arabes préislamiques et phénicien. *BiOr* 19.198–206.

Bratkowsky, J. G.

1974 *Sharpness in Yiddish, a fifth riddle in bilingual dialectology.* Doctoral dissertation, Indiana University. Ann Arbor, University Microfilms.

1981 *Yiddish linguistics: a multilingual bibliography*, 1959–1973, New York/London, Garland.

Bratkowsky, J. G. and Baviskar, V. L.
1975 *Dialectical studies of Slavic influence in Yiddish*, working papers in Yiddish and east European Jewish studies 7. New York, YIVO.
Brauner, R. A.
1974 *A dictionary of old Aramaic inscriptions*, Doctoral dissertation, Dropsie College.
Braverman, N.
1986 בין לשון המשנה ללשון התוספתא. *WCJS* 9, Division D, 31–38. Jerusalem.
Bravmann, M.
1961 Genetic aspects of the genitive in Semitic languages. *JAOS* 81.386–94.
1971 The Hebrew perfect forms: *qāṭ^{e}lā*, *qāṭ^{e}lū*. *JAOS* 91.429–30.
1977 *Studies in Semitic philology*. Leiden, Brill (collected studies).
Brenner, A.
1980 על מטה ושבט וסיווגם הסמנטי. *Leš* 44.100–108.
1982 Colour terms in the Old Testament. Sheffield (originally a doctoral dissertation, University of Manchester, 1979).
Breuer, M.
1958 פסוק הטעמים במקרא. Jerusalem, World Zionist Organization.
1970–71 נוסח הטעמים ב"כתר". *Leš* 35.85–98, 175–91.
1976 כתר ארם-צובה והנוסח המקובל של המקרא. Jerusalem, Mossad Harav Kook.
1979a לבירורן של סוגיות בטעמי המקרא: א. תמורת הזקף. *Leš* 43.243–53.
1979b לבירורן של סוגיות בטעמי המקרא ובניקודו ב. הגעיה. *Leš* 44.3–11.
1980 לברורן של סוגיות בטעמי המקרא ובניקודו: חילופי הניקוד בין בן-אשר לבן נפתלי. *Leš* 44.243–62.
1981 לבירורן של סוגיות בטעמי המקרא ובניקודו ד. כתיב וקרי ו'טעים'. *Leš* 45.260–69.
1985 לבירורן של סוגיות בטעמי המקרא ובניקודו ו. הצינורית וגלגולי לגרמיה. *Leš* 48–49.118–31.
Brichto, H.
1962 The problem of 'curse' in the Hebrew Bible. Doctoral dissertation, University of Pennsylvania. Ann Arbor, University Microfilms.
1963 *The problem of 'curse' in the Hebrew Bible*. *JBL* monograph series 13. Philadelphia [corrected reprinting, 1968].
Bright, J.
1973 The apodictic prohibition: some observations. *JBL* 92.185–204.
Brin, G.
1978–79 שימושי 'או' בטקסטים משפטיים במקרא. שנתון, an annual for biblical and ancient near eastern studies, 19–39.

1982 הנוסחה 'מ' . . . ומעלה/והלאה' במקרא. *Te^cudah* 2, Bible studies Y. M. Grintz in memoriam, ed. B. Uffenheimer, 287–97. Tel Aviv University.

1986 עיונים בלשונות לציון הזמן במקרא. *Te^cudah* 4, ed. M. A. Friedman and M. Gil, 37–54. Tel Aviv University.

Brisman, S.

1977 *A history and guide to Judaic bibliography.* Bibliographica Judaica 7, Jewish research literature, vol. 1. Cincinnati/New York, Hebrew Union College Press and Ktav.

1987 *A history and guide to Judaic encyclopedias and lexicons.* Bibliographica Judaica 11, Jewish research literature, vol. 2. Cincinnati, Hebrew Union College Press.

Broadribb, D.

1972 A historical review of studies of Hebrew poetry. *AN* 13.66–87.

Brock, S., Fritsch, C. and Jellicoe, S.

1973 *A classified bibliography of the Septuagint.* Leiden, Brill.

Brockelmann, C.

1908 *Kurzgefasste vergleichende Grammatik der Semitischen Sprachen, Elemente der Laut- und Formenlehre.* Berlin.

1908–13 *Grundriss der vergleichenden Grammatik der semitischen Sprachen*, 2 vols. Berlin.

1910 *Précis de linguistique sémitique.* Paris.

1916 *Semitische Sprachwissenschaft*, 2nd ed. Leipzig.

Broida, I.

1973 הנאום בספר דברים, סגנונו ואמצעיו הריטוריים. Tel Aviv.

Brongers, H. A.

1973 Die Partikel למען in der biblisch-hebräischen Sprache. *OTS* 18.84–96.

Brønno, E.

1943 *Studien über hebräische Morphologie und Vokalismus.* Leipzig.

1954 The Isaiah scroll DSIsa[a] and the Greek translations of Hebrew. *PICO* 23.110–11.

1967 The Hebrew laryngeals in non-masoretic traditions. *WCJS* 4, 1.113–15.

1968 Samaritan Hebrew and Origen's Secunda. *JSS* 13.192–201.

1970 *Die Aussprache des hebräischen Laryngale nach Zeugnissen des Hieronymus.* Doctoral dissertation, Kopenhagen. Universitetsforlaget, Aarhus.

Bronznick, N. M.

1976–77 הסמנטיקה של השרש "חלש" במקרא. *Leš* 41.163–75.

1977 Calque or semantic parallel, which? *HAR* 1.121–29.

1978 הערות לש"י עגנון כמעשיר הלשון העברית. *LLA* 30.117–23.

1979 'Metathetic parallelism'—an unrecognized subtype of synonymous parallelism. *HAR* 3.25–39.
1983 מלשון חכמים ללשון מקרא. *BM* 96.37–46.

Brovender, C.
1971 Hebrew language, pre-biblical. *EJ* 16.1560–68.

Brown, F., Driver, S. R. and Briggs, C.
1907 *A Hebrew and English Lexicon of the Old Testament.* Oxford, repr. 1966.

Brown, S.
1964 From Burney to Black: the fourth gospel and the Aramaic question. *CBQ* 26.323–39.

Brueggemann, W. A.
1973 Jeremiah's use of rhetorical questions. *JBL* 92.358–74.

Brunner, L.
1969 *Die gemeinsamen Wurzeln des semitischen und indogermanischen Wortschatzes.* Bern/Munich, Franke Verlag.

Bruno, C.
1979 The emergence of Hebrew biblical pointing, the indirect sources. Frankfurt am Main (offprint from *Judentum und Umwelt*, 1).

Brunot, L. and Malka, E.
1939 *Textes judéo-arabes des Fes.* Rabat.

Bubenik, V.
1973 Review of I. J. Gelb 1969. *Lingua* 31.85–92.

Bunis, D.
1974 *The historical development of Judezmo orthography: a brief sketch.* Working paper no. 2 of Working papers in Yiddish and East European Jewish studies. New York, The American Sephardi Foundation.
1975a *Problems in Judezmo linguistics.* New York.
1975b *A guide to reading and writing Judezmo.* New York.
1978 Response to D. Lida, in H. Paper, ed., *Jewish Languages: theme and variation*, 93–102. Cambridge, MA, Association for Jewish Studies.
1981a *Yiddish linguistics: a classified bilingual index to Yiddish serials and collections*, 1913–1958. New York/London, Garland.
1981b *Sephardic studies: a research bibliography.* New York, Garland.
1981c The Hebrew and Aramaic component of Judezmo: a phonological and morphological analysis. Doctoral dissertation, Columbia University. Ann Arbor, University Microfilms.
1985 Plural formation in modern eastern Judezmo. *Judeo-Romance Languages*, ed. I. Benabu and J. (G.) Sermoneta, 41–67. Jerusalem.

Burke, D. G.
1974 *The poetry of the book of Baruch: a reconstruction of the original Hebrew text of Baruch 3:9–5:9.* Doctoral dissertation, Johns Hopkins University. Ann Arbor, University Microfilms.

Burrows, M.
1956 *The Dead Sea scrolls.* New York.
1958 *More light on the Dead Sea scrolls.* New York.

Bush, F. W.
1960 Evidence from *Milhamah* and the massoretic text for a penultimate accent in Hebrew verbal forms. *RQ* 2.501–14.

Busi, G.
1984 *Horayat ha-qorè*: una grammatica ebraica del secolo XI. Frankfurt-am-Main, Peter Lang.

Butler, T. C.
1971 *'The song of the sea': Exodus 15:1–18; a study in the exegesis of Hebrew poetry.* Doctoral dissertation, Vanderbuilt University. Ann Arbor, University Microfilms.

Bynon, J. and T., eds.
1975 *Hamito-Semitics.* The Hague, Mouton.

Bynon, T.
1978 The Hamito-Semitic hypothesis and models of language relationship. *ACILCS* 2, 21–30.

Caird, G. B.
1976 Homophony in the Septuagint, in *Jews, Greeks and Christians, Essays in honor of William David Davies*, ed. by R. Hamilton Kelly and R. Scroggs, 74–88. Leiden, Brill.

Cantineau, J.
1950 Essai d'une phonologie de l'hébreu biblique. *BSLP* 46.82–122.

Cantor, H.
1980 ארגטיבציה של פעלים בלשון־הבינים של לומדי עברית. *HCL* 16.51–58.

Caquot, A. and Lemaire, A.
1977 Les textes araméens de Deir Alla. *Syria* 44.189–209.

Cardona, G. R.
1968 Per la storia fonologica de 'sade' semitico. *AION* 18.1–18.

Carmiel, Y.
1951 לשון הפייטנים. Masters thesis, Hebrew University.
1964–65 *A philological examination of the post-biblical vocabulary of Abraham Mapu's fictional writings and a study of its sources, with observations of the development of modern Hebrew.* Doctoral dissertation, University of Leeds. Ann Arbor, University Microfilms.
1967 ממלון ההשכלה. *Leš* 31.311–17.

Carmignac, J.
1974 L'emploi de la negation ʾēn dans la Bible et à Qumran. *RQ* 8.108–13.
1986 L'infinitif absolu chez Ben Sira et à Qumran. *RQ* 12.251–61.

Caspi, M.
1975 ישמש כמו דמה רץ במעלותיו (על שיר ותרבות השיר בשירה העברית בתימן). The Jews of Yemen, ed. by Y. Yeshᶜayahu and Y. Tobi, 333–46. Jerusalem, Yad Izhak Ben-Zvi.
1981 Saᶜadya ben Abraham al-Bashiri: a seventeenth century northern Yemenite Poet. *HUCA* 51.173–98.
1982 פיוטי המָרָנוֹת בסדר הרחמים. Tel Aviv, Sifriat Poalim.

Caspi, Z.
1952 לשון המגילות הגנוזות. Masters thesis, Hebrew University.

Cassuto, U.
1951/1965² האלה ענת. Jerusalem, Mossad Bialik.

Cathcart, K. J.
1973 *Nahum in the light of Northwest Semitic.* Rome, Pontifical Biblical Institute.

Cazelles, H.
1961 Hébreu, in *Linguistica Semitica, Studi di H. Cazelles*, ed. by G. Levi della Vida. *Studi Semitici* 4.91–113.
1973 Le sense du verbe *bᶜr* en hébreu. *Semitica* 25.5–10.

Ceresko, A.
1975 The A:B::B:A word pattern in Hebrew and Northwest Semitic with special reference to the book of Job. *UF* 7.73–88.
1976 The chiastic word pattern in Hebrew. *CBQ* 38.303–11.
1978 The function of chiasmus in Hebrew poetry. *CBQ* 40.1–10.

Chaney, M. L.
1976 HDL II *and the "Song of Deborah": textual, philological and sociological studies in Judges 5, with special reference to the verbal occurrences of* HDL *in biblical Hebrew.* Doctoral dissertation, Harvard University. Ann Arbor, University Microfilms.

Charlesworth, J. A.
1976 *The Pseudepigrapha and modern research* (with supplement, 1981). Septuagint and cognate studies 7. Missoula, Montana, Scholars Press.
1983/1985 ed., *The Old Testament Pseudepigrapha*, 2 vols. New York: Doubleday.

Chayen, M.
1969 *An investigation of the phonology of Modern Hebrew.* Doctoral dissertation, University of London.
1971–72 מבטאה של העברית הישראלית. *Leš* 36.212–19, 287–300.

1972 Vowels and transitions in a generative philology of Israeli Hebrew. *Linguistics* 86.31–40.
1973 *The phonetics of Modern Hebrew.* The Hague, Mouton.
1986 תורת החוזק בפונולוגיה לפתרון בעיות במורפולוגיה העברית. *WCJS* 9, Division D, 71–75. Jerusalem.

Chayen, M. and Dror, Z.
1976 מבוא לדקדוק תיצרוני עברי. Tel Aviv University.

Chernovsky, I.
1980 *Syntactic development of Hebrew speaking; Three to four year olds in conversational interaction.* Masters thesis, Tel Aviv University.

Chiesa, B.
1978 *L'antico testamento ebraico secondo la tradizione palestinense.* Torino, Bottega d'Ebraismo.
1979 *The emergence of Hebrew biblical pointing, the indirect sources.* Frankfurt am Main.

Chomsky, W.
1941–42 The history of our vowel system in Hebrew. *JQR* 32.26–49.
1945 How the study of Hebrew grammar began and developed. *JQR* 35.281–301.
1947–48 Some irregular formations in Hebrew. *JQR* 408–18.
1951–52 What was the Jewish vernacular during the Second Commonwealth? *JQR* 42.193–212.
1952 *David Kimhi's Hebrew grammar* (Mikhlol). New York (based on doctoral dissertation, Dropsie College, 1926).
1958–59 Toward broadening the scope of Hebrew grammar. *JQR* 49.179–90.
1962 The growth and progress of Modern Hebrew. *Studies and essays in honor of Abraham A. Neuman*, 106–27. Leiden.
1966 תרומת המדקדקים בימי הבינים לחקר הלשון העברית. פרקים, Organ of the American Hebrew Academy 4, ed. by S. K. Mirsky, 71–91. New York, Histadruth Ivrith.
1967 הלשון העברית. Jerusalem (Hebrew version and expansion of *Hebrew the eternal language*, Philadelphia, 1957).
1970 צורות מוקשות בדקדוק לשון המקרא והמשנה. *Zvi Scharfstein jubilee volume*, 176–83. Tel Aviv.
1971a Problems of pronunciation in Hebrew. *Gratz College 75th anniversary volume*, 21–27. Philadelphia.
1971b The pronunciation of the *shewa. JQR* 62.88–94.

Choueka, Y.
1966 Computers and grammar: mechanical analysis of the Hebrew verb. Proceedings of the 2nd conference of Information Processing Association of Israel, 47ff. Rehovoth.

1969 דקדוק יצירה פורמלי למלה השמנית בעברית. *Bar Ilan volume on humanities and social sciences*, Decennial volume 2.106–28.

Citron, A.

1965 *Love elements in the poetry of selected Hebrew poets of the Hebrew golden age in Spain.* Doctoral dissertation, New York University.

Citron, M.

1979 עיון תחבירי וסימנטי בפועלי חושים במקרא. Masters thesis, University of Tel Aviv.

Claasen, W. T.

1971–72 The declarative-estimative *Hiphᶜil. JNSL* 1.3–10, 2.5–16.

1978 Bibliographic problems and possibilities in the field of Semitics and Old Testament studies. *JNSL* 6.61–86.

Clarke, E. G.

1984 *Targum Pseudo-Jonathan of the Pentateuch: Text and concordance.* Hoboken, NJ, Ktav.

Clifford, R. J.

1972 *The cosmic mountain in Canaan and in the Old Testament.* Cambridge, MA.

Clines, D. J. A.

1974 The etymology of Hebrew *ṣelem. JNSL* 3.19–25.

Clurman, H.

1968 Ida Kaminska and the Yiddish theater. *Midstream* 14.53–57.

Cnaani, J.

1932–33a חדושי לשון בתקופת ההשכלה. *Leš* 5.57–72.

1932–33b משה שולבוים, חייו, עתוניו, ספוריו, מלונו וחלקו ביצירה הלשונית. *Leš* 5.299–332.

1936–37 השפעתם הלשונית של הפייטנים הקדומים על משוררי ספרד. *Leš* 10.173–82.

1960 לשון פיוטים כחומר למילון מודרני. *Sefer Tur-Sinai*, 303–10. Jerusalem.

1962ff. אוצר הלשון העברית לתקופותיה השונות. Jerusalem.

1977 חידושי הלשון של אברהם שלונסקי. מאזנים 45.236–39, 254.

1978–79 מתוך "מלון חידושי שלונסקי". *Leš* 43.121–47 (the dictionary was completed by R. Mirkin).

Coffin, E.

1968 *Ibn Janah's* Kitab al-luma: *a critique of medieval grammatical tradition.* Doctoral dissertation, University of Michigan. Ann Arbor, University Microfilms.

Cohen (Tawil), A.

1948 פירושי מלים עבריות על ידי מלים ערביות בפירוש המשניות להרמב"ם בהשוואה עם המיוחס לרב האי גאון. Masters thesis, Hebrew University.

Cohen, Amots
1968 מלרע במקום מלעיל. *Sinai* 32.180–81.
Cohen, Chaim (Harold Robert)
1972 Hebrew *tbh*: proposed etymologies. *JANES* 4.36–51.
1975 *Biblical* hapax legomena *in the light of Akkadian and Ugaritic*. Doctoral dissertation, Columbia University. Ann Arbor, University Microfilms. Published 1978 in the SBL dissertation series, Missoula, MT.
1978–79 Studies in extra-biblical Hebrew inscriptions 1—the semantic range and usage of the terms אמה and שפחה. שנתון, an annual for biblical and ancient near eastern studies 5–6. XXV–LV.
1982 עדויות אכדיות חדשות לגבי המובן והאטימולוגיה של המונח "משל" במקרא. *Teʿudah* 2, *Bible Studies Y. M. Grintz in memoriam*, ed. B. Uffenheimer, 315–24. Tel Aviv University.
Cohen, Daniel
1973–74 "כולל ומחובר" והדקדוק הגנרטיבי. *Leš* 38.195–205.
1986 ניתוח טקסטים לא־מנוקדים וניקודם על־ידי מחשב. *WCJS* 9, Division D, 117–22. Jerusalem.
Cohen (Ben Nathan), David
1957 נטיית פועלי ל"י בארמית שומרונית על פי התרגום השומרוני לתורה. Masters thesis, Hebrew University.
Cohen, David
1964a Remarques sur la dérivation nominale par affixes dans quelques langues sémitiques. *Semitica* 14.73–93.
1964b/1975 *Le parler arabe des juifs de Tunis*, vols. 1 and 2. Paris/the Hague, Mouton.
1970ff. *Dictionaire des racines sémitiques*. The Hague, Mouton.
Cohen, David and Zafrani, H.
1968 *Grammaire de l'hébreu vivant*. Paris.
Cohen, Haim
1981 הכינויים החבורים לפועל בלשון המשנה על־פי כתב־יד קאופמן. Masters thesis, Tel Aviv University.
1983 השימוש בכינוי המושא הדבוק לעומת השימוש "את+ כינוי" (אות־) בלשון המשנה. *Leš* 47.208–18.
Cohen, Marcel
1947 *Essai comparatif sur le vocabulaire et la phonétique du chamito-sémitique*. Paris, H. Champion.
1955 *Cinquante années de recherches linguistiques, ethnographiques sociologiques, critiques et pedagogiques*. Bibliographie complete, rééditions et éditions d'études diverses. Paris, Librairie C. Klincksieck.

Cohen, Menachem
1974 מגבשי כתיב במצחפי מסורה עתיקים ומשמעם לתולדות נוסח המקרא המקובל. Doctoral dissertation, Hebrew University.
1975–76 הכתיב של הנוסח השומרוני. *BM* 21.54–70, 361–91.
Cohen, Miles B.
1969 *The system of accentuation in the Hebrew Bible.* Honors thesis, University of Minnesota.
1972 The massoretic accents as a biblical commentary. *JANES* 4.2–11.
Cohen, Sol
1982 A note on the dual in Biblical Hebrew. *JQR* 73.59–61.
Cole, P. ed.
1976a *Studies in Modern Hebrew syntax and semantics.* North Holland linguistic series, 32. Amsterdam.
1976b An introduction to the generative study of Modern Hebrew syntax and semantics, in *Studies*, Cole, ed. 1976a.1–8.
1976c A causative construction in Modern Hebrew, theoretical implications. *ibid.*, 99–128.
1976d An apparent asymmetry in the formation of relative clauses in Hebrew. *ibid.*, 231–47.
Collins, O. E.
1977 *The stem* ZNH *and prostitution in the Hebrew Bible.* Doctoral dissertation, Brandeis University. Ann Arbor, University Microfilms.
Collins, T.
1978 *Line forms in Hebrew poetry.* Rome, Biblical Institute Press (see also *JSS* 23 [1978] 228–44).
Coogan, M. D.
1976 *West Semitic personal names in the* Murašû *documents.* Harvard Semitics monographs 7. Missoula, MT, Scholars Press.
Cooper, A. M.
1976 *Biblical poetics: a linguistic approach.* Doctoral dissertation, Yale University.
Cooper, R. L.
1984 A framework for the description of language spread; the case of modern Hebrew. *International Social Science Journal* 36.87–112.
Copeland, R. M. and Susskind, N.
1976 *The language of Herz's Esther: a study in Judeo-German dialectology.* University of Alabama Press.
Corré, A. D.
1956 The Anglo-Sephardic pronunciation of Hebrew. *JSS* 7.85–90.

1966–67 Phonetic problems in the Masora. *Essays presented to Chief Rabbi Israel Brodie*, 59–66. London.
1973 *ᵓelle, hēmma* = 'sic'. Biblica 54.263–64.
1975 *Wāw* and digamma. *AAL* 2/9.1–7 (149–55).
1982 Modern literary Judeo-Arabic and its contact with other languages. *WCJS* 8, Division D, English section, 13–17. Jerusalem.
1984 A bilingual processing program. *HCL* 21.v–xiii.

Corriente, F.
1969–70 A survey of spirantization in Semitic and Arabic phonetics. *JQR* 60.147–71.
1971 *Problematics de la pluridad Semitica—el plural fracto.* Madrid.

Couroyer, B.
1975 Un égyptianisme dans Ben Sira IV 11. *RB* 82.206–17.

Craigie, P. C.
1981 Ugarit and the Bible: progress and regress in 50 years of literary study, in Gordon D. Young, ed., *Ugarit in retrospect: 50 years of Ugarit and Ugaritic*, 99–111. Winona Lake, IN, Eisenbrauns.

Croatto, J. S.
1971 L'article hébreu et les particules emphatiques dans le sémitique de l'ouest. *PICO* 27, 88–89. Ann Arbor, MI.

Crews, C. M.
1962 The vulgar pronunciation of Hebrew in the Judeo-Spanish of Salonica. *JSS* 13.83–95.

Cross, F. M.
1954 The evolution of the proto-Canaanite alphabet. *BASOR* 134.15–24.
1956 A report on the biblical fragments of Cave four in Wadi Qumran. *BASOR* 141
1961 The development of the Jewish scripts. *The Bible and the Ancient Near East. Essays in honor of William Foxwell Albright*, ed. by G. Ernest Wright, 133–202. New York.
1967 The origin and early evolution of the alphabet. *EI* 8.8*–24*.
1973a Notes on the Ammonite inscription from Tell Siran. *BASOR* 223.43–53.
1973b Heshbon ostracon II. *Andrews University Seminary studies* 11.126–31.
1975 Ammonite ostraca from Heshbon. *Andrews University Seminary studies* 13.1–20.
1976 Heshbon ostracon XI. *Andrews University Seminary studies* 14.145–48.

1983 Studies in the structure of Hebrew verse: the prosody of Lamentations 1.1–12. *WLSGF*, 129–55.

Cross, F. M. and Freedman, D. N.

1952 *Early Hebrew orthography. AOS* 36. New Haven.

1953 A royal song of thanksgiving, II Samuel 22 = Psalm 18. *JBL* 72.15–34.

1972 Some observations on early Hebrew. *Biblica* 53.413–20 (Review of Goodwin 1969).

1975 *Studies in ancient Yahwistic poetry.* SBL dissertation series 21. Missoula, MT, Scholars Press.

Cross, F. M. and Lambdin, T. O.

1960 An Ugaritic abecedary and the origins of the proto-Canaanite alphabet. *BASOR* 160.21–26.

Cross, F. M. and Talmon, S., eds.

1975 *Qumran and the history of the biblical text.* Cambridge, MA, Harvard University Press.

Crown, A. D.

1976–77 הארות אחדות לחקר התעתיק של מלים איטלקיות באותיות עבריות. *Leš* 41.282–90.

1984 *A bibliography of the Samaritans.* Metuchen, NJ, and London, The American Theological Library Association and the Scarecrow Press.

Culley, R. C.

1970 Metrical analysis of classical Hebrew poetry. *Essays on the ancient world*, ed. by J. Wevers and D. B. Redford, 21–28. Toronto.

1976 *Studies in the structure of Hebrew narrative.* Philadelphia Missoula, MT, Fortress and Scholars Press.

Cuomo, L.

1974 *Le glosse volgari dell'Arukh di R. Nathan ben Jechjel da Roma.* Doctoral dissertation, Hebrew University.

1977 Antichisme glosse salentine nel codice ebraico di Parma, De Rossi 138. *MRA* 4.185–271.

Cutter, C. and Oppenheim, M.

1983 *Jewish reference sources: a selective, annotated bibliographical guide.* New York, Garland.

Dagut, M.

1972 ניתוח בלשני של בעיות סמנטיות בתרגום עברי־אנגלי. Doctoral dissertation, Hebrew University.

1976 המחסר הסימנטי כבעית תרגום מעברית לאנגלית. *Chaim Rabin volume*, ed. by B. Fischler and R. Nir, 36–43. Jerusalem, Council on the Teaching of Hebrew.

1978 *Hebrew-English translation.* Haifa.

1981 עיונים בבלשנות ובסמיוטיקה. מחסרים סמאנטיים וגבולות התרגומות, 71–82. Jerusalem.

Dahan, H.

1980 ניתוח בלשני של כמה מבעיות התרגום מעברית לערבית על פי מבחר תרגומים של פרוזה. Doctoral dissertation, Hebrew University.

Dahood, M.

1965/1968/1970a *Psalms I, II, III. Anchor Bible, New York.*

1966 Vocative *lamedh* in the Psalter. *VT* 16.299–311.

1967 Congruity of metaphors. *Hebräische Wortforschung, W. Baumgartner Festschrift*, Supplements to *VT* 16. 40–49.

1969a Ugaritic-Hebrew syntax and style. *UF* 1.15–36.

1969b Ugaritic and the Old Testament, in *nanaticium Iosepho Coppens septuagesimum annum complenti*, Vol. 1, ed. by H. Cazelles *et al.*, 14–33. Paris, P. Lethielleux.

1970 The independent personal pronoun in the oblique case. *CBQ* 32.86–90.

1971a Phoenician elements in Isaiah 52:13–53:12. *Near Eastern studies in honor of William Foxwell Albright*, ed. by H. Goedicke, 63–73. Baltimore/London.

1971b Causal *beth* and the root *nkr* in Nahum 3:4. *Biblica* 52.395–96.

1972 A note on third person suffix *-y* in Hebrew. *UF* 4.163–64.

1973a Vocative *lamedh* in 1 Kings 19:10, 14. *Biblica* 54.407–8.

1973b A note on *ṭôḇ* ‘rain’. *Biblica* 54.404.

1973c Northwest Semitic notes on Dt 32:20. *Biblica* 54.405–6.

1973d The breakup of two composite phrases in Isaiah 40:13. *Biblica* 54.537–38.

1975a Ezekiel 19:10 and relative *kî. Biblica* 56.96–99.

1975b The archaic genitive ending in Proverbs 31:6. *Biblica* 56.241.

1975c Isaiah 10:11 *hkmy* and I QIs[a] *hkmyh. Biblica* 56.420.

1976 *Ugaritic-Hebrew philology.* Rome, Pontifical Biblical Institute (a revision of the 1965 edition).

1978a Poetic devices in the book of Proverbs. *Studies in Bible and the ancient near East presented to Samuel E. Loewenstamm on his seventieth birthday*, 1.7–17. Jerusalem.

1978b Ebla, Ugarit and the Old Testament. Supplements to *VT* 29.81–112. Leiden.

1979a Third masculine singular with pre-formative *t-* in Northwest Semitic. *Or* 48.97–106.

1979b Eblaite, Ugaritic and Hebrew lexical notes. *UF* 11.141–46.

1982 Eblaite and Biblical Hebrew. *CBQ* 44.1–24.

Dahood, M., Deller, K. and Köbert, R.

1965 Review of Moscati 1964. *Or* 34.35–44.

Dalven, R.
1971 Judeo-Greek. *EJ* 10.427.
Dana, J.
1977 תורת השיר בספר העיונים והדיונים. Doctoral dissertation, Tel Aviv University.
1985 תעלומת השימוש בהשאלה במקרא ואצל חז״ל. *Sefer Avraham Even-Shoshan*, ed B. Z. Luria, 177–80. Jerusalem.
Daniel, S.
1983 צירופי ראש, פה, לב בתרגום השבעים לתורה. *ML* 161–72.
Darmesteter, A.
1909 *Leš glosses françaises de Raschi dans la Bible.* Paris.
Dascal, M. and Katriel, T.
1977 Between semantics and pragmatics: the two types of 'but'—Hebrew '*aval*' and '*ela*'. *ThL* 4.143–72.
David, Y.
1975 שירי עמיתי. Jerusalem (limited edition of 200 copies).
1977 פיוטי בר שמעיה. New York, American Academy for Jewish Research.
Degen, R.
1969 *Altaramäische Grammatik.* Wiesbaden, Harrassowitz.
1971 Zur neueren hebräistischen Forschung. *WO* 6.49–79 (review article of Jenni 1969).
Delcor, M.
1967 Two special meanings of the word *yad* in biblical Hebrew. *JSS* 12.230–40.
1975 Quelques cas de survivances du vocabulaire nomade en hébreu biblique. *VT* 25.307–22.
Demsky, A.
1977 A proto-Canaanite abecedary dating from the period of the Judges and its implications for the history of the alphabet. *TA* 4.14–27.
Devens, M.
1978 The phonetics of Israeli Hebrew: 'Oriental' versus 'general' Israeli Hebrew. Doctoral dissertation, UCLA.
1980 Oriental Israeli Hebrew: a study in phonetics. *AAL* 7/4. 25–40.
Devries, B.
1961 חלקה של העברית ביידיש ההולנדית. *Leš* 26.48–55.
De Vries, Simon
1965 Consecutive constructions in the 1Q sectarian scrolls. *Doron, Hebraic studies in honor of Prof. Abraham I. Katsh*, 75–87. New York.

Diakonov, I. M.
1965 *Semito-Hamitic languages. An essay in classification.* Moscow, Nauka, Central Department of Oriental Literature.
1975 On root structure in proto-Semitic. *Hamito-Semitica*, ed. by J. and T. Bynon, 133–53. The Hague, Mouton.

Diament, H.
1979 De la possibilité d'une structure semantico-syntactique hébraïque dans la langue des troubadours provençaux. *RN* 20/1.125–34.
1981 Diachronic and synchronic linguistics applied to stylistics. עיונים בבלשנות ובסמיוטיקה, 262–252 (English section continues the Hebrew numbering). Jerusalem.

Díaz, E. F.
1958 The *Sefer Okla W'Okla* as a source of not registered biblical textual variants. *ZAW* 70.250–53.
1974 Texto hebreo y targum arameo de un fragmento de la geniza dal Cairo con punctuacion babilonica, *BAEO* 10.201–13.

Diem, W.
1974 Das Problem von *š* im Althebräischen und die kanaanäische Verschreibung. *ZDMG* 124.221–52.

Diening, F.
1938 *Das Hebräische bei den Samaritanern.* Stuttgart.

Diethelm, M.
1977 *Grundlegung einer hebräishen Syntax.* 1. Neukirschen.

Dietrich, M.
1968 *Neue palästinisch punktierte Bibelfragmente.* Leiden, Brill.

Dietrich, M. and Loretz, O.
1977 Das Ugaritische in den Wörterbüchern von L. Köhler und W. Baumgartner (II). *BZ* 21.102–10.

Dietrich, M., Loretz, O., Berger, B. and Sanmartin, J., eds.
1973 *Ugaritisch-Bibliographie 1928–1966*, 4 vols. AOAT 20. Neukirchen-Vluyn.

Díez-Macho, A.
1957a Fragmento del texto hebreo y arameo del libro de Numerus escritto en una muy antigua megilla en el sistema babilonico. *Sefarad* 17.386–88.
1957b Importants manuscrits hébreux et araméens aux Etats-Unis. Supplements to *VT* 4.27–46. Leiden.
1958 Onquelos manuscript with Babylonian transliterated vocalization in the Vatican library. *VT* 8.113–33.
1960a The recently discovered Palestinian Targum: its antiquity and relationship with other Targums. *Congress volume*, Oxford, 1959. Supplements to *VT* 7.222–45.

1960b A new fragment of Isaiah with Babylonian pointing. *Textus* 1.132–43.

1963 A new list of so-called 'Ben Naftali' manuscripts. *Hebrew and Semitic studies presented to G. R. Driver in celebration of his seventieth birthday*, ed. by D. Winton Thomas and W. D. McHardy, 15–68. Oxford.

1968 A fundamental manuscript for an edition of the Babylonian Onkelos to Genesis. *BZAW* 103.62–78.

1968–78 *Neophyti I: Targum Palestinense MS de la Biblioteca Vaticana.* Tomos I–V. Madrid/Barcelona.

1971 *Manuscritos hebreos y arameos de la Biblia.* Rome.

1977–80 *Biblia polyglotta matritensia, series* IV: *Targum Palestinense in Pentateuchum, additur Targum Pseudojonatan ejusque hispanica versio.* Madrid.

Díez-Macho, A. and Meyer, R.

1965 *Recent progress in biblical scholarship.* Boars Hill, Oxford, Lincombe Lodge Research Library.

Díez-Marinos, L.

1977 Projects and achievements in the publication of the Onkelos Targum. *WCJS* 6, 1.77–87.

Dijk, H. J., Van

1969 Does third masculine singular **taqtul* exist in Hebrew? *VT* 19.440–47.

Di Lella, A.

1962 *A text-critical and historical study of the Hebrew text of Sirach.* Doctoral dissertation, The Catholic University of America. Ann Arbor, University Microfilms.

1966 *The Hebrew text of Sirach.* The Hague/Paris.

Di Marco, A.

1975/1976 Der Chiasmus in der Bibel, Ein Betrag zur struckturellen Stilistik. *LB* 36.21–97; 37.49–68.

Dion, P. E.

1979 Les types épistolaires hébreo-araméens jusqu'au temps de Bar Kokhbah. *RB* 86.544–79.

Diringer, D.

1960 *The story of the Aleph Beth.* New York/London.

1962 *Writing.* New York.

1967 Significance of the invention of the alphabet. *WCJS* 4, 1.219–21.

Diringer, D. and Brock, S.

1968 Words and meanings in early Hebrew inscriptions. *Words and meanings*, ed. by P. Ackroyd and B. Linders, 39–45. Cambridge.

Dodi, A.
1973 דקדוק תרגום אונקלוס על פי קטעי הגניזה. Masters thesis, Bar-Ilan University.
Dolgopolsky, A.
1977 Emphatic consonants in Semitic. *IOS* 7.1–13.
1978 On phonemic stress in Proto-Semitic. *IOS* 8.1–12.
Donag-Kinrot, R.
1969 המלים הנרדפות ב״תקוני סופרים״ של ש״י עגנון בספור ״והיה העקוב למישור״. Masters thesis, Hebrew University.
1978 לשון התלמידים בארץ—על שימושי לשון ועל תקן ונורמה בלשון התלמידים ילידי הארץ. Doctoral dissertation, Hebrew University.
1983 יחס הדוברים ללשון. *HCL* 17-28.
Donald, T.
1964 The semantic field of rich and poor in the wisdom literature of Hebrew and Akkadian. *OA* 3.27–41.
Donner, H. and Röllig, W.
1962–64. *Kanaanäische und aramäische Inschriften*. Wiesbaden (new edition, vol. 1, 1971; 2, 1973; 3, 1976; see *A concordance to the Aramaic inscriptions*, Aufrecht 1975).
Doron, D.
1964 לשונם העברית של דוברי ערבית בישראל על פי מבחני הבגרות. Masters thesis, Hebrew University.
Doron, E.
1984 *Verbless predicates in Hebrew*. Doctoral dissertation, University of Texas at Austin. Ann Arbor, University Microfilms.
Doron, P.
1964 מונחי ראליה בלשון ספרות ה״שאלות ותשובות״ במאות השבע־עשרה והשמונה־עשרה שבתחום לשונות אשכנזיות. Masters thesis, Hebrew University.
Dotan (Deutscher), A.
1951 שמות התנועות בדקדוק העברית עד המאה ה־11 במזרח ובספרד. Masters thesis, Hebrew University.
1954 שמותיו של השוא בראשיתו של הדקדוק העברי. *Leš* 19.13–30.
1957–58 האמנם היה בן־אשר קראי? *Sinai* 41.280–312, 350–62.
1963–64 השוא ומשרתי התביר לפי הנוסח המקורי של ״דקדוקי הטעמים״. *Leš* 27-28.189–213.
1964a ספר דקדוק הטעמים לרבי אהרן בן משה בן אשר. Doctoral dissertation, Hebrew University.
1964b The minor *gaʿya*. *Textus* 4.55–75.
1967 ספר דקדוק הטעמים לרבי אהרן בן משה בן אשר, 3 vols. Jerusalem.
1968 לבעית דחיק ואתי מרחיק. *WCJS* 4, 2.101–5.

1970 Prolegomenon to W. Wickes, *Two treatises on the accentuation of the Old Testament* (1881, 1887). New York, Ktav.
1971a Masorah. *EJ* 16.1402–82 (important bibliography 1479–82).
1971b *The Hebrew Bible according to the Aaron ben-Asher text of the Leningrad manuscript* (*H*). The School of Jewish Studies, Tel Aviv University.
1971c המקרא ותולדות. "סובאים"-עיונים בדרכי עבודתם של נקדני טבריה ישראל *Studies in Bible and Jewish history dedicated in the memory of Jacob Liver*, ed. by B. Uffenheimer, 241–47. Tel Aviv University.
1971–72 כתר ארם צובה ודקדוק הטעמים. *Leš* 36.167–85.
1973 תורה, נביאים וכתובים . . . . בכתב יד לנינגרד. Tel Aviv University.
1974 The beginnings of masoretic vowel notation, in H. M. Orlinsky, ed., *Masoretic studies* 1, 21–34. Missoula, MT, Scholars Press.
1975 Prolegomenon to C. D. Ginsburg, *The Massorah compiled from manuscripts* (Vienna, 1897–1905), XIX–XXXIV. New York, Ktav.
1977a אוצר המסורה הטברנית. Tel Aviv University.
1977b *Ben Asher's creed: a study of the history of the controversy*. SBL masoretic series. Missoula, MT, Scholars Press.
1977c *Wilhelm Bacher's place in the history of Hebrew linguistics*. Amsterdam.
1981 קטע חדש מספר אֱגרון. *Leš* 45.163–212.
1982 כתובת הא"ב מעזבת צרטה. *EI* 16.62–69.
1983 שקיעי הטעמת מלעיל עתיקה במסורת הטברנית. *ML* 143–60.
1985 פתחי חטפין. *Sefer Avraham Even-Shoshan*, ed. B. Z. Luria, 157–65. Jerusalem.

Doubles, M.
1968 Indications of antiquity in the orthography and morphology of the Fragment Targum. *BZAW* 103.79–89.

Dreessen, W. O.
1971 *Akedass Jizḥaḳ; ein altjiddisches Schrifttums im deutschen Sprachgebiet*. Stuttgart, J. B. Metzlersche Verlagsbuchhandlung.

Dreizin, F.
1981 Verbal nouns in Hebrew and other languages: a retreat from Montague. עיונים בבלשנות ובסמיוטיקה, 251–38 (English section continues the Hebrew numbering). Jerusalem.

Drinkard, J. F.
1980 *Vowel letters in pre-exilic Palestinian inscriptions*. Doctoral dissertation, Southern Baptist Theological Seminary. Ann Arbor, University Microfilms.

Driver, G. R.

1936 *Problems of the Hebrew verbal system.* Edinburgh.

1948 (1954[2],1976[3]) *Semitic writing.* Oxford University Press.

1953 Hebrew poetic diction. *Congress volume*, Supplements to *VT* 1, 26–39. Leiden, Brill.

1966 Forgotten Hebrew idioms. *ZAW* 78.1–7.

1967 Playing on words. *WCJS* 4, 1.121–29.

1969 Some uses of *QTL* in the Semitic languages. *PICSS*, 49–69. Jerusalem.

1970 Colloquialisms in the Old Testament. *Mélanges Marcel Cohen*, 233–39. The Hague, Mouton.

1973 Affirmation by exclamatory negation. *JANES* 5.104–14.

Dromi, E.

1979 More on the acquisition of locative prepositions: an analysis of Hebrew data. *JCL* 6/3.547–62.

Dror, Z.

1954 השמות הפרטיים המסתיימים ב־ם וב־ון במקרא. Masters thesis, Hebrew University.

Dubarle, A. M.

1966 *Judith*, Analecta biblica 24, 2 vols. Rome, Pontifical Biblical Institute.

Dubrow, M.

1973 *A generative-transformational contrastive analysis of English and Hebrew for selected grammatical structures that are difficult for the Hebrew speaking learner of English.* Doctoral dissertation, New York University. Ann Arbor, University Microfilms.

Dugma, Y.

1976 פעלים לוקאטיביים בעברית המקראית. Masters thesis, Hebrew University.

Edelmann, R.

1968 Soferim-Massoretes, 'Massoretes'—Nakdanim. *BZAW* 103. 116–23. Berlin.

Edrei, E.

1976 הטקסט, המסורה, הניקוד והטעמים בכתב יד לנינגרד 18 (אוסף פירקוביץ א, 59) לספר ירמיהו. Masters thesis, Hebrew University.

Edwards, R.

1975 *A Concordance to Q.* SBL, Sources for biblical study. Missoula, MT, Scholars Press.

Efratt, M.

1980 בכ״פ בראש שם אחרי מלת־שמוש מקושרת. *Leš* 45.40–55.

1986 ״ר׳ מחשב גאון״—ומניעות השורשים. *WCJS* 9, Division D, 109–16. Jerusalem.

Ehrlich, K.
1979 *Verwendungen der Deixis beim sprachlichen Handeln.* 2 vols. Frankfurt am Main, Berlin, Las Vegas, Peter Lang.

Ehrentreu, E.
1962 Ashkenazi and Sephardi pronunciations. *Jubilee volume presented in honor of the eightieth birthday of Rabbi Dr. Joseph Breuer*, 216–25. New York.

Eilers, W.
1978 Semitische Wurzeltheorie. *QS* 5.125–31.

Einhorn, I.
1940 שינוי הכתב העברי על פי המקורות התלמודיים. Masters thesis, Hebrew University.

Einspahr, B.
1976 Index to Brown, Driver and Briggs, *Hebrew lexicon*. Chicago.

Eisenbeis, W.
1969 Die Wurzel *šlm* im alten Testament. *BZAW* 113. Berlin.

Eisenstadt, S.
1967 שפתנו העברית החיה. Tel Aviv.

Eissfeldt, O.
1965 *The Old Testament, an introduction.* New York/Evanston, IL, Harper and Row.

Eitan, I.
1924 *A contribution to biblical lexicography.* Columbia University Press.
1928–29 Hebrew and Semitic particles. *AJSL* 45.48–63, 130–45, 297–311.

Eldar (Alder), I.
1974–75 ניקוד ההגדה של פסח במחזור ויטרי (כ״י ששון 535). *Leš* 39.191–216.
1975–76, 1976–77 שער נוח התיבות מתוך ״עין הקורא״. *Leš* 40.190–210; 41.205–15.
1976 חקר ועיון .לבירור מהותו וגלגוליו של ההניקוד הארץ ישראלי טברני 39–48. University of Haifa.
1977 מסורת קדם־אשכנזית על פי מחזורים אשכנזיים מן המאות הי״ב־הי״ג בתוספת בירור דרכי ניקודם. Doctoral dissertation, Hebrew University.
1978 מסורת הקריאה הקדם־אשכנזית. כרך א: ענייני הגייה וניקוד. כרך ב: ענייני תצורה. PHULTP 4. Jerusalem.
1978–79a מכתבי אסכולת הדקדוק האשכנזית: ״השמשוני״. *Leš* 43.100–111, 201–10.
1978–79b ההגייה המסורתית של יהודי בגדאד. *Leš* 43.217–23 (review article on Morag 1977).
1978–79c קטע מן ״הכתאב אלנתף״ לר׳ יהודה חיוג׳ לתרי־עשר. *Lěs* 43.254–59.

1979–80 טיבן של מסורות הקריאה העבריות בימה"ב והמקורות למחקרן. *LLA* 31/8.232–44.
1980 "אבות ותולדות" במערכת הבניינים. *Leš* 44.157–60.
1981a כתאב נחו אל עבראני. תקציר מדקדוקו של רב סעדיה גאון. *Leš* 45.105–32.
1981b שער בדבר מקומות החיתוך של העיצורים מתוך הדאיה אלקאר הארוך. *Leš* 45.233–59.
1981c עיונים .גילויים נורמאטיביים בספרות הדקדוק העברי של ימי הבינים בבלשנות ובסמיוטיקה, 13–19. Jerusalem.
1983 עיון מחודש בשאלת חלוקת התנועות העבריות־לדרך רום, דרך מטה, ודרך ניצב. *ML* 43–55.
1983–84 ההגייה הכפולה של הרי"ש הטברנית. *Leš* 48–49.22–31.
1986 ביאורי מלים אטימולוגיים בפרשנות המקרא ובמילונאות העברית בימי הביניים. *WCJS* 9, Division D, 49–53. Jerusalem.

Eldar, I. and Morag, S.
1986 תורת הלשון העברית בימי הבינים—מבחר פרקי עיון. Jerusalem, Akademon (reproduction of selected articles by various scholars).

Elitsur, M.
1977 תיאור מורפולוגי של גזרת הכפולים בלשון חז"ל על פי כתבי יד מנוקדים ובלתי מנוקדים בהשוואה ללשון המקרא. Masters thesis, Hebrew University.

Elitsur, S.
1981 פיוטי אלעזר בירבי קילַר ויחסם ליצירתו של אלעזר בירבי קַליר. Doctoral dissertation, Hebrew University.

Elkayam, S.
1983 מינם של שמות העצם במשנה על פי ההתאם התחבירי. Masters thesis, Bar-Ilan University.

Ellenbogen, M.
1962 *Foreign words in the Old Testament, their origin and etymology*. London, Luzac.
1969 The common pre-historic origin of certain non-synonymous Semitic roots. *JHS* 1.161–66.
1977 Linguistic archaeology, semantic interpretation, and the discovery of lost meanings. *WCJS* 6, 1.93–95.

Emerton, J. A.
1973 The problem of vernacular Hebrew in the first century A.D. and the language of Jesus. *JTS* 24.1–23.
1977 The etymology of *hištaḥ^{a}wāh*. *OTS* 20.41–55. Leiden.

Engel, E. and Sirat, C.
1982 המתודולוגיה של השוואת כתיבות ונסיון לאפיון יחסים גאומטריים בכתיבה. *WCJS* 8, Division D, Hebrew section, 77–81. Jerusalem.

Engel, J.
1941 מונחים צבאיים במקורות העברים. Masters thesis, Hebrew University.
Englander, H.
1937–38 Grammatical elements and terminology in Rashi. *HUCA* 12-13.505–21.
1942–43 A commentary on Rashi's grammatical comments. *HUCA* 17.427–98.
Enoch, P. and Kaplan, G.
1968–69 המהות הפיסיקלית של ההטעמה הישראלית. *Leš* 33.208–22.
Epstein, J. N.
1947–48 משנית וארמית בבלית. *Leš* 15.103–7.
1948/1964² מבוא לנוסח המשנה, 2 vols. Jerusalem.
Epstein, R.
1971 המשפטים המושאיים במקרא. Masters thesis, Tel Aviv University.
Epstein, Y.
1947 הגיוני לשון. Tel Aviv.
Erlich, R.
1973 Politics and linguistics in the standardization of Soviet Yiddish. *Soviet Jewish Affairs* 3.71–79 (reprinted in J. A. Fishman, ed., 1981a.699–708).
Eshel, B.
1960 להגים והגיות לפי שמות שבמקרא. *Sefer Tur Sinai*, ed. by M. Haran and B. Luria, 243–78. Jerusalem.
1967 לתצורת השמות הפרטיים—שמות אדם ושמות מקום—במקרא. Masters thesis, Hebrew University.
1971 מחקר סימנטי על תחום "המגורים" בעברית המקראית. Doctoral dissertation, Hebrew University.
Eshel, M.
n.d.(1975?) מלים וגלגוליהן. Haifa, Pinat Hasefer.
Eshel, R.
1982 *Effects of contextual richness on word recognition in pointed and unpointed Hebrew.* Doctoral dissertation, State University of New York at Albany. Ann Arbor, University Microfilms.
Even-Shoshan, A.
1944 ערכים מילוניים בתלמוד הבבלי. Masters thesis, Hebrew University.
1979 ספר שלום סיוון. בניינים חדשים-ישנים בלשון ימינו, ed. by A. Even-Shoshan, B. Z. Luria, C. Rabin and E. Talmi, 93–104. Jerusalem, Kiryath Sepher.

Even-Zohar, A.
1971 מבוא לתיאוריה של התרגום הספרותי. Doctoral dissertation, Tel Aviv University.
1972 ראשי־פרקים לתיאוריה של הטקסט הספרותי. הספרות 3/3–4.427–46.
Eybers, I. H.
1972 The root *ṣ-l* in Hebrew words. *JNSL* 2.23–36.
Eytan, E.
1967 ממלונו המקראי של רב סעדיה גאון. *WCJS* 4, 1.39–41 (English summary 253).
1971 Hebrew language: modern period. *EJ* 16.1642–57 (extensive bibliography: 1657–62).
Faber, A.
1980 *Genetic subgroupings of the Semitic languages.* Doctoral dissertation, University of Texas at Austin. Ann Arbor, University Microfilms.
1982 Early medieval sibilants in the Rhineland, South Central and Eastern Europe. *HAR* 6.81–96.
Fabry, H. J.
1975 Die Wurzel *šûḇ* in den Qumran-Literatur, zur Semantik eines Grundbegriffes. Bonner biblische Beiträge, Köln, Hanstein.
Falk, Z.
1956–57 "צאן ברזל" בתלמוד. *Tarbiz* 26.287–91.
1967 Hebrew legal terms II. *JSS* 12.241–44.
1969 Hebrew legal terms III. *JSS* 14.39–44.
1972/1978 *Introduction to Jewish law of the Second Commonwealth,* 2 vols. Leiden, Brill.
Farrar, C. and Hayon, Y.
1980 The perception of the phoneme /ᵓ/ in Modern Hebrew. *HAR* 4.53–77.
Fatihi, S.
1971 מבנים תחביריים בפתגמים מלשון חז"ל. Masters thesis, Hebrew University.
Federbush, S.
1965 מקום הארמית ביהדות. Jerusalem, Mossad Harav Kook.
1966–67 על הלשון העברית בספרות הרבנית. *OH* 16.103–8.
1967 הלשון העברית בישראל ובעמים. Jerusalem, Mossad Harav Kook.
Feigin, S.
1943 The original language of the Gospels. *JNES* 2.187–97.
Feinberg, C. L.
1945 *Ugaritic literature and the book of Job.* Doctoral dissertation, Johns Hopkins University.

Fellman, J.
1971 *The role of Eliezer ben Yehudah in the revival of the Hebrew language: a sociolinguistic study.* Doctoral dissertation, Harvard University.
1973a *The revival of a classical tongue: Eliezer ben Yehuda and the Modern Hebrew language.* The Hague, Mouton.
1973b The role of Eliezer ben Yehuda in the revival of the Hebrew language: an assessment. *Advances in language planning*, ed. by J. A. Fishman, 427–55. The Hague, Mouton.
1974 The Academy of the Hebrew Language: its history, structure and function. *IJSL* (*Linguistics* 120) 1.95–103.
1974–75 The consonantal phonemes of Israeli Hebrew. *AN* 15.18–19.
1975a A note on the phonemic structure of the ultra-short vowels in Tiberian Hebrew. *JNSL* 4.9–10.
1975b The Hebrew language on the eve of its renewal. *Orbis* 24.350–53.
1977a The linguistic status of Mishnaic Hebrew. *JNSL* 5.21–22.
1977b On the phonemic status of gemination in Classical Hebrew. *JNSL* 5.19.
1978a Sociolinguistic notes on the history of the Hebrew language. *JNSL* 6.5–7.
1978b (1976–77) The consonantal morphemes of Israeli Hebrew. *AN* 17.5–6.
1980 Linguistic nationalism: the case of Biblical Hebrew. *JNSL* 8.11–13.
Fellman, K.
1978 קטלוג התיעוד המוקלט של מפעל מסורות הלשון. *Catalogue of the recordings in the tape-archives of the Hebrew University language traditions project. PHULTP* 3. Jerusalem.
1982 עדה ולשון ח, חילופי צורה במסורות הלשון. Jerusalem, Magnes Press.
Fenton, T. L.
1970 The absence of a verbal formation **yaqattal* from Ugaritic and Northwest Semitic. *JSS* 15.31–41.
1973 The Hebrew 'tenses' in the light of Ugaritic. *WCJS* 5, 4.31–39. Jerusalem.
1980 שאלות הכרוכות בעדות הספרות האוגריתית על אוצר המלים של המקרא. *Leš* 44.268–80.
Fink, D.
1980 *The Hebrew grammar of Maimonides.* Doctoral dissertation, Yale University. Ann Arbor, University Microfilms.

Fischel, W.
1971 Judeo-Persian literature. *EJ* 10.532–39 (includes useful bibliography).
Fischler, Berakha
1983 לשונות התלמוד ב"עריכת" מאפו. *Leš* 47.278–84.
Fischler, B. Z.
1975 ב׳ כ׳ פ׳ דגושות ורפויות שלא כדין—בעברית הישראלית. *Rosen memorial volume*, ed. by U. Ornan and B. Fischler, 86–99. Jerusalem, The Council on the Teaching of Hebrew.
1976 הסופליציה ומקומה בהוראת שפה נוספת. *Chaim Rabin jubilee volume*, 110–19. Jerusalem, The Council on the Teaching of Hebrew.
1984 Ed. רשימת ספרים, מאמרים ועבודות דוקטור על העברית של ימינו. מן הסדנא 6. Jerusalem, The Council on the Teaching of Hebrew (with M. Riegler).
Fischler, B. Z. and Nir, R., eds.
1976 כלשון עמו. *Chaim Rabin jubilee volume, Studies in applied linguistics*. Jerusalem, Council on the Teaching of Hebrew (contains bibliography of Chaim Rabin up to that date, 163–74).
Fisher, L. ed.,
1972/1975 *Ras Shamra parallels*, vols. 1 and 2. Rome, Pontifical Biblical Institute (for vol. 3 in this series, see Rummel 1981).
Fisher, R. W.
1966 BŚR. Doctoral dissertation, Columbia University. Ann Arbor, University Microfilms.
Fisherman, H.
1972 The 'official' languages of Israel: their status in law and police attitudes and knowledge concerning them. *Language behavior papers*, 3–22 (mimeographed student journal of the Language Behavior section at Hebrew University); (appears also in *Multilingual political systems and solutions*, 498–535. Quebec City, Laval University Press).
1973 שמירת לשונות־אם בישראל. Masters thesis, Hebrew University.
Fishkin, A.
1976 אדם ולשונו. Tel Aviv, Anili.
Fishman, J. A.
1965a Yiddish in America. Publication 36 of the Indiana University Research Center in Anthropology, Folklore and Linguistics = *IJAL* 31/2.i–viii, 1–94. Bloomington and the Hague, Indiana University and Mouton.
1965b Language maintenance and language shift in certain urban immigrant environments: the case of Yiddish in the United States. *EE* 22.146–58.

1965c U.S. census data on mother tongues: review, extrapolation and prediction, in *For Max Weinreich on his seventieth birthday*, 51–62. The Hague, Mouton.

1966 Ed. *Language loyalty in the United States.* The Hague, Mouton.

1967 Bilingualism with and without diglossia; diglossia with and without bilingualism. *JSI* 23.29–38.

1969 Language maintenance and language shift: Yiddish and other immigrant languages in the United States. YIVO *Annual of Jewish social science* 14.12–26.

1972a הסוציולוגיה של יידיש בארצות הברית: עבר, הווה ועתיד. *Ḥug lidiᶜot ᶜam yisraʾel batfutsot* 6/3 (also abbreviated in *Goldene keyt* 75 [1972], 110–27).

1972b Language maintenance and language shift as a field of inquiry: revisited, in *Language and sociocultural change*, ed. by Anwar Dil, 76–133. Stanford University Press.

1973a Ed. *Advances in language planning.* The Hague, Mouton.

1973b The phenomenological and linguistic pilgrimage of Yiddish (some examples of functional and structural pidginization and depidginization). *KJS* 9.127–36.

1974 Introduction: the sociology of language in Israel. *Linguistics* 120.9–14.

1976 Yiddish and Loshnkoydesh in traditional Ashkenaz: on the problem of societal allocation of macrofunctions, in *Language in sociology*, ed. by A. Verdoodt and R. Kyolseth, 39–48. Louvain, Peters.

1977a Ed. *Advances in the creation and revision of writing systems.* The Hague, Mouton.

1977b The phenomenological and linguistic pilgrimage of Yiddish: some examples of functional and structural pidginization and depidginization, in Fishman, ed., 1977a.293–306.

1977–78 The sociology of Yiddish after the holocaust: status, needs and possibilities. *Gesher* 6.148–68.

1979 The sociolinguistic 'normalization' of the Jewish people. *Linguistic and literary studies in honor of Archibald A. Hill*, 4.223–31. Lisse, Peter de Ridder Press.

1980a Attracting a following to high-culture functions for a language of everyday life; the role of the Tshernovits conference in the 'rise of Yiddish', *IJSL* 24, *Sociology of Yiddish*, ed. by J. A. Fishman, 43–73. The Hague, Mouton (also appears in R. L. Cooper, ed., *Language spread: studies in diffusion and social change*, Arlington, 1981; appears also, with revisions, in J. A. Fishman, ed., *Never Say Die*, The Hague, Mouton, 1981, 369–94).

1980b The sociology of Yiddish after the holocaust: status, needs and possibilities, in *FY* 4, ed. by M. Herzog, B. Kirshenblatt-Gimblett, D. Meron and R. Wisse, 475–98. Philadelphia, Institute for the Study of Human Issues.

1980c Ed. Sociology of Yiddish. *IJSL* 24. The Hague, Mouton.

1981a Ed. *Never say die, A thousand years of Yiddish in Jewish life.* The Hague, Mouton.

1981b The sociology of Yiddish: a foreword, *ibid.*, 1–97 (important study and bibliography).

1981c Epilogue: contributions of the sociology of Yiddish to the general sociology of language, *ibid.*, 739–56 (revision and expansion of 1980b).

1985 *Readings in the Sociology of Jewish Languages.* Leiden, Brill.

Fishman, J. and Fishman, D.

1974 Yiddish in Israel. *Linguistics* 120.125–46.

1978 Yiddish in Israel: a case-study of efforts to revise a monocentric language policy, in *Advances in the study of social multilingualism.* The Hague, Mouton.

Fitzgerald, A.

1972 A note on G-stem *ynṣr* forms in the Old Testament. *ZAW* 84.90–92.

1978 The interchange of *L*, *M*, and *R* in biblical Hebrew. *JBL* 97.481–88.

Fitzmyer, J.

1961 The Aramaic inscriptions of Sefire I and II. *JAOS* 81.178–222.

1966 *The Genesis apocryphon of Qumran cave I; a commentary.* Rome, Pontifical Biblical Institute (second revised edition, 1971).

1967 *The Aramaic inscriptions of Sefire.* Rome, Pontifical Biblical Institute.

1971 *Essays on the Semitic background of the New Testament.* 1st edition, London, Geoffry Chapman; 2nd edition (1974), Missoula, MT, SBL and Scholars Press.

1975 *The Dead Sea scrolls: major publications and tools for study.* Missoula, MT, SBL and Scholars Press (second edition with addendum, 1977).

1979 *A wandering Aramean—collected Aramaic essays*, SBL monograph series 25. Missoula, MT, Scholars Press.

1980 The Aramaic language and the study of the New Testament. *JBL* 99.5–21.

Fitzmyer, J. and Harrington, D. J.

1978 *A manual of Palestinian Aramaic texts.* Rome, Biblical Institute Press.

Fleisch, H.
1947 *Introduction a l'étude des langues sémitiques.* Paris.
Fleischer, E.
1968–69 פיוט ליניי חזן על משמרות הכהנים. *Sinai* 33(64).176–84.
1970 נוספות למורשתו הפייטנית של רב האיי גאון. *Sinai* 67.180–98.
1971 יוצרים ויצירות בספרד ובפרובנס בדורות האחרונים שלפני הגרוש. Material for a seminar, Hebrew University, Faculty of Humanities, Department of Hebrew Literature. Jerusalem.
1971–72 מונח דקדוקי קדום בפיוט קלירי. *Leš* 36.263–67.
1973 פיוטי שלמה הבבלי. Jerusalem.
1974a פזמוני האנונימוס. Jerusalem, Israel Academy of Sciences and Humanities.
1974b לפתרונן של כמה בעיות יסוד. *H. Yalon memorial volume*, Bar-Ilan departmental researches, 2.444–70. Jerusalem.
1975–76 Review of Stern 1974 (*H*). *KS* 51.358–68.
1976 שירת הקודש העברית בימי הבינים. Jerusalem, Keter.
1977 עיונים בשירתו של רבי האי גאון in *A. M. Haberman jubilee volume*, ed. by Z. Malachi, 239–74. Jerusalem, Keter.
1983a חדשות ביצירתו של ר׳ יצחק בר לוי (אבן מר שאול). *ML* 425–50.
1983b The 'Gerona school' of Hebrew poetry. Rabbi Moses Nahmanides (Ramban): explorations in his religous and literary virtuosity, ed. by Isadore Twersky, 35–49. Cambridge, MA; Harvard University Press.
1984 היוצרות בהתהוותם והתפתחותם. Jerusalem, Magnes Press.
1985 בחינות בעליית שיטות השקילה המדויקות בשירה העברית. *Leš* 48–49.142–62.
1986 מחקרים במדעי יהדות. חקר השירה העברית בימי הביניים, ed. by M. Bar-Asher, 284–92. Jerusalem.
Florsheim, Y.
1973–74 כללי לשון המקרא בפרוש רש״י לתלמוד. *Leš* 38.243–56.
Fontinoy, C.
1969 *Le duel dans les langues sémitiques.* Bibliotheque de la faculté de philosophie et lettres de l'Université de Liege, Fascicle 179.
Forshey, H.
1973 *The Hebrew root* nḥl *and its Semitic cognates.* Doctoral dissertation, Harvard University (summary in *HTR* 66. 505–6).
Fortis, U.
1977–78 על מלים עבריות בתוך היצירה הספרותית בניבים האיטלקיים. *Leš* 42.125–35.
Fortis, U. and Zolli, P.
1979 *La parlata giudeo-veneziana.* Assisi.

Fox, A. J.

1984 *The evolution of the Hebrew infinitive, form and function: a diachronic study with cross-linguistic implications.* Doctoral dissertation, UCLA. Ann Arbor, University Microfilms.

Fox, M.

1973 *Ṭôḇ* as covenant terminology. *BASOR* 209.41–42.

Fraenkel, Gad

1950 הכתיבה בספרים ההיסטוריים של תנ"ך. Masters thesis, Hebrew University.

Fraenkel, Gerd

1960 Review of H. Rosén 1957. *JAOS* 80.142–45.

1963 Review of Morag 1962a. *JAOS* 83.120–22.

Fraenkel, M.

1949 קונטרס לשון העם. Jerusalem.

1970a *Zur Theorie der* Lamed-He *Stämme.* Jerusalem.

1970b *Zur Theorie der* Ayin-waw *und der* Ayin-Jud *Stämme.* Jerusalem.

Freedman, A.

1972 Italian texts in Hebrew characters. *MRA* 8. Wiesbaden, Harrassowitz.

Freedman, David

1980 *A study of the critical lexicographical methods of Yona ibn Janah.* Doctoral dissertation, University of California. Ann Arbor, University Microfilms.

Freedman, D. B. and Cohen, M. B.

1974 The Massoretes as exegetes: selected examples. *Masoretic studies* 1, ed. by H. M. Orlinsky, 35–46. Missoula, MT, Scholars Press.

Freedman, D. N.

1948 *The evolution of early Hebrew orthography, the epigraphic evidence.* Doctoral dissertation, The Johns Hopkins University. Ann Arbor, University Microfilms.

1960 Archaic forms in early Hebrew poetry. *ZAW* 72.101–7.

1962 The massoretic text and the Qumran scrolls: a study in orthography. *Textus* 2.87–102.

1971 The structure of Psalm 137. *Near East studies in honor of W. F. Albright*, ed. by H. Goedicke, 187–205. Baltimore/London, Johns Hopkins University Press.

1972a Prolegomena to George Buchanan Gray, *The forms of Hebrew poetry* (New York, 1915). New York, Ktav.

1972b The broken construct chain. *Biblica* 53.534–36.

1972c The refrain in David's lament over Saul and Jonathan. *Ex orbe religionum,* Widengren volume, 1.115–26. Lugdumi Batavorum.

1972d Acrostics and metrics in Hebrew poetry. *HTR* 65.367–92.
1975 Early Israelite history in the light of early Israelite poetry. *Unity and diversity*, ed. by H. Goedicke and J. J. M. Roberts, 3–35. Baltimore/London, Johns Hopkins University Press.
1978 Psalms 113 and the song of Hannah. *EI* 14. 14.58*–69*.

Freedman, D. N. and Greenfield, J.
1969 *New directions in biblical archaeology*. New York.

Freedman, D. N. and Ritterspach, A.
1967 The use of *aleph* as a vowel letter in the Genesis Apocryphon. *RQ* 6.293–300.

Freimark, P.
1971 Abkurzungen und univerbierende Verkürzungen im Neuhebräischen—ein Beitrag zur Wortbildung. *ZDMG* 121.7–36.

Friedlander, M.
1895 A third system of symbols for the Hebrew vowels and accents. *JQR*, o.s., 7.564–68.

Friedman, S.
1970–71 כל הקצר קודם. *Leš* 35.117–29, 192–206.

Friedrich, J.
1951 *Phönizisch-punische Grammatik*. Rome.

Fritsch, C. T.
1977 Homophony in the Septuagint. *WCJS* 6, 1.115–20.
1982 A study of the Greek translation of the Hebrew verbs 'to see', with Deity as subject or object. *EI* 16.518–68.

Fronzaroli, P.
1973 Statistical methods in the study of ancient near east languages. *Or* 42.97–113.
1974 Review of Corriente 1971. *JSS* 19.275–84.
1975 On the common Semitic lexicon and its ecological and cultural background. *Hamito-Semitica*, ed. by J. and T. Bynon, 43–53. The Hague, Mouton.
1984 Ed. *Studies on the language of Ebla. Quaderni di Semitistica* 13. Istituto de Linguistica e di Lingue Orientali, Universita di Firenze.

Fruchtman (-Agmon), M.
1970 האיחוי והשיעבוד כבוחן לסיגנונם של טיפוסי־כתיבה. *HCL* 2.46–29.
1973 יסודות הדקדוק ב״ערוגת הבושם״ לאברהם בן עזריאל. Masters thesis, Tel Aviv University.
1979 קטגוריות מיידעות ומתחמות בעברית הישראלית. Doctoral dissertation, University of Tel Aviv.
1980 שם־העצם הסוגי ומעמדו במשפטי משואה בעברית הישראלית בהשואה למקורות הקדומים של השפה ולשפות אירופיות אחדות. *Leš* 44.299–313.

1981 ספרות ילדים ונוער. עיון בשיר הילדים בגישה תחבירית 7/2–3.4–8.
1982 הידוע והסתום. Tel Aviv, Student Organization of Tel Aviv University.

Fuks, L.
1954 On the oldest dated Yiddish manuscript. *FY* 1.267–74.
1957 *The oldest known document of Yiddish literature.* Leiden, Brill.

Fulco, W. J.
1978 The ᶜAmmān citadel inscription: a new collation. *BASOR* 230.39–43.
1979 The Amman theater inscription. *JNES* 38.37–38.

Futato, M.
1978 The preposition '*beth*' in the Hebrew psalter. *WTJ* 41.68–81.

Gai, A.
1977 תיאורים אדנומינאליים בשפות שמיות. Doctoral dissertation, Hebrew University.

Galbraith, J. A.
1981 *A quantitative analysis of the parallelistic structures in Hebrew poetry.* Doctoral dissertation, Boston University. Ann Arbor, University Microfilms.

Gan, M.
1961–62 בין קודש לחול. *LLA* 13 (125).67–77.

Garbell (Chanoch), I.
1930 *Fremdsprachliche Einflüsse im modernen Hebräisch.* Inaugural dissertation, Friedrich Wilhelms Universität, Berlin.
1946 המבטא העברי ודרכי לימודו. *Leš* 14.39–47.
1947 מבטא העיצורים העבריים בפי יהודי איראן. *Leš* 15.62–74.
1950–51 שיטת חלוקת התנועות אצל המדקדקים העבריים ומקורותיהן. *Leš* 17.76–80.
1953–54 Review of Gumperz 1953 (*H*). *Leš* 19.83–92.
1954 The pronunciation of Hebrew in medieval Spain. *Homenaje a Millas Valicrosa*, 1.647–96. Barcelona.
1958 המבטא העברי, ראשי פרקים. The Faculty of Humanities,, Hebrew University, Jerusalem.
1959 מעמדם הפונימי של השווא ושל החטפים ושל בגד כפ״ת הרפויות בעברית המסורתית. *Leš* 23.152–55.
1961–62 Review of Kutscher 1959 (*H*). *Leš* 26.140–46.
1962–63 Review of Morag 1962a (*H*). *Leš* 27–28.73–76.
1965a *The Jewish Neo-Aramaic dialect of Persian Azaerbaijan. Linguistic analysis and folkloristic texts.* The Hague, Mouton.
1965b Review of Morag 1963 (*H*). *KS* 40.323–40.
1968 מסורות המבטא העברי של יהודי אסיה ואפריקה. *WCJS* 4, 2.453–54. Jerusalem (English summary 212).

Garbini, G.
1959 Unité et varieté des dialectes araméens anciens. *PICO* 24, 242–44. Wiesbaden.
1960 *Il Semitico di Nord-ouest.* Naples.
1965 La semitistica: definizione e prospettive di una disciplina. *AION* 25.1–15.
1970 La lingua della Ammoniti. *AION* 30.249–58.
1971 The phonemic shift of sibilants in Northwest Semitic in the first millennium B.C. *JNSL* 1.32–38. Leiden, Brill.
1974 Ammonite inscriptions. *JSS* 19.159–68.

Garfinkel, S. P.
1983 *Studies in Akkadian influences in the book of Ezekiel.* Doctoral dissertation, Columbia University. Ann Arbor, University Microfilms.

Garr, W. R.
1985a *Dialect geography of Syria-Palestine, 1000–586 B.C.E.* University of Pennsylvania.
1985b On vowel dissimilation in Hebrew. *Biblica* 66.572–79.

Garvin, P.
1965 The dialect geography of Hungarian Yiddish. *FY* 2.92–115.

Gates, J. E.
1972 An analysis of the lexicographical resources used by American biblical scholars today. SBL monograph series, dissertation series 8. Cambridge, MA, SBL and Harvard Divinity School.

Gealia, A.
1980 די עלטסטער יידישער גלאסאר צום תנ"ך. קאד. רייכלין 8, קארלייס־רוע. *WCJS* 6, Division D, 41–56.

Gehman, H. S.
1951 The Hebrew character of Septuagint Greek. *VT* 1.81–90.
1966 Adventures in Septuagint lexicography. *Textus* 5.125–32.

Geipel, J.
1982 *Mame loshn, the making of Yiddish.* London, Journeyman Press.

Gelb, I. J.
1952 *Morphology of Akkadian.* Chicago.
1963 *A study of writing.* Chicago, University of Chicago, Phoenix Books.
1969 *Sequential reconstruction of Proto-Akkadian.* AS 18, Oriental Institute, University of Chicago.
1977 Thoughts about Ibla. *Syro-Mesopotamian studies* 1/1. Malibu, CA, Undena Publications.

Gelb, I. J., Bartels, J., Vance, S. and Whiting, R.
1980 *Computer-aided analysis of Amorite.* AS 21. Oriental Institute, University of Chicago.

Geller, S.
1979 *Parallelism in early Hebrew poetry*, Harvard Semitic monographs 20. Missoula, MT, Scholars Press.
1982 Theory and method in the study of biblical poetry. *JQR* 73.65–77 (review of O'Connor 1980 and Kugel 1981).
Gerleman, G.
1948 Synoptic studies in the Old Testament. Lund.
1973a Die Wurzel *šlm*. *ZAW* 85.1–14.
1973b Die lärmende Menge. Der Sinn des hebräischen Wortes *hamon*. *Wort und Geschichte*, 71–75.
1974 Der Nichtmensch. Erwägungen zur hebräischen Wurzel *nbl*. *VT* 24.147–58.
1978 Das übervolle Mass: ein Versuch mit *haesed*. *VT* 28.151–64.
Gessman, A. M.
1967 The tongues of the Bible: an essay on biblical linguistics. *LQ* 6.19–30.
Gevaryahu, S. D.
1954 משנת הדקדוק של רבי אברהם דבלמט. Masters thesis, Hebrew University.
Gevirtz, S.
1963 *Patterns in early poetry of Israel*. Studies in ancient civilization 32. Chicago, University of Chicago.
1973a Evidence of conjugational variation in the parallelization of selfsame verbs in the Amarna letters. *JNES* 32.99–104.
1973b On Canaanite rhetoric. The evidence of the Amarna letters from Tyre. *Or* 42.162–77 (I. J. Gelb volume).
1982 Formative ע in biblical Hebrew. *EI* 16.57*–66*.
Gibson, A.
1981 *Biblical semantic logic: a preliminary analysis*. New York, St. Martin.
Gibson, J. C. L.
1966 Stress and vocalic change in Hebrew. *JL* 2.35–56.
1971–82 *Textbook of Syrian Semitic inscriptions*, 3 vols. Oxford, Clarendon Press.
1974 The Massoretes as linguists. *OTS* 19.86–96. Leiden, Brill.
Giesen, G.
1981 *Die Wurzel* שבע *"schwören"*. Bonn, Peter Hanstein Verlag.
Gil, J.
1973–74 בלשנות שמית משווה של חכמינו בימי הביניים. עיון ומעש, collected studies of the teachers of the Gordon Seminary, 188–92. Haifa.
1973–75 רבי יוסף קמחי כפרשן המקרא. *BM* 19.265–85; 20.369–77.

Gilboa, Y.
1982 *A language silenced.* New York, Herzl Press and Rutherford, NJ, Associated University Presses.
Giniger, C.
1954a Sainean's accomplishments in Yiddish linguistics. *FY* 1. 147–78.
1954b A note on the Yiddish Horant, *ibid.*, 275–77.
Ginsberg, H. L.
1936 כתבי אוגרית. Jerusalem.
1955 The classification of the Northwest Semitic languages. *PICO* 24, 256–57. Munich.
1970 The Northwest Semitic languages, in *The Patriarchs, WHJP*, ed. by B. Mazar, E. Fellman and A. Pelli, 102–24. Rutgers University.
Ginsburg, C. D.
1879 *Introduction to the Massoretico-critical edition of the Hebrew Bible.* Reprinted 1966 with prolegomenon by Harry M. Orlinsky. New York, Ktav.
Giora, R.
1981a תפקידי הטופיקליזציה ברמת המשפט והדיסקורס באנגלית ובעברית. Tel Aviv University.
1981b עיונים. המלים במשפט ויחסן לטקסט: ניתוח של משפטים ממוקדים בחקר השיח, ed. by S. Blum-Kulka, Y. Tobin and R. Nir, 263–308. Jerusalem, Akademon.
Givon, T.
1973 Complex NP's, word order and resumptive pronouns in Hebrew. Papers from the comparative syntax festival, ed. by C. Corum, T. Cedric *et al.*, 143–46. Chicago Linguistic Society.
1974 Verb complements and relative clauses: a diachronic case study in Biblical Hebrew. *AAL* 1/4.
1975 On the role of perceptual clues in Hebrew relativization. *AAL* 2/8.131–47.
1976a On the VS word order in Israeli Hebrew: pragmatics and typological change, in P. Cole, ed., *Studies in Modern Hebrew syntax and semantics*, 153–81. Amsterdam.
1976b The drift from VSO to SVO in Biblical Hebrew; the pragmatics of tense-aspect. *Symposium in the mechanisms of syntactic change*, ed. by C. N. Li, 181–254. Austin, University of Texas Press.
Glinert, L. H.
1974 *A generative study of peripheral categories in Modern Hebrew.* Doctoral dissertation, University of London.

1976 How OD: a study of a Modern Hebrew pseudo-quantifier, in P. Cole, ed., *Studies in Modern Hebrew syntax and semantics*, 249–63. Amsterdam.

1977 Number switch: a singular feature-change rule in Modern Hebrew. *AAL* 4/2.

1979 Linguistics and language teaching: the implications for Modern Hebrew. *HAR* 3.105–27.

1982a התנאי הבטל בעברית החדשה. *WCJS* 8, Division D, Hebrew section, 49–51. Jerusalem.

1982b המבנה ההדדי בעברית המדוברת. *Sefer David Gross*, ed. by S. Kodesh, 196–213. Jerusalem, Hamatmid.

Glück, J. J.

1970 Paronomasia in biblical literature. *Semitica* 1.50–78.

1971 Assonance in ancient Hebrew poetry: sound patterns as a literary device. *Essays in honor of Adrianus van Selms. POS* 9.69–84.

Gluska, I.

1981 שמות במשקל מַקְטֵל ובמקרא ובמשנה ומשמעויותיהם. *Leš* 45. 280–98.

Goddard, B. L.

1950 *The origin of the Hebrew infinitive absolute in the light of infinitive uses in related languages and its use in the Old Testament*. Doctoral dissertation, Harvard University.

Goetze, A.

1942 The so-called intensive of the Semitic languages. *JAOS* 62.1–8.

1953 A seal with an early alphabetic inscription. *BASOR* 129.8–11.

Goitein, S.

1930–31 היסודות העבריים בשפת הדיבור של יהודי תימן. *Leš* 3.356–80.

1962 סדרי חנוך בימי הגאונים ובית הרמב"ם. Jerusalem, The Ben-Zvi Institute.

Gold, D. L.

1974 Jewish intralinguistics: assumptions, methods, goals and sample problems. *Sociological abstracts* 22 (Suppl. 47-I, August): 344 (reprinted in the Newsletter of the Association for the Sociological Study of Jewry 1(3), Spring 1975: 12).

1977a Successes and failures in the standardization and implementation of Yiddish spelling and romanization. *The creation and revision of writing systems*, ed. by J. A. Fishman, 307–69. The Hague.

1977b Dzudezmo. *LangS* 47.14–16.

1978a The suffix *-nym*. *American speech* 53.238–39.

1978b Planning glottonyms for Jewish languages. *Language planning and language treatment: worldwide case studies* (special issue of *Word* 1979), ed. by R. E. Wood.
1978c Some contact problems in Yiddish lexicology. *Orbis* 29.
1980 The Spanish, Portuguese and Hebrew names for Yiddish and the Yiddish names for Hebrew. *IJSL* 24, *Sociology of Yiddish*, ed. by J. A. Fishman.
1981 Recent American studies in Jewish languages. *JLR* 1.11–88.
1982a The etymology of the Yiddish female given name *toltse*. *WCJS* 8, Division D, English section, 25–30. Jerusalem.
1982b Yiddish linguistic and Jewish liturgical boundaries as determinants of non-Jewish political boundaries? *JLR* 2.59–62.
1982c The official and unofficial use of Yiddish at a world conference: a microlinguistic study. *JLR* 2.63–65.
1982d The plural of Yiddish compounds with *ben-* and *bas-* and their significance for the study of Hebrew. *JLR* 2.66–71.
1983 From Latin *purgare* to British Jewish *porge*: A study in Jewish intralinguistics. *JLR* 3.117–55.

Gold, D. L. and Ornstein, J.
1976 Slave-Yiddish, a note on the Slavic impact on Yiddish: problems of multiple contact. *Orbis* 25.121–28.

Goldberg, A.
1961–62 לטיב ניב לשון המשנה. *Leš* 26.104–17.
1976–77 לטיב ניב לשון המשנה: "כיצד" כמלת הגבלה. *Leš* 41.6–20.
1983 "עירוב" ו"עיבור" ופתרון לשוני למשנה שאינה במקומה. *ML* 111–15.

Goldberg, B. Z.
1970 The American Yiddish press at its centennial. *Judaism* 20.224–28.

Goldberg, Donna and Choueka, Y.
1979 Mechanical resolution of lexical ambiguity; a combinatorial approach. *ICLLC* 149–64.

Goldberg, E.
1977 הפוליסמיה בלשון המקרא. Masters thesis, Hebrew University.

Goldberg, H.
1973–74 על לשונם ותרבותם של יהודי טריפוליטניה. *Leš* 38.137–47.
1980 *The Book of Mordechai, A study of the Jews of Libya.* Philadelphia, Institute for the Study of Human Issues.

Goldenberg, E.
1967 העשייה בלשון של רב סעדיה גאון בזיקה לתורתו הבלשנית. Masters thesis, Hebrew University.
1971 Hebrew language: medieval. *EJ* 16.1607–42.
1972–74 עיונים באגרון לרב סעדיה גאון. *Leš* 37.117–36, 275–90; 38.78–90.

1978–79 לוח הנטייה העברית הראשון. *Leš* 43.83–89.
1983 דוחק השיר בתורת־הלשון העברות בימי הבינים. *ML* 117–41.

Goldenberg, G.
1971 Tautological infinitive. *IOS* 1, 36–85. Tel Aviv.
1977 Imperfectly formed cleft sentences. *WCJS* 6, 1.127–33.
1980 על השוכן החלק והשורש העברי. *Leš* 44.281–92.
1985 על תורת הפועל והפועל העברי. מחקרים בלשון, ed. M. Bar-Asher, 295–348. Jerusalem, Department of Hebrew Language, Hebrew University.

Goldin, R.
1954 לשונו של נתן אלתרמן ומקורותיה. Masters thesis, Hebrew University.

Goldman, E., Smith, H. U. and Tannenbaum, R.
1971 Transliteration and a 'computer-compatible' Semitic alphabet. *HUCA* 42.251–78.

Goldschmidt, D.
1980 מחקרי תפילה ופיוט. Jerusalem, Magnes Press.

Goldsmith, E.
1975 Zhitlovsky and American Jewry. *Jewish Frontier*, November, 14–17.
1976 *Architects of Yiddishism.* Rutherford, Fairleigh Dickinson Press.

Goldwasser, E.
1957 תורתו הדקדוקית של פרופייט דוראן ("האפודי") על פי "מעשה אפוד". Masters thesis, Hebrew University.

Goldwasser, M.
1973 The language of a sixteenth century Yiddish text: *Azhoras Noshim. WCJS* 5, 4.41–44.
1980 די לאנגפארגאנגענע צייט אין יידיש (The pluperfect [plusquamperfectum] in Yiddish). *WCJS* 6, Division D, 33–39. Jerusalem.

Golomb, D. M.
1985 *A grammar of Targum Neofiti.* Decatur, Georgia, Scholars Press.

Good, E. M.
1965 *Irony in the Old Testament.* Philadelphia, Westminster.

Good, R. M.
1980 *The sheep of his pasture: a study of the Hebrew noun ᶜamm and its Semitic cognates.* Doctoral dissertation, Yale University. Ann Arbor, University Microfilms.

Goodstein, M.
1960 *The Judeo-Arabic book of philological comparisons between Hebrew, Aramaic and Arabic known as the* Risala *of Judah*

ibn Quraish (Hebrew text). Doctoral dissertation, Yeshiva University. Ann Arbor, University Microfilms.

Goodwin, D. W.
1969 *Text restoration methods in contemporary USA biblical scholarship.* Naples, Istituto Orientale de Napoli.

Gordis, R.
1937 *The biblical text in the making: a study of the* kethib-qere. Philadelphia (re-issued 1971).
1943 The asseverative *kaph* in Ugaritic and Hebrew. *JAOS* 63. 176–78.
1945 Studies in the relationship of biblical and rabbinic Hebrew. *Louis Ginzberg jubilee volume*, 173–99. New York.
1955 *Koheleth—the man and his world.* Texts and studies of the Jewish Theological Seminary of America 19. New York.
1960 לשון המקרא לאור לשון חכמים. *Sefer Tur Sinai*, 149–68. Jerusalem.
1971 The origins of the Masorah in the light of rabbinic literature and the Qumran scrolls. Introduction to re-issued Gordis 1937. New York, Ktav.
1983–84 השימוש ב״מ״ם המצב״ בעברית מקראית ומשנאית. *Hadoar* 63/16.246–47.

Gordon, A.
1983 *The structure of the Hebrew lexicon.* Doctoral dissertation, UCLA. Ann Arbor, University Microfilms.

Gordon, C. H.
1954 North Israelite influence on post-exilic Hebrew. *EI* 3.104–5. Jerusalem.
1955 North Israelite influence on post-exilic Hebrew. *IEJ* 5.85–88.
1965 *Ugaritic textbook.* Rome, Pontifical Biblical Institute.
1970 The accidental invention of the phonemic alphabet. *JNES* 29.193–97.
1982 Asymmetric janus parallelism. *EI* 16.80*–81*.

Goshen-Gottstein, M. H.
1950 Review of Weiman 1950 (*H*). *Leš* 17.231–40.
1951a תחבירה ומילונה של הלשון העברית שבתחום השפעתה של הערבית. Doctoral dissertation, Hebrew University.
1951b מה נוכל ללמוד מלשונן של מגילות ים המלח? *LLA* 5.3–18.
1957 The history of the Bible text and comparative Semitics. *VT* 7.195–201.
1958 Linguistic structure and tradition in the Qumran documents. *SH* 4.101–37. Jerusalem.
1959 מגילות קומראן ומעמדן הלשוני. Jerusalem, Schocken.
1960a *Text and language in Bible and Qumran.* Jerusalem.

1960b The authenticity of the Aleppo codex. *Textus* 1.17–58.

1963 The rise of the Tiberian Bible-text. *Studies and texts* 1, ed. by A. Altmann, 79–122. Cambridge.

1964 Semitic morphological structures. *Studies in Egyptology and linguistics in honor of H. Polotsky*, ed. by H. Blanc, 104–16. Jerusalem.

1965a לשון המקרא. in לקסיקון מקראי, ed. by M. Solieli and M. Bercuz, 442–50. Tel Aviv.

1965b שפות שמיות, *ibid.*, 865–76.

1965c *The book of Isaiah, sample edition with introduction*, The Hebrew University Bible Project. Jerusalem.

1968 חקר העברית המשוערבת בימי הבינים. *WCJS* 4, 2.109–12.

1969a מבוא למילונאות של העברית החדשה. Jerusalem/Tel Aviv.

1969b The system of verbal stems in the classical Semitic languages. PICSL, 70–91. Jerusalem.

1973 Hebrew syntax and the history of the Bible text. *ET* 84.124.

1975 *The Hebrew University Bible: The book of Isaiah*, Pt. 1, chs. 1–22. Jerusalem.

1976 *The Aleppo-Codex, edited, with critical apparatus*, limited facsimile edition. Jerusalem.

1978a The language of Targum Onkelos and the model of literary diglossia in Aramaic. *JNES* 37.169–79.

1978b לשונו של תרגום אונקלוס ומודל הדיגלוסיה הספרותית. *EI* 14.183–87.

1979 The Aleppo codex and the rise of the masoretic text. *BA* 42.145–63.

1980 תחביר העברית החדשה—הרהורים על דרכי מחקרה. *SHSL*, 189–201.

1981 *The Hebrew University Bible. The book of Isaiah*, Pt. 2, chs. 22–44. Jerusalem.

1983a Humanism and the rise of Hebraic studies: from Christian to Jewish renaissance. *WLSGF*, 691–96.

1983b שקיעים מתרגומי המקרא הארמיים, *Fragments of lost Targumim*, part 1. Ramat-Gan, Bar-Ilan University.

1985a מסורת פרשנית ומילונאית גזרונית (יח׳, ב, ו). *Sefer Avraham Even-Shoshan*, ed. B. Z. Luria, 295–300. Jerusalem.

1985b Problems of Semitic verbal stems: a review. *Bib Or* 42/3–4. 278–83.

1985c קורפוס, סוג ספרותי ושאלת אחדותה של העברית—היבטי המשגה והיבטי שיטה. מחקרים בלשון, ed. M. Bar-Asher, 57–73. Jerusalem, Department of Hebrew Language, Hebrew University.

Gottlieb, I. B.

1972 *Language understanding in Sifre-Deuteronomy: a study in language consciousness in rabbinic exegesis.* Doctoral dissertation, New York University. Ann Arbor, University Microfilms.

Grabbe, L.

1977 *Comparative philology and the text of Job: a study of methodology*. SBL dissertation series, Missoula, MT, Scholars Press.

Grande, B.

1969 הפונימה־ההברה בשפות השמיות, in הגות עברית באירופה, *Studies on Jewish themes by contemporary European scholars*, ed. by M. Zohori and A. Tartakover, 21–24. Tel Aviv, Yavneh.

1972 *Introduction to the comparative study of the Semitic languages* (Russian). Moscow.

Gray, J.

1965 *The legacy of Canaan*, Supplements to VT 5. Leiden, Brill.

Green, E.

1969 On accentual variants in the Slavic component of Yiddish. *FY* 3.216–39.

Greenberg, J.

1950 The patterning of root morphemes in Semitic. *Word* 6. 162–81.

1952 The Afro-Asiatic (Hamito-Semitic) present. *JAOS* 72.1–9.

1963 *Essays in linguistics*. University of Chicago Press, Phoenix books (originally published in 1957 as Viking Fund Publications in anthropology 24. Wenner-Gren Foundation for Anthropological Research).

Greenberg, M.

1965 *Introduction to Hebrew*. Englewood, NJ.

1970 Review of H. J. van Dijk, Ezekiel's prophecy on Tyre. *JAOS* 90.536–40.

Greenberg, Y.

1973 על לשונו של חיים הזז ביצירתו ״חתן־דמים״. Masters thesis, Hebrew University.

Greenfield, J. C.

1956 *The lexical status of Mishnaic Hebrew*. Doctoral dissertation, Yale University.

1964 Samaritan Hebrew and Aramaic in the work of Prof. Zev Ben-Hayyim. *Biblica* 45.261–68.

1967 Some aspects of treaty terminology in the Bible. *WCJS* 4, 1.117–19.

1968a Review of Wagner 1966. *JBL* 87.232–34.

1968b קווים דיאלקטיים בארמית הקדומה. *Leš* 32.359–68.

1969a Amurrite, Ugaritic and Canaanite. *PICSS*, 92–101. Jerusalem.

1969b The periphrastic imperative in Aramaic and Hebrew. *IEJ* 19.199–210.

1977 The prepositions *ʿad*/*ʿal* in Aramaic and Hebrew. *BSOAS* 40.371–72.
1978a The dialects of early Aramaic. *JNES* 37.93–99.
1978b Aramaic and its dialects, in *Jewish languages: theme and variation,* ed. by H. Paper, 29–43. Cambridge, MA, Association for Jewish Studies.
1978c The meaning of פחז. *Studies in Bible and ancient Near East, presented to Samuel E. Loewenstamm on his seventieth birthday*, 35–40.
1979 Early Aramaic poetry. *JANES* 11.45–51.
1981 *Aramaic studies and the Bible.* Supplement to VT 32, Congress volume, 110–30. Leiden.
1982 Some notes on the Arsham letters. *Irano-Judaica*, ed. by Saul Shaked, 4–11. Jerusalem, The Ben-Zvi Institute.

Greenfield, J. C. and Shaffer, A.
1982 הערות לכתובת הדו־לשונית מתל פח׳ריה. שנתון an annual for biblical and ancient near eastern studies, 5–6.119–29.

Greenfield, J. C. and Stone, M. E.
1979 Remarks on the Aramaic testament of Levi from the Geniza. *RB* 86.214–30.

Greenspahn, F. E.
1977 Hapax legomena *in biblical Hebrew.* Doctoral dissertation, Brandeis University. Ann Arbor, University Microfilms (reprinted by Scholars Press, Chico, CA, 1984).
1980 The number and distribution of *hapax legomena* in Biblical Hebrew. *VT* 30.8–19.

Greenstein, E.
1974 Two variations of grammatical parallelism in Canaanite poetry and their psycholinguistic background. *JANES* 6. 87–105.

Greenzweig, M.
1973 בחנים לשוניים בספר ״שבחי הבעל שם טוב״. Masters thesis, Hebrew University.

Greive, H.
1978 Die hebräische Grammatik Johannes Reuchlins (De rudimentis hebraicis). *ZAW* 90.395–409.

Grelot, P.
1962 La racine *hwn* en Dt. 1:41. *VT* 12.198–201.
1972 Deux tosephtas targoumiques inédites sur isaïe LXVI. *RB* 79.511–43.

Grintz, J. M.
1957 ספר יהודית. Jerusalem, Mossad Bialik.
1960 Hebrew as the spoken and written language in the last days of the second temple. *JBL* 79.32–47.
1972 מבואי מקרא. Tel Aviv, Yavneh.

1974–76 מונחים קדומים בתורת כהנים. *Leš* 39.5–20, 163–81; 40.5–32.

Gris, N.
1968 יידיש עלעמענטן אין עברית (Yiddish elements in Ivrit). *Zukunft* 73.568–72.

Gröndahl, F.
1967 *Die Personennamen der Texte aus Ugarit*. Rome.

Gropp, D. M. and Lewis, T. J.
1985 Notes on some problems in the Aramaic text of the Hadd-Yith^ci bilingual. *BASOR* 259.45–61.

Gross, Ben Zion
1941 קולות בעלי חיים בלשון העברית מתוך השוואה לשפות השמיות. Masters thesis, Hebrew University.
1971 משקלים בעלי סופיות —ון, —ו הכוללים שמות ממוצא שמי בלבד ומשמעויותיהם במקרא ובלשון חכמים. Doctoral dissertation, Hebrew University.

Gross, W.
1974 Die Herausführungsformel—zum Verhältniss von Formel und Syntax. *ZAW* 86.425–53.
1975 Das nicht substantivierte Partizip als Prädikat im Relativsatz hebräisches Prosa. *JNSL* 4.23–47.
1976 *Verbform + Funktion:* wayyiqtol *für die Gegenwart*. Ottilien, Eos Verlag.
1978 *Syntaktische Erscheinungen am Aufgang althebräischer Erzählungen: Hintergrund und Vordergrund*. Supplements to VT 32, Congress volume, 131–45.

Grossberg, D.
1977 *Nominalization in biblical Hebrew*. Doctoral dissertation, New York University. Ann Arbor, University Microfilms.

Grossfeld, B.
1972/1977 *A bibliography of Targum literature*, 2 vols. New York/Cincinnati.
1979 The relationship between Biblical Hebrew *BRḤ* and *NWS* and their corresponding Aramaic equivalents in the Targum—*ᶜRQ*, *ᵓPK*, *ᵓZL*: a preliminary study in Aramaic-Hebrew lexicography. *ZAW* 91.107–23.

Grossfeld, B. and Schiffman, L.
1978 *A critical commentary on Targum Neofiti I to Genesis*. New York, Ktav.

Gruber, M. I.
1980 *Aspects of nonverbal communication in the Ancient Near East*, Studia Pohl 12, 2 vols. Rome, Biblical Institute Press.

Guenther, A. R.
1977 *A diachronic study of Biblical Hebrew prose syntax: an analysis of the verbal clause in Jeremiah 37–45 and Esther 1–10*. Doctoral dissertation, University of Toronto.

Guggenheimer, E. and H.
1971–75 למילון התלמודי (הערות). *Leš* 35.207–10; 36.118–21; 37.23–25, 105–12; 39.59–62.
Guggenheim-Grünberg, F.
1954 The horse-dealer's language of Swiss Jews in Endingen and Legnau. *FY* 1.48–62.
1958 Zur Phonologie des Surbtaler Jiddischen. *Phonetica* 2.86–108.
1961 *Gallinger Jiddisch.* Göttingen, Vanderhoeck and Ruprecht.
1964 Überreste westjiddischer Dielekte in der Schweiz, im Elsass, und in Suddeutschland. *For Max Weinreich on his seventieth birthday*, 72–81. The Hague, Mouton.
1965 Place names in Swiss Yiddish: examples of the assimilatory power of a western Yiddish dialect. *FY* 2.147–57.
1969 Endinger Jiddisch. *FY* 3.8–15.
1973 *Jiddisch auf alemanischen Sprachgebiet.* Zurich.
1976 *Wörterbuch zur Surbtaler Jiddisch.* Zurich, Juria.
1980 Hebraisms in Swiss Yiddish: frequency and grammatical classes. *WCJS* 6, Division D, 1–5.
Guillaume, A.
1961, 1962, 1963, 1965a Hebrew and Arabic lexicography. *AN* 1.3–35; 2.5–35; 3 (1963 [1961–62]).1–10; 4 (1965a) [1963–64]).1–18.
1965b *Hebrew and Arabic lexicography.* Leiden, Brill.
Gumpertz, Y.
1942–43 הגיית אותיות בצרפת וגלגולה לאשכנז. *KLL*, Marcheshwan, 5703, 12–30.
1944–45 הערות פוניטיות לדקדוק נקדני טבריא. *Tarbiz* 16.210–30.
1953 מבטאי שפתנו. Jerusalem, Mossad Harav Kook.
1956 קריאת שמות בישראל. *Tarbiz* 25.340–53, 452–63.
Gundrey, R. H.
1964 The language milieu of first century Palestine, its bearing on the Gospel tradition. *JBL* 83.404–63.
Gunnel, A.
1980 *Determining the destiny:* PQD *in the Old Testament.* Doctoral dissertation, University of Uppsala. Coniectanea Biblica, Old Testament Series 16. Uppsala.
Gutman, A.
1974 הטעם בעברית מסורתית—גישה גנרטיבית. *HCL* 8.18–31.
Gutman, D.
1970 *The morphophonemics of biblical Hebrew.* Doctoral dissertation, University of Texas at Austin. Ann Arbor, University Microfilms.
1973 The phonology of massoretic Hebrew. *HCL* 7.1–52.

Guttel, H.
1971 Ladino. *EJ* 10.1342–51.

Habermann, A. M.
1947 שמואל הנגיד, דיואן. Tel Aviv.
1967 עתרת רננים. Piyyutim *and poems for Sabbath and holidays.* Jerusalem.
1968–69 עברית מפי פייטנים. *LLA* 20.35–38.
1970/1972a תולדות הפיוט והשירה. 2 vols. Ramat Gan.
1972b עיונים בשירה ובפיוט של ימי הביניים. Jerusalem.
1975 מלשונם העברית של יהודי אשכנז בימי הביניים. *LLA* 26.275–77.
1977 Bibliography of A. M. Habermann, compiled by Y. David, in שי להימן, *A. M. Habermann jubilee volume*, ed. by Z. Malachi, 1–36. Jerusalem, Rubin Mass.
1980 האם כתב יוסף פרל חיבורים ביידיש? *WCJS* 6, Division D, 57–61.

Hadas-Lebel, M.
1981 *Histoire de la langue hébraïque.* Paris.

Haephrati, J.
1981 *Disjunctive structure in the poetry of Saul Tschernichowsky, with special emphasis on his idylls* (Hebrew text). Doctoral dissertation, UCLA. Ann Arbor, University Microfilms.

Haines, B.
1966 *A palaeographical study of Aramaic inscriptions antedating 500 B.C.* Doctoral dissertation, Harvard Divinity School.

Haines, J. L.
1978 *The phonology of the Bovo-Bukh: a contribution to the history of east-Franconian Yiddish.* Doctoral dissertation, Columbia University. Ann Arbor, University Microfilms.

Hakak, L.
1974 *Modes of organization in modern free verse* (Hebrew text). Doctoral dissertation, UCLA. Ann Arbor, University Microfilms.

Hakkarainen, H. J.
1967–71 *Studien zum Cambridger Codex T-S 10.K.22, I-III.* Turku-Helsinki.

Halio-Torres, J.
1980 Writing the Spanish-Jewish dialect, in *Studies in Sephardic culture, The David N. Barocas memorial volume*, ed. by M. D. Angel, 95–106. New York, Sepher-Hermon.

Halkin, A. S.
1963 The medieval Jewish attitude toward Hebrew. *Texts and studies* 1, ed. by A. Altman, 233–48. Cambridge, MA.
1971 Judeo-Arabic literature. *EJ* 10.410–23.

1972–73 מולד. משה אבן עזרא ולשון השיר. 5.316–21.
1975 ספר העיונים והדיונים. Jerusalem, Meqise Nirdamim.

Hammershaimb, E.
1963 On the so-called infinitus absolutus in Hebrew. *Hebrew and Semitic studies presented to G. R. Driver*, ed. by D. Winton Thomas and W. D. McHardy, 85–103.

Hanani, P.
1975 דו־משמעויות תחביריות הנפתרות על־ידי הסמנטיקה. Masters thesis, Hebrew University.

Hanele, Y.
1971 חידושי העברית החדשה בתחום השם וחתואר וקשרם עם המשקלים. Masters thesis, Hebrew University.

Haneman, N. G.
1962 פרקים מתוך התצורה של הפועל של המשנה (מתוך כתב יד פארמה דה רוסי 138). Masters thesis, Hebrew University.
1965–66 תורת ההגה והצורות של לשון המשנה כפי שהיא מסורה במשניות כ״י פארמה. Proceedings of the Academy of the Hebrew Language. Jerusalem.
1968 שאילות מקראיות במקרא. *WCJS* 4, 2.95–96.
1972 תורת הצורות של לשון המשנה על פי מסורת כתבי־יד פארמה (דה רוסי 138) חלק א: הפועל. Doctoral dissertation, Hebrew University.
1974a למסורת הכתיב של כ״י הספרא המנוקד (כ״י רומי 66) *H. Yalon memorial volume*, Bar-Ilan departmental researches 2, 84–98. Jerusalem.
1974b האחדה ובידול בתולדות שני פעלים עבריים. *Archive of the dictionary of rabbinical literature* 2, ed. by M. Z. Kaddari, 24–30. Ramat Gan.
1975–76 על מלת־היחס ״בין״ במשנה ובמקרא. *Leš* 40.33–53.
1980a תורת הצורות של המשנה על פי מסורת כתב יד פרמה דה רוסי 138. University of Tel Aviv, (book form of 1972).
1980b על משמעות הביטוי ״בן כך וכך״ והדומים לו. *SHSL*, 103–9.

Hanson, K. C.
1984 *Alphabetic acrostics: a form critical study*. Doctoral dissertation, Claremont Graduate School. Ann Arbor, University Microfilms.

Hanson, R. S.
1963 *A paleographical study of Hebrew inscriptions of the Persian and Hellenistic periods*. Doctoral dissertation, Harvard University.

Haramati, S.
1963 הוראת העברית לאנאלפבתים. Doctoral dissertation, Hebrew University.

1968 הלכה ומעשה בהוראת הלשון העברית. Tel Aviv, Amichai.
1972 ניבים מספרים: תולדות ניבים וגלגולי משמעים. Jerusalem.
1973 דרכי הוראת העברית בתפוצות. Jerusalem, World Zionist Organization.
1976 יוסף הלוי: בלשן וחובב ציון. *LLA* 27.195–236.
1978 שלשה שקדמו לבן יהודה. Jerusalem, Yad Izkah Ben-Zvi Publications.
1979 ראשית החנוך העברי בארץ ותרומתו להחייאת הלשון. Jerusalem, Rubin Mass.
1981–82 יצחק אפשטיין איש הלשון. *LLA* 33/8–9 (328–29).195–248.
1982–83 ישראל חיים טביוב—תרומתו להחייאת הלשון ולהוחלתה בחפוצות. *LLA* 34/6–7 (336–37; entire fascicle).

Haran, M.
1972 The graded numerical sequence and the phenomenon of "automatism" in biblical poetry. VT Supplements 22 (Congress volume, Uppsala), 238–67. Leiden, Brill.

Harkavy, Z.
1972–73 על מבטאם העברי של עולי גרוזיה. *LLA* 24.168–69.

Harrington, D. J., S.J.
1980 Research on the Jewish Pseudepigrapha during the 1970s. *CBQ* 42.147–59.

Harris, T. K.
1979 *The prognosis for Judeo-Spanish: its description, present status, survival and decline, with implications for the study of language death in general.* Doctoral dissertation, Georgetown University. Ann Arbor, University Microfilms.

Harris, Z.
1936 *A grammar of the Phoenician Language.* New Haven, American Oriental Society.
1939 *Development of the Canaanite dialects*, AOS 16. New Haven, American Oriental Society.
1941 Linguistic structure of Hebrew. *JAOS* 61.143–67.
1948 Componential analysis of a Hebrew paradigm. *Language* 24.87–91.
1951 *Methods in structural linguistics.* Reprinted 1969 as *Structural linguistics*, Phoenix Books, University of Chicago.

Harviainen, T.
1977 On the vocalism of the closed unstressed syllables in Hebrew. *StudOr* 48/1. Helsinki.

Har Zahav, Z.
1930 לשון דורנו. Tel Aviv.
1951–56 דקדוק הלשון העברית, 6 vols. Tel Aviv.

Hasel, G. F.
1973 Semantic values of derivatives of the Hebrew root *š*ʾ*r*. *Andrews University Seminary Studies*. 11.152–69.
Hatab, G.
1977 השימושים השונים של מתאר־המצב ותרומתם לפתרון הדו־משמעות. Masters thesis, Hebrew University.
Hayman, L.
1980 *The meaning of the verb* Hošiaᶜ *in the Old Testament*. Doctoral dissertation, Claremont Graduate School. Ann Arbor, University Microfilms.
Hayon, Y.
1969 *Relativization in Hebrew: a transformational approach*. Doctoral dissertation, The University of Texas at Austin. Ann Arbor, University Microfilms.
1971a Relative clauses with verbal predicates. *HCL* 3.9–65.
1971b Relative clauses with non-verbal predicates. *HCL* 4.7–67.
1972 Having and being in Modern Hebrew. *HCL* 5.10–23 (English section).
1973 *Relativization in Hebrew*. The Hague, Mouton.
Hazan, E.
1984 רובדי הלשון בשירת רבי דוד בן אהרן חסין. *Massorot* 1.19–39.
Healy, J. F.
1976 Syriac *NṢR*, Ugaritic *NṢR*, Hebrew *NṢR* II, Akkadian *NṢR* II. *VT* 26.429–37.
Heckelman, Y.
1974 לשונם של חסידים כפי שהיא משתקפת ב״מגלה טמירין״ ליוסף פרל. Masters thesis, Hebrew University.
Heide, A. Van Der
1974 A biblical fragment with Palestinian-Tiberian ('Pseudo-Ben Naftali') punctuation in the Leyden University Library (Hebr. 259-1). *Museon* 87.415–23. 2 pls.
Heilman, S. C.
1981 Sounds of modern Orthodoxy: the language of Talmud study, in J. A. Fishman, ed., 1981a, 227–53. The Hague, Mouton.
1983 *The People of the Book*. Chicago/London, University of Chicago Press.
Heilprin, Y.
1946–47 לקט מלים מתחום־התרבות של היהדות האשכנזית. *Leš* 15.190–97.
Heinen, K.
1971 *Das Gebet im alten Testament: Eine exegetisch-theologische Untersuchung zur hebräischen Gebetsterminologie*. Rome, Pontificia Universitas Gregoriana.

Held, M.
1953a סתומה מקראית ומקבילתה באוגריתית (שרש "שרד" במקרא ובכתבי אוגרית). *EI* 3.101–3.
1953b עוד זוגות מלים מקבילות במקרא ובכתבי אוגרית. *Leš* 18.14–60.
1959 *MḪṢ/*MḪŠ* in Ugaritic and other Semitic languages. *JAOS* 79.169–76.
1961 A faithful lover in an Old Babylonian dialogue. *JCS* 15.1–26.
1962 The *YQTL-QTL* (*QTL-YQTL*) sequence of identical verbs in Biblical Hebrew and in Ugaritic. *Studies and essays in honor of Abraham A. Neuman*, ed. by M. Ben-Horin, B. Weinryb and S. Zeitlin, 281–90. Philadelphia.
1965a The action-result (factitive-passive) sequence of identical verbs in Biblical Hebrew and Ugaritic. *JBL* 84.272–82.
1965b Studies in comparative Semitic lexicography. *B. Landsberger Festschrift*. AS 16.395–406.
1968 The root *ZBL/SBL* in Akkadian, Ugaritic and Biblical Hebrew. *JAOS* 88.90–96.
1970–71 Studies in biblical homonyms in the light of Akkadian. *JANES* 3.46–55.
1973 Pits and pitfalls in Akkadian and Biblical Hebrew. *JANES* 5.173–90.
1974 Hebrew *maᶜgal*: a study in lexical parallelism. *JANES* 6.107–16.
1979 On terms for deportation in the Old Babylonian royal inscriptions with special reference to Yahdunlim. *JANES* 11.53–62.

Helmann, L.
1949 *Camito-Semitico e indoeuropeo*. Bologna.

Heltzer, M. and Ohana, M.
1978 *The extra-biblical tradition of Hebrew personal names from the First Temple period to the end of the Talmudic period.* Haifa.

Hermon, G.
1981 *Non-nominative subject constructions in the government and binding framework*. Doctoral dissertation, University of Illinois. Ann Arbor, University Microfilms.

Herr, L. G.
1977 *The scripts of ancient Northwest Semitic seals.* Missoula, MT, Scholars Press.

Herzberg, W.
1979 *Polysemy in the Hebrew Bible.* Doctoral dissertation, New York University.

Herzog, M. I.
1964 Channels of systematic extinction in Yiddish dialects. *For Max Weinreich on his seventieth birthday*, 93–107. The Hague, Mouton.
1965a The Yiddish language in northern Poland. Publication 37 of the Indiana University Research Center in Anthropology, Folklore and Linguistics = *IJAL* 31/2.i–xxix; 1–323. The Hague, Mouton.
1965b Review of J. Jofen, *A linguistic atlas of eastern European Yiddish*, New York, 1964. *Word* 21.154–59.
1969 Yiddish in the Ukraine: isoglosses and historical inferences. *FY* 3.58–81.
1978 Yiddish, in H. Paper, ed., *Jewish languages, theme and variation*, 47–58. Cambridge, MA, Association for Jewish Studies.

Herzog, M. I., Ravid, W. and Weinreich, U., eds.
1969 *The field of Yiddish* 3, London, The Hague, Paris, Mouton (abbreviated *FY* 3).

Herzog, M. I., Kirshenblatt-Gimblett, B., Miron, D. and Wisse, R., eds.
1980 *The field of Yiddish* 4. Philadelphia, Institute for the Study of Human Issues (abbreviated *FY* 4).

Hesbacher, P. and Fishman, J. A.
1965 Language loyalty: its functions and concomitants in two bilingual communities. *Lingua* 13.145–65.

Hestrin, R., and Dayyagi-Mendeles, M.
1978 חותמות מימי בית ראשון. Jerusalem, Israel Museum.

Hestrin, R., Yisraeli, Y., Meshorer, Y. and Eytan, E., eds.
1972 כתובות מספרות, *Inscriptions reveal*, Hebrew and English editions. Jerusalem, Israel Museum.

Hetzron, R.
1974 La division des langues sémitiques. *ACILCS*, 181–94.

Hill, A. E. III.
1981 *The book of Malachi: its place in post-exilic chronology linguistically reconsidered.* Doctoral dissertation, University of Michigan. Ann Arbor, University Microfilms.

Hill, D.
1967 *Greek words and Hebrew meanings.* Cambridge University Press.

Hills, S.
1954 *A semantic and conceptual study of the root* KPR *in Hebrew Old Testament with special reference to Akkadian* kuppuru. Doctoral dissertation, Johns Hopkins University.

Hintze, R.
1951 Zur hamitosemitischen Wortvergleichung. *ZPAS* 5.65–87.

Hirsch, R.
1951 A study of some aspects of a Judeo-Spanish dialect spoken by a New York Sephardic family. Doctoral dissertation, University of Michigan.

Hirschberg, H.
1961 Some additional Arabic etymologies in Old Testament lexicography. *VT* 11.373–85.

Hirschfeld, H.
1926 *Literary history of Hebrew grammarians and lexicographers.* Oxford.
1927 Kitab al Khazari *by Judah Halevi*, translated with introduction. New York, Bernard S. Richards (first published New York, 1906, reprinted 1964, New York, Schocken).

Hodge, C.
1954 Review of F. R. Blake 1951a. *Language* 30.177–80.
1971 *Afroasiatic, a survey.* The Hague and Paris, Mouton.

Hoffman, Y.
1982 The root *QRB* as a legal term. *JNSL* 10.67–73.
1986 לשונו של המקור הכהני ושאלת זמן חיבורו. *Teᶜudah* 4, ed. by M. A. Friedman and M. Gil, 13–22. Tel Aviv University.

Hofman, J.
1974a The prediction of success in language planning. The case of chemists in Israel. *Linguistics* 120.39–65.
1974b Predicting the use of Hebrew terms among Israeli psychologists. *Linguistics* 136.53–65.

Hofman, J. and Fisherman, H.
1981 Language shift and maintenance in Israel. *IMR*, 204–26.

Hoftijzer, J.
1965 Remarks concerning the use of the particle *ʾt* in classical Hebrew. *OTS* 14.1–99. Leiden, Brill.
1973 The nominal clause reconsidered. *VT* 23.446–510 (review article of Andersen 1970a).
1974 *Verbale vragen: Rede uitgesprochen bij de aanvarding van het ambt van gewoon hooglerar in het Hebreeuws . . . aan de Rijksuniversiteit te Leiden.* Leiden, Brill (deals with the problem of the verb in Biblical Hebrew).
1981 *A search for method: a study in the syntactic use of the* h-locale *in classical Hebrew* (with H. R. van Laan and N. P. de Koo). Leiden.
1985 *The function and use of the imperfect forms with* nun paragogicum *in classical Hebrew.* Assen, Van Gorcum.

Hoftijzer, J. and Kooij, G. Van Der, eds.
1976 *Aramaic texts from Deir Alla.* Leiden, Brill.
Holladay, W.
1958 *The root* šubh *in the Old Testament.* Leiden, Brill.
Holm-Nielsen, S.
1960 Hodayot-*psalms from Qumran.* Leiden, Brill.
Horowitz (Grebel), H.
1944 התפתחות שלש שיטות הניקוד, הארץ־ישראלית, הבבלית והטברנית. Masters thesis, Hebrew University.
Hospers, J. H.
1966 A hundred years of Semitic comparative linguistics. *Studia biblica et Semitica Theodoro Christiani Vriezen*, 137–51. H. Vageningen, Veenman and Zonen N.V.
1973/1974 *A basic bibliography for the study of the Semitic languages*, 2 vols. Leiden, Brill.
1978 Ed. *General linguistics and the teaching of dead Hamito-Semitic languages* (Groningen symposium, 7-8 Nov., 1975). Leiden, Brill.
Hoter-Yishai, R.
1944 מחקרים לשוניים אצל הרמב״ן. Masters thesis, Hebrew University.
Howard, G.
1982 Revision toward the Hebrew in the Septuagint text of Amos. *EI* 16.125*–33*.
Howard, J. A.
1972 *Hebrew-German and early Yiddish literature.* Doctoral dissertation, University of Illinois at Urbana.
Hrushovski, B.
1954 On free rhythms in Yiddish poetry. *FY* 1.219–66.
1964 The creation of accented iambs in European poetry and their first employment in a Yiddish romance in Italy (1508–9). *For Max Weinreich on his seventieth birthday*, 108–46. The Hague, Mouton.
1965 לשון פיגורטיבית בספרות: מקראה וביבליוגרפיה. Jerusalem.
1968 ׳ריתמוס הרחבות׳: הלכה ומעשה בשירתו האקספרסיוניסטית של אורי צבי גרינברג. הספרות 1.176–205.
Hudson, A. J.
1977 *Language attitudes in relation to varieties of Jewish identification.* Doctoral dissertation, Yeshiva University. Ann Arbor, University Microfilms.
1981 (Hudson-Edwards). Knowledge, use and evaluation of Yiddish and Hebrew among American Jewish college students, in J. A. Fishman, ed., 1981a.635–52.

Huesman, J.
1955 *The infinitive absolute in Biblical Hebrew and related dialects.* Doctoral dissertation, Johns Hopkins University. Ann Arbor, University Microfilms.
1956 The infinitive absolute and *waw* + perfect problems. *Biblica* 37.271–95, 410–34.

Huffmon, H.
1965 *Amorite personal names in the Mari texts.* Baltimore, Johns Hopkins.

Hughes, J.
1970 Another look at the Hebrew tenses. *JNES* 29.12–24.

Hulst, A. R.
1960 *Old Testament translation problems.* Leiden, Brill.

Hummel, H.
1955 *Enclytic 'mem' in early Northwest Semitic with special reference to Hebrew.* Doctoral dissertation, Johns Hopkins University.
1957 Enclytic 'mem' in early Northwest Semitic. *JBL* 76.85–107.

Hupper, W. G.
1977 *Bibliography of periodical literature on Semitic grammar and syntax.* Private printing, typescript copy.

Hurvitz, A.
1961 ניתוח בלשני של לשון השירה במקרא. Masters thesis, Hebrew University.
1965 Observations on the language of the third apocryphal psalms from Qumran. *RQ* 5.225–32.
1967a בחנים לשוניים לזיהוי מזמורים מאוחרים בספר תהילים. Doctoral dissertation, Hebrew University.
1967b לשונו וזמנו של מזמור קנ"א מקומראן. *Sefer Sukenik*, 82–87. Jerusalem.
1967c The usage of *šēš* and *bûṣ* in the Bible and its implications for the date of P. *HTR* 60.117–21.
1968 The chronological significance of Aramaisms in Biblical Hebrew. *IEJ* 18.234–40.
1971 המקרא ותולדות ישראל ."כיאזמוס דיאכרוני" בעברית המקראית, Studies in Bible and Jewish History dedicated to the memory of Jacob Liver, ed. by B. Uffenheimer, 248–55. Tel Aviv University.
1972 בין לשון ללשון. Jerusalem, Mossad Bialik (based on 1967a).
1974a The date of the prose tale of Job linguistically reconsidered. *HTR* 67.17–34.
1974b The evidence of language in dating the Priestly Code; a linguistic study in technical idioms and terminology. *RB* 81.24–56.

1982a A linguistic study of the relationship between the priestly source and the book of Ezekiel. *CRB* 20. Paris.

1982b ליקוטי "תרביץ"—מיקראה בחקר לשון המקרא. Jerusalem, Magnes Press.

1982c עיונים בלשונו של המקור הכהני—לשימושן של "שאר" ו"שכר" בספרי ויקרא ובמדבר. *Teʿudah* 2, *Bible studies in memoriam Y. M. Grintz*, ed. B. Uffenheimer, 287–97. Tel Aviv University.

1983a מחידושי לשונו של ספר יחזקאל—"מפה ומפה". *ML* 173–76.

1983b The language of the priestly source and its historical setting—the case for an early date. *WCJS* 8, Bible and language, 83–94. Jerusalem.

Hurvitz, M.

1945 לעזים רומיים ויווניים בקטעי התלמוד והמדרש מן הגניזה. Masters thesis, Hebrew University.

Hutterer, C. J.

1965 The phonology of Budapest Yiddish. *FY* 2.116–45.

1969 Theoretical and practical problems of western Yiddish dialectology. *FY* 3.1–7.

Ilani, N.

1977 הרחבת קבוצות הבחירה של פעלים מקראיים בלשון ימינו. Masters thesis, Bar-Ilan University.

1982 הרחבת קבוצות הבחירה של פעלים מקראיים בלשון ימינו. *HCL* 19.5–17.

Ish-Shalom, H.

1949 המליצה המקראית בשירת ר' שמואל הנגיד. Masters thesis, Hebrew University.

Isserlin, B. S. J.

1971 Ancient Hebrew pronunciation types in the light of personal and place names in Greek and Latin transcriptions. *PICO* 21, 100–101. Wiesbaden.

Izreʾel, S.

1978 The Gezer letters of the El Amarna archive; linguistic analysis. *IOS* 8.13–90.

1978–79 "את" ו"אל" בלשון המקרא. שנתון, an annual for biblical and ancient near eastern studies 3.204–12.

1986 ההיתה תחיית העברית נס? *WCJS* 9, Division D, 77–84. Jerusalem.

Jackson, K.

1980 *The Ammonite language of the iron age.* Doctoral dissertation, University of Michigan. Ann Arbor, University Microfilms.

1983 *The Ammonite language of the iron age.* Harvard Semitic Monographs. Chico, CA, Scholars Press (revised book form of 1980 dissertation).

Jacobowitz, J.

1968 לשון משותפת. Jerusalem.

Janssens, G.

1982 *Studies in Hebrew historical linguistics based on Origen's Secunda.* Orientalia Gandensis 9. Leuven.

Japhet, S.

1966–67 חילופי שרשי הפועל בטקסטים המקבילים בספר דברי הימים. *Leš* 31.165–79, 261–79, with marginal notes by E. Y. Kutscher, *ibid.*, 280–82.

1968 The supposed common authorship of Chronicles and Ezra-Nehemiah investigated anew. *VT* 18.330–71.

Jarden, D.

1949–50 עיוני לשון ומליצה במחברות עמנואל. *Leš* 17.12–18, 145–72.

1954 לשון המחברות של עמנואל הרומי. Doctoral dissertation, Hebrew University.

1956 מדרש לשון, ניבים ופתגמים בגלגוליהם. Jerusalem, Kiryath Sepher.

1966 דיואן שמואל הנגיד, בן תהלים. Jerusalem, Hebrew Union College Press.

1967 שפוני שירה. Medieval liturgical and secular poetry. Jerusalem, privately published.

1967–75 מלשונו של ר׳ שלמה אבן גבירול. *LLA* 19.218–20; 20.12–16; 21.28–36; 26.233–36.

1971/1973 שירי הקודש לרבי שלמה אבן גבירול. 2 vols. Jerusalem.

1975/1976 שירי החול לרבי שלמה אבן גבירול. 2 vols. Jerusalem.

Jean, C. and Hoftijzer, J.

1965 *Dictionnaire des inscriptions sémitiques.* Leiden, Brill.

Jeffrey, A.

1962 Hebrew language. *The interpreters dictionary of the Bible*, 2.553–60. Nashville.

Jellicoe, S.

1968 *The Septuagint and modern study.* Oxford University Press; reprinted, Eisenbrauns, 1978.

Jenni, E.

1967 Faktitiv und Kausativ um *ʾbd* 'zugrunde gehen'. VT supplement 16.143–57.

1968 *Das hebräische* Piʿel. Zurich.

1973 Zur Funktion der Reflexiv-Passiven Stammformen im Biblisch-Hebräischen. *WCJS* 5, 4.61–70.

1985 Hebräistische Neuerscheinung. *Theologische Rundschau* 50. 313–26 (survey of current developments).

Jochnowitz, G.

1968 Bilingualism and dialect mixture among Lubavitcher Hasidic children. *American speech* 43.182–200.

1970 Review of M. Herzog, W. Ravid and U. Weinreich, eds., 1969. *Language* 46.938–40.

1974 Parole di origine romanza ed hebraica en Giudeo-Italiano. *RMI* 40.212–19.

1978 Judeo-Romance languages, in *Jewish languages: theme and variation*, ed. by H. Paper, 65–73. Cambridge, MA, Association for Jewish Studies.

Joel, B. I.

1962–63 כתר משנת ה׳ אלפים ועשרים לב״ע. *KS* 38.122–32.

Joel, Y.

1971 תחביר ספר מלחמות ה׳ לרבי לוי בן גרשון Doctoral dissertation, Hebrew University.

Jofen, J.

1953 *The dialectical makeup of East European Yiddish: phonological and lexicological criteria.* Doctoral dissertation, Columbia University (resumé in *YS* 13 [1953], 157–60).

1964 *The linguistic atlas of Eastern European Yiddish.* New York.

Joffe, J.

1954 Dating the origin of Yiddish dialects. *FY* 1.102–21.

Joffe, J. and Mark, Y.

1961ff. *Comprehensive dictionary of the Yiddish language.* New York (being continued under the direction of M. Herzog [New York] and Ch. Shmeruk [Jerusalem]).

Jones, G. L.

1983 *The discovery of Hebrew in Tudor England: a third language.* Manchester University Press.

Jonge, M. de

1978 *The testaments of the twelve patriarchs.* Leiden, Brill.

Jongeling, B.

1971 *A classified bibliography of the finds in the desert of Judah.* Leiden, Brill.

Jouön, P.

1923 *Grammaire de l'hébreu biblique.* Rome (reprinted 1965).

1930 L'Évangile de notre seigneur Jésus-Christ. Paris.

Kaddari, M. Z.

1950 חקירות בלשון הארמית של הזוהר—הפועל והכינויים. Masters thesis, Hebrew University.

1960–61 לבדיקת המטפורה בעברית של ימינו. *Leš* 25.134–44.

1963–64 פרקי תחביר וסימנטיקה עבריים מלפני מאה שנה. *Leš* 27–28. 96–110.
1964–65a על הרכבי שם תואר בעברית של ימינו. *LLA* 16.195–206.
1964–65b שדות סמנטיים בלשון המגילות הגנוזות *Leš* 29.226–37.
1967–68 התקבולת המקראית מבחינה סימנטית. *Leš* 32.37–45.
1968a החיוב בלשון המגילות הגנוזות. Jerusalem, Kiryath Sepher.
1968b זיהוי יחידות סימנטיות. *WCJS* 4, 2.135–43.
1969a לדמותו של שד״ל כבלשן. *Bar Ilan volume in humanities and social sciences*, Decennial volume 2, 78–97. Jerusalem.
1969b Construct state and *di*-phrases in Imperial Aramaic. *PICSS*, 102–15. Jerusalem.
1970a מירושת לשון ימי הבינים. Bar-Ilan University, research monographs 7. Tel Aviv, Dvir.
1970b יחידות סימנטיות מורכבות בעברית הבתר־מקראית. Annual of Bar-Ilan University 7–8.204–10. Ramat Gan.
1971 מחקר תרגום אונקלוס בימינו: מעמד המחקר. *Studies in Bible and Jewish history dedicated to the memory of Jacob Liver*, ed. by B. Uffenheimer, 341–74. Tel Aviv University.
1972 פועל־יוצא המביע את גרימת פועל העומד בעברית המודרנית. ביקורת ופרשנות 2–3.103–6. Bar-Ilan University.
1973 פרקים בתחביר העברית המקראית. *WCJS* 5, 4.223–32.
1974a בדיקה תחבירית־סימנטית לקביעת גבולותיהן של תקופות בלשון העברית (מכל מקום). *H. Yalon memorial volume*, Bar-Ilan departmental researches 2, 471–98.
1974b מה־ל־צ(ירוף) ש(מני) הקודם למשפט בלשון חכמים. *Archive of the new dictionary of rabbinical literature* 2, ed. by M. Z. Kaddari, 85–95. Ramat Gan (see also *WCJS* 6 1973, published 1977, 1.171–81).
1975 סקירה על חקר הסמנטיקה והתחומים הסמוכים לה בעברית המודרנית. ביקורת ופרשנות 7–8.127–31. Bar-Ilan University.
1976 פרשיות בתחביר לשון המקרא. Ramat Gan.
1977 שנתון. ביטוי המשאלה מי־יתן, an annual for biblical and ancient near eastern studies 2.189–95.
1977–78 תיאור תחבירי־סימאנטי של ״מנע״ בלשון המקרא. *BM* 23(72). 86–92.
1978a ביקורת ופרשנות .עיון בתולדות הלשון העברית המודרנית 11–12. 5–17. Bar-Ilan University.
1978b המקור הנטוי כתיאור זמן בלשון המקרא. *EI* 14.132–36.
1978c נתפעל כבינוני בלשון העברית (השו״ת)—מה טיבו? *Leš* 42.190–202.
1978d ודאי (בודאי) בלשון חכמים. *Studies in Bible and the ancient near east presented to Samuel E. Loewenstamm on his seventieth birthday*, 2.383–95. Jerusalem.

1978–79 על הפועל היה בלשון המקרא. *Bar-Ilan* 16–17.112–25.
1980a ש״י עגנון רב סגנון. Bar-Ilan University.
1980b תיאור תחבירי־סמאנטי של ״מצא״ בלשון המקרא. *SHSL*, 18–25.
1981 לניתוח סגנוני של הדו־שיח ב״כיסוי הדם״ לש״י עגנון. עיונים בבלשנות ובסמיוטיקה, 152–70. Jerusalem.
1982 יחס הוויתור בלשון המקרה. *Te*ᶜ*udah* 2, Bible studies in memoriam Y. M. Grintz, ed. B. Uffenheimer, 325–48. Tel Aviv University.
1983a The existential verb *hwh* in Imperial Aramaic. *Arameans, Aramaic and the Aramaic literary tradition*, ed. by M. Sokoloff, 43–46. Bar-Ilan University.
1983b לתחביר הפועל היה בלשון המקרא. *ML* 459–72.
1984 Hebrew *mikol-makom*, *mamash-* and the *nitpa*ᶜ*el* in Responsa literature (with reference to probable or possible Yiddish influence on Hebrew). *JLR* 4.30–33.
1985a ממש בלשון השאלות-והתשובות. *Sefer Avraham Even-Shoshan*, ed. B. Z. Luria, 229–48. Jerusalem.
1985b עיון בתחביר דיאכרוני: מלת השלילה אל. מחקרים בלשון, ed. M. Bar-Asher, 197–210. Jerusalem, Department of Hebrew Language, Hebrew University.

Kagan, E.
1963–64 עיון בפוניטיקה של שלונסקי. *Tarbiz* 34.78–93.
1966–67 הפוניטיקה של השווא נע בשירת ימינו. *Tarbiz* 36.187–98.
1968–69 המפסיק בטור המשקל. *LLA* 20/8 (199).
1971–72 מכלי אל כלי. *Leš* 36.190–202, 268–81.
1976 מגלגולי משקל ההטעמות בשירתנו, חקר ועיון. 107–117.

Kahana, Y. Z.
1946–47 השפעה חיצונית באוצר המלים של ספרות התשובות. *Leš* 15. 198–203.

Kahle, P.
1902 *Der massoretische Text des alten Testaments nach der Überlieferung der babylonische Juden.* Leipzig, J. C. Hinrichs.
1913 *Masoreten des Ostens.* BWAT 15. Leipzig.
1927/1930 *Masoreten des Westens.* BWAT 33, 2 vols. Leipzig.
1928 Die hebräischen Bibelhandschriften aus Babylonien. *ZAW* 46.113–37, pls. 1–70.
1950 Treatise on the oldest manuscripts of the Bible, in L. Goldschmidt, *The earliest editions of the Hebrew Bible.* New York, Aldus Book Co.
1951a The age of the scrolls. *VT* 1.38–48.
1951b The Hebrew Ben Asher Mss. *VT* 1.161–65.
1951c *Die hebräischen Handschriften aus der Höhle.* Stuttgart, W. Kohlhammer.

1959 *The Cairo Geniza*, 2nd ed. Oxford.
1960 Die Aussprache des Hebräischen in Palästina vor der Zeit der tiberischen Masoreten. *VT* 10.375–85.
1961a Pre-masoretic Hebrew. *ALUOS* 2.6–10. Leiden, Brill.
1961b *Der hebräische Bibeltext seit Franz Delitzsch*. Stuttgart.
1962 Pre-masoretic Hebrew. *Textus* 2.1–7.

Kahle, P. and Weinberger, J.
1935 The Mishna text in Babylonia. *HUCA* 10.185–222.

Kamchi, J. D.
1969 *The adjective in Hebrew: an analysis of its morphology and function*. Doctoral dissertation, The University of London.
1973 The root *ḥlq* in the Bible. *VT* 23.235–39.

Kantor, H.
1980 ארגטיבציה של פעלים בלשון־הביניים של לומדי עברית. *HCL* 16.51–58.
1983 בעיות סימנטיות בהנחלת הלשון בשלב מתקדם. *Sefer David Gross*, ed. by S. Kodesh, 214–30. Jerusalem, Hamatmid.

Kantorowitz, S.
n.d. השפה העברית לכל סגנוניה. 2 vols. Warsaw (pre-World War II).

Kaplan, M. M.
1981 *The lion in the Hebrew Bible: a study of a biblical metaphor*. Doctoral dissertation, Brandeis University. Ann Arbor, University Microfilms.

Kara, Y.
1974 דקדוק לשון הארמית בבלית על פי כתב יד אנלאו 271 למסכת פסחים: הכתיב והפועל בגזרת השלמים. Masters thesis, Hebrew University.
1979 מסורות תימניות בלשון חכמים על פי כתב יד מן המאה השש עשרה. *Leš* 44.24–42.
1980 The way of preserving the Yemenite tradition. *WCJS* 6, Division D, 175–82. Jerusalem.
1982 לשונם הארמית של כתבי־היד התימניים של התלמוד הבבלי: הכתיב, תורת ההגה והפועל. Doctoral dissertation, Hebrew University.
1983 כתבי היד התימנים של התלמוד הבבלי: מחקרים בלשונם הארמית, הכתיב, תורת ההגה והפועל. *PHULTP* 10. Jerusalem.
1986 הערות לחקר הערבית שבפי יהודי תימן. *WCJS* 9, Division D, 123–30.

Kasher, A.
1969 פסוקי רמיזה—הערות ורמזים לוגיים. *Bar-Ilan volume in humanities and social sciences*. Decennial volume 2.129–51. Jerusalem.
1971 המעמד הלוגי של הפסוקים תלויי ההקשר. Doctoral dissertation, Hebrew University.

1974 האם לכל פסוק יש חוטר ביצוע עמוק?: סוגיה בפרגמטיקה של לשון ימינו ושל לשון המשנה. *H. Yalon memorial volume*, Bar-Ilan departmental researches 2.164–211. Jerusalem.

1976 Three notes on the pre-formative analysis, in P. Cole, ed., *Studies in Modern Hebrew syntax and semantics*, 183–91. Amsterdam.

1979–80 with I. Ibn Zohar, U. Ornan, E. Eytan and E. Rubinstein. עברית קדומה ועברית בת ימינו־לשון אחת—שיח בלשנים. *LLA* 31.107–36.

Kasher, R.

1973 תוספתא תרגומית לנביאים. Masters thesis, Bar-Ilan University.

Kashtan, M.

1949 שמואל דוד לוצאטו (שד"ל) כבלשן. Masters thesis, Hebrew University.

Katchen, A. L.

1979 *Christian Hebraists and Dutch Rabbis: seventeenth-century apologetics and the study of Maimonides' "Mishneh Torah.* Doctoral dissertation, Harvard University. Ann Arbor, University Microfilms (book, 1984, Harvard University Center for Jewish Studies).

Katsh, A. I.

1964 יגל חזון. Jerusalem.

1970 גנזי משנה. Jerusalem, Mossad Harav Kook.

1975–77 גנזי תלמוד בבלי, 2 vols. Jerusalem.

1977 *The biblical heritage of American democracy.* New York, Ktav.

Katz, D.

1978 *Genetic notes on Netherlandic Yiddish vocalism.* Unpublished paper, Department of Linguistics, Columbia University.

1980a Ber Borokhov, pioneer of Yiddish linguistics. *Jewish Frontier* 47.10–14.

1980b The wavering Yiddish segolate: a problem of sociolinguistic reconstruction. *IJSL* 24, *Sociology of Yiddish*, ed. by J. A. Fishman, 5–27.

Katz, E.

1963 *Six Germano-Judaic poems from the Cairo Geniza.* Doctoral dissertation, UCLA. Ann Arbor, University Microfilms.

1968 Review of *FY* 1, U. Weinreich, ed., 1965. *Language* 44. 137–41.

Katz, I.

1980 Stylized performances of a Judeo-Spanish traditional ballad. *Studies in Jewish folklore*, ed. by F. Talmage, 181–200. Cambridge, MA, Association for Jewish Studies (contains references to collections of Sephardic ballads).

Katz, K.
1968 קריאת המשנה במסורת יהודי ליטא: הפונולוגיה. Masters thesis, Hebrew University.
1975 מסורת הקריאה במקרא ובמשנה של קהילת ג׳רבה. Doctoral dissertation, Hebrew University.
1977 מסורת הקריאה של יהודי ג׳רבה במקרא ובמשנה. *PHULTP* 2, Jerusalem.
1980 Towards a description of the traditional pronunciation of the Jewish community of Djerba. *WCJS* 6, Division D, 115–19.
1981 מסורת הלשון העברית של יהודי ארם־צובא (חלב) בקריאת המקרא והמשנה: תורת ההגה. *PHULTP* 7. Jerusalem.
1983–84 הפיעל הקל במסורותיהן של שלוש עדות ספרדיות. *Leš* 48–49. 53–59.
Katzenelson, K.
1960 משבר העברית המודרנית. Tel Aviv, Anakh.
Kaufman, I.
1966 *The Samaritan ostraca, a study in ancient Hebrew palaeography.* Doctoral dissertation, Harvard University.
Kaufman, S. A.
1970 *The Akkadian influence in Aramaic and the development of the Aramaic.* Doctoral dissertation, Yale University. Ann Arbor, University Microfilms, 1971.
1974 *The Akkadian influence on Aramaic.* AS 19. Chicago.
1982 Reflections on the Assyrian-Aramaic bilingual from Tell Fakhariyah. *Maarav* 3.137–75.
1983 The history of Aramaic vowel reduction. *Arameans, Aramaic and the Aramaic literary tradition*, ed. by M. Sokoloff, 47–55. Ramat Gan, Bar-Ilan University.
1984 On vowel reduction in Aramaic. *JAOS* 104.87–95.
Kaye, A.
1980 Spinoza as linguist. *HAR* 4.107–25.
Kedar (Kopstein), B.
1977 Semantic aspects of the pattern *Qôṭēl. HAR* 1.155–76.
1981 *Biblische Semantik.* Stuttgart.
1982 משמעויות בנין ההתפעל במקרא והשתקפותן בתרגומים. *WCJS* 8, Division D, Hebrew section, 1–5. Jerusalem.
Kessler, M.
1973 Rhetoric in Jeremiah 50 and 51. *Semitica* 3.18–33.
Khanjian, J.
1974 *Wisdom in Ugarit and in the ancient Near East, with particular emphasis on Old Testament wisdom literature.* Doctoral dissertation, Claremont Graduate School. Ann Arbor, University Microfilms.

Khayyat, S.

1968 *Majmuʿat al-ʾAmthal al-ʿAmmiyyah, Harf Alif* (Arabic; A book of Iraqi Jewish proverbs). Jerusalem.

1972 המשפחה ופתגמיהם של יהודי בבל. *Folklore research center studies* 3.77–143.

1975 *Arabic folk songs among Iraqi Jews.* Doctoral dissertation, Dropsie University.

1979 Unpublished Judaeo-Iraqi folk songs from the manuscripts in the Sassoon collection. *JQR* 70.73–95.

Kim, Young Ihl

1981 *The vocabulary of oppression in the Old Testament:* ʿšq, ynh, lḥṣ *and congeners.* Doctoral dissertation, Drew University. Ann Arbor, University Microfilms.

King, R. D.

1980 The history of final devoicing in Yiddish. *FY* 4.371–430.

Kister, M.

1983 בשולי ספר בן־סירא. *Leš* 47.125–46.

Klar, B.

1942 עניני מסורה ומבטא אצל קרקסני. *KLL*, Marcheshwan, 5703, 31–38.

1947a לדרכי הרחבת הלשון העברית בימי הבינים. *Leš* 15.116–24.

1947b Ed. ספר השהם. שערי דקדוק ואוצר מלים לרבי משה בן יצחק בן הנשיאה מאנגלטירא. Jerusalem, Meqise Nirdamim.

1950–51 לתולדות המבטא העברי בימי הבינים. *Leš* 17.72–75.

1954 מחקרים ועיונים בלשון. Tel Aviv (collected essays).

Klarberg, F. Manfred

1970 Yiddish in Melbourne. *JJSoc* 12.59–73.

Klarberg, H.

1970 Stress patterns in spoken Israeli Hebrew. *AN* 10.129–33.

Klausner, J.

1949 ארמיסמים. *Leš* 16.192–95.

1957 העברית החדשה ובעיותיה. Tel Aviv, Massadah (collected essays).

Klausner, S. Z.

1955 Phonetics, personality and status in Israel. *Word* 11.209–15.

Klein, M.

1975 The extant sources of the fragmentary Targum to the Pentateuch. *HUCA* 46.115–37.

1979 Nine fragments of Palestinian Targum to the Pentateuch from the Cairo Geniza. *HUCA* 50.149–64.

1980 *The fragment-targums of the Pentateuch according to their extant sources*, vol. 1: *Texts, indices and introductory essays*; vol. 2: *Translation.* Analecta Biblica 76. Rome, Biblical Institute Press.

1982 Associative and complementary translation in the Targumim. *EI* 16.134*–40*.

1983 New editions of the Palestinian Targumim to the Pentateuch. *Arameans, Aramaic and the Aramaic literary tradition*, ed. by M. Sokoloff, 88–95. Bar-Ilan University.

Klibansky, M.

1941 מלים ומליות בעברית שנוצרו מתוך כ"ף החיזוק. Masters thesis, Hebrew University.

Klopfenstein, M. A.

1972 *Scham und Schande nach dem alten Testament. Eine begriffsgeschichtliche Untersuchung zu den hebräischen Wurzeln* boš, klm *und* ḥpr. Zurich, Theologischer Verlag.

Knisbacher, J.

1986 The limits of Hebrew-English machine translation. *WCJS* 9, Division D, English section, 85–92. Jerusalem.

Knudsen, E.

1969 Spirantization of velars in Akkadian. AOAT 1.147–55.

Knutson, F. B.

1971 *Literary parallels between the texts of Palais royal d'Ugarit IV and the Hebrew Bible.* Doctoral dissertation, Claremont Graduate School. Ann Arbor, University Microfilms.

Kochavi, M.

1977 An ostracon of the period of the Judges from Izbet Sartah. *TA* 4.1–13.

Kochman, T.

1981 השדה הסמנטי של הרצייה במקרא. Masters thesis, Tel Aviv University.

Koehler, L. and Baumgartner, W.

1953 *Lexicon in veteris testamenti libros.* 2 vols. Leiden, Brill.

1967ff. *Hebräischen und aramäischen Lexicon zum alten Testament*, 3rd ed. Leiden, Brill.

Kogut, S.

1968 משפטי התנאי בספר חסידים. Masters thesis, Hebrew University.

1970–71 בקורת ופרשנות, מצב המחקר של העברית של ימי הביניים 9–31.

1971 לשונה של מגילת איכה. *LLA* 22.213–19.

1976 המשפט המורכב ב"ספר חסידים". Doctoral dissertation, Hebrew University.

1977 על הכיאזם ועל תרומת ההבנה בו לבחינתם האכסיגטית במקרא של כתובים. שנתון, an annual for biblical and ancient near eastern studies 2.196–204.

1979–80 לדרכי החשיפה, ההגדרה והתיאור של כללים תחביריים של לשון המקרא. *Leš* 44.12–23, 109–23.

1980 שימושים מילוניים בעברית של "ספר חסידים" מתועדים במילונים או שתיעודם פגום. *WCJS* 6, Division D, 183–95.

1981–82 הכינוי היתר בלשון המקרא. *Leš* 46.9–26, 97–123.

1984a The Language of "Sefer Ḥasidim," its linguistic background and methods of research, in I. Twersky, ed., *Studies in Medieval Jewish History and Literature*, 2, 95–108. Cambridge and London, Harvard University Press.

1984b פסוקי התוכן—טיבם ומבניהם: פרק בתחביר העברית של ספר חסידים בזיקה לעברית המקראית וללשון חז״ל ובהשוואה לעברית החדשה. Jerusalem, The Hebrew University.

Komlosh, Y.

1971–72 Review of A. Díez-Macho, *Neofiti I, Targum Palestinense*, 1. Madrid, 1968. *KS* 47.84–88 (*H*).

1973a המקרא ותרגומיו. Jerusalem.

1973b תרגום ספר איוב. *WCJS* 5, 4.239–46.

1980 בירורים אטימולוגיים בתרגום יונתן לספרי תרי־עשר. *SHSL* 159–65.

1983 על פרשנותו של תרגום עמוס. *Arameans, Aramaic and the Aramean literary tradition*, ed. by M. Sokoloff, Hebrew section 6–9. Bar-Ilan University.

Kopelovitch(-Hanash), Z.

1982 *Modality in Modern Hebrew*. Doctoral dissertation, University of Michigan. Ann Arbor, University Microfilms.

1984 *ʾAval* and *ʾela* conjunctions in Modern Hebrew. *HS* 25. 132–40.

Kopf, L.

1976 *Studies in Arabic and Hebrew Lexicography*, ed. by M. H. Goshen-Gottstein. Jerusalem.

Kor, A.

1979 מחברת התי׳גאן העברית—מקורותיה . . . ויחסה למסורת תימן. Masters thesis, Tel Aviv University.

Kornblueth, I. and Aynor, S.

1974 A study of the longevity of Hebrew slang. *Linguistics* 120. 15–38.

Kosmala, H.

1964/1966 Form and structure in ancient Hebrew poetry. *VT* 14.423–45; 16.162–80.

1964 *Maskil. JANES* 5.235–41.

Kosover, M.

1966 *Arabic elements in Palestinian Yiddish.* Jerusalem, Rubin Mass.

Kosovsky, M.

1953 היחס הלשוני בין ״ברית דמשק״ והמגילות הגנוזות. Masters thesis, Hebrew University.

Kozodoy, N.

1977 Reading medieval love poetry. *AJSR* 2.111–29.

Krahmalkov, C.
1976 An Ammonite lyric poem. *BASOR* 223.55–57.

Krašovec, J.
1977 *Der Merismus im Biblisch-Hebräischen und nordwest Semitischen.* Rome, Biblical Institute Press.
1984 *Antithetic structure in biblical poetry.* Leiden, Brill.

Kraus, F. R.
1968 Sesam im alten Mesopotamien. *JAOS* 88.112–19.

Krauss, S.
1898/1900 *Griechische und lateinische Lehnwörter im Talmud, Midrasch und Targum*, 2 vols. Berlin.

Kremer, S.
1974–75 לשונם של סופרים; א. יעקב קלצקין ב. דב סדן. *LLA* 26/1 (256).

Kressel, G.
1981 כתבי דב סדן. Tel Aviv, Am Oved.
1983–84 הדיבור העברי בארץ בשלהי המאה הקודמת. *LLA* 35/7–8 (347–48).179–94.

Krupnick (Karu), B. and Silberman, A. M.
1927 *A dictionary of the Talmud, the Midrash and the Targum.* London. Reprinted 1970, London/Tel Aviv.

Kugel, J.
1981 *The idea of biblical poetry.* New Haven/London, Yale University Press.

Kuhn, K. G.
1960 *Konkordanz zu den Qumrantexten.* Göttingen.

Kuhnigk, W.
1974 *Nordwest semitischen Studien zum Hoseabuch.* Rome, Biblical Institute Press.

Kukenheim, L.
1963 *Judeo-Gallica ou Gallo-Judaica?* Groningen.
1967 Review of R. Levy 1964. *Lingua* 18.318–20.

Kuriakos, L.
1971 *Non-paradigmatic forms of weak verbs in biblical Hebrew.* Doctoral dissertation, University of Chicago (Published as a book, 1973, Kerala State, India).

Kuryłowicz, J.
1949 Le systeme verbal du sémitique. *BSLP* 45.47–56.
1961 *L'apophonie en sémitique.* Warsaw/Cracow.
1973a *Studies in Semitic grammar and metrics.* Warsaw/Cracow.
1973b Verbal aspect in Semitic. *Or* 42.114–20.

Kustár, P.
1972 *Aspekt im Hebräischen.* Doctoral dissertation, University of Basel, 1969. Basel, Friedrich Reinhardt.

Kutler, L.
1980 *Social terminology in Phoenician, Hebrew and Ugaritic.* Doctoral dissertation, New York University. Ann Arbor, University Microfilms.

Kutsch, E.
1970 Sehen und Bestimmen, Die Etymologie von ברית. *Archäologie und altes Testament, Festschrift für Kurt Galling*, 165–78. Tübingen, Mohr.

Kutscher, E. Y.
1939 אמד, עמד, עמדה. *Leš* 10.295–99.
1949–51 מחקרים בארמית הגלילית. *Tarbiz* 21.192–205; 22.53–63.
1950–51 הארמית המקראית—ארמית מזרחית היא או מערבית? *Leš* 17. 119–22.
1954 New Aramaic texts. *JAOS* 74.233–48.
1957 Role of Modern Hebrew in the development of Jewish-Israeli national consciousness. *PMLAA* 72, 2.38–42.
1957–58 לדיוקה של לשון מגילות ים המלח. *Leš* 22.98–106.
1958 The language of the Genesis Apocryphon. *SH* 4.1–36.
1959 הלשון והרקע הלשוני של מגילת ישעיהו השלמה ממגילות ים המלח. Jerusalem, Magnes Press.
1961 מלים ותולדותיהן. Jerusalem, Kiryath Sepher.
1960–61, 1961–62 לשונן של האיגרות העבריות והארמיות של בר כוסבא. *Leš* 25.117–33; 26.7–23.
1963a חנוך ילון—דרכו בחקר הלשון העברית. *H. Yalon jubilee volume*, ed. by S. Lieberman, S. Abramson, E. Y. Kutscher and S. Esh, 12–36. Jerusalem.
1963b לשון חז״ל, *ibid.*, 246–80.
1963–64 בבואה (CALQUE) של הארמית בעברית. *Tarbiz* 33.118–30.
1964–65 מחקר השמית הצפונית־מערבית בימינו. *Leš* 29.47–58, 115–28.
1965 Contemporary studies in northwest Semitic. *JSS* 10.21–51 (Review article on Garbini 1960).
1966–67a למילונה של לשון חז״ל. *Leš* 31.107–17.
1966–67b השפעת היונית על הלשון העברית. מחנים 112.54–57.
1966 Yemenite Hebrew and ancient pronunciation. *JSS* 11.217–25.
1967a כוך ובני משפחתה. *EI* 8.273–79.
1967b Mittelhebräisch und Judischaramäisch im neuen Köhler-Baumgartner. *Hebräische Wortforschung, W. Baumgartner Festschrift*, Supplements to VT 16, 158–75. Leiden, Brill.
1967c קטעי גניזה למכילתא דר׳ ישמעאל—אבות טקסטים. *Leš* 32.103–16.
1968 ביצוע תנועות u/i בתעתיקי העברית המקראית, בארמית הגלילית ובלשון חז״ל. *Benjamin de Vries memorial volume*, 218–51. Jerusalem.
1968–69a ״והוא משכירין והיא מזכירין״. *Leš* 33.78.

1968–69b כנענית־עברית פניקית־ארמית־לשון חז״ל־פונית. *Leš* 33.83–110.
1969a מחקרים בדקדוק לשון חז״ל (לפי כת״י קאופמן). *Bar-Ilan volume in humanities and social sciences.* Decennial volume 2, 51–77. Jerusalem.
1969b Two 'passive' constructions in Aramaic in the light of Persian. *PICSS*, 132–51. Jerusalem.
1969c Words and their history. *Ariel* 25.64–74.
1970 Aramaic. *Current trends in linguistics* 6, ed. by T. A. Sebeok, 345–412. The Hague, Mouton (important survey and bibliography).
1971a Hebrew language, Dead Sea scrolls. *EJ* 16.1584–90.
1971b Hebrew language, Mishnaic. *EJ* 16.1590–1607.
1972a מצב המחקר של לשון חז״ל (בעיקר במילונות) ותפקידיו. *Archive of the new dictionary of rabbinical literature* 1, ed. by E. Y. Kutscher, 3–28. Ramat Gan.
1972b מבעיות המילונות של לשון חז״ל (לרבות בעית השואת לשון חז״ל ללשון המקרא), *ibid.*, 29–82.
1976 *Studies in Galilean Aramaic.* Translated by Michael Sokoloff. Bar-Ilan studies in Near Eastern languages and culture. Ramat Gan.
1977 מחקרים בעברית ובארמית, ed. by Z. Ben-Hayyim, A. Dotan, G. Sarfatti and M. Bar-Asher. English and Hebrew sections. Jerusalem (includes bibliography of Kutscher, 19*–31*).
1982 *A history of the Hebrew language*, edited by Raphael Kutscher. Jerusalem and Leiden, Magnes Press and Brill.

Labuschagne, C. J.
1973 *Studies in Hebrew syntax and biblical exegesis.* Leiden, Brill.

Lafitte, P.
1957 Langue et musique chez les Israelites. *Gure Herria* 29.4–11.

Lambdin, T. O.
1971a The junctural origin of the West Semitic definite article. *Near eastern studies in honor of William Foxwell Albright*, ed. by H. Goedicke, 315–33. Baltimore/London, Johns Hopkins University Press.
1971b *Introduction to Biblical Hebrew.* New York.

Landau, D.
1974–75 המטונים והסינכדוכה. *Leš* 39.263–71.

Landau, J. M.
1970 Language study in Israel, in *Current trends in linguistics* 6, ed. by T. A. Sebeok, 721–45. The Hague, Mouton.

Landau, R.
1967 הצרוף הכבול בלשון ימינו. Masters thesis, Bar-Ilan University (summary appears in ביקורת ופרשנות, 1 [1970].80–85 [*H*], Bar-Ilan University).

1970 לדרכי היוצרותם של צירופים כבולים בעברית של ימינו. *Leš* 35.130–39.
1971 הפיצול הצורני כאמצעי של בידול משמעויות בעברית של ימינו. *Sefer Kamrat*, 104–7. Jerusalem.
1972 מהותה של הפוליסמיה בעברית של ימינו וקווים להתפתחותה. Doctoral dissertation, Hebrew University.
1975a משפט הזיקה ומשפט לוואי תוכן לסוגיו בעברית של ימינו. ביקורת ופרשנות, 7–8.132–36, Bar-Ilan University.
1975b על דרגות הכבילות הסימנטית של הלשון. *Rosen memorial volume*, ed. by B. Z. Fischler and U. Ornan, 45–58. Jerusalem, Council on the Teaching of Hebrew.
1976 הקולוקאציה בעברית של ימינו. *Chaim Rabin jubilee volume*, ed. by B. Fischler and R. Nir, 68–95. Jerusalem, Council on the Teaching of Hebrew.
1976–77 קולוקאטיביות הפועל בגזרה ובנטייה. *Leš* 41.243–69.
1980a על הסגנון המקראי של "בדמי ימיה" לש"י עגנון. *HCL* 16.26–50.
1980b הניב והשלכותיו על התרבות ומשמעויות המלים בעברית של ימינו. *WCJS* 6, Division D, 129–39. Jerusalem.
1980c מלים וצירופיהן: עיונים סמאנטיים בקולוקאציה העיתונאית. Ramat Gan, Bar-Ilan University.
1980d תהליכים סמאנטיים בצירוף הקולוקאטיבי בלשון העיתונות. *SHSL*, 202–16.
1983 בין חקר השיח לחקר הסגנון. *HCL* 20.61–77.

Landes, G. M.
1982 Linguistic criteria and the date of the book of Jonah. *EI* 16.147*–70*.

Landis, J. C.
1964 Who needs Yiddish? A study in language and ethics. *Judaism* 13.1–16.

Landmann, M.
1976 *Reform of the Hebrew alphabet.* Ann Arbor, University Microfilms.
1977 *Neugestaltung der hebräischen Schrift.* Bonn.

Landsberger, B.
1967 Akkadisch-hebräisch Wortgleichungen. *W. Baumgartner Festschrift.* Supplements to VT, 16.176–204.

Lapide, P.
1971 *Die Verwendung des Hebräischen in den Christlichen Religionsgemeindschaften mit besonderen Berücksichtigung des Landes Israel.* Inaugural dissertation, Köln.
1975a השפה העברית בכנסיות. *Rosen memorial volume*, ed. by B. Fleischer and U. Ornan, 59–63. Jerusalem, Council on the teaching of Hebrew.

1975b Insights from Qumran into the languages of Jesus. *RQ* 32.483–50.
1984 *Hebrew in the churches*. Grand Rapids, MI; Eerdmans.

Larrea Palacín, Arcadio de
1952 *Romances de Tetuán*, 2 vols. London.
1954 *Cancions rituales hispano-judías*. Madrid.

Lasery, Y.
1987 השירה היהודית־עממית במרוקו. Tel Aviv, Hakibbutz Hameuchad.

Lau, J.
1970 *Covenantal rhetoric of the eighth century* B.C. *Hebrew prophets*. Doctoral dissertation, UCLA. Ann Arbor, University Microfilms.

Laufer, A.
1968 פירוק הכינוי החבור לכינוי פרוד בלשון המשנה. Masters thesis, Hebrew University.
1972 *Synthesis by rule of a Hebrew idiolect*. Doctoral dissertation, University of London.
1975 A programme for synthesizing Hebrew speech. *Phonetics* 32.292–99.
1975–76 דבור עברי מלאכותי בעזרת מחשב. *Leš* 40.67–78.
1976–77 תיאור פונטי של תנועות. *Leš* 41.117–43.
1977 הנגינה של עברית מדוברת. Jerusalem, Hebrew University.
1983 השימוש בספקטוגראף לביסוס התעתיק הפונטי. *ML* 309–20.

Laufer, A. and Condax, I. D.
1981 The function of the epiglottis in speech. *LS* 24/1.38–61.

Lavian, M.
1975 כללי מקרא בתורת הפרשנות. Jerusalem.
1977–80 אותיות ומשמעותן במקרא, 3 vols. Jerusalem.
1978 טעמים ומשמעותם במקרא, vol. 1. Jerusalem.

Lavin, A. F.
1984 *The liturgical poems of Meir bar Isaac*. Doctoral dissertation, The Jewish Theological Seminary. Ann Arbor, University Microfilms.

Lazar, M.
1971 Ladino. *EJ* 10.1342–51.

Lazard, G.
1968 La dialectologie du judéo-persan. *SBB* 8.77–98.
1971a Judeo-Persian. *EJ* 10.429–32.
1971b Judeo-Tat. *EJ* 10.441–42.
1978 Note sur le jargon des juifs d'Iran. *JA* 266.251–55.

Lazarus, H. M.
1944 The rationale of the Tiberian graphic accentuation (xxi books). *Essays in honor of the very Rev. J. H. Herz*, 271–91. London.

Lederberg, S.
1948 שמות שווי־שורש בזכר ובנקבה והתפתחות הוראותיהם בלשון העברית. Masters thesis, Hebrew University.

Lehman, O. I.
1971 New light from manuscripts on the antecedents of the Tiberian system of vocalization. *PICO* 27, 102–3. Wiesbaden.

Lehmann, M. R.
1978–79 עיונים בו"ו הפירוש (EXPLICATIVUM). *Sinai* 85.200–210.

Leibel, D.
1965 On Ashkenazic stress. *FY* 2.63–72.

Lerner, M. B.
1986 לחקר הכונויים והתארים א. אבא. *Teᶜudah* 4, ed. M. A. Friedman and M. Gil, 93–113. Tel Aviv University.

Lerner, Y.
1981 חילופי ז/ד בייצוג/d̲/במסמכי יב: הסבר חילוף. *Leš* 46.57–64.

Leslau, W.
1946 Hebrew elements in the Judeo-Arabic dialect of Fez. *JQR* 36.61–78.
1958 *Ethiopic and South Arabian contributions to the Hebrew lexicon.* University of California publications in Semitic philology 20.
1962 An Ethiopian parallel to *ᶜlh* 'went up country' and *yrd* 'went down country'. *ZAW* 74.322–23.
1969 *Hebrew cognates in Amharic.* Wiesbaden, Harrassowitz.

Lettinga, J. P.
1962 *Grammatica van het bibjels Hebreeu.* Leiden, Brill (translated by A. and A. Schoars, *Grammaire de l'hébreu biblique*, 1980, Leiden, Brill).

Levenston, E. A.
1966 *A 'scale and category' description of the syntax of Israeli Hebrew, with special reference to English-Hebrew translation equivalence.* Doctoral dissertation, University of London.
1967–68 מבנה הפסוק העברי. *Leš* 32.389–98.
1971 Over-indulgence and under-representation—aspects of mother tongue interference. *Papers in contrastive linguistics*, ed. by G. Nickel, 115–212. Cambridge, University Press.
1976 לקראת סטיליסטיקה השוואתית של האנגלית והעברית. *Chaim Rabin jubilee volume*, ed. by B. Fischler and R. Nir, 59–67. Jerusalem, Council on the Teaching of Hebrew.

Levenson, E. R.
1972 *Moses Mendelssohn's understanding of logico-grammatical and literary construction in the Pentateuch. A study of his German translation and Hebrew commentary* (The *Biʾur*). Doctoral dissertation, Brandeis University. Ann Arbor, University Microfilms.

Levi, A.
1981 הגות עברית. הלאדינו והיצירה הספרותית בה בארצות האיסלאם. ed. by M. Zohory et al., 119–26. Jerusalem, Brit Ivrit Olamit.

Levi, Z.
1979 בעיית הנורמאטיביות ב"תקציר הדקדוק העברי" לשפינוזה. בקורת ופרשנות 13–14.217–50.

Levin, I.
1970 אברהם אבן עזרא—חייו ושירתו. Hakibbutz Hameuchad.
1973a על מות—הקינה על המת בשירת החול בעברית בספרד על רקע הקינה בשירה הערבית. Hakkibutz Hameuchad and Tel Aviv University.
1973b שמואל הנגיד—חייו ושירתו. Hakkibutz Hameuchad and Tel Aviv University.
1975 שירי הקודש של אברהם אבן־עזרא. Jerusalem, Israel Academy of Sciences and Humanity.

Levin, S.
1971 *The Indo-European and Semitic languages.* Albany, State University of New York.
1975 Greek occupational terms with Semitic counterparts. Reprinted for private circulation from the first LACUS (Linguistic Association of Canada and the United States) forum, 1974, ed. by A. and V. B. Malka. Columbia, SC.
1979 The מתג according to the practice of the early vocalizers. *HAR* 3.129–39.

Levine, B.
1962 *Survivals of ancient Canaanite in the Mishnah.* Doctoral dissertation, Brandeis University. Ann Arbor, University Microfilms.
1971 Review of Orlinsky 1966. *JAOS* 91.307–9.
1974 *In the presence of the Lord. A study of cult and some cultic terms in ancient Israel.* Leiden, Brill.
1978 פרקים בתולדות העברית המדוברת. *EI* 14.155–60.
1981 The Deir ᶜAlla plaster inscriptions. *JAOS* 101.195–220.
1982 לחקר המקור הכוהני—הבחינה הלשונית. *EI* 16.124–31.
1983 Late language in the priestly source: some literary and historical observations. *WCJS* 8, Bible and Hebrew language, 69–82. Jerusalem.

Levine, E.
1973 *The Aramaic version of Ruth.* Rome.
1975 *The Aramaic version of Jonah.* Jerusalem.
1976a *Ibn Ezra's commentary to the minor prophets.* Jerusalem.
1976b *The Aramaic version of Lamentations.* New York.

Levy, B.
1974 *The language of Neophyti I: a descriptive and comparative grammar of the Palestinian Targum.* Doctoral dissertation, New York University. University Microfilms, Ann Arbor, 1980.

Levy, I.
1959 *Chants judéo-espagnols.* London.

Levy, R.
1964 *Trésor de la langue des juifs français au moyen âge.* Austin, TX.

Libes, J.
1977 מחקר במילון ספר הזוהר. Doctoral dissertation, Hebrew University.

Licht, J.
1957 מגלת ההודיות. Jerusalem, Mossad Bialik.
1965 מגלת הסרכים. Jerusalem, Mossad Bialik.

Lida, D.
1975 Ladino. *AJSN* 14.7–8.
1978 Ladino language and literature, in *Jewish languages, theme and variation*, ed. by H. Paper, 79–92. Cambridge, MA, Association for Jewish Studies.

Lidovsky, Z. and Uval, E.
1979 *Bulletin No. 9, a listing of books on Hebrew grammar, Hebrew orthoepics and the history of the Hebrew language* (*H*). Jerusalem, Council on the Teaching of Hebrew.

Lieberman, S.
1931 תלמודה של קיסרין. *Supplement to Tarbiz* 2/4. Jerusalem.
1942 *Greek in Jewish Palestine.* New York, Jewish Theological Seminary.
1950 *Hellenism in Jewish Palestine.* New York, Jewish Theological Seminary.
1955–73 תוספתא: זרעים, 1955; מועד, 1962; נשים, 1967, 1973. New York, Jewish Theological Seminary.
1955–73 תוספתא כפשוטה, 8 vols. New York, Jewish Theological Seminary (notes on the critical edition of the Tosefta).
1965 מדרש דברים רבה, 2nd ed. Jerusalem, Wahrmann.
1967–68 הוראות נשכחות. *Leš* 32.89–102.
1968 ספרי זוטא (מדרשה של לוד). New York.
1970a שקיעין, מדרשי תימן, 2nd ed. Jerusalem.

1970b שש מלים מקהלת רבה, in memory of Gedaliahu Alon, מחקרים בתולדות ישראל ובלשון העברית, 227–35. Hakkibutz Hameuchad.

Lindenberger, J. M.

1974 *The Aramaic proverbs of Ahiqar.* Doctoral dissertation, Johns Hopkins University. Ann Arbor, University Microfilms.

Lipinski, E.

1980 Notes lexicographiques et stylistiques sur le livre de Job. *FO* 21.65–82.

Lipkin, S.

1975 יו"ד עיצורית במעמד סופי (או בין תנועות)—כתיבתה ומעמדה הפונולוגי בכתבי היד של לשון חכמים. Masters thesis, Hebrew University.

Lipschutz, J.

1931 רבי דוד קמחי כבלשן וכמילונאי. Masters thesis, Hebrew University.

Lipschutz, L.

1964 *Kitab al-khilaf.* The book of the *ḥillufim. Textus* 4.1–29.

1965 Kitab al-khilaf. *Mishael ben Uzziel's treatise on the differences between Ben Asher and Ben Naphtali.* Publications of the Hebrew University Bible Project, monograph series 1. Jerusalem (appeared earlier in *Textus* 2 [1962], Hebrew supplement 1–58).

Lisowsky, G.

1940 *Die Transkription der hebräischen Eigennamen des Pentateuch in der Septuaginta.* Doctoral dissertation, Basel.

Liver, J.

1972 חקרי מקרא ומגילות מדבר יהודה. Jerusalem, Mossad Bialik.

Loewenstamm, A.

1962 כתב יד קראי בלבוש שומרוני. Masters thesis, Hebrew University (see also *Sfunot* 8 [1964], 165–204).

1977–78 עיבוד ספרותם של הקראים במילון ההיסטורי ללשון עברית. *Leš* 42.37–50.

Loewenstamm, S. E.

1966–67 עבר לעבר בעברית של חז"ל. *Leš* 31.21–22.

1971 Grenzgebiete ugaritischer Sprach und Stilvergleichung: Hebräisch des zweiten Tempels, Mittelhebräischen, Griechisch. *UF* 3.93–100.

1973–74 הכינוי הדבק של השם כנשוא בעברית ובאוגריתית, *Leš* 38.149–50.

1974 עד היכן מגיעות הקבלותיה של ספרות אוגרית? *H. Yalon memorial volume*, Bar-Ilan departmental researches 2.212–20. Jerusalem.

1980 *Comparative studies in biblical and ancient Oriental literatures.* AOAT 204. Neukirchen-Vluyn, Neukirchener.

1982 עיונים במקרא לאור טקסטים אכדיים. *Teʿudah* 2, *Bible studies Y. M. Grintz in memoriam*, ed. B. Uffenheimer, 187–96. Tel Aviv University.

1983 עם סגולה. *ML* 321–28.

Loewinger, D. S.

1960 The Aleppo codex and the Ben Asher tradition. *Textus* 1.59–111.

1961 שרידי הניב המאורך במגילת ישעיהו הראשונה ובנוסח המסורה. Essays on the Dead Sea scrolls in memory of E. Sukenick, ed. by Y. Yadin and C. Rabin, 141–61. Jerusalem.

1968–69 כתר ארם צובה או דקדוקי הטעמים. *Tarbiz* 38.186–204.

1970 דקדוקי הטעמים, ed. by S. Baer and H. L. Strack, with prefatory note and appendix by D. S. Loewinger.

1978 *The Masora Magna to the Bible*, Ochla ve Ochla, *Codex Paris*, Bibliothèque Nationale 148. Paris (limited facsimile edition).

Loewinger, D. S. and Yahalom, J. (Y.), eds.

1973 *Sephardi collection of* piyyutim *for fast days and special Sabbaths from the year 1481* (Ms. Parma de Rossi 1192). 3 vols., limited edition, 390 numbered quarto volumes. Leiden.

Loprieno, A.

1979–80 The sequential forms in late Egyptian and Biblical Hebrew: a parallel development of verbal systems. *AAL* 7/5.

Loretz, O.

1971a, 1973, 1974 Psalmenstudien, I, *UF* 3.101–15; II, *ibid.*, 5.213–18; III, *ibid.*, 6.175–210; IV, *ibid.*, 211–40.

1971b *Studien zur althebräischen Poesie*. Neukirchen-Vluyn, Kevelaer.

Lowe, A. D.

1971 Some hellenistic features of the Hebrew wisdom on Ben Sira. *PICO* 27, 86–87. Wiesbaden.

Lowenstein, S.

1969 Results of atlas investigations among Jews of Germany. *FY* 3.16–35.

1973–75 Di šeyris-hapleyte fun yidiš in franken. *YS* 32.24–33; 33.37–45; 34.37–43.

Luc, Alexander To Ha

1982 *The meaning of* ʾhb *in the Hebrew Bible*. Doctoral dissertation, University of Wisconsin, Madison. Ann Arbor, University Microfilms.

Lund, S. and Foster, J. A.

1978 *Variant versions of targumic traditions within Codex Neofiti 1*. SBL Aramaic studies. Missoula, MT, Scholars Press.

Lundbom, J. R.
1973 *Jeremiah, a study in ancient Hebrew rhetoric.* Doctoral dissertation, Graduate Theological Union (published in 1975, Missoula, MT, Scholars Press).

Luzzatto, A. and Moldavi, M.
1982 *Bibliotheca Italia-Ebraica, Bibliografia per la storia degli Eorei in Italia.* Rome.

Maag, V.
1953 Morphologie des hebräischen Narrativs. *ZAW* 65.86–88.

Macdonald, J.
1963 The Leeds school of Samaritan studies. Notes compiled by the editor. *ALUOS* 3 (1961–62).115–18.
1966 New thoughts on a biliteral origin for the Semitic verb. *ALUOS* 5 (1963–65).63–85.
1975 Some distinctive characteristics of Israelite spoken Hebrew. *BiOr* 32.162–75.

Macuch, R.
1965 *Handbook of Classical and Modern Mandaic.* Berlin.
1969 *Grammatik des samaritanischen Hebräisch.* Berlin.
1973 Zur Grammatik des samaritanischen Hebräisch. *AO* 41.193–211.

Mafico, T. L.
1979 *A study of the Hebrew root* 'špṭ' *with reference to Yahweh.* Doctoral dissertation, Harvard University. Ann Arbor, University Microfilms.

Mahbub, H., ed.
1953 ספר שירי תימן. Jerusalem.

Maier, J.
1973 Serienbildung und 'numinoser' Eindrukseffekt in den poetischen Stücken der Hekalot Literatur. *Semitics* 3.36–66.

Mainz, E.
1982 Le libre de Daniel en Judéo-Persan. *Irano-Judaica*, ed. by Saul Shaked, 148–79. Jerusalem, The Ben-Zvi Institute.

Maitlis, Y.
1979 מדרש לפרקי אבות ביידיש קמאית לאנשל לוי. Jerusalem.

Malachi, S.
1966–67 עברית בתוך לשון לאדינו. *LLA* 18.11–18, 117–20.

Malachi, Z., ed.
1977a ספר הברמן. Jerusalem.

Malachi, Z.
1977b משלי חיות מחורזים לאברהם בר יעקב מרגנסברג, *ibid.*, 207–31.

Malamat, A.
1945 הלשון העברית וביקורת המקרא בדרשות חז״ל שבבראשית רבה. Masters thesis, Hebrew University.

1947 לחקר הלשון העברית ונוסח המקרא על יסוד דרשות חז״ל. *Leš* 15.151–60.

Mali, U.

1975 הבדלים בתרגום מילולי בין תרגום אונקלוס המיוחס ליונתן וכתב יד נאופיטי 1 לספר שמות פרקים א–ה. Masters thesis, Hebrew University.

1983 לשון השיחה בנביאים ראשונים. Doctoral dissertation, Hebrew University.

Malinowski, A. C.

1979 *Aspects of contemporary Judeo-Spanish in Israel, based on oral and written sources.* Doctoral dissertation, University of Michigan. Ann Arbor, University Microfilms.

Malisdorf, Z.

1975 *Sentential components in Hebrew.* Doctoral dissertation, City University of New York. Ann Arbor, University Microfilms.

1980 Love through death in modern Hebrew: a syntactic treatment. *AAL* 7/2.

Malkiel, S.

1950 לשונו של המדרש הגדול. Masters thesis, Hebrew University.

Malone, J. L.

1971 Wave theory, rule ordering and Hebrew-Aramaic segolation. *JAOS* 91.44–66.

1972 A Hebrew flip-flop rule and its historical origins. *Lingua* 30.442–48.

1975 Systematic vs. autonomous phonemics and the Hebrew grapheme dagesh. *AAL* 2/7.113–29.

1979 Textually deviant forms as evidence for phonological analysis: a service of philology to linguistics. *JANES* 11.71–79.

Maloney, E.

1981 *Semitic interference in Marcan Syntax.* SBL dissertation series 51. Scholars Press, Chico, CA (Doctoral dissertation, Fordham University, 1979).

Maman, A.

1979 העברית של טוביה בן משה הקראי. Masters thesis, Hebrew University.

1984a מסורת הקריאה של יהודי תיטואן במקרא ובמשנה. *Massorot* 1.120–51.

1984b השוואת אוצר המלים בחיבורי הבלשנות העברית למן רס״ג. Doctoral dissertation, Hebrew University.

Mandel, G.

1981 Sheelah Nikhbadah and the revival of Hebrew, in *Eliezer ben-Yehudah, a symposium in Oxford*, ed. by E. Silberschlag, 25–39. Oxford Centre for Postgraduate Hebrew Studies.

Mandel, S. B.
1978 *The development of Samaritan Hebrew: a historical linguistic view*. Doctoral dissertation, Harvard University. Ann Arbor, University Microfilms.

Mani, A. S.
1957 העברית לאור הערבית. Jerusalem.

Mansoor, M.
1958 Some linguistic aspects of the Qumran texts. *JSS* 3.40–54.
1961 The thanksgiving hymns. Leiden, Brill.
1962 The masoretic text in the light of Qumran. *Congress volume*, Supplements to VT 9.305–21.

Mansour, J.
1947 תוארי חכמים בתקופת המשנה, התלמוד והגאונים. Masters thesis, Hebrew University.
1955–56 הגיית הריש בפי יהודי בבל. *Leš* 20.47–49.
1965 הפסוק הפעלי ב״תמול שלשום״, פרק בחקר התחביר של ש״י עגנון. Doctoral dissertation, Hebrew University.
1968 עיונים בלשונו של ש״י עגנון. Tel Aviv.
1974–75 Anaptyxis in final clusters in the Judaeo-Arabic dialect of Baghdad. *AN* 15.20–25.
1975–83 העברית היהודית של בגדאד, 3 vols. (vol. 3 not complete). Haifa.
1980 בירור פונימי של התנועות בערבית היהודית של בגדאד. *WCJS* 6, Division D, 157–62.

Marbach, A.
1976 מחקרים בתרגומי יצירותיו של המינגוי לעברית. Masters thesis, Hebrew University.

Marchand, J. W.
1965 The origin of Yiddish, in *Communications et rapports du premier congrès international de dialectologie generale*, ed. by A. J. van Windekens, 248–52.

Marcus, D.
1970a *Aspects of the Ugaritic verb in the light of comparative Semitic grammar*. Doctoral dissertation, Columbia University. Ann Arbor, University Microfilms.
1970b The stative and the *waw*-consecutive. *JANES* 2.37–40.
1971 The *qal*-passive in Ugaritic. *JANES* 3.102–11.
1975 Review of Siedl 1971. *JNES* 34.146–47.

Marcus, S.
1965 השפה הספרדית־יהודית. Jerusalem, Kiryath Sepher.

Margain, J.
1973a Le '-*ah* de direction' en hébreu. *GLECS* 14 (1969–70).1–17.
1973b *Yakhol* et l'expression de la modalité "pouvoir". *ibid.*, 47–64.

1976a ʾ*Abhâl* et l'expression de l'adversatif en hébreu ancien. *GLECS* 15 (1970).17–38.
1976b Essais de sémantique sur l'hébreu ancien: monèmes fonctionels et autonomes, modalités. *GLECS*, Suppl. 4. Paris.

Margaliot, E.
1958–59 לשאלת הדיבור בזמן בית שני ובתקופת המשנה והתלמוד. *Leš* 23.49–54.
1962–63 עברית וארמית בתלמוד ובמדרש. *Leš* 27–28.20–33.
1970 היחסים שבין העברית התלמודית והעברית של ימינו. *Sefer Shmuel Yeivin*, 440–59. Jerusalem.

Margalit, B.
1975 Studia Ugaritica I: introduction to Ugaritic prosody. *UF* 7.289–313.
1976 Studia Ugaritica II: studies in *KRT* and *AQHT*. *UF* 8.137–92.
1981 The geographical setting of the *AQHT* story and its ramifications. *Ugarit in retrospect*, ed. by G. D. Young, 131–58. Winona Lake, IN, Eisenbrauns.

Margalit, Y.
1950 הברייתות שבמסכת שבת בתלמודים, בתוספתא ובמדרשי ההלכה— השוואה לשונית. Masters thesis, Hebrew University.

Mark, Y.
1954 A study of the frequency of hebraisms in Yiddish: preliminary report. *FY* 1.28–47.
1958 Yiddish-hebräish un hebräish-yiddishe nayshafungen (Yiddish-Hebrew and Hebrew-Yiddish coinages), in *S. Niger memorial volume*, ed. by S. Bickel and L. Lehrer, 124–57. New York, YIVO.
1969 The Yiddish language: its cultural impact. *AJHQ* 59.201–9.
1978 גראמאטיק פון דער יידישער כלל־שפראך. New York.

Markovitz, H.
1970 פסקות ההקדמה ללשון השיחה בספר בראשית. Masters thesis, Bar-Ilan University.

Martin, R. A.
1960 Some syntactic criteria of translation Greek. *VT* 10.295–310.
1974 *Syntactical evidence of Semitic sources in Greek documents.* SBL Septuagint and cognate studies 3. Society of Biblical Literature, Cambridge, MA (printed at Missoula, MT, Scholars Press).
1976 Syntax criticism of the Testament of Abraham, in *Studies on the Testament of Abraham*, ed. by G. W. E. Nickolsburg, Jr., 95–120. Missoula, MT, Scholars Press.

Martinez, E. R., S. J.
1967 *Hebrew-Ugaritic index to the writings of Mitchell J. Dahood.* Rome, Biblical Institute Press.

1981 *Hebrew-Ugaritic index II, with an Eblaite index, to the writings of Mitchell J. Dahood.* Rome, Biblical Institute Press.

Marwick, L.

1936 *The Arabic commentary of Salmon ben Yeruham the Karaite on the Book of Psalms, Chap. 24–72.* Philadelphia.

1957 *A handbook of diplomatic Hebrew.* Washington.

1980 *Diplomatic Hebrew, a glossary of current terminology.* Washington.

Maschler, H.

1966 דרכים להבעת מודליות בעברית החדשה. Masters thesis, Hebrew University.

Mashia, Y.

1972 *The terminology of Hebrew prosody and rhetoric, with special reference to Arabic origins.* Doctoral dissertation, Yeshiva University. Ann Arbor, University Microfilms.

Masson, M.

1967–69 La composition en hébreu israélien. *GLECS* 12–13, 106–30.

1973 A propos de l'origin du suffix *-nik* en hébreu israélien. *GLECS* 14 (1969–70).79–87.

1974 Remarques sur les diminutifs en hébreu israélien. *ACILCS* 1.256–79. Paris.

1975 Reactivation, emprunt, et morphologenes en hébreu israélien: le nom des éléments chimiques. *JA* 263.361–73.

1976a Remarques sur l'exploitation selective des schemes classiques en hébreu israélien. *GLECS* 15.47–54.

1976b Note sur les adjectifs verbaux en *CaCiC* de l'hébreu israélien. *GLECS* 15.111–15.

1976c *Leš mots nouveaux en hébreu moderne.* Publications Orientalistes de France.

Matalon, A.

1979 המבטא העברי במאבקו. Tel Aviv, Hadar.

Matenko, P. and Sloan, S.

1968 The Aquedath Jishaq: a sixteenth century Yiddish epic, in Matenko, P., *Two studies in Yiddish culture,* 3–70 + X. Leiden, Brill.

Mathews, K.

1980 *The paleo-Hebrew Leviticus scroll from Qumran.* Doctoral dissertation, University of Michigan. Ann Arbor, University Microfilms.

Mathews, K. and Freedman, D. N.

1985 *The Paleo-Hebrew Leviticus Scroll.* Winona Lake, IN, Eisenbrauns/American Schools of Oriental Research.

Matisoff, J. A.
1979 *Blessings, curses, hopes and fears: psycho-ostensive expressions in Yiddish.* Philadelphia, Institute for the Study of Human Issues.
Matmon-Cohen, Y.
1934–38 העברית אחרי גלות בבל. *Leš* 6.338–48; 7.136–44, 257–65, 349–55; 8.15–22, 123–30; 9.65–75.
Mazar, B.
1964 The Philistines and the rise of Israel and Tyre. *PIASH* 1, no. 7 (also appears in Hebrew in כנען וישראל, historical essays, 152–73, Jerusalem, 1974).
McCarter, P. K.
1974 The early diffusion of the alphabet. *BA* 37.54–68.
1975 *The antiquity of the Greek alphabet and the early Phoenician scripts.* Harvard Semitic monographs 9. Missoula, MT.
McCarthy, D. J.
1972 *Berit* in Old Testament history and theology. *Biblica* 53.110–21 (review article on Perlitt 1969).
McFall, L.
1982 *The Enigma of the Hebrew verbal system.* Sheffield, Almond Press.
McLaurin, E. W.
1952 *The influence of Hebrew and classical Septuagint and Hellenistic Greek elements in the redemptive terms of the Greek New Testament.* Doctoral dissertation, University of Texas.
McLean, M. D.
1982 *The use and development of palaeo-Hebrew in the Hellenistic and Roman periods.* Doctoral dissertation, Harvard University. Ann Arbor, University Microfilms.
McNamara, M.
1978 *The New Testament and the Palestine Targum to the Pentateuch,* Analecta biblica 27A. Rome.
Medan, M.
1950–51 מילונם של חכמי ישראל בספרד. *Leš* 17.110–14.
1969 The Academy of the Hebrew Language. *Ariel* 25.40–47.
1971 Elijah Levita. *EJ* 11.132–35.
Meehan, C.
1983 קרר לשון נוח בעברית ובארמית היהודית. *ML* 379–82.
Meek, T. J.
1955–56 Result and purpose clauses in Hebrew. *JQR* 46.40–43.
Melamed, E. Z.
1951–52 יעקב נחום הלוי אפשטיין כחוקר הלשון. *Leš* 18.37–53.
1956 על ה״תפסיר״ של יהודי פרס. *EI* 4.217–22.
1956–57 כפל אותיות כיסוד לדרשות חז״ל. *Leš* 21.271–82.

1961 Breakup of stereotyped phrases and an artistic device in biblical poetry. *SH* 8.115–53.
1966 ספר האונומאסטיקון לאבסביוס. Translated, with notes. *Tarbiz* 19, 21. Jerusalem.
1974 מסכת שביעית. *H. Yalon memorial volume*, Bar-Ilan departmental researches 2.385–417. Jerusalem.
1975 מפרשי המקרא: דרכיהם ושיטותיהם, 2 vols. Jerusalem.
1979 מאוצר לשון הקודש בלשון פרסית ויהודית. *Leš* 43.271–94.
1982 לשון נקייה וכינויים במשנה. *Leš* 47.3–15.

Melzer, A.
1972 *Asaph the physician: the man and his book.* Doctoral dissertation, University of Wisconsin (English up to page 91, rest Hebrew). Ann Arbor, University Microfilms.

Merchaviah, H.
1964–65 על תעתיק מלים עבריות בכתב־יד לאטיני מן המאה השלוש־עשרה. *Leš* 29.102–14; 30.41–53.

Mesch, B.
1975 *Studies in Joseph ibn Caspi, fourteenth century philosopher and exegete.* Leiden, Brill.

Mettinger, T.
1971 The nominal pattern '*qᵉtullah*' in biblical Hebrew. *JSS* 16.2–14.
1974 The Hebrew verb system: a survey of recent research. *ASTI* 9.64–84. Leiden, Brill.

Meyer, R.
1953 Zur Geschichte des hebräischen Verbums. *VT* 3.225–35.
1958a Bemerkungen zu den Handschriften vom Toten Meer. *ZAW* 70.39–48.
1958b Spuren eines semitischen Präsens-Futur in den Texten von Chirbet Qumran. Von Ugarit nach Qumran, Festschrift Otto Eissfeldt, *BZAW* 77.118–28.
1960 Das hebräische Verbalsystem im Lichte der gegenwärtige Forschung. *Congress volume, Supplements to VT*, 7.309–17.
1964 Aspekt und Tempus im althebräischen Verbalsystem. *OLZ* 59.117–26.
1965 A. Sperbers neueste Studien über masoritischen Hebräisch. A. Díez-Macho and R. Meyer, eds., *Recent progress in biblical scholarship*, 63–84. Boars Hill, Oxford, Lincombe Lodge Research Library.
1966, 1969, 1972 *Hebräische Grammatik*, vol. 1, *Schrift und Lautlehre*; vol. 2, *Formenlehre; Flexionstabellen*; vol. 3, *Satzlehre*, Sammlung Göschen 763, 763a, 764, 764a, 764b. Berlin, W. de Gruyter.
1979 *Gegensinn und Mehrdeutigkeit in der althebräischen Wort und Begriffsbildung.* Berlin (Sitzungsberichte der Sächsischen

Akademie der Wissenschaften zu Leipzig, Philol-Hist. Kl. Bd. 120, Heft 5).

Meyer, W. F.
1974 *Semitic significance of* 'padah' *in Old Testament Hebrew.* Doctoral dissertation, University of Wisconsin. Ann Arbor, University Microfilms.

Michel, D.
1960 *Tempora und Satzstellung in den Psalmen.* Bonn.

Michel, W. D.
1970 *The Ugaritic texts and the mythological expressions of and philological notes on the book of Job.* Doctoral dissertation, University of Wisconsin. Ann Arbor, University Microfilms.

Mierowsky, D.
n.d. *Hebrew grammar and grammarians throughout the ages.* A thesis approved for the degree of doctor of literature at the University of the Witwatersrand. Johannesburg.

Mieses, M.
1915 *Die Entstehungsursache der jüdische Dialekte.* Wien (reprint, Hamburg, 1979).

Mikam, M. I.
1965 בסוד הלשון. Haifa, Bet Sefer Reali (Mimeographed, limited edition, not for sale).

Milgrom, J.
1970 *Studies in levitical terminology* 1. Berkeley/Los Angeles, University of California.
1978 The temple scroll. *BA* 41/3.105–20.

Milik, J. T.
1955 Note additionelle sur le contract juif de l'an 134 après Jesus Christ. *RB* 62.398–406.
1956 The copper document from cave III, Qumran. *BA* 19.60–64.
1959 *Ten years of discovery in the wilderness of Judah*, translated by J. Strugnell. Naperville, IL.

Millard, A. R.
1962 Alphabetic inscriptions on ivories from Nimrod. *Iraq* 24. 41–51.

Millas Valicrosa, J. M.
1967 *Literatura hebraico-española.* Barcelona.

Miller, P. D. Jr.
1979 Vocative *lamed* in the Psalter: a reconsideration. *UF* 11. 617–38.

Miller, J. R.
1979 *A grammar of the type II marginalia within Codex Neofiti 1, with attention to other Aramaic sources.* Doctoral dissertation, Boston University.

Minkoff, H.
1975 Graphemics and diachrony: some evidence from Hebrew cursive. *AAL* 1/7.193–208.

Mirkin, R.
1957–58 על שלוש תופעות מורפולוגיות בעברית החדשה. *LLA* 9/10 (92).286–93.
1961–62 אי + שמות הפעולה בעברית הספרותית החדשה. *Leš* 26.217–19.
1966a משקל מפועל במקרא. במשנה ובתוספתא. Masters thesis, Hebrew University.
1966b Review of R. Sappan, מילון הסלנג הישראלי. *Leš* 31.72–74 (*H*).
1967–68 משקל מפועל. *Leš* 32.140–52.
1968 הבחינה הדקדוקית והסגנונית באוצר המלים של ינייי. *WCJS* 4, 2.437–42 (English summary 210–11). Jerusalem.
1972–73, 1974–75 פרקים בתולדות המלונות העברית החדשה. *Leš* 37.165–86; 39.73–98.
1974 שני קטעי משנה מן הגניזה. *H. Yalon memorial volume*, Bar-Ilan departmental researches 2, 371–84. Jerusalem.
1978a מסגנון אל סגנון. *Leš* 42.237–51.
1978b רישומי ריתמוס ותחביר מלשון המקורות בכתיבתו של מנדלי מוכר ספרים. *Studies in Bible and the ancient near east presented to S. E. Loewenstamm on his seventieth birthday*, 2.269–77.
1979 אוצר המלים בחיבוריו העבריים של ש״י אברמוביץ (מנדלי מוכר ספרים): ניתוח הבחינה המולונית הדקדוקית והסגנונית בסיוע מחשב. Doctoral dissertation, Hebrew University.
1980 אוצר המלים בספרות העברית העברית החדשה (1750–1920): הבחינה המילונית, הדקדוקית והסגנונית. *WCJS* 6, Division D, 223–32.

Miron, D.
1973 *A traveller disguised: a study in the rise of modern Yiddish fiction in the nineteenth century*. New York.
1980 Folklore and antifolklore in the Yiddish fiction of the Haskalah. *Studies in Jewish folklore*, ed. by F. Talmage, 219–49. Cambridge, MA, Association for Jewish Studies.

Mirsky, A.
1952–53 לפשוטה של לשון שירת ימי הבינים. *Leš* 18.97–103.
1956–57 עיון במשקלות בשירת ספרד. *Leš* 21.56–63, 206–11.
1957–58 ה״א החציצה. *Leš* 22.107–9, 266.
1958a מחצבתן של צורות הפיוט. Studies of the Research Institute for Hebrew Poetry, 7.1–129 (Published separately in 1968, Jerusalem, Schocken Institute).
1958b ילקוט הפיוטים. Jerusalem/Tel Aviv.
1958–59 הפיוט הספרדי, חומר לסמינריון. Hebrew University, Jerusalem.
1961 שירי יצחק אבן־כלפון. Jerusalem, Mossad Bialik.

1965 ראשית הפיוט. Jerusalem, The Jewish Agency.
1967 השירה העברית בתקופת התלמוד. 2.161–79. Jerusalem.
1968–69 משמעות החרוז בשירת ספרד. *Leš* 33.150–95.
1969 הזיקה שבין שירת ספרד לדרשות חז"ל. *Sinai* 64.248–53.
1974 דרכי המליצה של יוסי בן יוסי. *H. Yalon memorial volume*, Bar-Ilan departmental researches 2, 315–70. Jerusalem.
1977a פיוטי יוסי בן יוסי. Jerusalem.
1977b משמעות החרוז בשירי אזור, in *A. Habermann jubilee volume*, ed. by Z. Malachi, 175–206. Jerusalem, Rubin Mass.
1978 הפיסוק של הסגנון העברי. Jerusalem, Mossad Harav Kook.
1983 שירי הספרדים משער היחוד של ס' "חובות הלבבות" לר' בחיי. *ML* 383–406.
1985 סגולות ה־הא. *Sefer Avraham Even-Shoshan*, ed. B. Z. Luria, 199–206. Jerusalem.

Mishor, M.
1968–69 העדר ניגוד שורק/חולם בכ"י שניקודו טברני. *Leš* 33.309–11.
1969 לשון הכתובות העבריות מתקופת הבית הראשון. Masters thesis, Hebrew University.
1979 להבעת המודאליות בלשון חכמים. *Leš* 44.76–79.
1983a הזמן במַשלים הפסוקי בלשון התנאים. *ML* 407–18.
1983b מערכת הזמנים בלשון התנאים. Doctoral dissertation. Hebrew University.

Modena, M. M.
1986 Le choix "Hebraique" dans le lexique des langues Juives. *WCJS* 9, Division D, English section, 85–92. Jerusalem.

Monroe, J. T. and Swiatlo, D.
1977 Ninety-three Arabic *harga*-s in Hebrew *muwaššaḥ*-s: their Hispano-Romance prosody and thematic features. *JAOS* 97.141–63.

Moor, J. C. de
1978 The art of versification in Ugarit and Israel; I: the rhythmic structure, in *Studies in Bible and the ancient near east presented to S. E. Loewenstamm on his seventieth birthday*, 1.119–39. Jerusalem.

Morag, S.
1954 הכינויים העצמאיים לנסתר ולנסתרת במגילות ים המלח. *EI* 3.166–69.
1955–57 השווא בהגייתם של בני תימן. *Leš* 20.10–29, 112–34; 21.104–16.
1956 הגיית העברית בפי יהודי תימן. Doctoral dissertation, Hebrew University.
1956–57a לשון בגלותה ובתחייתה—עד אימתי דברו עברית. *LLA* 7.5–6.
1956–57b למחקר מסורות עדות לשון חכמים. *Tarbiz* 26.4–16.
1956–57, 1957–58 בנין פָּעֵל ובנין נִתְפָּעֵל. *Tarbiz* 26.349–56; 27.556.

1958 מישע. *EI* 5.138–44.
1959a The vocalization of Codex Reuchlinianus: is the 'pre-masoretic' Bible pre-masoretic? *JSS* 4.216–37.
1959b Planned and unplanned development in modern Hebrew. *Lingua* 8.247–63.
1960 שבע כפולות בגד כפרת״. *Sefer Tur Sinai*, 207–42. Jerusalem.
1961 Review of Kutscher 1959 (*H*). *KS* 36.24–32.
1961–62 קטע של משנה בניקוד שבין בבל לטבריה. *Leš* 25.27–30.
1962a *The vocalization systems of Arabic, Hebrew and Aramaic.* The Hague.
1962b Notes on the vowel system of Babylonian Aramaic as preserved in the Yemenite tradition. *Phonetica* 7.233–34.
1963 העברית שבפי יהודי תימן. The Academy of the Hebrew Language, Studies 4. Jerusalem.
1964–65 הערות לתיאור שיטת הניקוד של מחזור וורמייזא. *Leš* 29.203-9.
1965 *Oral traditions and dialects: towards a methodology for evaluating the evidence of an oral tradition.* Jerusalem.
1967a Uniformity and diversity in a language: dialects and forms of speech in Modern Hebrew. *PICL* 10, 1.639–44.
1967b Review of Schramm 1964 (*H*). *KS* 42.78–86.
1967–68 לתורת ההגה של הארמית הבבלית. *Leš* 32.67–88.
1968a Review of A. Sperber 1966 (*H*). *KS* 43.536–40.
1968b ניקודו של התלמוד הבבלי בתקופת הגאונים. *WCJS* 4, 2.89–94.
1968c העבודה במפעל מסורת הלשון של העדות. *WCJS* 4, 2.451–52.
1969 ניקוד. *EM* 5.837–57.
1969–74 המסורת הטברנית של לשון מקרא; הומוגניות והטרוגניות. *Perakim* 2.
1972–73 הערות אחדות לתיאורה של מערכת התנועות של העברית המדוברת בישראל. *Leš* 37.205–14 (reaction to Chayen 1971–72).
1973–74 מפעלם של ראשונים; על דרכם של חכמי המסורה ועל מונחים ארמיים שטבעו. *Leš* 38.49–77.
1974a On some terms of the Babylonian Massora, *Masoretic studies* 1, ed. by H. M. Orlinsky, 67–77. Missoula, MT, Scholars Press.
1974b On the historical validity of the vocalization of the Hebrew Bible. *JAOS* 94.307–15.
1974c On the historical validity of the vocalization of the Hebrew Bible. *HA* 15.85.
1974d כתב יד בבלי תימני של ספר דניאל. *H. Yalon memorial volume*, Bar-Ilan departmental researches 2, 221–74. Jerusalem.
1975a על ״מלות מפתח״ ו״מלות עדות״ בלשונו של ירמיהו. *Rosen memorial volume*, ed. by B. Fischler and U. Ornan, 64–73. Jerusalem, Council on the Teaching of Hebrew.

1975b יהודות תימן, מסורות הלשון של יהודי תימן, ed. by I. Yesh^c^ayahu and Y. Tobi, 357–66. Jerusalem, Yad Itzhak Ben-Zvi.
1977 Ed. מסורת לשון העברית של יהודי בגדאד בקריאת התורה והמשנה: תורת ההגה, with H. Allon, J. Fellman and K. Katz. *PHULTP* 1. Jerusalem.
1978 עיונים ביחסי משמעות. *EI* 14.137–47.
1979a 'דרך נצב'. *Leš* 43.194–200.
1979b Some notes on *muṣawwitāt* in medieval Hebrew and Arabic literature. *JANES* 11.85–90.
1980 בין מזרח למערב: לפרשת מסירתה של העברית בימי הבינים. *WCJS* 6, Division D, 141–56. Jerusalem.
1981 הגות עברית בארצות איסלאם. מסורות הלשון של יהודי תימן. ed. by M. Zohory *et al.*, 21–27. Jerusalem, Brit Ivrit Olamit.
1982 Some notes on Šelomo Almoli's contributions to the linguistic science of Hebrew. *Interpreting the Bible, essays in honor of E. I. J. Rosenthal*, 157–69. Cambridge University Press.
1983a הערות לסוגית הדו־תנועות בארמית הבבלית. *ML* 339–58.
1983b חקר לשון המקרא: אטימולוגיה וסימאנטיקה. *WCJS* 8, Bible and Hebrew language, 41–61. Jerusalem.
1984 לתולדות החשיבה הבלשנית בימי הביניים. *Massorot* 1.41–50.
1985 ראשיתה של העברית וייחודה של העברית. מחקרים בלשון, ed. M. Bar-Asher, 177–96. Jerusalem. Department of Hebrew Language, Hebrew University.
1987 *Studies in Contemporary Hebrew*, 2 vols. Jerusalem, Akademon (anthology of current articles).

Morag, S. and Sappan, R.
1966–67 מלשון הדייגים ויורדי הים בישראל. *Leš* 31.289–98.

Moran, W. L., S.J.
1950 *A syntactical study of the dialect of Byblos as reflected in the Amarna tablets.* Doctoral dissertation, Johns Hopkins University. Ann Arbor, University Microfilms.
1960 Early Canaanite *yaqtula. Or* 29.1–19.
1961 The Hebrew language in its Northwest Semitic background. *The Bible and the ancient near east, essays in honor of William Foxwell Albright*, ed. by G. Ernest Wright, 54–72. New York.
1975 The Syrian scribe of the Jerusalem Amarna letters. *Unity and diversity*, ed. by H. Goedicke and J. J. M. Roberts, 146–66. Baltimore/London, Johns Hopkins University Press.

Moreshet, M.
1966 הרמב"ן כבלשן על פי פירושו לתורה. Masters thesis, Hebrew University.
1966–67a הרמב"ן כבלשן על פי פירושו לתורה. *Sinai* 60.193–210.

1966–67b גלגולי משמעות של ניבים ושל צירופי לשון שמקורן במקרא. *LLA* 18/6–7.
1972a לקסיקון הפועל שנתחדש בלשון התנאים. Doctoral dissertation, Hebrew University.
1972b פעלים חדשים מחודשים בברייתות בבבלי ובירושלמי. *Archive of the new dictionary of rabbinical literature* 1, ed. by E. Y. Kutscher, 117–62. Ramat Gan, Bar-Ilan University.
1974a הברייתות העבריות בבבלי אינן לשון חכמים א׳. *H. Yalon memorial volume*, Bar-Ilan departmental researches 2, 275–314.
1974b נוספות ללשונן של הברייתות העבריות בבבלי ובירושלמי. *Archive of the new dictionary of rabbinic literature* 2, ed. by M. Z. Kaddari, 31–73. Ramat Gan, Bar-Ilan University.
1976 מורשת לשון חכמים ברובדי לשון מאוחרים. ביקורת ופרשנות 9–10.239–51.
1977–78 רש״י על הומונימים דקדוקיים בתורה. *BM* 23(72).93–117.
1979 הפועל בבינוני עם כינוי נושא חבור (אנקליטי). *Bar-Ilan* 16–17.126–48.
1980a לקסיקון הפועל שנתחדש בלשון התנאים. Ramat Gan, Bar-Ilan University (book form of 1972a).
1980b על בנין נופעל בעברית בתר־מקראית. *SHSL* 126–39.
1983 הנושא הקדום לשני נושאים בלשון חז״ל. *ML* 359–78.

Moreshet, M. and Klein, J.
1975–76 השורש כנון בלשון חז״ל באנלוגיה לאכדית. *Leš* 40.95–116.

Morgenbrod, M. and Serifi, E.
1976 Computer-analyzed aspects of Hebrew verbs. *HCL* 10.1–17.

Morrow, F. J., Jr.
1973 *The text of Isaiah at Qumran.* Doctoral dissertation, Catholic University of America. Ann Arbor, University Microfilms.

Moscati, S.
1951 *L'epigrafia Ebraica antica, 1935–1950.* Biblica et Orientalia 15. Rome.
1954 The plural in Semitic. *PICO* 23, 112–14. London.
1964 Ed. *An introduction to the comparative grammar of the Semitic languages.* Wiesbaden, Harrassowitz.

Moskona, I.
1971 About one of the components of the language of Djudezmo. *Annual of the public cultural and educational organization of the Jews in the People's Republic of Bulgaria (Sofia).* 6.179–220.
1979 Djudezmo. *LB* 22.53–69.

Moskovitch, W. and Ben-Oren, G.
1982 The Hebrew-Aramaic and Georgian documents in the spoken language of Georgian Jews. *WCJS* 8, Division D, English section, 19–24. Jerusalem.

Moskovitch, W. and Guri, J.
1982 לעקסיש־סעמאנטישע השפעה פון יידיש אויפן מאדערנעם העברעיש. (*Yiddish influence upon the lexico-semantic system of modern Israeli Hebrew*). *WCJS* 8, Division D, Hebrew section, 69–75. Jerusalem.

Muffs, Y.
1969 *Studies in the Aramaic papyri from Elephantine*. Leiden, Brill.

Muilenberg, J.
1953 A study in Hebrew rhetoric: repetition and style. *Congress volume*, Supplements to VT 1, 97–111. Leiden, Brill.
1961 The linguistic and rhetorical usages of the particle *kî* in the Old Testament. *HUCA* 32.135–60.

Müller, H. P.
1971 Die Wurzeln *ʿyq, yʿq, ʿwq*. *VT* 21.556–64.

Müller, W.
1975 Beiträge zur hamito-semitischen Wortvergleichung. *Hamito-Semitica*, ed. by J. and T. Bynon, 63–74. The Hague, Mouton.

Muraoka, T.
1969 *Emphasis in Biblical Hebrew*. Doctoral dissertation, Hebrew University.
1975 The *nun-energicum* and the prefix conjugation in Biblical Hebrew. *AJBI* 1.63–72.
1983 On the morpho-syntax of the infinitive in targumic Aramaic. *Arameans, Aramaic and the Aramaic literary tradition*, ed. by M. Sokoloff, 75–79. Ramat Gan, Bar-Ilan University.
1985 Emphatic words and structures in Biblical Hebrew. Leiden, Brill.

Murtonen, A.
1956–57 קטעי משנה בניקוד בבלי. *Leš* 21.1–6.
1958, 1960, 1964 *Materials for a non-masoretic Hebrew grammar*, vol. 1 (1958); vol. 2, *An etymological vocabulary of the Samaritan Pentateuch* (1960); vol. 3, *A grammar of the Samaritan dialect of Hebrew* (1964). Helsinki.
1959 On the influence of the development of vocalization upon the form system in Samaritan Hebrew. *PICO* 24.257–59. Wiesbaden.
1961–62 Spoken Hebrew from the tenth century A.D. *AN* 3.45–59.
1963–64 A historical-philological survey of the main Dead Sea scrolls and related documents. *AN* 4.56–95.
1966 The Semitic sibilants. *JSS* 11.135–95.

1967 *Early Semitic*. Leiden, Brill.
1968a Prolegomena to a comparative description of non-masoretic Hebrew dialects and traditions. *In memorium Paul Kahle*, ed. by M. Black and G. Fohrer, *BZAW* 103.180–87.
1968b The pre-historic development of the Hebrew verbal system. *WCJS* 4, 2.29–33.
1974 (1973–74) On the interpretation of the *matres lectiones* in Biblical Hebrew. *AN* 14.66–121.
1982 Methodological preliminaries to a study of Greek (and Latin) transcriptions of Hebrew. *AN* 20.60–73.
1986 *Hebrew in its West Semitic Setting*. Leiden, Brill.

Musaev, K. M.
1964 *Grammatika karaimskovo jazyka: Fonetika, morfologia*. Moscow.

Mussies, G.
1976 Greek in Palestine and the diaspora, in *The Jewish people in the first century*, ed. by S. Safrai and M. Stern, 2.1040–64. Philadelphia, Fortress.

Nahama, J.
1977 *Dictionnaire du Judeo-Espagnol*. Madrid.

Nahir, M.
1974a *Language academies, language planning and the case of the Hebrew revival*. Doctoral dissertation, University of Pittsburgh. Ann Arbor, University Microfilms.
1974b A study of the acceptance of the lexical work of the Hebrew Language Academy. *HA* 15.50–52.
1978 Normativism and educated speech in modern Hebrew. *IJSL* 18.49–67.

Nahum, Y. L.
1971 חשיפת גנוזים מתימן, ed. by S. Greidi. Holon, Israel.
1986 צהר לחשיפת גנזי תימן (edited by Y. Tobi). Tel Aviv.

Nathan, H.
1972 העיצור שי"ן בעברית. Masters thesis, Hebrew University.
1984 כלום נתבטל הניגוד נסתרת/נסתרות—נסתרים בתחום הכינויים הדבוקים?. *Massorot* 1.121–34.
1986 המונחים המשפטיים בלשון התנאים. *WCJS* 9, Division D, 23–29. Jerusalem.

Naveh, J.
1964–65 כתובות ארמיות קדומות. *Leš* 29.183–97.
1965a אלפבית in לקסיקון מקראי, ed. by M. Solieli and M. Berkuz, in 56–59. Tel Aviv, Dvir.
1965b כתובות. *ibid.*, 424–30.

1965c כתובות כנעניות ועבריות. *Leš* 30.65–80.
1967 התפתחות הכתב הארמי. Doctoral dissertation, Hebrew University.
1970 The development of the Aramaic script. *PIASH* 5. Jerusalem.
1971 Alphabet, Hebrew. *EJ* 1.674–89.
1973a Word division in West Semitic writing. *IEJ* 23.206–8.
1973b Some epigraphical considerations on the antiquity of the Greek alphabet. *AJA* 77.1–8.
1979 אותיות ותולדותיהן. Jerusalem, Keter.
1982 *Early history of the alphabet.* Jerusalem/Leiden, Magnes Press and E. J. Brill.

Naveh, J. and Shaked, S.
1985 *Amulets and magic bowls: Aramaic incantations of late antiquity.* Jerusalem: Magnes Press.

Naveh, P.
1969 כל שירי יעקב פרנסס. Jerusalem.

Nebe, G. W.
1972 Lexikalische Bemerkungen zu אוּשׁוֹן 'Fundament, Grundlage, Tiefe' in 4Q 184, Prov. 7, 9 und 20, 20. *RQ* 8/1 (29).97–103.

Neʾeman, P.
1973–74 היוצר ויצירתו. *LLA* 25/4–5 (244–45).

Neher, A.
1969 *De hébreu au français: la tradicion. Initiation et methodes* I. Paris, Klincksinck.
1984 The renaissance of Hebrew in the twentieth century. *Religion and literature* 16.21–35.

Nethanel, E.
1972 כתב־יד אנטונין לסדר טהרות—תיאור כללי, הפונולוגיה והפועל. Masters thesis, Hebrew University.

Netzer, A.
1982 An Isfahani Jewish folk song. *Irano-Judaica*, ed. by Saul Shaked, 180–203. Jerusalem, The Ben-Zvi Institute.

Netzer, N.
1969 הבחינות המילוניות בספר "אשכול הכופר" ליהודה הדסי הקראי. Masters thesis, Hebrew University.

Newby, G.
1972 The dependent pronoun in Semitic and Egyptian. *JQR* 62. 193–98.

Newsome, J. D.
1975 Toward a new understanding of the Chronicler and his purpose. *JBL* 94.201–17.

Nini, Y. and Fruchtman, M.
1980, eds. מעשה הרב, by Shem Tov ben Yitshaq Ardutiel or Don Santo De-Carrion. Tel Aviv University.

Nir, R.

1959 הניקוד הארץ ישראלי. Masters thesis, Hebrew University.

1967 הניב בחנוכו הלשוני של תלמיד בית־הספר התיכון בישראל. Doctoral dissertation, Hebrew University.

1975 The survival of obsolete Hebrew words in idiomatic expressions. *AAL* 2/3.11–17 (61–67).

1976 שקיפות לשונית ושקיפות פסיכו־לשונית בעברית החדשה. *Chaim Rabin jubilee volume*, ed. by B. Z. Fischler and R. Nir, 81–95. Jerusalem, Council on the Teaching of Hebrew.

1977 לחקר הסגנון של כותרות העיתונים העבריים. בלשנות שמושית 63–84.

1978 סמנטיקה של העברית החדשה. Tel Aviv, Amichai.

1979a חידושי לשון של אהרן מגד ב״עשהאל״. *LLA* 30.165–85.

1979b המבנה הסימנטי של שמות העצם המורחבים שבעברית החדשה. *HCL* 15.5–18.

1980a The semantic structure of nominal compounds in modern Hebrew. *BSOAS* 43.185–96.

1980b נסיון למיון הצירופים הלקסיקאליים שבעברית החדשה. *WCJS* 6, Division D, 163–68. Jerusalem.

1981a עיונים בחקר השיח. כותרות העיתון כיחידות־שיח, ed by S. Blum-Kulka, Y. Tobin and R. Nir, 75–116. Jerusalem.

1981b מה בין ״שימוש נורמאטיבי״ לבין ״שימוש קביל״ עברית החדשה? עיונים בבלשנות ובסמיוטיקה, 36–43. Jerusalem.

1982 השקיפות הלשונית של חידושי האקדמיה ללשון העברית. *HCL* 19.20–33.

1983 דרכי הצריכה של התרגום העברי בסרטי טלויזיה מיובאים. *Sefer David Gross*, ed. by S. Kodesh, 186–95. Jerusalem.

1986 תופעות של דו־משמעות בעברית העיתונאית בת־זמננו. *WCJS* 9, Division D, 55–62. Jerusalem.

Nir, R. and Nehemias, N.

1975 מדריך ביבליאוגרפי להוראת הלשון העברית. Jerusalem, Rubinstein.

Noble, S.

1940 *The survival of Middle High German and early German words in current Judeo-German translations of the Bible.* Doctoral dissertation, University of Ontario.

1958 Yiddish in a hebraishen levush (Yiddish in Hebrew garb), in *S. Niger memorial volume*, ed. by S. Bickel and L. Lehrer, 158–75. New York, YIVO Institute for Jewish Research.

1958–59 תרגומי שאילה מיידיש בעברית הרבנית. *Leš* 23.172–84.

1964 Hebraisms in the Yiddish of 17th century Ashkenaz (Yiddish). *For Max Weinreich on his seventieth birthday*, Yiddish section 120–30; English abstract 271–72.

Noffke, M. S.
1968 *The linguistic analysis of compared stylistic structures (on Isa 1–5).* Doctoral dissertation, University of Wisconsin.

Nöldeke, T.
1899 Die semitischen Sprachen, 2nd ed. Leipzig.
1904 *Beiträge zur semitischen Sprachwissenschaft.* Strasbourg.
1910 *Neue Beiträge zur semitischen Sprachwissenschaft.* Strasbourg.

Nysse, R. W.
1984 *A study of relationships between Greek and Hebrew witnesses to the text of 2 Samuel 1–9.* Doctoral dissertation, Harvard University. Ann Arbor, University Microfilms.

O'Connor, M. P.
1978 *Hebrew verse structure.* Doctoral dissertation, University of Michigan. Ann Arbor, University Microfilms.
1980 *Hebrew verse structure.* Winona Lake, IN, Eisenbrauns.

Ofek, U.
1951 זכר נקבה ברא אותם (בר׳ א, כד)—שמות העצם בלשון העברית ושמושם ה״מיני״ במקרא בתלמוד ובמדרשים. Masters thesis, Hebrew University.

O'Leary, D. E.
1923 *Comparative grammar of the Semitic languages.* London (reprinted Amsterdam, 1969).

Olshtain, E.
1981 קשרי גומלין בין כתיבה וקריאה וכשרותו של הקורא. עיונים בחקר השיח, ed. by S. Blum-Kulka, Y. Tobin and R. Nir, 51–73. Jerusalem.

Oppenheim, A. L.
1955 A note on *ṣôn barzel. IEJ* 5.89–92.

Orlinsky, H. M.
1960 *The origin of the* ketib-qere *system: a new approach. Congress volume*, Supplements to VT 7, 184–93. Leiden.
1965 Old Testament studies. *Religion*, ed. by P. Ramsey, 53–109. Englewood Cliffs, NJ, Prentice Hall.
1966 Prolegomenon to C. D. Ginsburg, *Introduction to the masoretico-critical edition of the Hebrew Bible*, 1897. New York, Ktav.
1974 *Essays in biblical culture and Bible translations.* New York.

Ornan, U.
1958 מלות היחס בשירתו של חיים נחמן ביאליק. Masters thesis, Hebrew University.
1958–59 ניתוח מכני והוראת התחביר. *Leš* 23.243–58.

1960–61 חלקי הדיבר. *Leš* 25.35–56.
1961–62 שיטת ניתוח מבני של דימויים ביצירות ספרותית: עיונים בבעית הסגנון. *Leš* 26.40–55.
1964a הצירופים השמניים בלשון הספרות העברית החדשה, בייחוד על פי הפרוזה של חיים נחמן ביאליק. Doctoral dissertation, Hebrew University (published as book, see below, 1965a).
1964b The Tiberian vocalisation system and the principles of linguistics. *JJS* 15.109–23.
1965a *The nominal phrase . . . with special reference to the prose of C. N. Bialik*. Published as *Technical report* no. 18, Educational Resources Information Center, Clearing House for Linguistics, May 1965, Cat. ED 011.644 (based on Ornan 1964a).
1965b תחביר העברית החדשה. Arranged from lectures by S. Bitterman. Jerusalem, Akademon (revised 1968 and 1973).
1967–68a כזה וכזאת. *Leš* 32.46–52.
1967–68b פרקי ייחוד (dealing with the compound nominal clause). מעלות 6.46–59. Tel Aviv, The Secondary Schools Teachers Association.
1968a תחביר העברית החדשה חלק א: המשפט הפשוט. Jerusalem.
1968b שימושם של כינויי קנין חבורים ופרודים בלשון ימינו. *WCJS* 4, 2.117–22. Jerusalem (English summary, 188).
1970–71 כולל ומחובר. *Leš* 35.272–91.
1971a Hebrew grammar. *EJ* 8.78–174.
1971b גישה חדשה לתיאור הפועל ולהוראתו והדגמתה בנטיית הבינוני. *Sefer Kamrat*, 32–11. Jerusalem, Council on the Teaching of Hebrew.
1971c בנינים ובסיסים, נטיות וגזרות. *Haᵓuniversita* 16 (June). 15–22.
1971–72 דקדוק יוצר (גנראטיבי וטרנספורמאטיבי)—מהו? 23/4 (224). 83–116 (entire fascicle).
1973a מקראה לתורת ההגה. Jerusalem, Department of Hebrew Language, Faculty of Humanities, Hebrew University.
1973b Ordered rules and the so-called phonologization of ancient allophones in Israeli Hebrew. *PICL* 11, Bologna, 2.1023–36 (reprinted in Hebrew translation in Ornan 1973a.333–59).
1975 פורמלי ופונקציונלי. *Rosen memorial volume*, ed. by B. Fischler and U. Ornan, 37–44. Jerusalem.
1976 על יצירת שרשים חדשים ועל כמה מלים מחודשות. *LLA* 27. 254–67.
1977 על המבטא העברי בכלל ובשידורי ישראל. *LLA* 28/10 (180). 259–70.
1980 עוד על הוראת הבניינים. *WCJS* 5, Division D, 1–9. Jerusalem.

1983a השערה הדבר בהגיים הנחציים. *HCL* 20.5–10.
1983b תצורת המלה העברית כיצד? *ML* 13–42.
1985a עברית אינה שפה יהודית. *Leš* 48–49.199–205.
1985b סיומו של תהליך תחיית הלשון. מחקרים בלשון, ed. M. Bar-Asher, 261–72. Jerusalem, Department of Hebrew Language, Hebrew University.
1985c ניקוד על ידי מחשב: לקח בלשני. *Sefer Avraham Even-Shoshan*, ed. B. Z. Luria, 67–76. Jerusalem.
1986 מפתחות וקונקורדנציות בכתב עברי פונמי. *WCJS* 9, Division D, 101–8. Jerusalem.

Ortega, M.
1977 *Estudio mesoretico de un menuscrito hebreo biblico espanol.* Codice nº 2 de la Biblioteca de la Universidad Complutense de Madrid. Madrid, Istituto 'Arias Montano'.
1980 *Texto hebreo biblico de Sefarad en* "Ôr Tôrah" *de Ménahem de Lonzanc. Madrid.*

Ouellette, J.
1980 An unnoticed device for expressing the future in middle Hebrew. *HAR* 4.127–29.

Pagis, D.
1962–64 מקורות לפעולתו של לוי אלתבאן במחקר הלשון. *Leš* 27–28. 49–57.
1967 שירי לוי אבן אלתבאן. Jerusalem, Israel Academy of Sciences and Humanities.
1970 שירת החול ותורת השיר למשה אבן־עזרא. Jerusalem, Mossad Bialik.
1972 Preface and bibliography in re-issued Yellin 1940 (*H*). Jerusalem, Magnes Press, Hebrew University.
1974–75 פיוטים מאוחרים מאיטליה. *KS* 50.288–312.
1976a Parallel theories in medieval Hebrew criticism. *AJSN* 17 (June, 1976), 5–6, 12.
1976b Trends in the study of Medieval Hebrew literature. *ibid.*, 7–9, 12.
1976c חידוש ומסורת בשירת החול העברית. Jerusalem, Keter.
1978 *Poesia secular* [*de*] *Selomo Ibn Gabirol.* Madrid (bilingual Hebrew-Spanish edition).
1979 Trends in the study of medieval Hebrew literature. *AJSR* 4.125–41.
1986 מחקרים במדעי. על המונח "ימי-הביניים" בחקר הספרות העברית היהדות, ed. M. Bar-Asher, 240–56. Jerusalem.

Pagis, D., Fleischer, E., and David, Y.
1983 כתבי פרופסור חיים שירמן (1904–1981). Jerusalem, Mossad Bialik.

Paper, H.
1958 *Yidiš un persiš: Cvey faln fun indoeyropeiš-semitišn cunoyf-tref.* New York, YIVO.
1964–68 The Vatican Judeo-Persian Pentateuch. *AcOr* 28 (1964).263–340; 29 (1965).75–181; 29 (1966).253–310; 31 (1968).55–113.
1968 Judeo-Persian Bible translations: some sample texts. *SBB* 8.99–113.
1972a *A Judeo-Persian Pentateuch.* Jerusalem, The Ben-Zvi Institute.
1972b Another Judeo-Persian Pentateuch translation: MS HUC 2193. *HUCA* 43.207–51.
1973a *Biblia Judeo-Persica: Edition variorum* (in microfilms). Ann Arbor, University Microfilms.
1973b Research in Judaeo-Persian: needs, deeds and prospects. *WCJS* 5 (1969) 4.85–89. Jerusalem.
1973c Ecclesiastes in Judeo-Persian. *Or* 42.328–37.
1976 A Judeo-Persian book of Job. *PIASH* 5/12. Jerusalem.
1978a Ed. *Jewish languages: theme and variation.* Cambridge, MA, Association for Jewish Studies.
1978b Judeo-Persian. *ibid.*, 103–14.
n.d. *Judeo-Persian as a source for Persian linguistic history.* Jerusalem, Institute of Asian and African Studies, Hebrew University.
1982 Proverbs in Judeo-Persian. *Irano-Judaica*, ed. by Saul Shaked, 12.2–47. Jerusalem, The Ben-Zvi Institute.

Pardee, D.
1978 Letters from Tel Arad. *UF* 10.289–336.
1981 Ugaritic and Hebrew metrics, in Gordon D. Young, ed., *Ugaritic in retrospect: 50 years of Ugarit and Ugaritic*, 113–30. Winona Lake, IN, Eisenbrauns.
1982 *Handbook of ancient Hebrew letters.* Chico, CA: Scholars Press (with S. D. Sperling, J. David Whitehead, and Paul-E. Dion).

Parfitt, T. V.
1972 The use of Hebrew in Palestine 1800–1882. *JSS* 17.237–52.

Parfitt, T. V. and Turčanová, M.
1981 Language revival: a comparison of the work of Eliezar Ben-Yehudah and L'udovit Štúr, in E. Silberschlag, ed., *Eliezer Ben-Yehuda, A symposium in Oxford*, 40–53. Oxford Center for Postgraduate Hebrew Studies.

Parker, S. B.
1967 *Studies in the grammar of Ugaritic prose texts.* Doctoral dissertation, Johns Hopkins University. Ann Arbor, University Microfilms.

Parks, M.
1979 *Teaching Hebrew to American students.* Doctoral dissertation, University of Wisconsin. Ann Arbor, University Microfilms.
Parunak, H. van Dyke
1975 A semantic survey of *nhm. Biblica* 56.512–32.
Passoni Dell'Aqua, A.
1984 La radice *jd*[c] ("il cognoscere/la conoscenza") nei documenti di Qumran. *Aevum* 58.20–37.
Patai, R.
1953 The phonology of Sabra Hebrew. *JQR* 44.51–54.
Patterson, D.
1981 Revival of literature and revival of language, in E. Silberschlag, ed., *Eliezer Ben-Yehuda, A symposium in Oxford,* 13–24. Oxford Centre for Postgraduate Hebrew Studies.
Patteson, R. K.
1967 *A study of the Hebrew text of Sirach 39:27–41:24.* Doctoral dissertation, Duke University. Ann Arbor, University Microfilms.
Peckham, B.
1968 *The development of the late Phoenician scripts.* Cambridge, MA, Harvard University Press.
Peladah, N.
1958–59 שכיחות ההגיים בעברית. Preface by C. Rabin. *Leš* 23.235–42.
Pelli, M.
1972 *The attitude of the first Maskilim toward the Hebrew language.* Beer Sheva, Israel.
1979 *The age of the Haskalah.* Leiden, Brill.
Penar, T.
1967 '*Lamedh vocativi*', exempla biblico hebraica. *VD* 45.52–46.
1975 *Northwest Semitic philology and the Hebrew fragments of Ben Sira.* Rome.
Penniachetti, F. A.
1968 *Studi sui pronomi determinativi semitici.* Naples, Istituto orientale de Napoli.
Pereira-Mendoza, J.
1940 *Rashi as philologist.* Manchester University Press.
Peres-Walden, Z.
1982 *The root of roots: children's construction of word formation processes in Hebrew.* Doctoral dissertation, Harvard University. Ann Arbor, University Microfilms.
Peretz, Y.
1961 עברית כהלכה. Tel Aviv, Sreberk.
1961–62 לדרכי ההדגשה בעברית החדשה. *Leš* 26.118–24.

1963–64 המחשה והפשטה. *LLA* 15/6 (148).
1964 בלשנות דרשנית. Tel Aviv.
1967 משפט הזיקה בלשון העברית לכל תקופותיה. Tel Aviv (includes 72 pp. of history of the Hebrew language with bibliography).

Perez, M.
1978 פרשנותו הפילולוגית של ר׳ יהודה אבן בלעם. Doctoral dissertation, Bar-Ilan University.
1981 הטיפול במלים יחידאיות בשורשן בפירושי ר׳ יהודה אבן בלעם. *Leš* 45.213–32.

Peri, Y.
1981 תורת הצורות של הארמית הגלילית על־פי שרידי התרגום הארצי־ישראלי. Masters thesis, Tel Aviv University.

Perlitt, L.
1969 *Bundestheologie im alten Testament.* Ramat Gan, Israel.

Perrot, C.
1969 Petuhot et setumot, étude sur les alinéas du Pentateuche. *RB* 76.50–91.

Perry, M.
1976 המבנה הסמאנטי של שירי ביאליק. The Israel Institute for Poetics and Semiotics, Tel Aviv University.

Pettinato, G.
1981 *The archives of Ebla: an empire inscribed in clay*, with an afterword by Mitchel Dahood. New York, Doubleday.

Phillipowsky, Z.
1895 Ed. מחברת מנחם. London/Edinburgh, reprinted Jerusalem, 1967.

Phillips, A.
1975 *Nebalah:* a term for serious disorderly and unruly conduct. *VT* 25.237–42.

Piamenta, M.
1960–61 השפעת הערבית על חידושי בן־יהודה. *LLA* 12.150–58.

Pilowsky, A. L.
1980 La querella Hebreo-Yiddish en Ereẓ Israel, 1907–1921, y sus proyecciones nacionales, politicas y culturales. *IJSL* 24, *Sociology of Yiddish*, ed. by J. A. Fishman, 75–108. The Hague, Mouton.

Pinchover, E.
1951 על הלשון של תרגום אונקלוס ותרגום הנביאים של "יונתן". Masters thesis, Hebrew University.

Pines, R.
1963 מונחי הצבע בעברית של המקרא ובלשון חכמים. Masters thesis, Hebrew University.
1975 הסתמיות במישור התחבירי. *Rosen memorial volume*, ed. by B. Z. Fischler and U. Ornan, 74–85. Jerusalem, Council on the Teaching of Hebrew.

Ploeg, J. van der
1959 *Le roleau de la guerre*. Leiden, Brill.
Ploeg, J. van der and Woude, A. S. van der
1971 *Le targum de Job*. Leiden.
Podolsky, B.
1981 הטעם כגורם מרופולוגי בעברית החדשה. *Leš* 43.155–56.
Poll, S.
1965 The role of Yiddish in American ultra-orthodox and Hassidic communities. *YIVO Annual of Jewish social sciences* 13.125–52.
1980 The sacred-secular conflict in the use of Hebrew and Yiddish among the ultra-orthodox Jews of Jerusalem. *IJSL* 24, ed. by J. A. Fishman, 109–25. The Hague, Mouton.
Polotsky, H.
1964a Semitics. *WHJP* 1, ed. by E. Speiser, 99–111. Rutgers University.
1964b Egyptian. *ibid.*, 121–34.
Polzin, R.
1976 *Late Biblical Hebrew: toward an historical typology of Biblical Hebrew prose*. Harvard Semitic monographs 12. Missoula, MT, Scholars Press.
Pope, M. H.
1949 A study of the Ugaritic particles *w*, *p* and *m*, with an excursus on *b*, *l* and *k*. Doctoral dissertation, Yale University. Ann Arbor, University Microfilms.
1964 The word *šaḥaṯ* in Job 9:31. *JBL* 83.269–78.
Porath, E.
1935–36 דרכי הלקסיקוגרפיה לספרות ההשכלה. *Leš* 7.356–61.
1938 לשון חכמים. Jerusalem.
Potchinsky, B. Z.
1943 שיטתו הלשונית של הסופר נפתלי הרץ וויזל. Masters thesis, Hebrew University.
Prager, L.
1974 Yiddish in the university. *The Jewish quarterly* 22 (1–2) 79–80).31–40 (reprinted in Fishman, ed., 1981a.529–45).
1981 מעמסו של המרכיב היידי במילונאות העברית. עיונים בבלשנות ובסמיוטיקה, 195–200. Jerusalem.
1982 *Yiddish literary and linguistic periodicals and miscellanies: a selective annotated bibliography*, published for the Association for the Study of Jewish Languages. Darby, PA and Haifa, Norwood Editions (with A. A. Greenbaum).
Price, J.
1969 *The development of a theoretical base for machine translation from Hebrew to English.* Doctoral dissertation, Dropsie University.

Price, R.
1977 *A lexicographical study of* "glh", "šbh" *and* "šwb" *in reference to exile in the Tanach.* Doctoral dissertation, Duke University. Ann Arbor, University Microfilms.

Prijs, L.
1950 *Der grammatikalische Terminologie des Abraham ibn Esra.* Basel.
1963 Der Ursprung des Reimes im Neuhebräischen. *BZ* 7.33–42.
1973 *Abraham ibn Esras Kommentar zu Genesis Kapitel 1.* Wiesbaden, Harrassowitz.

Prince, A. S.
1975 *The phonology and morphology of Tiberian Hebrew.* Doctoral dissertation, Massachusetts Institute of Technology. Ann Arbor, University Microfilms.

Puech, E.
1974 L'inscription du tunnel du Siloe. *RB* 81.196–214.

Puech, E. and Rofé, A.
1973 L'inscription de la citadelle d'Amman. *RB* 80.531–46.

Pummer, R.
1976–77 The present state of Samaritan studies. *JSS* 21:26–38; 22: 27–47.

Purvis, J.
1968 *The Samaritan Pentateuch and the origin of the Samaritan sect.* Harvard Semitic monographs 2. Cambridge, MA, Harvard University Press.

Putchinsky, B. Z.
1943 שיטתו הלשונית של הסופר נפתלי הירץ וויזל. Masters thesis, Hebrew University.

Qimron, E.
1970–71 מגילת תהילים מקומראן—סקירה לשונית. *Leš* 35.99–116.
1974–75 אלף־מצעית כאם קריאה בתעודות עבריות וארמיות מקומראן בהשוואה למקורות עבריים וארמיים אחרים. *Leš* 39.133–46.
1976 דקדוק הלשון העברית של מגילות מדבר יהודה. Doctoral dissertation, Hebrew University.
1976–77 נתפעל בינוני. *Leš* 41.144–47.
1977–78a לשונה של מגילת המקדש. *Leš* 42.83–98.
1977–78b לנוסחה של מגילת המקדש. *Leš* 42.136–45.
1978 ללשון בית שני בספר תהילים. *BM* 23(73).139–50.
1979 Review of Ben-Hayyim 1957–67 (*H*). *KS* 54.363–70.
1980a מקראה לסמינריון: בעיות בלשון המקרא. Jerusalem, Hebrew University, Faculty of Humanities, Department of Hebrew Language.
1980b למילונה של מגילת המקדש. שנתון, an annual for biblical and ancient near eastern studies 4.239–62. Jerusalem/Tel Aviv.

1981 המלות אשר, ש־, די בראש משפט עיקרי בעברית ובארמית. *Leš* 46.27–38.

1983 מלית השלילה אַל במקורותינו הקדומים. *ML* 473–82.

1986 *The Hebrew of the Dead Sea Scrolls*. Atlanta, GA, Scholars Press.

Rabi (Rabeeya), D.

1974 *Baghdadi Jewish proverbs and idioms with a linguistic and folkloristic commentary*. Doctoral dissertation, Dropsie College.

1975 Baghdadi Jewish proverbs and idioms: a study in linguistics and folklore. *GCA* 4.77–84.

1977 A critical analysis of a *nashid* by Shalem Shabazi and a Hallel found in an unpublished manuscript. *GCA* 6.79–92.

1978 A preliminary study of Hebrew forms in the Arabic dialect of the Jews of Baghdad. *GCA* 7.51–63.

Rabi, Y.

1977 שיחות על עברית. Sifriyat Poᶜalim.

1985 מצוקתה של העברית הישראלית המדוברת. *Sefer Avraham Even-Shoshan*, ed. B. Z. Luria, 249–53. Jerusalem.

Rabin, C.

1943 Saadya Gaon's Hebrew prose style. *Saadya studies*, 127–38. Manchester.

1945 ר׳ אברהם בר חייא ותחיית העברית במאה הי״א. מצודה 3–4. 158–70.

1951 *Ancient West-Arabian*. London.

1955 Notes on the Habakuk scrolls and the history of the O.T. text. *JTS* n.s. 6

1957 *Qumran studies*, Oxford (reprinted 1975, New York, Schocken).

1957–58a לחקר העברית הספרותית החדשה. *Leš* 22.246–57.

1957–58b הערות בלשניות לבעית תרגום דברי ש״י עגנון ללועזית. *Yovel Shay*, ed. by B. Kurtzweill, 13–25. Ramat Gan.

1957–58c עברית בינונית. *LLA* 9/3(85).88–92.

1958 The historical background of Qumran Hebrew. *SH* 4.144–61.

1958–59 הנחות יסוד לחקר לשונו של עגנון. לעגנון ש״י, 217–36. Jerusalem.

1960a התנועות הקטנות בעברית הטברנית. *Sefer Tur Sinai*, 161–206. Jerusalem.

1960b שמית והשתקפויותיה בעברית *ā*. Tarbiz 30.99–111.

1961–62 התיתכן סמנטיקה מקראית? *BM* 7.17–27.

1962 מלים זרות במקרא. *EM* 3.1070–80.

1963a Hittite words in Hebrew. *Or* 32.113–39.

1963b The origins of the subdivisions of Semitic. *Hebrew and Semitic studies presented to G. R. Driver*, 105–15. Oxford.

1964a מלים חתיות בעברית. *Sefer Segal* 151–79. Jerusalem (=Rabin 1963a).

1964b תחביר לשון המקרא, edited from lecture notes by S. Shkolnikov. Jerusalem, Akademon (reprinted 1974, 1979).

1964c Un phénomène d'alternance stylistique des constructions indéfinies en hébreu biblique. *GLECS* 10.34–35.

1965 יסודות הדקדוק המשוה של הלשון העברית. Lecture notes arranged by A. Hurvitz. Jerusalem, Akademon (expanded edition of same title, 1962–64. Reprinted 1973).

1967a גורמים סוציולוגיים בתולדות הלשון העברית. New York.

1967b Terms from the realm of social psychology. *VT* Supplement, 16.217–30.

1968a זמנים ודרכים בפועל שבלשון 'ספר חסידים'. *WCJS* 4, 2.113–16. Jerusalem (English summary, 188).

1968b Towards a descriptive semantics of biblical Hebrew. *PICO* 26, 2.51–52. New Delhi.

1968–69 תרגום השאילה ככוח יוצר בלשון. *LLA* 20.272–78.

1969a השפעל בעברית ובארמית—מהותו ומוצאו. *EI* 9.148–58.

1969b The structure of the Semitic system of case endings. *PICSS*, 190–204. Jerusalem, Israel Academy of Sciences.

1969c The revival of the Hebrew language. *Ariel* 25.25–34.

1970a Hebrew. Linguistics in Southeast Asia and North Africa. *Current trends in linguistics* 6, ed. by T. A. Sebeok, 304–46. The Hague, Mouton.

1970b מלים בעברית המקראית מלשון האינדו־ארים שבמזרח הקרוב. *Samuel Yeivin jubilee volume*, 462–97. Jerusalem.

1970c תורת ההגה של העברית המקראית. Mimeographed notes for lectures. Jerusalem, Hebrew University.

1971a תורת ההגה של העברית המקראית. Jerusalem.

1971b תולדות הלשון. Edited from lectures by R. Rosenberg, Jerusalem. Hebrew University, Faculty of Humanities, Department of the Hebrew Language.

1971c Semitic languages. *EJ* 14.1149–57.

1971d Loanword evidence in Biblical Hebrew for trade between Tamil Nad and Palestine in the first millenium B.C., in *Proceedings of the second international conference seminar of Tamil studies* (Madras, 1968), 1.432–40. Kuala Lumpur.

1971e Spelling reform—Israel 1968, in *Can language be planned? Sociolinguistic theory and practice for developing nations*, ed. by R. Rubin and B. H. Jernudd, Honolulu, University of Hawaii.

1972 Hebrew *zaḥal*. *IOS* 2.362–68.

1973a משמעותו של הצורות הדקדוקיות בלשון המקרא ובלשון של ימינו. Jerusalem, Akademon.

1973b Hebrew *baddîm* 'power'. *JSS* 18.57–58.

1973c עיקרי תולדות הלשון העברית. Jerusalem, The Jewish Agency.
1974a On enlarging the basis of Hebrew etymology. *HA* 15.25–28.
1974b La langue du Raschi, in *Raschi, ouvrage collectif*, 103–22. Paris.
1974–75a אבנט ופטדה. *Leš* 39.182–86.
1974–75b מהותו של הדיבור העברי שלפני התחייה. *LLA* 26.89–92, 227–33.
1975a Lexicostatistics and the internal divisions of Semitics. *Hamitosemitica*, ed. by J. and T. Bynon, 85–102. The Hague, Mouton.
1975b National language policy in Israel, in *Language policy and language development of Asian countries*, ed. A. Q. Perez and A. O. Santiago, 43–54. Manila.
1975c The ancient in the modern: ancient source materials in present-day Hebrew writing, in *Language and texts*, ed. by H. Paper, 149–79. Ann Arbor, Center for Coördination of Ancient and Modern Studies, University of Michigan.
1975d קשרים הודיים של שיר השירים. *Sefer Baruch Kurzweill*, 264–74. Tel Aviv, Schocken and The University of Tel Aviv.
1975e בעיות בהוראת הפועל העברי. ארחות 8/9.97–103. Jerusalem, Ministry of Education and Culture.
1976a Bibliography of C. Rabin in *Rabin jubilee volume*, כלשון עמו, ed. by B. Fischler and R. Nir. Jerusalem, Council on the Teaching of Hebrew.
1976b אטימולוגיות עבריות על סמך שפות כושיות־חמיות. חקר ועיון, 233–58. University of Haifa.
1976c Hebrew and Aramaic in the first century, in *The Jewish people in the first century* 2, ed. by S. Safrai and M. Stern, 1007–39. Philadelphia, Fortress.
1976d Language treatment in Israel, *Language planning newsletter*, 2/4.1–6. Honolulu, East and West Center.
1976e ראש ולענה. ראשי בשמים. ראש פתנים. *Leš* 40.85–91.
1976f הערות לשורש קנן/כנן. *Leš* 40.291–92.
1976g Liturgy and language in Judaism, in W. J. Samarin, ed., *Language in religious practice*, 131–55. Rowley, MA, Newbury House.
1977a Hamitic languages as a source of Semitic etymologies. *WCJS* 6, 1.329–40.
1977b Acceptability in a revived language, in S. Greenbaum, ed., *Acceptability in language*. The Hague, Mouton.
1977c הנורמטיביות והבלשנות. הד האולפן, 19.6–8.
1977d התעתיק העברי לשמות לועזיים. *LLA* 279.227–32.
1977e Ed. הבלשנות השימושית והנחלת הלשון, from the workshop 3–4. Jerusalem, The Council on the Teaching of Hebrew.

1977f הסמנטיקה והוראת לשון שנייה. *ibid.*, 185–98.

1977g אנחנו והלשון in מאסף ירושלים 11/12.37–49.

1978a The uniqueness of Bible translation, in E. Mveng and Z. Werbelowsky, eds., *Black Africa and the Bible*, 108–16. Jerusalem.

1978b ארחות. אוצר המלים בשלב מתקדם, 10.1–11.

1978c הערות מילוניות, in *Studies in Bible and the ancient near east presented to Samuel E. Loewenstamm on his seventieth birthday*, 2.397–407. Jerusalem.

1978–79 Review of Sarfatti 1978 and Nir 1978 (*H*). *Leš* 43.71–74.

1979a New words in an old language. רחובות 1/1.36–39.

1979b The emergence of Classical Hebrew, in *WHJP* 5.71–78, 293–95. Jerusalem.

1979c גיוון סגנוני בגוף הסתמי במקרא. Sefer Meir Wallenstein, 256–68. Jerusalem.

1979d הדקדוק שאנו מלמדים in מנחה... לשלמה קודש. 103–7. Jerusalem.

1979e מה היתה תחיית הלשון העברית? in ספר שלום סיון, ed. by A. Even-Shoshan *et al.*, 125–40. Jerusalem, Kiryat Sepher.

1979f Hebrew and Arabic in medieval Jewish philosophy, in *Studies . . . in honor of Alexander Altmann*, 235–45. University of Alabama.

1980a Strength or cheerfulness, in *Oriental studies presented to B. J. Isserlin*, 11–23. Leiden, Brill.

1980b מה היא עברית טובה? הד האולפן. 34.5–8.

1981a What constitutes a Jewish language? *IJSL* 30.19–28.

1981b Articles מילון and תרגום in אנציקלופדיה למדעי החברה, supplementary volume, cols. 592–601, 921–30. Jerusalem.

1981c עיסוק בלשני בלשון התפלה in מחקרים... לזכר יוסף היינמן, 163–71. Jerusalem.

1981d לשון המורה בכיתה. פרקים 3.3–10. Petah Tikva.

1981e מה בין תיכנון הלשון לבין נורמטיביות? in עיונים בבלשנות ובסמיוטיקה... לזכרו של מ. בן־אשר 44–51. Jerusalem.

1981f חקר השיח in עיונים בחקר השיח, ed. by S. Blum-Kulka, Y. Tobin and R. Nir, 1–15. Jerusalem.

1981g חקר שיח כעזר בחקר המקרא. יתʺר שאת, מנחת ידידות לכבוד הפרופ׳ יהודה ת׳ רדאי, ed. by N. Arrarat *et al.*, 72–89. Haifa, The Technion.

1982 Israeli research on Biblical Hebrew linguistics. *Immanuel* 14.26–33.

1983a אטימולוגיות קתבניות. *ML* 483–96.

1983b תקופותיה של הלשון העברית. *WCJS* 8, Bible and Hebrew Language, 19–25. Jerusalem.

1983c הוראת הלשון ומדעי הלשון. *Sefer David Gross*, ed. by S. Kodesh, 177–85. Jerusalem.
1983d The national idea and the revival of Hebrew. *Studies in Zionism* 7.31–48.
1985a מצוקתה של העברית הישראלית המדוברת. *Sefer Avraham Even-Shoshan*, ed. B. Z. Luria, 255–65. Jerusalem.
1985b תקופותיה של הלשון העברית. מחקרים בלשון, ed. M. Bar-Asher, 27–35. Jerusalem, Department of Hebrew Language, Hebrew University.
1985c לשון המקרא ולשון חכמים בעברית בת־ימינו. *Ibid.*, 273–85.

Rabin, C. and Fischler, B. Z., eds.
1979 מנחה לקודש, *Sholomo Kodesh volume*. Jerusalem, Council on the Teaching of Hebrew.

Rabin, C. and Raday, Z.
1974 אוצר המלים: מלים, צירופים ואמרות מסודרים לפי תחומי משמעות. 2 vols. Jerusalem.

Rabinovitz, J.
1951–52 νομοφύλαξ—מופלג. מופלא. *Leš* 18.25–26.

Rabinowitz, H. R.
1975–76 הרשב״ם כפרשן המקרא. *BM* 21.462–71.

Rabinowitz, I.
1971 The Qumran Hebrew original of Ben Sirah's concluding acrostic on wisdom. *HUCA* 42.173–84.

Rabinowitz, S.
1947 ספר המשקלים. New York.

Rabinowitz, Z. M.
1965 הלכה ואגדה בפיוטי יניי. Tel Aviv.
1976 גנזי מדרש. Tel Aviv (the oldest forms of rabbinic midrashim according to Geniza manuscripts).
1977 קרובת יניי לסדר ׳האזינו׳, in *A. M. Habermann jubilee volume*, ed. by Z. Malachi, 275–78. Jerusalem, Rubin Mass.

Radday, Y.
1970a עיונים לשוניים־סטטיסטיים בספר ישעיהו. Doctoral dissertation, Hebrew University.
1970b אקסצנטריות של מילון ואחדות ספר ישעיהו. *Tarbiz* 39.323–41.
1970c Two computerized statistical-linguistic tests concerning the unity of Isaiah. *JBL* 89.319–24.
1970–71 עיונים ברשימות השכיחות בעברית. *Leš* 35.218–34.
1973 *The unity of Isaiah in the light of statistical linguistics.* Hildesheim.

Radday, Y. and Schor, H.
1976 על שכיחות האותיות וההגאים בעברית המקראית והחדשה. *Chaim*

Rabin jubilee volume, ed. by B. Fischler and R. Nir, 120–29. Jerusalem.

1977 ר' החבור—קריטריון מבחין בין מחבר למחבר ובין סוג ספרותי לסוג בספרות המקראית. *WCJS* 6, 1.197–206.

Radday, Y. and Wickmann, D.

1975 The unity of Zachariah examined in the light of statistical linguistics. *ZAW* 87.30–55.

Rainey, A. F.

1969 The contribution of the Samaritan inheritance to research into the history of Hebrew. *PIASH* 3. Jerusalem.

1971 Verbal forms with infixed *-t* in the West Semitic El-Amarna letters. *IOS* 1.86–102.

1978a The Barth-Ginsburg law in the Amarna tablets. *EI* 14. 8*–13*.

1978b The scatterbrained scribe. *Studies in Bible and the ancient near east presented to S. E. Loewenstamm on his seventieth birthday*, 1.141–50. Jerusalem.

Rankin, O. S.

1930 Alliteration in Hebrew poetry. *JTS* 31.285–331.

Rappel, D.

1982 הצד הפרשני של הסטיות הדקדוקיות בתרגום אונקלוס. *Leš* 85–96.

Ratner, R. J.

1983 *Gender problems in biblical Hebrew*. Doctoral dissertation, Hebrew Union College-Jewish Institute of Religion. Ann Arbor, University Microfilms.

Ratzhaby, Y.

1956–57 עיונים בשירת ספרד. *Leš* 21.22–32.

1958–59 עיוני לשון בפיוטי ר' משה בן עזרא. *LLA* 10.9–16.

1966–69 עיוני לשון בשירת תקופת ספרד. *LLA* 18.195–203, 227–36; 20.67–75, 128–34, 164–69.

1968 ילקוט שירי תימן. Jerusalem.

1969–71 לשונות עבריים בדיבורם הערבי של יהודי תימן. *LLA* 21.227–32, 259–65; 22.43–46.

1970–71 שרידי ניקוד בבלי ב"כתר תורה" (תאג') תימני. *Sinai* 35(69). 225–45.

1971 שירי ר' שלם שבזי (מילואים ביבליוגרפיים). *KS* 46.338–42.

1971–72 מסורת לשון חכמים בשירתנו הספרדית. *LLA* 23.39–52, 119–25.

1972–73a הערות על מסורת לשון חכמים בשירה העברית בימי הביניים. *Leš* 37.311–12.

1972–73b עיוני לשון בשירתנו הספרדית. *Sinai* 73.50–62.

1973–74a לשונות עבריים בדבורם הערבי של יהודי תימן. *Leš* 38.269–85.

1973–74b לשונות עבריים באיגרותיהם של בני תימן. *LLA* 25/7 (247).175–82; 25/8 (248).212–19.

1974 לשון ודקדוק בשירת ר׳ שלם שבזי. *H. Yalon memorial volume*, Bar-Ilan departmental researches 2, 512–46.

1975–76 לשונות גנאי שבפי יהודי תימן. *LLA* 27.5 (265).139–50; 27/6 (266).177–85.

1977 לשונות עבריים בדיבורם של בני תימן. *LLA* 28/10 (180).270–74.

1978 אוצר לשון הקודש של בני תימן. Tel Aviv.

1979 קינות חדשות לרבי יהודה הלוי. *Sinai* 43(85).124–44.

1980 ״פ״א בלשון ישמעאל״ בכתובי מקרא. *SHSL*, 9–17.

1981 מקראות בדיבורם של בני תימן in הגות עברית בארצות האיסלאם, ed. by M. Zohory *et al.*, 28–43. Jerusalem, Brit Ivrit Olamit.

1981–82 לשונות בספרות שאלות ותשובות. *LLA* 33.99–104.

1984–85 משירת תימן (י״ג שירים חדשים). ביקורת ופרשנות 20.121–39.

1985 עיוני לשון בספרות ימי הביניים. *Sefer Avraham Even-Shoshan*, ed. B. Z. Luria, 267–88.

Redford, D. B.

1970 *A study of the biblical story of Joseph.* Leiden, Brill (includes a linguistic discussion on the dating).

Regev, Z.

1959 דרכי הקטנה בעברית של ימינו. Masters thesis, Hebrew University.

1983 טיפוח הלשון בתחום המשלבים במסגרת תכנון הלימודים במערכת החינוך. Doctoral dissertation, Hebrew University.

Reider, M.

1978 Spanish of United States Sephardim: state of the art. *Orbis* 27.33–43.

Reif, J. A.

1968 *Construct state nominalizations in Modern Hebrew.* Doctoral dissertation, University of Pennsylvania. Ann Arbor, University Microfilms.

Reif, J. A. and Levinson, H.

1965 *Hebrew basic course.* Foreign Service Institute, Department of State, Washington, DC.

Reif, S. C.

1973 A defense of David Qimchi. *HUCA* 44.211–46.

1979 *Shabbethai Sofer and his prayerbook.* Cambridge.

Reiner, E.

1970 Akkadian in *Current trends in linguistics* 6, ed. by T. A. Sebeok, 274–303. The Hague, Mouton.

Reiner, F.

1974 Masoretes, rabbis and Karaites: a comparison of biblical interpretations. *Masoretic studies* 1, ed. by H. M. Orlinsky, 137–47. Missoula, MT.

Rendsberg, G. A.
1980a *Evidence for spoken Hebrew in biblical times.* Doctoral dissertation, New York University. University Microfilms, Ann Arbor, Michigan.
1980b Janus parallelism in Gen. 49:26. *JBL* 99.291–93.
1980c Late Biblical Hebrew and the date of "P". *JANES* 12.65–80 (critical review of Polzin 1976).
1982a Double polysemy in Gen. 49:6 and Job 3:6. *CBQ* 44.48–51.
1982b Dual personal pronouns and dual verbs in Hebrew. *JQR* 73.38–58.

Revah, I. S.
1970 *Formation des parlers Judeo-Espagnols des Balkans.* Simposio de fiologia Romanica, Rio de Janiero, 20–28 August 1958, 141–60. Rio de Janiero, Ministerio da Educacio et Cultura.

Revell, E. J.
1969 A new biblical fragment with Palestinian vocalization. *Textus* 7.59–75.
1970a *Hebrew texts with Palestinian vocalization.* University of Toronto Press.
1970b Studies in the Palestinian vocalization of Hebrew. *Essays on the ancient Semitic world*, ed. by J. W. Wevers and D. B. Redford, 51–100. University of Toronto Press.
1971 The oldest evidence for the Hebrew accent system. *BJRL* 54.214–22.
1972 The placing of the accent signs in biblical texts with Palestinian pointing. *Studies in the ancient Palestinian world*, ed. by J. W. Wevers and D. B. Redford, 34–45. University of Toronto Press.
1973 A new sub-system of 'Tibero-Palestinian' pointing. *WCJS* 5, 4.91–107. Jerusalem.
1974a The relation of the Palestinian to the Tiberian Massora. *Masoretic studies* 1, ed. by H. M. Orlinsky, 87–98. Missoula, MT.
1974b Review of Allony 1969a. *JSS* 19.123–29.
1974c MdW II, MS M and other Palestinian MSS with defective accentuation. *Masoretic studies* 1, ed. by H. M. Orlinsky, 149–57. Missoula, MT.
1974d Aristotle and the accents: the categories of speech in Jewish and other authors. *JSS* 19.19–35.
1976 Biblical punctuation and chant in the second temple period. *JSJPHRP* 7.181–98.

1977 *Biblical texts with Palestinian pointing and their accents.* SBL massoretic studies. Missoula, MT, Scholars Press.
1980 Pausal forms in biblical Hebrew: their function, origin and significance. *JSS* 25.60–80.

Richter, W.
1975 Verbalvalenz und Verbalsatz. Ein Betrag zur syntaktischen Grundlegung einer alttestamentliche Literaturwissenschaft. *JNSL* 4.61–69.

Rickards, R. R.
1970 *The root* יָשַׁר; *a critical study of its derivatives in the Old Testament.* Masters thesis, University of Melbourne.

Rieder, D.
1974 *Pseudo-Jonathan: Targum Jonathan ben Uziel on the Pentateuch; copied from the London MS (British Museum add. 27031).* Jerusalem (see also M. L. Klein, *JBL* 94 [1975], 277–79).

Riesner, I.
1978 Der Stamm עבד im alten Testament. Berlin, De Gruyter.

Rimbach, J. A.
1972 *Animal imagery in the Old Testament. Some aspects of Hebrew poetics.* Doctoral dissertation, Johns Hopkins University. Ann Arbor, University Microfilms.

Rin, S.
1963 Ugaritic–Old Testament affinities. *BZ*, n.s. 7.22–33.
1967 Ugaritic–Old Testament affinities. *BZ*, n.s. 11.174–92.
1968 עלילות האלים, *Acts of the gods, the Ugaritic epic poetry.* Jerusalem, Israel Society for Biblical Research (with Shifra Rin).
1971 Review of A. F. Rainey, *A social structure of Ugarit* (*H*). *JNES* 30.225–26.

Ring, Y.
1971 חידושים לשוניים מתוך ״פנקס ועד ארבע הארצות״. Masters thesis, Hebrew University.
1973 צירופי היחס בלשון העברית החדשה. Doctoral dissertation, Hebrew University.
1981 תחביר הלשון העברית. Tel Aviv.

Rivlin, J.
1939 פעולתו של דוד ילין בלשון ובועד הלשון. *Leš* 12.237–40.
1956–57 משהו על יסודות עבריים ב״לשון תרגום״. *Leš* 21.308–13.
1959 שירת יהודי התרגום: פרקי עלילה וגבורה בפי יהודי כורדיסתן. Jerusalem.

Roberts, B. J.
1948 The evidence of the Tiberian massoretic text. *JTS* 49.8–16.

1979 The textual transmission of the Old Testament, in G. W. Anderson, ed., *Tradition and interpretation*, 1–30. Oxford.

Robertson, D. A.

1966 *Linguistic evidence in dating early Hebrew poetry*. Doctoral dissertation, Yale University. Published in 1972 in SBL dissertation series, no. 3, Cambridge, MA.

1969 The morphemes *-y* (*-ī*) and *-w* (*-ō*) in Biblical Hebrew. *VT* 19.211–23.

Roeh, I.

1982 *The rhetoric of news in the Israel radio*. Bochum, Studienverlag N. Brockmeyer.

Rooy, H. F. van

1986 Conditional sentences in biblical Hebrew. *WCJS* 9, Division D, English section, 9–16. Jerusalem.

Rosén, H. B.

1953 Remarques au sujet de la phonologue de l'hébreu biblique. *RB* 60.30–40.

1955–56 Review of R. Weiman 1950 (*H*). *Tarbiz* 24.234–47.

1956a העברית שלנו. Tel Aviv.

1956b אספקטים וזמנים בעברית המקראית. *Sefer Biram*, ed. by H. Y. Gevaryahu, B. Luria, and Y. Mehlmann, 205–18. Jerusalem.

1956c מְפֻעָל בעברית הישראלית. *Leš* 21.139–48.

1957 עברית טובה. Jerusalem (2nd ed. 1967).

1960 על תופעה תחבירית בשמית צפון־מערבית קדומה. *Sefer Tur Sinai*, ed. by M. Haran and B. Luria, 127–42. Jerusalem.

1961 Syntactical notes on Israeli Hebrew. *JAOS* 81.21–26.

1962 *Textbook of Israeli Hebrew*. 2nd corrected ed., 1976. Chicago, University of Chicago.

1969a The comparative assignment of certain Hebrew tense forms. *PICSS*, 212–34. Jerusalem.

1969b הרכבי שם־תואר ושמות תואר מורכבים בעברית הישראלית. *Bar-Ilan volume in humanities and social sciences*. Decennial volume, 2 (1955–1965), 98–105. Jerusalem.

1969c Israel language policy, language teaching and linguistics. *Ariel* 25.92–111.

1974 La position descriptive et comparative des formes contextuelles en hébreu. *ACILCS* 1, 246–55. Paris.

1976 הקנית נטיית הפועל העברי ה״רגולארי״—בסיסי—מוצא ומעברים סדורים. *Chaim Rabin jubilee volume*, ed. by B. Fischler and R. Nir, 130–39. Jerusalem, Council on the Teaching of Hebrew.

1977 *Contemporary Hebrew*. Trends in Linguistics 11. The Hague and Paris, Mouton.

1979a יוסי עבר דירה וכו׳ (עיון בתחביר ימינו). ספר שלום סיון, ed. by A. Even-Shoshan *et al.*, 141–44. Jerusalem, Kiryath Sepher.

1979b L'hébreu et ses rapports avec le monde classique, *GLECS*, Suppl. 7. Paris.
1982 אספקטים בחקר סדר חלקי המשפט בעברית הישראלית הכתובה. *WCJS* 8, Division D, 39–42. Jerusalem.
1985 קווים לתולדות מערכת זמני הפועל העברית. מחקרים בלשון, ed. M. Bar-Asher, 287–93. Jerusalem, Department of Hebrew Language, Hebrew University.

Rosenbaum, S. N.
1975 *The concept 'antagonist' in Hebrew psalmography*. Doctoral dissertation, Brandeis University. Ann Arbor, University Microfilms.

Rosenbaum, Y., Nadel, E. and Fellman, J.
1974 Related literature: recent, current and forthcoming. *Linguistics* 120.147–60.

Rosenfeld, M.
1974 הפיוטים הארמיים לשבועות—בחינתם הדיאלקטית ותרומתם למלון הארמי. Masters thesis, Bar-Ilan University.

Rosenthal, E. S.
1982 למילון התלמודי, Talmudica Iranica. *Irano-Judaica*, ed. by Saul Shaked, 38–134 (Hebrew section). Jerusalem, The Ben-Zvi Institute.
1983 פירושי סתומות בלשון חכמים. *ML* 507–14.

Rosenthal, F.
1961 *A grammar of Biblical Aramaic*. Wiesbaden, Harrassowitz.
1978 Aramaic studies during the past thirty years. *JNES* 37.81–91.

Rosner, D.
1974 The simile and its use in the Old Testament. *Semitics* 4.37–46.

Roth, L.
1961 Hebraists and non-Hebraists of the seventeenth century. *JSS* 6/2.204–21.

Rothenberg, P. D.
1942 שמות התנאים והאמוראים העבריים במקורות התלמודיים מבחינה בלשנית. Masters thesis, Hebrew University.

Rottenberg, M.
1979 כללי תחביר נעלמים של לשון המקרא. Tel Aviv, Reshafim.
1982 המלים אחד ואחת ככינויי זהות. *Leš* 46.141–42.

Rozenberg, M.
1963 *The term* špṭ: *an investigation of biblical and extra-biblical sources*. Doctoral dissertation, University of Pennsylvania.

Rubinkiewicz, R.
1977 *L'Apocalypse d'Abraham en slave*. Doctoral dissertation. Rome.

1980 Les sémitismes dans l'apocalypse d'Abraham. *FO* 21.141–48.
1983 The Apocalypse of Abraham, in J. H. Charlesworth, ed., *The Old Testament Pseudepigrapha* 1.681–705. New York, Doubleday.

Rubinstein, A.
1953 Hebraisms in the Slavonic 'Apocalypse of Abraham'. *JJS* 4.108–15.
1954 Hebraisms in the 'Apocalypse of Abraham'. *JJS* 5.132–35.
1963 The anomalous perfect with *waw*-conjunctive in Biblical Hebrew. *Biblica* 44.62–69.

Rubinstein, E.
1964 משפט הייחוד העברית של ימינו. Masters thesis, Hebrew University.
1968a המשפט השמני העברית של ימינו. Doctoral dissertation, Hebrew University.
1968b המשפט השמני, עיונים בתחביר ימינו. Hakibbutz Hameuchad.
1970–71 תיאור הנשוא ותיאור המשפט ומעמדם התחבירי. *Leš* 35.60–74.
1971a הצירוף הפועלי, עיונים בתחביר ימינו. Hakkibutz Hameuchad.
1971b המשפט המורכב ודרכי הוראתו. *Sefer Kamrat*, 181–85 (English summary xv–xvi). Jerusalem, Council on the Teaching of Hebrew.
1973–74 שָׁלַח—שִׁלַּח—עיון תחבירי וסימנטי בלשון המקרא. *Leš* 38.11–32.
1975a תזוזות קטיגוריאליות בצירופי שם התואר בלשון המדוברת *Rosen memorial volume*, ed. by B. Z. Fischler and U. Ornan, 100–106. Jerusalem, Council on the Teaching of Hebrew.
1975b Double causation in a sentence, a syntactic-semantic study in biblical Hebrew. *IOS* 5, 32–44.
1975–76 לפני + צ״ש: מסימון של מקום לסימון של ה״חושב״. *Leš* 40. 57–66.
1977 The verb *ṣiwwāh*—a study in the syntax of biblical Hebrew. *WCJS* 6, 1.207–12.
1978–79 ערכיות תחבירית ערכיות סמנטית. *Leš* 43.3–19.
1980a פעלים המביעים מצב רגשי: עיון תחבירי־סימנטי. *Leš* 45.5–16.
1980b העברית שלנו והעברית הקדומה. Jerusalem, Ministry of Defense (based on talks on Israel Defense Forces Radio).
1980c פעלים כמימוש פרופוזיציות ופעלים ככינוי לפעולות. *HCL* 15. 19–27.
1982b שקיפות סמנטית ואטימות סמנטית; עיון ב״פועלי מקום״ בלשון המקרא. *Te^cudah* 2, Bible studies Y. . Grintz in memoriam, ed. B. Uffenheimer. Tel Aviv University.
1983a עיונים בהצרכת הפועל. *ML* 497–505.
1983b פעלים שנושאם מימוש פרופוזיציה. *Leš* 47.147–54.

1983c מתחביר לסימאנטיקה: מדרכי העיון בלשון המקראית. *WCJS* 8, Bible and Hebrew Language, 69–78. Jerusalem.

1986 עיונים סמנטיים בפועל תיאורי בלשון המקרא. *Te^{c}udah* 4, ed. M. A. Friedman and M. Gil, 55–78. Tel Aviv University.

Rudolph, W.

1966 Eigentümlichkeiten der Sprache Hoseas. *Studia biblica et Semitica*, Theodoro Christiano Vriezen, 313–17. Wageningen.

Rüger, H. P.

1968 Zum Problem der Sprache Jesu. *ZNW* 59.113–22.

1970 Text und Textform im hebräischen Sirach. BZAW, 112. Berlin.

Ruiz, G.

1975 *Lamed* y *bet* enfaticos y *lamed* vocativo en Deuteroisaisas. Homenaje a J. Prado, 147–61. Madrid.

Rummel, S., ed.

1981 *Ras Shamra parallels: the texts from Ugarit and the Hebrew Bible*, vol. 3, Analecta Orientalia 51. Rome, Biblical Institute Press.

Rundgren, E.

1961a *Abriss des Aspektlehre.* Stockholm.

1961b *Das althebräischen Verbum.* Uppsala.

1963 *Erneuerung des Verbalaspekts im Semitischen.* Acta societas linguisticae Upsaliensis. Uppsala.

Rutherford, P.

1968 *Bibliography of American doctoral dissertations in linguistics 1900–1964.* Washington Center for Applied Linguistics.

Ryder, S. A.

1974 *The* D-*stem in Western Semitic.* The Hague, Mouton.

Sabar, Y.

1965–66 תפסירים למקרא ופיוטים בלשונם הארמית של יהודי קורדיסתאן. ספונות 10.335–410.

1973–74 היסודות הערביים בניב הארמי שבפי יהודי זאכו בקורדיסתאן. *Leš* 38.206–19.

1974a Nursery-rhymes and baby words in the Jewish Neo-Aramaic dialect of Zakho (Iraq). *JAOS* 94.329–36.

1974b First names, nicknames and family names among the Jews of Kurdistan. *JQR* 65.43–51.

1974–75 היסודות העבריים בניבים הארמיים של יהודי אזרביג׳אן. *Leš* 39.272–95.

1976 *Pešaṭ vayhi bešallaḥ*, a Neo-Aramaic midrash of the Jews of Zakho, Iraqi Kurdistan. *IJMES* 9.215–35.

1981 הגות. פירוש דרשני לספר יונה בארמית חדשה של יהודי כורדיסתאן עברית בארצות איסלאם, ed. by M. Zohory *et al.*, 130–43. Jerusalem, Brit Ivrit Olamit.

1981–82 A bibliography of secondary literature on New Aramic. *JLR* 1 (1981).123–25, *JLR* 2 (1982).98.

1982a על טיבם של התרגומים למקרא (ספר בראשית) בניבים של ארמית חדשה יהודית. *Leš* 46.124–40.

1982b The quadriradical verb in eastern Neo-Aramaic dialects. *JSS* 27.149–76.

1983a שני פירושים דרשיים להפטרת אסוף אסיפם (ירמיה ח:יג–ט:כג) לתשעה באב בניבים הארמיים שבפי יהודי כורדיסטאן (זאכו ועמדיה). Arameans, Aramaic and the Aramaic literary tradition, ed. by M. Sokoloff, Hebrew section 11–41. Ramat Gan, Bar-Ilan University.

1983b ספר בראשית בארמית חדשה בניבם של יהודי זאכו. *PHULTP* 9. Jerusalem.

Sadan (Stock), D.

1956 אבני שפה. Tel Aviv.

1965a סוגיות יידיש במסכת ביאליק, edited from lectures by D. Moshowitz. Jerusalem, Akademon.

1965b The midrashic background of "The Paradise" and its implications for the valuation of the Cambridger Yiddish Codex (1382). *FY* 2.253–62.

1974 ואף זו: סוגייה במסכת כלים. *H. Yalon memorial volume*, Bar-Ilan departmental researches 2, 418–43. Jerusalem.

1977 מכוחו של מקרא. Tel Aviv.

1979 בינה בלשונותיו של שמשון מלצר. *LLA* 30.129–58.

1981 Bibliography of C. Sadan, see Kressel, G., 1981.

1983a אווארט באשטייט. Tel Aviv.

1983b תג למסורת. *ML* 419–24.

1983c לבירור אחדותה של הלשון. *WCJS* 8, Bible and Hebrew Language, 69–78. Jerusalem.

1985 לבירור אחדותה של הלשון. מחקרים בלשון, ed. M. Bar-Asher, 37–43. Jerusalem, Department of Hebrew Languge, Hebrew University.

Sadka, Y.

1974 משלימי הפועל בעברית החדשה. Doctoral dissertation, Hebrew University.

1976–77 המרכיבים המחוברים. *Leš* 41.216–28, 270–81.

n.d. תחביר המשפט לאור תיאוריות חדשות. Jerusalem, Akademon.

1978 יש לי את . . . פרקים. 102–11.

1980 משפט ייחוד הנושא והכינוי הוא. *Leš* 44.224–39.

1981 תחביר העברית בימינו. Jerusalem.

Saebo, M.

1978 From pluriformity to uniformity: some remarks on the emergence of the massoretic text with special reference to its theological significance. *ASTI* 11.127–37.

Sáenz-Badillos, A.
1982 Linguistical components in Dunaš ben Labrat's *Tĕšubot*. *WCJS* 8, Division D, English section, 1–5. Jerusalem.
1986 A new critical edition of the "Maḥberet Menaḥem." *WCJS* 9, Division D, 31–36. Jerusalem.

Sager, N.
1954 *Transfer grammar, with special reference to translation procedure.* Masters thesis, University of Pennsylvania.

Sagi, H.
1976 ללשון העיתונות בימינו. Masters thesis, Hebrew University.

Saig, T.
1981 משפטי זיקה סינדטיים בלהג של יהודי בגדאד. Masters thesis, Tel Aviv University.

Sailhamer, J.
1981 *The translational technique of the Greek Septuagint for the Hebrew verbs and particles in Ps. 3–41.* Doctoral dissertation, UCLA. Ann Arbor, University Microfilms.

Sala, M.
1971 *Phonétique et phonologie du judéo-espagnol de Bucharest.* Janua linguarum, Series practica 142. The Hague/Paris, Mouton.
1976 *Le Judéo-espagnol*, Trends in linguistics, state of the art papers 7. The Hague, Mouton.

Sanders, J. A.
1965 *The Psalms scroll of Qumran cave 11.* Discoveries in the Judean desert 4. Oxford.
1967 *The Dead Sea Psalms scroll.* Ithaca, Cornell University Press.
1969 Cave 11 surprises and the question of canon. *New directions in biblical archaeology*, ed. by D. N. Freedman and J. C. Greenfield, 101–16. New York.

Samarin, W.
1967–68 Review of Fishman 1965. *Lingua* 19.111–12.

Sapir, Y.
1973 הארמית של התנאים על־פי אבות טקסטים של המשנה והתוספתא. Masters thesis, Hebrew University.

Sappan, R.
1961a Hebrew slang and foreign loanwords. *Ariel* 25.75–80.
1961b לסווגה הסימנטי של המטפורה. *Leš* 26.35–39.
1963/1972[2] דרכי הסלנג. Jerusalem.
1966 מילון הסלנג הישראלי. Jerusalem, Kiryath Sepher.
1967 מילון לחידושי הלשון ב״בן סירא״ העברי. Masters thesis, Hebrew University.

1974 הייחוד התחבירי של לשון השירה המקראית בתקופה הקלאסית. Doctoral dissertation, Hebrew University.
1979 (עיון תחבירי) ספר שלום סיון. אשרי, ed. by A. Even-Shoshan *et al.*, 113–20. Jerusalem, Kiryath Sepher.
1980 Nominal sentences with an abstract noun at head of the predicate phrase in Biblical Hebrew. *WCJS* 6, Division D, 169–73.
1981 הייחוד התחבירי של לשון השירה המקראית בתקופתה הקלאסית. Jerusalem, Kiryath Sepher (book form of 1974).
1983 *The logical-rhetorical classification of semantic changes.* Rehovot, Safra.

Sarauw, C.
1939 *Über Akzent und Silbenbildung in den älteren semitischen Sprachen.* Copenhagen.

Sarel, Z.
1984 מבנים של שיח בספרי לימוד עבריים במדעי הרוח והכשירות התקשורתית של פרחי הוראה. Doctoral dissertation, Hebrew University.

Sarfatti, G.
1957 מונחי המתימטיקה בספרי המתימטיקה העבריים של ימי הביניים. Masters thesis, Hebrew University.
1958–60 מונחי המתמטיקה של "משנת המדות". *Leš* 23.156–71; 24.73–94.
1960–61 המיכון של חקר הלשון. *Leš* 25.90–95.
1963 מונחי המתמטיקה בספרות המדעית העברית של ימי הביניים. Doctoral dissertation, Hebrew University.
1964–66 עיונים בסמנטיקה של לשון חז"ל ובדרשותיהם. *Leš* 29.238–44; 30.29–40.
1967–68a הצורות פעלהו יפעלהו והבעת הנושא הסתמי במגילת הסרכים. *Leš* 32.53–56.
1967–69b Review of Bendavid 1967 (*H*). *LLA* 19.93–100.
1968a מונחי המתמטיקה בספרות המדעית העברית של ימי הביניים. Jerusalem.
1968b שלבים בניתוח אוצר המלים של המכילתא בעזרת המיכון. *WCJS* 4, 2.433–36 (English summary 210). Jerusalem.
1969–71 שורש אחד או מלה אחת לדבר ולהפוכו. *LLA* 21.55–61, 181–87, 207–13, 270–74; 22.57–63.
1971–72 האטימולוגיה העממית. *LLA* 23.11–17, 141–43, 181–92.
1972–73 על הלעזים של רש"י. *Leš* 37.43–49.
1974–75, 1975–76 האטימולוגיה העממית בעברית המודרנית. *Leš* 39.236–63; 40.117–41.
1978 סמנטיקה עברית. Jerusalem, Rubinstein.
1980a על אודות היידוע של צירופי הסמיכות הכבולים בלשון חכמים. *SHSL*, 140–54.

1980b התפקיד הפרוסודי של ה"א הידיעה בלשון חכמים. *Leš* 44.185–201.
1980c Review of Moreshet 1980 (*H*). *Leš* 45.73–76.
1980d Ed. *Studies in Hebrew and Semitic languages: dedicated to the memory of Prof. Eduard Yechezkel Kutscher*, Bar-Ilan departmental researches. Ramat Gan, Bar-Ilan University Press (abbreviated *SHSL*).
1981 הגליונות של כתב־יד פארמה 138. *Leš* 45.93–94 (summarizes Cuomo 1977).
1982 Hebrew inscriptions of the first temple period—a survey and some linguistic comments. *Maarav* 3.55–83.
1983 מסורת לשון חכמים—מסורת של "לשון ספרותית חיה". *ML* 451–58.
1984 L'uso dell'articolo determinativo in esspressioni del tipo keneset ha-gedolah. *ASE* 10.219–28.
1985a צמודי מלים בסדר קבוע בלשון חכמים. *Sefer Avraham Even-Shoshan*, ed. B. Z. Luria, 301–13.
1985b התקרבות העברית ללשונות אירופה בתיווך העברית. מחקרים בלשון, ed. M. Bar-Asher, 251–60. Jerusalem, Department of Hebrew Language, The Hebrew University.

Sarig, L.
1981 בידול צורני כאמצעי לשקיפות מורפו־סמנטית בערבית היהודית של בגדאד in S. Moreh, ed., מחקרים בתולדות יהודי עיראק ובתרבותם, 35–39. Tel Aviv, Center for the Heritage of Iraqi Jewry.

Sasson, B.
1946 חידוש ומקור ביצירתו של אברהם שלונסקי. Masters thesis, Hebrew University.

Sasson, V.
1979 *Studies in the lexicon and linguistic usage of early Hebrew inscriptions*. Doctoral dissertation, New York University. Ann Arbor, University Microfilms.

Saulson, S. B.
1979 *Institutionalized language planning, Documents and analysis of the revival of Hebrew*. The Hague/Paris/New York, Mouton.

Saur, G.
1974 Die Ugaristik und die Psalmenforschung. *UF* 6.401–6.

Sawyer, J. F. A.
1967 Root meanings in Hebrew. *JSS* 12.37–50.
1972 *Semantics in biblical research. New methods of defining Hebrew words for salvation.* Studies in biblical theology 2. London, SCM Press.
1973a Hebrew words for the resurrection of the dead. *VT* 23.218–34.
1973b The place of folk-linguistics in biblical interpretation. *WCJS* 5, 4.109–13.

1975 A historical description of the Hebrew word *yšʿ*. *Hamito-Semitics*, ed. by J. and T. Bynon, 75–84. The Hague, Mouton.

Saydon, P.
1962 The conative imperfect in Hebrew. *VT* 12.124–26.
1964 The meanings and uses of the particle *ʾet*. *VT* 14.192–210.

Schaechter, M.
1969 The 'hidden standard': a study of competing influences in standardization. *FY* 3.284–304 (reprinted in J. A. Fishman, ed., 1981a.671–97).
1977 Four schools of thought in Yiddish language planning. *MGS* 3.34–66.

Schapira, Nathan
1974 השפעת היידיש על העברית ביצירותיו של מנדלי מוכר ספרים. Masters thesis, Hebrew University.

Schapira, Noah
1955–56 על הכוהל והיי"ש במקורות עבריים. *Leš* 20.62–64.
1959–60 התפתחות הטרמינולוגיה הכימית בעברית. *Leš* 24.95–106.
1961–62 שמות קנה־הסופר בספרות העברית. *Leš* 26.138–39.
1962–64 גלגולי העברית הטכנית. *Leš* 27–28.252–66, 340–53.

Scharbert, J.
1973 Die Geschichte der *baruk*-Formel. *BZ* 17.1–28.

Schertz, C. E.
1977 *Christian Hebraism in 17th century England as reflected in the work of John Lightfoot*. Doctoral dissertation, New York University. Ann Arbor, University Microfilms.

Schirmann, J.
1954–56 השירה העברית בספרד ובפרובנס. 2 vols. Jerusalem and Tel Aviv, The Bialik Institute and Dvir.
1965 שירים חדשים מן הגניזה. Jerusalem.
1967 *Problems in the study of post-biblical Hebrew poetry*. Israel Academy of Sciences and Humanities.
1979 לתולדות השירה והדראמה העברית, vols. 1–2. Jerusalem, Mossad Bialik (collected studies 1931–1978).
1983 Bibliography of J. Schirmann, ed. by D. Pagis, E. Fleischer, and Y. David, (1981–1904) כתבי פרופסור חיים שירמן. Jerusalem, Mossad Bialik.

Schlanger, J. E.
1967 La langue hébraique, problème de linguistique speculative. *RIP* 21.486–507.

Schlesinger, A.
1951 הניקוד המסורתי. Masters thesis, Hebrew University.
1954 טעמי אמ"ת וטעמי כ"א ספרים. *EI* 3.194–98.

Schlesinger, Y.
1975 תיאור פונטי של עברית שבפי דוברי אנגלית יוצאי ארצות הברית. Masters thesis, Bar-Ilan University.
Schmeltz, U. O. and Bachi, R.
1972–73 העברית כלשון דיבור יום־־יומית של היהודים בישראל. *Leš* 37. 50–68.
1974 Hebrew as the every-day language of the Jews in Israel—statistical appraisal. *Salo Whittmayer Baron jubilee volume*, 745–85. Jerusalem.
Schmelzer, M.
1981 שירי יצחק אבן עזרא. New York.
Schmid, H. H.
1971 Šalôm *"Frieden" im alten Orient und im alten Testament.* Stuttgarter Bibelstudien 51. Stuttgart, KBW Verlag.
Schneekloth, L.
1977 *The targum of the Song of Songs: a study in rabbinic biblical interpretation.* Doctoral dissertation, University of Wisconsin. Ann Arbor, University Microfilms.
Schneid, H.
1945 הצד הלשוני של דיוקי התנאים במדרשי ההלכה. Masters thesis, Hebrew University.
Schneider, W.
1974 *Grammatik des biblische Hebräisch.* München, Claudius Verlag.
Scholes, R. and Grossman, P. F.
1976 Utterance imitation by Hebrew-speaking children. *Linguistic and literary studies in honor of Archibald A. Hill*, 1.275–81. Lisse, Peter de Ridder Press.
Schottroff, W.
1969 *Der altisraelitische Fluchspruch.* Neukirchen-Vluyn, Kevelaer.
Schramm, G.
1956 *Judeo-Baghdadi: a descriptive analysis of the colloquial Arabic of the Jews of Baghdad.* Doctoral dissertation, Dropsie University.
1964 *The graphemes of Tiberian Hebrew.* University of California publications, Near Eastern studies 2. Berkeley.
Schultz, C.
1973 *ʿĀnî* and *ʿānāw* in Psalms. Doctoral dissertation, Brandeis University. Ann Arbor, University Microfilms.
Schuttermayr, G.
1971 Ambivalenz und Aspektdifferenz. Bemerkungen zu den hebräischen Prepositionen ב, ל und מן. *BZ* 15.29–51.

Schwarzwald (Rodrigue), O.
1969 הגזרות העלולות במשנה על פי המשנה מהדורת לוי בהשוואה לעברית המקראית וארמית הארץ־ישראלית. Masters thesis, Bar-Ilan University.
1973a *Lexical representations, phonological processes and morphological patterns in Hebrew.* Doctoral dissertation, University of Texas at Austin. Ann Arbor, University Microfilms.
1973b Roots and patterns in the Modern Hebrew lexicon. Proceedings of the conference on Hebraic studies held on April 1–2, 1973, at Ohio State University, Columbus, OH. *HA* 14.95–96.
1973–74 שרשים, בסיסים ומבנה המורפמות. *Leš* 38.131–36.
1975 עוד בעניין יחסי שורש ודגם במילון העברי. *HCL* 9.47–59.
1975–76 גישות תיאורטיות קונקרטיות ומפשטות בניתוח בגדכ״ת־בכ״פ בעברית. *Leš* 40.211–32.
1976a לשאלת תקינותם והווצרותם של משפטי הייחוד. *Bar-Ilan* 13. 321–40.
1976b על הוראת הנשוא־המורחב: הנשוא המורחב והאוגד. החינוך 48. 246–51.
1977 ייצוגם הלקסיקלי של הפעלים העלולים. *HCL* 12.25–36.
1978 תופעות בלשניות והשתקפותן בתחבירה של מלת השאלה ״מי״ בלשון המקרא. *BM* 24(76).81–88.
1978–79a הבררה: עיון בשאלה תחבירית לוגית ומורפולוגית. *Leš* 43.112–20.
1978–79b נורמאטיביות וטבעיות בתחולת חוק מורפופונמי בעברית החדשה. *Bar-Ilan* 16–17.171–92.
1979 מה בין משפט החסר למשפט הסתמי? *LLA* 30/1.15–21.
1980a בלשנות שימושית. מעלילות הפועל העלול. 2.63–76.
1980b תהליכים מקבילים בלשון חכמים ובלשון ימינו *SHSL*, 174–88.
1981a צורת הנקבה של השמות בסיומת —י בעברית. *Leš* 45.319–20 (response to Podolsky 1981).
1981b דקדוק ומציאות בפועל העברי. Ramat Gan, Bar-Ilan University.
1981c הגיית הע״ין בקהילות הספרדים המזרחיות. *Leš* 46.72–75.
1981d Frequency factors as determinants in the *binyanim* meanings. *HS* 22.131–37.
1981–82a על כמות המלים העבריות בספרדית־היהודית. *LLA* 33/3 (323). 80–87.
1981–82b לשונות סתרים עבריות בספרדית יהודית. *LLA* 33/10 (330).258–62.
1982a שילובן של המלים העבריות, מקורן ההיסטורי ודרכי התמזגותן. *WCJS* 8, Division D, Hebrew section, 63–67. Jerusalem.
1982b הערות אחדות על נטיות ״יש״ ו״אין״ קיומיות בעברית המדוברת. *HCL* 19.59–70.
1984 Markedness relations in the pronunciation of the prefixed particles in modern Hebrew. *AAL* 9/2 (entire fascicle).

1985a עיונים בתצורת המלים העבריות בספרדית־היהודית. *Leš* 48–49. 186–94.
1985b The fusion of the Hebrew-Aramaic lexical component in Judeo-Spanish. *Judeo-Romance languages*, ed. I. Benabu and J. (G.) Sermoneta, 139–59.
1986 דיאלקטים בספרדית־היהודית לאור התרגומים לפרקי אבות. *WCJS* 9, Division D, 139–46. Jerusalem.

Schweitzer, H.
1975 Was ist ein Akkusativ? Ein Betrag zur Grammatikstheorie. *ZAW* 87.133–46.

Scoggin, B. E.
1955 *Application of Hebrew verb states to a translation of Isaiah 40–55*. Doctoral dissertation, The Southern Baptist Theological Seminary. Ann Arbor, University Microfilms.

Scupak, N.
1977 על כמה מטבעות לשון משותפות לספרות החכמה המקראית ולספרות החכמה המצרית. שנתון, an annual for biblical and ancient near eastern studies, 2.233–36.

Seckbach, F.
1974 Attitudes and opinions of Israeli teachers and students about aspects of Modern Hebrew. *Linguistics* 120.105–24.

Segal, J. B.
1953 *The diacritical point and the accents in Syriac*. Oxford.
1955 Neo-Aramaic proverbs of the Jews of Zakho. *JNES* 14. 251–70.
1983 New Aramaic texts from Saqqara: an introduction. *Arameans, Aramaic and the Aramaic literary tradition*, ed. by M. Sokoloff, 23–29. Ramat Gan, Bar-Ilan University.

Segal, M. H.
1927 A grammar of Mishnaic Hebrew. Oxford.
1928 יסוד הפונטיקה העברית. Jerusalem.
1936 דקדוק לשון המשנה. Tel Aviv.
1958 ספר בן סירא השלם. Jerusalem.

Segert, S.
1960 Considerations of Semitic comparative lexicography. *AO* 28.470–87.
1961 Die Sprache der moabitischen Königsinschrifte. *AO* 29. 197–268.
1969 Hebrew Bible and Semitic comparative lexicography. *Congress volume*, Supplements to VT 17, 204–11. Leiden, Brill.
1978 Vowel letters in early Aramaic. *JNES* 37.111–14.
1984 *A basic grammar of the Ugaritic language with selected texts and glossary*. London and Berkeley, University of California Press.

Seikevicz, C.
1979 The possessive construction in Modern Hebrew, a sociolinguistic approach. Doctoral dissertation, Georgetown University. Ann Arbor, University Microfilms.

Sekine, M.
1973 The subdivisions of the Northwest Semitic languages. *JSS* 18.205–21.

Selinker, L.
1970 Basic clause types in Israeli Hebrew. *Word* 26.373–85.

Selms, A. van
1971 Some reflections on the formation of the feminine in Semitic. *Near Eastern studies in honor of William F. Albright*, ed. by H. Goedicke, 241–31. Baltimore/London, Johns Hopkins University Press.
1971–72 Motivated interrogative sentences in Biblical Hebrew. *Semitica* 2.143–49.
1975 Some remarks on the ᶜAmman citadel inscription. *BiOr* 32.5–8.

Semiloff-Zelasko, H.
1973 Vowel reduction and loss in Modern Hebrew fast speech. *HCL* 7.53–72.
1975 An accoustic-perceptual study of Modern Hebrew *ᵓalef* and *ᶜayin*. *JPh* 3.167–74.

Sephiha, H. V.
1972a Langues juives, langues calques, et langues vivantes. *La linguistique* 8.59–68.
1972b Ciclo de conferencias sobre el judeo-espanol, el ladino y la linguistica de las lenguas judias en el Institut des Langues et Civilisations Orientales. *Sefarad* 32.241–43.
1973a *Le Ladino (Judéo-espagnol calque): "Deuteronome," versions de Constantinople (1547) et de Ferrare (1553).* Édition étude linguistique et lexique, Éditions Hispaniques (Sorbonne), Paris.
1973b The present state of Judeo-Spanish in Turkey. *A Sph* 6. 22–29.
1974 Problematique du judéo-espagnol. *BSLP* 69, 1.159–89.
1975a Linguistique contrastive: traducion du *Hifᶜil* en Ladino (Judéo-espagnol calque). *GLECS* 16 (1971–1972).81–91.
1975b Theorie du ladino: additifs, in *Mélanges offertes à Charles Vincent Aubrun*, 2.255–84, Éditions Hispaniques. Paris, Sorbonne.
1975c Une bible Judéo-espagnole chrétienne, in *Hommage à André Neher.* Paris, Libraire Maisonneuve.

1975d Ladino (Judéo-espagnol calque) et commentateurs. *RHR* 4.117–28.
1976a Langues juives, langues calques, langues vivantes. *GLECS* 15 (1971).91–102.
1976b Le judéo-fragnol, dernier-né du djudezmo. *BSLP* 71, 1, xxxi–xxxvi.
1976c Diachronie du ladino, XIV Congresso Internazionale di linguistica e filologia romanza, *Atti*, 2.555–64. Naples.
1976–77 Judéo-espagnol. *EphE*, 217–31.
1977a L'intensité en judéo-espagnol. *Iberica* 1.285–94.
1977b *L'agonie des Judéo-Espagnols*, Editios Entente, Collection "Minorités." Paris.
1977c Archaïsmes lexicaux du ladino (judéo-espagnol calque). *CLHM* 2, 3.253–61. Paris, Klincksieck.
1978a Le colloque international: langues et civilisations juives contemporaines (Collège de France, Paris, 15–17 novembre 1977). *REJ* 137.479–81.
1978b Ladino (Judéo-espagnol calque) et Bibles espagnoles contemporaines, Université de Saint-Étienne, *Travaux* 22, Centre Interdisciplinaire d'Étude et de Recherche sur l'expression contemporaine, 163–73.
1978c Creations lexicales en ladino (Judéo-espagnol calque). *Estudios ofrecidos a Emilio Alarcos Llorach*, 2.241–55. Oviedo.
1978d Ladinismes dans la Fazienda de Ultra Mar, une Biblia Medieval Romanceada du XIIeme siècle—le ladino. *Actes du deuxieme Congrès international d'étude des cultures de la Mediterranée occidentale*, 220–26. Alger.
1980a Ladino (Judéo-espagnol calque) et sémantique. *Sfunot*, n.s. 1(16).XV–V. Jerusalem.
1980b Judéo-Espagnol-Ladino et Djudezmo. *WCJS* 6, Division D, 17–27. Jerusalem.
1981 הגות. הלאדינו—בבואה ספרדית־יהודית—או השאילה בכל הרמות עברית בארצות האיסלאם, ed. by M. Zohory *et al.*, 57–65. Jerusalem, Brit Ivrit Olamit.
1982 Le Ladino <judéo-espagnol calque>: structure et évolution d'une langue liturgique, vol. 1–2. Paris, Université de la Sorbonne-Nouvelle.

Seri, S. and Tobi, Y.
1976 שירים חדשים לר׳ שלום שבזי. Jerusalem, The Ben-Zvi Institute.

Sermoneta, G.
1967 'Il libro delle forme verbali,' compendie volgare del Mahalakh sevile ha-da^{c}ath di Moshe ben Josef Qimchi. *Scritti in memoria di Carpi*, 59–100. Jerusalem.

1969 *Un glossario filosophico ebraico-italiano del xiii° secolo.* Rome.
1971 Judeo-Italian. *EJ* 10.427–29.
1976 Considerazioni frammentari sul giudeo-italiano. *Italia* 1.1–29.
1978 Considerazioni frammentarie sul giudeo-italiano II, testi italiani in caratteri ebraici. *Italia* 1.62ff.
1985 The bilingual prose and poetry of Italian Jews. *Judeo-Romance languages*, ed. I. Benabu and J. (G.) Sermoneta, 161–88.

Sevenster, J. N.
1968 *Do you know Greek?* Leiden, Brill.

Sgerri, G.
1974 A propositi di origine de la langue ebraica. *Augustinianum* 14.223–57.

Shachevitz, B.
1966–67 ארבע לשונות: עיונים של ספרות בלשון המשכילים על פי "המאסף". *Molad* 1.236–42.
1967–68 רובדי אוצר מלים ב"דברי שלום אמת" לנפתלי הירץ ויזל. *Leš* 32.304–7.

Shaffer, D.
1972 The Hebrew revival myth. *Orbis* 21.315–26.

Shahadeh, H.
1969 הסמיכות הפרודה בכתבים של אהרן מגד וביחוד ב"חי על המת". Masters thesis, Hebrew University.
1971–72 האקדמיה הערבית בדמשק ובעית המודרניזאציה של הלשון הערבית. *Leš* 36.228–35, 301–7.
1983 מתי תפסה הערבית את מקום הארמית השומרונית? *ML* 515–28.

Shaked, S.
1982 Two Judeo-Iranian contributions: Iranian functions in the book of Esther and fragments of two Karaite commentaries on Daniel in Judeo-Persian. *Irano-Judaica*, ed. by S. Shaked, 292–303. Jerusalem, The Ben-Zvi Institute.

Shaked, Y.
1981 בעיות בחלקי הדיבר בעברית של המקרא. Masters thesis, Tel Aviv University.

Shalev, Y.
1973–74 על הסלנג הצברי. *KLL* 25/2–3 (242–43).61–79.

Shalom, D.
1979 ממשקעי הארמית בעברית החדשה. Doctoral dissertation, Bar-Ilan University.

Shamosh, A.
1971 מלים בעלות משמעויות מיוחדות בקבוץ. *Sefer Kamrat*, 193–217. Jerusalem, Council on the Teaching of Hebrew.

Shanbal, Y.
1977 בעיות לשוניות על פי העתונות העברית מראשית המאה עד קום המדינה. Masters thesis, Hebrew University.
Shapiro, M. and Choueka, Y.
1962–64 ניתוח מיכנוגראפי של המורפולוגיה העברית. *Leš* 27–28.354–72.
Sharvit, S.
1966–67 עיונים במילונה של מגילת הנחושת. *BM* 12.127–35.
1974a העדר ניגוד בין קמץ לחולם ובין סגול לפתח (בכתב יד שהגייתו בבלית). *H. Yalon memorial volume*, Bar-Ilan departmental researches 2, 547–55. Jerusalem.
1974b בעקבות המבואות לי״נ אפשטיין. *Archive of the new dictionary of rabbinical literature* 2, ed. by M. Z. Kaddari, 112–24. Ramat Gan.
1977 נוסחאותיה ולשונה של מסכת אבות. Doctoral dissertation, Bar-Ilan University.
1979–80 שמות במשקל קטלות, קטילה, קטילות. *LLA* 31.77–83.
1980 מערכת ה׳זמנים׳ בלשון המשנה. *SHSL*, 110–25.
1983 האפלולוגיה בלשון חכמים. *ML* 557–68.
Shashar, Y.
1963 היסוד הארמי בכתבי מנדלי מוכר ספרים ותפקידו הסגנוני. Masters thesis, Hebrew University.
Shavit, H.
1973 הזמנים ההפוכים בקובץ הסיפורים ״במדבר״ לדוד פרישמן. Masters thesis, Hebrew University.
Shay (Gershter), H.
1967 תנחום הירושלמי, אלמרשד אלכאפי—תרגום. Masters thesis, Hebrew University (see also *Leš* 33.196–207, 280–96).
1976 אלמרשד אלכאפי (המדריך המספיק) לרבי תנחום ברבי יוסף הירושלמי (האותיות ל־ש). Doctoral dissertation, Hebrew University.
1980 ממד חדש למלונות העברית בימי הבינים. *Leš* 44.202–18.
1983 פירושיו של תנחום הירושלמי למקרא בהשוואה למילונו למשנה תורה עפ״י דף שנמצא מפירושו לתהילים (כתוב בכתב ידו). *ML* 529–55.
Shazar, Z.
1929 גביות עדות בלשון יידיש בשאלות ותשובות, reprinted 1971 in אורי דורות, collected historical essays, 239–318. Jerusalem, Mossad Bialik.
Shea, W. H.
1977 Ostracon II from Heshbon. *Andrews University Seminary studies* 15.217–22.
1978 The Siran inscription: Amminadab's drinking song. *PEQ* 110.107–12.

1979 Milkom as the architect of Rabbath-Ammon's natural defenses in the Amman citadel inscription. *PEQ* 111.17–25.

1981 The Amman citadel inscription again. *PEQ* 113.105–10.

Shehadeh, L. A.

1968 *The sibilants in the West Semitic languages of the second millennium* B.C. Doctoral dissertation, Harvard University.

Shereshevsky, E.

1957 *Rashi as teacher, interpreter of text and moulder of character.* Doctoral dissertation, Dropsie University.

1981 *Rashi: the man and his world.* New York, Sepher-Hermon.

Shermon, M.

1966 *Systems of Hebrew and Aramaic orthography: an epigraphic history of the use of* matres lectionis *in nonbiblical texts to circa* A.D. *135.* Doctoral dissertation, Harvard University.

Shirman, D.

1977 פעלים המביעים מצב רגשי—עיון תחבירי־סימנטי על פי יצירתו של חיים נחמן ביאליק. Masters thesis, Hebrew University.

Shivtiel, Amichai

1971 השפעת הלשון הערבית על דרך כתיבת העברית בימי תחיית לשון. Masters thesis, Hebrew University.

Shivtiel (Ashbat, Damti). Y.

1937 מסורות התימנים בדקדוק לשון חכמים. *KLL* 1.8–15.

1938–39a הגיית הקיבוץ התימני. *KLL* 1.7–8.

1938–39b מסורות התימנים בדקדוק לשון חכמים. *KLL* 2.61–69.

1944 מסורות התימנים בדקדוק לשון חכמים. שבות תימן, ed. by Y. Yeshayahu and A. Sadok, 118–23. Tel Aviv.

1963 מסורות התימנים בדקדוק לשון המשנה. *H. Yalon Festschrift*, ed. by S. Lieberman, S. Abramson, E. Y. Kutscher and S. Esh, 338–59. Jerusalem.

Shmeruk, Ch.

1978 ספרות יידיש: פרקים לתולדותיה. Tel Aviv University.

1979 מחזות מקראיים ביידיש 1697–1750. Jerusalem.

1981 ספרות יידיש בפולין. Jerusalem, Magnes Press.

Shochet, A.

1985 יחסם של ראשי ההשכלה ברוסיה אל הלשון העברית. *Sefer Avraham Even-Shoshan*, ed. B. Z. Luria, 353–426. Jerusalem.

Shohamy, E. G.

1978 *Investigation of the concurrent validity of the oral interview with Cloze procedure for measuring proficiency in Hebrew as a second language.* Doctoral dissertation, University of Minnesota. Ann Arbor, University Microfilms.

Shtal, A.
1972 מבנה הלשון הכתובה אצל יהודים בני התרבות המזרחית והתרבות האירופיאית ומשמעותו לקידום ילדים טעוני טיפוח בישראל. Doctoral dissertation, Hebrew University.
1978 לשון וחשיבה של ילדים טעוני־טיפוח בישראל. Tel Aviv, Otsar hamoreh.

Shults, F. L.
1974 ŠLM *and* TMM *in Biblical Hebrew: an analysis of the semantic field of wholeness.* University of Texas at Austin. Ann Arbor, University Microfilms.

Shulvass, M.
1971 *From east to west: the westward migration of Jews from eastern Europe during the seventeenth and eighteenth centuries.* Detroit.
1973 *The Jews in the World of the Renaissance.* Leiden. Brill and Spertus College of Judaica Press.

Shunami, S.
1965 *Bibliography of Jewish bibliographies*, 2nd enlarged ed. Jerusalem, Magnes Press.
1975 *Supplement to the second edition enlarged, Bibliography of Jewish bibliographies.* Jerusalem, Magnes Press.

Shunarry, J.
1976 פרק בדרכה של העברית אל חידושי בן־יהודה. *Chaim Rabin jubilee volume*, ed. by B. Fischler and R. Nir, 140–49. Jerusalem, Council on the Teaching of Hebrew.

Shur, S.
1977 ההקשר החברתי־פוליטי של החייאת הלשון העברית בפרספקטיבה השוואתית. רבעון למחקר חברתי 12–19.109–16.
1979 Language innovation and socio-political setting: the case of Modern Hebrew. *HCL* 15.IV–XI.

Siedl, S.
1971 *Gedanken zum Tempussystem im Hebräischen und Akkadischen.* Wiesbaden, Harrassowitz.

Siegel, J. P.
1971 The employment of palaeo-Hebrew characters for the divine names at Qumran in the light of tannaitic sources. *HUCA* 42.159–72.
1972 *The scribes at Qumran. Studies in the early history of Jewish scribal customs, with special reference to the Qumran biblical scrolls and to the tannaitic traditions of* Massekheth Soferim. Doctoral dissertation, Brandeis University. Ann Arbor, University Microfilms.

1974 An orthographic convention of 1Q Isa^{a} and the origin of two masoretic anomalies. *Masoretic studies* 1, ed. by H. M. Orlinsky, 99–110. Missoula, MT, SBL and Scholars Press.
1975 The Severus scroll and 1Q Isa^{a}. Missoula, MT (see also *Masoretic studies* 1, 159–65, for abbreviated version).

Silberschlag, E., ed.
1981a *Eliezer Ben-Yehuda, a symposium in Oxford.* Oxford Centre for Post-Graduate Hebrew Studies.
1981b Critique of enlightenment in the works of Ahad-Haam and Ben Yehuda, in Silberschlag, ed., 1981a.54–68.

Silva, M.
1983 *Biblical words and their meanings: an introduction to lexical semantics.* Grand Rapids, MI, Zondervan.

Simonsohn, S.
1974 The Hebrew revival among the early medieval European Jews. *Salo Whittmayer Baron jubilee volume*, 831–59. Jerusalem.

Sirat, C.
1968a La paleographie hébraïque. *WCJS* 4, 2.173–74.
1968b Brèves remarques sur l'evolution de la langue poétique en hébreu. *Revue de l'école nationale des langues: orientales*, 27–48. Paris.
1974 Y-a-t-il un element ^{c}*Ain*$_{1}$ *Resh* commun à plusiers racines hébraïques? *ACILCS* 1, 234–45. Paris.
1976 תרגום ספרותי—הארות מתדולוגיות. *Chaim Rabin jubilee volume*, ed. by B. Z. Fischler and R. Nir, 104–9. Jerusalem.

Sirat, C. and Beit-Arié, M. eds.
1972/1979 *Manuscrits médiévaux en caractères hébraïques portant des indications de date jusqu'à 1540.* Part 1 (1972): *Bibliothèques de France et d'Israël—manuscrits de grand format*; part 2 (1979): *Bibliotheques de France et d'Israël—manuscrits de petit format jusqu'à 1470*, 2 vols., planches, notices. Centre national de la recherche scientifique and Académie national des sciences et des lettres d'Israël. Paris/Jerusalem.

Sivan, D.
1983 תרומת הטקסטים האכדיים מאוגרית לחקר האוגריתית ובעקיפין לחקר העברית המקראית. *Leš* 47.165–86.

Sivan, R.
1960–61 חידושי המלים של אליעזר בן יהודה. *LLA* 12/2–3 (114–15).
1964 צורות ומגמות בחידושי הלשון בעברית בתקופת תחייתה (מבוא כללי וחלק ראשון: הפועל). Doctoral dissertation, Hebrew University.

1969 Ben Yehudah and the revival of Hebrew speech. *Ariel* 25.35–39.
1970 שמנים שנה. *LLA* 21/4–5 (104–205).
1972–73 אליעזר בן יהודה ותחיית הדיבור העברי. *LLA* 24/3–4 (233–34).
1975 מדריך הכתיב המלא לפי כללי האקדמיה ללשון העברית. Jerusalem, Rubinstein.
1976 הדיבור העברי והסגנון הירושלמי. *Chaim Rabin jubilee volume*, ed. by B. Z. Fischler and R. Nir, 100–103. Jerusalem (English summary, xii–xiii).
1978 Ed. החלום ושברו. Jerusalem, Mossad Bialik (selections from the writings of Eliezer ben Yehudah, with introduction).
1979–80a בן יהודה, י״ל גורדון והרחבת הלשון. *LLA* 31.83–86.
1979–80b הלשון הירושלמית והתגבשות הסגנון החדש. *LLA* 31/2.3–68.
1979–80c חליפות ותמורות בלשון ימינו. *LLA* 31/9–10.251–308.
1981–82 ראשית הרחבת הלשון בימינו. *LLA* 33/1–2 (321–22).63–65.
1982 גורמים סוציולינגוויסטיים להצלחת החייאת העברית. *WCJS* 8, Division D, Hebrew section, 31–37. Jerusalem.

Sivan, R. and Kressel, G.
1970 לקט תעודות. Jerusalem, The Academy of the Hebrew Language.

Skaist, A.
1980 The background of the talmudic formula והכל שריר וקים. *SHSL*, XL–LIV.
1983 The *clausula salvatoria* in the Elephantine and Neo-Assyrian conveyance documents. *Arameans, Aramaic and the Aramaic literary tradition*, ed. by M. Sokoloff, 31–41. Ramat Gan, Bar-Ilan University.

Skehan, P. W.
1954 A fragment of the Song of Moses. *BASOR* 136.12–15.
1957 The Qumran MSS and textual criticism. VT Supplements 4.148–60. Leiden, Brill.
1959 Qumran and the present state of Old Testament text studies. *JBL* 78.21–25.
1969 The scrolls and the Old Testament text. *New directions in biblical archaeology*, ed. by D. N. Freedman and J. Greenfield, 89–100. New York.

Skoss, S.
1928 *The Arabic commentary of Ali ben Suleiman the Karaite on the book of Genesis*. Philadelphia.
1936/1945 *The Hebrew-Aramaic dictionary of the Bible known as* Kitab Jami al-alfaẓ (Agron) *of David ben Abraham al-fasi the Karaite*. *YOSR* 20, 21. New Haven.
1955 *Saadiah Gaon, the earliest Hebrew grammarian*. Philadelphia.

Slingerland, H. D.
1977 *The testaments of the twelve patriarchs: a critical history of research.* SBL monograph series. Missoula, Montana.

Slobin, D.
1963 Some aspects of the use of pronouns of address in Yiddish. *Word* 19.193–202.

Smith, J. C.
1968 *Elia Levita's* Bovo-Buch: *A Yiddish romance of the early 16th century.* Doctoral dissertation, Cornell University.

Smith, M.
1950 היסודות העבריים והארמיים של טקסט האוונגליונים. Doctoral dissertation, Hebrew University.
1951 *Tannaitic parallels to the Gospels.* JBL Monograph series 6. Philadelphia (corrected reprint, 1968).

Snaith, N.
1968 Prolegomenon to *Jacob ben Chajim ibn Adonijah's Introduction to the rabbinic Bible* by C. D. Ginsburg, 1867, reprinted in *Library of biblical studies*, ed. by H. M. Orlinsky, VII–XXXVI. New York, Ktav.

Snijders, L. A.
1953 *The meaning of* zār *in the Old Testament.* Leiden, Brill.

Soden, W. von
1952 *Grundriss der akkadischen Grammatik*, Analecta orientalia 33. Rome, Pontifical Biblical Institute.
1959 Tempus und Modus im Semitischen. *PICO* 24.263–65.

Soggin, J. A.
1966 Tracce di antichi causativi in *Š*-realizzati come radici autonome in ebraico biblico. *AION* 15.17–30.
1968 Akkadisch TAR *Berîti* und hebräisch כרת ברית. VT 18. 210–15.
1972 *KLH-KLL:* osservazioni sull'uso di due radici in ebraico biblico. *AION* 32.366–71.

Soisalon-Soininen, I.
1972 Der infinitivus constructus mit ל im Hebräischen. *VT* 22. 82–90.

Sokoloff, M.
1967 העברית של אמוראי ארץ ישראל לפי מדרש בראשית רבה כתב־יד ואטיקן 30. Masters thesis, Hebrew University.
1968–69 העברית של בראשית רבה לפי כתב־יד ואטיקן 30. *Leš* 33.25–42, 135–49, 270–79.
1971 שרידי כתבי־יד ופלימפססטים של בראשית רבה מן הגניזה וכתב־יד ואטיקן 60 של בראשית רבה. Doctoral dissertation, Hebrew University.

1978 The current state of research on Galilean Aramaic. *JNES* 37.161–67.
1980 הערות למילון של הארמית-גלילית. *SHSL*, 166–73.
1983 Ed. *Arameans, Aramaic and the Aramaic literary tradition.* Ramat Gan, Bar-Ilan University.

Solá-Solé, J. M.
1961 *L'infinitif sémitique.* Paris.

Sollamo, R.
1979 *Renderings of Hebrew semi-propositions in the Septuagint.* Annales academiae scientarum fennicae, dissertationes humanarum litterarum 19. Helsinki, Suomalainen Tideakatemia.

Souroudi, S.
1982 *Shirā-ye Hatani.* A Judeo-Persian Wedding Song. *Irano-Judaica*, ed. by Saul Shaked, 204–64. Jerusalem, The Ben-Zvi Institute.

Spak, R.
1975 טכניקות התרגום של י"ד ברקוביץ וח' ברנר בפרק הראשון של "טוביה החולב" לשלום עליכם. Masters thesis, Hebrew University.

Spanier, A.
1927 *Die massoretische-Accente—Eine Darlegung ihres Systems nebst Entwicklung.* Berlin.

Speiser, E. A.
1925–26, 1932–33, 1933–34 The pronunciation of Hebrew according to (based chiefly on) the translations in the Hexapla. *JQR* 16. 343–65; 24.9–46.
1951 A note on alphabetic origins. *BASOR* 121.17–21.
1952 The elative in West Semitic and Akkadian. *JCS* 6.81–92.
1955 The durative hithpa^{c}el: a *tan* form. *JAOS* 75.118–21.
1964a Akkadian, in *WHJP* 1, ed. by E. A. Speiser, 112–20. Rutgers University.
1964b The expanding orbit. *ibid.*, 246–66, notes, 371–72.

Sperber, A.
1959a *A grammar of Massoretic Hebrew.* Copenhagen.
1959b כתבי הקדש בארמית, vol. 1, תרגום אונקלוס לתורה. Leiden, Brill.
1959c כתבי הקדש בארמית, vol. 2, תרגום יונתן לנביאים ראשונים. Leiden, Brill.
1962 כתבי הקדש בארמית, vol. 3, תרגום יונתן לנביאים אחרונים. Leiden, Brill.
1966 *A historical grammar of Biblical Hebrew.* Leiden, Brill.
1968 כתבי הקדש בארמית, vol. 4A, תרגום לכתובים.
1973 *The Bible in Aramaic*, vol. 4B, *the Targum and the Hebrew Bible.* Leiden, Brill.

Sperber, D.
1971–72, 1973–74, 1974–75 חקרי מלים וגרסאות. *Leš* 36.257–62; 38.44–48; 39.55–58.
1973–75 חקרי מלים וגירסאות. *Sinai* 74.273–74; 76.200–203; 77.13–16.
1974 חקר מלים וגירסאות. *Archive of the new dictionary of rabbinical Hebrew* 2, ed. by M. Z. Kaddari, 102–7. Ramat Gan.
1975–76 חקרי מלים וגרסאות. *Leš* 40.167–71.
1980 פויטינון (**phoitenon*). *SHSL*, 155–58.
1982 יוונית ולטינית בספרות התנאים והאמוראים, קובץ מחקרים. Jerusalem (Hebrew section, 114 pages; English section, 194 pages).
1984 *A dictionary of Greek and Latin legal terms in rabbinic literature.* Ramat Gan and Leiden, Bar-Ilan and Brill.
1986 *Nautica talmudica.* Ramat Gan and Leiden, Bar-Ilan and Brill.

Sperling, D.
1969 The Akkadian legal term *dīnu* u *dabābu. JANES* 1.35–40.
1972 Akkadian *egerrû* and Hebrew *bt qwl. JANES* 4.62–74.
1973a Late Hebrew *ḥzr* and Akkadian *saḫāru. JANES* 5.397–404.
1973b *Studies in late Hebrew lexicography in the light of Akkadian.* Doctoral dissertation, Columbia University. Ann Arbor, University Microfilms.

Spichansky, Y.
1972–73 הלשון העברית לאור ההלכה. *OH* 22.98–117.

Spiegel, S.
1958 קרובות יניי בניקוד בני בבל. Studies of the Research Institute for Hebrew Poetry 7.137–43. Jerusalem, Schocken Institute.

Spitaler, A.
1954 Zur Frage der Geminaten-dissimilation im Semitischen—Zugleich ein Betrag zur Orthographie des Reichsaramäischen. *IF* 61.257–66.

Spomer, H. C.
1972 *Some concerns in the semantics of Biblical Hebrew.* Doctoral dissertation, University of Michigan. Ann Arbor, University Microfilms.

Stankiewitz, E.
1964 Balkan and Slavic elements in the Judeo-Spanish of Yugoslavia. *For Max Weinreich on his seventieth birthday*, 229–36. The Hague, Mouton.
1965 Yiddish place names in Poland. *FY* 2.158–81.
1975 Max Weinreich's History of the Yiddish language and its contribution to linguistics. *Yiddish* 1.26–39.

Starinin, V. P.
1963 *Struktura semitskovo slova prejivistji morfemi (The structure of the Semitic word: interrupted morphemes).* Moscow.

Steiner, R. C.
1977 *The case for fricative-laterals in Proto-Semitic.* New Haven, AOS.
1979 From Proto-Hebrew to Mishnaic Hebrew: the history of ךָ and ךְ—ָ. *HAR* 3.157–74.
1983 *Affricated* ṣade *in the Semitic languages.* American Academy for Jewish research, monograph no. 3. Winona Lake, IN, Eisenbrauns.
Stern, N.
1971 שם הפועל בעברית הישראלית. Masters thesis, Bar-Ilan University.
1983 חג״מ ודמוי־פועל + שם־פועל בעברית הישראלית. *Leš* 47.248–63.
Stiasny, V.
1971 בעיות בלשונו של קהלת מוסר. Masters thesis, Hebrew University.
Storm, S.
1974 *Modern Hebrew phonology, a generative approach.* Doctoral dissertation, University of Wisconsin. Ann Arbor, University Microfilms.
Strelcyn, S.
1974 Review of Fontinoy 1969. *JSS* 19.92–97.
Stuart, D. K.
1971 *An approach to the meter of early Hebrew poetry.* Doctoral dissertation, Harvard University.
1976 *Studies in early Hebrew meter.* Harvard Semitic monographs. Missoula, MT, Scholars Press.
Studemund, M.
1975 *Bibliographie zum Judenspanischen.* Hamberg, Buske.
Suder, R. W.
1973 *The functional syntax of the Hebrew verb clause in the sectarian scrolls from Qumran, Cave 1.* Doctoral dissertation, University of Wisconsin, Madison. Ann Arbor, University Microfilms.
Susholtz, S.
1976 Who needs Yiddish? *The Jewish Observer*, June, 18–20 (reprinted in J. A. Fishman, ed., 1981, 219–24).
Sutcliffe, E. F., S. J.
1948 St. Jerome's pronunciation of Hebrew. *Biblica* 29.112–25.
Swiggers, P.
1981 The word *šibbolet* in Jud. xii.6. *JSS* 26.205–7.
Szajkowski (Shaykovski), Z.
1939 Der kamf kegen yidish in frankraykh. (The struggle against Yiddish in France). *Yivo-bleter* 14.46–77.

1948 *Dos loshn fun di yidn in di arbe kehiles fun komta venesen (The language of the Jews in the four communities of Comtat Venaissin).* With a preface by Max Weinreich. Published by the author with the aid of the Yiddish Scientific Institute—YIVO.

1964a The struggle for Yiddish during World War I: the attitude of German Jewry. *Leo Baeck Institute Yearbook* 9.131–58.

1964b Notes on the languages of the Marranos and Sephardim in France. *For Max Weinreich on his seventieth birthday*, 237–44. The Hague, Mouton.

1966 *Catalogue of the exhibition: The history of Yiddish orthography from the spelling rules of the early sixteenth century to the standard orthography of 1936.* New York, YIVO Institute.

1970 *One hundred years of the Yiddish press in America, 1870–1970: catalogue of the exhibition.* New York, YIVO Institute for Jewish Research.

Sznejder, M. B.

1922–23, 1939 תורת הלשון בהתפתחותה, 2 vols. Vilna.

1933–35, 1935–36 הלשון העברית הספרותית. *Leš* 7.52–73.

Szulmajster, A.

1980 *Étude des structures linguistiques du Yidich à travers la chanson populaire: les éléments non germaniques du Yidich.* Paris.

Tadmor, H.

1982 ברית ושבועת אמונים במזרח הקדום. שנתון, An annual for biblical and ancient Near Eastern studies, 5–6.149–73 (see original English version in G. W. Tucker and D. A. Knight, eds., *Society of Biblical Literature Centennial Addresses*, 1980. Chico, California, 1982).

Tal (Rosenthal), A.

1966 הפיוטים הארמיים לשבועות—בחינתם הדיאלקטית ותרומתם למילון הארמי. Masters thesis, Hebrew University.

1971 לשון התרגום לנביאים (על פי החומר של נביאים ראשונים) מעמדה בכלל ניבי ארמית. Doctoral dissertation, Hebrew University.

1975 לשון התרגום לנביאים ראשונים ומעמדה בכלל ניבי ארמית. Tel Aviv.

1976 The Samaritan targum to the Pentateuch, its distinctive characteristics and its metamorphosis. *JSS* 21.26–38.

1978 Towards a critical edition of the Samaritan Targum of the Pentateuch. *IOS* 8.107–28.

1978–79 רבדים בארמית היהודית של ארץ ישראל. *Leš* 43.165–84.

1979 בירורים בארמית של ארץ ישראל. *Leš* 44.43–65.

1980–81 התרגום השומרוני לתורה, vol. 1, 1980; vol. 2, 1981. University of Tel Aviv.

1982 מילון הארמית השומרונית עכשיו—על שום מה? *WCJS* 8, Division D, Hebrew section, 15–19. Jerusalem.
1983 המקור לצורותיו ברובדי הארמית היהודית בארץ ישראל. *ML* 201–18.

Talmadge, F. E.
1975 *David Kimchi, the man and the commentaries.* Harvard Judaic monographs 1. Cambridge, MA/London.

Talmy, G.
1975 *On the role of perceptual clues in Hebrew relativization. AAL* 2/8. Undena, Malibu, CA.

Talmon, S.
1955 לשאלת חילופי הגירסה במגילת ישעיה א. *Sefer Urbach*, 147–56. Jerusalem.
1963 The Gezer calendar and the seasonal cycle of ancient Canaan. *JAOS* 83.177–87.
1968 מגילת המזמורים מקומראן. *Tarbiz* 37.99–104 (review of Sanders 1965).
1969 Prolegomenon to Romain Butin, *The Ten Nequdoth of the Torah*, 1906, reprinted 1969, I–XXVII. New York, Ktav.
1977 בין חקר הסגנון ובין חקר נוסח המקרא. שנתון, an annual for biblical and near eastern studies, 1.116–63.
1978 'יגיד עליו רעו'—ביאורי כתובים ותיקוני נוסח במקרא על סמך מקבילות מספרות אוגרית. *EI* 14.117–24.

Talmon, Z.
1984 בחנים לשוניים בפתגם הארמי שבתלמוד הבבלי. Doctoral dissertation, Hebrew University.

Talshir, D.
1982 אמת־מידה לקירבה בין דיאלקטים (תרגומיים)—עיון בשדה סימאנטי משותף לתרגומים הארמיים. *WCJS* 8, Division D, Hebrew section, 21–24. Jerusalem.
1983a אנקה שהיא גמלה. *ML* 219–36.
1983b שמות בעלי החיים בתרגום הארמי של השומרונים. Doctoral dissertation, Hebrew University.

Tannenblatt, M.
1963–64 משה שולבוים—חוקר ובלשן. *LLA* 15.221–72.

Tawil, H.
1980 Two notes on the treaty terminology of the Sefire inscriptions. *CBQ* 42.30–37.

Tene, A.
1972 השלילה בספר בראשית. Masters thesis, University of Tel Aviv.

Téné, D.
1956 ענייני התחביר שב"כתאב אלתנקיח" לרבי יונה אבן ג'נאח. Masters thesis, Hebrew University.

1962 המשך הנמדד של התנועות בעברית. *Leš* 26.220–68.

1967–68 האם תוכנו של השורש העברי ערוך? *Leš* 32.173–207.

1968 L'hébreu contemporaine. *Le langage*, ed. A. Martinet, 975–1001. Paris, Éditions Gallimard.

1969 Israeli Hebrew. *Ariel* 25.48–63.

1971 (1969) L'articulation du signifié de monème en hébreu contemporaine. *Word* 25.289–320.

1971–72 Review of Allony 1969a (*H*). *KS* 47.545–600.

1983 השוואת הלשונות וידיעת הלשון. *ML* 236–87.

1985 לענין אחדותה ההיסטורית של העברית וחלוקתה לתקופות. מחקרים בלשון, ed. M. Bar-Asher, 101–55. Jerusalem, Department of Hebrew Language, Hebrew University.

1986 תקופת הביניים בדברי ימיה של ידיעת הלשון העברית. מחקרים במדעי היהדות, ed. M. Bar-Asher, 226–39. Jerusalem.

Tennenbaum, J.

1958 Die yiddishe sprakh oif der tog-ordenung fun der sholom-konferents in Pariz, 1919 (The Yiddish language on the agenda of the peace conference at Paris in 1919). *S. Niger memorial volume*, ed. by S. Bickel and L. Lehrer, 217–29. New York, YIVO Institute for Jewish Research.

Thacker, T. W.

1954 *The relationship of the Semitic and Egyptian verbal systems.* Oxford University Press.

Thiessen, J.

1973 *Yiddish in Canada, the death of a language?* Leer, Verlag Schuster.

Thompson, D. L.

1973 *The order of adverbial modifiers in Genesis and Proverbs: a study of the syntax of Hebrew poetry.* Doctoral dissertation, The Johns Hopkins University. Ann Arbor, University Microfilms.

Thompson, H. O. and Zayadine, F.

1973 The Tell Siran inscription. *BASOR* 212.5–11.

1974 The works of Amminadab (the Tell Siran bottle inscription). *BA* 37.13–19.

Thompson, S.

1985 *The Apocalypse and Semitic syntax.* Society for New Testament Studies Monograph Series 52. Cambridge University Press.

Thorion, Y.

1968 תעתיקי השמות הפרטיים העבריים בפאפירוסים ובכתובות היווניים והלטיניים. Masters thesis, Hebrew University.

1977 המשפט המורכב בפרוזה המקראית של תקופת בית ראשון. Doctoral dissertation, Hebrew University.

1982 Die Sprache der Tempelrolle und die Chronikbucher. *RQ* 11.(43).423–26.
1984 *Studien zur klassischen hebräischen Syntax*. Berlin, Dietrich Reimer Verlag.

Thorion-Vardi, T.
1985 The use of tenses in the Zadokite documents. *RQ* 12.65–88.

Tobi, Y.
1966–67 צירי וחולם במבטא יהודי תימן in בואי תימן, *Researches and documents in the culture of the Yemenite Jews*, ed. by Y. Ratzhaby, 52–57. Tel Aviv.
1972–73 על מסורת לשון חכמים בשירה העברית בימי הבינים. *Leš* 37. 137–53.
1975 יהדות תימן. בין שירת תימן לשירת ספרד, ed. by Y. Yesh^cayahu and Y. Tobi, 303–32. Jerusalem, Yad Izhak Ben-Zvi.
1977 יצחק בן ישראל—פייטן בבלי בן המאה הי״ג. *A. M. Haberman jubilee volume*, ed. by Z. Malachi, 125–37. Jerusalem, Rubin Mass.
1980 פיוטי רב סעדיה גאון, חלק א–ב. Doctoral dissertation, Hebrew University.
1981 שירים חדשים למשוררי בבל מן המאות הי״ב–הי״ג, in S. Moreh, ed., מחקרים בתולדות יהודי עיראק ובתרבותם, 5–72. Tel Aviv, Center for the Heritage of Iraqi Jewry.
1982 כתבי היד התימניים במכון בן־צבי. Jerusalem, The Ben-Zvi Institute.

Tobin, Y.
1981 עיונים בחקר־השיח. חקר השיח ותהליך התרגום הספרותי, ed. by S. Blum-Kulka, Y. Tobin and R. Nir, 213–61. Jerusalem, Akademon.
1986 Aspectual markers in Modern Hebrew. *WCJS* 9, Division D, English section, 53–60. Jerusalem.

Toledano, B.
1961 ספר אלמרשד אלכאפי (המדריך המספיק) מהפרשן . . . ר׳ תנחום ב״ר יוסף הירושלמי. Jerusalem.

Toll, T.
1972 Die Wurzel *PRṢ* im Hebräischen. *OS* 21.73–86.

Tollenaere, F. J.
1963–64 האוטומציה בשירות מדע הלשון. *Leš* 27–28.148–69.

Toury, G.
1977 נורמות של תרגום והתרגום הספרותי בשנים 1945–1930. The Porter Israeli Institute for Poetics and Semiotics, Tel Aviv University.
1981 עיונים בבלשנות ובסמיוטיקה. לשאלת היחסים בין תרגום ומקור, 83–96. Jerusalem.

Tov, E.
1972 Lucian and proto-Lucian—toward a new solution of the problem. *RB* 79.101–13.
1975a *The book of Baruch, also called I Baruch (Greek and Hebrew): Texts and translations*, Pseudepigrapha series 6. Missoula, MT, Scholars Press.
1975b *Lexical and grammatical studies on the language of the Septuagint.* Jerusalem, Akademon.
1976a The three dimensions of LXX words. *RB* 83.529–44.
1976b *The Septuagint translations of Jeremiah and Baruch—a discussion of an early revision of Jeremiah 29–52 and Baruch 1:1–3:8*, Harvard Semitic monographs 8. Missoula, MT, Scholars Press.
1978 עיונים באוצר המילים של תרגום השבעים—הזיקה בין אוצר המלים לטכניקת התרגום. *Tarbiz* 47.120–38.
1978–79 אופיה הטקסטואלי של מגילת ויקרא מקומראן. שנתון, an annual for biblical and ancient near eastern studies 3.238–44.
1980 ביבליה הבראיקה—מהדורת שטוטגרט החדשה. שנתון, an annual for biblical and ancient near eastern studies 4.172–79.
1981 *The text-critical use of the Septuagint in biblical research.* Jerusalem, Simor, Ltd.

Trevor, D.
1963 The semantic field of 'folly' in Proverbs, Job, Psalms and Ecclesiastes. *VT* 13.285–92.

Trommer, P.
1975 עיון סימנטי ותחבירי בפועל אמר המקראי. Masters thesis, Hebrew University.
1983 פועלי התנועה בעברית בת־ימינו: עיון סמנטי ותחבירי. Doctoral dissertation, Tel Aviv University.

Tronik, R.
1974 *Israeli periodicals and serials in English and other European languages.* Metuchen, NJ, The Scarecrow Press.

Trost, P.
1965 Yiddish in Bohemia and Moravia: the vowel question. *FY* 2.87–91.

Truper, M.
1941 הכתיב שבמדרשי ההלכה. Masters thesis, Hebrew University.

Tsanin, M.
1983 פולער העברעיש־־יידישער ווערטערבוך. Bnai Brak.

Tsevat, M.
1955 *A study of the language of the biblical Psalms.* JBL monograph series 9. Philadelphia.

Tsumura, D. T.
1973 *The Ugaritic drama of the good gods—a philological survey*. Doctoral dissertation, Brandeis University. Ann Arbor, University Microfilms.
1983 Literary insertion (A × B Pattern) in biblial Hebrew. *VT* 33.468–82.

Tsur, R.
n.d. עיונים בשירה העברית בימי הביניים. Tel Aviv.

Turniansky, N.
1980 היצירה הדו־לשונית באשכנז—קוים לאופיה *WCJS* 6, Division D, 85–99. Jerusalem.

Tur-Sinai, N. H.
1954–59 הלשון והספר, 3 vols. Jerusalem, Mossad Bialik (collected studies).

Twersky, I.
1980 *Introduction to the code of Maimonides*. New Haven and London, Yale University Press (chapter 5, "Language and style," 324–55, is a richly annotated and detailed discussion of Maimonides' language).

Tyloch, W.
1975 The evidence of the proto-lexicon for the cultural background of the Semitic peoples. *Hamito-Semitica*, ed. by J. and T. Bynon, 55–61. The Hague/Paris, Mouton.
1980 Quelques remarques sur l'hébreu contemporain. *FO* 21. 175–77.

Ullendorff, E.
1954 The Semitic languages of Ethiopia and their contribution to general Semitic studies. *PICO* 23.117–18. London.
1956 The contribution of south Semitics to Hebrew lexicography. *VT* 6.190–98.
1957 Modern Hebrew as a subject of linguistic investigation. *JSS* 2/3.232–61.
1958 What is a Semitic language? *Or* 27.66–75.
1967 *Ethiopia and the Bible*. London.
1971 Comparative Semitics, in *Afroasiatic*, ed. by C. T. Hodge, 27–38. The Hague/Paris, Mouton.
1977 *Is Biblical Hebrew a language?* Wiesbaden, Harrassowitz (collected papers).

Ulrich, C. E.
1978 *The Qumran text of Samuel and Josephus*, Harvard Semitic monographs 19. Missoula, MT, Scholars Press.

Ungar, E. M.
1984 *A syntactic and semantic model for the analysis of relative*

clauses in English and Hebrew. Doctoral dissertation, Cornell University. Ann Arbor, University Microfilms.

Unger, M.

1968 Yiddish words in Hebrew (*loshn qodesh*) texts of 'wonder tales' (Yiddish). *YS* 28.11–21.

Urbach, E.

1967–68 לשון ועניין. *Leš* 32.122–28.

Valle Rodriguez, C. del

1976 *Grammatikos hebreos Espanoles.* Salamanca.

1977 Sefer Ṣaḥot *de Abraham* ibn Ezra, I. Salamanca.

1981 *La escuela hebrea de Córdoba.* Madrid.

Vardy, M.

1950 השפעה לשונית בין הברייתות שבמסכת פסחים בתלמוד בבלי, בתלמוד הירושלמי, בתוספתא ומדרשי ההלכה. Masters thesis, Hebrew University.

Vardy, T.

1967 משפטי הוויתור בעברית החדשה. Masters thesis, Hebrew University.

Varughese, A.

1984 *The Hebrew text underlying the Old Greek translation of Jeremiah 10–20.* Doctoral dissertation, Drew University. Ann Arbor, University Microfilms.

Vattioni, F.

1969–78 I sigilli ebraici. *Biblica* 50 (1969).357–88; II. *Augustinianum* 11 (1971), 447–54; III. *AION* 38 (1978).227–54.

Veenhof, K. R.

1972 De Amman citadel inscriptie. *Phoenix: Bull. uitgegeven door het Vooraziatisch-Egyptisch Genootschap EOL* 18.170–79. Leiden.

1973 Een ammonietische incriptie. *Phoenix* 19.299–300.

Veetil, P. K.

1982 *Declaration and Covenant.* Analecta Biblica 88. Rome, Biblical Institute Press.

Vergote, J.

1975 La position intermediaire de l'ancien égyptien entre l'hébreu et l'arabe. *Hamito Semitica*, ed. by J. and T. Bynon, 193–99. The Hague, Mouton.

Vetter, D. and Walther, J.

1971 Sprachtheorie und Sprachvermittlung. *ZAW* 83.73–96.

Vidislavsky, D.

1980 אספקטים תחביריים ומילוניים בלשונם המדוברת של תלמידים ממוצא מערבי וממוצא מזרחי. Masters thesis, Bar-Ilan University.

Vivian, A.
1981 *Studi di sintássi contrastiva: dialetti aramaici.* Istituto di Linguistica e di Lingue Orientali, Università di Firenze.

Wächter, L.
1971 Reste von *Šafᶜel* Bildungen im Hebräischen. *ZAW* 83.382–89.

Wagner, M.
1966 Die lexicalischen und grammatikalischen Aramäismen im alttestamentlichen Hebräisch. Berlin.
1967 Beiträge zur Aramäismenfrage im alttestamentlichen Hebräisch. *Hebräische wortforschung. W. Baumgartner Festschrift.* Supplements to VT 16, 355–71. Leiden.

Waldman, N.
1969 Akkadian *kaṣāru* and semantic equivalents. *JNES* 28.250–54.
1970 A note on Canticles 4:9. *JBL* 89.215–17.
1971 Rabbinic homilies and cognate languages. *Gratz College Anniversary volume*, 269–73. Philadelphia.
1972a Akkadian loanwords and parallels in Mishnaic Hebrew. Unpublished doctoral dissertation, Dropsie College.
1972b Hebrew עז and the divine aura. *GCA* 1.6–8.
1973 On עבר, הפליג and Akkadian parallels. *ibid.*, 2.6–8.
1974a Notes on Mal. 3:6, 3:13 and Ps. 42:11. *JBL* 93.543–49.
1974b Words in the Aramaic lexicon. *JANES* 6.125–32.
1974c Words for 'heat' and extended meanings. *GCA* 3.43–48.
1975a The Hebrew tradition. *Current trends in linguistics* 13, ed. by Thomas A. Sebeok, 1285–1330. The Hague, Mouton.
1975b On 'shout, litigate and challenge.' *GCA* 4.3–8.
1976 A comparative note on Exodus 15.14–16. *JQR* 66.189–92.
1977a A note on excessive speech and falsehood. *JQR* 67.142–45.
1977b The heavenly writing. *GCA* 6.93–97.
1979a The breaking of the bow. *JQR* 69.82–88.
1979b A biblical echo of Mesopotamian royal rhetoric, *Essays on the occasion of the seventieth anniversary of the Dropsie University*, 449–55. Philadelphia.
1979c The *DĀḆĀR RAᶜ* of Eccl. 8:3. *JBL* 99.407–8.
1981 The wealth of mountain and sea: the background of a biblical image. *JQR* 71.178–80.
1982 The sprinkling of venom. *HAR* 6.199–203.
1984 A note on Ezekiel 1:18. *JBL* 103.614–18.
1987 Noise and disorder in the Bible and the Ancient Near East, in *Community and Culture*, ed. by Nahum M. Waldman, 233–41. Philadelphia, Gratz College and Seth Press.

Waletzky, J.
1980 Topicalization in Yiddish. *FY* 4.237–315.

Walters, Y.
1981 עיונים בחקר .תפקידם של גורמי הקשר בשימוש בהערכה לשוניים השיח, ed. by S. Blum-Kulka, Y. Tobin and R. Nir, 17–50. Jerusalem, Akademon.
Ward, W.
1960 Some effects of varying phonetic conditions in Semitic loan-words in Egyptian. *JAOS* 80.322–27.
Wartsky, Y.
1970 לשון המדרשים. Jerusalem.
Watson, P. L.
1970 *Mot, the god of death at Ugarit and in the Old Testament.* Doctoral dissertation, Yale University. Ann Arbor, University Microfilms.
1972 Archaic elements in the language of Chronicles. *Biblica* 53. 191–207.
Watson, W. G. E.
1975 Verse patterns in Ugaritic, Akkadian and Hebrew poetry. *UF* 7.483–92.
1984 *Classical Hebrew poetry: a guide to its techniques.* Journal for the Study of the Old Testament Supplement Series, 26. Sheffield, JSOT Press.
Watts, J.
1959 Remarks on Hebrew relative clauses. *PICO* 24, 190–91. Munich.
1964 *A survey of syntax in the Hebrew Old Testament.* Grand Rapids, Eerdmans.
Wechter, P.
1964 *Ibn Barun's Arabic works on Hebrew grammar and lexicography.* Philadelphia. Dropsie College.
Weich-Shahak, S.
1985 Towards a study of the linguistic features of the Judeo-Spanish romances. *Judeo-Romance languages*, ed. I. Benabu and J. (G.) Sermoneta, 169–88. Jerusalem.
Weil, G.
1962 Propositions pour une étude de la tradition massoretique babylonienne. *Textus* 2.103–19.
1963a *Élie Lévita, humaniste et massorète (1469–1549).* Leiden, Brill.
1963b Un fragment de Okhlah Palestinienne. *ALUOS* 3.68–80.
1963c La nouvelle édition de la Massorah (BHK IV) et l'histoire de la Massorah. Supplements to VT 9, 266–84.
1963–65 Fragment d'une Massorah alphabetique du Targum Babylonien du Pentateuch. *ALUOS* 5.114–34.

1964 *Initiation à la Massorah: l'introduction au* Sefer Zikhronot d'Élie Lévita. Leiden, Brill.

1968 Prolegomenon to S. Frensdorff, *Die Masora Magna*, 1876, Library of biblical studies, ed. by H. M. Orlinsky, I–XXXIII. New York, Ktav.

1971 *Massorah gedolah iuxta codicem Leningradensem B 19a*; 1, catalogi. Rome, Pontificium Institutum Biblicum.

1972 La Massorah. *REJ* 131.5–104.

1978a Ed. *The international dictionary of manuscript collections, libraries, private collections, repositories and archives*, vol. 1, The manuscript collections. Paris, Berger-Levrault.

1978b *Concordance de la cantilation du Pentateuque et des cinq Megillot*. Nancy. (with P. Rivière and M. Serfaty).

1979 Trilitéralité fonctionelle ou bilitéralité fondomentale des racines; verbales hébraïques: une essai d'analyse quantifiée. *RHPR* 59 (3/4).281–311.

1982 *Concordance de la cantilation des premiers prophetes Josue, Juges, Samuel et Rois*. Paris.

Weiman, R.

1950 Native and foreign elements in a language: a study in general linguistics applied to modern Hebrew. Philadelphia (originally doctoral dissertation, Columbia University, 1950; reprinted 1977, Folcroft, PA, Folcroft Library Editions).

Weinberg, E. and Polani, H.

1975 Bulletin No. 7, *A bibliography (annotated) of: Hebrew-Hebrew, Hebrew-bilingual and multilingual dictionaries, published since 1948 in Israel and abroad* (*H*). Jerusalem, Council on the Teaching of Hebrew.

Weinberg, W.

1966 Spoken Israeli Hebrew: trends in the departures from classical phonology. *JSS* 11.40–68.

1968 The *qamaṣ qaṭan* structures. *JBL* 87.151–65.

1969–70 Transliteration and transcription of Hebrew. *HUCA* 40–41. 1–32.

1970–71 בשולי הפרסום החדש של ״כללי הכתיב חסר הניקוד״. *Leš* 36. 203–11.

1972 תיקון הכתב העברי. Jerusalem.

1973 Towards a world standard in the transliteration of Hebrew. *WCJS* 5, 4.137–51. Jerusalem.

1974 Biblical grammar/Israeli grammar: accepted and unacceptable changes. *HA* 15.32–41.

1975–80 The history of Hebrew plene spelling. *HUCA* 46.457–87; 47.237–80; 48.301–33; 49.311–38; 50.289–317.

1980 Method and results of an inquiry into the acceptability of non-normative forms in spoken Hebrew. *WCJS* 6, Division D, 29–46.
1985a *The history of Hebrew* plene *spelling*. Cincinnati. Hebrew Union College Press (collected studies from *HUCA*, 1975–80).
1985b Observations about the pronunciation of Hebrew in rabbinic sources. *HUCA* 56.117–43.

Weinberger, L.
1973 *Samuel Ha-Nagid, Jewish prince in Moslem Spain*. Judaic studies 3. University of Alabama.
1975 אנתולוגיה של פיוטי יון. אנאטוליה והבלקנים. Cincinnati, Hebrew Union College Press and University of Alabama Press.
1983 Bulgaria's synagogue poets: the Kastoreans. Cincinnati. Hebrew Union College Press.

Weiner, G.
1975–76 על העברית שביידיש האמריקנית לעומת הלעז שבעברית הישראלית. *LLA* 27.113–21.

Weinfeld, M.
1972 *Deuteronomy and the deuteronomic school*. Oxford, Clarendon Press.
1982a נבואת בלעם בכתובת מדיר עלא(סוכות). שנתון, an annual for biblical and near eastern research, 5–6.141–47.
1982b The counsel of the "Elders" to Rehoboam and its implications. *Maarav* 3.27–53.
1983 חילול, כבישה ומרמס רגל. *ML* 195–200.

Weinfeld, S.
1972 טעמי המקרא. Jerusalem.

Weingreen, J.
1939/1959² *A practical grammar for classical Hebrew*, 2nd ed. Oxford.

Weinreich, M.
1931 Vos volt yidiš geven on hebraiš? *Zukunft*, March, 194–205.
1936 Form vs. function in Yiddish. *Occident and Orient: Gaster anniversary volume*, ed. by Bruno Schindler, 532–38. London, Taylor's Foreign Press (Spanish version in *Judaica* 5(58).145–52, 1938).
1938 Jiddisch als Gegenstand de allgemainen Sprachwissenschaft. *ACIL* 4, 226–27. Copenhagen, Munksgaard.
1953 *Yidishkayt* and Yiddish: on the impact of religion on language in Ashkenazic Jewry. *Mordecai M. Kaplan jubilee volume*, ed. by Moshe Davis, 481–514. New York, Jewish Theological Seminary (Reprinted in *Readings in the sociology of language*, ed. by J. A. Fishman, 382–413. The Hague, Mouton, 1968).

1954 Prehistory and early history of Yiddish: facts and conceptual framework. *FY* 1.73–101.

1954–55 Ikorim in der geshikhte fun yidish. *YS* 14.97–110; 15.12–19.

1956a The Jewish languages of Romance stock and their relation to the earliest Yiddish. *RPh* 9.403–28.

1956b Yiddish, Knaanic, Slavic: the basic relationships, in *For Roman Jakobson: essays on the occasion of his sixtieth birthday*, ed. by M. Halle *et al.*, 622–32. The Hague, Mouton.

1958 Bnai het uvnai ḥet in Ashkenaz: die problem und vos zi lozt uns heren (Yiddish phonology as a clue to medieval Hebrew: the aspirate and the velar and palatal spirants). *S. Niger memorial volume*, ed. by S. Bickel and L. Lehrer, 101–23. New York, YIVO Institute for Jewish Research.

1959a בני הית ובני חית באשכנז: הבעיה ומה היא באה להשמיענו. *Leš* 23.85–101.

1959b Ineveynikste cveyspraxikeit in askenaz biz der haskole: fakten un bagrifen. *Die goldene keyt* 35.80–88.

1960 Old Yiddish poetry in linguistic-literary research. *Word* 16. 100–18.

1963–64 ראשית ההברה האשכנזית בזיקתה לבעיות קרובות של היידיש ושל העברית האשכנזית. *Leš* 27–28.131–47, 230–51.

1965 On the dynamics of Yiddish dialect formation. *FY* 2.73–86.

1967 On the dynamics of Jewishness versus the ghetto myth: the sociolinguistic roots of Yiddish. *To honor Roman Jakobson* 3.211–21. The Hague, Mouton (reprinted in J. A. Fishman, ed., 1981a.103–17).

1973 געשיכטע פון דער יידישער שפראך (*History of the Yiddish language: concepts, facts, methods*). 4 vols., New York, YIVO Institute for Jewish Research (partial English translation, 1980, by S. Nobel, with the assistance of J. A. Fishman. University of Chicago and Hebrew Union College—Jewish Institute of Religion).

Weinreich, U.

1949 *College Yiddish.* New York, YIVO (5th revised edition, 3rd printing, 1976).

1953 *Languages in Contact.* New York, Linguistic Circle of New York (2nd ed., 1963, The Hague, Mouton).

1954a Ed. *The field of Yiddish* 1. New York (abbreviated *FY* 1).

1954b Stress and word structure in Yiddish. *FY* 1.1–27.

1956 Notes on the Yiddish rise-fall intonation contours. *For Roman Jakobson: essays on the occasion of his sixtieth birthday*, ed. by M. Halle, 633–43. The Hague, Mouton.

1959–61 העברית האשכנזית והעברית שביידיש: בחינתן הגיאוגראפית. *Leš* 24.242–52; 25.57–80, 180–96.

1961–62 על ממדן הגיאוגראפי של לשונות יהודיות ושל תרבות ישראל. *Leš* 26.125–37.
1964 Western traits in Transcarpathian Yiddish. *For Max Weinreich on his seventieth birthday*, 245–64. The Hague, Mouton.
1965 Ed. *The Field of Yiddish* 2. The Hague, Mouton (abbreviated *FY* 2).
1968 Modern English–Yiddish—Yiddish–English dictionary. New York, McGraw-Hill and YIVO.
1969 The geographic makeup of Byelorussian Yiddish. *FY* 3. 82–101.
1971 Yiddish. *EJ* 16.789–98.

Weinreich, U. and B.
1959 *Yiddish language and folklore: a selective bibliography for research.* The Hague, Mouton.

Weinstein, Y.
1939 המילון המקראי של רש"י לפי פירושו לספרי הנביאים. Masters thesis, Hebrew University.

Weinstock, L.
1979 *Onomatopoeia and related phenomena in Biblical Hebrew.* Doctoral dissertation, University of Pennsylvania. Ann Arbor, University Microfilms.
1983 Sound and meaning in Biblical Hebrew. *JSS* 28.49–62.

Weisberg, D.
1968 Some observations on late Babylonian texts and rabbinic literature. *HUCA* 39.71–80.

Weiser, A.
1955 עטור סופרים. *Sefer Urbach*, 216–21. Jerusalem.
1965 דקדוק לשון העברית. Jerusalem.

Weiss, I. H.
1867 *Studien über die Sprache der Mischna.* Wien, reprinted in Hebrew translation, 1969. Jerusalem, Carmiel.

Weiss, R.
1960–61 שיטתו של אליעזר בן יהודה בחידושיו. *LLA* 12.199–106, 232–40.
1961–62 חידושים ומחדשיהם. *LLA* 13.84–90.
1962–63 על לשונו של יל"ג. *LLA* 14.95–104.
1962–64 חמל, חוס = פסח. *Leš* 27–28.127–30.
1973–74 פרופ' יוסף קלוזנר כמחיה הלשון העברית. *LLA* 25.167–74.
1975 שימושי לשון מן הימים ההם בזמן הזה—לקט ממאמריו העממיים בענייני לשון. *LLA* 27/1-2 (261–62).
1976–77 מקודש לחול—לקט שני ממאמריו העממיים בענייני לשון. *LLA* 28/1 (271).
1977 לא—מושך עצמו ואחר עמו־(על שימושה של מלת שלילה בתקבולת). שנתון, an annual for biblical and near eastern studies 2.82–92.
1978 הערות על שימושה של מלת השלילה "לא" במקרא. *EI* 14.148–54.

1982 בשוט לשון. Jerusalem, Kiryat-Sefer.

Weissblüth, S.

1983 עיונים בלשונו ובסגנונו על רבי נחמן קרוכמאל (רנ"ק) בספרו "מורה נבוכי הזמן". *HCL* 20.29–59.

Weissert, D.

1971 המקרא ותולדות ישראל. תרגום השבעים לפועל "חדל", *Studies in Bible and Jewish history dedicated to the memory of Jacob Liver*, ed. by B. Uffenheimer, 279–88. Tel Aviv University.

Weitzman, E.

1981 עיונים בחקר השיח. פיענוח אינפרמציה בעיתונות והשלכות תרגום, ed. by S. Blum-Kulka, Y. Tobin and R. Nir, 117–46. Jerusalem, Akademon.

Welch, J. W., ed.

1981 *Chiasmus in antiquity: structures, analyses, exegesis.* Hildesheim, Gerstenberg Verlag.

Weller, P.

1971 התערבות לשון האם בלימוד שפה חדשה. Masters thesis, Hebrew University.

Wernberg-Møller, P.

1957 *The manual of discipline*, Leiden, Brill.

1958a Studies in the defective spellings in the Isaiah scroll of St. Marks monastery. *JSS* 3.244–64.

1958b 'Pleonastic' *waw* in Classical Hebrew. *JSS* 3.321–26.

1964 The contribution of the Hodayot to biblical textual criticism. *Textus* 4.133–75.

1974 Aspects of masoretic vocalization. H. M. Orlinsky, ed., *Masoretic studies* 1.121–30. Missoula, MT, Scholars Press.

Werner, F.

1982 האפשרויות השונות של תצורת המלים בעברית בת זמננו. *WCJS* 8, Division D, Hebrew section, 57–62. Jerusalem.

Werses, S.

1980 יוסף פרל כמתרגם ליידיש של טום ג'ונס לפילדינג. *WCJS* 6, Division D, 63–84. Jerusalem.

Wertheimer, Y.

1968 לשונו של יוסף ריבלין. Masters thesis, Bar-Ilan University.

1975–76 על אמנם וצירופיה כמלות ויתור. *Leš* 40.233–49.

1983 לשונו של מ"ל ליליינבלום: תיאור סינכרוני של המלות בלשונו. Doctoral dissertation, Bar-Ilan University.

Wevers, J. W.

1970 *Heth* in classical Hebrew. *Essays on the ancient Semitic world*, ed. by J. W. Wevers and D. B. Redford, 101–12. University of Toronto Press.

Wevers, J. W. and Redford, D. B., eds.

1971 *Studies on the ancient Palestinian world.* University of Toronto Press.

Wexler, P.
1964 Slavic influences in the grammatical functions of three Yiddish verbal prefixes. *Linguistics* 7.83–92.
1975 Review of Fellman 1973a. *Lingua* 36.370–73.
1977 Ascertaining the position of Judezmo within Ibero-Romance. *VR* 36.162–95.
1978 The terms ‘Sabbath food’: a challenge for Jewish interlinguistics. *JAOS* 98.461–65.
1979 Jewish onomastics—achievements and challenges. *Onoma* 23/1.96–113 (review article on B. Z. Kaganoff, *A Dictionary of Jewish names and their history*, New York, Schocken, 1977).
1980 Periphrastic integration of Semitic verbal material in slavicized Yiddish and Turkish. *FY* 4.431–73.
1981 Jewish interlinguistics: facts and conceptual framework. *Language* 57/1.99–149.
1985 Linguistica Judeo-Lusitanica. *Judeo-Romance languages*, ed. I. Benabu and J. (G.) Sermoneta, 189–208. Jerusalem.
1987 *Explorations in Judeo-Slavic linguistics.* Leiden, Brill.

Wheeler, S. B.
1970 Review of Sperber 1966. *JANES* 2.66–73.
1971 The infixed *-t-* in Biblical Hebrew. *JANES* 3.20–31.

Whitaker, R. E.
1972 *A concordance of the Ugaritic literature.* Cambridge, Harvard University Press.

Whitley, C. F.
1972 Some functions of the Hebrew particles *Beth* and *Lamedh*. *JQR* 62.199–206.
1974 Has the particle *šām* an asseverative force? *Biblica* 55.394–98.
1975a The Hebrew emphatic particle ‘*l*’ with pronominal suffixes. *JQR* 65.225–28.
1975b Some remarks on *lû* and *lōʾ*. *ZAW* 87.202–4.
1975c Some aspects of Hebrew poetic diction. *UF* 7.493–502.

Wieder, A.
1965 Ugaritic-Hebrew lexicographic notes. *JBL* 84.160–64.

Wieder, N.
1964 הצורה רבּוּן במקורות עבריים. *Leš* 27–28.214–17.

Wiesenberg, E. J.
1976 Rabbinic Hebrew as an aid in the study of biblical Hebrew, illustrated in the exposition of the rare words *rahat* and *mezareh*. *HUCA* 47.143–80.

Wilch, J. R.
1969 *Time and event, an exegetical study of the use of* ʾeth *in the Old Testament*. Leiden, Brill.

Wilcher, A.
1940 מילות ההכללה בעברית. Masters thesis, Hebrew University.
Wildberger, H.
1967 "Glauben," Erwägungen zu האמין. Supplements to VT 16. 372–86.
Wilensky, M.
1978 מחקרים בלשון ובספרות. (collected studies, edited by S. Abramson, A. Eliner and M. Medan). Jerusalem, Academy of the Hebrew Language.
Wilensky, M., Téné, D. and Ben-Hayyim, Z.
1964 ספר הרקמה לר׳ יונה אבן ג׳נאח, 2 vols. Jerusalem.
Willi, T.
1974 Christliche Hebräisten der Renaissance und Reformation. *Judaica* 30.78–85, 100–25.
Williams, R. J.
1965/1976[2] *An outline of Hebrew syntax*. Toronto.
1970 The passive Qal theme in Hebrew. *Essays on the ancient Semitic world*, ed. by J. Wevers and D. B. Redford, 43–50. University of Toronto Press.
1972 Energic verbal forms in Hebrew. *Studies on the ancient Palestinian world*, ed. by J. W. Wevers and D. B. Redford, 75–85. University of Toronto Press.
Willis, J. T.
1979 The juxtaposition of synonymous and chiastic parallelism in tricola in Old Testament Hebrew psalms. *VT* 29.465–80.
Windfuhr, G.
1970 The cuneiform signs of Ugarit. *JNES* 29.48–50.
Wistansky, H.
1944 האוצר הלשוני בספר משלי. Masters thesis, Hebrew University.
Wolf, C. U.
1942 *Toward an understanding of the vocalization of pre-massoretic Hebrew*. Doctoral dissertation, University of Hartford.
Wolf, M.
1969 The geography of Yiddish: case and gender variation. *FY* 3.102–215.
Wolf, S.
1962 *Jiddisches Wörterbuch*. Mannheim.
Wolff, H. W.
1974 *Anthropology of the Old Testament*. Philadelphia.
Wunderlich, H.
1973 מלים בעברית בתוספת ת״ו לפני השורש. Masters thesis, Hebrew University.

Würthwein, E.
1979 *The Text of the Old Testament: An introduction to the* Biblia Hebraica. Grand Rapids, Eerdmans (translated from the expanded and revised fourth edition of *Der Text der alten Testaments*, Stuttgart, 1973).

Yadin, Y.
1962a *The scroll of the war of the sons of light against the sons of darkness*. Oxford University Press.
1962b Expedition D—the cave of the letters. *IEJ* 12.227–57.
1967 The Ben Sira scroll from Masadah. *EI* 8.1–45.
1969 *Tefillin from Qumran*. Jerusalem.
1977 מגילת המקדש, 3 vols. in 4. Jerusalem.

Yahalom (Lehmann), B.
1951 הקווים האופייניים בתרגומו של רבי יהודה אבן־תיבון ל״ספר השרשים״ לרבי יונה אבן ג׳נאח. Masters thesis, Hebrew University.

Yahalom, Y.
1966 הניקוד הארץ־ישראלי בקדושתות חדותה למשמרות ותופעות הלשון העולות ממנו. Masters thesis, Hebrew University.
1969–70 הניקוד הארץ־ישראלי בקדושתות חדותה למשמרות ותופעות הלשון העולות ממנו. *Leš* 34.39–41.
1974 תחביר הפיוט הקדום (כולל ינייי) כיסוד לסגנונו. Doctoral dissertation, Hebrew University.
1980a שמעון בירבי מגס—הפייטן ויצירתו. *AJSR* 5, Hebrew section, 25–37.
1980b הפאסיב בפיוט. *Leš* 45.17–31.
1982 ראשיתה של השקילה המדויקת בשירה העברית. *Leš* 47.25–61.

Yahuda, A.
1982 *Hebrew is Greek*. Oxford, Beckett Rieblestein.

Yalon, H.
1937a שוא שאחרי שורוק בראש מלה. *KLL* 1.16–19.
1937b שבילי מבטאים. *KLL* 1.62–78.
1942a הגייה ספרדית בצרפת הצפונית. *KLL* (Iyyar, 5702), 16–31.
1942b על הגיית החטפים והקמץ החטוף באשכנז. *KLL* (Iyyar, 5702), 31–36.
1959–60 נימוקים למשניות מנוקדות. *Leš* 24.15–46, 157–66.
1962–64 מה בין ר׳ שלמה אלמולי לר׳ אליהו בחור (כלל יסודי בנטיות השם והפועל). *Leš* 27–28.225–29.
1963 הקמץ בניקוד הבבלי ובתימן. *Tarbiz* 33.129–35.
1964 מבוא לניקוד המשנה. Jerusalem.
1964–65 הגיית תנועות. *Tarbiz* 34.129–35.
1966–67 במקרא ובסידור. *Leš* 31.283–86.
1967 מגילות מדבר יהודה—דברי לשון. Jerusalem, Kiryath Sepher.

1971 פרקי לשון. Jerusalem, Mossad Bialik (collected studies).
1974 Bibliography of H. Yalon, compiled by R. Weiss, in *H. Yalon memorial volume*, Bar-Ilan departmental researches 2, 1–7.

Yannai, I.
1970 *The quardiliteral verb in the Hebrew language.* Doctoral dissertation, UCLA. Ann Arbor, University Microfilms.
1973–74 פעלים מרובי עצורים בלשון העברית. *Leš* 38.118–30, 183–93.
1974 Augmented verbs in Biblical Hebrew. *HUCA* 45.71–95.
1978 (1976–77) החזרת עטרה ליושנה, 'Restoring the crown to its original form.' Hallowed words in Hebrew and their development in modern times. *AN* 17.20–34.
1980 Secularization in Modern Hebrew, a chapter in the semantics of the language. *WCJS* 6, Division D, 101–13. Jerusalem.
1986 שובו של הניקוד העברי. *WCJS* 9, Division D, 85–92.

Yarkoni, R.
1973 כתר התורה של שלמה בן־בויאעא (משנת 930 למנין הרגיל)— ניקודו וטעמיו. Masters thesis, Hebrew University.

Yaron, J.
1976 תרומתו של שמואל כהן ללקסיקולוגיה השומרונית. Masters thesis, Hebrew University.

Yaron, R.
1961 *Introduction to the law of the Aramaic papyri.* Oxford University Press.

Yarshater, E.
1977 The hybrid language of the Jewish community of Persia. *JAOS* 97.1–7.

Yeivin, I.
1956 הקפת התיבות הזעירות במקרא (כ״א ספרים). Masters thesis, Hebrew University.
1958 מגילויי המלרעיות בלשון העברית. *EI* 5.145–49.
1958–59 השפעה תחבירית והשפעה מוסיקלית על דרכי הקפת תיבות זעירות. *Leš* 23.35–48.
1959–60 הטעמת תורה שבעל פה בטעמים. *Leš* 24.47–69, 167–78, 207–31.
1960 קטע מקרא בניקוד טברני לא־מסורתי. *Tarbiz* 29.345–56.
1962 A Babylonian fragment of the Bible in the abbreviated system. *Textus* 2.120–39.
1963 A Palestinian fragment of Haftareth and other mss. with mixed pointing. *Textus* 3.121–27.
1965 הניקוד הבבלי ומסורת הלשון המשתקפת ממנו. Doctoral dissertation, Hebrew University.
1969 כתר ארם צובא: ניקודו וטעמיו. Jerusalem.
1971 הצורות ״יקטלנו, יקוטלנו״ במגילות מדבר יהודה לאור מסורת הניקוד הבבלי. המקרא ותולדות ישראל, *Studies in Bible and Jewish history dedicated to the memory of Jacob Liver*, ed. by B. Uffenheimer, 256–76. Tel Aviv University.

1972–73 עוד למונח מסורה הבבלית "בע". *Leš* 37.154–56.
1973a מסורת לשון העברית המשתקפת בניקוד הבבלי. Jerusalem, Akademon (abridgment of Yeivin 1965); expanded, 2 vols., 1985, Jerusalem, Academy of the Hebrew Language).
1973b מבוא למסורה הטברנית. Jerusalem, Akademon.
1973c Ed. *Geniza Bible fragments with Babylonian Massorah and vocalization*, 1. *Pentateuch* (2 vols.). Leiden, Brill.
1974a קטע מחבור מסורתי בבלי למקרא ותרגום אונקלוס. *H. Yalon memorial volume*, Bar-Ilan departmental researches 2, 99–163.
1974b אוסף קטעי הגניזה של המשנה בניקוד בבלי. Jerusalem.
1978 א דגושה במקרא. *Studies in Bible and the ancient near east presented to Samuel E. Loewenstamm*, 2.223–27. Jerusalem.
1979–80 מלים אחדות וניקודן במסורת־הלשון הבבלית. *LLA* 31/4.148–55.
1980a שינוי איכות של חטפים. *Leš* 44.163–84.
1980b ניקודי מלים וצורותיהן בכתבי־יד ותרומתן למילון ולדקדוק. *WCJS* 6, Division D, 215–22. Jerusalem.
1981 הגעיות ותפקידן. *Leš* 46.39–56.
1982a נוסח ניקוד וטעמים בדף החדש מתוך כתר ארם צובא. *Tarbiz* 51.174–76.
1982b המסורה הבבלית לנבאים. *EI* 16.112–23.
1983 משמעות סימן הדגש בניקוד הטברני ה"מורחב". *ML* 293–307.

Yelin, Y.
1973 הדקדוק כיסוד בהלכה. Jerusalem, Mossad Harav Kook.

Yellin, D.
1933–34 הצמוד השלם בתנ"ך. *Leš* 5.276–94.
1939 המשקלים בשירת שמואל הנגיד. Studies of the Research Institute for Hebrew Poetry 5.181–208.
1940 תורת השירה הספרדית. Reprinted, Jerusalem, 1972, with bibliography and preface by D. Pagis.
1945 תולדות התפתחות הדקדוק העברי. Jerusalem.

Yeshᶜayahu, Y.
1975 ייחודה ושליחותה הלאומית של שירת רבי שלם שבזי, in *The Jews of Yemen*, ed. by Y. Yeshᶜayahu and Y. Tobi, 285–301. Jerusalem, Yad Itzhak ben Zvi.

Yitzhaki, Y.
1970–71 דעותיהם של סופרי ההשכלה על הלשון העברית. *Leš* 34.287–305; 35.39–59, 140–54.

Yizhar, M.
1967 *Bibliography of Hebrew publications on the Dead Sea scrolls 1948–1964*. Harvard theological studies 23. Cambridge, Harvard University Press.

Yoder, P. B.
1970 *Fixed word pairs and the composition of Hebrew poetry.*

Doctoral dissertation, University of Pennsylvania. Ann Arbor, University Microfilms.
1971 A-B pairs and oral composition in Hebrew poetry. *VT* 21.470–89.
1972 Biblical Hebrew, in *Versification, major language types*, ed. by W. Wimsat, 52–65. New York, Modern Language Association.

Yoel, Y.
1967 מגמות בתרגומי ימי הביניים. Masters thesis, Hebrew University.
1972 תחביר ספר מלחמות ה׳ לרבי לוי בן גרשום. Doctoral dissertation, Hebrew University.

Zadok, R.
1982 Remarks on the inscription of *HDYS*ᶜ*Y* from Tall Fakhariya. *TA* 9.117–29.

Zafrani, H.
1971 Judeo-Arabic and Judeo-Berber. *EJ* 10.409–10.

Zand, M.
1965 Idiš kak substrat sovremennogo ivrita. *Semitiskie yazyki* 2/1.221–46. Moscow.

Zbili, J.
1981 קולוקאטיביות ונרדפות בתחום משמעותו של הפועל נשא בלשון המקרא: עיון פרשני־סמנטי. Masters thesis, Bar-Ilan University.

Zeiberg, R.
1981 עיון תחבירי וסימנטי בפועל ידע. Masters thesis, Tel Aviv University.

Zeidman, I.
1956 עיונים בלשון. על לשונן העברית של הרמב״ם. *LLA* 6.3–10.
1963–64 דוד ילין, מורה הלשון וחוקרה. *LLA* 15(150).

Zeidner, M.
1978 אספקטים פסיכולינגוויסטיים של משלב שפת התינוקות בעברית. עיונים בחינוך 10.105–22.

Zeldis, J.
1973 *A classification of container words in Hebrew*. Doctoral dissertation, University of Pennsylvania. Ann Arbor, University Microfilms.

Zeliger, H.
1940 למילונו המקראי של רבי אברהם אבן־עזרא על פי פירושיו לספרים בראשית־שמות. Masters thesis, Hebrew University.

Zelikovitz, Y.
1953 שימושי לשון בספר היכלות רבתי. Masters thesis, Hebrew University.

Zevit, Z.
1975 The so-called interchangeability of the prepositions *B*, *L* and *M* (*N*) in Northwest Semitic. *JANES* 7.103–12.

1980 *Matres lectionis in ancient Hebrew epigraphs.* Cambridge, MA, American Schools of Oriental Research.

Zijl, P. J. Van

1972 Baal, a study of texts in connection with Baal in the Ugaritic epics. AOAT 10, Neukirchen-Vluyn.

Zilkha, A.

1970 *Negation in Hebrew.* Doctoral dissertation, University of Texas at Austin. Ann Arbor, University Microfilms.

1976 Contradictions in deep structure in Hebrew. *HS* 17.165–67.

Zilkha, R.

1981 פרופוזיציה הגורמת לפרופוזיציה. Masters thesis, Tel Aviv University.

Zimels, A.

1972 *The Palestinian Targum MS Neofiti on Genesis and Noah in comparison with Pseudo-Jonathan and Targum Onkelos.* Doctoral dissertation (written in Hebrew), Yeshiva University. Ann Arbor, University Microfilms.

Zimmels, H. J.

1958 *Ashkenazim and Sephardim.* London, Oxford.

Zimmerman, F.

1975 *Biblical books translated from the Aramaic.* New York, Ktav.

1978 *The Aramaic origins of the four Gospels.* New York, Ktav.

Zimmern, H.

1915/1917^2 *Akkadische Fremdwörter als Beweis für babylonischen Kultureinfluss.* Leipzig.

Zimrani (Singmann), A.

1938 מילונו המקראי של רש״י לפי פירושו לנביאים. Masters thesis, Hebrew University.

Ziv, Y.

1976 On the re-analysis of grammatical terms in Hebrew possessive constructions, in P. Cole, ed., *Studies in Modern Hebrew syntax and semantics*, 129–52. Amsterdam.

1981 עיונים in חקר השיח והתרת בעיות "קיום" אחדות בעברית החדשה בחקר השיח, ed. by S. Blum-Kulka, Y. Tov, R. Nir, 303–16.

Zivy, A., ed.

1966 *Elsäser Jiddisch: Judisch-deutsche Sprichwörter und Redensarten.* Basel, Victor Goldschmidt.

Zlotowitz, B.

1981 *The Septuagint translation of the Hebrew terms in relation to God in the book of Jeremiah.* New York, Ktav (with an introductory essay on anthropomorphisms and anthropopathisms in the Septuagint and Targum by H. M. Orlinsk-

Zohory, M.
1969 לחקר יסודותיה של לשון אבות in הגות עברית באירופה, ed. by M. Zohory and A. Tartakover, 25–40. Tel Aviv.
Zuckerman, R.
1969 Alsace: an outpost of western Yiddish. *FY* 3.36–57.
Zulay, M.
1936 מחקרי יניי. Studies of the Research Institute for Hebrew Poetry 2.213–391.
1938 פיוטי יניי. Berlin, Schocken.
1946 עיוני לשון בפיוטי יניי. Studies of the Research Institute for Hebrew Poetry 6. Jerusalem, Schocken Institute.
1964 האסכולה הפייטנית של רב סעדיה גאון. Jerusalem, Schocken.
Zuntz, G.
1956 Greek words in the Talmud. *JSS* 1.129–40.
Zurawel (צורבל), T.
1980 חילופי בנינים בין החומש השומרוני לחומש הטברני. Masters thesis, Hebrew University.
1984 נטישת בניין קל בעברית נוסח שומרון; לבירורה של סוגייה בדקדוק. *Massorot* 1.135–51.

INDEX OF NAMES

The United Library
Garrett-Evangelical/Seabury-Western Seminaries
2121 Sheridan Road
Evanston, IL 60201